Lydia Maria Child

Lydia Maria Child
Selected Letters, 1817-1880

Edited by Milton Meltzer and Patricia G. Holland

Francine Krasno, Associate Editor

THE UNIVERSITY OF MASSACHUSETTS PRESS *Amherst, 1982*

The publisher gratefully acknowledges the support of
the following in the publication of this work: the
National Endowment for the Humanities, the Aaron
Diamond Foundation, the Foundation of Jewish Philan-
thropies/Greater Miami Jewish Federation, the
Theodore and Shirley Libby Fund of the Combined
Jewish Philanthropies of Greater Boston, the Schocken
Foundation, Samuel Chavkin, Ann McGovern, Allan
Meltzer, Ralph E. Shikes, and the Associate Alumni of
the University of Massachusetts, Amherst.

To Sidney Kaplan, friend and mentor,
in tribute to his influence as a scholar of history,
literature, and art

Contents

Acknowledgments

Research for this project would have been impossible without the generous support of the National Historical Publications and Records Commission and the University of Massachusetts at Amherst. The W. E. B. Du Bois Department of Afro-American Studies and the University of Massachusetts Press were the project's sponsors here, and the editors owe special thanks to John H. Bracey, Jr., professor of Afro-American Studies, and to Leone Stein, director of the Press.

For making publication of this work possible, the editors and publisher gratefully acknowledge the support of the National Endowment for the Humanities, the Aaron Diamond Foundation, the Foundation of Jewish Philanthropies/Greater Miami Jewish Federation, the Theodore and Shirley Libby Fund of the Combined Jewish Philanthropies of Greater Boston, the Schocken Foundation, Samuel Chavkin, Ann McGovern, Allan Meltzer, Ralph E. Shikes, and the University of Massachusetts Alumni Council.

We would like to thank the university's Graduate Research Council for supporting a research assistant for this work and the staff of the library for a great deal of help of all kinds. Our two graduate research assistants, Altina Waller and Doris Lamica, worked with unfailing care and resourcefulness, and we are most grateful for the volunteered last-minute help of Lois Ahrens.

For permission to publish letters in their holdings, we thank the directors of the following libraries: American Antiquarian Society, Worcester, Mass.; American Philosophical Society, Philadelphia, Pa.; Boston Public Library; Brown University, John Hay Library, Providence, R.I.; Buffalo and Erie County Public Library, Buffalo, N.Y.; Columbia University Library, New York, N.Y.; Cornell University Library, Ithaca, N.Y.; Dartmouth College, Baker Library, Hanover, N.H.; Essex Institute, Salem, Mass.; Glassboro State College, Glassboro, N.J.; Harvard University, Houghton Library, Cambridge, Mass.; Huntington Library, San Marino, Calif.; Iowa State Historical Department, Des Moines; Kansas State Historical Society, Topeka; Library of Congress, Washington, D.C.; Massachusetts Historical Society, Boston; University of Michigan, Clements Library, Ann Arbor; New-York Historical Society, New York; New York Public Library; Historical Society of Pennsylvania, Philadelphia; Princeton University Library, Princeton, N.J.; Radcliffe College, Schlesinger Library, Cambridge, Mass.; University of Rochester Library, Rochester, N.Y.; Scripps College Library, Claremont, Calif.; Smith College, Sophia Smith Collection, Northampton, Mass.; Swarthmore College, Friends Historical Library, Swarthmore, Pa.; Syracuse University Library, Syracuse, N.Y.; University of Virginia, Clifton Waller Barrett Library, Charlottesville; Wayland (Mass.) Historical Society; Wellesley College Library, Wellesley, Mass.; Western Reserve Historical Society, Cleveland, Ohio; West Virginia Department of Culture and History, Charleston; Williams College Library, Williamstown, Mass.; Worcester (Mass.) Historical Society; Yale University, Beinecke Rare Book and Manuscript Library, New Haven, Conn.

We would also like to thank Walter G. Perry and William Phillips, Jr., for permission to publish Child letters in their personal possession. Many letters included here are from the collection of Lydia Merrill, Child's great grand-niece, and thanks to her generosity are now in the Schlesinger Library. Finally, we would like to acknowledge Houghton Mifflin for our use of Child letters from two books published by that firm, *Letters of Lydia Maria Child* (1882) and *James and Lucretia Mott: Life and Letters* (1884).

The suggestions of the members of our advisory board were most helpful, and we are grateful for those scholars' support: Nancy Cott, Yale University; Herbert Finch, Cornell University; Andrea Hinding, University of Minnesota; Florence Howe, State University of New York, Old Westbury; Janet Wilson James, Boston College; John Kendall, University of Massachusetts; Linda Kerber, University of Iowa; Walter Merrill, Drexel University; Eva Moseley, Radcliffe College; Mary-Elizabeth Murdock, Smith College; Benjamin Quarles, Morgan State University.

Preface

Lydia Maria Child is of lasting importance for her role in the nineteenth-century struggle for racial equality. Born in 1802, in her outlook Child was one of the most eighteenth-century of the nineteenth-century women reformers, virtually all of whom were younger than she. She confronted a rapidly industrializing society with the values of the earlier Republican age, believing in the natural rights of all people and the wisdom of the "common man." She considered herself one of those common people and remained throughout her life staunchly antiaristocratic. In her view, education and rational persuasion were the means to an egalitarian society.

She became a schoolteacher while in her teens, and, consistent with an eighteenth-century esteem of education, she wrote two educational historical novels using American settings and published a magazine for children that included articles on history and science as well as moral tales. Though interested in the religious movements of the time, especially liberal Christianity and Swedenborgianism, she was essentially a secularist. One of her brothers was the Unitarian minister and scholar Convers Francis: though she shared his interest in Transcendental theories, she never accepted his Unitarian doctrines. Her study of the common ground of the world's religions, *The Progress of Religious Ideas* (New York, 1855), reflected her nonsectarian ideas and was rooted in the tradition of eighteenth-century rationalism.

Although many of the characteristically nineteenth-century concerns intrigued Child, only a few absorbed her, and those that did can be seen as outgrowths of Enlightenment questioning and the egalitarian ethos. Developments in the arts—literature, music, painting, sculpture—and ideas in history and science were of great attraction, as was the movement to abolish slavery and eliminate racism. But industrial development held little interest for her, and her attitude toward the world of finance and capitalism was chiefly one of contempt. Westward expansion did not greatly interest her either, and when the possibility of a move west arose, she was only dismayed. Though attentive to communitarian experiments like Brook Farm, and a friend of many who joined them, she was skeptical about their survival, and a fear of restraint on her individuality kept her from joining.

Her eighteenth-century values were to a great extent responsible for her ambivalence about her role as a woman and an activist. Though she and her husband never had children, she held to the post-Revolutionary ideal of the "Republican mother," the view of woman as the cultivator of those who, with reason and ethical sense, would carry forward the principles of the Republic.[1] She adhered in many ways to eighteenth-century customs of woman's place. She would not speak in public despite considerable evidence that she was eloquent and witty in conversation. She thought the abolitionist Grimké sisters should simply *exercise* their right to speak but not make an issue of it. She was ambivalent about all-women societies: of the many female antislavery groups organized in the 1830s, she commented to Lucretia Mott, "They always seemed to me like half a pair of scissors."[2] And despite the many strains imposed by her own marriage to an intellectually compatible but financially luckless lawyer, she remained committed to the eighteenth-century view of the wife as "help-meet," as long as her freedom to act according to her conscience was not restricted in this role.

It was her insistence on this freedom of conscience that led to her discomfort with the earlier visions of woman. When the idea of the "Republican mother" became influenced by evangelical Christianity in the 1830s and faded into the "moral mother" confined in her "female sphere" of home and—if unmarried—schoolroom, Child resisted. Like a number of the other women in the abolition movement, Child claimed her right to express her views on slavery and organize to end it. She supported the other women who chose to speak in public, and in 1840 she joined Maria Weston Chapman and Lucretia Mott as the first female members on the executive board of the American Anti-Slavery Society. By the 1850s she was supporting women's right to vote. Even though Child stayed on the periphery of the woman's rights movement of the 1860s and 1870s, Elizabeth Cady Stanton and Susan B. Anthony recognized her achievement. In their *History of Woman Suffrage* (1881), published the year after Child died, she was one of the nineteen women to whom they dedicated the volumes, women "whose earnest lives and fearless words, in demanding political rights for women, have been, in the preparation of these pages, a constant inspiration."

The year after William Lloyd Garrison organized the New England Anti-Slavery Society (David Lee Child, her husband, was a founding member), her analysis of slavery, *An Appeal in Favor of that Class of Americans Called Africans* (Boston, 1833), helped bring such notables as William Ellery Channing, Charles Sumner, Thomas Wentworth Higginson, and Wendell Phillips into the movement. Already a popular and critically esteemed author, Child's lucid writing and her public commitment to the cause became major and long-lasting assets to the antislavery movement. She saw it as her task to make factual

[1] For a thorough and thoughtful description of this ideal view of woman, see Linda Kerber's study *Women of the Republic: Intellect and Ideology in Revolutionary America* (Chapel Hill: University of North Carolina Press, 1980).
[2] 5 Mar. 1839; see p. 106.

truth and ethical principles known in a straightforward, vivid way, trusting to the public's ordinary sense of decency to accomplish the needed change. Her views merged well with those of the antislavery movement because in the 1830s the Garrisonians saw their primary task as eliminating racism in the minds of the populace while at the same time aiming for the concrete goal of immediate emancipation. Without a changed public sentiment toward blacks, freedom from slavery would, they felt, be largely meaningless.

Although sharply attacked by the regular press for activity in the radical abolition movement, Child was able to sustain her lifelong career as a professional author. She wrote tales for children, advice books for wives and mothers, biographies of heroic women, accounts of blacks struggling for freedom, reports of the latest works of artists, musicians, and writers, as well as novels, stories, and poetry. For two years she edited a weekly newspaper, the *National Anti-Slavery Standard*.

While her published works—the books and pamphlets she wrote and the journals she edited—are in themselves a fascinating representation of her multifarious efforts to shape American character, it is her letters that are most extraordinary for their reflection of the times. Addressed to both public figures and intimates, they express in vivid, humorous, and eloquent ways an entire range of concerns, from writing books to curing with dandelion tea, from marriage and prostitution to the relations of labor and capital, from abolitionism to spiritualism. Where her prescriptive writings—her advice to women—convey what she thought *ought* to be, her letters reveal how life actually *was*. In *The Frugal Housewife* (Boston, 1829), she explains her ideas on how people ought to manage on a small income and maintain their self-respect, but her letters convey her discouragement with her own poverty and her frustration at the recurrent failures of her husband's enterprises. Her novels suggest what love between men and women should be; her letters describe how difficult those relations really were. On political reforms, her publications are characterized by a calm and measured tone; her letters, if always lucid, are often angry and denunciatory. In sum, her letters are a frank and thoughtful commentary on her times from the point of view of one still trying the experiment of the new republic. As a writer, reformer, journalist, and editor, Child was able to express her strength and extend her freedom to a remarkable degree, given the liabilities of being female in her century. Paradoxically, though Child earned her living largely as an author working at home, within women's "appropriate" sphere, her voice became one of the most well known, distinguished, and respected in nineteenth-century America.

Editorial Method

Child's letters were recognized while she was still alive as documents valuable for their eloquence as well as their content. In 1882, two years after her death, Houghton Mifflin published the *Letters of Lydia Maria Child*, edited anonymously by Child's feminist friend Harriet Sewall. Useful as this edition has been (it contains several letters whose originals are now lost), its editorial practices were far below modern standards, and Sewall evidently did not have access to several collections since located.

Aware of the richness of Child's letters and the inadequacy of the 1882 edition, the present editors in 1977 began a project to locate and publish the two-way correspondence of Lydia Maria Child so that it would be readily available to students and scholars. In 1980 *The Collected Correspondence of Lydia Maria Child, 1817–1880*, was published on microfiche by Kraus Microform of Millwood, New York. Including 2,604 letters, the edition has a guide that contains extensive biographical and bibliographical information as well as an index to the contents of the letters and all correspondents.

Out of that comprehensive collection the editors have chosen the letters most revealing of Child's character and the times in which she lived. No letters to Child are included; few exist, since she regularly burned large batches of received correspondence, and the important passages of those that survive are quoted in notes. Most of the letters chosen comment on social and political concerns; many reflect on books she read, on art, music, and drama. Also included are many letters—though by no means all—describing the Childs' financial straits, her periodic sense of isolation and despair, and her daily household labor, thus bringing forth an aspect of women's lives that is usually hidden. To avoid the tedium of repetition and triviality, the editors have made considerable use of extracts; complete texts are available in the microfiche edition, the exact location described in the note to each letter.

Wherever possible, the text of each letter has been established from the original handwritten document. To convey a text as close to the original as possible and thus allow the reader to read what Child's correspondents would have read, the editors have retained her spelling and occasional misspelling, abbreviations, italicizations, punctuation, and all slips of the pen. The term *sic* is used only when the text is incomprehensible. Perhaps because Child was an experienced and exacting editor, her writing is normally clear and precise; when it is not, the reader can reasonably infer unusual haste or anxiety on Child's part.

The only silent changes made by the editors are the lowering of superscriptions and the inclusion of inserted words into the line of text. Cancelled words or letters are given in angle brackets. Supplied words, letters, and punctuation are in square brackets. Ellipses within square brackets indicate words or letters illegible or torn away; the nature of these gaps is described in notes. Ellipses without square brackets indicate portions of the text omitted by the editors.

The name of Child's correspondent is given in a headnote. Placement of the date is standardized, and dates missing, incomplete, or in error, are supplied or corrected in square brackets. Paragraph indentations are also standardized. Child sometimes indicated a change in subject by leaving a wide space between sentences rather than starting a new paragraph; this extra spacing has been imitated. Postscripts and marginal writings are indented—even if this was not done in the original—and placed according to the editors' best guess about the order in which they were written. Child's page numbers and addresses, if any, are omitted. Also omitted are endorsements or notations by others on the letters; when of special interest, these are described in the notes.

Most of the letters are transcribed from the original document. A note following each letter describes the original text and gives its location. In several instances the source of the text is a transcript of a Child letter made by someone other than Child, probably in preparation of the manuscript for the 1882 edition of her letters. In other instances the source is that 1882 edition itself or a newspaper. In both cases, page numbers in the source are omitted from the citation: letters in the 1882 edition are in chronological order, and the date of the newspaper issue is sufficient. The letter's location in the microfiche edition is given so that readers may consult the complete manuscript text: "microfiche 18/509," for example, means that the letter appears on fiche card 18 and is letter number 509.

Symbols and Abbreviations Used

[ ]	Editorial insertion
[[ ]]	Child's brackets
⟨ ⟩	Words or letters cancelled by Child
ALS	Autograph letter, signed
AL	Autograph letter, the signature omitted or cut off
L	A later copy or printed text of a letter

Footnotes to letters are keyed numerically, beginning with 1 each new letter. Footnotes to headnotes are keyed symbolically, * † ‡.

Chronology

1802   11 February   Birth of Lydia Francis in Medford, Massachusetts.

1814   Death of her mother; she moves to Norridgewock, Maine.

1820   Moves to Gardiner, Maine, to take teaching position.

1822   Moves to Watertown, Massachusetts, to live with brother Convers Francis; adds name *Maria*.

1824   Publishes first novel, *Hobomok*.

1826   Opens girls' school in Watertown; founds and edits *Juvenile Miscellany*.

1828   19 October   Marries David Lee Child, editor of *Massachusetts Whig Journal;* moves to Boston.
        3 December   Whigs defeated in election of Andrew Jackson.

1832   6 January   David becomes founding member of the New England Anti-Slavery Society.

1833   Publishes *An Appeal in Favor of That Class of Americans Called Africans;* begins career as antislavery activist.

1835   Publishes *The History of the Condition of Women, in Various Ages and Nations*.

1837   9–12 May   Delegate to first Anti-Slavery Convention of American Women, New York.

1838   Moves with David to Northampton, Massachusetts, to raise sugar beets.

1839   May   Returns to Boston until April 1840.

1840   Split within American Anti-Slavery Society; appointed to society's executive committee.

1841   May   Moves to New York City to edit *National Anti-Slavery Standard*.

1843   May   Resigns as editor; separates financial affairs from David's.
        Publishes *Letters from New-York, First Series*.

1850   June   Childs move to West Newton, Massachusetts.

1853   December   Childs move to permanent home in Wayland, Massachusetts.

1855   Publishes *The Progress of Religious Ideas Through Successive Ages*.

1856   Kansas-Nebraska Bill passed; works for antislavery settlers in Kansas.

1859   16–18 October   John Brown's raid on Harpers Ferry, Virginia; raises funds for families of John Brown and his men.

1860 Publishes four antislavery pamphlets.
1865 Publishes *The Freedmen's Book*.
1866 Works on letter campaign for freedmen.
1874 17 September   Death of David Lee Child, Wayland.
1880 20 October   Death in Wayland.

1

1817-1832

The letters of the early years of Lydia Maria Child concern her reading, her work as a teacher and author, and—after her marriage—her struggle with poverty. She was fifteen when these letters begin. She was Lydia Francis then, living in Norridgewock, Maine, on the Kennebec River. Her mother had died three years before, and Lydia was staying with an older sister. This sister, Mary Preston (1793–1847), was married to a lawyer, and the household was lively with several small children and visiting neighbors. Abnaki Indians also lived nearby, some of whom Lydia came to know. Her earliest letters are to her older brother and intellectual mentor, Convers Francis (1795–1863), who in 1815 had graduated from Harvard College and gone on to study at Harvard Divinity School.

Lydia Francis had spent her childhood in Medford, Massachusetts, just outside Boston. Born 2 February 1802, she was the youngest of the five children of David Convers Francis (1766–1856) and Susannah (Rand) Francis (1766–1814). Her father was a prosperous baker whose products were distributed in America and Europe. Despite his success, the family had no aristocratic pretensions. Lydia attended a local dame school rather than an academy, and of her two brothers, one became a farmer and the other—Convers—was the first in the family to go to college.

Although Lydia Francis would later write the popular sentimental verse about Thanksgiving Day, "Over the river and through the wood to grandfather's house we go," she felt no nostalgia for her own early years. At the age of forty-five, she wrote Lucy Osgood, a lifelong resident of Medford. "You ask what would I give to have been with you on your pilgrimage to my old homestead," she said. "Alas, my friend, I would have given a good deal to have been spared the pain. Cold, shaded, and uncongenial was my childhood and youth. Whenever reminiscences of them rise up before me, I turn my back on them as quickly as possible."* She never hints at the nature of her unhappiness. The letters of her later youth reveal no sorrow but only a lively independence of mind and an occasionally teasing manner toward her serious brother.

* 26 Mar. 1847, Lydia Maria Child Papers, Anti-Slavery Collection, Cornell University.

To Convers Francis

Norridgewock, September, 1817.

I perceive that I never shall convert you to my opinions concerning Milton's treatment to our sex.

Whether the ideas I have formed of that author be erroneous or not, they are entirely my own. I knew Johnson was a violent opponent to Milton, both in political and religious concerns; but I had never seen, or heard, of any of his remarks upon his poetical productions. Much as I admire Milton, I must confess that Homer is a much greater favorite with me. "Paradise Lost" is unquestionably the sublimest effort of human genius. It fixes us in a state of astonishment and wonder; but it is not characterized by that impetuosity and animation which, I think, gives to poetry its greatest charm.

L, extract; *Letters of Lydia Maria Child*, 1882 (microfiche 1/2).

To Convers Francis

Winslow [Maine], March 12, 1820.

I can't talk about books, nor anything else, until I tell you the good news; that I leave Norridgewock, and take a school in Gardiner, as soon as the travelling is tolerable. When I go to Gardiner, remember to write often, for " 'tis woman alone who truly feels what it is to be a stranger." Did you know that last month I entered my nineteenth year?

I hope, my dear brother, that you feel as happy as I do. Not that I have formed any high-flown expectations. All I expect is, that, if I am industrious and prudent I shall be *independent*. . . .

L, extract; *Letters of Lydia Maria Child*, 1882 (microfiche 1/7).

To Convers Francis

Gardiner [Maine], May 31, 1820.

You need not fear my becoming a Swedenborgian. I am in more danger of wrecking on the rocks of skepticism than of stranding on the shoals of fanaticism. I am apt to regard a system of religion as I do any other beautiful theory. It plays round the imagination, but fails to reach the heart. I wish I could find some religion in which my heart and understanding could unite; that amidst the darkest clouds of this life I might ever be cheered with the mild halo of religious consolation. . . .

L, extract; *Letters of Lydia Maria Child*, 1882 (microfiche 1/9).

Late in 1821 or early 1822, nineteen-year-old Lydia Francis moved from Maine back to Massachusetts to live with her brother Convers, by then the minister of the Unitarian Church in Watertown, near Boston. The social life was active there, and she met many of the young intellectuals who were her brother's friends. Ralph Waldo Emerson and Theodore Parker were among those to discuss ideological controversies in the Francis house.

Still in search of a religion, she decided to be baptized in her brother's church and gave herself a new name. The name *Lydia*, she later vaguely explained, was unpleasant for some childhood associations (see her letter of 27 May 1866), and she added on *Maria*. She was *Maria* from then on, with *Lydia* generally reduced to an initial in her signature. The Unitarian faith was less to her liking than her new name, however, and the search for a religion went on.

She became a writer at this time, publishing her first novel—*Hobomok, a Tale of Early Times*—in 1824, when she was twenty-two. The story was set in seventeenth-century Massachusetts and told of a white woman who marries a Pequod Indian, Hobomok, and has their child; in the end, her banished Church of England lover returns, and Hobomok walks off into the forest, relinquishing her. The theme was a plea for racial and religious tolerance. She wrote the novel in six weeks, according to later account, after she had read an article in the April 1821 *North American Review* calling for the use of local historical events and characters in American fiction. John Gorham Palfrey's article was a review of a narrative poem, *Yamoyden*, by James W. Eastburn, about a Nipnet married to a white woman. In that story, the couple and their child survive the white men's attacks during King Philip's War and remain together at the end.

Like most writers in the 1820s in New England, Maria Francis published and distributed the book at her own expense. The *North American Review* of July 1824 found the plot in poor taste because of the interracial marriage and birth, and sales at first were low. She went on to publish a book for children, *Evenings in New England*, also in 1824, but the following two letters to George Ticknor reveal the difficulties of being an entrepreneur. Ticknor (1791–1871), professor of modern languages at Harvard, was an influential figure in the literary world. His angry opposition to abolitionism later ended his connection with Child.

To George Ticknor

                                         Watertown. March 29'th, 1825.
   Sir,
   With trembling diffidence, which I in vain struggle to subdue, I venture to address this letter to you; and with all my confidence in the generosity and refinement of your character, I cannot feel assured that you will forgive the presumption. A simple statement of facts must form my excuse.   A few weeks since, I heard from Mrs. Curtis the flattering observations you made concerning

"Hobomok,"—and no one who has been accustomed to the broad blaze of encouragement and patronage, can form the faintest idea of the impulse it gave to my mind.[1] There is nothing in life like the beatings of pure, youthful ambition,—of a soul excited by praise and expanding over its own glorious visions. To have been praised by such a man was sufficient to urge me on to mightier efforts; and, under the influence of this inspiration, I had already commenced a new work, when a letter from my publisher informed me that the sale of Hobomok had left me considerably in debt. 1000 were printed, and only half sold. It is not wonderful surely, that the energy and enthusiasm of youth should be checked by such news, and that the volume commenced with so much eagerness should be committed to the flames. I felt as if my rashness had been too severely punished, and that something must be done to give a new currency to the unfortunate book. But my brother could not with propriety take active measures in my behalf, and I was too sensitive to apply to any of my acquaintance. There are but few to whom we can make a frank avowal of disappointed hope, of a heart chilled and a mind prostrated by discouragement. To make such a disclosure to most men, would be like scattering the fragrance of the violet in the path of the hurricane. I will not use language, which, however sincere, your modesty might construe into idle flattery—suffice it to say, that all my associations with you[r] name are such as induce me to apply to you.

You may ask, what do you wish, or expect me to do? I answer, your influence in the literary and fashionable world is very great, and a few words timely spoken by you would effect more than my utmost exertions. Your judgment would have much weight with those whose taste is law, and your notice would induce many to purchase, who would otherwise regard the subject with a very natural indifference. This sort of influence is all that I wish, and more than I expect. Indeed my vanity would hardly have formed such a *wish*, had you not voluntarily praised my trifling production. I am aware that it is almost unpardonable to obtrude myself upon you, amid all the cares that unavoidably wait upon a station like yours; but I am certain it will afford you some pleasure to revive the hopes of a young and disappointed author.   Regard for my brother's feelings has induced me to keep him in ignorance of this presumptuous action; and from the same motives I have been silent before my old friend Mrs. Curtis.   Trusting you will at least pardon me, I am

Very Respectfully,
L. Maria Francis.

ALS; George Ticknor Autograph Collection, Dartmouth College (microfiche 1/11).

---

[1] Lois (Robbins) Curtis (d. 1866) was a widow whose husband had been George Ticknor's half-brother.

To George Ticknor

Watertown. March 31'st. 1825.

I cannot tell you, indeed I cannot, Professor Ticknor, how much I thank you for your prompt and kind attention; but I feel somewhat distressed lest you should mistake the *nature* of my application to you. My affectionate brother, ever active for my interest, will do all that he can do—I have only hoped for that sort of influence from you which it would be improper for him to exert. To bring the book into notice,—to resuscitate its mushroom existence, is *all* I have wished from you. However, I send you the statement you requested, with no other fear than that your ready kindness will induce you to devote too much time and attention to my affairs.

Cummings Hilliard & Co. are my publishers,—and Mr. Carter is the only one with whom I have transacted any business. 1000 copies were printed, to be sold at 75 cts., which would have amounted to 750 dollars. Printing, paper, and binding 245$; commission &c. 250, making all expences about 500$. A few more than half the edition are sold, which, allowing for the deduction of misprinted volumes, leaves 98$ against me.

With mingled feelings of gratitude, embarrassment and confidence,

I am, with great respect,
L. Maria Francis.

ALS; George Ticknor Autograph Collection, Dartmouth College (microfiche 1/12).

In July 1825, the *North American Review* carried a favorable notice of *Hobomok,* and Maria Francis thereupon asked Ticknor if she might dedicate her next novel, *The Rebels,* to him.

At this time, she met David Lee Child, whom she married in 1828. Born 8 July 1794, he was the son of a farmer in West Boylston, Massachusetts. A graduate of Harvard College in 1817, he taught at the Boston Latin School from 1817 to 1822 and then became secretary to the American legation in Portugal. He fought in a liberal uprising there and then returned from Portugal in 1824 to study law with an uncle in Watertown, where he and Maria Francis met for the first time. She recorded her impressions in her diary:

Dec. 2, 1824. Mr. Child dined with us at Watertown. He possesses the rich fund of an intelligent traveller, without the slightest twinge of a traveller's vanity. Spoke of the tardy improvement of the useful arts in Spain and Italy. They still use the plough described by Virgil. . . .

Jan 26 [1825]. Saw Mr Child at Mrs Curtis's. He is the most gallant man that has lived since the sixteenth century; and needs nothing but helmet, shield, and chain armour to make him a complete knight of chivalry. . . .

5

May 3d One among the many delightful evenings spent with Mr. Child. I do not know which to admire most the vigour of his understanding, or the ready sparkle of his wit. Talked of the political position of England—said war was necessary to her existence. Spoke of the tendency to decline which marks all institutions, particularly republican. Laughed as he mentioned the tremendous *squirearchy* of America.

In May 1825 David noted in his diary "the ethereal, high-souled, high-reaching Maria! the elegant, pure, powerful-minded Maria! . . . I know of no mind with which it seems to me, my soul could hold such sweet converse as with the elegant, susceptible, correct, & brilliant spirit which animates the pleasing beautiful form of [Maria]. . . . She is the only lady in W[atertown], who has made any impression upon me of a serious & enduring kind, i e to say of *a tender kind*." *

As the following letters to her sister in Maine show, Maria Francis visited often in Boston, where Child had moved to begin his law practice, while she was teaching school in Watertown. In the fall of 1826 she began publishing her bimonthly magazine for children. The *Juvenile Miscellany*, which was the first periodical for children in the United States, contained educational articles as well as poems and stories, many of which she wrote herself. The magazine was popular and financially rewarding; she went on publishing it for eight years.

To Mary Preston

Chestnut St. June 11'th—1826—

Dear Sister,
    What with the crowding occupations of pleasure and of duty, I think I have a right to expect two letters for one, from you, this winter,—though you are the mother of "a numerous offspring, lovely like yourself," and I a poor, isolated spinster.   I have a million things, which I wish to say to you, every day,—but I cannot put them in a letter— They are too personal, would betray too many secrets—&c—By the gentleman who will bring this, I hope to send my portrait—1 I have had much trouble to get it on board some vessel, with a trusty captain,—but have not yet succeeded. I should have sent it by Mr. Sawtell, had not Abbá insisted upon seeing it, before it went,—and her *gentle* wrath is

---

* Unpublished memoir of David Lee Child by L. Maria Child, 1 July 1875, incorporating extracts from their diaries in the original hands, Lydia Maria Child Papers, Anti-Slavery Collection, Cornell University Library.
1 Francis Alexander (1800–80), portrait painter and lithographer, had recently painted Maria Francis's portrait, and the two became friends. He married in 1831 and continued working in Boston until 1853, when he retired to Florence, Italy. The painting now hangs, poorly restored, in the Medford (Mass.) Historical Society.

usually of long duration.[2] I hope you will like the picture. If it has any fault, it is because the artist has *too much* genius— He wanted to make a Sappho of me, and to pour over my very ugly face the full tide of inspiration. Do not openly find fault, if you *are* disappointed.—It might reach his ears,—and he has all the susceptibility of genius. Do not smile! he is young, unmarried,—and my *especial* friend. If you catch any look of mine, I am sure it will be valuable to you,—for the slightest glance of yours would be so to me. How I wish Mr. Alexander could take a likeness of you and your husband—All heads of families should leave behind them inanimate, as well as living likenesses. . . .

You know, I suppose, that I am going to take a large school in Watertown, almost the very day that I leave Boston? I do not like it, very much; but this winter's campaign has cost me a good deal, and I must earn something immediately. I should like it better if I could board any where but at brother's. Relations never ought to live together, unless they keep debt and credit, like strangers; and to tell the truth, Abbá with all her apparent gentleness, is not always comfortable to get along with. She is jealous of every compliment paid to my talents, of every attention I receive, even from my brother—However, all this is between ourselves. I have been attending to French and drawing, with the view of fitting myself for a large and genteel, and perman[en]t school. As I shall probably never marry, this is peculiarly desirable to me. Oh, how I wish *that* a *first rate one* could be established at Hallowell under the patronage of Sprague, and Mann, &c.[3] I do not know of a place I would sooner choose, in the whole United States, for a constant residence, than that town. However, I should be afraid to give up a profitable certainty at Watertown, for an honourable uncertainty there.   I mentioned to Abba, about the caps—She has not opened her heart very wide, I think; but they may be useful to you. I wish very much that I had time to work you some; but at present, it is a sheer impossibility.   Father has not been so happy this many a long year as he is now— I do hope it will last.

I was much delighted yesterday with visits and presents from my Portsmouth friends, accompanied with an earnest request to visit them. I supposed they had all forgotten me years ago. Oh, the world is too good to me, by half. I have had a good many trifling presents this winter—Books, rings, pictures, trinkets, and an elegant India comb, 11$— But you must not think, dear sister, that I have not had vexations and afflictions. Just in proportion to my conspicuousness, I have had enemies, as well as friends,—and I have deserved them both. Oh, how often I have wanted you to fly to, for advice and assistance. If people knew half the extent of my vehement, and impetuous temperament,

---

[2] Mr. Sawtell was probably Cullen Sawtell (1805-87) from Norridgewock, Maine, who later became a congressional representative. Abby Bradford (Allyn) Francis (1796–1860) had married Convers Francis in 1822.

[3] Sprague is unidentified; Mann may be Horace Mann (1796–1859), the well-known educator, then living in Boston.

they would give me credit for governing myself as well as I do. "What's *done*, we partly may compute, but know not what's *resisted*."

. . .

ALS; Walter G. Perry Collection, Westfield, N.J. (microfiche 1/18).

To Mary Preston

Watertown January 6'th 1827—

My dear Mary,

A happy new year to you and yours! As prosperous and delightful as you deserve, and that is saying enough, in all conscience. The New Year here was ushered by a dolorous day—Cold and stormy and every way unpleasant. I was cross when I first waked, and continued so till night. And yet no young lady in Christendom can look back upon a year of pleasanter reminiscences. Friends kind, generous, and attentive, where I least expected it—Fortune smiling beyond my utmost hopes. Only think, the subscription for my Miscellany[1] stands now at 850 names, and is every day increasing. The rich and fashionable people, who I thought would consign me to oblivion as soon as I left Boston, and the first novelty had worn off,—continue as attentive as if I were their equal. I sometimes ask myself can I be the same individual I was in Dorchester, two years ago? Can it be that I am on terms of intimacy—nay that I even regard with contempt some of these great people, who used to frighten me at a distance? I cannot be sufficiently grateful to a kind Providence for the mercies wherewith he has loaded me.   I do not mean by this, that I have not causes of uneasiness. Few get along in this life without meeting with tempers they can neither please, nor manage,—but those are only spots on the sun—shadows, which flit across the sunshine of every-body's path, and which ought not to depress my spirits so much as they sometimes do. My hand begins to grow stiff; for I am writing in my school-room, and it is terribly cold.   It is a good many weeks since I have heard from you. I was told I had a letter somewhere in Boston, from Maine; but I have not obtained it yet. I do wish you could find it in your heart to write oftener. I know you have many cares—So have I—though of a different kind—Six hours of the day I am in my school—and the remainder of the time I have to write for the Miscellany, to receive and answer all the numerous letters connected with it, to write for various other publications, see company—and do my sewing. . . .

Have you seen any No—of the Miscellany—and how do you like it? Tell N. Deering that children's books are more profitable than any others, and that I am American enough to prefer money to fame—Especially as I having [*sic*] reasonable prospect of being always single.[2]

[1] *Juvenile Miscellany.*
[2] Nathaniel Deering (1791–1881) was an editor and dramatist in Maine.

Give my best love to Warren and the children—I want to see their little shining heads very much. I sometimes think I will start right off on a visit to Maine; but a thousand inconveniences start up,—and I doubt whether the Kennebec will ever look me in the face again; however I will *hope* otherwise. Good Night—

Yours Affectionately
Maria—

N.B. Bro. C. and Abbá are well—She is not as she wishes to be; and oh, strange perversity of fate, Mrs. Bigelow is as she does not wish to be.

ALS; Walter G. Perry Collection, Westfield, N.J. (microfiche 1/23).

Maria Francis and David Lee Child became engaged ten months later. David described Maria to his mother as "one who possesses the intellect of Johnson, the goodness & learning of Lady Jane Gray; & the gentleness & attraction of Aspasia."* David, who was practicing law in Boston and serving as a state legislator, was also editor of the *Massachusetts Whig Journal,* a thrice-weekly and later daily political paper founded by John Quincy Adams and Daniel Webster in 1826.

To Mary Preston

Boston—Oct—28'th 1827—

Dear Sister,

I blush that I should have been absolutely engaged more than a week without having found a moment to tell you of the important news. Mr. Child's extreme devotion, and my own excess of happiness, must form my excuse for this negligence.   Indeed, dear sister, I am happy,—happy, *beyond my own imagination,*—and that is saying much.   The how, and the why, and the when, and the wherefore, I cannot tell you by letter. Suffice it to say that on Friday, the 18 of October, 1827 I received an epistle from D. L. Child Esq,—and that on the same day an answer was returned, which sealed my fate—A fate which every hour's acquaintance with Mr. C. leads me more and more to think will be a happy one. May Providence, in his mercy, help me to deserve so rich a blessing.   Since an explanation has taken place, I find that mutual interest has long existed between us and that we have both been playing hide and go seek, for various idle reasons; but it is all ended, now,—and I am happier than ever any woman was in reciprocated affection.   I was surprised and pleased

* David Lee Child to Lydia (Bigelow) Child, 20 Oct. 1827, typed transcript, Simison Papers, Beinecke Rare Book and Manuscript Library, Yale University.

to see Mrs. F. Swan, here—Have you seen her since her return? Abba's little babe grows large and beautiful. She has plenty of milk for it,—and I am in hopes all will go on well, so far as that is concerned.

I have removed into Boston,—and shall board at my old French boarding house during the winter. Mr. C. boards a few houses further down the street.

I received much attention in Cambridge, and left it with regret. I am hardly settled here yet,—and late events have taken up my attention so much, that I am dreadfully hurried in writing. Give my love to Warren and the children. I am, in prodigious haste,

Your Affectionate Sister,
Maria—

ALS; Walter G. Perry Collection, Westfield, N.J. (microfiche 1/25).

Maria Francis probably wrote the following letter in 1827, when Margaret Fuller (1810–50) was seventeen and living at home in Cambridge. Fuller was already an enthusiastic intellectual; the two had made plans to study Madame de Staël's ideas on empiricist John Locke. Maria Francis here refers to a review article by William Ellery Channing (1780–1842), the eminent Unitarian, in the *Christian Examiner* (July–August 1827), in which he describes Napoleon as ruthless and without moral feeling.

To Margaret Fuller

[After October 1827?]

Dearest Margaret,

I received your very characteristic note with great pleasure. Like you, it was full of thought, raciness, originality, and queerness; and like you it excited the pleasantest emotions in my heart. I am far from mourning over our separation as one of the disappointments of this delusive world; for I have strong hopes that we shall have many and pleasant years of acquaintance yet. I shall never be a woman of leisure,—because my own character is opposed to rest; but I hope to be *more settled* than I now am some time or other. "And how settled?" you will ask—"With all your time, wishes, and thoughts, at the disposal of another, how are your friends to have any good of you"?

My dear Margaret, the passion of love is very exclusive in a woman's heart, I acknowledge—It *ought* to be so,—nay, if it exist at all, it *must* be so;—but do you suppose all other avenues of kindly feeling are shut up? Oh, I assure thee no! "I do not love Ceasar less,—but I love Rome more."   The rain, which broke bridges, and brought the frost out of the ground is answerable for my brother's disappointment,—not my own selfishness, as you insinuate. The stage in which we were, instead of passing through W. at 8 o'clock in the eve, passed at 4 o'clock on Sabbath morning. Now prove Cupid guilty of treason against "natural affection," if you can! And yet—but, I won't confess. I shall avail myself of your kind invitation at no distant day; and so strange a thing *may* happen as for me to keep my promise concerning a week's visit.

How do you like Doct. Channing's Review? if you are not tired of being asked—   Eloquent I certainly think some passages; but I am not prepared to give it the unqualified praise, which many bestow. Neither do I think its spirit sufficiently impartial. I like his high *theory* exceedingly; but is there no injustice in comparing Bonaparte with a certain abstract, ideal excellence, rather than with any of his species?   If the credit of Bonaparte's bridges and codes of law belong entirely to architects and civilians, may not the same thing be said of every emperor under heaven? If the Ithuriel touch of Napolean's energetic genius wakened a whole mass of slumbering talent into life, what more, in the name of all that is candid, do we need to prove his intellectual might?[1]

Do you think the style, beautiful as it is, sufficiently condensed? I think there is great repetition of ideas. He seems to move round and round in a ring.   How dare I talk thus of a man I venerate like Doct. C—when, too, I am not an unqualified admirer of Bonaparte?

I have no room to say more than that I am always glad to see you. Respects to your charming mother.

Your Affectionate
Maria.

ALS; Simison Papers, Beinecke Rare Book and Manuscript Library, Yale University (microfiche 1/33).

Maria Francis and David Lee Child were married on 19 October 1828. The couple quickly found themselves in unfamiliar financial difficulties. Subscriptions to the *Massachusetts Whig Journal*, David's newspaper, dropped off after the Whig defeat in the 1828 election of Andrew Jackson. As editor, David had publicly accused John Keyes, a state senator and chairman of the committee of accounts, of handing over a state printing contract to a Jacksonian press before opening the sealed bids. Keyes accused him of libel, David was indicted, and on 16 January 1829 he was convicted—two days after the following letter. He promptly appealed.

To raise money for the newspaper, Maria wrote letters on David's behalf, used up savings, and borrowed money from her father. She also tried to earn as much as she could from her writing, and found her success with a new audience of female readers. Most New England women were literate by then (records suggest that only half the female population was literate fifty years before), and

---

[1] In *Paradise Lost* (4.810–19), the angel Ithuriel touches Satan with a spear, startling him—in Milton's image—like a spark suddenly igniting gunpowder.

there was a new emphasis on the importance of women in shaping the republic's citizenry. As urban populations grew rapidly and husbands found work outside the household, wives began to carry greater responsibility for the home and children. Women were deemed crucial in running households that would not bankrupt their husbands and in raising intelligent, responsible children. Child capitalized on a market for writing that would help women in their tasks.

Her books for children and her magazine, *Juvenile Miscellany*, were in a sense educational aids for mothers. In 1829 Child published her immensely popular book *The Frugal Housewife*, aimed specifically at women who were not wealthy and not "ashamed of economy." She included recipes for inexpensive dishes; advice on restoring and cleaning carpets, drying feathers, cleaning mattresses, making shampoo, and preparing herbal medicines; and a chapter titled "How to Endure Poverty." She wrote from her own experience. She followed up this book with one of advice to mothers and another for young girls, and in 1832 she began issuing the *Ladies' Family Library*. Its first three volumes contained historical accounts of women, both famous and obscure, noted for their devotion to their husbands and to political or religious principles. In volumes four and five, she wrote a history of women throughout the world up to the present time.

Lydia Bigelow Child (1807–78) was David's sister; she lived all her life at the home of their parents, Zachariah (1763–1845) and Lydia (Bigelow) Child (1764–1849), in West Boylston, Massachusetts.

To Lydia B. Child

Wednesday—Jan 14th [1829]

My dear Lydia,

I was much gratified by your kind letter,—for I began to think the folks at home did not care anything about us. The lots of good things father brought down were very acceptable to us. I never tasted anything sweeter and nicer than the pork. Tell mother I believe I have put up every bag and string she sent down. The brown bread was all the better for being made by her hands,—and I was much gratified by the thoughtful attention.

I have found out that your brother is fond of it,—and we bake a loaf every week. John is boarding with us a few weeks now.[1] It is a great comfort to me to have him here. I never saw anybody so kind and obliging. Your brother's libel suit (or rather one of them) came on last Monday. It is not yet decided. I expect to know, when he comes home to supper tonight. I believe he would die, if he had not John to help him. You don't know how irregular we are obliged to live—half the time he does not eat a mouthful from breakfast time

[1] John Child (1802–58), David's brother, graduated from West Point in 1827, served with the Army Corps of Engineers in 1835, and later worked in the railroad industry. He added a final *e* to his name later in life.

till nine o'clock at night. You know he has a *Daily* paper now. Your brother wanted to make his mother a new year's present,—and since she mentioned the tea-pot, he told me to buy one for her. I hope it will suit you. You must be careful about putting it where the balls will melt off.

Your cap is very beautiful! I was in hopes to be able to send you some recompense by your father; but I never was so short of money since I can remember,—and I do not like to ask your brother, because I am likely to have a little store of my own from the Savings bank, in a few days. I am going to try to sell one of the caps,—and if I can get a good price you shall have the proceeds; but the market is so full of such things that I can't tell what chance there will be. The caps look too handsome for me,—I find myself looking more carefully to personal economy than I did before I was married.

I have picked up all the books I can find, which I think will prove interesting to you; but we don't seem to have many now.

I am glad Lucretia is coming down,—though I am afraid she will not find me very good company,—I have so much writing and copying to do.[2] Many and many a time, when I have been sitting here alone a whole evening, I have wished she was living with us. This is sincere—though I have sometimes been afraid you would think I did not wish her to come. I have not spoken, because I felt a little embarrassed on the subject,—but the plain truth often saves heart-burnings among relations. The fact is, I mentioned the subject to your brother, when I was first engaged to him; and he entered warmly into it,—you know it is in his nature to be generous and kind. Afterward, disappointment in several places where he had vested money, some debts on his hands, and three libel-suits coming one after another, (and even if he gains his case with Keyes, it must cost him over three hundred dollars) made us both question whether it were not best to put off our marriage. At one time we concluded to do so—but I had purchased a good deal of my furniture,—we should both be obliged to board out,—and we did not feel happy about it. I am in the receipt of 300 a year for the Miscellany, and we concluded that this sum added to what your brother had yearly expended while a batchelor, would support us, if we were economical—and so we married—and I do not believe we shall repent it.

I have tried to be as saving as possible—I certainly have denied myself every superfluity. I have dropped *all* my acquaintance. I neither visit, nor receive visits. We never ride—never go to the theatre, or any place of public amusement. It seems queer to me,—I used to go about so much; but after all, I am happier than I ever was.   To return to Lucretia—your brother tried to get a school for her; but Boston folks have taken the idea that nobody can teach a school so well as a gentleman, and so many girls of the first rate education are willing to teach, that it seems impossible to get a school here.

Then it was a question whether Lucretia had better stay with us without

2 Lucretia Child (1804-48) was David's sister; she married Robert Webster Haskins (1804-81) in 1833 and had three children.

any employment; and your brother said honestly he could not afford it; that if for a year or two we could get along with very little expense, he hoped then to feel a free and unembarrassed man. I need not say you must not think him selfish,—for you know his natural disposition is as open as the day. He is doing very well—people who would not flatter me, assure me his paper is thought the best in New England. His subscribers constantly increase, and they are highly respectable men. So you must not think we have rushed thoughtlessly into matrimony and ruin. The only object is, to be saving for a time, lest the pressure of too many untoward circumstances meeting together should destroy prospects otherwise flattering. I have spoken freely—and the communication must be kept a secret between your mother, yourselves, and John. Best love to Mother & Lucretia. I shall write again soon, by John.

Your[s] affectionately, L. Maria.

ALS; Child Letters, MC 305, Schlesinger Library, Radcliffe College (microfiche 1/35).

Carey and Lea, the prosperous Philadelphia publishing house, issued an annual gift book, *The Atlantic Souvenir,* which from 1827 to 1829 included Child's stories and poems. They did not, however, publish her works in book form, as she suggests in the following letter. In 1831 she issued such a collection, *The Coronal,* through the Boston firm of Carter and Hendee.

To Carey and Lea

[Before 25 July 1829?]

Messrs. Carey & Lea,

The gentlemanly and generous manner, in which you have always transacted business with me, leads me to apply to you with something of the confidence of friendship; for I am sure your advice will be disinterested.   Since I first began to write I have written a great number of stories, essays, &c. for various publications. Better writers than myself have set me the example of collecting these into a volume. I have always disliked such a step during an author's life-time; but the heavy pressure of these discouraging times, leads me to think of it as a source of some profit. Will you tell me candidly if you think I can make anything? And if so, on what terms you will publish it? Which would be most for my interest to sell the copy-right, or take so much on each volume? I should think I had as many as forty stories &c.; but I should only take what

I thought the best. I should think a volume about the size of the "Rebels" might be made. Do not advise me to it unless you think I can make *something*.

I am very Respectfully,
L. M. Child.

ALS; Simon Gratz Collection, Historical Society of Pennsylvania (microfiche 1/38).

To George Ticknor

[1829?]

Mr. Ticknor,

Writing this letter is the most painful task I ever imposed upon myself. It is so for various reasons; but it is peculiarly so, from my extreme reluctance to trouble you with my wretchedness. But the fact is, I have been in a state little short of insanity, for the last fortnight; and this must be my excuse for pouring out my heart where it is *safe* to do so.   Owing to the temporary pressure of circumstances, my husband is very much involved, and must speedily be ruined, unless five thousand dollars can be raised to assist him. Mr. Crowninshield, Doctor Barstowe, Mr. H. G. Otis, and Mr. Israel Thorndike jr. have all consented to advance money—but they wait—and wait—and want to see how much each is willing to do; and the misery is, my husband cannot stand it a fortnight longer.[1] The necessity of appearing cheerful before him, produces such a reaction when I am alone, that I can neither eat, nor sleep. There is no mental suffering equal to the hourly dread of losing all the little, one has earned by years of hard exertion. I have tried to think what *I* could possibly do. But the curse of poverty is upon me; and it will be long before my exertions could raise half the small sum, which would save us. Would you be willing to advance one thousand dollars on my furniture and books? For my furniture I gave eleven hundred dollars last October; and our books are probably worth two hundred, or more.   I would not make this request to save myself, if I thought there was danger of your losing by it. Indeed if I have my health, you shall not lose, if I pay it by ten dollar instalments.

After a careful and cool investigation of the state of affairs, I am convinced Mr. Child is right in thinking his paper will be valuable property by and bye, if we can but weather this stormy cape. Whereas if we are obliged to give it up now, it will do nobody good, and my husband will be paid for three years prodigiously hard labour by bringing his best friends into debt. I know you take little interest in political affairs; and I likewise know a man is himself

[1] Benjamin W. Crowninshield (1772–1851), Gideon Barstow (1783–1852), Harrison Gray Otis (1765–1848), and Israel Thorndike, Jr., were all prosperous Whigs in the Boston area. Daniel Webster, one of the paper's founders, had in January 1829 dropped his support.

answerable for the risks he chooses to run; but again I repeat the paper is every month becoming more valuable; and there is a fair and reasonable prospect of its paying those who will assist us now. If five gentlemen could be found, who would advance one thousand a piece, and that speedily, it would be worth twenty thousand to us; because the very means of doing anything by our own exertions depends on present help.

If living on bread and water would prevent the necessity of such application, I would do it cheerfully: but Mr. Child's unwearied exertions, and my own rigid economy will avail us nothing now, unless somebody will assist us through present trouble.

A variety of causes have produced this embarrassment. The extreme anxiety of the Jackson men to put down the paper; the annoying tricks they have resorted to; the alarm of creditors occasioned by their busy report that Mr. C. must fail; and the loss of two or three hundred subscribers at the first news of the election,—some from disgust of politics,—some from vexation at being deceived in their expectations,—and some from a foresight of the pecuniary trouble likely to result to themselves from political defeat.

Those that fell off, fell off *suddenly;* but the increase of subscribers is steadily progressive.

However, I am sure all the property we possess in the world (excepting the Journal establishment) will make your thousand dollars safe. I will put *every thing* into your hands, if you will unite with Mr. Thorndike, Otis &c in this thing. Your assistance will do no good without theirs; for unless *all* can be done, a *part* is of no use. I know not but I may express myself too earnestly; but I am sick with anxiety,—and feel as if a whole life of gratitude would not be enough toward those who should assist us.

I have written this letter without the knowledge of my husband; merely because I wished to conceal from him how much I am distressed. You will not of course mention the letter, excepting to those who already know the circumstances.

My most respectful affection to Mrs. Ticknor. If you are kind enough to answer this, please send it to the Massachusetts Journal Office Congress St.

Very Respectfully,
L. M. Childe.[2]

ALS; George Ticknor Autograph Collection, Dartmouth College (microfiche 2/41).

To Lydia B. Child

[February? 1830]

Dear Lydia,

I have not neglected to write to you because I did not think of you affectionately; but because I have not had spirits to do anything. I have kept think-

---

[2] This spelling of her name with an *e* occurs nowhere else in her letters or publications. Whether Ticknor made the loan or not is unknown.

ing the darkest time had come, and that the clouds must break away; but still a darker one would come. I have been in good health—blessed by Providence we have both been in extremely good health; and have no prospect of having anybody but ourselves to take care of.   I have had serious thoughts of taking a school; and perhaps I shall do so. But it is uncertain whether I could get one large enough to be profitable, under two or three years—schools are so very numerous here—and if my poor brain will but hold out to meet the demands of booksellers from various parts of the Union, I can do better than I can with a common-sized school.   If it be possible to dispose of our lease, I have come to the determination to dispose of part of my furniture, and board out. It will be cheaper, and we shall not be subject to so many unpleasant things—But I do hate to give up *home*.

I have had two boarders all winter; and I now have one, who is likewise a scholar. This has taken up my time very much. I long for Spring to come, that I may clear up; for the house is all dirt.   If Lucretia will come, I will try to make it as pleasant as I can for ⟨you⟩ her. I should love to have her come; though I am afraid she would not have much to enjoy—I wish I had something good and pretty to send you—I should send the Frugal Housewife; but it is entirely out of print; and the 2d edition will not be out for some days. I shall send it soon.

Your brother was delighted with your pretty purse; and the kind little note in it—He kissed it with much fervor. Love to Lucretia—Poor girl! She has had a hard winter of it. I wish my means were equal to my will.

Yours most affectionately
Maria.

Remember me with much kindness to Susan, when you write—

ALS; Child Letters, MC 305, Schlesinger Library, Radcliffe College (microfiche 2/42).

In March 1830 David Lee Child went to prison. His appeal of the Keyes libel conviction had been unsuccessful. How long a sentence he served is not known, but the next letter shows him to have been at home in August. In October 1832 the state supreme court found that the original indictment could not be sustained.

While he was in prison, Maria lived with a friend, Emily Marshall, and took over editing the *Massachusetts Whig Journal*. By 1831, however, the *Journal* had folded. Child wrote to her mother-in-law on 23 June 1831: "I do wish I could be a mother. . . . Sometimes I get a little fidgetty, because I want to go to housekeeping so much,—and it is such a long, long way out of the woods yet."[*] The Childs never did have children—none of her letters reveal any sign of pregnancy—and the financial troubles lasted until the 1860s.

* Child Letters, MC 305, Schlesinger Library, Radcliffe College.

———

To David Lee Child

Phillips's Beach. Orient St. August 8 [1830]
Sunday Evening.
Dearest Husband,

Here I am in a snug little old fashioned parlour, at a round table, in a rocking chair writing to you; and the greatest comfort I have is the pen-knife *you* sharpened for me just before I came away—As you tell *me* sometimes (I don't believe you, though) it makes my heart leap to see anything which you have touched. The house here is real old-fashioned, neat, comfortable, rural, and quiet. There is a homespun striped carpet, very much like the one at West Boylston,—two profiles over the mantelpiece, one of them a soldier placed in the frame rather one-sided, with a white shirt-ruffle, a white plume, and a white epaulette;—a vase of flowers done in⟨to⟩ water colours, looking considerable sickly, and straggling about as if they were only neighbours in law;—and Ophelia with a quantity of carroty hair, which must have cost oceans of bear's grease,—(which hair is thrown over three or four rheumatic trees,—) and one foot ankle deep in water, as if she were going to see which she liked best, hanging, or drowning. These with an old fashioned table and desk form a schedule of the furniture. The old lady is just like your good mother—just such honest shoulders—just such motions, a face very much like her,—and precisely the same kind, motherly ways—I am sure you would be struck with the resemblance. I like the whole family extremely. They are among the best specimens of N. England farmers—as simple and as kind as little children. I have not seen anything that savored of affectation, except a hen that sidled up to her husband, and then ran off in a great fright, when he came near— And the old lady here has caused *Orient* St. to be nailed on a tree at the corner of the house, because, as she told the selectmen, it was a very proper name, being as they lived in the most eastern part of the town.

The food is excellent. The butter is as sweet as strawberries; and every thing is "*nice*", hard gingerbread and all. I have taken nothing but milk as yet— morning, noon, and night. In the stillness of the evening we can hear the sea dashing on the beach, "rolling its eternal bass" amid the harmony of nature. I went down to a little cove between two lines of rocks, this morning, and having taken off my stockings, I let the saucy waves come dashing and sparkling into my lap. The water was very cold but very refreshing; but I was a little sad, because it made me think of the beautiful time we had, when we washed our feet together in the mountain waterfall. How I do wish you were here! It is nonsense for me to go a "pleasuring" without you. My sleep don't do me any good; and every pleasant sight makes my heart yearn, because you are not with me. I am very homesick for you, and my private opinion is that I shall not be able to stand it a whole week. As for the place itself, it is in all respects exactly what I wanted to find. Oh, how I do wish we had a snug little cottage here and just income enough to meet very moderate wants. Tomorrow I am going to take my night-gown down to the beach, and seat myself in the cove, where the waves can gallop over me. I have walked about a mile a day, and seen a flock of geese, that acted as [. . .]¹ as a drove of Killarney pigs. I got well mudded by plunging into the meadow after that brightest of all bright blossoms, the Cardinal Flower. There is no one here with me but Margaret Read and Marian. The Wildses could not come. Mrs. Marshall, Priscilla, and perhaps Emily will come in the stage tomorrow.² I was *so* sorry not to have a chance to bid you good bye,—but the driver would not wait. If I do tough it out to stay all the week, I wish you would bring me a No. of the Miscellany, which you will find in the lower drawer of the Secretary. No matter what No. it is, provided it has a pinkish cover. I want it for a little girl there is here. The ladies desire a kind remembrance to you. My dear husband, I *cannot* stay away a week. We lost a great deal of life by not being married sooner, and I am determined to waste no more precious hours of happiness. Don't forget,

Your loving wife,
Maria

. . .

ALS; Lydia Maria Child Papers, Anti-Slavery Collection, Cornell University (micro-fiche 2/44).

To Lydia B. Child

Boston. August 2 1831.

My Dear Lydia,

. . .

We are very well; but not very happy just now. The house in which Mrs. Talbot lives has been sold at auction,—and we are obliged to remove, day after tomorrow. The house she is going to take will not be ready for several weeks. In the meantime I must hire some place to pack my furniture, and must stay about here and there, dependent upon the hospitality of my friends. Oh, dear! how I do wish we could go to housekeeping. This makes the *fifth* time my furniture has been removed, since we began to board out— It is already half ruined. Dear Lydia, I feel in a discouraged mood to-day. Every thing we can earn goes to pay debts—and yet it seems as if we never should get out of difficulty. The prime of our life must be spent in one perpetual struggle with poverty.   However, it is wrong to feel so. Divine Providence has blessed me with a most remarkable degree of success during the last year; and I wonder I do not always trust in His goodness.

¹ The letter is torn here, with one or two words missing.
² The Wildses were probably the family of Marshall's partner, Dixey Wildes. The Marshalls were Priscilla (Waterman) Marshall, wife of Boston China trade merchant Josiah Marshall, and their daughters Priscilla and Emily. The young Priscilla was married to John M. Read of Philadelphia, perhaps related to Margaret Read.

I wish you would send down by the first safe opportunity, Abbott's Letters from Cuba, and the gold cross and heart I loaned Lucretia.[1] I happen to be in want of them this fall.

I rejoice at John's prospects. From all I can hear of the young lady, she is every way worthy of him. I want to see her very much. I hope she will not come to Boston while I am without a home; but I fear the chance is she will; and I shall thus miss of seeing her. She is *not* handsome, I understand, but every thing else that is good and desirable. Do not blame John for being too happy. I should be afraid to marry a man who was very wise when he was in love— It is not *natural* that it should be so.

I am glad you like the Mother's Book.[2] It sells with astonishing rapidity. They cannot get another edition ready soon enough. I have never received so many congratulatory letters on the publication of any book.

. . .

ALS; Child Letters, MC 305, Schlesinger Library, Radcliffe College (microfiche 2/50).

To David Lee Child

Lancaster Sunday Eve—[2 October 1831]

My dear, dear Husband,

It is now the 2d of October; and it melts my heart to think what we said, and thought, and felt, three years ago, at this time. It was about this time that I went to bespeak "Fanny's Fairings"; and your look then is present to me now. In all that relates to external circumstances, our married life has been a stormy journey. But in all other respects, my dear husband, have we not realized all, and *more* than we then hoped? *I* at least have; and by the blessing of ⟨g⟩God, I will try to be a more "perfect wife" than I have been. I need not be alarmed about the decay of my love, according to the criterion I told you; for I *am* miserable here alone. It has been in my heart more than once to leave the printing here to take care of itself, jump into the stage, and come right back home; but alas, I *have* no home to come to—no corner in which to fix up my things for the winter. Oh, how I do long to be settled! I will have everything so snug and bright when you come home. Your slippers and stockings warm by the fire; and I with "a whole Iliad in my face", and a Paradise Regained in my heart.

If you get the lamp painted, be sure to have it *verdigris* green, and the inside of the shade painted bluish white. Who do you think can mend that chair?

[1] In 1828 an American, Abiel Abbot, spent four months in Cuba trying to recover from tuberculosis and became interested in the living conditions of the slaves there. His book *Letters Written in the Interior of Cuba* (Boston, 1829) describes those conditions.
[2] Child's book on child management was published in 1831 in Boston; a second edition appeared the same year.

Don't go to an expensive place, and make your bargain before-hand. Kiss little Nony; but not her dog, for me.[1] I love you. Do you love me?

Yours affectionately,
Maria.

ALS; Lydia Maria Child Papers, Anti-Slavery Collection, Cornell University (microfiche 2/52).

The first volume of the *Ladies' Family Library* was *The Biographies of Madame de Staël, and Madame Roland,* published in 1832. Child's research led her to the memoirs of Napoleon, including those by his Irish physician, Barry Edward O'Meara, and his private secretary, Louis Antoine Fauvelet Bourrienne; she also used the work of Madame de Staël's cousin, Albertine Adrienne de Saussure.

To George Ticknor

[1831?–1832?]

Mr. Ticknor,

I am very much obliged to you for attending to my request, though I had finished copying the Memoir of Madame de Staël before it arrived. It was strangely stupid in me not to look at the title-page of the Ten Years' Exile, for the date,—but so it was—I looked everywhere but in the right place. I came to the same conclusion that you express concerning O'Meara; and my remarks are much the same as they would have been, had I received your note. There is still one thing on the subject of the two millions, which I must find and insert— I mean a very interesting conversation between Bonaparte and the young Baron de Staël. I have seen it somewhere—I thought it was in Bourrienne; but it is not there. Don't trouble yourself to attend to it—I shall find it.

I have heard that Mr. Allston saw and heard much of Madame de Stael— I remember something about a procession to St. Peters, in which she carried a wreath of flowers, and was wrapt in one grande enthusiasm, but what it was all about I don't know.[1]

I wrote a letter to Mr. Allston on the subject; but did not send it; partly because I was afraid to address an artist, who is almost deified in my imagination,—and partly because I thought the twelve Tribes of Israel would all be comfortably settled at Grand Isle, before I received an answer.

[1] Nony was Anna Loring (1830–96), then ten months old, the daughter of the Childs' close friends Ellis Gray Loring and Louisa (Gilman) Loring.
[1] Washington Allston (1779–1843), the artist, had studied in Europe and was then living in Boston.

I am very much ashamed of the state of M.S— but badly as they look, they have all been copied, and several pages twice copied; and I am so much hurried, that I cannot repeat the labour. I would not *trouble* with them, were it not for the use I have made of your Lectures; although I should feel grateful for any suggestions you may please to make.   I have sometimes abridged your remarks, because detailed criticisms would be out of place in such a work as mine. I did not like to call Lafayette a *"less guilty*["] leader of the Revolution, and I therefore merely said "Lafayette, and other popular leaders"; but I will restore the line if you prefer it.

In the description of Madame de Staël s last illness, I inserted two sentences of Madame Saussure's, against which you will see pencil-marks. Perhaps you will not like such mosaic-work; but it is difficult to avoid it in a work of this kind.

I have derived much information from your beautiful lectures, which I could not enclose within marks of quotation; and this I shall signify in the Preface.

If I have made any use of your observations, which you do not approve, have the goodness to let me know.

I hope you will like the Memoir. The deuce is in it, if I have not done well, with your Lectures and Madame Saussure before me, and my own warm interest in the subject. Madame de Stael might have wished a more able biographer; but she could not have desired a more partial one. As for the style, I have chiselled, and rubbed with sand-paper, and polished, and done everything to bring out the beauty of the wood, except *varnishing* it so much as I used to do. After all, I may have weakened it in the process.   I wish I dared to send a copy to the Duchess de Broglie! But then if I live to be very old, in this Charlestown-Bridge-Country, I may be beheaded for sending a book to a Duchess.

Have the goodness to thank Mrs. Ticknor for her very kind note.[2] A word of encouragement animates me; for I have been afflicted with such a mental lethargy, for sometime past, that "I whiles think I am dead; but then again I jalouse I am living"—particularly when I receive such notes as Mrs. Ticknor's two last.   Pardon this long letter—I am sure I don't know how I came to write such a long one; it was quite unintentional.

With Much Respect & Gratitude,
L. M. Child

P.S. In one of Byron's Letters, page 90 of M.S. the words, *Macoronico Tedescho* occur. I do not understand Italian, neither does my husband; and I am afraid to trust a phrase of Byron's for fear of some *concealed wickedness*. I

---

[2] Anna Eliot, of a wealthy Boston family, married George Ticknor in 1821.

thought the first word must be the diminutive of Macoroni—and that the phrase was something equivalent to *stupid coxcomb;* but I cannot tell why I thought so.[3]

ALS; George Ticknor Autograph Collection, Dartmouth College (microfiche 2/56).

[3] "Macoronico Tedescho" means "bastard German."

2

1833-April 1838

By mid-1833, Child was in the ironic position of being poorer than she had ever been in her life, even though the *North American Review* (July 1833) acclaimed her as the foremost woman writer in America. The prestigious Boston Athenaeum, a private library, gave the honor of free privileges to her, only the second woman so recognized. In the next five years, she published one-fourth of her entire oeuvre—a novel, a historical survey, several anthologies, a guide to child care and another to nursing, and, most significantly, six books and pamphlets on the institution of American slavery. This intense intellectual activity was a result, in part, of her becoming an abolitionist at a time when the movement for immediate emancipation was just gaining national prominence.

After several years of antislavery work, Child would use the legend of the sorcerer's apprentice to describe the nature of the controversy surrounding women reformers. Like the apprentice's broom, woman had been changed into a "living, energetic being," and nothing could turn her back into a household utensil. The 1833 publication of her first antislavery book, *An Appeal in Favor of That Class of Americans Called Africans,* marked her entrance into a movement that would be the focus of her political activism for the rest of her life. William Lloyd Garrison (1805–79) "got hold of the strings of my conscience, and pulled me into Reforms," she wrote late in life. "Old dreams vanished, old associates departed, and all things became new" (25 May 1879). She may have met Garrison at the office of David's *Massachusetts Whig Journal*, where in 1827 Garrison worked as a journeyman. In January 1831 she almost certainly read the first issue of his newspaper, *The Liberator*, which heralded the start of the abolitionist movement in the North.

An Appeal in Favor of That Class of Americans Called Africans was one of the first books of its kind published in the United States and is still a classic in the literature. Child calls for immediate emancipation without compensation to owners, argues against colonization in Africa, defends innate racial equality, and indicts racism in the North and the South. Wendell Phillips, William Ellery Channing, Thomas Wentworth Higginson, and Charles Sumner later credited *An Appeal* with having a significant influence on the development of their own antislavery ideas. Child's lucid writing style and the strength of her arguments made the book a major piece of propaganda, and it was required reading for agents of the American Anti-Slavery Society. The *North American Review* (October 1835), in an about-face, attacked her abolitionism and her entrance into the "male" world of politics.

Slavery had been abolished in Massachusetts in 1783, and the importation of slaves to the United States became illegal in 1807. Yet, in the first thirty years of the century, there had been a dramatic increase in the domestic slave trade. At the time of Child's entrance into the antislavery movement, there were over two million slaves in the United States, constituting one-sixth of the entire population. The Denmark Vesey slave plot in 1822, the publication of David Walker's *Appeal to the Colored Citizens of the World* in 1830, and the Nat Turner insurrection in 1831 led to the tightening of Southern laws and the imposition of severe restrictions on the lives of slaves and free blacks.

The themes of Child's letters address many of the major issues of the abolition societies during these years: the use of moral persuasion as an agitating tool, the right of Congress to abolish slavery in the District of Columbia and to end the domestic slave trade, the role of women reformers, the rescue of fugitives, the right of free inquiry and discussion, and the Texas Revolution. In addition, there are scattered references to her own publications, including her *Ladies' Family Library* with its two-volume *History of the Condition of Women* (1835). International in scope, this was her only work to focus exclusively on women. Sarah Grimké, author of *Letters on the Equality of the Sexes and the Condition of Woman* (Boston, 1838), a primal American feminist document, quoted liberally from Child's *History*. Child's book is not a treatise on woman's rights—she specifically denies this intention in the preface. However, her denial attests to her awareness of the issue and its growing prominence in the public mind.

In 1833 she and David lived at Cottage Place in a small house with a garden overlooking South Boston and the harbor. In jest they called their house "Le Paradis des Pauvres" but they were soon to be plunged into real poverty. That Child was not overcome by this unexpected reversal and subsequent isolation from friends suggests her personal stamina and commitment to reform. As she herself realized, involvement in the urgent work of antislavery saved her from prolonged melancholy. Years later, she would single out this period as one of the happiest in her life.

To Convers Francis

Boston Nov. 22d 1833

Dear Brother,

. . .

That most agreeable of all agreeable men, Mr. Crawford, of London, was here last night.[1] He popped in most unexpectedly; for I thought he was half across the Atlantic. He was indeed on the wing—and goes to N. York to night to embark. I wish I could have managed to have had you seen him; but he has been flying from one public place to another, on government business, and we never knew six hours beforehand of his visits.

He tells harrowing stories of what he has seen at the South during his inspection of prisons there. Slaves kept in readiness to join their coffle were shut up in places too loathsome and horrid for the worst of criminals. He says had any one told him such things as he has seen and heard, he should have considered it excessive exaggeration. Yet we talk of mild epithets, and *tenderness* toward our Southern brethren. Curse on this "smooth barbarity of courts." Of the various cants now in fashion, the cant of charity is to me the most disagreeable. Charity, which thinks to make wrong right by baptizing it with a sonorous name— that covers selfishness with the decent mantle of prudence— that glosses over iniquity with the shining varnish of virtuous professions— that makes a garland bridge over the bottomless pit— and calls the devil an "archangel ruined."

If evil would manifest itself as it really is, how easy it would be to overcome it; but this it cannot do, simply because it *is* evil.

Hoping to have the pleasure of seeing you all next week, I remain,

Your Affectionate Sister,
Maria.

P.S. Can you bring in as well as not the Foreign Review that has the article about young Bonaparte in it?

ALS; Washburn Papers, Massachusetts Historical Society (microfiche 2/61).

The Boston Female Anti-Slavery Society, one of the first women's abolitionist groups, was formed in October of 1833. The society met weekly, distributed *The Liberator,* and circulated petitions asking Congress to abolish the slave trade and slavery in the District of Columbia. Charlotte (Brown) Phelps (ca.

[1] William Crawford (1788–1847) was a British prison reformer. When Child saw him, he was serving as a commissioner to the United States for the London Prison Discipline Society.

27

1803–38) was married to the abolitionist Reverend Amos Phelps and was the society's first president.

In this letter to her, Child reveals her characteristic uneasiness with organizational activity and her ambivalence about membership in all-female groups of any kind. However, she did join the Boston society sometime during this year, 1834.

To Charlotte Phelps

[2 January 1834]

Dear Madam,

Upon further consideration, I have felt that I might do wrong in attempting to influence the opinions of others, by any expression of my own views. My opinions concerning the formation of a distinct female society have remained unchanged since my first conversation with Mrs. Shipleigh; but I may be in the wrong, and others in the right.[1] In this, and all other matters, each one must act in freedom, according to his own perceptions of right and wrong, advisable or unadvisable—being, first of all things, careful that he is not guided by selfishness.   Being therefore equally desirous of preserving my own freedom and the freedom of others, I have concluded not to suggest any arguments, which may prevent others from doing what appears to them advisable. The plain truth is, my sympathies do not, and never have, moved freely in this project; but this is no reason why others may not effect a great deal of good by it, and do it in all sincerity. I am willing to pay my subscription, and to increase it by donations, as soon as we have fewer pecuniary difficulties to struggle with; but I had much rather not, in any way be connected with the government.

Both the infant school, and the Anti Slavery Society already formed, are good objects for the funds; and so far as my little pittance is concerned, I am willing it should go to either—or to assist in any other project which the ladies think proper.

Very Respectfully,
L. M. Child.

ALS; Anti-Slavery Collection, Rare Books and Manuscripts, Boston Public Library (microfiche 2/63).

By May 1835, the Boston Athenaeum had cancelled Child's membership in disapproval of the political views of *An Appeal*. The official records of the Athenaeum do not show the cancellation, but evidence for it is found in a letter from Deborah Weston to Anne B. Weston dated 8 May 1835: "Maria [(Wes-

---

[1] Mrs. Shipleigh was probably the wife of the Quaker abolitionist Thomas Shipley.

ton) Chapman] is very busy about Mrs. Child. The facts are these. Mrs. Child is writing a book & she can't go on with it, because the directors of the Athaeneum library have revoked the permission which they gave her some years ago to take out what books she chose. As these books she *must* have, or give up her book. So Maria has taken it in hand. The price of a share is $100. & Maria has raised $75 since yesterday morning, so we think she will succeed."* The book Child was researching may have been *The History of the Condition of Women.* She referred to this event, years later, as an example of her ostracism by the intellectual elite of Boston.

The relationship between Maria Child and Maria (Weston) Chapman in the 1830s was one of admiration and mutual support. Child was also a friend of the Weston family in Boston, including the sisters Deborah, Caroline, and Anne, all active reformers. Maria Chapman (1806–85) was an early supporter of Garrison and an important political protégé. Her skills as organizer, editor, and fund raiser made her one of the most outstanding figures in the beginning days of the movement.

To Maria (Weston) Chapman and Other Ladies

Cottage Place. June 1'st 1834 [1835?].[1]

Dear Ladies,

Please accept my warmest acknowledgements for the generous present you have made me, and the delicate manner in which it was offered. I have never in my whole life, met with anything that gratified me more, or affected me so deeply. It would have excited strong emotion at any time; but coming, as it did, while I was under the influence of many discouraging circumstances, I was moved even to tears.

A letter of thanks would have been sent immediately, according to my first intention, had it not been for peculiar circumstances. We are obliged to leave our present residence; and when my husband left home, he was quite undecided between several plans, some of which would remove us to an inconvenient distance from the Athaeneum. I wished to inform you distinctly how the money, so kindly bestowed, would be appropriated; but at present I can only assure you, that, if we go out of the city, it shall be used as nearly as possible in the manner you intended; and if we remain here, the original purpose shall be literally fulfilled.

---

* Anti-Slavery Collection, Rare Books and Manuscripts, Boston Public Library.
[1] This letter should probably have been dated 1835, the year the Childs moved from Cottage Place. This date is consistent with the date of Deborah Weston's letter about the revocation of Child's Athenaeum membership.

God bless you all, and make me worthy of the good opinion so kindly expressed by you.

Yrs. Most Respectfully & Gratefully,
L M. Child.

ALS; Anti-Slavery Collection, Rare Books and Manuscripts, Boston Public Library (microfiche 2/64).

The year 1835 was called the "mob year" because proslavery sentiment broke out in violence in several major cities. Garrison narrowly escaped being lynched. George Thompson (1804–78), the leading British abolitionist, who was in the United States on his first lecture tour, was also attacked. When he was forced to cancel his speaking engagements because of threats to his life, the Childs were instrumental in spiriting him to New York and hiding him in the homes of friends.

The following group of letters, evidence of mounting resistance to antislavery ideas, is, at the same time, testimony to the effectiveness of Child's and others' propaganda. During this proslavery backlash, abolitionist editors and agents were thrown out of the South. A Georgia law applied the death penalty to publishers of material that allegedly incited slave insurrections. Another sign of the mood of the country was the near passage of a bill that would give postmasters the right to intercept antislavery mail. Child was convinced that letters addressed to her were sometimes "lost."

Child's *Authentic Anecdotes of American Slavery* was published in 1835, and in October of that year the American Anti-Slavery Society commissioned her to write for the commercial and political papers and periodicals. By this time, David's law practice had disappeared. Maria's association with George Thompson promised a way out of their financial troubles. When he offered them positions as agents for the antislavery societies in England, they accepted and made plans to sail.

The next two letters are addressed to Louisa (Gilman) Loring (1797–1868) and her husband, Ellis Gray Loring (1803–58). They and their daughter, Anna, were close friends of Child's; Ellis became her legal and financial adviser as well. Louisa was a member of the Boston Female Anti-Slavery Society but did not take a consistently active role in the movement. Ellis, the only son of an apothecary, was a successful lawyer who frequently litigated antislavery cases. He helped found the New England Anti-Slavery Society and, like Child, was a moderate Garrisonian. Child's letters to him are characteristically confidential in tone and wide-ranging in subject matter; the correspondence lasted twenty-three years.

To Louisa Loring

New York. August 15th. [1835]

Dearest Louisa,

I am at Brooklyn, at the house of a very hospitable Englishman, a friend of Mr. Thompson's.[1] I have not ventured into the city, nor does one of us dare to go to church to day, so great is the excitement here. You can form no conception of it—'Tis like the times of the French Revolution, when no man dared trust his neighbor. Private assassins from N. Orleans are lurking at the corners of the streets, to stab Arthur Tappan; and very large sums are offered for any one who will convey Mr. Thompson into the slave states.[2] I tremble for him, and love him in proportion to my fears. He is almost a close prisoner in his chamber—his friend deeming him in imminent peril the moment it is ascertained where he is. We have managed with some adroitness to get along in safety so far; but I have faith that God will protect him, even to the end.— Yet why do I make this boast? My faith has at times been so weak, that I have started, and trembled, and wept, like a very child; and personal respect and affection for him has so far gained the mastery over my trust in Providence, that I have exclaimed in anguish of heart, "Would to God, I could die for thee"! "Would to God, I could die for thee"!

Your quiet-minded husband could hardly been made to realize the terrible state of fermentation now existing here. There are 7000 Southerners now in the city; and I am afraid there are not 70 among them, who have the slightest fear of God before their eyes. Mr. Wright was yesterday barricadoing his doors and windows with strong bars, and planks an inch thick.[3] Violence, in some form, seems to be generally expected. Alas poor fools! They are building up the very cause they seek to destroy. "Woe to the rebellious children saith the Lord, that take counsel, but not of me; and that cover with a covering, but not of my spirit, that they may add sin to sin."

The steam-boat to Newport was full of Southerners; and Mr. Thompson and the fire-brands with him, soon attracted their attention, and became the permanent objects of their malignant looks and scornful jests. Had I committed some monstrous crime, I could not have performed this journey with more uncomfortable sensations. God grant a fair breeze, that I may soon be wafted out

[1] Henry Ibbotson (ca. 1797–1849), a merchant in the steel and cutlery trade in New York City, was also an abolitionist who with his wife put up the Childs at his home in Brooklyn.

[2] Arthur Tappan (1786–1864), a wealthy merchant and abolitionist, provided financial support for *The Liberator* and the American Anti-Slavery Society until he broke with Garrison in 1840.

[3] Elizur Wright, Jr. (1804–85), resigned his professorship at Western Reserve College in 1833 to become president of the New York Anti-Slavery Society. He was also one of the founders of the American Anti-Slavery Society and served as its corresponding secretary until 1839.

of sight of this wicked city. I hope we shall sail tomorrow; but we *may* not; for Mr. Child has been arrested here at the suit of George Snelling, who not content with leaving the whole burden of the Journal debts to his partner, has been advised by somebody to annoy him in this way.[4] If we are obliged to pay for our places in the packet of tomorrow, and Mr. C. cannot arrange this affair, as he hopes, I shall cross the Atlantic alone, and he will follow, as soon as we can. This is a bad alternative, to make the best of it.

At Newport, I called to say farewell to Dr. Channing;[5] and I gladly said farewell; for during our brief interview, my remaining respect for him diminished rapidly. He said the abolitionists *ought* in their publications to advocate peace principles with peculiar care. I told him they *did* so, to a remarkable degree. He said he was glad to hear it— he did not know anything about their books—he never read them. What right then had he to judge and advise? He then gave similar advise [*sic*] about abolition meetings, add[ing][6] that he never attended any of them.

We returned from Doct Channing's by the way of the beach—and a most magnificent beach it was—with farm-houses and verdant fields lying almost on its very bosom—I never beheld a more lovely marriage of land and sea. Several boats were lying on the beach, waiting for the tide to waft them on its sparkling surface. I thought of Doct. Channing, and sighed, that he too was a tide-waiter.

Our aristocratic sister-in-law (Bro. John's wife) was at first a little annoyed at our intimacy with the "wandering insurrectionist," Thompson; but before we parted, she said, "What a gentlemanly, delightful man he is! If he staid here another day, he would make me an abolitionist"![7] I found your persevering card-case in my bag. I have just written the name of my English entertainer in it; for she is exceedingly kind to me, and I dare not go into the city to buy a present for her, lest some one should follow me to our retreat. Just before I left Boston, I received a silver card-case, wrought with great neatness and elegance—a mutual present from Mr. Thompson & Mr. Garrison. It will be the last thing I voluntarily part with in life.

I am sorry to find that the lace handkerchief I lent Susan was not put up—I have wanted it— But, however, that's a trifle. Give my kindest, my most grateful remembrance to Mr. Loring, and kiss Nony's sweet little face for me. Perhaps I may yet see you again, before we get off to England. How I do want to see you! Remember me affectionately to Susan, and tell old Mrs Loring I often think of her kind care of us. Remember me with my whole heart to good Henrietta & her

[4] George Snelling had been the legal partner of David Child; Child was arrested for nonpayment of a debt at his suit.

[5] William Ellery Channing.

[6] The paper is torn away here.

[7] Laura (Dwight) Childe (1809–54) was the daughter of James S. Dwight, a wealthy industrialist from Springfield, Mass. She married John Childe, David's brother, in 1832.

sister.[8] When the History of Women comes out, I want a copy sent to Catherine Sargent, from her affectionate friend L. M. C.

God bless & preserve you. I fear I shall never find such another friend in any part of the world. Yrs most affectionately,

L M C.

P.S. The copper plate of the kneeling slave may be sent to the Anti Slavery office N. York, care of Elizur Wright.[9]

Please pay Mr. Thompson one dollar for Irving's prairies, and tell him I left it for him.[10] Charge it to me. Do be kind, very kind to him.

ALS; Loring Family Papers, Schlesinger Library, Radcliffe College (microfiche 3/80).

To Ellis Gray Loring

Brooklyn, Aug. 22d 1835

Dear Friend,

. . .

I wish Mr. Ticknor could likewise settle his bill; for this unpleasant delay in a city where everything is expensive, diminishes my funds.[1] Before Mr. Child left he took me to Bath, about ten miles from the city, which was considered a safe distance from mobs. Mrs. Ibbotson of Brooklyn, in whom I have found a very kind friend, was good enough to come down and insist upon my returning to her house. I shall probably stay here till Monday, when I intend to go to the house of a Quaker in New Rochester, who has often sheltered persecuted abolitionists.[2] There is to be an immense pro-slavery meeting in the open Park at N. York this afternoon. The Southerners have given out that after this meeting the "fanatics" may expect to have their houses demolished. The time and place chosen are admirably calculated to excite riots; for on Saturday evening, the workmen will all be at leisure to hear and to do. Poor fools! they are shooting poisoned arrows at

[8] Susan may be Susan Bigelow, daughter of James Francis, who married Jackson Bigelow. Nony is Anna Loring. Relief Loring (ca. 1774–1848) was the mother of Ellis Gray Loring. Henrietta Sargent (1785–1871), pioneer in the antislavery movement, was an officer of the Boston Female Anti-Slavery Society, and, with her sister Catharine (1774–1852), a good friend of Child's.

[9] The engraving was by the black artist Patrick Henry Reason (b. 1817).

[10] Washington Irving's *Tour of the Prairies* (Philadelphia, 1835) was an account of his trip to the land of the Osage and Pawnee Indian tribes.

[1] William Davis Ticknor (1810–64) was the publisher of several of Child's books, including the *Appeal* and *The Freedmen's Book* (1865). In the 1850s he became partner to James T. Fields and published Hawthorne, Longfellow, and other leading New England writers, as well as the *Atlantic Monthly*. Ticknor and Fields ran the Old Corner Bookstore in Boston, a gathering place for many authors.

[2] The home of Joseph Carpenter (1793–1872) and his wife, Margaret (Cornell) Carpenter, in New Rochelle, New York, was a station in the underground railroad.

the Rock of Ages. "Men may be destroyed—*principles* never"! I see H. G. Otis is filling the measure of his iniquities, and adding another item of shame to the Hartford Convention for his posterity to blush at.[3] What a half rotten, half petrified thing is that man's heart!

I trust all our friends will be very, very cautious concerning Mr. T.[4] Let his movements be kept a profound secret—let no letters be addressed to him through the P. Office—do not talk about him to strangers, even if they appear friendly. Above all, hasten his departure for some part of his Majesty's dominions, by an *unusual* route. These are not idle, womanly fears. God knows I would be *the* last to shrink, or to advise others to shrink, in times like these. But his life is worth far more to the cause, than his death; and emissaries are abroad, who grow more ferocious, the more they are baffled. The tone of the papers here would almost make you smile, painful as the subject is. "We cannot," says one, "find words to express our hatred of this foreign felon, this common swindler, who driven from England, probably escaped here from Botany Bay. We rejoice to see that all the respectable people of Boston have called a meeting to put him down. The only building in Massachusetts that ought to be open to him is the State Prison at Charlestown." A virulent little paper is buzzing about here, called the Anti-Abolitionist. Over it is a large wood cut, representing men and women, black and white, hugging and kissing each other; and on the table are decanters marked A. T. B.—which signifies Arthur Tappan's Burgundy.

I am not expecting Mr. Child until Tuesday, though he [. . .][5] that he shall return by Sunday. I wish I had gone with him, notwithstanding his remonstrances; for I feel unhappy thus separated; particularly when he is in trouble.[6] If he is in Boston, when you receive this, please tell him I am going to New Rochester, from the idea that it will be cheaper than at Bath, and more quiet. How is Louisa? What a comfort it would be to me to see her! For in spite of myself, my heart is somewhat sad. I would I were in England!

> "What is left for patriots here?
> For Greeks, a blush—for Greece, a tear."

. . .

Yours Most Gratefully & Truly
L. M Child.

. . .

[3] Harrison Gray Otis, mayor of Boston, 1829–31, was a delegate to the Hartford (Conn.) Convention in January 1815. This group of Federalists met to write constitutional amendments that would reassert state and regional rights. Otis, who was present at the Faneuil Hall meeting the day before this letter was written, was one of the prominent Bostonians who reprimanded the abolitionists and reassured Southerners that Boston would not support immediate emancipation.
[4] George Thompson.
[5] The paper is torn away, with one word missing.
[6] She refers to David's arrest on 13 Aug.

34

The Carolinians are in a great fuss because some mustard has arrived there done up in English newspapers containing Parliamentary Speeches against slavery! They are as badly off as the man who feared the atmosphere would fall in.[7]

ALS; Loring Family Papers, Schlesinger Library, Radcliffe College (microfiche 3/81).

To George Thompson

New Rochelle 22 miles from N. York
Sep. 18th 1835.

Dear Friend,

It has very often been in my heart to write to you, but I have delayed, and delayed, in hopes of being able to give some certain information concerning our departure; and now I have determined to wait no longer, though I can only say that we shall *probably* sail on the 1'st of Oct. Though the delay has been accompanied with inconveniences and useless expense, we have reason to be glad on the whole; for we have, through quite unexpected channels, received information that may prove very important. But in these days, our motto must be *vigilance, activity*, and *silence.*   After I heard of your safe arrival in Hartford, I began to feel easy in my mind, and to sleep as usual. The following placard was taken down from one of the public buildings, and handed to me by E. Wright,[1] the day after you left.

To the people of the City and County of N. York, greetings:

Know ye that information hath this day reached me that *George Thompson,* the Envoy Extraordinary and Minister Plenipotentiary, duly sent out by the old women of Scotland, to lecture the Americans on the subject of slavery, is now in this city, at the house of *Lewis Tappan, 40 Rose St,* and about to lecture in this city:[2] I therefore command you, my trusty and well-beloved, that you take his body forthwith and bring him before me, at the Merchants' Exchange, in said city, to be dealt with according to my code of laws.

Judge Lynch.

This pitiful ebulition of spleen, of malice as impotent as it is infernal, was printed in huge letters—particularly the name of yourself and Lewis Tappan. A mob was in fact regularly organized to attack his house at midnight, the Thursday after you left; but the names of the individuals, and the line of operations, were confided to a man secretly attached to the abolitionists; the result was the

[7] On 29 July, in Charleston, S.C., a mail packet of abolitionist literature from New York, possibly containing some of Child's work, was impounded by the postmaster; it was publicly burned the next day.
[1] Elizur Wright, Jr.
[2] Lewis Tappan (1788–1873), philanthropist and reformer, was one of the founders of the New York and American Anti-Slavery Societies in 1833. The following year, his house was destroyed by an antiabolitionist mob.

mayor informed them that they were all known by name, and if they did it, they must proceed at their peril. This put a stop to their magnanimous project. I believe we have many more secret friends than any of us imagine; and though their motives for remaining secret are certainly none of the noblest, yet in such a crisis as this, they can work for us more effectually than we can work for ourselves. Both in New York and Philadelphia the tide is obviously turning in our favor. Sly jokes at the South, and serious disapprobation of slavery, continually find their way into the papers, though the editors *do* preface their remarks by saying, "We don't like the abolitionists." When I read such things, I smile to think of the Roman historian, (Tacitus, I believe) who says: "Nero accused the *Christians* of being the incendiaries that set fire to the city; but though they are undoubtedly a turbulent and mischievous sect, we believe they cannot be justly accused of *this* enormity."

At Philadelphia a circumstance occurred, which pleased me much. A man by the name of Conrad stopped a box of abolition, and tried to "set the river on fire" by emptying the contents into the Deleware.[3] At a meeting, a short time after, this individual was nominated as a representative to the Legislature, with sanguine hopes of success. When his name was read, a man rose and asked, "What has Mr. Conrad done to gain the confidence of the people? He has combined his exertions with violent men, who make some of our best citizens afraid to sleep in their own houses—he has broken open and torn in pieces a letter addressed to a worthy private citizen—and he has thrown into the Deleware a small portion of dry goods consigned to a poor widow! Whenever his name is placed on a nomination list, I motion that it be torn in pieces, as he tore Thomas Shipleigh's letter."[4] This motion was received with applause, and Conrad lost his election. In New York, bad as it is, something of the same spirit is at work. Stone, of the Commercial Advertiser, has received so many letters from country towns, telling him that he will ruin his party if he abuses the abolitionists, that he was fain to copy Abbott's article on that subject, from the Religious Magazine, as a salvo.[5] The Evening Post has lost all chance of favor with the South; and the aristocratic N. York American, when it speaks at all, speaks in a candid, friendly tone. Into the columns of both these papers, your humble servant has gained admission, under a very thin disguise, assumed for mischievous purposes. If you should not hear of me by name for a year to come, you may rest assured that I am *busy*.[6]

And now I want to bestow upon you a little of what everybody is willing to give—viz. advice. What if you and Mr. Kimball of N.H., or you and Henry

[3] This was possibly Robert Taylor Conrad (1810–58), Philadelphia lawyer and writer.
[4] Thomas Shipley (1787–1836), Quaker abolitionist, joined the Pennsylvania Society for the Abolition of Slavery in 1817 and helped found the American Anti-Slavery Society. His home in Philadelphia was an important link in the underground railroad.
[5] She refers to William Leete Stone (1792–1844), journalist and historian, who advocated the emancipation of slaves by Congress.
[6] Child's articles in the *Evening Post* and the *New York American* have not been identified.

Benson, should go into the interior of Vermont (not into large towns first) jogging along in your own wagon, stopping wherever you see a school-house, and asking the use of it to deliver a lecture gratis.[7] In the course of half a day an audience could be collected, by the active exertions of Mr. Kimball. Let him go round and tell people that George Donisthorpe of Scotland is travelling along that way, and would like to tell them how slavery was abolished in Great Britain, and how they find the plan works. I mention Mr. Kimball, because I think he would take wonderfully with the country people, and because his spirits need to be recruited by some comical adventures. I wish the abolitionists would be more *concealed* in their operations—not for the sake of avoiding danger, but for the sake of doing a greater amount of good.

I have had many anxious moments on your account; but I have a strong faith, that God will restore you safely to your native land. The following lines I wrote while staying at Bath alone, during the absence of Mr. C.

. . .[8]

We have had a delightful visit of eight days at Philadelphia. Mr. Child went to collect certain items of information, and I went, rather than be left alone. I was charmed with the city—it is such a pleasant contrast to N. York. *You* were spoken of with the warmest affection; and there as elsewhere, the few who do you justice are worth all the rest of the population. Mrs Pervis requested me to ask you to return the Bow in The Clouds, by the first convenient and safe opportunity.[9] I began in a very small hand, from a pre-sentiment that I should write a great deal; but still I am pinched for room. Please present my kindest regards to your wife and children. Dont place them in any city this winter—pray dont. My watch keeps excellent time; but its publicity sometimes embarrasses me a little.[10]   I wish it may seem good in your eyes to pursue the plan above sug-

---

[7] Joseph Horace Kimball (1813–38) was editor of the *Herald of Freedom* in Concord, N.H., where Thompson was staying. He travelled to the West Indies with James A. Thome and coauthored the report *Emancipation in the West Indies: A Six Months Tour in Antigua, Barbadoes and Jamaica in 1837* (New York, 1838). Henry Benson (1814–37) helped found the Providence (R.I.) Anti-Slavery Society and was an agent for *The Liberator*. Benson's sister, Helen Eliza, was the wife of William Lloyd Garrison.

[8] Child's "lines" were cut out, leaving a gap in the original letter of approximately four inches. The address leaf is marked to John Greenleaf Whittier in Haverhill, Mass., who would have forwarded the letter to Thompson in Concord, N.H. Child probably chose this circuitous mailing route to protect Thompson's whereabouts.

[9] Harriet (Forten) Purvis (d. ca. 1875) was the daughter of the black leader James Forten. She was one of four black signers of the founding charter of the Philadelphia Female Anti-Slavery Society. In 1834 she married Robert Purvis, a prominent Philadelphia abolitionist. Child probably met her at a meeting of the Philadelphia society when Child spoke on the importance of opening channels of communication with abolitionist women in Boston and England.

[10] Thompson and Maria (Weston) Chapman were responsible for purchasing the watch, a gift in honor of Child's antislavery work.

---

gested, until all the *white hats* are "over the border;"—or, in other words, till the snakes get into their winter holes.

May the blessing of God be with you to strengthen and preserve.

Yours with the truest respect & affection,
L M. C.

In this closing sentiment, my husband, who is writing by my side, most warmly unites. He visits N. York every few days to receive & bring the news.

ALS; Whittier MSS, Friends Historical Library, Swarthmore College (microfiche 3/82).

To Convers Francis

New Rochelle, September 25, 1835.

We are boarding in the family of an honest Hicksite Quaker, in this quiet secluded village, which we chose both for economy and safe distance from cities.[1] There is nothing in the neighborhood worthy of a traveller's attention except the grave of Tom Paine, in the corner of a field, near the road-side. It is surrounded by a rough stone wall, two or three feet high. In one place the stones are broken down and lying loose, where Cobbett entered to carry off his bones.[2] He was buried in this lonely manner, because all the churches, and even the Quakers, refused him admittance into their burying-grounds. And we who boast of living in a more liberal age, are carrying on the same petty persecution under different forms!

I agree with you most cordially that man, without a "principle of reverence for something higher than his own will, is a poor and wretched being;" but I would have that reverence placed on principles, not on persons; and this in a true republic would, I believe, be the case. I believe our difficulties grow out of the fact that we have in reality very little republicanism. A principle of despotism was admitted in the very formation of our government, to sanction which our consciences have been continually silenced and sealed. In our social institutions, aristocracy has largely mingled. The opinion of a great man stands in the place of truth; and thus the power of perceiving truth is lost. We should be little troubled

[1] They were boarding with Joseph Carpenter. The Hicksite group of Quakers, under the leadership of Elias Hicks, split off from the more orthodox Quakers in 1828. The Hicksites advocated boycotting slave-made products.
[2] Thomas Paine (1737–1809), revolutionary political pamphleteer and agitator, the author of *Common Sense*, spent his last years socially ostracized, ill, and poor. Supposed an atheist, he could not be buried in consecrated ground, and he was interred on his farm in New Rochelle. In 1819 his house was burned, and his remains carried off by William Cobbett (1763–1835), the political journalist from England. Cobbett intended to sell Paine's bones to raise money for a monument to him. The monument was never built, and after Cobbett's death the remains passed into the hands of a receiver in probate; they were acquired by a furniture dealer in 1844—then lost to history.

with mobs if people called respectable did not give them their sanction. But you will say a true republic never can exist. In this, I have more faith than you. I believe the world will be brought into a state of order through manifold revolutions. Sometimes we may be tempted to think it would have been better for us not to have been cast on these evil times; but this is a selfish consideration; we ought rather to rejoice that we have much to do as mediums in the regeneration of the world. . . .

You ask me to be prudent, and I will be so, as far as is consistent with a sense of duty; but this will not be what the world calls prudent. Firmness is the virtue most needed in times of excitement. What consequence is it if a few individuals do sink to untimely and dishonored graves, if the progress of great principles is still onward? Perchance for this cause came we into the world.

I have examined the history of the slave too thoroughly, and felt his wrongs too deeply, to be prudent in the wordly sense of the term. I know too well the cruel and wicked mockery contained in all the excuses and palliations of the system.

L, extract; *Letters of Lydia Maria Child*, 1882 (microfiche 3/83).

As the Childs' plans to go to England were further postponed, New Rochelle continued to be the base from which they carried on their antislavery work. At this time, Child met Lucretia (Coffin) Mott (1793–1880) and Angelina Grimké (1801–79). A Quaker minister, Mott was an early activist in the abolitionist movement and later a pioneer of women's rights. Grimké also distinguished herself early in the history of antislavery as a brilliant lecturer. She left her aristocratic, slaveholding family in South Carolina and came to the attention of Northern abolitionists with the publication of a letter denouncing slavery in *The Liberator* in September 1835. With her sister, Sarah, she reported on the horrors of that institution, her observations based on firsthand experience. The American Anti-Slavery Society published Angelina's *Appeal to the Christian Women of the Southern States* (New York, 1836), the only abolitionist document written by a Southern woman expressly for other women of that region.

The following letter was published in the first annual report of the Boston Female Anti-Slavery Society. At issue was the appropriateness of women's taking *public* roles in the abolition of slavery.

To the Boston Female Anti-Slavery Society

[October?—before 19 November 1835]

Dear Sisters:—

. . .

With regard to our righteous cause, the indications are already numerous, that what has happened to individuals, has "fallen out rather to the *furtherance* of

39

our principles." I think there never was such cause for hope—such encouragement for renewed energy, as at the present moment. The tide is rapidly turning in our favor. Before it *is* turned, some may suffer in reputation, property, and person; but of what consequence is it, if we do sink to untimely and dishonored graves, if the sacred cause of freedom and humanity is advanced by our humble instrumentality.

In Philadelphia, I attended an interesting meeting of the Female Anti Slavery Society, and suggested to them the propriety of writing to the ladies of England and Scotland, as you had done. They very cordially assented to the proposition. I think you might find it profitable to open a correspondence with this society; for their vicinity to the southern states, makes them very frequently, eye-witnesses to painful scenes connected with the system of slavery. The name of the President is Mrs. Sidney Ann Lewis; the Secretary, Mrs. Lucretia Motte—both of the society of Friends. The former keeps a little shop for the sale of anti slavery documents, and free cotton goods. The mayor called and advised her to take down the sign, which she had boldly hung up at the door. She quietly replied, "I thank thee for thy friendly advice, but do not feel disposed to follow thy suggestion."

I wish this spirit were more universal among the Quakers; but many excuse themselves, by saying they must not mix with the world—that Israel must dwell in his tents. If *our* way does not seem right, why can they not work in their own way? Assuredly, they would, and so would others that make similar objections, if they truly loved the work for Christ's sake. Assuredly, they would, if they remembered "those who are in bonds as bound with them." They do not realize the condition of the oppressed; and the spirit of the world is with them in this very fear of acting *with* the world. I was very much pleased with an answer made by Angelina Grimké, who was born and educated at the south. A lady told her that she suffered her heart to be too much engrossed with the subject of slavery—that the suitable time had not yet come, for action of the subject. She replied, very mildly, "If thou wert a slave, toiling in the fields of Carolina, I apprehend thou wouldst think the time had *fully* come."

. . .

In Philadelphia, there lived a very worthy, honest couple, who had a right to their freedom, even according to our wicked laws; for they had been manumitted in their youth. But the heirs of their master, refused to carry their wills into effect, and after several years of unavailing remonstrance and entreaty, they ran away. They reached Pennsylvania in safety, and soon gained respect and confidence, by their examplary deportment, and strong affection for each other. For several years, all went on well; but a few months ago, hired agents found the way to their quiet abode, under pretence of searching for a horse that had been lost. Soon after, a set of ruffians broke into the house at midnight, and dragged the man off, amid the shrieks of his family—beating him so cruelly that the snow was stained with his blood for a long distance. His poor wife had an infant eight or ten days old—she sprung from her bed and rushed out into the snow to plead for her husband. Alas! it was unavailing—for our laws *compel* us to deliver the bond-man to his oppressor. The family by whose orders this monstrous outrage was committed, was the aristocratic, and highly respected family of T*** in Baltimore. James was soon after sold, and his new master wrote to James Motte, of Philadelphia, in the most hypocritical tone, begging him to persuade the wife to follow her husband into slavery—saying he was willing to pay any price for her, *merely* for James' sake; because he was such a pious, exemplary man, and had an affection for his wife as strong as he had ever seen in any human being.[1] The woman's friends, of course, advised her not to go, for her children's sake; but she, poor creature, seems completely broken hearted. Yet in the face of facts like these, some will tell you that *women* have nothing to do with this question!

> "When woman's heart is bleeding,
> Shall woman's voice be hushed?"[2]

When Bonaparte told a French lady that he did not like to hear a woman talk politics, she replied,—"Sire, in a country where women are beheaded, it is very natural they should like to know the reason." And where women are brutalized, scourged, and sold, shall we not inquire the reason? My sisters, you have not only the right, but it is your solemn *duty;* and may God bless you, according to the firmness with which you perform that duty.

In fullness of affection,

L. M. Child

L; *Right and Wrong in Boston* (Boston: Boston Female Anti-Slavery Society, 1836), pp. 90–94 (microfiche 3/84).

To Convers Francis

New Rochelle, December 19, 1835.

In your last letter you charge democracy with being the mother of evil. I do not wonder at it; for these are times when its best friends have need of faith. But I believe the difficulty ever is in a lack of republicanism. The aristocratic principle, unable to act openly, disguises itself, and sends its poison from under a

---

[1] James Mott (1788–1868) was a Quaker abolitionist who gave up a prosperous cotton business in Philadelphia to sever his connection with the slave labor system. He married Lucretia Coffin in 1811. In the 1850s, their home on Arch Street was a refuge for fugitive slaves.

[2] These lines come from a poem by Elizabeth Chandler, sometimes mistakenly attributed to Garrison. "Shall we behold, unheeding, / Life's holiest feelings crushed? / When woman's heart is bleeding, / Shall woman's voice be hushed?" (*The Liberator*, 8 Jan. 1831).

mask. What is the root of the difficulty on this great question of abolition? It is not with the farmers, it is not with the mechanics. The majority of their voices would be on the right side if the question were fairly brought before them; and the consciousness that such would be the result creates the earnest desire to stop discussion. No, no! It is not these who are to blame for the persecution suffered by abolitionists. Manufacturers who supply the South, merchants who trade with the South, politicians who trade with the South, ministers settled at the South, and editors patronized by the South, are the ones who really promote mobs. Withdraw the aristocratic influence, and I should be perfectly easy to trust the cause to the good feeling of the people. But, you will say, democracies must always be thus acted upon; and here, I grant, is the great stumbling-block. The impediments continually in the way of bringing good principles into their appropriate forms are almost disheartening; and would be quite so, were it not for the belief in One who is brooding over this moral chaos with vivifying and regenerating power. What can be more beautiful than the spirit of love in the Christian religion? Yet where shall we find Moslem or pagan more fierce and unrelenting than Christians toward each other?

L, extract; *Letters of Lydia Maria Child*, 1882 (microfiche 3/85).

The Childs were among the few eastern abolitionists to consider joining the free-labor colony at Matamoros, Mexico (now Texas), planned by Benjamin Lundy (1789–1839) as a refuge for free blacks from persecution in North America. Lundy hoped that if blacks were given a chance to work and establish their own communities, they would disprove ideas of racial inferiority and lessen racial prejudice. The colony would also further the free-produce movement by employing blacks to raise sugar, cotton, and rice.

The plan met with coolness in the East. Matamoros was in a politically volatile area. The Mexican government had abolished slavery in September 1829, and frequently clashed with the proslavery Texans who were eager to establish Texas as an independent republic. Garrison objected to the proposed settlement because he thought that it was a form of colonization, that the Mexican government was unstable, and that the emigration of a few hundred families was too limited in scope to affect prejudice significantly.

The Childs' decision to join was a coup for Lundy and, to some extent, an indication of how desperate the Childs were to get out of debt. The long journey and creation of a new settlement augured hard, dangerous work. David was offered a sizable portion of land and a way to make additional money by employing farm laborers. He had a genuine interest in the free-produce movement and, in three years' time, would be growing sugar beets in his own experiment in undermining the Southern slavery economy.

To Ellis Gray Loring

New Rochelle Jan 30th 1836

Very Dear Friends,

The long uncertainty is over. To-day my husband writes a formal resignation of the mission to England. We are aware that Mr. Thompson's returning so much sooner than was expected *does* make a difference, though we have reason to believe that the Society[1] generously wish us to proceed, without taking that into the account. I informed my brother Convers that we should not probably go to England, and he answered by blaming the Society; which he probably was not *very* reluctant to do. This blame was entirely gratuitous on his part, and I shall endeavour to convince him of his error. I mention it, because I wish to have it distinctly understood that we do not, even in our hearts, find any fault with the Society. Our not going is entirely a matter of our own decision, founded on the conviction that the mission is not now so much needed, as was at first supposed. In addition to this, the expenses into which this unpleasant affair has unavoidably plunged us, would leave us more entirely dependent on the Society's funds than we should like to be, for clothing, and incidental expenses, which one *must* incur in such a place as England.   As for the *pleasure* of the excursion, I found I could give it up very easily; for I do not love to travel, I have been bored-to-death with Album-writing, in New York and Philadelphia. Every time this task was imposed upon me, I thought of England, and sighed; for "coming events cast their shadows before." I *did* hope to make some profitable literary arrangements, by which we could have been enabled to pay the debts we so much desire to pay; but, after all, that is a ⟨uncertain⟩ lottery—and wherever I am, if my health is spared, I can write books. So far as giving up the mission is concerned, I can truly say I felt no pain in giving it up, except what was occasioned by the circumstance that the enemies of the cause would triumph in it.   But the state of *inaction* and *uncertainty* in which we have been placed has, I acknowledge, been a very severe trial. I have not always borne it as a Christian should. Such seasons are useful to teach us how habitually we lean upon the world, and how little we trust in God. I have been nearer to losing all faith and hope in Divine Providence than I remember ever to have experienced. And why was this? It was because temporal good was more desired than spiritual good.

You[r] first desire will be to know what we intend to do with ourselves. I have been reluctant to tell you, because I know it will, at first, occasion a pang in Louisa's heart. We have made all our arrangements to join Benj. Lundy's Free Labor settlement, in Tamaulipas, Mexico. When you reflect upon our situation, you will, I think, see the necessity of our going into *some* new country. We have deliberated anxiously, during the last four months, and have come to the conclusion that this move offers greater advantages than any other. Our friends will generally cry out against it; but this I think they would not, if they had examined

[1] The American Anti-Slavery Society.

43

the premises as carefully as we have. The unsettled state of the country will be the first idea that presents itself;—but Lundy's Grant is four or five hundred miles from the scene of disturbance; it is far up from the sea, and not in the way of direct communication between any great towns. Lundy is a man of sterling integrity and worth. We became acquainted with him in Philadelphia, and had this confirmed by our own observation, and by the cordial and unqualified testimony of many who had known him for years. In religion he is a Quaker—of course will not be always officiously meddling with the creeds of others. Besides, in many respects my own views are so similar to the Friends, that I can have better sympathy with them than with any others. Joseph and Mary Beale (the Irish Quakers, of whom I wrote to Maria Chapman) propose to accompany us. I have become much attached to Mary Beale, this winter. She seems very frank and warm-hearted; and has an unusual share of talent and vivacity. Perhaps you remember in the Appeal, the mention of a man from Vermont, who ⟨afterward⟩ became a planter, first in Mississippi, and afterward in Matamoras—and who pronounced from experience that free-labor was cheaper? This gentleman is Richard Pearce—a man of considerable property and influence, who is now waiting to join our Colony. Benj. Lundy tells me his wife is a very friendly, cultivated, excellent woman. These things I mention for *your* comfort; that you may remember the picture has lights as well as shadows. That there will be many privations and difficulties to encounter, especially, at first, I am well aware; but I hope I shall be enabled not to magnify them unnecessarily. My dear husband would fain have me wait, and follow him when he gets settled. But the French war may make it difficult to follow him—he needs me to comfort him—and I should not be happy away from him. I expect to remain at Mr. Pearce's house, till some comfortable arrangements are made.—and now for business. We want you to collect every cent you can for us, consistently with reserving payment & security for yourself. The picture of the Capitol I should like to have sold for us, by some bookseller. The plate originally cost 5 dollars, and the frame ⟨for⟩ 5. It ought to sell for five or six, I think. When I paid you the 119 dolls, you said I need not do it, unless I chose. I am reluctant to ask the favor of borrowing it again; but if you can conveniently, it will indeed be a great obligation to us. If you please, you can let us know, *as soon as you can,* what you have in your hands for us; it being understood that in all transactions, Mr. Child receives as the *agent* of my father. You know there are 500 dollars in the hands of Hen. Ibbotson of Pearl St. New York; if you think proper you could give us an order on him for the sum you wish to send us, and then *you* could settle with the Society. If you do write to Henry Ibbotson, remember we are to receive it as *agents* of Mr. Convers Francis. Mr. Child will draw up a paper resigning into your hands & father's, all right and title to the copy-rights, or profits, of the Oasis, Frugal Housewife, Girl's Book, Family Library, and Philothea.[2] From there, pay yourself and Mr. Sewall, as soon as you

[2] As a married woman, Child could not hold property, including copyrights on her own books, apart from her husband. She edited *The Oasis* (1834), a collection of antislavery pieces. *Philothea* (1836), her third novel, was a romance set in ancient Greece.

can; reserving only fathers yearly interest on 890 dollars, half due in June, the other in September.[3] The copy-rights will be sent back to you, unincumbered. We have heard of Ticknor's failure; and are of course prepared to hear that what was due to us there is lost. I went 7 times to his store, and waited long, several times before I came away, in hopes of effecting a settlement, without leaving you the trouble of it. I wish you would ask Timothy H. Carter first, and Russell second, what they will pay for the right of printing 5000 copies of the Mother's Book; and let him have it, who will give the most, and pay *now*.[4] I should be unwilling to dispose of such a right under 100 dolls; it *ought* to be more than twice that,—but I do not expect it. I wish I knew whether Mr. Hastings, Ticknor's binder, *lost* what was due to him for binding the Oasis. Mr. Child left a volume of The Weekly Massachusetts Journal at Ticknor's store. I want it sent to H. Sargents,[5] to be put in one of the trunks. The trunks are to be sent to New York, to John Rankin, No 8 Cedar St.[6] His name, and *not* ours to be on them. Please make a cross on each superscription, that he may identify them as belonging to Convers Francis. You will smile, perhaps, to see how a burnt child dreads the fire. I wish you would pay for removing the trunks from Poplar St—also for a woman to re-pack one of them, according to directions I sent to Henrietta. One bottle of Mrs Kidder's medicine, and two of Cocoa oil, which I left in Louisa's chamber, may be packed in the trunk at your house, and sent, provided they are of no use to you—otherwise, it is not of the slightest consequence.

. . . As for us, be assured we shall labor for this cause, let us be where we may. One thing that reconciles me to this Mexican project, is the reasonable prospect of being extensively useful to the oppressed. We have lately pretty much given up writing for the papers, in this quarter. One half of the articles they wont put in; and the remaining copy is half of it lost. I have persuaded the widow Turpin to place her children here at Joseph Carpenter's, to go to the small schoolhouse, of which I was so much enamored. I conducted them thither the first day they went; and an honest farmer, who met me, inquired what little white girl that was with three colored children walking with her. One scholar was removed on account of these children; but no further difficulty has yet occurred. They are bright likely children; and I am in hopes the next generation will profit by having been their school-mates. At *our* table the blacks, domestics and all, have a majority of one. It is a solid satisfaction to see prejudice so entirely forgotten. The Quakers in general here are much infected with the pride of caste; and Joseph Carpenter has a hard struggle of it. He has borne a faithful and consistent testimony on this subject, and the inevitable effects are already beginning to follow—

---

[3] Samuel Sewall (1799–1888) loaned Child at least one hundred dollars for publication of *The Oasis.* An abolitionist and attorney, he defended many fugitive slaves. He served in the Massachusetts Senate as a Free-Soiler and was the Liberty party candidate for governor in 1842.
[4] Timothy H. Carter ran a printing supply house in Boston.
[5] Henrietta Sargent.
[6] Rankin was a New York merchant and reformer.

arrangements to join B. Lundy's Free Labor Colony, and shall go, as soon as the ice clears out of the harbour. His grant is several hundred miles from the scene of difficulty in Texas.[1] It is fairly and fully guaranteed to him by government; so there is no danger of being cheated with regard to claims, as many were in Texas. B. Lundy is a Quaker, and those who have known him from his boyhood all agree in describing him as a man of great integrity and moral worth. Several gentlemen of property and respectability have formed a joint [stock][2] company to erect mills, and other useful work. . . .

Richard Pearce, my friend from Boston, and B. Lundy, all describe the climate healthy. For the sake of our names and influence in the beginning, Mr. Lundy is desirous to give us privileges, which we could not obtain in any of the new states of *this* country. Somewhere we must go, if we ever hope to get out of debt; and we shall not in *reality* be more separated from you, than we should be in Ohio, or Indiana. The communication between N. York and Matamoras is frequent and constant.

Two things are required of those who join our Colony; viz not to bring a drop of ardent spirits, or a particle of prejudice against color. Even if the Mexicans were as savage as Lydia thinks, abolitionists had better run their chance among them, than trust to the tender mercies of their own countrymen. If father means to join us, I wish he would make up, out of his good walnut timber, some ox-bows, and [. . .]les. Such things, and all kinds of seeds will be [. . .] a new settlement. It will not do for him to [. . .]*and*, unless things should be in a more quiet [. . .] Texas. We steer first for Matamoras; from which [. . .] will not be very far distant. Richard Pearce [. . .] agency in that city, where information concern[ing our m]ovements can always be obtained. If father comes, [. . .] to buy a bill of exchange with all the money he [. . .]ant to spend; ⟨and have the bill sent after him to Matamoras.⟩ He will receive it ⟨there⟩ at Matamoras, with 20 per ct profit; and it will be more safe than to take it with him. Isaac Pearce No. 478 Broadway, N. York, is Lundy's agent in that city, and he will advise him what steps are prudent, if he tells him who he is.

. . .

ALS; Child Letters, MC 305, Schlesinger Library, Radcliffe College (microfiche 4/93).

[1] On 10 Mar. 1835, Lundy signed a contract with Mexico for a tract of 138,000 acres between the Rio Grande and the Nueces rivers. He had permission to colonize two hundred fifty families within a two-year period, but he could not fix the actual site of the colony until he brought in the settlers.
[2] The margins of several pages of this letter are worn away, cutting off the ends of lines; bracket words are supplied by the editors.

To Louisa Loring

West Boylston. May 3d—[1836]

Dearest Louisa,

Of many changes there is no end. We have again resolved to go to England! and that immediately. But keep this strictly to yourself for the present. The state of the case is this. Difficulties increase so much in Mexico, and the probability of a war between that country and our own, seems to be so probable, that I found Mr. Child somewhat disheartened and unsettled with regard to our original scheme. Three days after I arrived here, we received a long letter from George Thompson; in which he says the friends of abolition in England are determined to have us there. They want us to edit a periodical, which they are about to establish, and which he says will be liberally supported. For fear the expense of coming will be an objection with us, they have already subscribed fifty pounds sterling to meet us on our arrival, to be at our service if we wish it. The Westminster & Edinburgh Reviews are said to want an able American writer very much. Our friend Mr. Appleton, who has lived a good deal in England, has been here for a few days past, and will bring you this letter in person.[1] He has been calculating our expenses and prospects, and he thinks we can do well in England. This encourages me—for I know he is a very calculating, prudent man, with great experience of the ways of the world. The reason we want you to say nothing, is that we desire to get away *noiselessly*.

Please tell Mr. Loring that Mr. Child's client, of whom he spoke to me, recovered a judgment in the justices' court, for his small debt; some 2 or 3 years ago.

Concerning the type-Foundry business, Mr. C did not write, because he wished it to be left to take its course.

I think I shall be with you next week. Mr. Child desires his best and most grateful affection to you both; with a kiss for dear Nony, and thanks for her transparent heart of oak.

With a settled prospect of doing *something somewhere*, I find hope again springing up in my heart. I do not wake up, as I have for months past with a load on my heart.

God bless you, my precious friend.

Yrs Truly,
Maria.

Love to Henrietta & M. Chapman, but do not speak of our plans yet.

ALS; Loring Family Papers, Schlesinger Library, Radcliffe College (microfiche 4/95).

[1] John James Appleton (1792–1864) served in a number of diplomatic posts, spending most of his life in France. He was a frequent correspondent of David's during this time.

———

Esther Carpenter (1815–1900) was the daughter of the Quakers Joseph and Margaret Carpenter, with whom the Childs had stayed in New Rochelle. She subsequently married Moses Pierce of Pleasantville, N.Y.; they named their daughter after Child.

To Esther Carpenter

West Boylston, May 9, 1836.

Abolitionism is rapidly growing respectable here, because the abolitionists are becoming more and more numerous. Since truth is thus made to depend on the voice of the majority, what a comfort it is to reflect that all majorities were minorities in the beginning.

I cannot forbear to repeat to you an interview between Miss Martineau and Mrs. _____, formerly a fashionable friend of mine, deeply skilled in the small diplomacy of worldly wisdom.[1] Mrs. _____ said some things in disparagement of Maria Chapman, accompanied with the wise remark that women were not capable of understanding political questions. My friend Mrs. _____, wishing Miss M. to take up the cudgel in defence of the rights of women, put her mouth to her ear-trumpet, and said, "Ask Mrs. _____ to repeat her remark to you!" The lady somewhat reluctantly observed, "I was saying, Miss M., that women ought to attend to their little duties, and let public affairs alone." "Believe me, Madam," replied Miss M., "that those who perform their great duties best are most likely to perform their little duties best." "Oh, certainly, of course," said Mrs. _____, "but Mrs. C. is so enthusiastic. She told me she felt she had a mission to perform on earth. Now, if I felt so, I should think I ought to be sent to Bedlam." "Madam," replied Miss M., "it appears to me that those of us who think we have no mission to perform on earth ought to be sent to Bedlam."

L, extract; *Letters of Lydia Maria Child*, 1882 (microfiche 4/96).

With the defeat of the Mexican army by the Texans in April 1836, Texas began operating as the independent Lone Star Republic. The Mexican troops had retreated south of the Rio Grande, placing Lundy's land within Texas boundaries. By June, Lundy abandoned plans for the colony, since an antislavery settlement would never be tolerated in Texas's predominantly proslavery atmosphere. Lundy and David Lee Child each wrote articles on the threat of Texas to free-soil advocates; their arguments were cited often during congressional debates on the annexation of Texas.

During the summer of 1836, the Childs lived apart, Maria at her father's house in Natick, David with his family in West Boylston, apparently to econo-

[1] The British writer and abolitionist Harriet Martineau (1802–76) travelled in the United States from 1834 to 1836.

mize and to allow David to litigate Snelling's law suit. Their letters to each other reflect her deepening despair over their poverty and David's discouragement over his business failures. Their sole income now came from her writing.

To David Lee Child

Natick July 28th 1836.

Dear Husband,

I have just received your sad letter. It went straight to my heart, and renewed the temptation, against which I have struggled for several days: viz. to jump into the cars and come straight up to West Boylston. You and I are like two drops of quick-silver placed a few inches apart on a level surface—there is a continual restlessness and agitation, till at last they get together, in spite of the perfect level.   Dear husband, do not be discouraged. "Better days are coming"—even in *this* world. And for another, who can tell with how much gratitude we may hereafter look back upon the fiery trials sent to purge away the dross and purify the gold? I think I can already perceive that they have done me good. Can not you perceive the same? Shall we not hereafter be more tender-hearted toward our suffering species? more considerate? more forgiving? I weep when I think how selfish and unreasonable I have often been. Dear husband, let us *profit* by our misfortunes, and thus turn them into gain.   Your feelings exaggerate both the past and the present. Few men have done more good in the world than you have done. Few are more *truly* respected, though thousands are more popular. The errors you have committed have been entirely errors of judgment. How much more bitter would be the retrospection, if you had to look back upon crime, and wilful wrong! God knows that I consider my union with you his richest blessing. It has made me a better and a happier woman than I ever was before. I had rather be your wife without a cent in the world, than to possess millions, and not be your wife. I have deep reason to say and feel this; for you have been to me a most kind, considerate, and forgiving husband; and I have ever loved and respected you with my whole heart. How many times have you guided me when I was wrong! How many times have you strengthened me, when I have been weak! How often restored me to my balance, when I have been perverse and unreasonable!   God bless you, my best-beloved friend! How I *do* want to fold you to my heart.

I am not surprised that the case has gone over to September. When I wrote to Louisa, last week, I told her I did not expect it would be finished till late in the fall, or early in the spring. But after all, what great matter is it? We *must* wait till the middle, or last, of September, at all events, to hear from Thompson. It will take you all that time to prepare the law-book you spoke of. You must come here, dearest, to do it. I have bargained with father about your board, and I can do your washing. Father resisted the mention of board and said you would be welcome here at all times; but I thought *you* would feel more independent to pay cheap board. The last of August some money will become due to me for the History of Women. You *must* come to me—and that *right off*. If you don't, I shall come to you; and that would look very foolish, you know. *Do* come, if you love me. Why should we be wandering apart, in melancholy mood, when we *can* be together? Letters can be sent after you immediately, you know. My heart aches to see you. I believe I should take the cars to morrow, if you had not written that Persis has come back. I wrote to you day before yesterday; (that is, on Tuesday) but when I received[1]

I sent for a letter Tuesday night, and felt down-hearted to learn there was none there; but my heart jumped this afternoon, at sight of your hand-writing.

Susan and father desire love to you.

AL; Lydia Maria Child Papers, Anti-Slavery Collection, Cornell University (microfiche 4/102).

In August 1836, Child learned the story of the slave child Med Sommersett, who had been brought north by a white woman from New Orleans. Child and other members of the Boston Female Anti-Slavery Society went as a delegation to Med's mistress to try to convince her to free the slave. After her refusal, the society secured a writ of habeas corpus, setting in motion a case that came before the Massachusetts Supreme Court late in August. Chief Justice Lemuel Shaw (1781–1861) made an unprecedented decision in favor of a slave's right to remain in a free state into which he had been brought temporarily—and hence to become free. Had this occurred two decades later, when the country was thoroughly roused over the issue of fugitive slaves, its importance would have been instantly and widely recognized. Abolitionists, of course, hailed the decision as a significant victory. Med remained in Massachusetts and was adopted by Isaac Knapp, copublisher of *The Liberator*.

To Esther Carpenter

South Natick, September 4, 1836.

I have lately had a most interesting case brought under my observation. When in Boston I was entreated to exert myself concerning a little child, supposed to be a slave, brought from New Orleans, and kept shut up at No. 21 Pinckney Street. The object was to persuade the child's mistress to leave her at the colored asylum, and failing to effect this object, to ascertain beyond doubt whether the child was a slave, whether there was intention to carry her back to New Orleans, and to obtain sight of her in order to be able to prove her iden-

---

[1] The letter breaks off here, the remaining pages lost. The last two paragraphs are postscripts on earlier pages.

tity. . . .[1] I will not fill this sheet with particulars. Suffice it to say, the way was opened for us. We obtained all the evidence we wanted, carried it to a lawyer, who petitioned for a writ of habeas corpus; the judge granted the petition; and the man who held little Med in custody was brought up for trial. In consequence of the amount of evidence ready to be proved by three witnesses, the pro-slavery lawyers did not pretend to deny that the intent was to carry the child back into slavery; but they took the new and extraordinary ground that Southern masters had a legal right to hold human beings as slaves while they were visiting here in New England. Judge Wild expressed a wish to consult with the other judges; and our abolition friends, finding the case turn on such a very important point, resolved to retain the services of Webster, for want of a better man. He was willing to serve provided they would wait a few days. Rufus Choate, a man only second to him in abilities, and whose heart is strongly favorable to anti-slavery, was employed.[2] The opposite counsel were full of sophistry and eloquence. One of them really wiped his own eyes at the thought that the poor little slave might be separated from its slave mother by mistaken benevolence. His pathos was a little marred by my friend E. G. Loring, who arose and stated that it was distinctly understood that little Med was to be sold on her way back to New Orleans, to pay the expenses of her mistress's journey to the North. The judges decided unanimously in favor of Med and liberty!

The "Commercial Gazette" of the next day says: "This decision, though unquestionably according to law, is much to be regretted; for such cases cannot but injure the custom of our hotels, now so liberally patronized by gentlemen from the South." Verily, Sir Editor, thou art an honest devil; and I thank thee for not being at the pains to conceal thy cloven foot.

L, extract; *Letters of Lydia Maria Child*, 1882 (microfiche 4/106).

A new phase of the Childs' married life began when David decided to travel to Europe in the fall of 1836 to study the farming of sugar beets. At that time, the manufacture of beet sugar was virtually unheard of in the United States. David's idea was to employ free labor to undersell Southern growers, reduce the value of slave labor, and undermine the Southern economy.

In the following letter, Child refers to two members of the influential

---

[1] The ellipses are from the 1882 edition of Child's letters. The owner of Med accused the women's delegation of gaining entrance to the house under the pretense of looking for Sunday school children.
[2] Samuel Sumner Wild (1771–1885) became a judge on the Massachusetts Supreme Court in 1815 and served until 1850. Daniel Webster (1782–1852) was U.S. senator and secretary of state under Presidents William Henry Harrison and John Tyler. His reputation with the abolitionists had not yet been ruined by his support of the Compromise of 1850. Choate (1799–1859), a prominent Boston lawyer, later in his life became hostile to the antislavery movement.

Beecher family. Lyman Beecher (1775–1863), eminent Presbyterian minister, was the father of nine children, including Harriet (Beecher) Stowe, the author; Catharine, the educator; Henry Ward, the Congregationalist minister; and Isabella (Beecher) Hooker, the suffragist. Lyman was president of Lane Theological Seminary in 1834 when the trustees forbade the organization of antislavery groups and the discussion of abolition on campus. He supported the colonization of blacks and regarded abolitionists like Child as fanatics.

Her reference to Lyman's oldest son is actually to the second-born son, Edward Beecher (1803–95), who was the only active abolitionist in the family at this time. Approximately one year after the date of this letter, he helped Elijah Lovejoy defend his press in Alton, Illinois, from the pro-slavery mob that killed Lovejoy. Edward Beecher published his *Narrative of the Riots in Alton* (Alton, Ill.) in 1837.

The story of Charity Bowery (d. ca. 1838) describes the frequently cruel treatment of slaves by their masters. Shortly before this letter was written, Charity had been trying to earn money to buy the freedom of her son, Richard, by taking in laundry. All of her sixteen children were sold away from her.

To Lydia (Bigelow) Child

Boston Oct. 19th 1836

Dear Mother,

I arrived in Boston yesterday, after a rapid passage from New York. I did not *forget* my promise to write soon, neither was I *negligent;* but immediately on our arrival at N. York our prospects were thrown into uncertainty by unexpected circumstances, and I waited to *know* something concerning what we were to do, before I wrote. Five minutes after we landed, we found our friend George Kimball, formerly of New Hampshire.[1] He was just on the point of seeking my husband in Boston, to convey to him certain proposals of some wealthy gentlemen, provided he would learn the process of making Beet Sugar. I thought I would delay writing, till it was decided whether those propositions would be accepted. They were accepted—and we expected to spend the winter in Philadelphia to learn the process. I resolved to write the moment we were settled there in a comfortable boarding-house. But, as if disappointments and uncertainty were *always* to be our portion, the Philadelphia manufacturers retracted their own solemn promise to teach, and resolved to keep the secret to themselves. Then all was afloat again, till Mr. Kimball urged Mr. Child to go to France to acquire the desired knowledge. After some demurs, this was decided upon, and a passage was engaged. But a dispute arose between those who freighted the vessel and those who chartered her, in consequence of which the captain was obliged to give up carrying passengers. This occasioned eight days' delay. Passage was engaged in

[1] Kimball was a lawyer who had practiced in Canaan, N.H., and then moved to Alton, Ill. He had made plans to join Lundy's free-labor colony in Mexico.

another vessel, the Solon, for London; and my dear husband sailed in her on Monday last at 11 o'clock.

He went by way of England in order to transact some law-business there, which he hopes will prove profitable; but he intends to cross over to France as soon as possible, and hopes to return to me in May.

My poverty, but not my will, consented to remaining behind, while one I loved so much was going where I so much wished to go. I shall probably spend most of my time with my friends in Boston, where I can most easily procure the books that I want to use for writing. I think the prospect is that my dear husband can get a good living by this new business, in almost any part of the country. If it is the Lord's will, I hope I shall be spared from going to the West. I have an exceeding dread of such a destination; but I hope I shall be willing to do my duty.

In New York, I heard the Revd Mr. Ludlow, a Presbyterian minister, who is the heartiest abolition preacher I ever heard. In one of his sermons, he spoke of the reluctance to make sacrifices in the service of God. "There are few like Moses, that good abolitionist," said he, "who preferred rather to suffer persecution with the people of God, than to enjoy the pleasures of sin for a season". They have five preachers in New York, who openly and boldly manifest their abolition tendencies, both in sermons and prayers. Doctor Beecher's eldest son has come out a warm abolitionist, and is said to be laboring with his jesuitical father. At the Tabernacle in New York, when invitations are given to partake the sacrament, they always except those "who vend or distil ardent spiri[ts] or keep their fellow men in bondage."   Old Charity Bowery was much pleased at the attention of sending her the night-caps. She thanked me a hundred times over, and prayed over and over again that the Lord would bless me, and my husband, and my father, and my sister Lydia, who was so kind as to think of poor Charity. I asked her if she had received tidings of any of her children since I saw her. The poor creature groaned as she answered, "Yes maam I have heard that poor Richard is no longer a slave. I heard that he was bought by a Mr. Mitchell of Mobile. Will, a gentleman who has been very kind to me was going to Mobile; so I asked him to inquire for poor Richard. When he come back, he did not love to tell me what he had heard; but I begged so hard, that at last he let me know the truth. Mr. Mitchell ordered poor Richard to come to be flogged. Richard said he had done nothing to be flogged for, and he would not come. His master said, "If you dont come immediately, I'll shoot you." "Shoot then," replied Richard; "I dont deserve to be flogged, and I wont come". Mr. Mitchell pointed his pistol, fired, and in two hours after my boy was dead. He told the gentleman of this himself, and boasted of what he had done."

.   .   .

L; Simison Papers, Beinecke Rare Book and Manuscript Library, Yale University (microfiche 4/108).

Child confronted Boston aristocracy directly in the person of William Ellery Channing, the preeminent Unitarian minister. In the next letter, she gives a vignette of one of their many discussions on slavery. She refers to a petition headed by Channing, part of a steady flow sent to Congress that reached a peak in 1836. Child's *Appeal* was an important early influence on Channing's antislavery ideas, but he remained a gradualist.

To Henrietta Sargent

South Natick Nov. 13th 1836.

Dearest Friends,

I suppose you heard of me on my way to Doctor Channing's? The reason I did not call for you to accompany me, was just this. I did not *intend* to go, before I left Boston; but when Mr. Loring came home to dinner, he urged it as a duty, both to politeness and to abolition. He had, moreover, a good deal to say about the absolute *necessity* of my mixing with people of the world—for the want of which, he said I was growing intolerant and unsocial. Aware that there was considerable truth in his arguments, "I up and went;" but it was too late in the afternoon, to think of coming round for you.

I found the Rev. Doctor walking down Mount Vernon; but he insisted so strongly upon going back, that I at last consented. He was very kind and complimentary, in manners and conversation. He soon began to talk of Anti Slavery. I could see that he had progressed (as we Yankees say) considerably since I last conversed with him; but he still betrayed his characteristic timidity. Almost every sentence began with, "I am doubtful," or "I am afraid." He was "doubtful" of the policy of sending out seventy agents.[1] He was "afraid" there would be among them some indifferent men. I told him that they gave pretty good evidence they were not indifferent to the *cause*. He did not mean *that*—he meant there would be some among them of indifferent intellectual and moral gifts. I urged that their willingness to go was strong presumptive evidence in favor of their *moral* character; and expressed a reasonable doubt whether the seventy sent out by the apostles were all equally gifted. He replied, "But *they* went out on a very simple errand." I rejoined, "And the abolitionists go out on a very simple errand. Their principles are a resuscitation of doctrines preached by the apostolic seventy." He admitted that the foundation principles of Christianity and abolition were identical; but still *this* subject was so intertwisted with politics, prejudice, and interest—and the manner of *illustrating* it might be so injudicious, that he thought it every way desirable to have agents peculiarly qualified. I answered that we had good reason to suppose the early opposition to *Christianity* was inter-

[1] These agents were trained by Theodore Weld and were single-handedly responsible for abolitionizing Ohio, New York, Pennsylvania, and Rhode Island. The nucleus of the "Seventy" was the men who withdrew from Lane Seminary in the fall of 1834 when they were forbidden to discuss abolitionism.

woven with the prejudices and interests of nations. If it were not so, why had the apostles been persecuted even unto death. We, like the apostles, could only choose the willing-hearted, and trust that God would bless their mission. Even if it were desirable to select the "wise and prudent" of this world, there was abundant reason to suppose that now, as then, they would not be in *readiness* to perform the Lord's mission.

I don't know how much longer we might have "argufied" about the seventy, if we had not been interrupted by Mrs. William Minot, who was soon followed by several other ladies.[2] From courtesy, I forebore to renew a subject, which might be embarrassing to mine host, in the presence of visiters, who doubtless would not so much as touch it with a pair of tongs; but I was much pleased to have the Doctor interrupt some general remarks, which I made on literature, with this question—"But, Mrs. Child, I want you to tell me something more about the progress of Anti-slavery." I related several anecdotes illustrative of the progressive movement of the public mind—assuring him that all ranks and classes *had* been moved, in spite of themselves—nay even while many cursed the *steam* which propelled them. I did not forget to relate how many Southerners in N. York, during the past summer, had been into the Anti Slavery office to inquire for the best books on emancipation. He seemed much affected by the story of the anonymous fifty dollars sent to the Society, as "the *Master's* mite toward the relief of those in bondage."

On the whole, I trust I helped him on a *little*. When I again come into the city, the busy *mouse* will again go to work gnawing away the net-work, which aristocratic family and friends are all the time weaving around the *lion*. Next time, I wont cheat *you* of your visit. I wish you had been with me this time, to help me remember; for the first part of his conversation I cannot recall, for the life of me.

. . .

Yrs most affectionately, L M. Child.

I suppose you have heard ere this that Doct Chaning [*sic*] promptly headed the Boston Petition for the abolition of slavery in District of Columbia. The one in Norfolk County is headed by J. Q. Adams.[3] It will sound well in Congress to read aloud, "The petition of W'm. E. Channing & others". "The petition of J. Q. Adams, & others"!

ALS; Lydia Maria Child Papers, Anti-Slavery Collection, Cornell University (microfiche 4/110).

[2] Louisa (Davis) Minot (1787–1858) was a contributor to the *North American Review*, an art educator, and the author of a book on perspective and several works for children. She and her husband, William, lived on Beacon Hill in Boston.

[3] Former president John Quincy Adams (1767–1848), then representing the Plymouth District, Mass., in the Congress, led the fight for the right of petition. He opposed the congressional gag rules tabling antislavery petitions because they obstructed the right of free speech.

The Anti-Slavery Fairs mentioned in the following letter were a major source of funds for the movement. In 1834, Child and Louisa Loring organized the first bazaar, which was held at the Massachusetts Anti-Slavery Society office in Boston. The Boston Female Anti-Slavery Society took over the sponsorship in 1835 and continued the annual fairs for many years. They offered a wide range of items, such as free-labor sugar, gift books, handcrafts, and clothing. During the 1840s and 1850s, the fairs netted an average of four thousand dollars a year for the abolitionists.

While David was in Europe, Child would continue to live with her father until the winter of 1838. During this period, when she was separated from her husband and anxious about money, her aversion to the "bustling world" intensified. Her reclusiveness—a sharp contrast to the delight she had shown in the attention paid to her as an aspiring author in Boston—would become a part of her legend.

To Louisa Loring

South Natick Nov 27th 1836

Dear Louisa,

. . .

Since I came here I have been as busy as a bird building her nest. Writing, pasting, sewing, and knitting—sometimes for myself, sometimes for the Fair. I suppose I have accomplished at least twice as much as I should have done in the same space of time in Boston. To my surprise, I found father had provided wood, and sawed it short, for a fire *in my chamber*. I never doubted his kindness and generosity to me; but I did not expect that he would be willing to be thus *put out of his way*, and have the arrangements of his household altered.

Before I left you, I was much inclined to spend a large portion of the winter in Natick; and this circumstance has decided me. After various argumentations, father has consented to let me pay for my wood, and a dollar a week for board, provided I insist upon it. My washing I can do myself; and thus I can be as independent as a lordling, for trifling expense. The absence of all intellectual excitement I do feel—sometimes oppressively; but I have great kindness and temporal comfort, and it is a good place to *work*.

If I had nothing to do but to take my pleasure, I know of nothing I should like better than to read to you, and "play with Ellis;" but I have been so long afloat, with a mind harrassed by the vexatious minutiæ of pecuniary difficulties, that I *must* work. I am so anxious to earn something for Mr. Child before he comes home, that I should be sorry just at this time to have any of those renowned German Satans appear before me with a large offer for myself. The sentence startles me since I have written it—for I have of late been siezed with such a novel thirst for money, that I do not know but some of those imps are indeed at work. Well, if he is at work upon me, he wont let me stay on abolition ground—that's clear. *That* will make him show his horns and hoof, however much he may be enamored of darkness.

Another advantage attending a residence in Natick is, that I shall be free from occasional contact with the bustling world, which is so inconceivably irksome to my wearied spirit. I know such intercourse has its advantages, and that faults of character are increasing for want of this salutary check. If ever I again have a *home*, I will cultivate society, in spite of my teeth. The tedious taxes of etiquette shall be duly paid; and I will endeavor to be a polished marble, without any obtruding corners to jostle other polished marbles, or any roughnesses to prevent its rolling smoothly along the path of life.

But at present, I cannot find motive to make this exertion; because I feel all the time in a *migratory* state. With all the busy machinery of society, I have nought to do. The puppets, and those that move them, are all strangers to me; and I cannot find any reasons why I should seek to make acquaintance with them. To do good, and receive good, would indeed be a sufficient reason; but then I feel that I shall not be among them long enough to effect this purpose. For opportunities lost and influence wasted, I have many bitter regrets; but this is foolish—if I were to live life over again (which God in his mercy forbid!) I should make the same mistakes, or worse ones.

Brother Convers spent the day here last week. He was in one of his pleasantest and brightest moods. He came to invite me to Thanksgiving, and to spend at least a portion of the winter with him. I promised to go for a few days. I am glad he came. By being separate, the distance would only be increased by a thousand imaginary causes.

I intend to come to Boston the latter part of the week after Thanksgiving, and stay about three weeks; then I retire into my den for the winter.

Give my most affectionate regards to Mr. Loring, and my little friend Anna. Tell old Mrs Loring that I have thankful recollection of various warm doses, tucking up of the bed-clothes, and divers other "creature comforts," which I owed to her careful hands.

Farewell.   Your affectionate & grateful friend, L. M. C.

ALS; Loring Family Papers, Schlesinger Library, Radcliffe College (microfiche 4/111).

To Lydia B. Child

South Natick. Jan 17'th 1837.

Dear Sister,

Half an hour ago, I received my first letter from David, and I hasten to inform you, as I know you must be anxious. It contained little information, except that he had been well during the voyage, and had arrived safely in Liverpool. As the letter was sent off as soon as he got on shore, he, of course, could tell me little about his prospects. He sailed from New York on the 17'th of Oct, and arrived in Liverpool on the 13'th of Nov. A pretty good passage, considering he went in a merchant ship.

When we shall be re-united, I know not, nor where we shall go, when we do meet. I have so much lost my interest in all things connected with this life, that I care but little about anything.

You have doubtless learned the success of our Fair from the Liberator. My cradle-quilt sold for $5. Mr. Garrison bought one of David's oak hearts for abolitionists. He said the idea was so much like Mr. Child that he *must* have one of them. A sort of half-abolition party seems to gain ground in Boston, but the thorough abolitionists are at a stand. One of the most remarkable steps in the progress of the cause is the publication of a novel called Archy Moore.[1] The hero purports to be a runaway slave, and tells his own story with all the eloquence of genius aided by fiery indignation. It is a very powerful book, both in the truths it contains, and the genius with which it is written. The author betrays such a minute knowledge of all the local peculiarities of the South, that he must have resided there. If the book were not very high priced, I would purchase half a dozen to send round the country. It is *conjectured* to be from the pen of a young lawyer in Boston, named Hildreth. He is the partner of Richard Fletcher, of odious Fanieul Hall memory; but differs from him widely in his opinions of slavery.[2] He has lived a good deal at the South.   (I have spelt the old Hall wrong—Never mind—I always forget how to spell it.)

I was in Boston a few weeks, to help them about the Fair. The day before I returned, as I was coming out of an apothecary's shop, where I had been to buy some cough-drops, I heard somebody calling, "Mrs. Child! Maria Child!" I turned and saw Mrs. Bigelow of Watertown.[3] ["]How d'ye do? Did you write Archy Moore?" "No. I did not." "I told Mr. Bigelow I didn't believe a woman wrote it; but he said nobody but you *could* write it." "What do people say of it?" "Say! Why it's moving Heaven and Earth!" "I am glad of it. Heaven and earth *ought* to be moved on this subject." "Good-bye."   I thought this interview carried on at the top of our voices, in a keen wind, on a slippery side-walk, was quite characteristic.

---

[1] Richard Hildreth's *The Slave; or, Memoirs of Archy Moore* (Boston, 1836) was a significant antislavery work and went through several editions. Hildreth (1807-65), lawyer, historian, and editor, later wrote *Despotism in America* (Boston, 1840), a discussion of the effects of slavery.

[2] Fletcher (1788-1869) was a distinguished trial lawyer in Massachusetts and a congressman from 1837 to 1839. Child is referring to the 21 Aug. 1835 meeting at Faneuil Hall in which Fletcher and others criticized the abolitionists. He later supported abolition in the District of Columbia and an end to the domestic slave trade. Child appealed to him in December of 1836 for money for the Boston Samaritan Asylum for Indigent Colored Children, but there is no record of his response.

[3] Clarissa Bigelow and her husband, Tyler, were David Child's aunt and uncle.

There is no particular news stirring, that I know of; though a vast deal might stir without my knowledge; for I live very much the life of an oyster, now-a-days.

. . .

ALS; Child Letters, MC 305, Schlesinger Library, Radcliffe College (microfiche 5/115).

The year 1837 was a turning point for the abolitionists. Up to that time, their main goal had been to get a public hearing. Differences among them in social philosophy, tactics, and personalities had been submerged. But by the middle of 1837, these differences were becoming more critical. The role of women changed dramatically as Angelina and Sarah Grimké began lecturing to "promiscuous audiences" (men and women), raising the issue whether women should leave their private "sphere" and enter the world of politics. At the end of the year, Elijah Lovejoy was martyred by a proslavery mob in Alton, Illinois. On the East Coast, the Massachusetts Anti-Slavery Society withdrew its financial support of *The Liberator*, a move that gave Garrison the freedom to discuss non-resistance and antisabbatarianism in the paper. Increasingly, his radical ideas became the focus of criticism from the clergy and from many national leaders of the antislavery movement.

In the next letter, Child's picture of harmony at the annual meeting of the Massachusetts Anti-Slavery Society glosses over the debate which took place over the issue of political action versus moral persuasion.

To Lydia B. Child

Boston. Jan 27th 1837

Dear Sister,

Expecting to meet the Revd Mr. Sinclair this evening, I cannot forbear, though in a great hurry, to say a few words to you.[1] I took a sudden resolution to come down to the Annual A. Slavery meeting, and arrived in the middle of the first day. When I learned that they were obliged to meet in a *Stable*, in this city of churches, I was doubly glad that I encountered cold weather and bad travelling, for the sake of being there.[2] It is not the *first* time (I speak it reverently) that Divine Truth has been placed in a stable. On the evening of the second day we obtained the Representative's Hall, by a majority of *one* vote. Small as this

[1] Alanson St. Clair (1804–77), or Sinclair, as Child calls him, was a pastor in Universalist and Unitarian churches in Worcester, Mass., and an agent for the Massachusetts Anti-Slavery Society.
[2] Efforts to find a meeting space in a church for the anniversary meeting of the Massachusetts Society were futile, and the members finally settled for a loft in a stable.

majority is, it shows that our friends are coming up near enough to our enemies at least to *measure swords*. We owe this chance to the *country* members. "God bless the yeomanry of Massachusetts! How they make the enemy fly!"

By the blessings of God, we improved this opportunity to address the people gloriously—most gloriously! I really thought I should depart from the body, with sheer extatic delight. Mr. Loring made a clear, logical, persuasive, and somewhat witty speech; Amos Dresser told his narrative in a very simple and affecting manner; and Stanton blared forth like a volcano.[3] I thought I could almost *see* the fiery sparkles of his eloquence falling into the hearts of men all over the house there to do its work, until they were "purified by fire." The meeting was crowded to suffocation, and it was thought more than a thousand went away for want of room. Some hissing and a good deal of noise; but this latter seemed principally occasioned by efforts to get in. One country representative who had violently opposed our having the use of the Hall, came to Mr. May,[4] after the meeting, and put ten dollars in his hand, for the Society. "I have been mistaken["] said he, "and there is my acknowledgment of it." "Will you put your name down as a member?" asked Mr. May. "Not *yet*," was the significant reply.

To day we have had a small meeting, intended for business; but nevertheless, there has been a great deal of speaking—much of it highly interesting and affecting. Mr. Sinclair astounded me with his whole-hearted zeal. Mr. May listened to him till his expressive face fairly mantled all over with joy. "How I rejoice," said he, "that there exists such union in the Abolition Church. Bro. Such a one, is a clergyman of the *Calvinistic* church; that one, of the *Methodist;* this one of the *Baptist;* & I am a *Unitarian:* yet we have all uttered the same principles—all breathed the same spirit." Here he was informed that Mr. Sinclair was not a Baptist. He turned and shook hands, as he exclaimed "A Unitarian! Welcome, most welcome, another in the ranks of righteousness"! I whispered, "Ah, brother May, he was so *warm*, that you thought he could not be a Unitarian." The frank-hearted man replied, "Your joke is no joke, because it is true. That *was* the reason I did not suppose he was a Unitarian."

I have had no letter from Mr. Child since I wrote to you; but a letter from Miss Martineau to Mr. Loring speaks of a party which she made for him, where everybody was listening to his account of slavery & anti-slavery in America.

---

[3] Amos Dresser (d. 1904) and Henry Brewster Stanton (1805–87) were among the group of "Lane Rebels," from Lane Theological Seminary, in the American Anti-Slavery Society. Dresser was publicly flogged in Nashville, Tenn., for having abolitionist material in his suitcase. Stanton organized the Rhode Island Anti-Slavery Society. An excellent orator, he was one of the most articulate critics of Garrison in the late 1830s. He married Elizabeth Cady in 1840, shortly before they went to London as delegates to the World Anti-Slavery Convention. Later Stanton became active in the Liberty party and then the Republican party.
[4] Samuel Joseph May.

Oh, I *do* hope we shan't have to go to the West. I dread it worse than any other catastrophe that I can imagine.

Best love to Mother & Lucretia.

Yrs Truly
Maria.

L; Simison Papers, Beinecke Rare Book and Manuscript Library, Yale University (microfiche 5/116).

To Louisa Loring

South Natick. Saturday Eve.
[March? 1837]

Dear Louise,

Mr. Child's long, long expected letter came to day. All but one sheet of it was a copy of communications to Mr. Kimball[1] about machinery &c. It was written under the mistaken impression that the Illinois Company was formed, and beginning operations.

He appears to enter into this new subject with all his heart and soul, as he generally does. His letter to me, though rather business like, is more loving than the first one; and I am consequently less out of sorts with matrimony than I was. He does not say when he went to France, nor tell a word what he did in England. His letter is dated from Arras in Belgium. He says friends seem to rain down upon him, and he has been prospered far beyond his expectations in prosecuting the objects of his voyage. He names the whole of May and June as the time of his probable return. He does not tell me anything about his "*pecunary*" affairs, though how he is to stay abroad so long is more than I can imagine, without he "adds in the Year of our Lord into the sum of his profits."—He desires love to you and yours.

Since I left Boston I have received a proposal for him from the State of New York, which I am in hopes may prove a good thing.

When I came up to Natick, I had rather an odd scene in the stage. For several miles I sat reading Ion, without looking up. But there were five representatives in the stage, and anon they began to speak of abolition petitions. I laid down my book and listened. Two praised Mr. Adams warmly. A third doubted the propriety of agitating that subject. I asked him why? He said it made the Southerners angry. I told him it was a pity he had'nt been on the carpet to have advised St Paul not to offend people. He said the North was all right on that subject. I told him "oh yes—that was the reason, when two slaves ran away from Baltimore, merchants in State St were ready to subscribe thousands to catch them & send

[1] George Kimball.

63

them back." He said that when people committed a crime it was right to sieze them. I asked him what crime had been committed? He said they had broken the law in running away from their masters. "This is a fresh proof of the soundness of opinion at the North," said I—"when a representative of Massachusetts, who it must be supposed has read the Declaration of Independence, declares it a *crime* for a slave to run away"! The other representatives laughed, & clapped their hands. I asked him what he would do if thrown on the Algerine coast, and sold to an Arab. He said he supposed he should try to regain his liberty. "Oh no," replied I, "it would be a *crime* to run away from your master." He said colored people were inferior to us, and were *made* for slaves. I told him that position was not susceptible of proof; but one thing *was* clearly proved to my mind; viz. that a man who thought it a *crime* for a slave to run away, was unquestionably fit for a slave.

At every turn I threw that word *crime* in his teeth. His brethren laughed and clapped. The poor man winced under it, and said "he was unfortunate in his mode of expression—it would perhaps have been better to have chosen another word" &c.   Who this Northern "sky-ophant" was, I know not; but I burnt him up like a stroke of the sun, and swept his ashes up after him. I was not the least mite angry; but never in all my life was I half so brilliant and witty. It seems to have produced the effect of an electric shock upon the members in the stage. Every day or two some new echo comes back to me from the neighboring towns.

Oh, if I was a man, how I *would* lecture! But I am a woman, and so I sit in the corner and knit socks.

. . .

Yrs L. M. C.

I have been gloomy almost to madness for these last three weeks; but my dear husband's letter has enlivened me.

ALS; Lydia Maria Child Papers, Schlesinger Library, Radcliffe College (microfiche 5/121).

The convention Child mentions in the next letter is the first Anti-Slavery Convention of American Women held 9–12 May 1837 in New York City. Child refused to be a delegate. Perhaps she balked at accepting money from the society. She was fiercely proud of her financial independence, or the appearance of it, and was loath to accept help except in circumstances of extreme need. She may also have thought, as did Lucretia Mott and others in the Philadelphia Female Anti-Slavery Society, that women were better off as equal members in the American Society than as members of a sexually segregated organization.

To Lydia B. Child

South Natick. April 2d 1837

Dear Sister

I last week received a letter from my precious husband, after waiting more than three months in anxious suspense, without hearing a single word. I have received but three letters in the whole; one from England, and two from Belgium. He says "friends have seemed to rain down upon him, and he has been blessed beyond expectation in the objects of his voyage." I shall begin to expect him about the last of May. What his prospects will be after his arrival, is very uncertain. I have a sort of superstition that his customary bad luck will follow him in every thing. The fact is, I no longer have any hope concerning these matters. But it seems to me I can be content to have him with me in the poorest and dreariest corner of the world. He writes in a full flow of spirits, for he has been continually busy, and his whole soul is taken up with the objects of his mission. I have sent a few extracts from his last letter to the Liberator. If they have room to publish them, you will see that he is not too much hurried, to keep his eyes open to all that concerns the slave.

I think the recent tidings from Mount Vernon will not increase Lucretia's attachment to that place.[1] Who would have thought that the demon of slavery had taken such entire possession of this people? But is it not wonderful how fast the Lord is doing this work?—not only in spite of enemies, but by the very instrumentality of enemies? Stanton is a giant in the cause. He goes up to Goliah 'in the name of the living God,' and strikes him in the very forehead. His late able and eloquent defence before the House of Representatives is thought to have given a prodigious impulse to the cause.[2] I do not like to be shut up in Natick in these stirring times, I assure you. I am trying to write an abolition novel; but it must be a sort of argumentative affair; for anything that took the *same* ground as Archy Moore would seem utterly tame in comparison.[3] The Revd Ira Blanchard here thinks it must be over-wrought; for, like most of his tribe, he is very ready to believe the robber, but slow to believe the robbed.[4]

You remember I told you of Charity Bowery's daughter, who was obliged to promise on the Bible that she would not run away; and then "for her honor and her Christianity's sake, went back into slavery." It seems that her mistress, Mrs. Orme, was in Boston this autumn and winter, superintending the education

[1] Child probably refers to Martin Van Buren's inauguration speech, in which he refused to support efforts to abolish slavery in the nation's capital and the rest of the South.
[2] In the spring of 1837, the Massachusetts legislature gave abolitionists permission to speak to committees in the House of Representatives. Henry Stanton and William Lloyd Garrison were among the speakers.
[3] Child never published the abolition novel, and the manuscript has not been found.
[4] Ira Henry Thomas Blanchard (1797–1845) graduated from Harvard in 1817 in the same class as David Child.

of her nieces.[5] Some friends in N. York gave notice of this circumstance to the Female Anti-Slavery Society of Boston, and requested their aid for the poor slave; that is, to procure permission for Maria to come and stay with her aged mother, before she dies. Mrs. Southwick, Mary S. Parker, and Catherine Sullivan waited upon Mrs. Orme, with a letter from certain New York ladies, who were friendly to poor Charity Bowery.[6] Mrs. Southwick is the Quaker lady, who rebuked Turner, the Baltimore slave agent; and you may well believe that her remarks were uncompromising and searching. Our excellent President was solemn and impressive, as she always is; and Miss Sullivan pleaded with her characteristic gentleness and persuasion. But Mrs. Orme was unmoved and incredulous. She said Maria was now residing with her brother at the South, and if his consent could be obtained, she might perhaps be allowed to visit her old mother. She could not possibly give Maria her freedom, because she was very much attached to the woman, and the woman very much attached to her, and entirely unfit to take care of herself. For the same reason, she civilly declined the offer of the New-York ladies to purchase Maria. She would not be so unkind as to deprive the woman of her protection. What mockery!   Like James and John, I am sometimes tempted to call down fire from Heaven. But why do I say this? Fire *has* come down from Heaven. It is kindling men's hearts, and will yet purify this guilty nation.

With the exception of attending the Annual Meeting two months ago, I have been entirely separated from *the brethren*. The Liberator, and now and then a letter from Mrs. Chapman, keeps me in their track. The death of Ann Chapman is a *very* severe loss to us.[7] It seems a mysterious Providence that one so much needed should have been taken, while so many 'cumberers of the ground' remain. But the 'Lord's ways are not as our ways,' and his doings are wisely hid from us.

It seems there is to be a Female Convention, in New York. The Boston Society are to send Mary S. Parker and Susan Paul (colored) as delegates.[8] Both the individuals are extremely well chosen. I was appointed as a third delegate, and a vote passed to pay all my expenses; but I declined going. I had rather put money

[5] Unnoted names could not be identified.

[6] Thankful (Hussey) Southwick (1791–1867), a Quaker, hosted George Thompson during his American tour and in 1838 served on the executive board of the New England Non-Resistance Society. Mary Stockwell Parker (1801–41) was president of the Boston Female Anti-Slavery Society at this time.

[7] Ann Greene Chapman (1802–37), daughter of Henry Chapman, the antislavery merchant, and sister-in-law of Maria (Weston) Chapman, was an active member of the Boston Female Anti-Slavery Society and bequeathed more than a thousand dollars to the antislavery cause.

[8] Susan Paul (1809–41) was the daughter of Thomas Paul, pastor of the African Baptist Church in Boston. A teacher in a black primary school in Boston, she became a life member of the New England Anti-Slavery Society. She was secretary of a black women's temperance society, an active member of the Boston Female Anti-Slavery Society, and vice-president of the second Anti-Slavery Convention of American Women. She died of tuberculosis at thirty-two.

into their pockets, than take it from them. My cheerfulness and patience have been very severely tried this winter; especially while waiting so long for a letter from my husband. Father is extremely kind, and *wants* to make me happy; but he so habitually looks on the dark side, that I believe he would keep the very larks from singing. To contend with his gloom and my own too, has sometimes seemed a hopeless task.   I was very much obliged to you for your long, kind letter. I should like to come to West Boylston very much; but am at present too economical to travel much. I do not know whether Mr. Child will come here, on his return, or whether he will send for me to meet him in N. York. His future plans are involved in entire uncertainty. . . .

. . .

The people in this village are dead while they live—about slavery and everything else. The fact is, their priest is a mere feeder on husks. In the upper village of Natick, Mr. Moore, the clergyman, has always had his heart open on the subject. As a natural result, there is a large anti-slavery society formed there, of which he is a member. How fearful are the responsibilities of the clergy at this time!   I wrote Mr. Thompson word that Mr. Hard did not dare to christen Lucretia's baby.[9] Has she heard from her good husband? What are his prospects? It appears to me if I can only be with my husband again, I shall never more express any dissatisfaction with him ⟨again⟩, if he shoots all the birds in the country, and sets the house afire beside.

Remember me to Betsy Keyes. Ann Chapman was very much pleased with her sincere, direct letter about the petitions. Pray get up an *enormous* petition this year; and in order to do it, begin in right good season. Van Buren seems to suppose that he and Jackson are going to countervene the Almighty. He will find himself mistaken.

Remember me to Mrs. Newton and the Nash family. I *hope* they will spare no pains to scatter abolition broadcast through town and country.

Farewell. Your affectionate sister,

Maria.

I wish when you write, you would inform me when the butter-nuts ought to be *gathered* to make pills & syrup.

ALS; Child Letters, MC 305, Schlesinger Library, Radcliffe College (microfiche 5/120).

To Henrietta Sargent

South Natick. April 17'th [1837?]

Dear Henrietta,

Do you think, and does Mrs. Chapman think, I do wrong in not going to the Convention? Do either of you think I am refusing to do what I can to assist the

---

[9] Mr. Hard may have been a minister in South Boylston. Lucretia (Child) Haskins' baby was named for George Thompson. A later son was named for William Lloyd Garrison, a daughter for Lydia Maria Child.

cause? If so, tell me frankly. I have various misgivings. My reluctance to go is great, and it may blind my perceptions of duty. Besides I am in a vacillating and discouraged state of mind. I feel as if I had no more to do in the world—or at least no *power* to do any more.

This state of mind, being wrong in itself, is unfavorable to clear views of duty.

Tell me what you and Mrs. Chapman think of my refusal. I do not ask this from mere solicitude about the *opinions* entertained of me, even by those whom I respect and love so much as I do you two; but perhaps your moral vision is clearer than mine. I *want* to do what is right.

When is Mrs. Loring going into the country? I do not want to come to Boston till May, on account of being occupied; but if she goes soon, I must either come at an earlier date, or not see *her* all summer.

With kind remembrance to Catherine,

Yrs Affectionately
L. M. Child.

ALS; Lydia Maria Child Papers, Schlesinger Library, Radcliffe College (microfiche 5/122).

The Boston Juvenile Anti-Slavery Society started a children's petition campaign for the abolition of slavery in the District of Columbia (boys under twenty-one years and girls under sixteen years could sign), and *The Liberator* advised parents to encourage their children in this work. The following letter was the only one in the newspapers to register disapproval; it called forth strong rebuff from Oliver Johnson, who was editor during Garrison's absence. He argued that all people, not only citizens, had the right of petition, and that children were capable of comprehending simple truths of right and wrong. Presumably, petitions from children continued to be collected and sent to Congress.

To William Lloyd Garrison

[Before 11 August 1837]

To the Editor of the Liberator:

Your paper of the 14th ult. contains a notice of Children's Petitions to Congress, and an exhortation to abolition parents to encourage their circulation. I regret this measure exceedingly, and cannot but hope that it will not be carried into effect. I consider it an error of judgment, because the inevitable tendency will be to throw contempt on *all* our petitions; and it seems to me improper, because children are of necessity guided by others, and because this step is involved with questions evidently above juvenile capacities.

Abolition parents ought thoroughly to prepare the hearts and minds of their children for the conscientious discharge of duties that will come with their riper years; but this haste to invest them with the attributes of citizenship appears premature, and almost ridiculous. I have not as yet conversed with an abolitionist, who did not view the subject in the same light.

Respectfully and truly yours,
L. M. C.

L; *The Liberator*, 11 Aug. 1837 (microfiche 5/125).

Drawing on her fame as a writer and her connections with people of the middle and upper classes, Child often wrote to possible benefactors. The wealthy bachelor Jonathan Phillips (b. 1778), a relative of Wendell Phillips, was especially co-operative. Child wrote to him several times: for the Boston Samaritan Asylum for Indigent Colored Children, for Susan Paul, for a young prostitute Child befriended in New York, and lastly for the artist Horace Kneeland. Phillips responded to the following letter almost immediately by sending thirty dollars to Susan Paul.

To Jonathan Phillips

Washington St. 671. Jan. 23d 1838

To Jonathan Phillips Esq.
Dear Sir,

Having learned by experience that your benevolence is like a full, free fountain, my reluctance to again address you in behalf of the destitute is increased almost to painfulness. Never but twice in my life have I ⟨ever⟩ begged money of any person, for any purpose; and on both these occasions I have felt constrained to apply to you, who, from reputed wealth and tenderness of heart, must necessarily be overwhelmed with similar applications.

But without further apology, I will tell a plain story and leave you to judge whether the case I lay before you is worthy of claiming any share of your attention among more important objects of charity.

Miss Susan Paul is the daughter of the Revd Mr. Paul, late colored clergyman in this city. From personal knowledge of her character, I believe her to be very worthy, industrious, and well-informed. For several years she has taught a primary school, the proceeds of which have supported her, and assisted in the maintenance of a widowed mother. Since her father's death, up to the present time, they have, by scrupulous economy, avoided incurring the slightest debt. About a year ago, they were obliged to leave the house they had a long time occupied, because its ruinous condition rendered it uninhabitable in storms. The few streets where colored people are allowed to live were so much crowded, that she could obtain no tenement at the humble price suited to her finances. At last, she hired

69

a small building in a street occupied by white people; but the neighbors assured her that the family would not be allowed to remain there in comfort and safety.   She could hear of no other house, except one in Grove St. in the midst of a colored neighborhood. The rent ($200) was more than she could pay; but the family of a respectable and worthy colored man offered to take half the house, and did so. It appears probable that they honestly meant to pay their proportion of the rent; but sickness, and the loss of money due to him in various directions, reduced them to such distressing poverty, that the whole burden came upon Miss Paul.

In addition to this, her sister died about a year since, leaving four helpless children, that may be termed orphans; for their worthless father is leading a profligate and miserable life at N. Orleans. To these children Miss Paul performs a mother's duty in the most exemplary manner. The few hours when she is not in school are diligently employed in sewing for their support. Her mother is aged, and can do little more than the family work. Her only brother (almost white) formerly earned something as a printer in the Liberator Office; but he is now a charity student at Dartmouth, where he obtained admission after being rejected, under one pretence or another, by nearly every literary institution in N. England. He cannot assist his family at the present time, being himself very much straitened for the necessary supply of books and clothing.

Miss Paul is high-spirited, and I believe suffered much before she complained. Day before yesterday, she sent for me, and told me her distress, and how she had struggled with it, rather than make it known to the abolitionists, who were called to sacrifice so much for the colored people. She said she abhorred the idea of depending upon others—she felt that negroes ought to struggle with their own difficulties as they best could—she had never before incurred debt—nor should she have done so in this instance, could she have foreseen that the whole responsibility of paying the rent would come upon her. Her mind appeared to be in a state of pitiable anxiety and perplexity. The lease of the house had nearly expired, and if she could but obtain a hundred dollars, she could pay present debts, and not exceed her income in future. She was desirous to borrow this sum, and pay it slowly, by small installments; but her ability to do this, with four orphans to support, appears to me very precarious.

I have spoken to a few abolitionists, who have contributed five dollars a piece; and I shall ask others. But I will candidly tell you why I apply to *you*, rather than collect the sum, as I probably could do, from abolitionists.

Most of them have very limited means; the demands upon them are incessant; and what they give to collateral objects must generally be deducted from their annual donations to the Anti Slavery cause.   If *you* think proper to give anything, it will not, I presume, diminish the treasury of the Anti Slavery Society.

You will appreciate my frankness; for this avowal would deter nearly every gentleman in the city from giving a cent; but I prefer that you should understand all the bearings of the case, and do as seemeth to you good.

With sentiments of the highest respect & esteem,

L. M. Child.

P.S. If you think proper to communicate with me on this subject, a line will reach me either at the house or office of Ellis G. Loring Esq.

ALS; William Phillips, Jr., Collection, Salisbury, Conn. (microfiche 96/2532).

When David returned from Europe during the late fall of 1837, he found that a serious backlash against abolitionists had begun. In a series of letters and appeals, the Massachusetts clergy denounced the Grimkés as abolitionists and as women. At issue was the right of free speech as well as the propriety of women's lecturing. Theodore Weld, who later married Angelina, and John Greenleaf Whittier thought that women should base their defense of their right to speak on the Quaker tradition of women addressing mixed assemblies. The Grimké sisters insisted on basing their right simply on their being women and human beings.

On 21 February 1838, Angelina delivered an impassioned speech on slavery to the Massachusetts state legislature and presented petitions with the signatures of twenty thousand women. She was the first woman to speak before a U.S. political body. The effect of her eloquence on Child is described in the following letters. The Grimkés' lectures on slavery at the Odeon Theater in Boston that spring also included specific mention of a widening woman's "sphere." They were among the first American women to articulate publicly the concept of woman's rights, and Child responded warmly to their courage. Her own thoughts on woman's rights were molded by long discussions with the Grimkés in June of 1837.

At this time, David and other male abolitionists urged Maria to lecture in public. David wrote to Angelina on 12 February 1838: "Much has been said to my dear wife to engage her in the same line of labor, which you have fortunately chosen. I am persuaded that if the time shall come, when the internal monitor shall indicate that way as the most useful for her to walk, she will not in any event be disobedient to the commandment."* Child chose, instead, to use her writing to make herself heard.

To Esther Carpenter

March 20, 1838.

I thought of you several times while Angelina was addressing the committee of the Legislature. I knew you would have enjoyed it so much. I think it was

* Weld-Grimké Papers, Clements Library, University of Michigan.

a spectacle of the greatest moral sublimity I ever witnessed. The house was full to overflowing. For a moment a sense of the immense responsibility resting on her seemed almost to overwhelm her. She trembled and grew pale. But this passed quickly, and she went on to speak gloriously, strong in utter forgetfulness of herself, and in her own earnest faith in every word she uttered. "Whatsoever comes from the heart goes to the heart." I believe she made a very powerful impression on the audience. Boston, like other cities, is very far behind the country towns on this subject; so much so that it is getting to be Boston *versus* Massachusetts, as the lawyers say. The Boston members of the legislature tried hard to prevent her having a hearing on the second day. Among other things, they said that such a crowd were attracted by curiosity the galleries were in danger of being broken down; though in fact they are constructed with remarkable strength. A member from Salem, perceiving their drift, wittily proposed that a "committee be appointed to examine the foundations of the State House of Massachusetts, to see whether it will bear another lecture from Miss Grimké."

One sign that her influence is felt is that the "sound part of the community" (as they consider themselves) seek to give vent to their vexation by calling her Devil-ina instead of Angel-ina, and Miss Grimalkin instead of Miss Grimké. Another sign is that we have succeeded in obtaining the Odeon, one of the largest and most central halls, for her to speak in; and it is the first time such a place has been obtained for anti-slavery in this city.

Angelina and Sarah have been spending the winter at the house of Mr. P____, about five miles from here.[1] The family were formerly of the Society of Friends—are now, I believe, a little Swedenborgian, but more Quaker, and swinging loose from any regular society; just as I and so many hundred others are doing at the present day. I should like earnestly and truly to believe with some large sect, because religious sympathy is so delightful; but I now think that if I were to live my life over again I should not outwardly join any society, there is such a tendency to spiritual domination, such an interfering with individual freedom.

. . .

L, extract; *Letters of Lydia Maria Child*, 1882 (microfiche 5/131).

Since David's return from Europe in 1837, he had been making plans to raise sugar beets and manufacture the sugar. In 1838 he formed a partnership with Maximin Isnard, the French vice-consul in Boston, and Edward Church, whose 1837 book on sugar beets recommended the valley of the Connecticut River in Massachusetts as the best location in America for their growth. Accordingly, the Childs made plans to move to Northampton, Mass. in the Connecticut Valley.

[1] The reference is to the home of the Quaker abolitionist Samuel Philbrick (1789–1859) in Brookline, Mass.

To Lydia (Bigelow) Child

Boston April 6th 1838

Dear Mother,

I should have written before, but have been waiting, waiting, waiting, hoping to have something certain to tell concerning our prospects. It seemed to be our fate to be tried with every form of discouragement; but at last, a ray of light seems to break through the darkness. A Company at Northampton have employed Mr. Child on terms that will give us a comfortable living; and I assure you we think it no small blessing not to be obliged to leave old Massachusetts. We expect to proceed to our place of destination about the first of May. For this summer, we intend to board in some plain economical family, and try to pick up our crumbs [a] little. For the last two years it has been all losses and expenditure with little or nothing coming in. I think it very lucky that all our trunks and boxes are safely collected together, scattered to the four winds, at New York and elsewhere, and lodged in Hartford on the way to Northampton. I think we shall continue to look in upon you just for one night, as we go along; for our route will lie through Worcester.

Last night I went to the Odeon, to hear Angelina Grimké. It is a very large hall, capable of holding more than three thousand people. It was crowded, gallery after gallery up to the very ceiling, and through a lecture of two hours there was perfectly hushed attention. Think of this, compared with the time when a few women were mobbed in their small room at 46! The Odeon is the first good central hall that we have been able to obtain. Angelina spoke most eloquently; and the whole audience seemed to hang upon her words. They laughed but once; and that was when she told them that in a few years a Northern woman would be as ashamed to marry a slave-holder as a horse-thief. They leave Massachusetts soon, on their way to Pennsylvania. It is said they intend to push into Maryland, and try their eloquence there. It is truly a wonderful dispensation of Providence, that these two women should come forth from the bosom of a proud and fashionable family in South Carolina, and by becoming Quakers should prepare themselves for the great work, which the Lord had for them to do in the unseen future.

. . .

L; Simison Papers, Beinecke Rare Book and Manuscript Library, Yale University (microfiche 5/133).

3

July 1838–February 1841

The last two years of the 1830s were a critical time in the growth of the antislavery movement. By 1840, men and women favoring political action and objecting to Garrison's radical ideas about religion and woman's rights split off, forming the American and Foreign Anti-Slavery Society and the Liberty party. The major antislavery issues—economic ties between the North and South, proslavery clergy, nonresistance, "the woman question," the boycott of slave-labor products, moral persuasion versus political action—are all discussed by Child with characteristic eloquence in her letters.

In May 1838, the Childs moved to Northampton, Massachusetts, a hundred miles west of Boston, to begin their sugar beet experiment. Child's intermittent stay in Northampton between May 1838 and May 1841 was one of the bleakest periods of her life. The farm was a difficult venture. In addition to strenuous manual labor she continued writing—the couple's only source of income. Because the farm work in Northampton took up so much of Child's time, she often was not able to go to the state and national antislavery meetings. Instead, she influenced others through correspondence.

Isolated as she was, she kept abreast of political developments in the movement through the newspapers and by word of mouth. Her removal from the circle of abolitionists in Boston meant that she could see her coworkers from the vantage point of the ordinary citizen. What she saw distressed her: the sectarian fighting was enervating, and it discredited the movement in the public eye. Undoubtedly, her pessimism was affected by the political conservatism of Northampton. There was a small, active antislavery movement in western Massachusetts, of which she was a part, but she seems to have been disheartened by the atmosphere of social and political orthodoxy. As difficult as it was for her to live in this "iron-bound Valley of the Connecticut," as she called the region (see her letter of 18 November 1838), her contact with a conservative populace tempered her political vision, bringing to it a new realism. She at this time predicted that emancipation would come only through violence.

Northampton, the county seat, had a population of thirty-seven hundred in 1838. In radical, postrevolutionary times, it had been a focal point for the Shays

Rebellion of 1786, the revolt of debt-ridden farmers. By the time the Childs arrived, Northampton and the surrounding mill towns had become a conservative, Federalist stronghold. Most of the people were of Yankee stock: day laborers, skilled craftsmen, farmers, merchants, and mill owners, with a handful of lawyers, doctors, and ministers. A stagecoach, and a canal completed in 1835, were the means of transportation linking the insulated self-dependent town to the outside world. The farmland was some of the state's richest and lay within sight of the Berkshire Mountains to the west. It was a beautiful village—later in the century Jenny Lind would dub it the "Paradise of America"—but in her letters Child notes her increasing indifference to its aesthetic charm.

When Child wrote the following letter, she and David were boarding at a house on one of the town's wide, elm-shaded streets. Ironically, her neighbor, Thomas Napier, was a slave auctioneer from South Carolina. She also mentions Joseph Lyman (1767–1847), a "River God," one of the social and intellectual elite of the Connecticut Valley, and sheriff of Hampshire County. His second wife, Anne Jean (Robbins) Lyman (1789–1867), and their daughter, Susan, became close friends of Child. Years later Child wrote of her friendship with Mrs. Lyman, "Both of us were as direct and energetic as a loco-motive under high pressure of steam."* They admired each other's "earnestness of conviction" and directness of speech, in spite of their political differences, although Child never gave up trying to persuade her friend to endorse antislavery.

To Ellis Gray and Louisa Loring

Northampton July 10'th 1838

Dearest Friends,

Having an opportunity to send to Boston I gladly improve it in writing to you for my own pleasure; for my life is too monotonous to furnish any details interesting to you. I have actually but just finished mending the old clothes that have been packed up in N. York, or traversing Europe. Mr. Child has hired about an acre of land, and planted it with sugar-beets himself, fearing the supply of that article would be deficient. I often go and help him weed three or four hours night and morning. In the morning I go out sometimes at 3 o'clock, sometimes at 4; when all the world, except the birds, are asleep. Think of that Mrs. Remarkable Lazy-bones! Mr. Child says, "What do you think would tempt Louisa to bestir herself at this hour?" "Nothing short of saving Ellis' life," said I, laughing. "Oh, I guess she would try it twice, for little Med's life." ["]Maybe she would try it *once* to save little Med," said I; "Ellis having a strong desire that Med should survive." Thus we jibed and jeered about you; but you know (though you once forgot it) that our jokes come from hearts filled with the deepest respect and affection for you both—and that they are uttered unrestrainedly, in perfect con-

* 3 Aug. [1874], J. Peter Lesley Collection, American Philosophical Society Library.

76

fidence that you cannot misunderstand us, and that you will pay us well in the same light coin.

While boasting of my Herculean labors, I must not omit that before I received any money from Wilkins, I became so "careful & troubled about many things," that I actually undertook to cut & make a frock-coat to save the expense, which is as great here as in Boston.[1] It was a toilsome job, but I really succeeded quite tolerably, considering.

We have been treated with a good deal of politeness here. Once more I have it in my power to be the favorite of the class denominated first. I am punctilious in attending to the demands of courtesy, and all will go on smoothly between us and the grandees, until I bring the Anti Slavery Petitions "between the wind and their nobility"; and then I shall be, as I have before been, like the man who had spent a night, that seemed years, revelling in fairy palaces, and awoke in the morning to find himself alone on a cold and barren heath.   The metaphor is exaggerated, for two reasons; first because the aforesaid world no longer seems like fairy-land to me, because "men cannot build palaces from cinders"; and secondly, because seclusion is not a cold and barren heath, but is ever and anon visited by the flowers, birds, and bees of the inner creation. So even in the disagreeable task of carrying around petitions, it will not cost me a very severe struggle to obey the "Stern Daughter of the Voice of God."

It would amuse you to see how we are annoyed by a rich slave-auctioneer, who lives almost under our windows. . . .

Mrs. Judge Lyman asked me the other day whether I had become acquainted with this neighbor. I told her that a slave-auctioneer and a warm abolitionist would not be likely to find much pleasure in each other's society. "Oh," said she, "no doubt Mr. Napier would treat you with great politeness." "I was not thinking of *his* opinion," replied I. "We could extend to him the kindness due to every member of the human family; but *we* could have no pleasure in intimacy with a man living on the wages of the poor, kept from them by the power of the strongest." Mrs. Lyman seemed not a little surprised to have the saddle put on *that* horse; she had evidently been accustomed to another arrangement. She accused me of being as bigoted as Mr. Napier himself, who felt too good to associate with Unitarians. I endeavored to show the difference between errors of opinion and sins in actual practice. This launched the vessel at once, and we were out at sea forthwith. In the discussion which followed, concerning whether slave-holding was, or was not sin, the natural earnestness of our characters was kept in check by mutual politeness; but I assure you Anti Slavery did not strike her colors. Mrs. Lyman seems determined that she *will* get acquainted with me, though she is the very embodiment of aristocracy. Hates republics, hates democracy in every form, of course hates reforms of all sorts, and loves to have woman a graceful

---

[1] Wilkins was probably associated with American Stationers' Co., the Boston publishers of *The American Frugal Housewife*. The title of *The Frugal Housewife* had been changed in 1832 to distinguish it from editions published abroad.

vine that droops and dies, unless it can find some stately oak around which to twine itself. But she is a fine-looking woman (anything but a drooping and twining vine) of noble impulses, and a brave, imprudent frankness; and I like her, notwithstanding her distorted views of men and things. If she can manage to like me, anti-slavery, rights-of-woman, and all, it must be because she respects the daring freedom of speech which she practices. Judge Lyman having expressed a wish to see Thome & Kimball's book, I have sent it to him, with a brief but somewhat emphatic letter. As Mrs. Lyman interspersed her praises of slave-holders with the usual Selah, "I am in favor of Colonization," I thought it best to send Jay's book likewise; but I shall not urge the subject upon them against their inclination.[2] I think I have found the place in *Judge* Lyman's mind whereon to rest the lever; and let me once get it placed, and then— "First mad the Gods— first get the Gods mad—and they'll destroy themselves."

. . .

With a kiss for dear Ænoniana, I am your most grateful and attached friend, till death do us part. L. Maria Child

P.S. I hereby acknowledge the receipt of an order on the Eagle Bank, for one hundred and fifty dollars, from Ellis Gray Loring, Esq.

I was particularly pleased with the Petition for Abner Kneeland,—not a word too much or too little, or out of place.[3]

A kind remembrance to Caroline Sturgis.[4] Tell her that her sketch of Mrs. Chapman has given me much pleasure.

Please subscribe for Carlyle's Miscellanies in my name, and take pay out of Wilkins' money for F. H. If you dont pay with *my* money, I shall not feel free to ask any similar favor.

How like a malicious ⟨demon⟩ madman Brownson acts![5] Is the man sane?

A young Quaker bookseller from N. York called the other day to inform me that he had bought the Frugal Housewife, and that Mr. Loring thought I should

---

[2] William Jay, *An Inquiry into the Character and Tendency of American Colonization and American Anti-Slavery Society* (New York, 1835). The book went through ten editions.

[3] The atheist Abner Kneeland (1774–1844) was the last person to be imprisoned in Boston for blasphemy. A petition for his pardon, based on the right of free speech, was signed by many Bostonians, including Ellis Gray Loring. Kneeland was released and later moved to Iowa.

[4] Caroline Sturgis (1819–1888) was a Transcendentalist writer and an early admirer of Margaret Fuller. She later married William Tappan, son of the abolitionist Lewis Tappan.

[5] Orestes Augustus Brownson (1803–76), a Unitarian minister, in 1838 started the *Boston Quarterly Review*, a Democratic reform journal. In the second number of the quarterly, Brownson published an article supporting John C. Calhoun's argument that mailing antislavery publications to the South was a violation of the "law of nations," because it interfered with the internal affairs of an independent political community. Brownson supported Garrison in his fights with conservative clergy, but refused to join any anti-slavery organization.

---

be satisfied with his references. I am glad to have it plague Mr. Loring no longer; otherwise I am rather sorry to have it go to N.Y.[6]

Mr. Child desires his heart's best love to you both, and to Nony in particular. Will you *never* be unfortunate, so that we can help you? It would be *such* a satisfaction!

ALS; Loring Family Papers, Schlesinger Library, Radcliffe College (microfiche 5/137).

Abolitionists were victims of all kinds of harrassment, even in towns the size of Northampton, where Southerners came to vacation in the summer. The Childs found a leaflet on their door that said, "First of August! ON THIS DAY ABOUT 500,000 Persons in the British West Indies, will be emancipated from Slavery." The words "persons" was scratched out and "Niggers" put in its place. Maria saved the leaflet and wrote on the bottom of the paper, "Stuck on the door of David L. Child's room, at Northampton, August 1st 1838; the word in pencil being one of the unanswerable pro-slavery, or pro-colonization arguments, considered to be even more rational and efficacious logic, than brick-bats, or rotten eggs." *

One of the most devastating proslavery riots occurred in Philadelphia on 16–17 May 1838. Maria (Weston) Chapman collapsed after braving the rock-throwing, window-smashing mob to address the second Anti-Slavery Convention of American Women at Pennsylvania Hall. The building, financed by abolitionists and friends of free speech, was burned to the ground by rioters just three days after the opening ceremony. Chapman's sister Caroline Weston (1808–82), an abolitionist and woman's rights advocate, taught in a school which she and her sisters founded on Boylston Street. In this letter to her, Child responds to rumors about Chapman's collapse.

To Caroline Weston

Northampton July 27'th 1838

Dear Caroline,

Many thanks for your two kind letters, detailing so many particulars, which no one else would have thought to communicate, even if they knew of them. Your second letter did not reach me till three days ago, more than a month after date; but I was glad to receive it, for all that.

I have had no opportunity to refute misrepresentations concerning your

[6] Samuel S. and William Wood of New York published *The American Frugal Housewife* from 1838 to 1860.
* Lydia Merrill Collection, Oroville, California.

high-souled and ill-understood sister.[1] Mrs. Judge Lyman is the only one here likely to abuse her, and she would not venture to speak disparagingly of her before me. My own testimony I lose no opportunity of bearing; and whoever speaks of her in my hearing know that they do it in the presence of a very warm friend and admirer.   This world-babble is of little consequence. Can one be deep, or high, or even simply true, without misrepresentation?

For the state of abolition here, I refer you to my letter to Mrs. Chapman. It seems to me lifeless enough. Orthodoxy has clothed most of the community in her straight-laced garments. There is organing, and psalm-singing, and praying, and preaching, and reverence for "the divine ambassadors of Christ," and saving of souls, &c more than enough; but of genuine love to the neighbor, as a child of one common Father, the manifestations seem to be of the smallest.   I don't mean they are worse than other people. You know what I mean.

Our room is within call of a rich slave-auctioneer, who prays so loud that Mr. Child has to strike up his accordion to drown sounds so discordant to our feelings. ⟨Whether the Lord⟩ "Hear him! Hear the pious old thief, trying to come paddy over the Lord!" exclaims Mr. Child, in the vexation of his spirit. Whether the Lord hears him or not, I cannot tell; but he takes care that the *neighborhood* shall. I have felt half disposed to repeat the advice of the heathen philosopher: "Dont pray so loud. It's safer for you not to let the gods know where you are."   The other day his grand-daughter came out to play, and her mother said to her, "Come in and get your sun-bonnet; by and bye, they'll take you for a little black girl." I called out (not loud enough to be heard, except by Mr. Child) "And then, likely as not, your grandfather will sell you!" Another of the children sat singing from a book: "He jumped on a nigger, and *thought* he was a horse!" Whereupon I wrote to Mrs. Loring, to know if her sister Gilman had been preparing infant literature suited to the "peculiar institution" of South Carolina.[2] A curious incident happened at the school where his oldest grand-daughter attends. On the afternoon devoted to reading, a little girl brought a Juvenile newspaper. The young Southerner saw in it an article headed, "The Happy Slave rejoiced to return to his Master." With sparkling eyes, she exclaimed, "Oh may I read this aloud?" Having obtained permission, she read the well-known story of the slave, who *pretended* to go back into slavery, in order to carry his wife off with him. Toward the last, her tones were rather less exulting than at the beginning.

[1] Child was especially angered by insinuations that Chapman neglected her domestic duties for the sake of reforms. To repudiate the gossip that Chapman "went crazy because she could not have everything her own way," Child offered the interpretation that Chapman's "naturally feeble" health had been seriously weakened by her last pregnancy and her inability to breastfeed her child. (See letter to Lydia B. Child, 7 Aug. 1838, Child letters, MC 305, Schlesinger Library, Radcliffe College.)
[2] Caroline (Howard) Gilman (1794–1888) was one of Child's contemporaries in children's literature. In 1832 she began to publish the *Rose-Bud, or Youth's Gazette*, a magazine for children, in Charlestown, S.C. She was married to Louisa Loring's brother, Samuel Gilman.

This same Mr. Napier (who published a letter in Charleston S.C. indignantly contradicting the charge of being opposed to slavery) is deacon of the church here, and Sunday teacher. In this last capacity he takes occasion to teach that Africans are the descendants of Ham, and God has especially ordained them to perpetual slavery. His minister, Rev. Mr. Mitchell, (one of the "divine ambassadors of Christ"—Oh thou insulted Nazarine!) refuses to permit an anti-slavery lecture in his meeting-house, and gives as a reason that "it might drive Mr. Napier, and his Carolina son-in-law, Mr. Hibbins, out of town"; for the same reason, I presume, his family refuse to sign petitions.[3] Every day or two, I see baskets of vegetables and fruit carried over to him from Mr. Napier's garden; a part of the price for which the Judas betrays his master.

Recently I was told that Mrs. Napier's sister was coming from S.C. and was going to bring a slave with her; but she was "so happy that there was no danger of her taking her freedom. They expected trouble from the abolitionists, but the slave couldn't be tolled away" &c This, and more of the same import was ostentatiously proclaimed beforehand. At last Mrs. Gadson and the slave came. The woman was repeatedly pointed out by the Southern household, with the triumphant assertion, "You see how happy our slave is. She is a sample of the general condition of the slaves. The abolitionists in Troy tried to coax her away, but could not."   The woman passed frequently under my window, and appeared sleek and contented. She repeatedly hemmed very loud, when near me. Being suspicious that she was instructed to throw herself in my way, in order to boast of her happy slavery, and laugh at my useless efforts to make her in love with freedom, I resolved that they should not "catch old birds with chaff." But I wrote a searching letter of eight pages to Mrs. Gadson herself accompanied by the Anti S. Catechism, and A E. G.'s Appeal[.][4] These were sent back in about two hours, in great wrath; but I afterward learned that the whole family had the benefit of hearing the letter, except Mr. Napier who *would* not hear it.

The colored woman afterward came in, and complained that Mrs. Gadson told her that I called her a well-fatted pig, and her children puppies. I easily convinced her, by reading the letter, that I had said nothing about her, but compared the happiness of slaves to that of well fed pigs; and spoke of them as liable to be sold like dogs, and their offspring, like puppies, sold to another purchaser. Many more things had the false woman tried to make her believe were contained in the letter. But the influence of truth and kindness on my part had its effect. She seemed more than satisfied. She has since been to see me, and promises to accom-

[3] Clergyman and author John Mitchell (1794–1870) was pastor of the Edwards Church in Northampton until 1842, when he resigned because of poor health. James Hibbin (1799–1871) studied law in South Carolina, moved to Northampton in 1832, and served as deacon of Edwards Church.

[4] Child's *Anti-Slavery Catechism* (1836) and Angelina Grimké's second pamphlet, *An Appeal to the Women of the Nominally Free States: Issued by an Anti-Slavery Convention of American Women and Held by Adjournment from the 9th to the 12th of May, 1837* (New York, 1837).

pany me to the Monthly Concert. She assures me most solemnly that she is not a slave— That she is a free woman— That she and Mrs. G. agreed before they left S.C. to *say* she was a slave; but that she certainly is free, and that is the *reason she feels so easy*. Here is a pretty piece of duplicity somewhere.

I wish I had some co-operators to hammer on that Mrs. G's conscience; but I cannot rouse anybody. The slave auctioneer is too rich—employs too many people.

Did you notice that Resolution of the Maternal Association of Clergymen's Wives, in the last Friend of Virtue? I wanted to amend it thus: ["]Resolved, That we will sustain the Friend of Virtue, if it contains nothing likely to diminish the reverence paid to our husbands, or to encourage women, who probably will preach cheaper than they."

I have written in great haste, but will not (like somebody I wot of) take up my paper with apologies.   If you go to see *Henritt*, just take this letter. It may serve to amuse the dear woman.

Mr. Child desires his best love to you and your sisters. You dont know how we *do* long for a Boylston St. to run to.

I want to say a thousand things about Mrs. Chapman (God bless her) and sundry other matters; but I must defer to another opportunity

Best love to your sisters; the Chapmans of Chauncey Place—Wendall Phillips, &c.

With true friendship, L. M. Child.

ALS; Anti-Slavery Collection, Rare Books and Manuscripts, Boston Public Library (microfiche 6/141).

The "woman question"—whether women should be allowed to become equal members in the societies—was the topic of so much debate in 1838 that the American Anti-Slavery Society published a position paper urging the public not to identify the movement wtih a few people's unorthodox ideas about woman's "sphere." But it went on to say that as an organization it had no right to interfere with its members' ideas and that diversity of opinion was a sign of strength, a position with which Child and Garrison agreed.

Abby Kelley (1810–87), on 31 May 1838, became the first woman to be elected to a committee of the New England Anti-Slavery Society. Kelley came to the attention of the movement's leaders when she spoke for the first time at the 1837 Women's Convention. Afterwards, she was urged to pursue a career as a lecturer. At the time she was elected to the committee, a resolution was passed calling for full participation of women in the society. On the basis of the passage of this resolution, Child probably thought that the "woman question" had been settled, which impression may have led to her decision not to attend the 1838 or 1839 antislavery women's conventions. But the issue was not settled—after

Kelley was elected, eight clergymen left in protest. Not until 1840, when women were finally accepted as equal members in the American Anti-Slavery Society, did separate women's conventions cease.

To Caroline Weston

Northampton August 13th 1838

Dear Friend,

I received your interesting letter by the Philadelphians with great pleasure. By a series of unfortunate mischances we saw very little of the travellers, though we were eager to do so, and took great pains to effect it. When a Quaker *has* a soul, what large ones they have! Pity that a sect founded on such high and broad principles should be buried in the mere shell of lifeless forms! But when they are free, like the friends that brought your letter, they are free indeed.   I rejoice to hear how pleasantly you are situated. Being deprived of the "sympathy and popularity to which I had been accustomed" has likewise rested on my spirit like an invisible incubus, and I knew not what it was that impeded my utterance. When I first came here, "the upper circles" were decidedly disposed to patronize me. I made use of my position to place the anti-slavery lever, and I *think* I can already discern symptoms that I shall eventually go to Coventry. It is a healthy, bracing place, that same Coventry, and particularly well calculated to preserve strength of vision.

A week ago, we visited our brother at Springfield.[1] My sister, who really has much natural kindness and integrity, imbibed nothing but aristocratic influences from the hour of her birth to the day of her marriage. Whenever I see her, she receives a slight impulse toward abolition, and falls gently back upon her velvet cushions long before I have an opportunity to see her again. With her I found it necessary to do battle for Mrs. Chapman. Sarah T. Smith, the Moral Reform woman, who attended the Philadelphia Convention, told her that Mrs. Chapman was in the Insane Hospital, because at the Convention a majority opposed certain views of hers, and she could not carry her point. I have on the stocks a letter to Sarah T. Smith, in which I shall very kindly try to convince her that her statements are erroneous, and somewhat rashly made. Our private opinion is that she received her information from "one of the round substances"; but of this I say nothing. What Dr. Osgood is it whose name you mark with two notes of admiration? There is a Calvinistic minister by the name of Osgood in Springfield, who⟨m⟩ my sister says "injures the abolition cause by his imprudence; being a man that goes to the extreme in everything." Such evidence, from such a source, of course led us to the conclusion that he was a man after our own hearts.

You say you shall always think I failed to follow the leadings of Providence, in not going to the Convention. I can only reply that I *saw* no such leadings; per-

[1] John Childe of Springfield, Mass.; his wife was Laura ⟨Dwight⟩ Childe.

haps my mind was not in a state so quiescent as to be *willing* to perceive them. The plain fact is, I never did enter with a free and cordial spirit into Societies and Conventions. Their machinery oppresses me. I want to say *what* the Spirit moves, and *when* it moves. I am sorry to see that another Woman's Convention is to be held. I was in hopes Abby Kelly had settled all that for us on better ground.

I beg of you not to publish my last letter; and I ask it for manifold reasons. One is, that the colored woman is in a delicate and embarrassed position. By *right* she ought, even in the legal sense, to be free; and she thinks herself so; but on account of informalities we fear she is in the power of oppressors. She opens her heart fully to me; and oh, what a tissue of meanness and falsehood her disclosures reveal! I have been dropped into the midst of this tangled skein in a strange way. What will come of it, I know not. My straight-forward way of proceeding has done better than the most adroitly planned *ruse de guerre* to confound all their schemes for gulling the credulity of the North. I wish I could tell you some of the odd crooks and turns in this affair; but it takes so long on paper!

. . .

Have you read Carlyle's Miscellanies?[2] They are full of rare and racy things, and there is a delightful tone of magnanimity and candour pervading them all.

Speaking of magnanimity, I would our friend Oliver Johnson (whom you know I really like in the main) had more of it.[3] Why cannot he rise more serenely above the dirty and dingy atmosphere of personalities? If Hatteck (junior editor of Stone) desecrates the principles of abolition, or any other great principles, lay his fault before him & the world with Christian boldness; but why circulate gossip about his domestic or personal affairs, such as his being angry concerning his wife's conversation?[4] Brother Oliver does not appear to me always to give his hard knocks in a good spirit. I sometimes feel in a similar state of mind myself; but I soon hear the monitory voice, "It is not good to be here. *Arise*, let us go hence." Will you procure one of my printed Addresses to the Senators & Representatives, do it up with the enclosed letter, and send it to the old patriot, by Edmund Quincy jr.?[5]

[2] Thomas Carlyle, *Critical and Miscellaneous Essays* (Boston, 1838–39).
[3] Editor and reformer Oliver Johnson (1809–89) supported the equal participation of women in the societies. Like Garrison, he began his career as a printer's apprentice. He helped found the New England Anti-Slavery Society and frequently edited *The Liberator* in Garrison's absence.
[4] Child probably refers to Fitz-Greene Halleck (1790–1867), not Hatteck, and William Leete Stone (1792–1844); both were writers and journalists.
[5] Rather than serve as a delegate to the 1838 Women's Convention, Child may have volunteered to write abolitionist material. "I think as M. L. Child told us she was willing to write an Address to Northern Senators & Representatives that it would be a pity to give her anything else to do . . ." (Angelina Grimké to Anna Weston, [1838], Anti-Slavery Collection, Rare Books and Manuscripts, Boston Public Library). The patriot is probably John Quincy Adams. Edmund Quincy, Jr. (1808–77) joined the Massachusetts Anti-Slavery Society in 1837 and devoted most of his life to reform causes. During the controversy over the "woman question," he supported the proponents of women's full membership.

I must hasten to say good bye; for company waits in the parlour.   God
bless you.

Yrs most truly,

L.M.C.

Sarah T. Smith said she merely repeated what she had heard.

ALS; Anti-Slavery Collection, Rare Books and Manuscripts, Boston Public Library
(microfiche 6/143).

Francis George Shaw (1809–82) and Sarah (Sturgis) Shaw (1815–1902) were
among Child's closest lifelong friends. They became active in the antislavery
movement and in this formative period debated abolitionism with Child and
were undoubtedly influenced by her views. Sarah married her cousin, Francis,
in 1835. He left his father's prosperous Boston business in 1840 to pursue literary
and reform work.

To Francis and Sarah Shaw

Northampton August 17th 1838

Dear Friends,

A gentleman on his way to Boston has promised to call in an hour or two to
take a package for me; and I cut short letters to other friends in order to say that
I received your very kind note from Greenfield, and should have acknowledged
its reception, had I not expected to see you in a few days. A letter received last
night informs me that you have returned without taking Northampton in the
way. I was grievously disappointed, for I lotted upon seeing you. However, I
should have been sorry to purchase the pleasure at the expense of any incon-
venience on your part, or any neglect of business.

The reasons which influence your mind with regard to joining the Anti-
Slavery Society appear to me good and satisfactory; and in your case I have not
(as I have sometimes been compelled to have) the slightest suspicion of their
insincerity.

With regard to intercourse with slave-holders, far from shunning it myself,
I seek it diligently. Many and many an hour's argument, maintained with candour
and courtesy, have I had with them; and they have generally appeared to like me,
though my principles naturally seemed to them stern and uncompromising. I am
not so intolerant as to suppose that slaveholders have not many virtues, and many
very estimable qualities; but at the same time, let me caution you against believing
all their fair professions on the subject of slavery. Men who are true and honorable on all other subjects will twist, and turn, and deceive, and say what they
must absolutely know to be false, on this subject. I account for the inconsistency

and tergiversation of such men, partly upon the supposition that conscience perpetually whispers to them that the system is wrong, but is not sufficiently revered to overcome the temptation of apparent interest. Still more do I attribute it to the fact, that by education and habit they have so long thought and spoken of the colored man as a mere article of *property*, that it is almost impossible for them to recognize him as a *man*, and reason concerning him as a *brother*, on equal terms with the rest of the human family. If, by great effort, you make them acknowledge the brotherhood of the human race, as a sacred and eternal principle,—in ten minutes, their arguments, assertions, and proposed schemes, all show that they have returned to the old habit of regarding the slave as a *"chattel personal."*

Has the Virginian gentleman, of whom you speak, ever read "An Inquiry into Colonization, by the Hon. William Jay"? If he has not, I wish he might be persuaded so to do. It is written in a clear and candid manner; and I should think it must convince any mind of the impolicy (to speak of no other consideration) of shipping off laborers from a country where laborers are so much needed.

Does he not know that the reason the free colored people of the South do not stand up erect in the full stature of men, is that because while they live in the midst of enslaved brethren they are inevitably objects of dislike, and jealousy, and dread to the white man, and therefore cannot be *really* free? Let him look impartially at Antigua, and see what is the result where *all* are free. Virginia, with her great natural advantages of soil and stream, and her abundant supply of laborers, might grow rich faster than any state in the Union, if she would only make those laborers efficient friends by an act of simple justice.

You make a mistake concerning the Anti Slavery Society in one respect, and I allude to it, merely that you may be correct about it as a matter of fact. The Society do not require abstinence from slave-labor; and very few of their members have any conscientious scruples about it. I am among those few; but with me it is more a matter of *feeling* than of principle. The sugar does not taste good, because it brings before me the image of the toiling slave. The few friends of abstinence from slave-labor have written and published a great deal on the subject; but nearly all the friends of the cause view it in the same light as you do. Among this majority are Garrison, E. G. Loring, Francis Jackson &c &c.[1] I have heard of but two instances of anti-slavery men who have discontinued business with the South from conscientious scruples on the subject. James Mott, a Quaker merchant of Philadelphia, and the Chapmans of Boston. These things are matters of individual conscience, with which the Society have nothing to do.   Do you think our forefathers did wrong in trying "to force men to do right" by refusing to use taxed tea and stamped paper? I suppose you know that the distress occasioned to British manufacturers and merchants by that movement in the Colonies

[1] The abolitionist Francis Jackson (1789–1861), who was active in Boston government, was a lifelong supporter of Garrison. During the 1835 riots in Boston, he opened his home to the Boston Female Anti-Slavery Society when it could not find a safe meeting place.

was so great that they perfectly besieged Parliament with Petitions to repeal the offensive laws. *If* it was right to do this for our own freedom, it is surely right to do as much, and more, for the freedom of an enslaved brother.

When I said that I was disappointed in the church, I meant in the individuals that compose the church; or in other words, the Society. As for the doctrines, I in vain try to find any others that so well satisfy my reason and my heart.

I received the Proceedings of the Convention, for which I am much obliged to you. What *wonderful* exclusiveness is shown in that Report on Schools! This cannot be the right spirit. After all, that religious belief which is the mere result of education and habit, and not the deliberate conviction of our own minds, is weak, and little calculated to endure conflict.

. . .

ALS; Houghton Library, Harvard University (microfiche 6/146).

The marriage of Angelina Grimké and Theodore Weld on 14 May 1838 had caught the imagination of the movement. In the wedding vows, Theodore renounced all legal authority given him as a male over Angelina. The sisters retired from lecturing the following year (Sarah joined the Weld household) and became involved, instead, with the responsibilities of child care and housekeeping. They never altogether resumed their active public lives.

In a letter to Angelina, Child elaborates on the story of Rosa, the slave brought north by a neighbor's niece, on vacation from Charleston, South Carolina. It is not known whether Rosa and her children were eventually freed.

To Angelina (Grimké) Weld

Northampton Aug. 26 1838

Dear Sister Angelina,
. . .

Mrs. Martin, the wife of a clergyman in S.C. was left with two slaves, which she manumitted immediately after her husband's death. Her son held several slaves, among whom was the mother of my heroine Rosa, or Rosy. When Rosa was 3 or 4 years old, her mother died; and Mr. Martin, not knowing what to do with the child, told his mother she might have her, if she would take care of her. Old Mrs. Martin brought Rosy up as a little pet; and there was a peculiarly affectionate attachment between the child and Susan Martin, one of the old lady's grand-daughters. With this Susan Martin, Rosa says Angelina Grimké was well acquainted. When the old lady died she left a Will, that provided for Rosa. She was to serve *Susan* during her life-time, but after Susan's death, neither Rosa nor her children were to serve anyone. They were to be free. Hereupon quarrels arose between Susan Martin and her married sister, Mrs. Wagner. Mrs. Wagner had a large young family, and she thought it very hard that she could not have Rosa to wait upon her. Their daily domestic life was embittered by squabbles about their grandmother's partiality, and Rosa was made constantly uncomfortable. In the meanwhile, Susan became somewhat straitened in pecuniary circumstances, and her health failed. Physicians advised a voyage to Europe. At this juncture, Mrs. Anna Bennet, sister of Mrs. Napier, proposed to take Rosa under her protection, in order to keep her from the dreaded Mrs. Wagner, and to advance Susan Martin seven hundred dollars for Rosa and her children. Rosa was assured that neither she nor her children could be held as slaves after Susan's death. She inquired of Mr. Bentham, a lawyer, and *he* assured her she was perfectly safe. He had seen old Mrs. Martin's will, and he knew for a certainty that nobody could hold her after Susan's death. These assurances, united to a confidence in Mrs. Bennet's goodness and sincerity, induced Rosa to consent to the transfer. Susan took the $700. Before she went to Europe she made a Will, ratifying all her grandmother had promised, and giving similar directions for the comfort of Rosa and her family. This Will and old Mrs. Martin's were, very imprudently, left with Mr. Wagner. Susan returned from Europe with renovated health, contrary to her expectation. Her father died, and during his illness was very desirous to see his mother's Will; but Mr. Wagner said it was lost; and it has never been found to this day. Rosa still continues with Mrs. Bennet, who is reputed to be a kind woman, religious, and sometimes is *thought* to be a little uneasy in conscience about holding slaves. How deep, or sincere this feeling is, I know not.   Rosa came to Northampton this summer with Mrs. Bennet and her daughter, Mrs. Gadsden. She is called Rosa *Gadsden*. I am afraid that among them they will play her false, and that neither she nor her 3 children will obtain the boon, which old Mrs. Martin thought she had effectually secured to her. Mr. Gadsden is an infidel and a slave-auctioneer, with every good feeling deadened by the love of gold. What can she expect from him?

    She thinks it might do good if *you* would write an earnest letter to Susan Martin, impressing upon her what she owes to the memory of her grandmother. I should think she would be afraid of the old lady's ghost, unless she does something without delay to secure Rosa's freedom, and that of her children, by abundant witnesses, and with all the formalities of the law. If she is too poor to pay their expenses in leaving Carolina (as they must do, you know, if they are emancipated) has not Gerrit Smith offered to defray such expenses?[1] I am afraid Rosa is sold outright and forever to Mrs. Bennet; but she herself feels very sure that she *could* not be thus sold.   Perhaps a letter to Mrs. Bennet, *after* you have written to Susan Martin, might not be amiss.   Mrs. Bennet is old, and has of *late* been scrupulous that her slaves should have their own earnings. She is reputed kind & pious. I ought to mention that Susan Martin tried to settle matters amicably with Mrs. Wagner by offering her the services of Rosa's *children* dur-

[1] Gerrit Smith (1797–1874), of Peterboro, N.Y., was a wealthy philanthropist, abolitionist, and reformer who provided financial support for fugitive slaves.

ing her (Susan's) life time; but this did not suit; and Rosa had invincible repugnance to being transfered to Mrs. Wagner.

I write in great haste; for the Revd Dr. Cox, who carries the letter leaves in this morning's stage.[2]

God's best blessings be with you and Sarah, & Theodore.

Yrs truly,
L. M. Child

Rosa says her mistress's name is spelt Gadsden. We rather had the impression that it was Gadson. You probably will know.

My husband desires a most affectionate remembrance to you all.

ALS; Weld-Grimké Papers, Clements Library, University of Michigan (microfiche 6/147).

Like many abolitionists, Child opposed both defensive and offensive wars, including slave insurrections. The Peace Convention discussed in the next letter was held on 18 September at the newly erected Marlboro Chapel in Boston. A resolution that denounced human government was drafted by Garrison and passed; the resolution urged that the use of the franchise and other civic duties be given up. Child and many others could not sanction this position.

To Abigail Kelley

Northampton. Oct. 1'st 1838.

Dear Friend,

. . .

You are quite out in your conjectures concerning me. My present situation is not one of my own choosing. A succession of trying circumstances led us here, and I ought to be thankful for the blessings with which I am surrounded; but I am in fact more home-sick than I ever was in my whole life. You suppose me to be in a delightful rural retreat, luxuriating in the beauties of Nature and Art. The plain truth is, we are living in the most secluded and frugal manner, with a plain honest farmer and shoe-maker, remarkably (and to me somewhat painfully) out of the atmosphere of literature and taste. Kindness, integrity, and plain good sense are around us; and were it not so difficult to change habits once formed, I should feel no deficiency. You seem to take it for granted that I am glad to be away from the din and activity of Boston. But oh, how I have hungered and thirsted after the good, warm abolition-sympathy, which I found only there!

I have not been called to labor much in the cause this summer; though some

[2] Child probably refers to the Reverend Dr. Samuel Hanson Cox (1793–1880), one of the few staunch antislavery ministers in the Presbyterian church.

disagreeable duties have come in my way—just enough to make me odious to the pro-slavery neighborhood. The abolitionists here, with very few exceptions, are wonderfully enamored of that imitation of Peace, which can exist for awhile without Righteousness for its foundation. "Let there be peace in the church—peace in the neighborhood"—is the burden of their song. So they support, and appear to reverence, a minister who receives $250 a year from a rich slave-auctioneer here, and in return preaches against all reforms, and puts as many obstructions in the way of reformers as possible; and the slave-auctioneer is Deacon of said minister, and teaches in his Sunday School that the Africans are descendants of Ham, fore-ordained to perpetual slavery; ergo, he, the pious Deacon, is justified in carrying into execution the decrees of the Almighty. There are many abolitionists belonging to that church; but they never open their lips—so highly do they value "the peace of the church."

This town is a great resort for Southerners in the summer season; and never in my life have I witnessed so much of the lofty slave-holding spirit. Will moral influence ever reach these haughty sinners? Never. Much as I deprecate it, I am convinced that emancipation must come through violence.

I wanted to be at the Peace Convention very, *very* much. I think an occasion can never again occur that can tempt me so much. I wanted to go for my own edification & instruction, not because I thought I could do the least good by being there. Up to a certain point my perceptions are clear, and my convictions strong, on this subject. I follow the straight road, till I see the no-government question in the distance, dimly, "like men as trees walking"; and there I stop. It brings the old problem that has puzzled the world eighteen hundred years—*Can* individuals living in the midst of a wicked world conduct precisely as they would, if Christ's kingdom had really and universally come, and earth was made a Heaven? The conviction returns upon me, and daily gains strength, that if but *one* human being earnestly and perseveringly sought to reach perfect holiness, the emanation from him would purify the world. There is overwhelming solemnity in this thought of our individual responsibility. The Peace Convention, little as will be thought of it at present, is unquestionably the greatest event in the 19th century.[1] Posterity will marvel at the early adoption of such transcendental principles, looking down on all the wider as well as narrower forms of human selfishness, and perceiving so clearly that under no disguise can they ever be admitted to Christ's kingdom. I was sorry so much was said about the "meek's *inheriting* the earth." Unquestionably there is an exceeding great reward *in* doing the will of God; but it should follow, as the shadow follows the substance; not be presented as a *motive*. It is a very refined form of selfishness, still it seems to me it is selfish. For this reason I have ever felt some objection to hearing the joys of Heaven represented as a *reward* for virtue.

You will ask why I was not at the Peace Convention, if I deemed it such an

[1] Child probably read the report of the proceedings in the 28 Sept. issue of *The Liberator*.

important movement, and so much wished to come. The simple reason is that we must be very economical, and travelling is expensive. I would not let this stand in the way of what seemed to me a duty; but, as I tell you, in this case I wanted to go for my own sake.

I am far from thinking you correct in saying "the experiment failed last Spring at the N. England Convention."[2] I wanted to thank you for your spirited conduct on that occasion; and I have no doubt that great good was done.

I thank you for your hearty invitation, which it would give me uncommon pleasure to accept, were it in my power. If ever I have a domicil, which I can call my own, I shall reciprocate the invitation most cordially. I have had a letter from Angelina, giving a charming picture of their happy domestic life, "serving one another in love," and dispensing altogether with hired service.

My respects to your mother; for I have internal evidence that she is a good woman.

Farewell. The blessing of God be with you.   Yrs most truly, L.M.C.

My husband unites with me in affectionate and respectful remembrance. He wished me to go to Boston, though he did not, according to your wicked advice, make use of his legal right to command.

ALS; Abigail Kelley Foster Papers, American Antiquarian Society (microfiche 6/149).

To Angelina (Grimké) Weld

Northampton Oct. 2'd 1838.

Dear Friend,

Your interesting letter of August 8'th was gladly received; it being the first tidings we had of your existence since your marriage. I began to think it was with you as with a girl, who being met by a person with whom she had formerly lived at service, was asked, "Where do you live now, Nancy"? "Please, ma'am, I dont live anywhere now; I'm married."

Your letter, however, gives indication that you *do* live somewhere, and that right happily. If I were to speak according to common parlance, I should say the world was for you all rose-colored with the honey-moon; but ten years' experience has taught me that the honey-moon is in fact the least happy part of married life.

The message that letters of congratulation were entirely "within a woman's sphere" was meant playfully. My husband thought you knew too well how much he despised the idea of any distinction in the appropriate spheres of human beings, as classes. However, I am glad you took him in earnest, since it drew forth such an eloquent defence.

2 The "experiment" refers to the election of Abby Kelley to a committee of the New England Anti-Slavery Society in May 1838. At the Peace Convention she was placed on a business committee, and when she used her authority to call to order one of the male members, several clergy and laity walked out.

Rosa, I am sorry to say, had returned to So. Carolina before I received your letter of Sep. 16th; or rather she had left Northampton, to sojourn in various cities before her mistress returned to the South. The struggle in her mind between her children and freedom was evidently severe & painful. At one time, I think the balance would have turned in favor of remaining in Massachusetts, had she not received a pathetic letter from her daughter in slavery, containing these words: "Dear mother, do come back to us; for you know we have nobody but God and you to pity us. Little Johnny says, 'Tell dear mother she must come back soon' "

For my own part, I did not say a word to sway her mind, from first to last; for she was evidently a very fond mother, and I felt afraid she would be very wretched if separated from her children. I merely assured her that I would be her friend, and get a good home for her, if she chose to take her freedom.

Two slaves from Georgia were brought here by Mr. John Stoddard. (nephew of Arthur Tappan.)[1] I understand from Rosa that the younger of the two was half a mind to take her freedom, though she left children behind her; and not being able to obtain communication with them myself, I asked Rosa to do it. The elder of the Georgians, a bold, pert, disagreeable girl, directly informed Rosa's mistress; which of course made a great deal of difficulty. After that, she was so closely watched, even after she went to bed, that she found opportunity but for one short, stolen interview with me. She was then sad enough, and her heart seemed almost torn in two by the struggle between contending feelings. I saw her no more, until I saw her follow her mistress into the stage-coach that conveyed her away from freedom.   To the last, she evidently entertained hopes in connection with old Mrs. Martin's Will; though to us they seemed perfectly groundless; and we told her so. I do not know how she would answer the queries in your last letter. I confess it was rather a relief to me to hear that you had *not* written; for I felt afraid of involving the poor creature in fresh difficulties. How would it do to write to Mr. Bentham, saying merely that you have heard (without alluding to any source) that old Mrs. Martin willed Rosa to be free, after the death of her grand-daughter Susan? I do not know whether he wrote the Will, or merely witnessed it; but Rosa said he was quite familiar with its contents, and often told her to be easy, for he had seen the Will, and she might trust to him. You might mention your presumption that he wrote the Will, as a good reason for addressing him for information. Whether such a step would do good or harm, you are the best judges. Do as you think proper. Mr. Napier's family are boasting that I tried very hard to persuade Rosa to take her freedom, but that I could not coax her away from her beloved mistress. They must know this is untrue; but Christians that will steal will lie also. I do not believe the South will voluntarily relinquish her slaves, so long as the world stands. It must come through violence. I would it might be averted; but I am convinced that it cannot be.

[1] John Stoddard (b. 1809) married Mary Morgin of Savannah, Ga., and settled on a large plantation in the South.

When Charles Stuart returned to Europe, did he leave with your husband a copy of Abdy's Travels, given to us by the Author? We lent it to him, and we want it very much.[2]

. . .

My best love to Sarah, and to your excellent husband. I wish you were all coming here to Convention this week.[3] If I kept house, I would not take no for answer. Situated as I am at present, I could not make you comfortable.

Yours Most Truly,
L. M. Child

P.S. My suspicions fixed on J. G. Whittier, because I took it into my head that he evinced an unusual and very peculiar interest in you.[4]

My dear husband unites in most affectionate & respectful remembrance for you all.

ALS; Weld-Grimké Papers, Clements Library, University of Michigan (microfiche 6/150).

To Henrietta Sargent

Northampton Nov. 18'th 1838

Dear Friends,

. . .

My husband and I are busy in that most odious of all tasks, that of getting signatures to Petitions. We are resolved that the business shall be done in this town more thoroughly than it has been heretofore. But, "Oh Lord, sir!"

I have never been so discouraged about abolition, as since we came into this iron-bound Valley of the Connecticut. I have ceased to believe that public opinion will ever be sincerely reformed on the question, till long after emanci-

[2] The anticolonization views of Charles Stuart (1783–1865) had a significant impact on the U.S. and British antislavery movements. This British author of the influential *West India Question* (London, 1832) became a lecturer for the American Anti-Slavery Society in 1834. But toward the end of the decade, he sided with the anti-Garrisonian faction. The book Child refers to is by Edward Strutt Abdy: *Journal Book of a Residence and Tour in the United States* (London, 1835).

[3] An Anti-Slavery Convention for the Western Counties was held in Northampton on 5 Oct. Its resolutions reflected the widening debate over the relationship of the movement to mainstream politics. Members of the convention claimed the right to organize a political party, but "we decline forming a political party by ourselves, and carefully avoid merging ourselves, as a body, in either of the political parties of the day" (*Hampshire Gazette*, 17 Oct. 1838).

[4] No evidence confirms Child's conjecture that Angelina might have married Whittier. The Quaker poet and abolitionist John Greenleaf Whittier (1807–92) was a founder of the American and Foreign Anti-Slavery Society. In 1838, he edited the *Pennsylvania Freeman*. In 1837 Whittier and Theodore Weld had vowed never to marry, a vow Whittier kept. A myth grew that they had pledged celibacy until slavery was abolished.

pation has taken place. I mean that, for generations to come, there will be a very large minority hostile to the claims of colored people; and the majority will be largely composed of individuals, who are found on that side from any and every motive, rather than hearty sympathy with the down-trodden race. Public events, probably of the most unexpected character, will help along the desired result. The injudicious course of the South has identified the claims of emancipation and free discussion, and thus thousands have already been roused, who care little or nothing for the poor slave. The stupidity and recklessness of Stevenson, in his mad encounter with O'Connell, have fairly laid before the gaze of Europe that most disgusting feature of slavery, which abolitionists have been obliged to leave partially veiled, for decency's sake.[1] What God is preparing for us along the Indian frontier, in Mexico, Cuba, & Hayti, I know not; but I think I see "coming events cast their shadows before." We certainly have done all we could to secure the deadly hostility of the red man and the black man, everywhere. I think God will over-rule *events* to bring about a change, long before the moral sense of this nation demands it as a matter of justice & humanity. . . .

. . . We talk of the *doing away* of the slave-trade, and say that the moral sense of *all Christendom* unites in branding it as piracy; yet was the infernal traffic *ever* so active as it now is? And if the moral sense of all Christendom was really so universally hostile to it, *could* it be so active? No. The fact is, many are still willing to make money by it, and the majority do not care a sixpence about it.

The abolition of slavery in this country will certainly come; but I despair of a regenerated public sentiment, till God has brought about the event in his own way. The abolitionists are His chosen instruments in this great work; and we must labor diligently according to the light we have, though the desired end may be produced in ways totally different from *our* calculation.

I never hear from Maria Chapman. Is she quite recovered? Has Wendall Phillips gone to the West Indies? Has Manlius Sargent ever heard anything about the tracts he sent to Queen Victoria? Did Mr. Pierpont compromise with his people?[2] Oh how much I should have to talk about, if I *could* but see you! How

---

[1] The Southerner Andrew Stevenson (1784–1857), minister to Great Britain, challenged Daniel O'Connell (1775–1847), Irish leader in the House of Commons and abolitionist, to a duel. O'Connell had accused Stevenson of being a breeder of slaves for traffic.

[2] Wendell Phillips (1811–84) was highly admired by Child. Of a socially prominent Boston family, he credited his wife, Ann Greene, with inspiring him to join the abolitionist movement in 1837. Quickly distinguishing himself by his eloquence, he became general agent for the Massachusetts Anti-Slavery Society in 1839. He did not go to the West Indies in 1838. Lucius Manlius Sargent (1786–1867), one of the leaders of the temperance movement in the antebellum years, may have sent temperance tracts to England. In the 1850s he published *Ballad of the Abolitionist Blunderbuss* (Boston), a satire on Emerson and other antislavery advocates. John Pierpont (1785–1866), pastor of the Hollis Street Church in Boston, had stood trial in July 1814 for his views on temperance and antislavery but he held his pulpit until 1845.

I do dread this long, lonesome winter! My dear husband is obliged to be at the Factory most of the time, evenings and all; and I am *entirely* alone.

. . .

ALS; Lydia Maria Child Papers, Anti-Slavery Collection, Cornell University (microfiche 6/152).

To Ellis Gray and Louisa Loring

Northampton Dec 5'th 1838

Dearly Beloved Friends,

Of the money that becomes due from Woods & Co early in January, please to make the following disposal.[1] To Mr. S. E. Sewall pay a note for One Hundred Dollars, which I owe him for Oasis. To yourself, pay the remains of a note, which, if my recollection serves me right, is now about Ninety Dollars, likewise borrowed for the Oasis. To yourself likewise pay Seventy Dollars, for four months board of my husband and myself, last winter; and with the balance of the money, pay interest on the two Oasis notes, if it will hold out for the same.

With regard to the *board*, I trust you will do as I say. It was always our intention to pay you, at least as much as we actually caused you to expend. I submitted to Louisa's kind juggling *for the time being*, because it was *then* inconvenient for me to spare the money. As it is, we shall remain under great obligations; for we could not have boarded decently elsewhere, during that time, for the small sum I mention. The fifteen dollars that I paid Louisa is a cheap remuneration for *fuel*. I *asked* to board with you, because I foresaw that many disagreeable things would attend our staying with Father, though he is a kind and good old man as ever lived. We are very grateful to you for consenting to the arrangement; but if you love us, you *must* consent to be paid. Remember that it is not judicious or kind to insist upon obliging people in a way that pains them. My strongest peculiarity is pride of personal independence. This made my situation last winter perfectly suffocating to my soul. It changed my nature—I was no longer myself. Take the fetter off, I pray you—restore me the free air. Suppose that I want to scold you?—how can I feel free to do it, till that Seventy dollars is paid? In sober earnestness, I shall be deeply *grieved* & *wounded*, unless you consent to make the proposed settlement. As for what little writing and teaching French we did, you yourself know that it was not a cent in a dollar toward paying for the continual trouble you have with my business. If you really have any regard for me, oblige me in *my* way, not in your own.

Charles Sedgwick & wife lately visited her mother, who resides in this town.[2]

[1] She refers to the publishers of *The American Frugal Housewife*.
[2] Charles Sedgwick (1791–1856) was clerk for the Supreme Court of Massachusetts and brother of the author Catharine Sedgwick. His wife, Elizabeth (Dwight) Sedgwick (1801–64), ran a school for young women in Lenox, Mass., for over thirty years and wrote several educational books.

We spent a very pleasant evening with them. They talked a good deal of Fanny Butler, who has been boarding in Stockbridge the past summer.[3] It seems she keeps tugging at her husband's conscience all the time, about his slaves. One day he begged her to spar[e] him—saying, "You know, Fanny, we don't feel alike on that subject. If I objected to it in my conscience, as you do, I would emancipate them all." "Pierce!" exclaimed she, "look me full in the face, and say that in your conscience you think it right to hold slaves, and I will never again speak to you on the subject." He met her penetrating glance for a moment,—lowered his eyes,—and between a blush and a smile, said, "Fanny, I cannot do it." Mrs. Butler has some habits of mind, which the Sedgwicks call incipient insanity. Sometimes she makes it a rule in all her rides and walks, for a whole season, always to take the right-hand road; and no picturesque scenery, or pleasant company, can divert her from this plan. In a collection of biographies, if she wants to read any particular one, she *must* begin at the beginning, and read till she arrives at it. This winter she is reading all the books in her library the names of whose authors begin with a particular letter; and she is determined to read no other.

Judge & Mrs. Shaw called to see me this summer. He asked whether Med were in a comfortable situation, and was surprised when I told him of her death.[4] He repeated a conversation with a New-Orleans gentleman about the cruelty of separating a child from its parents—how dreadfully the mother felt about it, &c   I mention this, thinking you may put Dr Jackon, or some other person, in the way of convincing the Judge that Med received every possible kindness.   He was very reserved on all subjects connected with Anti-Slavery. I suppose on account of his official station.

At Springfield I met with a letter from Bancroft to Mrs. Jonathan Dwight, in which he says, "Last evening went to H. G. Chapman's, where I found a squad of blue-stockings and abolitionists; both of whom are my abhorrence."[5] The letter was written last winter, and refers to that evening when we saw him

---

[3] Frances Anne (Kemble) Butler (1809-93) was born in London into a theatrical family and, as Fanny Kemble, was a highly successful actress. In 1834, at the height of her career, she married Pierce Butler (1807-67), a lawyer and owner of a plantation in Georgia.

[4] Lemuel Shaw was the judge in the Med case; his wife was Hope (Savage) Shaw and their daughter Elizabeth later married Herman Melville. Judge Shaw was settling the estate of Thomas Melville, an old friend of David Child and the grandfather of Herman Melville; Shaw may have visited the Childs to discuss payment of a debt. Med had died within the previous two weeks. Ellis Loring took responsibility for erecting a gravestone and asked Child to supply him with an inscription.

[5] The historian and diplomat George Bancroft (1800-1891), a Democrat, was married to Sarah Dwight, daughter of Springfield lawyer Jonathan Dwight and Sarah (Shepard) Dwight. Bancroft founded the Round Hill School, an influential experiment in education, in Northampton in 1821. He stayed until 1832 teaching and writing his history of the United States. Henry Grafton Chapman (1804-42), wealthy Boston merchant, abolitionist, and husband of Maria (Weston) Chapman, contributed large sums of money to the antislavery movement.

in West St.   All classes and conditions of men in this region describe him as a selfish, treacherous man, who will desert his best friend the moment he ceases to be of use to him. Brother John says the very day after he published his democratic address advocating the rights of working-men & slaves, which elicited a poetic tribute from Whittier, he had offered him a petition for abolition in the D.C. and refused to sign, on the ground that he did not think it right to throw such an apple of discord into Congress.

I send our dear Nony a pair of stockings and some popping-corn. I am afraid the first I sent was too green to parch well. I wish I knew whether the stockings fit, and whether another pair would be desirable this winter; if so, it is only to say the word; for I have the yarn in readiness. The only ground for hesitation is that it is not well to knit too many ⟨pairs⟩ when she is growing so fast. As for getting any reply to this, or any other question, from my beloved Mrs. Remarkable Lazy-bones, I despair of it. What is the matter, Louisa? Do you know you have not written me a single line since I came here? Surely, none of my *badinage* has offended?

I thought Mrs. Chapman's letter to the R.I. Convention was uncommonly eloquent. Did it not strike you so? I was so much pleased with the conclusion, "For God and the Human Race," that I mean, some time, to have it cut on a seal.

She sent me up the last Report of the Female A S. Society sealed with Dominie Sampson, exclaiming "Prodigious!"[6]

Farewell. The blessing of God be with you all.

Your grateful & attached friend, L.M.C.

. . .

In making the settlement, take pay for any postage that you may have paid, for Reed's Growth of the Mind, &c—[7]

ALS; Manuscript Division, New York Public Library (microfiche 6/154).

Theodore Dwight Weld (1803–95), to whom the following letter is addressed, trained many agents, including the Grimkés, for the American Anti-Slavery Society. The rigors of lecturing destroyed his voice, and he gave up public speaking shortly before his wedding. Child's information about Southern slaveholding influence in Northampton probably contributed to the exhaustive research done by the Welds and Sarah Grimké that culminated in *Slavery As It Is.* This definitive book, published by Weld in 1839, was the most widely read abolitionist tract of its time; it included extracts from Southern newspapers and eyewitness accounts of slavery by black and white abolitionists. Weld continued working in

[6] Dominie Sampson is a character in Sir Walter Scott's *Guy Mannering.*
[7] Sampson Reed's *Observations on the Growth of the Mind* (Boston, 1826) was an essay on Swedenborgian thought.

New York for the American Anti-Slavery Society and was an antislavery lobbyist in Washington in the early 1840s but soon after retired from the movement. He found a second vocation as a schoolteacher.

To Theodore Dwight Weld

Northampton. Dec. 18th 1838

Dear Friend & Brother,

Though almost a stranger here, I have been deputed to answer the interrogatories in your letter to Mr. Williston.[1] The result of my inquiries is as follows.   Miss Margaret Dwight, Principal of the Gothic Seminary for young ladies, has resided considerable at the South.[2] She generally has 5 or 6 Southerners among her pupils; and she is engaged to educate a constant supply of teachers for a similar school, established under her auspices, in Georgia. She is very fond of the Southern institution, and strongly prejudiced against abolitionists. Her situation entitles her to influence the young a good deal.

Sarah Brackett, Lucy Dewey, and Harriet Clark have gone from here to teach in Georgia. Roxana Hunt went to teach in Alabama. Thankful Wright went as teacher to Virginia, and married a slave-holder there.[3]

Mr. Sheldon went from here for his health, and now teaches in S. Carolina.[4] Says he acts on the strictly non-committal system. He was however rejected in one school, because he would not go quite so far as to say he should be willing to *buy* slaves.

Mr. H. A. Dwight is a teacher in Georgia.[5]

Elizabeth Long married Stebbins Lathrop, a N. England man, who now keeps store in Savannah, Georgia.[6] Her half-brother Joseph Stebbins is in the same store.

Frances Dickenson married Mr. James Lyman, both of Northampton.[7] He now keeps store ⟨at Fort Gibson, Mississippi.⟩ in St. Louis, Missouri. Her brother is in the same store. His partner is a slave-holder; whether he is or not, is un-

---

[1] The home of John Payson Williston (1804–72), reformer and abolitionist, was a station on the underground railroad. He founded the first antislavery newspaper in western Massachusetts, the *Hampshire Herald*, in 1845.

[2] The school of Margaret Dwight (1804–45) was one of the best in western Massachusetts.

[3] Unnoted names could not be identified.

[4] Possibly this was George Sheldon (1813–81), pastor of the Presbyterian Church in Summerville, S.C.

[5] This was probably Henry A. Dwight (1804–79), native of Northampton, 1829 graduate of Williams College, and founder of a military academy in Norfolk, Va.

[6] The owner of a successful dry goods business in Savannah, Ga., J. Stebbins Lathrop (1816–94) returned to Northampton during the Civil War and became one of its leading businessmen.

[7] Frances Pomeroy Dickenson married James B. Lyman (b. 1813) in 1838. They moved to St. Louis for the first few years of the 1840s and then returned to Northampton.

known. He is quite furious on the subject. Told Mr. Williston "he was glad Lovejoy[8] was shot—he deserved death."

Deacon Luther Clark's daughter married Wm Wells, both of Northampton.[9] He now keeps store at Fort Gibson, Mississippi. Her brother is in the store with him. He began by buying a woman from compassionate motives, as he said, to prevent her from being separated from her husband. Has since increased his stock of slaves, and speculated in Texas lands. Hates abolitionists, and has mightily influenced his own and his wife's relations against them.

David Jewett is in business in Vicksburg, Mississippi. His father here is perfectly furious against abolitionists.

Dr. Legur of this place has a son in Vicksburg. According to his own story, he was active in the mob there—boasted of having shot the first gambler that was killed.

King Hunt, son of the late Doctor Hunt, a drinking, bad-tempered young man.[10] More than suspected of setting fire to his uncle's barn, and breaking open his store. He ran off, and became a slave-overseer somewhere South.

John Stoddard, nephew of Arthur Tappan, married a Georgian lady, rich in slaves. He carries on a large plantation near Savannah. His influence on this subject is very pernicious. He brought on two slaves, (not his own, but hired) and was parading the streets, with them walking behind him, all last summer. One of these slaves was a pert, wanton woman, evidently trained to go about in the shops and taverns, preaching up the exalted merits of slavery, telling how she pitied and despised free negroes, how easily she could make her $12 a week &c. The other slave appeared sad and unhappy, and was very vigilantly guarded. John Stoddard told his sister-in-law that they had serious scruples about bringing her to the North, because she looked so discontented.[11] His lordship was in a high state of excitement after visiting the High School here. He could not become reconciled to the monstrous fact that the children of *poor people* were allowed to learn chemistry, botany, &c.

Lyman Hinkley, grandson of Judge Hinkley, married a South Carolinian, rich in slaves.[12] They reside here. All the family connexions have a bitter hostility to abolitionists.

The son of Judge Lyman edits the Brunswick Advocate in Georgia.

---

[8] Elijah Lovejoy.
[9] Luther Clark (1767–1855) was deacon of the First Church in Northampton from 1805 until his death.
[10] The physician David Hunt (1773–1837) was active in the Massachusetts Medical Society.
[11] Stoddard's sister-in-law was Francis Bradish, who was married to William Stoddard. For more information on John Stoddard see note 1, p. 92.
[12] Samuel Lyman Hinckley (1810–71) worked in the law firm of his grandfather, Samuel Hinckley (1757–1840). The elder Hinckley was judge of the probate court from 1816 to 1834 and president of the Northampton Bridge Corporation.

Edward Lyman, merchant in Natchez[13]

Mr. Whitney, merchant in Alabama.

James Greenwood, merchant, Alabama. He was a poor orphan helped along by William Stoddard, by whom he was treated like a very brother. I lately heard a most insolent letter from him to Mr. Stoddard, forbidding him to write or send anything to him about emancipation.[14]

Lyman Clapp, in a Bank at Natchez.

Mr. Parsons, dentist in Natchez.

Edward Storrs clerk in Georgia.

Eli Lovel & wife, cabinet maker, Georgia.

Franklin Parsons, d'o   do

Mr. Thomas Napier, formerly a slave-auctioneer in Charleston S.C. Owns a large establishment here; and having the name of being a good, pious man, does the more mischief on this subject. Very irritable on the subject of slavery. Rose and answered Arnold Buffum with a good deal of warmth when he first lectured here. Being about to go South on business, he published a letter assuring his friends that he was uncontaminated by Northern abolition. Said to have sold all his slaves, when he came here. Holds landed property at the South, and was concerned in a Rice business between Northampton & Charleston; but that failed. Has a great deal of Southern company at his house. Deacon of Mr. Mitchell's church, and Sunday School teacher. He teaches his class that the negroes are descendants of Ham, ⟨fore⟩ordained by God to be forever "servants of servants." There are many abolitionists in the same church and Sunday school; but they keep as whist as a mouse when a cat is about the premises. Deacon Napier admired and patronized Gurley greatly, during his late visit here.[15]

Mr. Hibbins, son-in law of Mr. Napier, resides here. Was formerly a slave-holder in S.C. Said to have sold his slaves when he came away. Said to have come North because he did not like to educate his children in a Southern state of society. Less irritable upon the subject than Napier, but contrives to slip smoothly over it. Deacon at Mr. Mitchell's, and Sunday School teacher.

Mr. Mitchell has a salary of $800; of which $250 was formerly paid by a Messrs Napier & Hibbin. In consequence of pecuniary losses, they now pay him but $100. Mr. Mitchell opposed to all reforms; but seldom comes out in any form

---

13 Possibly this was Edward Bellows Lyman (1811–54), son of Theodore Lyman, who married a woman from Mobile, Ala.

14 An active temperance worker and abolitionist, William Stoddard (1804–84) was a partner in the local business firm of Stoddard, Lathrop and Co.

15 Arnold Buffum (1782–1859) was a Quaker abolitionist and one of the founders of the New England and American Anti-Slavery Societies. Ralph Randolph Gurley (1797–1872), director of the American Colonization Society, travelled widely, lecturing and debating with New England abolitionists. Child heard him in a debate with George Thompson in Boston and noted Gurley's "jesuitical evasions, hair-splitting subtlety, and cunning appeals to popular prejudice" (Letter from New-York #33, *National Anti-Slavery Standard*, 18 Aug. 1842).

that can be met by open discussion. Refuses to sign petitions; makes inuendoes in his sermons; thinks slavery wrong in the abstract, but finds something very lovely in slave-holding Christians— ⟨refuses to sign petitions,⟩ and diligently circulates Dr. Wayland's Limitation. When Moses Breck, one of his parishioners, tried to get leave for Mr. Colver to lecture in his pulpit, after starting various objections, he at last said, "Why Mr. Breck, if such things are done, it will drive Mr. Napier and Mr. Hibben out of town."   He was not even willing that Mr. Colver should preach for him on Sunday, though he promised to say nothing about abolition. Mr. Mitchell replied he was afraid his people would not like his exchanging so often; but a very few weeks after, Dr. Leland of S. Carolina, who was staying at Deacon Napier's, preached for him all day.[16]

Mr. Church, who resides on Round Hill, was formerly a slave-holder in Kentucky. Said to have sold his slaves when he came North. Has a son now a slave-holder, and owns landed property at the South. Attached to the Southern institution; but a timid, quiet man, who says little.

The Hotels here full of Southern travellers, attracted by the beauty of the scenery. Landlords have no love for abolitionists. Partridge, of the Mansion House, was quite angry with Mr. Child for asking a colored man there if he were free. "I dislike slavery as much as you do," said Mr. Partridge; "but then I get my living by slave-holders."

Since the Rice-Hulling manufactory failed, I know of no establishment here connected with the South. Mr. Whitmarsh of the Silk Factory, has a good many Southern customers in the way of eggs and mulberries; but I never heard of anything like partnership.[17]

Of the numbers who have gone from here to the South, I have *heard* of but two, who do not apologize for slavery, and dislike abolitionists. Two of the female teachers write to their friends that they think worse of slavery than ever; but what they say there I know not.

If any individuals here know cases of cruelty by their own observation, they are not those who choose to tell.

[16] Francis Wayland (1796–1865), president of Brown University, wrote *The Limitations of Human Responsibility* (Boston, 1838), stating that it was possible to be both a Christian and a slaveholder. An activist in abolition and temperance, Moses Breck (1793–1882) was one of the original members of Edwards Church and a master builder with a large business. Nathaniel Colver (1794–1870) was an abolitionist, orator, and agent for the American Anti-Slavery Society. After the Civil War, he helped establish the Colver Institute for the training of black ministers in Richmond, Va.
[17] Founder of the Northampton Silk Company, Samuel Whitmarsh (d. 1875) was the first businessman outside Northampton to invest large sums of capital in local industry. "Mulberry Fever"—cultivating mulberry trees for silk—was the rage when the Childs lived here. The company suddenly went bankrupt in 1840, and the land was sold to a socialistic community, the Northampton Association of Education and Industry.

So endeth my testimony. Disgusting as the picture is, we are probably freer from the pollution than most large towns in N. England, because little business is done here, and manufactories and [*sic*] small and few.

Very Respectfully,
L. M. Child.

ALS; Weld-Grimké Papers, Clements Library, University of Michigan; published in Gilbert H. Barnes and Dwight Dumond, eds., *Letters of Theodore Dwight Weld, Angelina Grimké Weld and Sarah Grimké, 1822–1844*, vol. 2 (New York: D. Appleton-Century Co., 1934), pp. 726–30 (microfiche 6/156).

To Convers Francis

Northampton, December 22, 1838.

If I were to choose my home, I certainly would not place it in the Valley of the Connecticut. It is true, the river is broad and clear, the hills majestic, and the whole aspect of outward nature most lovely. But oh! the narrowness, the bigotry of man! To think of hearing a whole family vie with each other, in telling of vessels that were wrecked, or shattered, or delayed on their passages, because they sailed on Sunday! To think of people's troubling their heads with the question whether the thief could have been instantaneously converted on the cross, so that the Saviour could promise him an entrance to Paradise! In an age of such stirring inquiry, and of such extended benevolence—in a world which requires all the efforts of the good and wise merely to make it receptive of holy influences, what a pity it is that so much intellect should be wasted upon such theological jargon! No wonder that the intelligent infidel, looking at mere doctrines and forms, should be led to conclude that religion had done more harm in the world than good. The really inward-looking find in these no language by which they can give even a stammering utterance to their thoughts and feelings; yet the incubus of forms, from which the life has departed, oppresses them, though they dare not throw them off. Something is coming toward us (I know not what), with a glory round its head and its long, luminous rays are even now glancing on the desert and the rock. The Unitarian, busily at work pulling down old structures, suddenly sees it gild some ancient pillar, or shed its soft light on some moss-grown altar; and he stops with a troubled doubt whether *all* is to be destroyed; and if destroyed, wherewith shall he build anew? He looks upward for the coming dawn, and calls it transcendentalism. The Calvinist at work with strong arm and sincere heart at his fiery forge, fashioning the melted metal in time-honored moulds, sees a light, before which his fires grow dim, and the moulded forms seem rigid and uncouth. Perplexed, he asks if the martyred fathers *did* die for a faith that must be thrown aside like a useless stove of last year's patent. His grim iron forms return no answer, for there is not in them that which *can* answer the earnest questionings of the human soul. He too looks upward, sees the light, and calls it Perfectionism.

Having accidentally fallen into this vein of thought brings Emerson to my remembrance. How absurdly the Unitarians are behaving, after all their talk about liberality, the sacredness of individual freedom, free utterance of thought, etc.[1] If Emerson's thoughts are not their thoughts, can they not reverence them, inasmuch as they are formed and spoken in freedom? I believe the whole difficulty is, they are looking outwardly to what the logical opponents will say, not inwardly with calm investigation. I am not at all disturbed by what any man believes, or what he disbelieves; and as for the Unitarian views, they arise from doubts too familiar to my own mind to be intolerant at this period of my life. But I do like to have men utter their thoughts honestly, and not be afraid that it will not do to break down old forms. Of the many who make an outcry about Emerson's scruples concerning the sacrament, what proportion do you suppose really regard that institution as sacred? "What can be more unprofitable than to see men struggling with their whole force and industry to stretch out the old formula and phraseology, so that it may cover the new, contradictory, entirely uncoverable thing? Whereby the poor formula does but crack, and one's honesty along with it. This stretching out of formulas till they crack is, especially in time of swift changes, one of the sorrowfullest tasks poor humanity has."

I by no means charge the Unitarians with being the only ones that strive to stretch out old formulas; but it is more observable in them, because so inconsistent with their own free theories.

L, extract; *Letters of Lydia Maria Child*, 1882 (microfiche 6/157).

To Theodore Dwight Weld

Northampton Dec. 29'th 1838

Dear Brother Weld,

Since we sent our last letter to you, Mr. Samuel F. Lyman, son of Judge Lyman, of this place, has returned from a visit to N. Hampshire. He has just told my husband that in Walpole, N.H. he met with an abolitionist more fiery than any he had yet seen. He knew nothing of the progress of Anti Slavery; had not seen the publications; had not seen, and I believe not heard of, Thome and Kimball; his abhorrence of slavery was founded upon what he had himself witnessed. His name was Seth Hunt.[1] He was born somewhere in the vicinity of Northamp-

[1] Child refers to the angry response to Emerson's "Divinity School Address," delivered before the senior class of Divinity College, Harvard, on 15 July 1838. Emerson appealed for an original, intuitive spiritual experience and charged the formal church with being false and moribund. William Ellery Channing and Theodore Parker enthusiastically supported his ideas, but strict Unitarians attacked the address as irreverent and atheistic and ostracized Emerson.

[1] Samuel Fowler Lyman (b. 1799), a Northampton lawyer, was register of probate. Seth Hunt (1780–1846) was a native of Northampton and a lawyer and businessman whom Thomas Jefferson had appointed to the governorship of the Territory of Alabama.

ton, and is known here. He is now about 60 years old. He was originally a lawyer. For a short time he had the government of Alabama, while that was a Territory. He is now carrying on Copper Works in Indiana; but will remain in Walpole N.H. till February. He says that, three years ago, he had the care of a Steam-boat, passing either up or down (probably the latter) the Mississippi. On their way, at one of their stopping places, they saw a poor slave with an iron mask over his face, fastened with a ⟨a locked⟩ padlock behind. A space was left for the eyes, and two gimblet-holes at the mouth, to breathe, and suck in water, as through a straw. This he was obliged to wear all the time, because suspected of a desire to run away. He could taste no food, except when his overseers un-locked the mask for him.   This instrument of tyranny was once brought on board the steam-boat, by the sailors, who had a great curiosity to find out who made it, who was the man that used it, &c. But Mr. Hunt said, "Take it away! Take it away! The sight of it pains and disgusts me; and I advise you all to be cautious about your inquiries into it, lest we should get lynched."

I was sorry they could not have brought away this specimen of the American Inquisition; for I have often wished you could collect a variety of the instruments of torture used, and deposit them at the A. S. Office. I believe such a collection would do a vast deal of good.

But to return to Mr. Hunt, his indignation is unbounded. He says it disgusts him to hear about generosity and chivalry; for, judging by his own opportunities for observation, nothing can exceed the general meanness and rapacity of the South. He says it is all nonsense to talk about the Union; there *can* be no good results from union with so much tyranny and crime.

I have written all this, thinking you might like to communicate with the N. Hampshire abolitionists, in order to obtain Mr. Hunt's evidence. It may turn out to be of importance, and it may not. Am I wrong in thinking you would rather pay the postage of this letter, than not to be informed of Mr. Seth Hunt?

Some time when you are writing to us, will you mention what has become of James Bradley, whose story is in the Oasis?[2] When I say *you*, I mean Angelina; for your writing is so much like *les pieds de mouches*, that the famous decypherer of the hieroglyphicks would give it up in despair.

What think you of the prospects of Anti Slavery, dear brother. Shall we keep the steam up till the work is done? I am disheartened sometimes to see how few of the *nominal* abolitionists are *real* ones. Many in this region, for instance, have "their dander up" (as some express it) about their own rights of petition

[2] The ex-slave James Bradley had sent Child a narrative of his life four years earlier. He describes his capture in Africa by "soul destroyers," his sale to different owners in the United States, and his work and mistreatment in the fields. He raised three hundred dollars to buy his freedom by selling hogs and horse collars he plaited from corn husks. Free in 1833, he taught himself to read and write and was accepted into Lane Seminary, where he met Theodore Weld. (James Bradley and Theodore [Dwight] Weld to Child, 3 June [1834], Anti-Slavery Collection, Rare Books and Manuscripts, Boston Public Library.)

&c; but few really sympathize with the slave. I know of but one man here, except my husband, who I should feel quite sure would, under all circumstances, consider Anti Slavery paramount to the interests of his own religious sect, or political party. I should not even dare to *hope* it, except from a very few. Here, I apprehend, lies the difficulty of which the good Gerrit Smith so earnestly complains. Men take narrow and superficial views, centering in self, instead of standing firmly on those eternal principles, which embrace the rights and happiness of every human being. To you and I, who look on the *foundations* upon which slavery rests, it is not of the slightest consequence whether James Williams told the truth or not; yet the doubt thrown on his narrative is doing incalculable mischief.[3] For this reason, I long for some further light on the subject.

Had I known any abolitionist by name in Walpole, I would have written directly there.

It may need some argument to persuade Hunt to let his name be published. Of his character we have no information.

AL; Weld-Grimké Papers, Clements Library, University of Michigan; published in Barnes and Dumond, *Letters of Theodore Dwight Weld, Angelina Grimké Weld and Sarah Grimké*, 2:734–36 (microfiche 6/159).

The first split in the antislavery movement occurred at the January 1839 meeting of the Massachusetts Anti-Slavery Society, ushering in a year of dissension. A group led by the Reverend Charles T. Torrey (1813–46) submitted a resolution to exclude women from the meetings. At the New England Convention in May, a similar resolution was voted down, and the antifemale minority left to form the Massachusetts Abolition Society, referred to as the New Organization by Garrisonians.

Child and other supporters of Garrison wanted the societies open to all abolitionists. Petitioning, testifying before legislatures, nominating antislavery candidates on a local level, and, on occasion, voting—were the most effective means of agitation, they said. They looked toward a reformed public opinion as the only way to change politics. Their opponents, including Alanson St. Clair, Amos Phelps, and Henry Stanton, did not want abolitionists with unorthodox ideas about religion and women in the societies. They thought abolition was a political issue, and only an abolitionist avant-garde could regenerate politics.

The attitude Child expresses toward separate women's societies in the next

---

[3] Child refers to the controversy surrounding the slave narrative of James Williams, as related to John Greenleaf Whittier. *The Narrative of James Williams, an American Slave* . . . (Boston, 1838), was one of nearly a hundred slave stories used as propaganda by the abolitionists. Some critics dismissed them as unreliable because they were not documented and they allegedly exaggerated atrocities. There were many factual discrepancies in Williams's narrative, and the American Anti-Slavery Society discontinued its sale in 1838.

letter is similar to the official position of the 1837 National Anti-Slavery Convention of American Women. A national women's society and a women's newspaper would be inexpedient; according to the report, "the best hope of the sexes are in each other; and . . . the plan of separate sources of knowledge, and separate means of mental and moral improvement is likely to produce characteristic difference, fatal to the happiness and usefulness of both" (Annual Report of the Boston Female Anti-Slavery Society, 1837, p. 40). After the 1838 convention, a significant number of women questioned, as Child did, whether a convention should be held the following year.

What Child underestimated at the time was the real influence of the women's conventions on abolitionism. By pressing the issue of overcoming racial prejudice and setting an example of courage and level-headedness in the midst of violent proslavery mobs, they made a unique contribution to the movement. After the conventions, several delegates also reported increased membership in their local societies. Harriet Martineau captured some of the spirit of the women in "The Martyr Age of the United States," published in the December 1838 issue of *The Westminister Review;* the article also mentions the public censure of the Childs after they gave legal counsel to a black family in Boston.

To Lucretia Mott

Northampton, March 5th, 1839.
My dear friend,—Your letter was received a few days since, and it gave us great pleasure to hear from you once more. My husband wanted me to write a letter expressing sympathy when we heard of your pecuniary losses last summer.[1] I tried; but I threw it up in despair, saying, "I *cannot* compassionate such souls for the loss of worldly goods. Have they not each other? Have they not inward peace, which the world giveth not, and cannot take away?" I could only feel sorry that they who would give liberally to the Anti-Slavery cause, and other benevolent projects, should have less to give away; but even in this point of view, I could not express condolence; for was not money the least of your *doings?* Could its absence impair your moral influence?

As to your request, I think it more than doubtful whether I can comply with it.[2] There are several obstacles in the way. Besides, as I am growing very scrupulous about exact truth, I will not disguise that I do not want to go to the convention, much as I should like again to visit Philada. I never have entered very earnestly into the plan of female conventions and societies. They always seemed to me like half a pair of scissors. This feeling led me to throw cold water on the project of the Boston Female Anti-Slavery Society. You will remind me of the great good done by that society. I admit it most cordially. I am thankful there

1 James Mott was part owner of Penn Factory, which was severely damaged by fire.
2 Mott may have asked Child to come to the convention as a delegate from the Boston Female Anti-Slavery Society.

were those who could work heartily in that way. To pay my annual subscription, and occasionally make articles for sale, was all I ever could do freely and earnestly. I attended the first convention because I was urged by friends, and I feared I might fail in my duty if I obstinately refused. But I then thought the large sum necessarily expended in getting the delegates together might be otherwise expended with far more profit to the Anti-Slavery cause. This opinion has been confirmed by the two conventions already held. For the freedom of women, they have probably done something; but in every other point of view, I think their influence has been very slight.

I should think an Address to the Women of the U.S. would be somewhat stale, unless written with peculiar originality and piquancy. What think you of a letter to the Women of Great Britain, written by yourself, on the subject of abstaining from U.S. cotton? A discriminating duty between free and slave labor produce in England would strike a heavier blow to slavery here than anything else in the wide world.

In my opinion, the convention last year, in rejecting Maria Chapman's "Address to the Clergy," threw away a gem "richer than all their tribe." I have long considered Mrs. Chapman as one of the most remarkable women of the age. Her heart is as large and magnanimous as her intellect is clear, vigorous, and brilliant. I am glad Harriet Martineau has done her justice in England, for very few appreciate her here. The Westminster article, though abounding in small mistakes, appears to me discriminating and forcible. I am sorry, however, that it is published. Persecution is much better for the abolitionists than praise. The immortal radiance of the Truths they are commissioned to maintain may be mistaken for a glory around their own brows. Just at this particular time, too, they are not behaving quite well enough to have the gaze of the world fixed upon them. Oh! how my heart is grieved by these dissensions! I wish our dear and much respected friend Garrison would record them more sparingly in his paper; but I suppose he thinks it necessary. In addition to disguised enemies of sound Anti-Slavery, I think there is now a large class of sincere abolitionists, with narrow views of freedom, who require some other paper than the "Liberator." They are frightened, sincerely frightened, at new and bold views. They think the mere utterance of them is in danger of resolving all shapes back to chaos. It requires great faith to trust truth to take care of herself in all encounters.

. . .

My dear husband unites with me in kind and grateful remembrance to your husband, yourself, and children. Farewell.   Yours very truly,   L. M. Child.

L, extract; Anna Davis Hallowell, ed., *James and Lucretia Mott: Life and Letters* (Boston: Houghton Mifflin, 1884), pp. 135–38 (microfiche 7/171).

To Caroline Weston

(Not to be published in any part.)   Northampton. March 7th 1839

Dear Caroline,

It is lucky that no very important affairs of state are dependant on the punc-
tuality of our correspondence. My last letter it seems was some months in reaching you; and yours of Nov. 25th came into my hands on Jan. 11'th.

I have had a most eager desire to see you. My yearnings to be in Boston have
been checked only by a feeling of relief at being distant from the scene of con-
tention. The present state of things is exceedingly painful to my mind. This
difficulty is a far more complicated affair than was the clerical appeal. It is too
evident now, that with real enemies of the cause, and half-and-half abolitionists,
are mixed up a *large* class of sincere friends of emancipation, according to their
honest but limited views thereof. I watch the aspect of things carefully, according to my circumscribed opportunities; and I am convinced that every move
Garrison can make against the Abolitionist re-acts against the Liberator.[1] Friends
at a distance *will* not believe that such men as Stanton and Phelps are plotters
against the cause; and if you prove their narrow sectarianism, nothing is gained,
at least for the present; for this seems a virtue in their eyes. I think I may say I do
not know of *one* Garrison abolitionist here. Moses Breck, the carpenter, is so,
when left to his own good sense and spontaneous feeling; but he is very easily
influenced by the members of his church. Two individuals here, Mr. Stoddard,
(nephew of Arthur Tappan) and Mr. Williston, became responsible for a hundred copies of the Abolitionist. They are both good, conscientious men, but
much fettered with sectarian bigotry; especially Mr. S. At the first Monthly Concert after the Anniversary, they gave an account of their visit to Boston. I think
their manner of telling the story gave the *impression* that a very large proportion
of the Society felt the need of a new paper, but forbore to urge its being the
organ of the Society, because they did not want to make trouble; "all Lynn being
there—most of them Quakers, and Mr. Garrison's personal friends." They said
3000 were subscribed for on the spot; but they did not tell that this was effected
by 30 individuals' becoming responsible for a hundred each. Garrison was spoken
of with respect, and restrained, and I thought *con*strained praise. I had a sort of
suspicion (perhaps entirely unfounded) that the few words of eulogy were uttered to keep *us* quiet. The friends present were urged to take the new paper,
only on the ground that Mr. Garrison could not advise political action consistently with his "new light." In all that was said, there was nothing to contradict,
or deny; yet we both felt that the *impression* given was not at all the same we
received from the delegates when they first arrived from Boston. They *then* told
Mr. Child that the opposition to a new organ of the Society was overwhelming—
that only *one* (Mr. Torrey) stood in favor of it;—and this did not seem at all

[1] The *Abolitionist* was the organ of the Massachusetts Abolition Society.

like all Massachusetts' reluctantly yielding to Lynn, for the sake of quiet. I dont believe they have many subscribers here; for there is not life enough on the subject to get up an interest of any kind. The abolitionists are honestly, sincerely frightened at the bearing of the Peace principles on governments; but more than that, I suspect they dimly perceive that these ideas are shaking a belief in the literal sense of the Old Testament to its very foundations. Everything must be rejected that will not combine with the savage customs of the half-civilized Jews. For eighteen hundred years they have been amalgamating Christianity and Judaism—and a strange compound salt they have made of it! It is marvellous that they do not see that every enormity under the sun may be sanctioned by the literal sense of the Old Testament.

With regard to the Liberator, we let no opportunity slip of talking in its favor, and urging the very few who take it to continue it. I often attack bigotry with "a troop of horse shod with felt"; that is, I try to *enter* the wedge of general principles, letting inferences unfold themselves very gradually. Calvinism grates and creaks harsher and harsher discord in the ears of my soul. If it were the Lord's will, I would I might be out of the hearing of it. It is doubtless performing a great use in the world, or it would not have taken such strong hold of the minds of men. How beautiful it would be to live in a world where it was not needed! I will not say I am trying to be tolerant; for I have learned to abominate that proud, self-sufficient word. What right have I, or any other fallible mortal, to be *tolerant* of others?

Sinclair's[2] recent "devel-opements" bring to my recollection his conversation last summer, when I saw him at the Convention here and in Greenfield. He would not hear anybody praised without disparagement. When we spoke affectionately of Garrison, he told us he had changed very much; that he had grown indolent and self-sufficient—unfit to edit a paper &c &c. When Johnson[3] was mentioned, he said he was a noisy tin-kettle tied to Garrison—that he was a servile imitator of Garrison—that anything under the heavens, that was real, was better than an imitation. We admitted the truth of his maxim, but were not aware that it peculiarly applied to O. J.; he might adopt Garrison's views from the sincerity of conviction. This Sinclair would not admit. He insisted that O. J. thought Garrison a prodigious great man, and was trying to get a little gleam of his fame reflected upon himself. He denied that Thompson[4] was eloquent—said he could throw up pretty fire-works, but was totally incapable of argument. Some slur was thrown by him upon Stanton; but I forget what. At Greenfield he invited *all* abolitionists, who were present, to take part in the Convention; and laid a strong emphasis on the word. He afterward told me, at Mr. Parkman's, that he had done it to bring in the women; and he rather reproved me, that I did not act upon the hint. Said he wished women could go to the polls. I told him I

2 Alanson St. Clair.
3 Oliver Johnson.
4 George Thompson.

thought they had as good a right there as men; but that politics rested on such a thoroughly bad foundation, that I, for one, should feel no inclination to use the right. He replied, "Then you are *fit* to be a slave." He said the Peace Convention had greatly strengthened his predelictions in favor of resistance—he was ten times as much a war-man as ever. I expressed my regret, particularly on account of the bearing of such principles on slave-insurrections; I was not willing to harm a hair of the slave-holder's head. He said that was all fudge—that the time would soon come when all the free states would think the negroes had as good a right to fight for freedom as the old Revolutionary fathers had. I told him I hoped it would be so; but I hoped it would be the belief that *neither* of them had the right. He, however, maintained that if there were a chance of *success* for the negroes, it would be a *duty* to help them fight. I was frightened. A great gulf seemed to be yawning beneath my feet.

. . .

Neither of us knew what to make of Sinclair's harsh state of mind; and we could only explain it by supposing him envious.

. . . Goodbye. Yrs. Truly, L. M. Child.

. . . Notwithstanding Sinclair's low estimate of Johnson, he insisted that he edited the Liberator much better than Garrison; and held a long argument with Mr. Child to that effect.

ALS; Anti-Slavery Collection, Rare Books and Manuscripts, Boston Public Library (microfiche 7/172).

Massachusetts was one of the free states that had inherited a colonial law barring intermarriages between free blacks and whites. The state reenacted the law in 1786 and did not repeal it until 1843. In the *Appeal*, Child argued against the prohibition and made the additional point that children of interracial marriages could not inherit property because they were illegitimate.

To the Legislature of Massachusetts

Northampton, March 20, 1839.

The undersigned believes that the law barring intermarriages between people of different complexions has no tendency whatever to restrain vice; that its uselessness is virtually acknowledged by your Report, which declares 'if no such regulation had been placed on the statute book, it might be doubtful, at least, whether its pages should be *encumbered* with any provision on the subject;' that it is an unjustifiable interference with domestic institutions—inasmuch as it attempts to control by legislative action a connexion which, above all others, ought to be left to private conscience and individual choice; that its influence on the rights and good name of innocent children may be most cruel; that it is as obviously a violation of the great principles of freedom, on which our institutions rest, as a law prohibiting marriages between Catholics and Protestants—and more absurd—inasmuch as religious opinions have a more important bearing on character and happiness, than gradations of complexion; that it is strongly tinged with the vile system of slavery, in which it originated; that this legalized contempt of color in Massachusetts has a direct tendency to sustain slavery at the South, and is publicly quoted for that purpose; that posterity will look back with as much wonder to the excited discussions on this subject as we now do to the proceedings of learned lawyers and judges, who hung witches for raising a storm; and finally, that it is in all respects a disgrace to the statute book of a free and intelligent Commonwealth. Therefore, your petitioner prays that it may be immediately repealed; and that her name may be publicly recorded with the honorable women of Lynn, as protesting against said law.[1]

Your petitioner can offer no certificate that she *understands* her own petition; but she begs respectfully to offer her sincere assurance that she fully comprehends the origin of the law, its bearings past and present, the strong prejudice by which it is sustained, and the consequent unpopularity of her proceeding.[2] That she is not made the ignorant tool of evil-designing persons, during the recent excitement, is evident from the fact that she six years ago published a book, in which she mentioned this very law, as a violation of the principles of justice and freedom.

Lastly, your petitioner, as a free-born woman, sharing moral and intellectual advantages with all the sons and daughters of this intelligent Commonwealth, begs leave, dispassionately and respectfully, to protest against the contemptuous treatment offered to her sisters in Lynn. To sustain this protest she appeals to no law of 'chivalry,' which had its use in a barbarous age, and should pass away with barbarism. As far better suited to the age and country in which she lives, she prefers a plain appeal to the respect due from the representatives of a free and enlightened people to the decorous expression of any conscientious views and opinions from any member of the community.

Lydia Maria Child.

L; *The Liberator,* 26 Apr. 1839 (microfiche 7/174).

---

[1] In February 1839, Carolina Augusta Chase and 785 other women from Lynn, Mass., petitioned the state legislature to repeal all laws that recognized a distinction between races. When a second petition signed by Samuel Curtis in support of the first petition was submitted, legislators called it a "burlesque" and tried unsuccessfully to have it thrown out of the Committee of the Judiciary.

[2] Presumably, a petitioner could be asked to present a certificate showing that he or she understood the contents of the petition.

Philosophical and tactical differences quickly spread to the national level. Conferences about forming a political party of abolitionists resulted in the birth of the Liberty party in time for the 1840 elections. At the May 1839 meeting of the American Anti-Slavery Society, a test vote in favor of seating women passed. James G. Birney, who would be the Liberty party's nominee for president the following year, protested the vote, setting the stage for the final split at the 1840 annual convention.

To Louisa and Ellis Gray Loring

Northampton April 30th 1839

Dearest Louisa,

Your kind letter arrived last night and was a cordial to my sinking heart. My desire to come to Boston is stronger than I can express. It seems to me I would undergo almost any penance, if I could but start this very hour. In the first place, my desire to be with you is intense; and in the next place, there would be satisfaction in turning my back on Northampton, to go in *any* direction. If we were keeping house, and less trammelled and plagued in business, I suppose I should not feel so strongly the inconveniences of the narrow and bigotted spirit around me; but in our boarding-place, and in every other respect, we are in what the French call a *false position*. This hint must account to you for my not being more urgent to have you visit us here.

But while it seems as if I *should* fly, I am so anxious to get away—I am tied by considerations, which you will admit should have weight with me. Mr. Child has returned, after being detained in N. York ten days. When Snelling's[1] lawyer became convinced that he really intended to go through the insolvent process, he took his note for $150, and let him return. Planting time approaches so near, that the loss of these ten days is a serious disaster; especially as Mr. C. is obliged to drag along with the help of one man, when he ought to have six. He is anxious, and more depressed than I have ever seen him. I am the only person in this region to whom he can open his heart; and I do not feel as if I ought to leave him till he gets some sugar into the market, and feels in better spirits. As soon as we can have profits coming in from the sugar, it will oil the wheels a little. The present difficulty is that syrup will not grain well without the whole process of manufacturing is done very *rapidly;* and in order to do this, there should be many hands. Were it not that Palmer's theory commends itself to my mind as much the more elevated of the two, I would lay down the maxim that *poverty* is the origin of all evil.   Another reason for delaying, is that it is not yet decided whether we remain in Northampton; and until I know this, I cannot make suitable arrangements concerning all the baggage that has been brought here from the four corners of the earth. I am *afraid* I cannot get away until the last week in May; and then you will be gone in the country—shall you not? What

[1] George Snelling.

a privilege I should consider it, to be able to comfort or cheer you! But how can *you* need cheering! I think I guess the secret. If my conjectures are right, I do hope you will be able "persevere unto the end." I never felt so forcibly as within the last year, that to a childless wife, life is almost untenanted.

Rest assured that I will come sooner than I say, if it be possible to do it without violating duty to my dear husband.

I have written to Henrietta about coming to make candy at her house.[2] I did it, because I took it for granted you would be out of Boston. I mention it, lest you should think it strange that I did not make the proposition to you. My present idea is to work pretty *largely* at that business if I can make profitable arrangements; but, for manifold reasons, I want as little said about it as possible. Let it rest between you and Henrietta. I must *earn* something this summer. I am willing to do *anything*. I should be cheerful, notwithstanding all trials, if it were not for self-reproach. Well as I am, I have no right to be living on the bounty of friends. *What* to do I know not. I cannot take a school, while liable to be called away to follow Mr. Child's fortunes; and I am afraid my "false position" toward the "spirit of the age," will cut off profit as an author. I have, however, written to S. G. Goodrich, to see if I cannot get some sort of editing, or compiling, or writing, or coloring maps; but I have not yet sent the letter.[3] It waits for a private conveyance next week. In the meantime, dearest and best of friends, I have no "naughty pride" to swallow. I am willing to be under obligation; only it is a *principle* with me that a person in good health ought to avoid it if they can. There are sick and imbecile enough in the world to be helped, without my entering on the charity list.   God bless your kind heart. You are a great comfort to me.

To E. G. L.

Dear Friend,

If it be true that we love others according to the amount we have to do and sacrifice for them, we must be very dear to you. I cannot bear to tax you so continually; but still, I had rather be under the obligation to you than to any other mortal.

With regard to that unlucky machinery, Mr. Child had no idea it had arrived in N. York, until he received a dunning letter from Turnbull, which occasioned the call upon you for the $200. *Why* he was not informed of its arrival seems strange. If Mr. Suffern knew his entire ignorance of that fact, he probably would not be prejudiced. By and bye, when the beet sugar business gets a going,

---

[2] Maria had a plan to help David meet expenses by manufacturing some of his beet sugar into barley and rock candy and peppermints. There is no record that she carried out the experiment.

[3] Samuel Griswold Goodrich (1793–1860) was publisher of *The Token*, a literary gift annual (1818–42) that included stories by Child and Nathaniel Hawthorne. Goodrich was known for his *Tales of Peter Parley* series, children's instructional stories.

the machinery will probably bring a high price. I hope we can contrive to save it from being sacrificed.[4]

I too am most deeply pained by the anti-slavery dissensions. They make me sick at heart, discouraged, and ashamed. I think pretty much as you do; though I probably believe in more real *Jesuitism* against the Mass. Board than you do.

Unitarians, or any of the liberal sects, have but small idea of the sectarian zeal, and cunning, and obstinate perseverance, with which Calvinism seeks to build itself up, and shut others out. But the spirit is manifestly wrong on both sides; fierce excitement, and exaggerated suspicion. My sympathies go with the Mass. because I think they are jealous *for* freedom, and the others *against* it. A most malignant spirit prevails here; although there is nothing to oppose; for they are all dead set against the Mass. Board.   Last night I attended a *prayer* meeting, where I supposed this odious controversy would not arise. But Mr. Williston[5] (a very bigotted Calvinist) without any fitness or propriety in so doing, opened the meeting by saying, "It is a lamentable fact, and ought to be known, that as Abolition has become somewhat popular and flattered, certain men want to claim the rank of leaders, and lord it over God's heritage. You are aware that there is an unhappy division between the Mass. and American Societies. The Mass. is governed by Garrison, and a few like him, who are determined to drag in the Woman question, and non-resistance as a part of Anti Slavery—these things are to be made *tests*. These men want to rule in this Commonwealth; but the Mass. Society expresses merely the opinion of Lynn and a few in Boston." He then said there was room for others to speak. A young man arose, and spoke in a conciliatory vein, though evidently believing Mr. W.'s statement. He closed by offering a prayer in a truly Christian spirit. It was Lyman Parsons, the poetical Spectacle Mellen, to whom I have before alluded. Then Mr. Williston made a signal to Mr. Hubbard, the schoolmaster, who began to state that "the Mass Board were determined to sustain the theory that women ought to go to Congress, speak in Legislatures &c—that they likewise abjured human governments, saying men ought to obey no ruler but Jesus; and these things they were determined to force upon others as *tests*. What if Baptists should be determined to make belief in immersion a test of abolition &c?"[6] It was a small meeting consisting of ten or 12 men, and as many women. My husband was not there. I felt as if I *ought* to check this full tide of misrepresentation. So, in a very mild and polite tone, I told Mr. Hubbard I believed he was under a wrong impression. That "I had attended

[4] David had ordered beet sugar machinery for the Illinois Company while he was in Europe, and the company apparently defaulted on the payment. Its representative, Mr. Turnbull, befriended David in Europe. Turnbull arrived in New York with a bill of four hundred dollars for the machinery.

[5] Probably John Payson Williston.

[6] George (Spectacle) Mellen, a chemist, often disrupted antislavery meetings. His book on the unconstitutionality of slavery was published in 1841. Fordyce Mitchell Hubbard (1809–88), a teacher and minister, was a frequent contributor to the *North American Review* and author of several historical works.

about all the A. Slavery meetings in the vicinity of Boston, and never heard the theory of women's going to Congress mentioned there; that a few individuals favored that theory, but most of them did not; and it was *never* brought forward as a part of Anti Slavery. That of the Mass. Board I believed he would not find two who sympathized with Mr. Garrison's scruples about government; so far from making it a *test*, they did not even think favorably of the theory." &c &c.

I was throwing words away—Mr. W. said an individual of good information on the subject, (probably Wm Stoddard, just returned from Boston) told him they were determined there to urge the question of women's voting, at the next Anniversary at N. York—Then came excited voices about the Sabbath, the clergy! the clergy! and Mr. Williston having said contemptuously that people in the Western part of the State had never thought or talked about the equality of women, and he did not consider it desirable that they should; ⟨and⟩ then ⟨he⟩ prayed that those who, in the pride of their hearts, desired to be leaders, might have humility given them &c.

Does not this remind you of what Carlyle says about a "pre-ternatural state of suspicion"? I believe there is no help for it. The Societies must split. Farewell to another cherished illusion!

Mr. Child was surprised by the prejudice and bitterness at N. York, though he expected to find a good deal—Colver *boasted* of his sacrifices, in comparison with Garrison.[7] It was the first time Mr. C. had ever heard such things from the mouth of an abolitionist. It pained and disgusted him. He says the determination evidently is to rule the Mass. Society or annihilate it. He thinks neither side is doing just right; but he thinks there is far more *openness* on the part of the Mass. Society.

What a pity it is that Johnson has so much to do with the Liberator, just at this crisis. I like to have selfish priests reproved, like other men; but Johnson seems to delight in throwing the word "clerical" in the teeth of his opponents, without rhyme or reason, just as boys pelt each other with offensive nick-names. I conclude with Mr. Burton's remark, "This sin is a dreadful thing—What *shall* we do with it?"

AL; Loring Family Papers, Schlesinger Library, Radcliffe College (microfiche 7/179).

Child moved to Boston about the first week of June 1839 to find work, preferably a teaching job. The sugar crop had brought in no profit for the year, although fifteen hundred pounds of sugar were manufactured. David joined her in rented rooms at the end of October, but he had not completely given up on the farm.

[7] At the anniversary meeting the Reverend Nathaniel Colver submitted a resolution that delegates be male. Ellis Loring offered an amendment recognizing female and male delegates, which was approved by the convention.

She remained in Boston until May 1840, anxious for a permanent home, but freed from the farm work and considerably more cheerful than she had been in years.

To David Lee Child

Dearly Beloved Husband,

Now what do you think? Tired of waiting for *your* movements, and finding a person in great despair about obtaining a room for a few weeks, I have taken up with a new companion, and gone to house-keeping without your lordship. But I wont tell you who the new companion is. I leave you to guess. "There's a bone for *you* to pick."

Seriously, I last week began to feel in a forlorn condition. I was quite ill, from repeated attacks of cholera, but I tried to conceal it, because I had nowhere to be sick. Louisa was boarding in the country; and the old lady, though very kind and friendly to me, I know in her heart never considers a visiter any great god-send when they are gone away. Mrs. Dixwell is staying at Henrietta's—her house being repaired and embellished from garret to cellar for the bringing home of Epes's new wife this autumn.[1] In fact, I began to have an uncomfortable feeling that I had staid among my friends too long; for even to the best of friends a visit is more perfectly and untiringly agreeable when there is no suspicion that you *have* to stay for your own convenience. In this mood, I encountered a companion in distress; and here we are! The first night I came here I was all alone. How lonesome I *did* feel! How I *did* long for you! How many pleasant and tender scenes came floating up from the cloudy bosom of the past! Do *you* ever look back to the bird's nest, the sacred Saturday night of the little white image, and other seasons of similar soul-refreshment? Even now, when I have suffered my spirit to become cankered and fretted by vulgar cares, such memories come like blessed angels in my path, and I fervently thank God for the rich experience of your tenderness. Dearest and best of friends, shall we *ever* again, "in the wide sterility of this world lay out a garden of household love, and fill it with flowers, forgetful of the wind that scatters, and the frost that kills?" I am weary, weary of separation. My soul yearns again to experience "that life *within* life which two persons know together,—which one knows not without the other,—which ceases to both the instance they are divided." But *you* dont think it ceases; for Mr. Collins tells me you seemed *very* happy when he saw you.[2] I felt at first a good mind to be stuffy about it; but my second thought was to feel glad that if you really must stay at Northampton, you were not so discontented under it as my-

[1] Child had been rooming with Henrietta Sargent. Henrietta's sister, Esther (Sargent) Dixwell (1776–1865), was the mother of Epes Sargent Dixwell (1807–99), headmaster at Boston Latin School. He married Mary Ingersoll Bowditch.
[2] John Anderson Collins (1810–79) was active in the Massachusetts Anti-Slavery Society and founder of a short-lived Fourierist colony at Skaneateles, N.Y.

self. To me it has been a very grievous disappointment; for it upset as pretty a little arrangement of plans as I have imagined this many a day; and besides it seemed as if in everything connected with *you* I was to be forever disappointed; and you know very well that what is *not* connected with you has very little interest in my eyes.

My reason and inclination tug different ways dreadfully at the present time. My inclination insists upon having you here; but my reason clearly decides that, now autumn is so near, you had better work up all this year's beets before you come; that is, if it is going to be an object for you to undertake to work them up at all. Take Cassandra's advice this time. Will you?

I yesterday bought some sugar at a Grocer's, who in answer to my inquiry for free-labor sugar, replied that we should soon have enough of it of our own; for they "were making beet sugar on a *great scale* in the western part of the state." I could not help smiling at men's facility at exaggeration.

Mr. Scoble from England has been in Boston a few days.[3] He called to see me, and the same evening I heard him address a very large audience in Marlboro Chapel. He told little that was new to the readers of Thome and Kimball; but the fact that he had just come from the W. Indies rendered it interesting, and his manner is in the highest degree gentlemanly and pleasing. I will tell you an incident that illustrates characters well. Mr. Phelps introduced the speaker as Rev. John Scoble from England, who was on his return from the W.I. to England, and had taken the U.S. in his way.[4] "It is quite providential that he is here," said he. "He merely intended to be present at the Albany Convention; but being disappointed about his passage, he quite unexpectedly has a few days to visit Boston. I mention this, that the audience may be aware that he did not come here for the purpose of instructing us. He would, however, be very happy to hear any questions that any one may have the curiosity to ask."   After several little preliminaries of business were settled, Mr. Garrison arose and asked leave of the chairman (Mr. Geo Odiorne, of new organization) to speak;[5] which being obtained, he said, in his deep, clear, strong voice, "I am strongly impelled to say a few words to inform this audience who the Rev. John Scoble is. As republicans and Christians, it *ought* to be enough for us that he is a Man! He is not an Englishman, he is a man! He is not a subject of Victoria, but of the King of Kings! He is not a resident of the British Islands, he is a Citizen of the World!" And then he went on to tell in a few eloquent words, how well Scoble had fought the Anti Slavery

---

[3] British abolitionist and minister John Scoble (b. 1799) toured the United States in 1839 to lecture on emancipation in the West Indies.
[4] Abolitionist minister Amos Augustus Phelps (1805–47) dropped out of the Massachusetts Anti-Slavery Society when his resolution proscribing women delegates was defeated at the May 1839 convention. In 1839 he was pastor of the Free Church in Boston and editor of the *Emancipator*.
[5] George Odiorne (1764–1846), a merchant in Exeter, N.H., moved to Boston and eventually became a bank president.

battle in England, and how he was now striving to have ⟨it⟩ slavery abolished throughout the world.

When I mentioned this incident to Collins, he answered, "How plainly it reveals the character of the two men. One moving in a tea-cup, and the other in the World." By the way, I have never been able to guess why St Clair (a Universalist and a Unitarian) had joined the schismatics; but Mr. Jackson[6] tells me he was greatly provoked and disappointed because Collins was appointed General Agent, instead of himself. The Mass. Society knew his wishes; but they heard of so many errors of judgment, and of his own best lectures defeated by his private conversation, that they did not dare to trust him. I am much pleased with Scoble, because he has fought well in England, and because he is a very finished gentleman; but if he was in the midst of *our* battle, I think he would be a clerical appealer; for I can see that his soul is in the strait jacket of Calvinism.

I suppose you saw in the paper that Dr. Bemis of Watertown blew his brains out with a gun. He had been threatened with the house of correction, as a means of keeping him in some decent order; and he was so terrified about it, that he carried a loaded gun to his chamber. When the milk-man's cart stopped at the door early in the morning, they suppose he must have imagined it had come for him; for he instantly shot himself. Such was the Fifth Act of this domestic tragedy, called the Drunkard's Progress.

Dearest *do* you love your forlorn little wife? or do you feel just about as happy without her as with her? I dont know what I *shall* do if you dont love me. Your affection is all my comfort in this world. I sent you Right & Wrong.[7] Have you received it? Tell me what you think about Cassandra's advice, and whether you think I had better make an effort for a school here this winter.   I suppose you think it is good enough for me if I do feel forlorn, since I took it in my head to go off and leave you; but indeed I should not have thought of such a movement, had I thought there was the remotest probability of being separated so long.

Yrs most truly, Maria

I feel quite well now; but I was dreadful sick while it lasted.

ALS; Lydia Maria Child Papers, Anti-Slavery Collection, Cornell University (microfiche 7/184).

In a letter published in *The Liberator*, Child sums up her ideas on the widening split within the movement. She watched with increasing alarm the intensified

---

[6] Probably Francis Jackson.
[7] Maria Weston Chapman, *Right and Wrong in Massachusetts* (Boston, 1839), or John A. Collins, *Right and Wrong amongst the Abolitionists of the United States* (2d ed. Glasgow, 1841).

efforts of New Organization followers to proscribe membership in the anti-slavery societies. Her coolness toward the women's conventions of the previous two years changed to active determination to keep the Boston Female Anti-Slavery Society intact. Splits within local societies were not unusual at this time, but the Boston experience was especially ugly, perhaps owing to the tenacity and organizational expertise on each side.

In the fall of 1839, the issue of raising funds for the national society, perceived as anti-Garrisonian, brought sectarian feelings about religion and non-resistance to the forefront. Child, Maria (Weston) Chapman, and other supporters of Garrison wanted to pledge money to the state society and organized a separate fair to do this. At the fall meeting when annual elections were held, near chaos reigned. Child and others denounced the proceedings as unconstitutional. Mary Parker, the New Organization president, ordered the Boston Female Anti-Slavery Society dissolved by fiat. Child and others refused to participate in the meeting, arguing that Parker had never been legally elected. Eventually Parker and her supporters resigned and formed the Massachusetts Female Emancipation Society. Child served as president pro tem of the Boston Female Anti-Slavery Society until its April quarterly meeting, when Thankful Southwick replaced her.

To William Lloyd Garrison

Boston, Sept. 2d, 1839.

Dear Friend:

You ask me what I am thinking about the anti-slavery controversy, and whether I am not disheartened by recent divisions.

I reply that I think the Massachusetts Anti-Slavery Society clearly in the right; so clearly, that I am amazed when any mind I have deemed honest finds the least difficulty in perceiving it. To most whose vision is imperfect on the subject, I am constrained for want of any better solution, to apply the old proverb, 'None are so blind as those that *won't* see.'

Let us inquire into the charges. First, it is said that the Constitution of the Anti-Slavery Society pledges its members to political action; and that the Mass. Society are recreant to this duty, because they favor the non-resistants, or no-government men, as they are sometimes called. The Board of the Mass. Society have denied this charge in terms very distinct and decided. The documents issued by them during the present controversy appear to me uniformly distinguished for plain truth, good sense, and good temper: and whoever will take the trouble to glance at facts, will find them abundantly sustained thereby.

The Board consists of 28 men, of whom 4 only have any conscientious scruples about voting. I believe it may be said with truth that ninety-nine hundredths of the Mass. Society go to the polls; and many of them are very active in the exertion of political influence. Resolutions passed by them on the subject of political action, during the last year or two, have been more peculiarly strong and searching, than those of former years; and never have they been more actively interested in elections likely to have a bearing on the anti-slavery cause.

The whole difficulty lies in a nutshell. It is simply this. From the very commencement of our enterprise, there were a few, such as Effingham L. Capron, Samuel J. May, &c. who had scruples about using the elective franchise.[1] The principles on which these scruples were founded, at first obscure in many minds, became clearer under the strong light cast upon them by anti-slavery; until in a few souls they at last found satisfactory utterance in the doctrines of Non-Resistance.

It is not my purpose here to discuss the merits of those doctrines. The Mass. Society, in its anti-slavery capacity, had no right to decide upon them, any more than it had to arraign John G. Whittier for scruples about stated seasons of prayer. It has turned neither to the right hand nor the left, either to sustain Non-Resistants, or to condemn them. It called upon them, in common with all other men, to do for the *slave* whatsoever their hearts would prompt and their consciences permit them to do for their *own brother in the flesh*, under similar circumstances.

But by and bye some required that the Society should declare it the imperious duty of every abolitionist to go to the polls, and advise any man to withdraw from the Association, who failed to do this. The Mass. Society, of course, replied, 'This cannot be done without violating an obvious *principle of freedom*. Every man has a right to adopt his own opinions, and choose his own mode of action on any given subject. All *we* ask of him is whether he works as heartily and consistently for the slave, as for any other object.'

When the point was urged of its being an imperious duty for every abolitionist to go to the polls, and Non-Resistants replied that their consciences would not permit this mode of action, it became necessary to word resolutions on this subject in such a manner as not to violate any man's freedom of conscience, while it urged every man to labor for the slave in modes consistent with his own convictions of duty. That is, men who voted on *any* occasion were solemnly conjured to carry their *abolition principles* to the polls, triumphant over every consideration of interest or party.

It has been untruly represented that a change has come over the Society. It is not so. They are just what they were in the beginning. At their very first meeting, they would have worded their political resolutions just as they now do, had they known there was even one member, whose conscience might be fettered by a contrary course. When it is now brought up before them, and in the shape of a test too, they cannot, as honest men, act otherwise than they do. They are re-

---

[1] Effingham Lawrence Capron (1791–1859) became the first president of the Non-Resistance Society in 1838. A Quaker, he was among the founders of the American Anti-Slavery Society and served as president of the Massachusetts Anti-Slavery Society in 1836.

quired to violate a plain principle of freedom, because some of their brethren assume to think that such a course would hasten the abolition of slavery. They reply, 'Our faith is in broad, eternal principles, which by their own unchanging and harmonious nature, can never by any possibility interfere with each other. We are clearly persuaded that no good can ever come of giving up one principle for the apparent chance of advancing another. We will strive with all our might, mind, and strength, to overthrow slavery; but we see, as clearly as the simplest problem in mathematics, that this object cannot be advanced by violating freedom of conscience; and even if we saw this result less clearly than we do, it would be impossible for us to set aside a sacred principle deeply fixed in our own convictions.[']

It is strange to me that men do not perceive there is no other alternative for free and honest minds. Yet at the New York meeting, some persons were exceedingly surprised at the votes. They exclaimed, 'These Non-Resistants must be increasing very fast!' When the simple fact probably was, that there were not ten in the whole meeting; but there were a hundred who, without any sympathy in their peculiar views, saw it to be a duty to respect the individual freedom of those ten.

How ridiculous it would seem to apply a similar test to other forms of opinion. Some think abstinence from Slave Labor the surest and speediest way of abolishing a system of legalized theft. What if they should demand that all who differed from them should be officially advised to withdraw from the Society? Some think much of the efficacy of Monthly Concerts of Prayer for the enslaved. What if they should insist upon expelling Quakers, who have scruples about stated seasons of prayer? When resolutions have been passed maintaining it to be a duty to exclude slaveholders from the communion, Unitarian members have always voted against them, saying, 'It is contrary to our ideas of church government, and seems to us a violation of religious freedom. If any man evinces a wish to partake of any of the privileges or ordinances of the gospel, we feel that no human being has authority to exclude him; but we are glad to see our Orthodox brethren passing such resolutions in anti-slavery meetings, because it is consistent with *their* principles. They would exclude a person for stealing a horse, and certainly ought not to do less for stealing a man.' What if the Orthodox had said, 'These Unitarians ought to withdraw from the Society. The Constitution demands of them the exertion of *religious* influence; and it is plain to our minds that religious influence cannot be faithfully exerted without refusing to commune with slaveholders.[']

Non-Resistants simply wish to exercise the same right that has been used by Unitarian members with regard to church government. That is, they are content to be a minority, voting against any thing which happens to clash with their own convictions of right, and giving a brief explanation why they do so. They never introduce the subject of non-resistance into anti-slavery meetings, but on the contrary scrupulously try to keep it out. They have never expressed or evinced a desire that their opponents should be advised to withdraw from the Anti-

Slavery Society because they *do* go to the polls; but their opponents have shown a vehement wish to expel them because they do *not* go. This is a note-worthy difference; in as much as the latter actively interferes with freedom, and the former lets it alone.

You will perhaps remind me that the Liberator usually contains two or three columns about non-resistance. True; the editor puts them there by the same right that any other editor publishes his own opinions in his own paper. The Liberator is not and never, was the organ of the Mass. Anti-Slavery Society. For a very short time, the Society was connected with it in a pecuniary way. I was present at the meeting where it was decided to appropriate funds to assist the Liberator, then considerably involved in debt; and I well remember how earnestly Mr. Garrison protested against being considered the organ of any Society. He said he could not be the organ of other men's opinions, nor could he be impeded in the free utterance of his own. The society, on their part, were equally desirous to have it distinctly understood that the editor alone was responsible for what appeared in the columns of the Liberator.—But it is urged that the world *will* consider Garrison our leader, and therefore hold us responsible for his opinions. We cannot help this. He is *not* our leader. No man is our leader. We agree in the wish to abolish slavery, and differ, in a friendly manner, concerning all other subjects under the sun. We respect and love Mr. Garrison, because we believe him to be an honest and true man, unusually gifted with the power of seeing principles clearly in their own light. We should regret the decline of the Liberator, because we think its boldness, sincerity, clear-sightedness, and unfettered freedom of spirit, render it very valuable to the anti-slavery cause. Beyond this, there is no identity between the Massachusetts Society and Mr. Garrison. Probably no six individuals of them would agree with him, or any other man, in all his opinions. They simply accord to him, what they would accord to men far less worthy of their esteem; viz: the right to hold and express his own opinions. They cannot consent to exclude him, Effingham L. Capron, Isaac Winslow, Samuel J. May, and other faithful coadjutors, simply because the world choose to hold all abolitionists responsible for each and every one of Mr. Garrison's opinions.[2]

If there were individuals who could not tolerate the Liberator, by reason of their dislike to non-resistance, or for any other cause, I should have been glad to have had them supplied with another anti-slavery paper more suited to their views. But I wish it had been done in an open and friendly manner, instead of resorting to such secret machinery and veiling real feelings under assumed pretences.

With regard to the Woman Question, as it is termed, the case is much the same. The Massachusetts Society have simply refused to take action upon it when the minority have urged them to do it. In the beginning, we were brought together by strong sympathy for the slave, without stopping to inquire about each

[2] A wealthy sea captain and merchant, Isaac Winslow (1787–1867) was an early supporter of antislavery and a delegate to the World Anti-Slavery Convention in 1840.

other's religious opinions, or appropriate spheres. Then, women were hailed by acclamation as helpers in the great work. They joined societies, they labored diligently, and they stood against a scoffing world bravely. When the two Grimkes came among us, impediments in the way of their lecturing straightway arose, particularly among the clergy. The old theological argument from St. Paul was urged, and the Grimkes replied in their own defence. A strong feeling of hostility to woman's speaking in public had always been latent in the clergy, and this incident aroused it all over the country. The sisters found obstacles so multiplied in their path, that they considered the establishment of woman's freedom of vital importance to the anti-slavery cause. 'Little can be done for the slave,' said they, 'while this prejudice blocks up the way.' They urged me to say and do more about woman's rights, nay, at times they gently rebuked me for my want of zeal. I replied, 'It is best not to *talk* about our rights, but simply go forward and *do* whatsoever we deem a duty. In toiling for the freedom of others, we shall find our own.' On this ground I have ever stood; and so have my anti-slavery sisters. Instead of forcing this 'foreign topic' into anti-slavery meetings or papers, we have sedulously avoided it. The Liberator has not meddled with the discussion, except when attacks upon the Grimkes seemed to render replies on their own part absolutely necessary. From that day to this, the clergy, as a body, have been extremely sensitive on the subject. Different minds assign different causes for this sensitiveness. Some respect it, as occasioned by a conscientious interpretation of Scripture; others consider it an honest but narrow bigotry; while others smiling say, 'They are afraid the women will preach better and charge less.' Without imputing motives, I simply state an obvious fact.

If there are clergymen, or others, in our ranks, who conscientiously believe it wrong for a woman freely to utter her thoughts and impart her knowledge to any body who can derive benefit from the same, I should be the last to put any constraint on his opinions. I should agree with the Massachusetts Society that it would be a monstrous violation of freedom to request or to advise him to withdraw from the society because some of his views seemed likely to retard the progress of the cause. I would have such a minority do exactly what the Unitarians did in the question of church discipline; viz. vote against what they disapprove, and briefly explain their reasons; and should they become a majority, I should then esteem it our duty to do the same, in all kindness and courtesy.

Our opponents insist that the society shall introduce a 'foreign topic,' by acting *against* what is called woman's rights. The society very properly answer, 'We have never meddled with this subject, in our anti-slavery capacity; nor can we now consent to take any action upon it, one way or another. From the beginning, women, by paying their money, have become members of anti-slavery societies and conventions in various free states. They have behaved with discretion and zeal, and been proverbially lavish of exertion. We claim no authority to prescribe or limit their mode of action, any more than we do that of other members. In this, there is nothing peculiar to Massachusetts; the same course having been pursued in various parts of the Union, in the unconscious *oneness* of our anti-slavery zeal.'

For my individual self, I now, as ever, would avoid any discussion of the woman question in anti-slavery meetings, or papers. But when a man advises me to withdraw from a society or convention, or not to act there according to the dictates of my own judgment, I am constrained to reply, 'Thou canst not touch the freedom of my soul. I deem that I have duties to perform here. I make no onset upon your opinions and prejudices; but my moral responsibility lies between God and my own conscience. No human being can have jurisdiction over that.'

But, my dear friend, these questions of Non-Resistance, Woman's Rights, &c. are only urged to effect a secret purpose far more important in the eyes of our opponents, viz. to get Garrison formally disowned by the abolitionists of Massachusetts. The causes which lead to this desire lie deep and spread wide. Many men can talk of the necessity of an Isaiah among the Jewish priests, who are unwilling to acknowledge the need of a prophet among a time-serving priesthood now.

To your second question, I answer that I am *not* discouraged by these dissensions. Disagreeable they unquestionably are; so much so, that we would be willing to give up any thing but principle to avoid them; but, under God's Providence, they will mightily promote the cause of general freedom. Those early reformers, the apostles, had similar experience. Very early in the history of the Christian church, Paul writes of 'false brethren unawares brought in, who came in privily to spy out our liberty which we have in Christ Jesus, that they might bring us into bondage: To whom we gave place by subjection, not for an hour; that the truth of the gospel might continue with you.' [3]

In the words of an eloquent friend, I bid you 'Take courage, for truth always has been, and always will be, most effectually propagated by *cuttings*.'

I have no disposition to fight against the American Society; but I cannot conscientiously work for it; because I believe its Executive Committee are at present arrayed against free principles; and I am convinced that any money sent to them from Massachusetts would be most diligently used against the Massachusetts Society, who now, by the force of circumstances, are standing as the representatives of great and free principles. For these reasons, I am working diligently for the October Fair, and exhort others to work. God bless the Massachusetts Anti-Slavery Society! Good men and true women from the beginning until now!

Yours affectionately,

L. MARIA CHILD.

L; *The Liberator*, 6 Sept. 1839 (microfiche 8/186).

[3] Gal. 2:4–5.

To Lydia B. Child

Boston Nov. 18th 1839

Dear Lydia,

. . .

I cannot give any good reason for not writing, except that I have been very much out of spirits, and have struggled in vain with feelings of discouragement. I now feel happier than I have for several years, though our pecuniary fortunes are at the lowest ebb. Your brother was obliged to be near the State-Library in order to finish his long contemplated Slave Law-Book; so we have hired two cheap rooms, where we board ourselves, and with borrowed furniture play keep house. Even this humble imitation of a home is exceedingly pleasant, after our long wanderings & separations.

Dec. 12th 1839

Dear Lydia,

I was interrupted when I reached the bottom of the first page; and what with old clothes to mend, washing, cooking, superintending Lowell Fair, attending Anti Slavery Committees, and three different courses of lectures, to which we were invited, the time has unconsciously slipped away, without my resuming this letter.[1]

. . .

Your brother has received a medal and a Diploma from the Mechanics' Institute, for the first Beet Sugar made in America. We *hope* he will likewise receive the 100 dollar premium, from the Agricultural Society; but this we know not yet. It is time something was coming in; for as yet it has been all outlay. But I have a comfortable pre-sentiment that the tide is soon going to turn.

The scenes in our Female Anti Slavery meetings are painful and disgusting. I came down from Northampton cool and unbiassed. I saw that the Massachusetts Society were on the right side, but I was exceedingly afraid of becoming a partizan in spirit. In this state of mind, I could not but think Mrs. Chapman somewhat unjust toward Mary Parker, the Balls &c.[2] I knew she did not *mean* to be so; but it was easier for me to think her somewhat blinded by her zeal, than it was to believe they were deliberately carrying two faces. But personal attendance on the meetings has convinced me, even against my will. I trust I am still free from a partizan spirit; but it is no longer possible for me to doubt that the Board of the F. Society wish to *appear* friendly to the old organization, or at least neutral,

[1] One of the series of lectures was Margaret Fuller's Conversations. Lecture topics included fine arts, mythology, ethics, and education. Child was one of twenty-five women present at the first lecture and attended several weekly meetings.
[2] Martha V. Ball, like Mary Parker, was a New Organization partisan and leader of the Massachusetts Female Emancipation Society. Lucy M. Ball, probably Martha's sister, had been treasurer of the Boston Female Anti-Slavery Society in 1836.

while they ingeniously *contrive* to have their funds and influence support the new organization. If they would *honestly* come out, and say that what appears to us the wrong side seems to [th]em³ the right one, I should be the last to interfere with their freedom of opinion, or to put obstacles in the way of its free expression. But the difficulty is, many of the *Society* are blinded by the smooth pretences of the *Board*, and are doing the work of Phelps and Torrey, while they know it not. Hence those ge[nt]leman [*sic*] are determined the Board shall keep in office.   Dr. Mansfield of Lowell told me that St. Clair borrowed, or rather begged, some money of him, on the plea that he had none to pay his passage to Boston in the cars; and that afterward, to his surprise and regret, he saw it set down in the Abolitionist, against his name, as a contribution to the New Organization, with which he had no sympathy whatever. To such tricks will men rapidly descend, when they take counsel of time-serving ministers how to render the cause popular, and strive to [g]ain power by endeavoring to draw into the ranks the poli[tica]lly ambitious. I trust the good ship Anti Slavery will soon right herself; but this is the toughest gale she has been out in. Pray keep your eyes open, and see that none among you who *wish* to sustain the Old Massachusetts, are deceived by fair, false words into giving their money so she will never receive it.

Tell Mrs. Newton I received her letter, for which I am much obliged. I have no wish to dictate to others, or to put any obstacles or discouragements in their way, when it seems to them right to step forward. But my *own* feeling is, as it has been, that it is not judicious to petition on the subject she names; at least, not at present. We can *do* whatsoever seems to us right, with a modest freedom, as if none would question. If duty calls us into unusual modes of action, the world will best become accustomed to it and prepared for it, by simply *seeing* it done. In the meantime the word and act of every reflecting woman should show that she considers herself an individual, responsible being—not the passive tool, or sensual plaything, of man.

Our Fair, as you have seen, went off successfully. If we could only have sold all our things, we should have made twice as much as we did. The number and variety of articles was exceeding great—immense.

When I send this to the P. Office, I shall send a copy of the Liberty Bell for you to the Office of Ellis Gray Loring. State St. nearly opposite South side of Post Office. If you have a chance, send for it. I wrote the story of Charity Bowery for it. Good bye. Yrs truly, Maria.

. . .

ALS; Child Letters, MC 305, Schlesinger Library, Radcliffe College (microfiche 8/190).

³ Several letters are missing where the paper has crumbled at the fold.

In the following letter, again to *The Liberator*, Child analyzes how the issue of woman's rights became a tactical weapon in the battle between Garrisonians and anti-Garrisonians. Differences over political activism and religion came to dominate the struggle in these last years of the decade, somewhat eclipsing the earlier emphasis on women's equal participation in the societies.

Child's letter struck a nerve. On 14 March, Caroline Weston wrote to her sister Anna, "Mrs. Child came in & brought a letter she has just got from Mr. Birney—in which he is very indignant at her statements in the last Lib. & says that he never *thought* or *said* that a change must be made in the American A.S.S.—on account of the Woman Question—& then goes on to establish every word she has said as true—he appeals to the *magnanimity* of women—to keep them out of the Societies—!!—& intimates in a sprightly manner—that the wrongs & sufferings of the slaves are greater than those of women . . . you never saw such a piece of malicious twaddle as his letter was. . . ."* Birney's letter to Child has not been found.

To William Lloyd Garrison

[Before 6 March 1840]

To the Editor of the Liberator:

Anniversaries are seasons peculiarly favorable to reminiscence; therefore it is not singular, that at the late Annual Meeting of the Massachusetts Anti-Slavery Society my thoughts reverted to the secession from our ranks, and to the probable causes which led to it.

For the thousandth time, it occurred to me as an odd circumstance, that either you or I had ever been charged with a wish to use anti-slavery as a tool to advance what are called woman's rights. It needed, indeed, but a common portion of far-sightedness to foresee that a struggle for the advancement of any principle of freedom would inevitably tend to advance *all* free principles; for they are connected like a spiral line, which, if the top be put in motion, revolves even to the lowest point. But farther than this general proposition, I never thought of connecting the two subjects, even in my own ideas. I by no means believe this unconsciousness was peculiar to myself. Even those, who are now loudest in their opposition to what is called the Woman Question, are, I apprehend, warmed by a zeal of somewhat recent date; at least, the following reminiscences seem strongly to imply it.

I well recollect the first time I ever saw James G. Birney.[1] It was on the occasion of his first visit to New England abolitionists, and at the house of Francis Jackson. After some conversation about anti-slavery at the West, I said, 'On some

* Anti-Slavery Collection, Rare Books and Manuscripts, Boston Public Library.
[1] Birney (1782–1857) was a slaveholder and state legislator in Alabama. He moved to Kentucky and set his slaves free in 1834. He then moved to Cincinnati and in 1837 to New York City.

points, you seem to be in advance of the East. At the recent State Anti-Slavery Convention in Ohio, I see that a very considerable number of the delegates were women. The fact attracted my attention, because, as far as I am informed, it is the first instance of the kind. Were you aware of being so much in advance or was it accidental?'

Mr. Birney replied, 'Purely accidental, I presume. It never occurred to me there was anything strange in such a measure. It seemed so natural and proper that the abolition of the women should be represented, as well as that of the men.'

These were his very words, without addition or diminution. Yet I am told Mr. Birney now declares some change must be insisted on, if women are allowed to vote at the meetings of the National Society.

During one of my visits to the city of New York, (I think it was in the autumn of 1836) Mr. Lewis Tappan called a meeting for pro-slavery and anti-slavery discussion. Owing to circumstances, which it is useless to recapitulate, the meeting was a failure. No one came prepared to speak. There was a good deal of embarrassment, and long intervals of silence. Three successive times, Mr. Tappan came to urge me to address the audience; of which, I think, a majority were men. I told him I had never spoken in public, and should feel very much embarrassed. He replied, 'You will doubtless recover from your embarrassment in a few moments; and you really ought to make an effort to overcome your reluctance, when you reflect how much good you can do, and how much the audience will be interested, if you allow me to announce that Mrs. Child of Boston is about to address them.' I persisted in my refusal, on the ground that I really had nothing to say. He then appealed to my husband, not only to fulfill his own promise of speaking, but to persuade me to speak. Mr. Child replied that he wished me to act in perfect freedom, and the subject was then dropped.

Mr. Lewis Tappan now declares his determination to have a New Society formed, unless the American Society rescinds its vote to allow women a participation in its meetings; and this opposition I understand to arise from conscientious scruples, founded on St. Paul. I am not aware that he has altered his religious opinions in the course of three years, or that any reason exists for a change in his estimation of St. Paul. Yet if Mr. Tappan then deemed it a sin for women to speak in promiscuous assemblies, how could he reconcile it to his conscience to urge me to do it?

If I mistake not, it was the summer following this incident, that Theodore D. Weld was sent into Massachusetts for the express purpose of procuring agents for the American Society. Having announced that he wished to secure my services, he was informed that I was absent in the country, but that my friend Henrietta Sargent could give all needful information. He waited upon her, and told his errand. When she suggested that I might feel some reluctance to take a step so new to me, he laughed at the idea. 'It is wrong,' said he, 'to let any foolish scruples stand in the way of doing so much good. The Grimkes are a glorious example, and the women of Massachusetts ought not to be slow in following it.'

With much earnestness, he sought to impress it upon her mind how very desirable it was, that I should consent to the proposal of the Executive Committee, and engaged her to use her utmost influence to persuade me to this step. During the whole of this conversation, not a syllable was said about addressing meetings of women only; nor did I ever hear such a qualification suggested, until this winter.

Who would have thought that, in the course of two brief years, that same Executive Committee would have sought to make war upon the Massachusetts Society, even to annihilation, on the charge of their being advocates for women's rights.

In the autumn of 1838, being invited to visit a friend in Greenfield, I happened to be present at the Franklin County Anti-Slavery Convention.[2] I was totally unconscious of any other motive than a common friendly interest in any anti-slavery gathering; but I was afterward surprised to learn that my presence occasioned considerable uneasiness among some of the brethren. One whispered to another, 'I hope she didn't come to introduce Boston notions into the valley of the Connecticut. I trust she is not going to advocate women's rights!' They might have spared their fears; for I was no more thinking of women's rights, than I was of the coming in of the Jews.

All *gentlemen* present were invited to join the Convention. So sleepy was I at the post of the woman question, that I did not even notice this phraseology (though I probably should notice it now) until Mr. St. Clair emphatically proposed to amend it by introducing the word *persons*. After the meeting, Mr. St. Clair asked me if I did not understand what he meant by placing emphasis on the word *persons;* and if so, why I had not voted.

I replied that I did not vote, simply because I saw no occasion that required it; and that I was a stranger. Thereupon, he rebuked me, in language that seemed to me, at the time, bordering on rudeness; but which I attributed merely to an honest zeal for freedom.

Six months after, Mr. St. Clair joined those who left the N.E. Convention to form a New Organization, on the declared ground that they could not conscientiously unite with men who allowed women to vote at their meetings.

I leave these facts for each one to interpret as seemeth to him good. I can only testify that they are verily true.

Yours with much esteem,
Lydia Maria Child

L; *The Liberator,* 6 Mar. 1840 (microfiche 8/198).

The date of the next letter was also that of the anniversary meeting of the American Anti-Slavery Society at which the final organizational split occurred. Antici-

[2] Greenfield, Mass., is about twenty miles north of Northampton.

pating a fight, both sides had worked behind the scenes to have their supporters present. The Massachusetts society offered to pay the Childs' expenses for the trip, but they did not go. They were completely absorbed with settling in on a small rented farm in Northampton to which they had moved at the end of April. Although Child was not at the convention, she did have a role in the proceedings.

The entire executive committee, except James Gibbons, withdrew from the convention when Abby Kelley was appointed to serve on a business committee. Lewis and Arthur Tappan, Amos Phelps, and other supporters of political action left to form the American and Foreign Anti-Slavery Society. Lucretia Mott, Maria (Weston) Chapman (who was in the West Indies), and Child were appointed to take the places of those who had resigned from the executive committee. The American Anti-Slavery Society, now firmly Garrisonian, issued several resolutions abjuring political action and condemning churches that were not actively antislavery.

In western Massachusetts, the Childs began their second year of beet farming with two oxen, two horses, a cow, and two laborers. Maria had no help with housework at first, but by the middle of July, a young Irish woman joined the household to help her in the kitchen. The Childs planned to rent until the following year, when they would move to a farm her father had bought for them in Northampton.

To Ellis Gray Loring

Northampton May 7th. [1840]

Dear Friend,
To day is the eventful day! and you are at N. York! With all my other anxieties, I feel very anxious about the cause. Mr. Child has been so busy, and I have been so very secluded, that we have luckily been out of the way of infectious excitement; but echoes now and then reach our ears, that convince us of a very extensive and active agitation on the part of the Ex. Committee. The degree of diligence and tact manifested would exceed your belief. No opportunity, great or small, has been omitted in this region, to preoccupy the minds of people against the Massachusetts Board. *Every* minister, influential deacon, or active sectarian, for miles and miles and miles round, has been furnished with the N. York side of the case, without any chance of hearing the Mass. side. Private letters *innumerable* have been written in every direction, especially by Phelps. He has been in Northampton at work, within a week; but *we* never heard of his visit, until it came to us by the way of a friend from Hatfield. Nothing is more observable in all these transactions than the effort at secresy.

Rely upon it, my friend, there is sectarianism at the bottom of all this. A large proportion no doubt act honestly, because they have been misinformed as to the premises, and therefore draw false conclusions; but "They that know the very nerves of state, have givings out that are an infinite distance from their true meant design"!

If you want to hate sectarianism with all your soul, come and spend a year in Hampshire County. If I can't get to a freer atmosphere very soon, it seems to me I shall die of it. It is enough to overthrow all faith in progress, to hear such talk as I hear, in the 19th century.

I send you a copy of a letter, which Mr. Child intended to have sent to the Anniversary. We should like to have you get it copied in the Mass. Abolitionist; but if they decline doing so, request them to return the copy to you. In which case, we wish to have it inserted in the Liberator, stating (without any *fling*, or any remark whatever) that the Abolitionist declined to publish it. If they allege its length as a reason for not printing it, let the Liberator simply state the alleged reason, without comment.

My dear husband cannot quite give up his good opinion of war in certain cases; but he is continually writing and saying things that make grand pegs for me to hang future arguments upon. I smiled to see these symptoms of a laboring state of mind in the letter I send you. He complains that I have spoiled him for a soldier, without making him a Christian.

With the earnest hope of seeing you soon, I remain Yrs Gratefully & Affectionately,

L. M. Child.

ALS; Manuscript Division, New York Public Library (microfiche 8/204).

To Lydia (Bigelow) Child

Northampton June 7'th 1840

Dear Mother,

. . .

I have been here six weeks. I received a letter from dear Lydia the very day before I left Boston. I had then made all my arrangements to come to West Boylston in two days; but a letter from Mr. Child summoned me to Northampton, saying that he should come with a horse and wagon to Wilbraham Depôt, and there wait for me. And lucky it was, that I did come, without stopping by the way; for I found father with his leg bolstered up in a chair, severely bruised by a fall from a wagon. For three weeks, it needed to be dressed two or three times a day. He bore it more patiently than could have been expected; but with his active habits you may well suppose it was a severe trial.

After sleeping on the floor 8 or ten days, and eating on the tops of barrels, our furniture came at last. It was tumbled in heaps on the floor. I had it to set up, as I could; in the mean time father's leg to dress, and cooking and washing to do for him, Mr. Child, and a stout Irish laborer, who works and eats as much as two other men.

I never got so weary in my life. At night my feet ached so that I could not sleep, and I almost cried with the pain. It made me think of you, and your wearisome, laborious life, and how you used to complain of the feet ache.   Through all this, I could not find anyone to give me a helping hand; and up to this moment, I am alone. But, God be praised, father has quite recovered from his lameness, and I have got things about the house into *somewhat* comfortable train; so I am not quite so overwhelmed with work as I was.   Father has bought an excellent farm for me, on what he considers very good terms; but the buildings are all to be erected, and in the meantime we hire house and land for the present year, with John's[1] assistance. I hope we shall prosper; we work hard enough for it, at any event. I have been afraid poor David would break down laboring in the hot sun, day after day. He has in fact been very unwell; but I think he will soon get seasoned. He keeps up his spirits and energy wonderfully. No tongue can tell the difficulties he has had to struggle with in this new business. From his pecuniary embarrassment, he has labored under every conceivable obstacle, but I hope and trust it will be the means of bringing us out of the mire at last. I do not think continued adversity does good to *my* character, whatever may be its effects on others. I know prosperity is considered a dangerous trial; but I should like to have it; and I say, as the old woman did, "I dont care how fiery the trial may be."

. . .

ALS; Child Letters, MC 305, Schlesinger Library, Radcliffe College (microfiche 8/205).

During this period of hard physical work and intellectual isolation, Child sought spiritual consolation. Like many of her contemporaries, she was attracted to the writings of Goethe and the Swedish mystic Emanuel Swedenborg. Her religious philosophy at this time was indebted to Swedenborg's doctrine of correspondence, the belief that each object in the material world was an emblem of a spiritual state.

To Convers Francis

Northampton Oct. 20th 1840

Dear Brother,

Your letter gave me exceeding great pleasure, although it humbled me. Your visit was a great satisfaction to me, as any renewal of our intimacy always is; and I had full purpose of heart to write by father and tell you so. But he and Mr. Child started for Boston nearly together, and as both went unexpectedly soon,

[1] John Childe.

there was a hurried call for autumn clothing, not in readiness to meet the demand. As there was but one pair of female hands in the house, I was reluctantly obliged to give up writing the letter, which I had written in my mind. Thank God that you are not a woman! *Great* labors do but strengthen the intellect of a well-balanced character; but these million Lilliputian cords tie down the stoutest Gulliver that ever wrestled in their miserable entanglement.

As for letters, I write exceedingly few, though I carry a whole mail of them in my head often for several days, waiting in vain for a leisure hour to pen them in. Oh, for that land of spiritual Daguerrotype, where thoughts and affections write themselves spontaneously in the angels' language of types & symbols![1] Yet to most, if not to all of us, such spiritual Daguerrotype were one of the fearfullest things!

And speaking of this, I will, in the random vein I am now in, ask you if you do not *see* that the spiritual idea, in all things of science, art, social forms, &c flows into its appropriate correspondence, even down into the lowest, ultimate forms? Is not the *idea* of this present age written in the fact that any man can have his likeness taken in a minute, by machinery? In the "philosophy of clothes," has it ever occurred to you that in those Eastern nations where a belief in fatalism stops the activity of human *thought*, the fashion of the *garments* changes not? While in France, where churches and governments are demolished in three days, the fashion of the garments is forever changing? I apprehend the clothing of a nation reveals much to the inhabitants of the aforesaid spiritual Daguerrotype region. We *borrow* our fashions. How is it with our thoughts? By the way, did you hear that excellent joke, that Louis Phillipe had written to Dr. Channing to *manufacture* a religion for the French people?

My thoughts run on in the wildest way. For the first time these six weeks, I have somebody in the kitchen to do my work; and there is a whole boys' school let loose in my brain, kicking up heels, throwing up caps, hurraing, chasing butterflies—everything in short except drowning kittens. So you must not look for anything like coherence. To go back to my hobby of twenty years, i.e. the forms of ideas. See you not how that old jangling pair, necessity and free-will, are shown in the tendency of all things to decay and re-production? in mysticism and rationalism? in conservatism & reform? Forever in the Universe, and in the universe-containing man, there is one hand winged and the other chained. Because of necessity and free-will the revolving worlds keep their places. The Sun is their necessity, centrifugal force their strong free-will. And those two opposing ideas which regulate the motion of the stars, are constantly taking form in the most trivial actions of my daily life. By my soul, though, free-will has a hard battle in these latter times; necessity presses like a patent screw.   A plague on my roving imagination to-day! That patent screw, simple as the phrase is, has set me out on a new chace of thought; but I will not follow it; for "verily all things

[1] The first practical process of photography was invented by the Frenchman Louis Daguerre in 1839.

are quite infinite"; and he that looks *into* a word will ever find that it contains volumes.

. . .

My many cares leave little time, and less fitness of mind, to amplify "Gospels of Beauty"; besides I want to keep still, out of sight and hearing of the bustling world; moreover, I do not think the editors of the Dial have the least wish for such an article; and lastly, I have no particular sympathy with the clique here called transcendentalists.[2] I want them to *have* their say; but I have never thought they had *much* to say, that would enlighten or bless the world. In no form of negation does my soul delight; it craves affirmation.

In these trying times, my dear husband retains a very large portion of the sentiment and romance that characterized our early love. Father, when he perceives it, calls it "childish folly". How should he know, as we do, that it transcends all wisdom?

. . .

Your sermons produced a great sensation here; which I look upon as no small thing, in a town where John Dwight preaches.[3] He finds much spiritual mindedness in Northampton. He takes what he gives, and thinks the reflection is a primal ray.

. . .

AL; Lydia Maria Child Papers, Anti-Slavery Collection, Cornell University (microfiche 9/215).

Child spent the winter completely occupied with the household work of sewing, cooking, and caring for her father. She and David anticipated one more growing season as the test of whether they should maintain or abandon the farm.

To Ellis Gray Loring

Northampton Feb. 9'th 1841.

Dear Friend,

What ails you all in Boston? Have you gone *en masse* to the world of spirits? or entered a Convent of La Trappe? or only moved to Iowa? For all useful purposes, I dont see but one might as well be true as the other; for not a syllable can

[2] The *Dial*, the quarterly magazine of Transcendentalist philosophy, literature, and religion, began publication in July 1840. Margaret Fuller and George Ripley edited it until 1842, and Emerson until it ceased in April 1844, but none of Child's works ever appeared in it.

[3] John Sullivan Dwight (1813–93) met Child when he served as pastor for a Unitarian church in Northampton in 1840. He resigned a year later and shortly after left the ministry. A Transcendentalist, he lived at Brook Farm and frequently contributed to the *Dial*.

be obtained in answer to any questions addressed to you. Some æons ago a string of rhymes was sent to Nony; whether they ever arrived, St. Bernard's dog knows as well as I do. Father sent a paper, which he says is of importance, but whether it ever reached E. G. L. the fisherman of Bagdad can tell as well as we. Then Mr. Child sent a letter asking legal advice for the satisfaction of my mind, with requests written inside and out to answer soon; whether said letter is still at the Depot, to be "met in a bag of beans," wherein it was sent, may be known to Prince Cream-Categorie koolie-khan,—but *we* are totally in the dark.

Some centuries have now passed since morning, noon, and night I have been in a raging fever to see "The Hour and the Man."[1] I thought *every*body must know I was in a fever; and I thought *some*body would have lent me the book, for a few weeks, when they had done with it. Again and again we have inquired for it at the bookstore and the library. We might have as well gone to the Dead sea to catch whales. I am ready to "stand up against a post and d____ *every*body." What ails you all? May you live on White Pigeon Prairie ten years, to eat wild buffalo, of your own catching and cooking; and may you never see a new book all the time, but only an Ouisconsin Trumpet now and then, or a Blast from the Rocky Mountains, containing a bit of an extract, with editorial comment! Then when you come back, see if you will leave me waiting another century on hackle-teeth, for The Hour and the Man!

To fall into a somewhat slower method, we sent about a fortnight since, a box, by our representative, Charles P. Huntingdon, which he promised to leave at the Depot, with timely information to you of the same. It contained beans, buck-wheat flour, and sundry books and letters, to one of which we are desirous of receiving an answer. Did the box ever arrive? Did a letter from father reach your hands, some eight or ten days before that? If so, have you been practising Beethoven's waltzes ever since? Or what is the reason you haven't a civil word to throw to a dog?   Charles P. Huntingdon is expected at Northampton in the course of next week. I have named the Hour and the Man—see to it.

I should like to know if there is any anti-slavery news stirring; but it were better to interrogate the spirit of Oceola, than any of you dumb dogs in Boston. I want to know what you think of Geo. Ripley's plan. I want to know what his plan *is*.[2] Mrs. Shaw promised to send it up by my Irishman at Christmas; but they are just like all the rest of you; siezed by a dumb spirit of late. I wish you might all have some experience, White Pigeon or otherwise, to teach you the value of living in such a place as Boston. As for this Connecticut Valley, I dislike it more and more and more, every week I live. If I buy a pound of butter, it is sure to fall

[1] Harriet Martineau's *The Hour and the Man: A Historical Romance* (London, 1841) was a novel about the Haitian liberator Toussaint L'Ouverture.
[2] Unitarian minister and Transcendentalist George Ripley (1802–80) founded Brook Farm in West Roxbury, Mass. Ripley was president of the farm for its entire existence from 1841 to 1847.

short an ounce; and every quart of milk lacks a gill of true measure. Thus Faith without Works shows itself in *ooltimates,* as Mr. Graeter used to say. Calvinism sits here enthroned, with high ears, blue nose, thin lips, and griping fist. I would I had lived in an age when the gaunt spectre had *done* his mission. It were wiser, however, to wish for that quiet liberality of spirit, which cannot be disturbed by spectres.

Should anything be said, at the meetings of the Mass. Board, about appointing Rev. Abel Brown of this place an Agent, please put in your veto. If you do not, mischief will ensue, unless I am greatly mistaken. If Garrison had had even the small chance to observe him, which I have had, he would not have headed his letter in the Liberator, "Recantation." The sentence which led him to consider it so, is *very* equivocal; and was doubtless meant to be so; for I think I do not wrong him, when I say he is well used to creeping in and out of equivocal sentences. He is a political and theological manager; therefore his natural place is in the New Organization. To speak in Alcott phrase, he is it, and it is he. He is a Baptist, and if the sectarian hate, which is very rife here between the two Societies, leads him to chastise Calvinistic N. Org. justly, let him do it; but do not trust him in anything where double dealing might do mischief. For *you* it will be enough that he is a Baptist; but less enlightened judges might demand more.[3]

We are all well in bodily health, except father, who has suffered severely from rheumatism. The good old gentleman has tried to bear it patiently, and has made the least possible outward trouble; but his perpetual restlessness and gloom, arising from early mistakes, now out of his power to rectify, have at times almost driven me crazy. I have tried to do my duty faithfully, and have struggled and prayed for a cheerful equanimity of soul; and I have not found it altogether in vain. So far, everything works well in Mr. C.'s business. He has been disappointed only in two things. Father's discontent knocks up the plan of living with us. I see it is absolutely necessary to his comfort to have a place *by himself;* and I know he cannot do this, if I consent to receive as much money as he originally proposed to vest for my benefit. I therefore conceived it to be a duty to stop short at half the sum; this is the reason Mr. C. wants to mortgage the *improvements* on the farm to John, on who he must depend. The other disappointment is that the land hired of the Silk Company (because our own farm was not purchased till too

[3] Abel Brown (1810–44) was one of the founders of the Eastern New York Anti-Slavery Society and publisher of the *Tocsin of Liberty.* Brown's recantation was published in *The Liberator* on 22 Jan. 1841. The Hampshire County Anti-Slavery Society had become a New Organization auxiliary in 1840. Brown's letter, written from Northampton, was critical of members who professed to be antislavery but who had not worked for abolitionist political candidates or tried to change the policies of proslavery churches.

late) proved more exhausted by previous tenants than we expected.   Give my best love to dearest Louisa and Nony, and a kind & grateful remembrance to your mother. Yrs **Truly,**

L. M. C.

ALS; Loring Family Papers, Schlesinger Library, Radcliffe College (microfiche 9/225).

4

May 1841–May 1843

In April 1841 Child and her husband were appointed editors of the *National Anti-Slavery Standard*, the weekly newspaper of the American Anti-Slavery Society. They replaced Nathaniel P. Rogers, who had resigned when the Massachusetts Society objected to the publication of his personal nonresistant views as the society's. The Childs agreed to take the job on the understanding that David would spend a great part of the time in Northampton. On 12 May 1841 Child went to New York City. The masthead on their first issue, 20 May 1841, listed Lydia Maria Child as editor and her husband as assistant editor, and she thus became the first woman in the United States to take charge of a newspaper oriented to an issue of public policy.

When she took on the post, she accepted the charge of keeping the paper on neutral ground between the two abolitionist camps—the Garrisonians, relying on "moral" appeal, and the New Organization, the political abolitionists relying on political pressure and the ballot box. The *Standard*, she felt, should be addressed not to the already committed abolitionist but rather to those only beginning to wonder about slavery. Using the paper to fight out ideological differences within the movement not only discredited the cause, she believed, but gave undeserved attention to the New Organization.

Although some of the internal controversy was reflected in the paper, Child tried to concentrate on public matters. The paper reported in detail the congressional debate over the admission of Texas to the Union and the struggle led by John Quincy Adams to overturn the gag laws barring discussion of the slavery issue. Not long after the Supreme Court's 1841 decision freeing the slaves who revolted aboard the *Amistad* in 1839, there was another shipboard uprising: in 1842 slaves on the *Creole*, en route from Norfolk, Virginia, to New Orleans, took the ship to Nassau, where the British freed all but a few held on criminal charges. When Joshua Giddings, Whig congressman from Ohio, used the occasion to attack slavery and the coastal slave trade, the House censured him. He resigned, but his district soon returned him triumphantly to Congress. Other issues of the time were the movement against capital punishment, discrimination against Irish Catholic immigrants, and cases concerning fugitive slaves.

Child lived throughout her stay in New York in the home of Isaac T. Hopper (1771–1852), a Quaker active in antislavery work and prison reform. The year Child moved in—1841—the Quakers disowned Hopper for his anti-slavery views. His son John (1815–64), a lawyer and agent for the New England Life Insurance Company, was thirteen years younger than Child but became her intimate friend; her letters are full of references to their companionship. The business manager of the *Standard*, James S. Gibbons (1810–92), was married to Isaac Hopper's daughter Abigail (1801–93), who was also active in social reform.

In a letter to Frank Shaw, Child explains the circumstances of her move to New York.

To Francis Shaw

N. York May 27th 1841

Dear Friend,

It was very characteristic of you to write me such a kind letter, so early after my arrival here. A letter is never so refreshing as during the *first* days after we have left home, when the heart is desolate with remembrance of the past, and un-accustomed to its new relations. To me your friendly words were peculiarly cheering; for I feel anxious, responsible, and *alone*. The few acquaintances I ever had in this disagreeable city now belong to the new organization, and consider me a Samaritan, with whom the Jews have no dealings. I board with an excellent Quaker family, (Isaac T. Hopper's) who are as kind to me as if I were daughter and sister; but you may well suppose that a very large proportion of my thoughts can find no echo here.

You do me injustice in praising my "moral courage" and "devotion to the cause" in coming here. I would I deserved the praise; but I must disclaim it, be-cause it does not belong to me. It was a *driving*, not a *leading* of Providence, which brought me into this position. And though details of personal affairs are wearisome,—and though I had much rather indulge in mystical theories about the sun and the planets, light and music, the sky and the ocean,—yet that you may understand my position, and not misconstrue my motives, I will give a brief ac-count of my *affairs*.

My father is a conscientious and kind-hearted, but very peculiar man. His restlessness is remarkable. During the twenty years since he left business, he has removed thirteen times. Of late years, he has been full of the idea that if he could only live with *me*, he should be perfectly contented. I more than doubted it, and greatly dreaded the experiment. But duty to him, in his old age, required it; and if he only *could* be contented, it would be advantageous to both, in an economical point of view, to unite our households. He agreed to expend $3000 on a farm for me; that being about the sum he expected to leave me at his decease; but the doing of this would diminish his own small income so much, that he could no longer keep house by himself as he had done. He bought a hundred acres of remarkably fine land, for $1000 dollars; but it was in a very neglected state, having belonged to minors. There were scarcely any fences, a barn in ruins, and an old shantee with two little rooms and a low garret. It was father's intention to expend the remaining $2000 in buildings, and many a pleasant vision I had of a quiet, rural home at last. But, he soon became restless, complained of being away from old friends and familiar scenes; told the domestics and neighbors that he was a poor wanderer now, having done so much for his daughter as to deprive himself of a home &c. This grew worse and worse; and you may well suppose was well nigh intolerable to a spirit like mine; for my leading fault is a stubborn pride of independence. At last Mr. Child and I both agreed that we must decline the expenditure of another dollar by father; that he *must* be left free to choose his residence where he would. We did so. He returned to the vicinity of Boston, leaving us with a barn unpaid for, no house to live in, no fences to our fields. Carpenters pressed for payment; it was a small sum to be sure; for the frame of the old barn had been used, and most of the timber cut from the farm; but we had it not. Then there was no use in planting, without fences to guard the crop; and stone wall could not be laid without money. I still clung to the idea of a *home*, and had pleasant visions of quiet days in the white-washed shantee, with my little garden; but the barn and the fences, and man's wages—what was to be done? I resolved to go abroad and seek my fortune, if it were to take a school in Iowa. Just then came renewed intreaties that we would edit the Standard; saying that the very existence of the paper depended upon having a judicious editor, warmly interested in the cause. Mr. Child could not leave, unless he gave up farm and manufactory altogether, and sold for little or nothing, the tools and machinery he had so much trouble to obtain. There seemed nothing left but for *me* to take the responsible and irksome situation. So you see it is love for my husband, and the hopes of earning a home, as Jacob did Rachel, which brought me to N. York. I am indeed thankful that since I must leave home to work, I am working for ⟨the⟩ anti Slavery; ⟨cause;⟩ and that is all the praise I deserve, for "devotion to the cause."   Perhaps you will think it would have been wise in Mr. Child to have left his present business, and come with me. But, in the first place, the editorship of this paper is a very precarious support; and in the next place, he has never yet fairly tried the Beet Sugar experiment. He has never had the machinery to do so, until now. His brother offered the loan of a few hundreds to enable him to purchase it; But as it suited his convenience to loan it in small instalments at intervals, Mr. Child was not able to get up his machinery late in the season; especially as the change in our pecuniary relations with father made it necessary to expend some of the loan for farming-tools. Mr. Child, therefore made no sugar this year; for when the works were completed, the spring freshets produced a back-water that entirely stopped the wheel. Had it not been so, he would have made but little; because he had only a few hired acres of poor land to raise his beets on. Last year was mainly spent in *preparing* the farm for this year. A good many acres are now well prepared for sowing, and the machinery is all in readiness. In this state of things, I could not bear to have him throw all up, without having even tried the experiment. I do hope it will at least be profitable enough to give us a moderate living. A quiet, rural home, I care not how humble, is all I ask. All I have suffered in my whole life would not I believe equal my ⟨harassed feelings⟩ suffering from harassed, anxious, and wounded feelings during the past year. One star only has shone through the clouds—the star of domestic affection. Yes, there *was* another—the star of friendship, with healing in its rays. I know not what I *should* have done without the continued sympathy of you and the precious Lorings. Mr. Alcott would consider this shameful weakness; but the woman greatly predominates in me. I cannot live without being beloved.

The first familiar face I met in N. York streets was Barrett's. He is preaching here with great effect. Grenville Mellen and Rufus Dawes are among his proselytes.[1] John Hopper, a very intelligent son of mine host (who was mobbed at N. Orleans, and barely escaped with his life) has his curiosity a good deal excited about the doctrines, and wants to go to church under the plea of "showing Maria the way." I am almost superstitious about it. Wherever I go, the N. Church by some means keeps a faint outward hold on me, on one side, while reforms grasp me strongly on the other. I wish the two could be reconciled, or else that I could escape from one of them. This standing between is painful business. If conscience would let me, I would quit reforms, and nestle quietly under the wings of mother church; but as Luther says, "God help me. I cannot do otherwise. Here I stand." I hear there is to be a New Church Convention here next week. Give my best love to Sarah. I should have written to you both, before I left Northampton, had I not hoped, even to the last day, that I should pass through Boston, and have a talk with you. I fear it will now be a long time before I have that pleasure.

A Package is weekly sent from the Anti Slavery office in Boston to the office in N. York. You can slip a letter in any time, and save the postage to help the next runaway slave. Dont forget that a letter from either of you always comforts my soul.   "I thank my God for every remembrance of you."   Yrs with strong affection, L. M. Child.

If any little incident bearing upon slavery, or the general topic of human freedom, comes to your knowledge from the East or West Indies, the North or the South, why wont you send it to the Standard? I wish you would write an article on the commercial relations between the North and the South.

If in the course of your reading, you meet with anything peculiarly interesting, will you just signify chapter and verse to me? An Anti Slavery editor comes in for none of the loaves and fishes of the booksellers. I am a *black* sheep in the flock.

I wish you would freely find fault with the Standard, if you see anything in bad taste, or likely to injure the cause.

[1] Benjamin Fiske Barrett (1808–92) was minister at the Swedenborgian New Church Society in New York. Mellen (1809–41) and Dawes (1803–59) were both poets and editors.

My engagement here is for one year. Then for the green fields and the pure air! I never envied you till now, that you are fitting up a rural home.

Furness is turned away from Philadelphia for preaching abolition![2] How the ice melts!

Three cheers! N. York has repealed her 9 month's law, and the slave brought here is free![3]

P.S. Since writing this Thomas Worcester has sent for me to come & see him.[4] I want to go, yet dread to go. They will attack my freedom forthwith, & I shall resist forthwith.

ALS; Houghton Library, Harvard University (microfiche 10/233).

Child quickly grasped the precarious financial state of the *Standard*, as well as the joylessness of editing in an atmosphere of steady and conflicting criticism.

To Ellis Gray Loring

N. York. June 17'th 1841

Dearly Beloved Friend,

I am under *inexpressible* obligation to you for your communications and suggestions for the Standard. I almost break down sometimes, under the disagreeableness of the employment, and the utter want of interest manifested in the paper. I have not received a line of encouragement from any mortal but yourself. *Personally* I do not want it; but for the sake of the *cause*, I should like to see more interest manifested for the continuance of the paper. J. S. Gibbons says he won't go on in this way, unable to meet the pecuniary demands of each month and mortified by continual dunning. Nobody knows what sacrifices of feeling and of money he has made to sustain this paper. He and I both agree that next January ought to close it, unless the Society show more interest to have it sustained. I am casting an anchor to the windward concerning other employments here in N. York, and can probably succeed in finding those more to my mind. This reading of papers and pamphlets, and poring over Congressional documents, is perfectly intolerable, unless sustained by the conviction that I am doing some good to the anti slavery cause, and that the abolitionists think it worth while for me to practise this self-denial, for the sake of keeping up the Standard. If there was any warmth and earnestness of feeling about it, that would carry me very lightly over

[2] William Henry Furness (1802–96), from Child's hometown of Medford, Mass., was a Unitarian minister and abolitionist in Philadelphia.
[3] A law had permitted slaveholders to bring slaves into New York for up to nine months without the slaves losing their slave status. Slavery had ended in the state in 1827.
[4] Worcester (1795–1878), a Swedenborgian minister, founded the first New Church Society in Massachusetts in 1821.

all disagreeableness, but this *dragging* along is very irksome.   Abby Kelly, in one of her letters, says, "The Standard gives good satisfaction *in the main*." She then goes on to express a wish that I could feel free to write something declaring that I approved of Rogers's editing, and thought it necessary *at the time* for him to publish all he did; but this I cannot do conscientiously. I have great respect and regard for him, but I think he showed a wonderful deficiency of judgment.

Dont fail to tell me whether you thought the review of The Hour and the Man anything like what it should be. How provoking that they should have printed the "union of two *infirmities*," instead of two *infinities*.

You bid me praise O'Sullivan and other democrats—I have accordingly tried to find out what they have done and said.[1] I sent to O'Sullivan himself to inquire what were the best things said and done by his party concerning the nine-months law; but he has not given me any information; and J. S. Gibbons does not know where to find it.

Mr. Child regrets that I put in Hudson's account of the Hartford Meeting.[2] But what can I do? A great many would feel displeased if there was no record kept of these public meetings.

As for your Committee of Vigilance, my deliberate conviction, unbiassed by the opinion of any one, is that Garrison did right. I have no objection to Charles T. Torrey's doing as much good as he likes in the world, and I have no objection to praising him for it; but in the present state of things, I should have insurmountable objections to having my name connected with his.[3] Such union with the old organizationists is sought only to gain additional influence to do mischief with. You have not so bad an opinion of New Organization as you ought to have, in my humble opinion. If we want to retain *any* degree of vitality, we must keep our skirts clear of it; and we cannot do this, while our names appear side by side with the supporters of it. A pang shot through my heart when I saw your name by the side of Torrey's; for I know better than you do, what insidious use is made of such concessions. If we could only let N. Organization *entirely* alone, it would die out, and reappear by and bye in some new pro-slavery form; but as long as our violent spirits will continually attack it, and our mild and candid spirits will

---

[1] John Louis O'Sullivan (1813–95) founded the *U.S. Magazine and Democratic Review* in 1837 to promote nationalistic and expansionist views; he is credited with coining the phrase *manifest destiny* in 1845.

[2] Erasmus Darwin Hudson (1805–80) was a physician in Northampton, Mass., and an agent for the American Anti-Slavery Society. In the *Standard*, 3 June 1841, he described the proceedings of the Connecticut Anti-Slavery Society, 21 May 1841, where a rule against women speaking was enforced and Abby Kelley denied the floor. "Bigotry was the presiding genius at the meeting," he wrote.

[3] Torrey, who in 1840 had joined the American and Foreign Anti-Slavery Society, had just organized the Boston Vigilance Committee in response to the capture in Boston of fugitive slave John Torrance. Garrison commented in *The Liberator*, 18 June 1841, that it was "unfortunate" that "one so decidedly objectionable" as Torrey should be the committee's agent and secretary.

acknowledge it as anti-slavery, there is no hope for us. Between the two, old organization may as well go mute; yet the truth is on its side.

Perhaps I speak with more freedom than kindness; if so, the words belie my heart, which loves and respects you, I had almost said beyond any other human being. Therefore it is, that I am vexed to have your goodness made the dupe of artful men. Here on this private sheet of paper there is no need of mincing the matter; and here I declare my belief that Torrey and Leavitt are both artful and treacherous as the _____ Do you suppose it is accident, that they still keep the heading of *American* Anti S. Society over Birney's nomination?[4] Nay, verily. The Washington Globe was never guilty of anything more completely a party trick.

I rejoice to hear of your anticipated visit to N. York. If you could ever be free in a private house, you could here at Isaac Hopper's. There would be no restraint of times or seasons, with regard to rising or going to bed, or anything else. John and I are promenading the Battery four nights in the week, until 12 o'clock; and the old gentleman makes no objection to these outlandish hours. John has been in the habit for years; he urges me to go with him, and as I like his company extremely, and am glad enough to escape from my solitary confinement all day, I never refuse to go. You surely wont want greater freedom than license to be about all night, and to lie abed all day. Friend Isaac sends you a most hearty and pressing invitation to make his house your home. If it does not suit your independence to accept this invitation, you can pay board, you know. But if, on account of callers, or for any other reason, you want *genteel* lodgings, you cannot find them in greater beauty than at the Globe Hotel. There are private rooms and tables furnished for all who like. A great many bachelors and gentleman travellers put up there; of course, it would not be chosen as lodgings for a *young* lady, if she were *alone;* but for a person of Louisa's *great* respectability I cannot conceive any impropriety, if she remained there without you, as I understood your question to imply. . . .

　. . .

AL; Child Papers, Clements Library, University of Michigan (microfiche 10/235).

Discouraged by her job as editor, Child took a brief holiday in Massachusetts at the end of June 1841. She stayed with the Lorings at their summer house in Brookline and visited with many old friends before coming back to New York by 4 July. The holiday was not refreshing for long, however. On 21 September 1841 she wrote bitterly to Ellis Gray Loring, "How I do long to get out of this infernal treadmill! How I do long to be re-united to my dear husband, and have

4 Joshua Leavitt (1794–1873), a founder of the American Anti-Slavery Society, had joined the political abolitionists and was editing their newspaper, the *Emancipator*. James Birney was the Liberty party's candidate for president.

145

some quiet, domestic days again! It makes me groan to think that only four months of the stipulated year have passed. Nothing *but* Mr. Child's pecuniary distress would keep me here another month. I hate it, with an inconceivable and growing hatred."*

A week later, she wrote the following letter, explaining some of the background to her outburst, in particular the resentment felt by two New York abolitionists that they had not been made the *Standard*'s editors. Oliver Johnson, then a member of the executive committee of the American Anti-Slavery Society, had occasionally filled in for Garrison on *The Liberator*. James C. Jackson (1811–95) had assisted the previous editor of the *Standard;* shortly after the date of this letter, he moved to Cazenovia, New York, to edit the *Madison County Abolitionist*, a New Organization newspaper.

To Ellis Gray Loring

New York Sep. 28th. [1841]

Dear Friend,

. . .

I do not allow home-sickness to get the better of me often; and when I do, it is but temporary. My lot could not have been cast in a kinder family, though it might in one more interesting; for there is a tedious monotony about Quaker life. A few things connected with the Standard have given me pain. I will merely say that Oliver Johnson and James C. Jackson thought *they* ought to have been editors, and that there was no call for the Society to throw away its money in paying me. How far Johnson has become reconciled to the arrangement, I know not; but Jackson is full of jealousies and heart-burnings; and will probably become N. Org. From all other quarters, I hear of nothing but encouragement and approbation. Hudson, Burleigh, and Foster, all write most heartily concerning the success they have with the paper, and the approbation generally bestowed upon it.[1] The subscription list increases steadily; if it will only go on for a year, as it has the last two months, we shall be quite above board. In ⟨a⟩ an editorial note this week, you will see why your mother did not receive her paper; a reason which I have no doubt will be highly satisfactory to you.

I am glad to find myself thus sustained; for I felt anxious about my own inexperience; especially when I discovered that there had not been unanimity in wishing me at this responsible post. I am rather doubtful whether the *gritty* school quite approve of me now. I observe Garrison gives no indication, public or private, of interest in the Standard; the Westons commend nothing, except

---

* Manuscript Division, New York Public Library.
[1] Charles Calistus Burleigh (1810–80) was then editing the *Pennsylvania Freeman*. Stephen Symonds Foster (1809–81) was an antislavery lecturer; in 1845 he married the abolitionist Abby Kelley.

my answer to Leavitt about Rogers;[2] and Mrs. Chapman, in her letters, gives no opinion whether the paper is now advancing the good of the cause, or not—she merely seems very anxious that something should turn up to bring me into *"rough water."* I can tell her, however, that if by rough water, she means controversy and personalities, the ship must find another pilot. I am willing to do *hard* work, but not *dirty* work, for any cause.

. . .

Whenever you come, I hope sincerely that Augusta will come with you.[3] She will be most cordially welcome to share my humble apartment, and John I know will do all in his power to make her visit pleasant. By the way, I do not plead guilty to Louisa's implied charge, when she talks about "geniuses like Mrs. Follen and I dressing up common subjects in romantic garb."[4] I never represented that John Hopper was particularly distinguished above hundreds of other intelligent young men. I simply spoke of his *kindness* as very remarkable, and of my pleasant surprise to find a Quaker sympathize so much with my literary tastes. As for his kindness, I never saw anything like it; I think he lives for nothing else but to devise ways and means for my happiness. The best joke of all is, he calls me his *daughter*, and says he feels bound to take fatherly care of me.

This New York is a frightful place. What is the reason the proportion of crime is so much greater than in London? For a good while past, I have walked but little after 10 o'clock at night. I am afraid to. I never met with anything disagreeable myself; but the penny papers, every now and then, frighten me out of my wits.   I am sorry the moon will not shine while you are here, if you come on the 2d. You never will see the Battery in its glory, till you see it by moonlight, and at full tide. The Belle Poule is lying near it now, with her tricolor flying; and once in a while the Prince's band regale the populace with most celestial music. It is the same band that played requiems and dirges when the remains of Napolean were conveyed to Paris.

Dont let your interest in the Standard subside; for I have no doubt that I shall be chained to the oar two or three years at least; and while I work at all, I shall try to work well. I will not dishearten you by running from my post; and don't you dishearten me by *seeming* to join hands with N. Org. Do it out and out, if you do it at all.

. . .

ALS; Manuscript Division, New York Public Library (microfiche 11/265).

[2] Joshua Leavitt had published in the *Emancipator*, in an editorial praising Child's editing of the *Standard*, a backhanded attack on N. P. Rogers; Garrison reprinted her defense of Rogers in *The Liberator*, 11 June 1841.
[3] Augusta G. King, of Salem, Mass., was Louisa Loring's niece.
[4] Eliza Lee (Cabot) Follen (1787–1860) was a writer, editor, and abolitionist. She wrote mainly for children and women, and in 1841 published a memoir of her husband, Charles Follen (1796–1840), a German-born scholar, Unitarian minister, and abolitionist.

A sign of Child's effort to heal the breaches in the antislavery ranks by giving credit where credit was due was her publication in the *Standard* of 30 September 1841 of a front-page article on Gerrit Smith, the political abolitionist who founded the Liberty party in 1840. The article recounted in detail how he had bought a family of slaves in Mississippi—Sam and Harriet and their seven children, price thirty-five hundred dollars—and freed them near his home in Peterboro, New York. In asking Smith's opinion on the Constitution and slavery, she was raising an issue current among abolitionists: whether the Constitution was basically a proslavery document, as Garrison had decided, or, as some Liberty party people felt, an antislavery document that gave Congress the right to abolish slavery in the states.

To Gerrit Smith

N. York. Tuesday Sep. 28'th [1841]

To Gerrit Smith.
Dear Sir,
. . .

Although it is far less agreeable to work for the anti-slavery cause, than it was a few years ago, I still think the good work is going on more rapidly than ever. The roots which then struck down straight and deep, are now branching out extensively, and sending up shoots in all directions. Among the various agencies at work, few are more likely to bring forth abundant fruits than your redemption of Sam and Harriet. May God's best blessings be with you and your excellent wife!

What are your opinions concerning an early effort to revise the U.S. Constitution? There is a party who contend that slavery is not *in* the Constitution. That it is not there, according to the legitimate construction of language, is most true; but that it was conceded to be there by the North, and so understood by the South, appears to me evident. Others think it is not time *yet* to move in this matter; but I confess I am always in a hurry to clear my own skirts of anything I consider wrong. Certainly the Free States are more directly implicated in slavery by this clause, than by anything else; in their civil relations, at least. I should like very much to know your views upon it.

With renewed expressions of gratitude for your kind tokens of encouragement and approbation,

I am with the sincerest sentiments of respect and esteem,

L. M. Child.

ALS; Gerrit Smith Collection, George Arents Research Library, Syracuse University (microfiche 11/266).

Child's reawakened interest in the arts appears in this next letter to Frank Shaw, then living near Brook Farm in West Roxbury, Massachusetts.

In July 1841, Child sat for the French silhouettist Auguste Edouart (1789–1861). Edouart had come to the United States two years before and while on this visit cut with extraordinary delicacy more than thirty-eight hundred silhouettes of people both eminent and obscure.

Child refers to the artist William Page (1811–85), then working on the painting *Jepthah's Daughter*, which he never finished. Noted for portraits and historical paintings, Page was president of the National Academy from 1871 to 1873; his works, however, were plagued by a darkening of the pigment so severe that the figures quickly became nearly indistinguishable. His marital difficulties were chronic. At this time, his first wife had recently left him, leaving behind three young daughters.

Orson Fowler's phrenological examination of Child's head that July had resulted in an analysis of her character in the September 1841 issue of the *American Phrenological Journal*. The account described her "more than ordinary degree of ambition to . . . bring about moral, social, and intellectual reforms" and noted, "Combativeness is large." When William Lloyd Garrison announced in *The Liberator* of 17 September 1841 that he would reprint the account, he wrote: "It is stated that she was induced to visit Mr. F's office from curiosity; that she was a perfect stranger to him; that he had no means whatever of conjecturing her name or character; and that not a word was spoken by her until after the examination of her head was completed, and the results written down. The *hit*, it seems to us, is very remarkable, and serves to demonstrate the truth of phrenology as an accurate and valuable science."

To Francis Shaw

New York October 12th 1841

Dear Friend,

I seldom *tease* my friends to do what they seem adverse to doing; but I *do* want your profile and Sarah's; and I send this by Mons. Edouard, who cuts with remarkable genius. He is a real *artist*. He is to remain in Boston a few weeks. Will you go to his room, and both have your likenesses taken on the same paper, in some familiar, household attitude? I never teased you for anything before, and I never will tease you for anything again, if you will just do this to oblige me. I don't wish to have you taken with either hoe or spade in your hand; nor would it be exactly the thing to have you playing with an opera glass. Suppose you and Sarah should both be training flowers on a trellis? That would be delightfully emblematic of your young family, you know.

I should like to have you look at M. Edouard's collection of cuttings. They are very numerous, and comprise the greater part of the distinguished people of Europe and America. He has seen all sorts of places and persons, and is very full of entertaining anecdote. He is a gentleman in character and manners, and the farthest possible from being intrusive. He has always been remarkably successful and popular wherever he has been. Charles 10'th was so much pleased with his cuttings, that he gave him a diamond ring, and the king of Austria presented him with a gold snuff-box. I mention these things, hoping it may induce Anna, and your other friends, to look in upon him, and speak of his cuttings to others, if they are pleased with them. I do not mean that you should make any *effort;* but just look in upon him, and if you think he is an artist in his way, just say so; that is all. *I* think he is, very decidedly; and that is a decision you will, of course, deem important.

I have been to see Page's poor little children, and shall do so often if he remains in New York this winter. I have likewise given him a ticket of admittance to my own private room, throughout the season. I did it because I thought he might like to come where he could talk or not talk, as he liked, without being looked at by people, who do not know his sufferings, and of course cannot sympathize with them. I thought he seemed pleased with the idea, and I am in hopes I shall be able to soothe him. If I do not, it will not be for want of trying; for I pity him most sincerely. How is he to live during the six or eight months that he is finishing his great picture?

I received Sarah's pleasant letter with much thankfulness; but was quite surprised to find you were still at Savin Hill. When shall you get into your new house?

My heart is just now throbbing with pleasant anticipations; for I expect to start for Northampton on Saturday, to make my husband a visit of three or four weeks. It seems so odd to *visit* him. I do hope that circumstances will be so ordered as to bring about a re-union soon. I am the worst of all temperaments to live without being beloved. If I were to begin life again, with all my sobering experience, I should risk all for love again, and consider the world well lost. What has wealth or fame to offer, compared with a friend whose welcoming smile and kiss is always ready, and who verily *thinks* you the wisest, best, handsomest, and above all, the dearest person in the world? Did you receive the Phrenological Journal? If so, what did you think of my head? And what did Sarah think of it?

I am curious to hear what are the prospects of Ripley's Community. I have supposed that it would fail, and Adin Ballou's likewise; because the *beginnings* of such things always do.[1] But whether it succeeds or not, I think it will do much good; for these plans are unquestionably the nucleus of a great idea, destined to work important social reforms.

A sort of a jackanapes was telling me the other day, that the Chinese made their hair black by something they eat; and that foreigners afflicted with red hair had availed themselves of this skill, which was kept a profound secret. I laughed

[1] George Ripley's Brook Farm lasted until 1847. Adin Ballou (1803–90), a Universalist minister, started Hopedale in Milford, Mass., in 1841; it prospered until 1856, then languished until its final close in 1869.

at it, as a most absurd hoax; especially as he maintained that the hair never changed, after this process of dieting for a few weeks. Did you ever happen to hear of such a thing?

You never tell me what you are reading. For my part, I cannot find anything worth reading. Either I grow fastidious, or literature grows vapid. The world needs a vigorous, stirring religious sentiment to dawn anew upon it. The old formulas will not cover the new ideas. 'Tis a wearing age to live in; nevertheless I am happy and hopeful.

With sincere affection for you all, Yrs truly, L. M. C.

ALS; Houghton Library, Harvard University (microfiche 11/273).

In November 1841 Child returned from a four-week visit to David in Northampton, the first since leaving in May. Now determined to keep control over the *Standard*, she firmly opposed an effort by the more politically minded Philadelphia abolitionists to unite their paper, the *Pennsylvania Freeman*, with the *Standard*, believing that it would jeopardize her paper's neutrality among the antislavery factions.

To Ellis Gray Loring

New York Nov. 24 1841

Dearly Beloved Friend,

My very soul yearns to hear from you in the good old friendly way; it seems so long since I have had any communication with you, except in the way of business. My visit to Northampton was one of almost unmixed pain. David looked so thin and over-worked, that I should hardly have known him; and the woman who had promised to look after his comfort, had proved most negligent and unfaithful. I was so overwhelmed with hard work while there, that I did not take a single walk, or even step out to look at the calves. I managed to leave things in a very comfortable train, and I expect to send on a colored goody soon, to cook and wash for him. Moreover, his health and spirits mended astonishingly during the short time of my sojourn. We have plans in which both of us agree, which I think will have a happy result. They involve long separation; but at the end of the road, I see a light.

I thought you would have sent some communications for the Standard, while I was gone; and I looked for them anxiously. I thought it would be just *like* you. My dear friend, between us there can be no sham—no assumed gloss, merely to please each other. You know I speak truly, when I say that there is not an individual in the anti slavery cause (or out of it either, for that matter) except perhaps Wendall Phillips, upon whom I could place such high value as a correspondent for the Standard, as yourself. If I have not said it, it was because I thought you *knew* it, beyond a doubt, and partly because I felt delicate about urging you up to what I supposed to be a disagreeable job, done mainly for *my* sake. But this delicacy I will now throw aside. The ruling idea of my life, at this present showing, is to make the Standard a first-rate paper; and you *must* help me—both with counsel and communications. It is a lucky *accident*, that by serving me, you may likewise serve the cause of freedom.

Just now, I want you to write an article in a most especial manner, and to do it *soon*. A good deal of excitement is prevailing here about the Catholic school question; and you are aware that the Catholics have adopted the infallible method of curing all evils—that is, they have formed a political party, and set up mainly Catholic candidates. Having, as they urge, tried all other means for their rights without success. On the opposite side, is the hue and cry of "Catholic usurpation"—the "Pope seizing the government" &c.   They have the same right in the public schools that the other sects have; but they complain and with more justice than Protestants are generally aware of, that this common benefit is made the vehicle, both in books and teachings, to render the faith of their fathers odious and ridiculous in the eyes of the children; & that therefore they cannot conscientiously avail themselves of it. Protestants deny the charge; but, without being aware of it, they are continually stabbing Catholics, in school-books, &c. A large class *are* indeed aware of it, and *purposely* persecute the Catholics, in such insidious ways as the spirit of the age compels them to adopt. All is party zeal, and sectarian fury. Cannot you say a calm, wise word? I would write an article myself; but I do not see quite clearly how this school fund *ought* to be managed. The Quakers, you are aware, pay the common tax, and support their own schools beside; in consequence of objections to the spirit of the school books &c. Yet do they not in some sort violate their consciences? For the tax that pays for the publication of military odes and eulogiums on heroes, does in effect support the navy and the army, more efficiently than it could be done in any other manner. If other sects won't support schools for *their* doctrines, why should they be taxed to teach opinions *opposed* to their own? Untie this knot, will you?

I moreover want the long review of the constitutional question which you promised to divide into sections, and send; and I want a letter about the visit to Springfield Armory; but first and foremost, I do greatly want an article on the Catholic question.

You will observe an article in to day's paper on Transcendentalism. It is the beginning of a series of merely *popular* explanations of subject[s] much talked of and little understood. I shall take up Homeopathy, Puseyism &c.[1] Where can I find a good, and clear account of the origin, rise, progress, and character, of the last mentioned? I have merely general ideas about it. . . .

Sub rosa. The Penn. Freeman talks of uniting with the Standard. The difficulty in the way is, that they want to insert 3 columns per week, on their own

[1] Edward Bouverie Pusey (1800–82), an English Anglican, became a leader of the Oxford Movement, a liberal form of English Catholicism.

hook. That is, on such subjects, and in such a way, as they choose. To this I cannot conscientiously consent. While I have the entire responsibility of the paper, I must have the entire control. The Freeman is filled with twaddling articles, without intellectual life and spirit, generally; and moreover, it is always betwixt & between on points of principle. It holds out a hand to both organizations, and gives encouraging glances to 3d party. If *such* communications are to be admitted into the Standard, I cease to be its editor the next day. They propose to give $1000 for one thousand papers—of which they are to have the distribution in Pennsylvania, and on which *they* are to make sufficient profit to support office expenses. Would it not be better to drop the Freeman at once, and let those who like subscribe for the Standard, at the usual price and others for the Emancipator?

I smiled to see how soon the Standard got into hot water as soon as my back was turned. The Free American upon me for an extract from the Herald of Freedom, which *I* certainly should not have admitted. and the Madison Co. Ab[olitionist] out upon another article, which *I* should not have written, but am called to answer for.

I got home just in time to knock out of type a short editorial triumphing over the fall of the A. & F. Reporter. How good and sensible men do lack judgment & taste!

They were all rejoiced to see me at Friend Hopper's. *One* in particular talked of bouncing through the ceiling; and that was J. S. Gibbens, rejoiced to throw off the paper.

Farewell, dear friend, God fold you in his arms! Yrs truly, L. M. Child. Write to me soon, do. To me, *myself*, I mean.

. . .

ALS; Manuscript Division, New York Public Library (microfiche 11/286).

To the Eastern Pennsylvania Anti-Slavery Society and its secretary, James Miller McKim (1810–74), Child set forth her editorial policy, insisting that it would apply as well to columns sent from the Philadelphia society. The society reluctantly agreed to Child's terms, and in December 1841 publication of the *Pennsylvania Freeman* was suspended in favor of the *Standard* and the subscription lists combined. In January 1844 the *Freeman* was reestablished in Philadelphia and continued publication until June 1854.

To James Miller McKim and Philadelphia Friends

New York. Nov. 24th [and 25th] 1841

Dear Philadelphia Friends,

I intended to have answered your letter, written by J. M. McKim, the day after I received it; but on my return from Northampton, business pressed upon me almost to distraction. If you find it difficult to realize this, have the goodness to remember that in addition to what men editors have to perform, I am obliged to do my own washing and ironing, mending and making, besides manifold stitches for my husband's comfort.

In the first place, my coming to Philadelphia is altogether out of the question. It would give me very great pleasure to do so; but I am too earnest to write up the Standard, "high," if not "*dry*," on a large subscription list, to make any excursions from home, not absolutely necessary. In the present case, I think a letter will answer all purposes, except the pleasure of talking with each other.

With regard to the three columns of communications from Pennsylvania, I cannot, consistently with my freedom as an editor, receive them on different terms from other communications; that is, I will insert them if they seem to me for the good of the cause, and otherwise reject them. I think you will not consider this an undue assumption, when you recollect that all the responsibility of the paper rests upon my name. If I have the entire responsibility, particularly at a crisis like this, which demands discretion far more than ability in an editor, I surely ought to have the entire control. If the Society deem that I exercise it injudiciously, I am more than ready to withdraw at any moment.   If you wish to know what I shall be *likely* to reject, I will state what you already have the means of knowing. I could not conscientiously edit a paper that advocated, or even partially favored, a political *party* among abolitionists. Neither would my conscience let me admit anything implying, or *seeming* to imply, that the old and new organization were equally worthy of support. Neither could I admit anything that sanctioned, or excused, an abolitionist in voting for a pro-slavery man, either whig or democrat. As a matter of judgement, I would not admit any thrusts, or side-hits, at either Whigs or Democrats, *as such;* any sarcasms upon any sect, *as such;* anything involving controversial points of theology; or anything either to attack or sustain the doctrines peculiar to non-resistants, women's rights, Grahamism, &c.[1] Do I explain distinctly enough?

When you call upon me "to define my position," I do not clearly understand whether you mean me, L. M. Child, or me, the editor of the Standard. If you mean individual me, I answer, in all respect and courtesy, that I am amenable to no man, or association of men, for my opinions. If you mean the editor of the Standard, I will say that I respect the freedom of the American Society full as much as I wish it to respect my freedom. The views of a large majority are by no means coincident with my own, on many subjects; but there is sufficient identity for me to manage their organ without interfering with their conscientious freedom, or in any degree violating my own. I have neither the right, nor the wish, to make the paper a vehicle of my own opinions, as distinct from theirs; therefore I am silent about many things which I should probably advocate in a paper of my own. It is true indeed, that the general *bias* of the mind is inevitably betrayed by

[1] Grahamism, a program of dietary reform emphasizing the use of whole-grain flour, was started by Sylvester Graham (1794–1851), after whom the graham cracker is named.

every writer, unless he in[tends]² to disguise. Thus alm[ost a]ny page I ever wrote would show plainly enough that I w[a]s not a Presbyterian; though I might not be thinking of Presbyterianism when I wrote it, any more than of the depth of water in Symnes's Hole.³

The position which I understand the American Society to stand upon, is precisely the same it stood upon from the beginning. If you dont understand this position *now*, as well as formerly, pardon me the pleasantry if I say I think you are in the case of the drunken man, who ran round the room to catch his motionless bedstead, because his own head was dizzy. The political buzz has bewildered you. It is its nature to do so.

An immense majority of the American Society, nearly all of them approve of voting. Non Resistance, they merely recognize as a matter believed in by a few of its members, who have as good a right to their opinions, as anti-bank men have to theirs. Further than this, it has nothing to do with non-resistance. Therefore I do not understand how any can have been "shut up to the necessity of choosing between Liberty Party Policy and Non Resistance Policy." Has a word ever dropped from my editorial pen involving that paper in non-resistance doctrines? The American opposes the Liberty Party, not because it is political *action*, but because it is an organized *party*, and therefore likely to do harm. You ask to have rules given for voting. How can this be done, when the duties of individual voters change with every election, and in every County. This year, Mr. Child voted for one whig senator, and one loco-foco; because they were both abolitionists, and he had confidence in both; but he would by no means pledge himself to vote for *every* abolitionist set up by the democratic party; even if he liked the man, some unforseen point of duty might come in the way. For Governor, he gave a scattering vote.

The Liberty Party question each can soon settle for himself. Is a distinct *party* likely to injure our cause? If so, the man who holds that opinion, yet cooperates with the party, on the ground that he sees no other mode of political action, is as inconsistent as a Calvinist would be in sustaining a Unitarian church, because there was no other place of worship in his neighborhood.

I cannot state whether the policy of Pennsylvania will conflict with the policy of the Standard, or not; for I cannot clearly ascertain what Pennsylvania policy *is*. My dislike of 3d party and N. organization is too strong and settled, to admit of anything like "accommodation" with them.

With sentiments of the highest respect and esteem, I am truly yr friend Maria Child.

25th

Since writing this I have seen a letter from J. M. M. to J. S. Gibbons; in reply to which I must again say it is impossible for me to come to Philadelphia.

---

² The paper is torn.
³ Symmes' (not Symnes's) Hole was supposedly in the ocean's floor, leading to the center of the earth.

ALS; Lydia Maria Child Papers, Anti-Slavery Collection, Cornell University (microfiche 12/290).

To Maria (Weston) Chapman

New York ⟨Nov⟩ Dec. 1'st [1841]

Dear Friend,

. . .

You don't know how I am plagued with the Third Party. From all quarters come requests to *explain* what the old organization are to do about politics—the opposition seek by all subtle and well [. . .]ed[1] schemes, to get me editorially committed on non-resistance; James C. Jackson is coaxing all he can to stop the Standard, (at least, I *think* so) and Garrison is helping him with puffs innumerable. The Liberator lauds the Liberty Party, and inserts its notices; Francis Jackson and *Wendell Phillips,* (I would have coined my blood for gold, rather than he should have done it) are flourished forth on the Liberty ticket; and I expect daily to see Garrison put up for governor, and Edmund Quincy for congress.

Am I to hold up the Standard of moral influence *all* alone? Or does nobody care whether it is held up or not? I can assure you my position is a puzzling and discouraging one.   The Penn Freeman is seeking union with the Standard, but wants mightily to sift in something in favor of what they call *concentration,* though *not* Liberty Party. What they mean, the Lord may know, though "his servant doth not."

It looks to me like a cat from the meal tub, and I'm shy of it. Those Penn. abolitionists are everlasting betweenities.

It is late at night, and I have proof to read. So, with the most affectionate remembrance to your good husband, and his parents, and Mary, and love to your sunny tribe of sisters, especially my dar[ling] Lucia, I will bid you a hurried farewell.

Yours truly,
L. M. Child.

I rejoice that you approve my editing. I thought I was too *cautious* to please you; but I can tell you, my caution plagues New. Org. worse than anything.

Why don't you write ⟨an⟩ a description of articles for the Fair, and send it to me?

My coming to Boston is out of the question. My business at this present time is to write up the Standard, in spite of 3rd Party, or the _____ and I will put my *whole* strength into it.

ALS; Anti-Slavery Collection, Rare Books and Manuscripts, Boston Public Library (microfiche 12/292).

[1]A single word is heavily cancelled and unrecovered.

The day after Child wrote the following analysis of political abolitionism the *Standard* published the resolutions of the Liberty party convention of December 1841, held in Williamsburg, New York. One resolution applauded the recent slave uprising on the *Creole*, asking that this "noble example" be "imitated by all in similar circumstances"; another supported slave rebellion in the South. In response, the American Anti-Slavery Society—of which Child was secretary—said that the society's constitution did not countenance physical force by slaves in claiming their rights. Violence, Child believed, not only was wrong in itself but also would stimulate more violence in reprisal.

To James Miller McKim

New York Jan 26'th 1842.

Dear Sir,

. . .

I sincerely hope that no coolness is growing up between me and the Philadelphia friends, on the annoying question of 3d Party. My views on this subject are very clear, and very decided; but I believe them to be *entirely* unmixed with partizan or personal feelings. You are very much mistaken if you suppose I am looking at the subject merely through non-resistance spectacles. I see as plainly as Thomas Earle, or any other politician can see, that public sentiment *must* act through politics.[1] In the present state of the world it is neither possible nor desirable to avoid this. But I likewise see plainly that public sentiment cannot be made *by* political machinery; though political parties *can* be changed by public sentiment. The fifteen gallon law is a good illustration of this. A temperance public sentiment could not be *made* by passing that law; but the Washington Temperance association, if it keep on diligently working with its spiritual weapons, will ere long so completely change public sentiment, that it will spontaneously embody itself in law.

I desire to see an anti-slavery Congress as earnestly as Joshua Leavitt, or Thomas Earle can desire it; and one of my strongest reasons, if not *the* strongest, for opposing 3d Party, is that it will inevitably tend to retard that desirable event. We should have held the balance of power very much sooner, in all the free states, by perseverance in the old method; and it is my opinion that we never shall hold it, till we return to that method. However, to show you that I am uninfluenced by party feeling, I can truly say that I should be very glad to have my prediction prove false; because, since the party experiment *will* be fully tried, I should be sorry to have so much hard work wasted.

Two things were foreshown to me from the beginning; and most sincerely do I hope that the voice prophesied falsely. The party which has assumed so many names, and which now, by a strange hurricane of circumstances, has glued

[1] Earle (1796–1849), a Philadelphia lawyer and editor, had been the Liberty party's vice-presidential candidate in 1840.

157

together with it so many heterogeneous materials, (none of them in a state of *fusion*) under the name of the Liberty Party, will I think separate from, and oppose, old organized anti-slavery on two important questions; whenever those questions become prominent. New Org. under whatever name it may then bear, will come out in favor of compensation to the masters; and I think also, in favor of helping the slaves by physical force. vide the Williamsburg Resolutions. If I am not mistaken, this spirit will develope itself more and more.

I come to these conclusions, from the following general premises. It is the maxim of politics that ends may be brought about by means of the greatest present expediency; therefore whenever compromise of principle will secure great accession of numbers, compromise will [be] made. This will be the case with regard to the question of compensation. Any given principle brings forth offspring with features resembling its own; therefore, I think there will be a tendency to appeal to military power, ultimately. Politics and war both arise from want of faith in spiritual weapons; both start with the idea that the outward can *compel* the inward; both seek to co-erce and restrain rather than to regenerate; hence in emergencies, their choice of weapons will be similar. You may name this non-resistance, if you choose; but the deductions are philosophic, and the premises are universal principles of our nature. I saw these principles, and argued from them, years and years before I ever heard, or thought, of non-resistance.

I thank the Philadelphia friends very cordially, for their many invitations to visit them. Few things would give me greater pleasure; for my recollections of that city are most agreeable. But I am continually hurried by the pressure of editorial duties, and others in connection with personal economy, family relations, &c. I live in a perpetual whirl, which is to me most unpleasant. As for the state meeting, *that* was altogether out of my line. I never speak, and am therefore of no use in such a place; and as a matter of inclination, I am always reluctant to go to public meetings. I was peculiarly averse to coming to the Penn. meeting; because, as editor of the Standard, I must be talked about; and my presence might fetter freedom.

I should be much grieved to have any portion of this letter published; so please not to give any copy, of any part of it, to anybody. My most affectionate and grateful remembrances of James Mott and his family, and believe me

Your friend most truly, L. M. Child.

My heart's best offering to that excellent old couple, Robert and Esther Moore.[2]

ALS; Lydia Maria Child Papers, Anti-Slavery Collection, Cornell University (microfiche 13/328).

---

[2] Robert Moore (ca. 1763–1844), a physician, and his wife, Esther (ca. 1774–1854), both belonged to the Society of Friends in Philadelphia and were active in the antislavery movement.

Abolitionist criticism of American slavery policy intensified suddenly on 24 January 1842. On that day, Congressman John Quincy Adams presented a petition from Haverhill, Massachusetts, calling for the dissolution of the Union in protest of the gag rules against discussion of slavery. A Southern caucus led by Thomas F. Marshall of Kentucky tried to have Adams censured and expelled. After nearly two weeks of furious debate, the resolution of censure was tabled in return for Adams's dropping the call for dissolution. Adams continued opposing the gag rule, which was finally lifted in December 1844.

The call for dissolution of the Union was taken up by William Lloyd Garrison, and on 24 February 1842 Child published an editorial supporting disunion.

To Ellis Gray Loring

N. York Feb. 15th 1842

Dear Friend,

Many thanks even for the few lines you sent. "I thank my God for *any* remembrance of you." I wish I could see you. I greatly *need* to talk with you. The feeling grows stronger and stronger with me that I am not the person to uphold the Standard at this crisis. I do not allude to my own weariness and utter distaste for the work, but to the bearings on the *cause*. I think the friends would be better satisfied with another hand at the helm in this political storm. Rogers I know has never liked the Standard since I had it; Garrison's want of cordiality is obvious enough; and Abby Kelly is out of sorts with it. She highly disapproves my conciliatory tone toward the Free-Will Baptists of R. Island; yet sure I am, that I pursued a Christian course; though the organ of that sect treats my concessions with contemptuous silence, and goes on as ever railing about the false charges brought against them.[1] It is a 3d party paper; and those papers, almost without exception, will not take even a paragraph from the Standard, if they can help it; or in any way recognize its existence. I take from them whenever I find anything good.

Bolles of Connecticut has dropped his paper; giving as a reason that "a paper nobody quarrels with, cannot be doing any good."[2] He thinks even Garrison does not quite tow the mark, and that Rogers is the only *real* abolitionist. For my own part, I am grievously tried with Abby Kelly's resolutions, and Rogers's editorials.[3] It seems as if the devil helped her to drive away all the tender-spirited

[1] The *Standard*, on 23 Dec. 1841, had run a letter from Abby Kelley charging the Free-Will Baptists in Rhode Island with being proslavery. Kelley later apologized for the accusation (*Standard*, 13 Jan. 1842), and a week later Child wrote that she regretted not having deleted that portion of Kelley's letter.

[2] William Bolles (1800–60) was an abolitionist in New London, Conn.

[3] On 30 Dec. 1841, the *Standard* published Abby Kelley's account of a Rhode Island convention resolution stating that "every person who is not an out-spoken and out-acting abolitionist . . . is a dangerous member of the community." N. P. Rogers had returned in 1841 to editing the *Herald of Freedom* in Concord, N.H.

and judicious from our ranks; and helped him to make precisely the admissions, and state precisely the premises that the enemy would wish him to do. How pitifully one-sided and unphilosophical he *is*! Yet is he honest and true, and as such must be borne with. But in view of all these things I am thinking, I am thinking some person can be found for this post fitter than I am, and that will give better satisfaction. Who can you think of?

There are two things I wish might be done in Boston. I suppose you have seen that the Washington Correspondent of the N. York American thinks your Faneiul Hall Resolutions were more calculated to do harm than good. The fact is, I think they were disappointed at Washington, because they had received the idea that the meeting was to be a general gathering of *citizens*, to sustain J. Q. Adams; not an *abolition* meeting. Cannot such a meeting be got up to pass a vote of thanks to the brave old man?

The other thing is to have Dr. Channing write a letter to Marshall of K'y.

The Congressional, and the pressure of all sorts of speeches, public meetings &c has plagued me dreadfully. I have tried my best to attend to them as well as a man; but after all, it is not my work.

For two weeks I have been trying to get in Gerrit Smith's Address to the Slaves; which in some respects I like, and in others do not like. You need not be at all concerned about my barking in answer to Le Roy Sunderland, Isaac Knapp, or any other cur.[4] It is altogether contrary to my system.   I do not fear dear Louisa's third partyism much; should she get involved in it, her gentle spirit would soon retire in disgust. Its doings make me, for the first time, deliberately sorry that I ever had anything to do with anti-slavery associations; and it has given me a warning I shall not forget with regard to all other associations; unless indeed it be Geo. Ripley's.

. . .

ALS; Manuscript Division, New York Public Library (microfiche 13/333).

To Francis Shaw

New York Feb. 15th 1842.

Dear Friend,

. . .

You seek to draw me into a non-resistance argument; and if I answer, pray bear in mind that it is of your own seeking. I have never read arguments on the

[4] Gerrit Smith's article in the *Standard*, 24 Feb. 1842, called on slaves to do whatever was required in order to flee, including steal. Child noted that the object of antislavery work was to "destroy the system," not encourage escape or stealing; such encouragement, she said, would only inflame the slaveholders. La Roy Sunderland (1804–85) edited *Zion's Watchman* at this time. Isaac Knapp had owned a half interest in *The Liberator* until 1840. In Dec. 1841 he publicly accused Garrison of defrauding him and announced that he would publish the "true" *Liberator*. Only one issue of *Knapp's Liberator*, 8 Jan. 1842, was printed.

subject, in my life. I seldom see anything from professed non-resistants that is not distasteful to me; unless indeed it be Edmund Quincy's articles, and now and then something from C. K. Whipple.[1] The idea has grown up spontaneously and gradually in my mind, like a flower. That it's application in all departments of life, social and civil, is the *only* cure for a disordered world is very clear to me. It is in fact *the* idea which distinguishes the gospel of Christ from all other wise and philosophic utterance; it is this which makes it *holy*.

You admit my argument that it is better to lay down your own life than to take another's, when the question is solely between him and yourself; but you say you would feel justified in taking his life, if it stood in the way of the spiritual and moral, as well as physical, welfare of a whole race; you consider your own life as a breath, and another's is no more.

This statement of yours gives rise to several reflections in my mind. In the first place, your vision seems to me somewhat obscured by the old entanglement between man's *social* responsibility, and his *individual* responsibility. It is this which keeps many a timid slaveholder from acting individually right, lest he should do injury in his social position. It is this very idea, looked at in a religious light, which gives rise to the question ought the church (spiritually) to come out from the world, and live above it? Or will she do more good by conforming in some degree to the world?

Now my own opinion is that the perfection of the *individual* is the sure way to regenerate the *mass*. I am to obey my highest instincts; and in no other way can I possibly do so much to bring discordant social relations into harmony. "If *I* am lifted up, I will draw *all* men unto me."

In the next place, I would remind you that you lay down *your* life to *sustain* a principle; but when you *take* life you *violate* a principle. In the third place, to attempt a cure of *spiritual* evils, by taking *material* life, is a violation of the order of the universe. The *physical* cannot cure the *spirit*. It is like the old Bishops, who advised George Fox to drink beer to allay his *spiritual* thirst. You may have killed the outward man, but you have not destroyed the principle of which he was the active agent. The spirit which made *him* dangerous is still abroad in this world; and his unregenerated soul in another world is imparting the same bad influence. Had you by love cured his *soul*, then had you indeed killed that which made him dangerous to society.

In the fourth place, what influence has *your act* of killing that sinner's body, on the spiritual and moral condition of society? Observe with a quiet, unprejudiced eye the state of popular feeling about the time of an execution; then tell me whether the angel or the devil in man is most aroused. Tell me whether prosecuting attorneys, constables, &c bear any resemblance whatever to your ideal of the disciples of Christ. If they do not, what has your spirit in common with them? and should it not dwell altogether apart? Let them try to "cast out devils by

---

[1] Both Quincy and Charles King Whipple (1808–1900) were active in the New England Non-Resistance Society and wrote for its paper, the *Non-Resistant*.

Beelzebub the prince of devils." The Master has said, "If I be lifted up, I will draw all men unto me." Let the world take care of its balance of evils, according to its own wisdom; if the Christian obeys the highest wisdom, there will be no evils to balance.

Give my best love to Sarah, with thanks for her refreshing letter, and tasteful little memorial of her visit to the Fair.   Yrs with true affection, L. M. C.

What would you think of the *safety* of the pecuniary investment of $2000 in Geo. Ripley's establishment?[2] I mean the person's labor put in likewise.

ALS; Houghton Library, Harvard University (microfiche 13/334).

Child's letters to Ellis Gray Loring trace her growing displeasure with her position at the *Standard*.

To Ellis Gray Loring

N. York Feb. 28th 1842.

Dear Friend,

. . .

I will write no more desponding letters; at least, I resolve not to, let me feel as I may. The flood of consoling epistles that came made me quite ashamed. Maria Chapman, in the midst of her hurry and anxiety, though she had already written to say farewell; Wendell Phillips, in the queerest strain of banter; John King, sui generis; Henrietta Sargent in stern reproof; E. G. Loring in a few calm quieting words; and Mrs. Follen, most encouraging. I did feel ashamed, when I reflect how much I had to comfort and sustain me, and how much misery and desolation of all sorts there was around me. I was wrong; and will complain no more. I will just edit the paper conscientiously, till the way opens plainly for me to leave it, and trouble nobody with my misgivings.

Just in the way of business, I will, however, state that the influences here are not calculated to make one strong and cheerful, as they are in Massachusetts. We (I mean the Committee) see by too plain indications that there is not much confidence in us, either in our judgment or efficiency. Else, why are friends so tardy in getting us out of embarrassment? I am clear, and so is James S. Gibbons that the office here ought to close, and the stock be sold to pay debts, rather than go on so another year. I do not speak personally; for my salary is paid up to two months; and if it were not, I would not speak for myself. But it is dreadful to drag along so, and be dunned by the workmen and others. I shall not take any of the $500, for the following reasons. Mr. Doughty, who lent us $200 without interest, some time ago, now is driven for money. $137 is due for our rent. $100 is due

2 Brook Farm.

to our printers, who have families, and must have it. $150 of arrears is due to N. P. Rogers, and he is suffering for it. $150 more is due to Wm C. Rogers, arrears for most faithful services; and he is in great need of it.

The friends who expect efficient action at our hands, should bear in mind that the *old* executive Committee here had never less than four people who gave their *whole* time to the work of the office, beside three or four clerks to help them; all well paid, and therefore willing to give their *whole* time and attention. Some were most lavishly paid. $18000, in one year, divided between 4 persons— Birney, Stanton, Benedict, the fourth I forget.[1]   In Mass. you are out of debt, and have two smart agents, to give their *whole* attention to the business of the office; therefore, you can have everything attended to, and work with a strong heart. *We* have no efficient person to give their *whole* time to business, because we have no means whereby to secure such services. Isaac T. Hopper is very attentive, and does good work in the office, in many ways; but he is old, and has a very moderate salary. James S. Gibbons has his own business to attend to, which takes nearly all his time. Yet he has worked harder than any agent we have in the field, and taken more responsibility than any other man in the cause, be he who he may. Instead of receiving a cent, he has expended liberally, and would do and risk more, if it were not for justice to his family.   Mrs. Chapman wrote me that the Mass. Society would probably send $1000. We had expected something from the Fair; especially as the Irish Friends stipulated that *their* donations should be given to the *American* Society; but we concluded that this donation was to be included in the $1000. Collins writes that we must employ forty-dozen agents, and drive business ahead; but adds we must not rely on Massachusetts.[2] On what then are we to rely. Massachusetts established the Standard. It is in a great measure her own work. I do not say she is bound to support it; but I say unless she does, it ought to stop, and the office be shut up. If we were once out of debt, we could go on nicely, I think; if we could not, we ought to stop. But you must remember that ever since the division, we have had a mill-stone of debts about our necks. As for agents, with few exceptions, they eat up all they get, and so are no *pecuniary* help, though they do do good to the cause. I strongly oppose hiring more, for fear of increasing debt, and so does J. S. G.

In great haste,
Yrs. Most affectionately,
L. M. C.

ALS; Manuscript Division, New York Public Library (microfiche 13/340).

[1] S. W. Benedict, like the others, became a political abolitionist in 1840.
[2] John A. Collins was then general agent of the Massachusetts Anti-Slavery Society.

To Ellis Gray Loring

New York March 9'th. 1842

Dear Friend,

Many thanks for your kind letter. You would be amply paid for the trouble of writing, if you knew how much good it did me. I *thought* you would like the last Standard. I cannot manage the paper at all as I would. Puplic [*sic*] documents of one kind or another crowd upon me so, and since the union with the Freeman I am flooded with communications, mostly of an ordinary character.[1] Entre *nous*, almost every communication I put in is re-written entirely by me, for the sake of condensation. I had rather write three editorials than one such job; and after I have done all, they are not worth much. But they are sent by individuals and societies interested in the cause, and I fear to injure the interests of the cause and the paper by omission. I have an increasingly uncomfortable sense of being fettered by being the organ of a *Society*. I am not certain whether one *can* fill such a position without injury to his own soul. At all events, it injures mine. The Philistines bind me with cords. Have not *societies* done about all they *can* do for this cause? Do not understand me as having changed my views with regard to organizations. I have the same faith in the efficiency of combined action that I ever had; but I see many signs that make me think it has nearly *done* its work on this subject. One sign is that there is now so little vitality in our associations; they are an appearance rather than a reality; and of this, there never comes a regenerating power. Another sign is, that the whole community are now at work, in one way or another, to keep the ball in motion; and they can be kept at it to the end, by an occasional nudge from you and me &c, even to the end. Should you do any the less, if you were not a member of any society? I should not.

How wonderfully strong the N.Y. American comes out! Who *is* the Washington Correspondent? My suspicions fall on Theodore Weld.[2] He is evidently an out and out abolitionist; and I believe Theodore is a whig. I knew of his secret mission to Washington to work with Giddings[,] Slade &c before he went; but he allowed me to be told only on condition of perfect secresy; therefore I made no allusion to it, in my letters.[3]   He promised to correspond with the Standard; but has since pleaded constant hurry as an excuse. You ask what this means? I will tell you my own crude thoughts, which may or may not have foundation. Take them for what they are worth. Giddings, Slade, &c are abolitionists at heart, but

---

[1] The *Pennsylvania Freeman* had suspended publication in Dec. 1841; its subscription list was transferred to the *Standard*.

[2] Child had reprinted an article by the *New-York American*'s Washington correspondent in the *Standard* of 24 Feb. 1842, about the tabling of a petition on behalf of black seamen. In fact, the correspondent for the *American* was not Weld but David Bacon (1813–66), a U.S. physician who had served in Liberia.

[3] Joshua Reed Giddings (1795–1864) was an Ohio lawyer and one of abolition's staunchest spokesmen in Congress, where he served from 1838 to 1859. William Slade (1786–1859) was a Vermont lawyer and antislavery Whig representative in Congress, 1831–43.

strongly attached to the principles of their political party. They cannot co-operate with Leavitt & Co; because they are seeking to destroy the old parties. They *can* co-operate with Weld, who is about as much opposed to 3d party as I am. During the whole winter, Weld has been sending to J. S. Gibbons for documents facts &c for *their* use. Some with a view to sustaining J. Q. Adams's defence, others about Texas &c.[4]

You will say, "A fig for *her* political sagacity"! Nevertheless I will venture to suggest a crotchet that has entered my brain. I *think* a portion of the whigs are about forming themselves into a party *distinctly on abolition grounds;* (being careful, of course, not to identify themselves with the old fanatics) Vide, the present position of the N.Y. American! I think there are political reasons, which would suggest such a move, apart from any conscientious considerations in the minds of such individuals as Giddings &c. 1'st the Loco focoes have monopolized the *Southern* influence; nobody can hope to outbid them in *that* game.[5] 2d There is obviously enough a strong under-current of feeling opposed to slavery daily increasing, and already strong enough to be of importance to the party that chooses to throw itself on its tide. 3d The "Liberty Party," not only compels men to renounce *all* their ⟨other⟩ political predilections, except opposition to slavery; but it is in grain loco-foco. Leavitt, Wright, Goodell, Jackson, Smith[,] Stewart, are democrats, in the technical sense;[6] and the papers of that party throughout the country betray a decided lurch toward that side; therefore, as a *general* thing, abolition whigs, that have one eye open, are shy of it; and the question naturally occurs, shall we let them use up all the abolition material of the country, or shall *we* come in at turn of tide, and let *our* vessel ride on the swell?   I have said my say—I don't know whether it ever entered another head than my own; but you need'nt laugh.   I like your views about the Union much. They give a form to my own undefined feelings. With regard to the letter to Everett, Dr Channing is the man! the *very* man—made on purpose.[7]   I have never intended to endorse Fourier's system. But is he unphilosophical in saying that *every* passion and emotion of the human heart was made to be exercised in a healthy sphere, and no one made to be stifled? In the Swedenborgian heaven there is every thought and affection that there is in hell,—only they are all turned *right side up;* and this has always seemed to me beautiful. I have never liked the term "non-resistance," for I have felt that the instinct for fighting was not wrong; that it only needed to

[4] Child refers to the attempted censure of Adams for submitting the disunion petition.
[5] The Locofocos in 1840 had joined with states'-rights Southerners to pass an independent treasury bill over strong Whig opposition. That bill, repealed in 1841, would have established federal depositories to replace the use of state banks and private businesses in holding federal funds.
[6] Joshua Leavitt, Elizur Wright, Jr., William Goodell, James C. Jackson, Gerritt Smith, and Alvan Stewart were all Liberty party members; Goodell (1792–1878) was an early associate of Garrison and later editor of the *Friend of Man* in Utica, N.Y., and Stewart (1790–1849) was a lawyer in Utica.
[7] The nature of the proposed letter is not known; Edward Everett (1794–1865) was then ambassador to Great Britain.

be *rightly directed*. Resist we ought, and that with all our might. The irrationality lies in stabbing and strangling *bodies* to cure *souls*. We fight spiritual evils with material weapons, to which they are entirely impassive. Military *music* will last always. It is the voice of active resistance to evil. I think Fourier means that society ought to be so constructed that every passion will be excited to healthy action on suitable objects; that the activity which now produces so much evil, should not be lost, but simply changed in its direction. I wish you would read this part of my letter to Dr. Channing, and tell me what he says. This question of communities is interesting my mind very much at this time.   I have not been to hear Emerson; though Mrs. Shaw wished to give me a ticket, and Edmund Benzon, a young German in whose company I find great delight, has been *determined* that I should go with him, and has followed me up night after night.[8] Your account of Emerson's lectures in Boston put me out of sorts with him somewhat; and I am so terribly hurried, that I find it difficult even to get time to comb my hair. Besides which I must acknowledge an increasing aversion to going at all into public, or seeing anybody but old and beloved friends. I shrink into my shell more and more. I do hope I shall see you at the Anniversary, and have a chance to have a long confidential talk. I have many things to say. . . .

I had written to Judge Jay, before the receipt of your letter, begging an article from his pen on the late decision of the Supreme Court.[9] The judge appears quite friendly, and often steps into the office. The Notes on 3d Party were from his pen; written while he was member of the Ex. Com, and lately sent to me. I wish I could hear John Dwight. Mrs. Shaw tells me he is going to join the Community at Roxbury. Ripley has written me an urgent letter to join; but I am drawn two ways.

. . .

AL; Manuscript Division, New York Public Library (microfiche 13/345).

To Ellis Gray Loring

N. York March 22d [1842]

Dear Friend,

I write in haste, a few words merely on business. An editorial article in a late Liberator, on Third Party, extracted from the 11'th Report of the Mass. Society, contains a sentence which I am *very* earnest to have altered, if the Report has not yet come out of the press.

[8] Edmund Benzon (d. 1873), born in Germany, was at this time a young businessman in New York City. While not active as an abolitionist, he gave financial aid to the cause.
[9] The Supreme Court decision Child refers to is *Prigg* v. *Pennsylvania*, in which the Court held that the execution of fugitive slave laws was under federal rather than state power. Consequently, some Northern states passed "personal liberty" laws forbidding state officials to help federal authorities seize and remove fugitive slaves. Judge William Jay's article appeared in the *Standard* on 10 Mar. 1842.

I refer to the question, "Are the editors of the Liberator, the Herald of Freedom, and the Anti Slavery Standard, less efficient agents in the cause, because their editors cannot vote?"

In the first place, it is unjust and impolitic to rank the Standard with Non Resistance papers. I have been particularly careful that it should *not* be so. My life is already fretted out of me, by inquiries whether I endorse Rogers's mad proceedings; and by long, argumentative communications, taking it for granted that I do endorse them; and behold the Mass. Society steps forth, and officially places Rogers and I in the same category! While in point of fact, I consider the Herald of Freedom as doing incalculable mischief to our cause.

Moreover, there is *one* of the editors of the Standard who believes in the elective franchise, and is very fond of using it. It is not very delicate or respectful, to leave him out of the account. My peculiar situation is sufficiently disagreeable to me, without adding anything which seems like giving me the superiority over my gifted and beloved husband.

Pray have the sentence changed, if *possible*.

You need not trouble yourself about Ripley's Community. I have not the slightest thought of joining it. I have had quite enough of hard work without any pay, in the course of my life.

I do want to see you mightily to talk over my plans. If you hear of anything, in *any* part of the world, which seems like a good opening for us, dont let the desire to keep me in the anti slavery treadmill prevent your giving the information. But let this request be strictly between ourselves.

Heart's love to Louise and Anna.

Yrs most affectionately & gratefully,
L.M.C.

P.S. The Washington Correspondent of the N.Y. American is David Bacon, formerly on the coast of Africa, in the Colonization service, but sick of that scheme now.

Don't read to anybody, what I say about the Herald of Freedom. You and I jump in judgment. The extract from your letter about the Union was in type before your next letter came.

ALS; Manuscript Division, New York Public Library (microfiche 14/357).

In January 1842, Charles Lenox Remond (1810–73), a black abolitionist from Salem, Massachusetts, brought back from Ireland a document signed by the patriot Daniel O'Connell and sixty thousand other Irish citizens. Known as the Irish Address, it petitioned Irish Americans to support the antislavery movement and treat blacks as equals. In response, the Catholic archbishop of New York, John Hughes, signified his antiabolitionism by doubting the authenticity of the petition. An April 1842 resolution from the Hibernian Anti-Slavery Society in

Dublin affirmed that the petition was genuine, but abolitionist efforts among the American Irish were nevertheless unsuccessful. The connection between Garrisonian abolitionists and Irish advocates of independence from England was a long-standing and mutually influential one.

To Ellis Gray Loring

N. York April 6th [1842]

Dearest Friend,

I meant to have written a good long letter this week, but again must limit myself to a few words on business, in haste.

Judge Jay wishes to have some suitable, responsible, influential persons write to O'Connell, enclosing a copy of Bishop Hughes Letter; and requesting him to certify the authenticity of his signature to the Irish Address, attested by the city authorities of Dublin; or in any other way to make assurance doubly sure. It would probably be well, too, to state that no trickery was used to obtain it from him. Judge Jay considers some step of this kind very necessary, and that it ought to be done in Boston. I want you to ask Garrison (and *soon*) to take my name off the Call for the World's Convention; on the ground that I feel no call whatever to the work, and probably should not attend such a Convention, if I were in Boston at the time. I intended to have taken it off when I first saw it appended, but neglected it.

I am sorry they are going to send H. C. Wright to England.[1] He appears to me as little calculated to do good, as almost any person ⟨I⟩ they could select. However, let everybody work in their own way.

I gave offence by refusing to publish "Liberty Party" notices; and now I suppose I shall give offence in another quarter by refusing to publish the Non Resistance Resolutions. I cannot help it. It seemed to me that impartiality required such a course. I have no pleasure in the paper since it united with the Freeman. It was always drudgery; and now it is *unmitigated* drudgery. Such a set of fussy, ignorant old women as the Pennsylvania abolitionists are, I never sa[w.] One complaining that I dont put in editorial enough!! Another that I write about subjects not strictly anti-slavery; another that I am intolerant to "Liberty Party"; another that I neglect non-resistance and women's rights; another that I don't quote more from Garrison and Rogers—&c &c. and *all* sending me thousands of the dullest communications, bad grammar, and detestable spelling. *Good* communications I rarely get; because *Boston* don't send me any. The Washington letter is from Gates.[2]

[1] Henry Clarke Wright (1797–1870), formerly an agent for the American Anti-Slavery Society, was an active nonresistant.
[2] Seth Merrill Gates (1800–77) was an abolitionist congressman from New York State.

Best, best love to dear Louisa, and tell her I shall not come to Boston, unless there is *great* emergency, for a year to come.   Yrs Most truly,

L.M.C.

ALS; Manuscript Division, New York Public Library (microfiche 14/358).

To Maria (Weston) Chapman

New York, April 26th. [1842]

Dear Friend,

. . .

In your parting letter, you seemed to forebode some new division among us; and Caroline's letter seems to imply some such thought in her own mind. Rest you easy. No division will ever come through *my* agency. It is my earnest wish to have all true friends of the slave stand in as close a phalanx as possible. I am indeed fretted, at times, with Rogers's remarkable want of judgment; for it does seem as if the Evil-one helped him to say just the very things, and in the very way, our opponents want him to. But these things can in no degree alter my high respect for his moral worth, and my confidence in his unchangeable truth. I shall be glad when he leaves off palavering that hypocritical whiffler and traitor, J. C. Jackson. That man is the worst enemy old organization has. He uses his old friendships for the most insidious party purposes; that is, according to *my* belief. He is all the time spreading honey-drops on his web, and Garrison and Rogers catch them up, and make their best bow to him. I am *glad* our friends got insulted at the Albany Convention.[1] The next time they are gulled into co-operation with Third Party, I hope they will get kicked bodily, as well as spiritually. I am weary of seeing the honest and the true cajoled by the artful and the treacherous. Why on earth can't they let them alone? neither giving them notoriety by invective, nor countenance by standing on the same platform. I felt insulted to be invited to the Massachusetts Anniversary together with J. C. Jackson; yet you in that quarter have the same opportunities to judge of his moral obliquities that I have. I do not think James is a *worse* man than many others, who are opposed to the old organization; but I do think his peculiar position, as the professed friend of both sides, gives him peculiar facilities for doing mischief; facilities, which he by no means omits to use.

I hope we shall have a good, inspiriting anniversary. But above all things, I hope there will be no attempt to call the Irish together. In the first place, their moral and intellectual state is such, that they might about as well attempt to call the *dogs* together for any purpose of reform; and in the next place the present crisis is peculiarly unfavorable. The state of excitement on the Catholic School Question is intense; and war is liable at any moment to break out between the

[1] The Liberty party held a convention in Albany, N.Y., on 20–21 Apr. 1842; the nature of the insult is not known.

Catholic and Protestant Irish.[2] Bishop Hughes, as you know, has come out against abolition; and this would bring us into the dance at once. We have already had one frightful mob, and a battle between the contending factions; and everybody expects a worse one, election week. I should have no objection to running this risk, if any *good* were likely to result from it. But this system of exciting the ignorant Irish by the use of O'Connell's name, strikes me as work that peculiarly belongs to the Third Party. Both the tools and the materials belong to *them*. If the Address has *any* effect on that excitable population, it will be merely to drive them to the polls to vote for third party, or to the hotels to knock down slave-holders; and this will send the opposite faction to knock down abolitionists; for voting and beating are all the *moral* agencies they have any idea of. For my part, I want no such materials for our cause.

You must excuse me for burning the sonnets from Ireland, which you had the kindness to copy for the Standard. I try not to be over-fastidious in my literary taste, as you may well imagine by some things I consent to put in the paper; but really those were *too* execrable. They should be sent to Geo. Bourne, or any-body else that likes "devil's broth, with sulphur fixins," as John King says.[3]   I thought it not unlikely that some in Massachusetts might think I did wrong in declining to publish the non-resistance resolutions. I can only say that the very *existence* of the Standard depends on its not being identified with the Non Resistance movement. The only way it can be made to sustain itself, is as an acceptable family newspaper. It is obvious enough that *we* cannot rely on extraneous support. It must either support itself, or stop.

I rejoice to hear of Mr. Chapman's amended health. I *do* hope we shall see you both at the anniversary. I believe James Gibbons will go crazy, if you don't come. I am glad Caroline & Anna are coming.

Remember me with most affectionate respect to the excellent family in Chauncy Place; and give sincere love to your sunny troop of sisters.

Do come to the anniversary.

Yrs truly, L. M. Child.

Dont forget a most kind and respectful remembrance to your good husband.

ALS; Anti-Slavery Collection, Rare Books and Manuscripts, Boston Public Library (microfiche 14/365).

In *The Liberator*, 22 April 1842, Garrison requested the American Anti-Slavery Society to take up dissolution of the Union at its May meeting in New York.

[2] See Child's explanation of the school question in her letter of 24 Nov. 1841, p. 152.
[3] George Bourne (1780–1845), English-born minister and member of the American Anti-Slavery Society, was vindictively anti-Catholic. He had helped write the popular but defamatory *Awful Disclosures of Maria Monk . . . in the Hotel Dieu Nunnery of Montreal* (New York, 1836).

Given the tense political atmosphere in the city, Child feared mob action if Garrison's request were heeded. She published a notice in the city press that this request did not mean that the American Anti-Slavery Society had already committed itself to disunion. Garrison was outraged at this "Extraordinary Disclaimer," as he called it, even though he finally decided not to attend the meeting.

To Wendell Phillips

New York May 3d 1842

Dear Friend,

I must have seemed ungrateful for your kindness, in writing me a cheering letter, when I had the perversity to complain of my editorial treadmill; but I was *not* ungrateful. I felt it deeply, and it did me much good. I did not suppose any mortal would see or hear of my letter, but Ellis and Louisa; and I am in the habit of laying open my soul to them in *all* its moods, reasonable and unreasonable. I seldom record such a state of feeling; for I acknowledge that we have no right to intrude our sadness upon others.

As for the Standard, I dislike the charge of it extremely; but I am usually in a very quiet state about it—content to do the best I can, and leave it in better hands as soon as possible. I am by no means "so unreasonable as to expect Dr. Channing and N. P. Rogers to eat with equal satisfaction from the same dish." My course has been dictated by the deliberate conviction that we greatly needed *one* paper that would not disgust or repel minds slightly acquainted with our principles. Whether the National organ ought to be such a paper is another question. Many of our friends think it ought; and I should like right well to have them a majority; for I feel an increasing aversion to being the organ of *any* Society. As for changing my course, that is out of the question. Taste, principle, and philosophy would alike forbid me to prepare such hyena soup with brimstone seasoning, as suits many of our friends. And I never have believed that such dishes were a benefit to our cause; Mrs. Chapman to the contrary notwithstanding. Anti slavery might have made ten times the progress it has, if plain-speaking had been mixed with kindness, and zeal tempered with discretion. With non-resistance it is faring even worse than with anti-slavery. Think of Henry C. Wright in *such* a cause! A wild boar rooting among pearls. However, I possess my soul in patience, and laughing call to mind one of Mrs. Chapman's significant sayings: "The Lord does his work by many instruments that *I* would not touch with a pair of tongs."

Perhaps the Circular of the Committee here may surprise you. It seemed necessary for the freedom of *our* opinion, and is I trust so worded as not to clash with any of *yours*. We would not have done it merely to avoid a mob, with which all appearances combined to threaten us; but most of us would feel obliged to withdraw from the American Society, if it took any direct *society* action for the dissolution of the Union. We do not understand as yet what are the *means* proposed to dissolve the Union; they may be of a character in which we could not conscientiously participate, though we should not feel called upon to oppose others, who could. The turning-point with us, is not whether it is any harm to dissolve the union; but whether the *means* employed will strictly come within *moral influence*. I confess I do not at present see how they can; perhaps I may see plainer, after hearing other minds discuss it. Garrison's unguarded editorial seemed to hand us all over to a line of policy, which we had had no time to examine. If precisely the same ideas had been *worded* a little differently, they could not have been made such effectual use of by our enemies. The mob-fever has been rising, since that document was transferred to our city papers. The permission to use Broadway Tabernacle has been partially recalled; but I rather think we shall have it, if the mayor will promise to keep a look-out in that quarter. My present impression is that there will be no popular violence; but I think there would have been, had we not inserted our circular in the daily papers. As it is, I shall remove my few valuables to a place of safety. I was extremely pleased with Remond, whom I saw the other day for the first time. He is the first colored person I have met, who seemed to be altogether such an one as I would have him. He carries ballast enough for his sails; and that is unusual.

The letter of introduction for your friend I never sent. Can you pardon this? It was hard for me to refuse anything you asked, I assure you. Had he not been a *resident* in N. York, I certainly should have complied with your request. But the fact is, I live in a continual hurry; and the only two visiting acquaintance I have, often incommode me, though I like them particularly well. In the first place, it is a greater labor for me to edit the paper, than it would be for a man; because my previous habits unfit me for it. Then I have to wash, iron, mend, and sweep my room; all of which the privileged men-editors avoid. The fact is, I can scarcely snatch an hour for exercise absolutely necessary to the preservation of my health. This must be my excuse for declining to make acquaintance.

I am intending to take a run to Northampton for three or four weeks, as soon as the anniversary is over. Could you not come and take charge of the Standard, meantime?[1] It would be a great relief to my mind, if I could leave it in good hands. James S. Gibbons would gladly do his best (which is *very* good) but he is so immersed in business, that he cannot. I *do* wish you could. If Mrs. Phillips could come with you, she would find beautiful places of sojourn about N. York. Staten Island, for instance. If you came alone, I think you could find very agreeable and comfortable quarters with J. S. Gibbons. I would leave things so arranged as to make you as little trouble as possible. When you come to anniversary, we will talk about it. In fact, I did not mean to have mentioned it till then; but I thought it would perhaps be well to have time to think upon the propo-

[1] Phillips did not take charge of the paper, and Child did not go to Northampton.

sition. I think it is important, just at this juncture, that the Standard should be well kept up.

With most affectionate respect & gratitude,
L. M. C.

Remember me most kindly to Mrs. Phillips, and to the excellent family in Chauncey place; especially dear, good Mary.

ALS; Houghton Library, Harvard University (microfiche 96/2535).

To Ellis Gray Loring

New York May 6th 1842

Dear Friend,

I received your letter about an hour ago. I was not surprised at the light in which you viewed the Circular of our Executive Committee; but I think you would have viewed it differently, had you known the excited state of our city, and our extreme difficulty in getting a place to meet in. In consequence of Garrison's article, no place has as yet been obtained, though we have deemed it best to promise indemnification for any losses that might be incurred by a mob.   Your opinion does not in the least depress me, my dear friend; so feel no concern on that score. I have acted according to my own convictions of duty; and in such a case even *your* opinion does not disturb me.

I write thus speedily, not because I am in the least degree excited, but because it may be useful to our Massachusetts friends to know that on one subject my mind is made up, *beyond all power of change*. Under no circumstances whatever, let who will urge it, will I ever go to Philadelphia to reside. I do not utter this as a threat; but that they may have the fact in their possession, to have such influence as it may on their arrangements. Neither should I be willing to edit it at Boston. On many accounts it would be most desirable; but there is a clique there who would continually draw me into much that my reason, taste, and conscience increasingly disapprove. I grow more and more doubtful whether this system of perpetual agitation is the best wisdom, or the truest expediency. For a change in the editorship of the Standard, I am *more* than willing; therefore let arrangements be made as may seem for the best interests of the society, without reference to me.

What *object* there can be in removing to Philadelphia, I cannot imagine. A half dozen milk-and-water abolitionists, who need somebody to tell them whether they belong to the old or the new organization; without energy enough to sustain the tuppenny Freeman, what on earth can they do for the Standard?

The expenses incurred for the American Society you must be aware were to pay *old* arrearages; things were never so promising as they are now, since Birney's regency with $42000 a year to back him. ⟨as now.⟩ We have 4000 subscribers; and they steadily, though not rapidly, increase.

———

That the policy of our Committee is opposite to yours is visible. We are for quiet, persevering appeals to the good sense and good feeling of the judicious and reflecting; you are for agitation.

How this can be reconciled, I know not; and I shall be perfectly content with any arrangement that may be thought desirable. But one thing no argument or persuasion shall ever induce me to do. I never will go to Philadelphia.

The office here has been engaged for another year, and some pecuniary embarrassments would result from a change. We have an admirable set of men, printers and clerk; and *I*, for one, cannot see how things could be bettered by a change. But I repeat that personally I am very willing that any change should be made, which may seem best. I would thank the Society to remember that I am an individual, however, and neither their property, nor their hireling.

I shall be glad to see your mother, for the sake of "auld lang syne," and Friend Hopper will almost jump through the roof; but I am afraid the excited state of things will mar the pleasure of her visit.

Best love to all,

Yrs most affectionately,
L. M. Child.

P.S. I dont *hardly* think we shall have a mob, unless the dissolution of the Union is broached; if it is, we unquestionably shall.

N.B. *Agencies* have been very expensive. Not more than two of the agents have paid their own way. Were it not for this, I think the paper might very nearly support itself now.

ALS; Child Papers, Clements Library, University of Michigan (microfiche 14/372).

Maria (Weston) Chapman endorsed this letter from Child: "Mrs. Child. Evidence the influence of Dr. Channing, William Jay & the Tappans, in alienating her mind from the line of duty."

To Maria (Weston) Chapman

New York May 11th [1842]

I received your vehement letter of the 8th, and smiled at the great fluster you were in, where it seemed to me there was not the slightest occasion. There is no separation whatever between us and the Massachusetts friends, and never has been. There is probably very slight, if any, difference between my views about the Union and those of Wendell Phillips. If we differed at all, it would be merely as to the choice of *means* to dissolve our partnership with guilt; and I cannot tell whether we differ even on that; for I do not know what mode of operation he proposes. You fight with a man of straw altogether, when you suppose I have any unwillingness to have the subject fully and freely discussed in the Standard; provided it is done in a rational and manly style, and not with the cat-hauling of Henry C. Wright. With regard to the Circular of the Committee, you seem to consider that it was intended to rebuke Garrison; when its sole purpose was to correct a *false* impression in the minds of citizens of N. York. Had I not deemed the impression *untrue*, the mobs might have sacked the city, for all my explaining to them. It was imprudent in Garrison to state that the chief business of our anniversary was to dissolve the union; it was incorrect to state *that* as the leading object of operations for the Society for the coming year, *before* the Society had at all deliberated what was best on a subject so very important; it was rash to throw out such an enunciation, without any explanation of the *means to be used* for the purpose. I considered the circular not only proper and justifiable, but absolutely necessary; and my opinion has undergone no iota of change. I should do just the same thing next week, under similar circumstances; you, and Ellis G. Loring, and D. L. Child, to the contrary, notwithstanding. Mr. Child says we must "back out of the mistake as well as we can." I reply, that if other members of the Committee, see their way clear to call it a mistake, I have no objection; but I shall come out with my individual protest.

I thank you for your kind exhortation not to "*cry* off my vexation"; albeit it made me smile. In the first place, I feel no vexation. In the next place, I know not where you received your impression that I was so sensitive to the opinions of others. I care not the turning of a copper, whether the Channingites and the Quakers approve my course, or not; and I care *as* little whether the Chapmanites and the Garrisonites, and the Henry C. Wright-ites, give me a blowing up; I am glad that they should do it, if it is any relief to their minds. Every day that I live, I thank God more and more, that he gives me the power and the will to be an *individual*. I am obliged to the Society for being willing to do my thinking for me, and graciously decide whether I shall live in N. York, Philadelphia or Boston. The *Standard* is theirs to move where they will; *I* am my own; and shall never consent to edit, except where I now am; and under circumstances of the same un-impeded freedom. An agitator I am not, and never will be. I find no fault whatever with those who *are;* nay, I acknowledge their great usefulness. But whenever the Standard becomes the organ of agitation, the adaptation of character to employment will require another editor. For myself, I would like to leave it to-morrow, and accept the propositions of booksellers here; but my attachment to anti slavery principles would lead me to wish to stand by it, so long as the Society were content to have it a good family anti-slavery newspaper, not intended to meet the wants of ultra abolitionists, but to gain the ear of the people at large. I told Abby Kelly this, when she first urged me to take the paper; a step which I most deeply regret ever having been urged into. I do not agree with your proposition that we have "no right to wash our hands of each other." If I thought my connection with the society implied any such fetter, I should leave it tomorrow. I feel at liberty to wash *my* hands of anybody, and anything, I please; though I do not feel at liberty to prescribe to *them*. I have no *disposition* to "wash my hands of Garrison"; for the simple reason that I have the highest respect for his ability, the most perfect confidence in his integrity of purpose, and a general unity with his principles. I am not willing to be mobbed for *him*, though I am for any *principle* that we hold in common. Neither do I ask him to be willing to be mobbed for any and every unguarded or injudicious thing *I* may say or do. You say we "must not *prescribe* to each other." I thought so too, when I read that a set in Massachusetts were going to measure every man's "humanity, patriotism and piety," by their willingness to dissolve the union; but though my individuality rose in resistance, and made me *want* to oppose what I in the main agreed with, I took no exceptions to Garrison therefor; because I knew he wrote in the earnestness of his heart, and with purity of purpose. Nevertheless, for myself, I do not acknowledge his, or any other person's, measurement; albeit they are welcome to measure to their heart's content. I regard it as I do the Presbyterian's measure of my creed; a thing altogether harmless, though somewhat assuming.

You say "if the Standard cannot face up to Judge Noah and Watson Webb, you see no use in its existing."[1] Whenever the Society require such facing up, I hope they will inform me, and I shall send my resignation by return of mail; for I never will hold controversy with any such chaps. You can buy Jimmy Jackson back for a trifle, whenever you want such work done. *I* do not adopt *his* theory of yielding my judgment to a majority. I hope you will not think this letter is in a threatening spirit, originating in an undue estimation of my own importance. No such thing. I merely wish it understood that I am emphatically an *individual;* and that you must choose your agent with reference to the work you want done. Remembering always that I am eager to jump out of the tread-mill.

I regret extremely to hear of Mr. Chapman's feeble health. Give my most affectionate remembrance to him; and to his good father's family.   Yours with undiminished regard,

L. M. C.

ALS; Anti-Slavery Collection, Rare Books and Manuscripts, Boston Public Library (microfiche 14/373).

The anger Child aroused by her handling of Garrison's call for dissolution quieted over the summer. She wrote for the *Standard* of 7 July 1842 an eloquent exposition of moral reform entitled "Talk about Political Party." In the form of a dialogue between a political abolitionist and a Garrisonian, the article indirectly expressed Child's own Garrisonian views. Garrison reprinted the article in *The Liberator* and endorsed her position.

[1] Mordecai Manuel Noah (1785–1851), at this time judge of the New York Court of Sessions, was rabidly antiabolitionist. James Watson Webb (1802–84), also antiabolitionist, was then editor of the *Morning Courier and New York Enquirer.*

She stayed all summer in New York, temporarily troubled with pain in her eyes. When the Lorings invited her to Boston for a visit, she declined: "I feel more and more inclined to slink into an unobserved corner, perform my duties as well and as quietly as I can, and be dismissed from early service as soon as possible."*

Writing to Frank Shaw, she talks once again about William Page.

To Francis Shaw

N. York. Oct. 12. 1842

Dear Friend,

I should be sorry to have you measure my affectionate remembrance by the frequency of my letters. I think of you often, and always with my heart's blessing. But in addition to the necessity of constant writing, and the consequent aversion to the pen, I have all this summer been troubled with a disease of the eye, similar to that which arrested Mr. Dana's studies.[1] I have at times been very sad, lest the disease should prove chronic; but a wash made of sulphate of zinc has been a great help to me. If they continue to improve as they have done, I shall set up a little image of zinc before my eyes, for them to worship.

I write now, especially, to tell you that I think Mr. Page *needs* to go to Europe. His friends here try to laugh him out of the humour, by reminding him that he used to say it was absurd for artists to go abroad. But it is not growth in Art that he needs to seek—it is renovation of mind, and relief from the pressure of external circumstances. He is a proud man; and even his best friends have to guess half of what he suffers. I think I do not mistake, or exaggerate his state of mind. His soul is lacerated, and the atmosphere of N. York keeps the wound open. That woman torments him with threats to bring a new suit. She probably could not recover anything for her support, but she can goad and mortify him.

I wish he were in Rome, with Powers.[2] He says the times are so bad, that he could not get orders for pictures; but I tell him the times are equally bad to get orders for pictures at home. He talks about finishing his great picture first, and going to Europe with the proceeds. But *when* will he finish it, if he is constantly depressed and irritated? Could he not carry the drawing with him, and do it in Rome?

You will observe that *I* did not put into his head the idea of going. He has been from time to time recurring to it, whenever his heart was heavy within him, and mourning that he could not make arrangements to go soon. The difficulty in his mind seems to be the need of staying here a year longer, to make money

---

* 18 Sept. 1842, Manuscript Division, New York Public Library.
[1] Charles Anderson Dana (1819–97), later a reformer and editor of the *New York Sun*, in 1841 dropped out of Harvard College because of eye trouble.
[2] Hiram Powers (1805–73), American sculptor, had established a studio in Florence.

enough to go. I tell him that he will make more money in Rome in the course of the next year, and live cheaper. Am I wrong? I think he will at once be in portraits what Powers is in busts; and with this demand upon his genius, will come fresh spirit to meet it.   Think over this matter will you, and give him such advise as you think best. I have long thought that he greatly needed change of scene.

. . .

What a set they had to bury the old clothes of a living man, there in Federal St. Lathrop, Young, Parkman, and Gannett.[3] The dead burying the dead, with a witness. I like Parker's article on Pierpont mightily.[4] What a cheering thing is a *living* soul.

. . .

ALS; Houghton Library, Harvard University (microfiche 15/414).

The next three letters to Ellis Gray Loring reveal the details of the *Standard*'s and Child's personal financial difficulties and suggest her growing detachment from antislavery concerns. David left Northampton in October 1842, preparing for bankruptcy proceedings. He stayed in New York briefly and then went to Washington, D.C., sending reports to the *Standard* and *Liberator* on political activity there until April 1843.

To Ellis Gray Loring

[29? October 1842]

Dear Friend,

James S. Gibbons returns your money according to the bond; but being agonized with a screaming tooth ache employs me to write.

My dear friend, I hate to trouble you; for you have had expense and trouble enough, Heaven knows; but really, things grow desperate with poor James. He would not tell you himself; but I will tell you that the above check is procured by drawing his own salary a month ahead. He receives but $1500 a year, and has five children to support, beside keeping a caravansery for all travelling abolitionists. In addition to the above check, he has lately paid the printers a hundred dollars of his own money. David has been here a week, and left day before yesterday. He was under *pressing* necessity for $100; and John was obliged to lend it

3 William Ellery Channing died 2 Oct. 1842, and Child refers to his Unitarian colleagues at the funeral.
4 The article by Theodore Parker (1810–60), the antislavery clergyman and Transcendentalist, appeared in the *Dial* of Oct. 1842. It concerned the controversial ministry of John Pierpont, the abolitionist, at the Unitarian Hollis Street Church in Boston.

to the Society out of his own pocket. For myself, I have had only 37½ cts in my purse for 3 months past, and now have but one cent. I have great need of some decent winter clothes, but will go in rags, before I ask poor James to pay up my salary.

I do not say this to *you;* but because the Massachusetts folks ought to know how we are situated. James has calmly and quietly resolved to discontinue the Standard, if relief does not come before the end of the year. Collins promises to bring $400 on the 13 of Nov. Of this, $300 is already due to James and John for money loaned; and the family is just now in peculiarly straitened circumstances. Collins promises to make a great bluster, and take us out of our pecuniary difficulties. James says he will wait a reasonable time, but will not much longer be bamboozled with big talk. I am as calm as a June day, about the Syracuse address, and the Volley opened upon us all round, by the Liberty Party papers.[1] I have long expected this. But I am *not* calm about our unpaid printers, my own unpaid board, poor James's continual vexations, &c. It is not *right* to have things go on so.

David is going to take advantage of the bankrupt act immediately.[2] The farming tools were bought with John's money, and immediately pledged to him a year and half ago, before the bankrupt law was passed. The same of what little furniture we have, which belongs to father. Will these mort[g]ages hold against other creditors. My anti slavery watch, two rings from my husband, various little keepsakes of very trifling value, and some forty or fifty books, *gifts* to me, can I not honestly save them to myself, somehow?

Many, many thanks for Jean Paul. It is one of the most delightful books I ever read. I have had no other copy sent; but am *very* willing to return it to you, after I have made copious extracts. Gunderode I have not seen.[3] Please ask the publisher to send it, and I will send the pay. I would send it now; but I have already borrowed $10 of John, on my own account, and I will not borrow more.

Best love to Louise and Anna and believe me Most affectionately,

Maria.

. . .

ALS; Manuscript Division, New York Public Library (microfiche 15/419).

[1] An article from the *American Citizen,* reprinted in *The Liberator* on 21 Oct. 1842, called the American Anti-Slavery Society as much an obstacle to abolition as the colonization societies.
[2] A new federal bankruptcy law passed in 1841 allowed anyone to declare voluntary bankruptcy and thereby cancel financial obligations. The law was repealed in 1843.
[3] Eliza Buckminster Lee edited and translated the *Life of Jean Paul Frederic Richter* (Boston, 1842). Margaret Fuller translated Bettina Von Arnim's *Gunderode* (Boston, 1842).

To Ellis Gray Loring

Dearest Friend,

. . .

Dickens's book has, of course, brought down upon him all the wrath and patriotism of the penny press.[1] They have already got out out [sic] a caricature of him, dancing at Five Points, with a great, fat splay-footed "nigger." Witty, is it not? I am sorry that Dickens, in the funny parts, yielded so much to his irresistable propensity to caricature; for it casts a suspicion of exaggeration over the whole. John was in a great fever because he could not send you a copy on the road; I believe he would have chartered an express, if he had known where to find you. The hits at slavery almost tickled him out of his wits. As for Page, I don't like him at all. He was vexed with Dickens for saying anything about slavery. He said he had no patience with it in an *Englishman*, who had so much despotism at home. I rowed him up salt river. I told him *he* held his peace, and that was one, among a thousand reasons, why foreigners had *occasion* to cry out. I moreover cautioned him never to let me hear him say another syllable about English factory-children and working-men; (a theme on which he is very apt to enlarge) for that such remarks were unseemly in "a foreigner, who had so much despotism at home." I am sorry he said it; for it is just one of those things that permanently effect my estimate of a man's character. There is something so narrow and clannish about it.

. . .

Osgood came to spend the evening night before last; and I found, to my dismay, that he was going to be in N.Y. all winter.[2] He is such a *spectral* man! One always has the feeling that he *affects* to admire a thing, *affects* to understand, &c. Mrs. Charles Sedgwick was here last week. She tells me that Dr Channing became very much interested in animal magnetism, during his last visit to Lennox, and was utterly astounded at some facts in relation to Mrs. Mowatt, of N.Y. who was there on a visit.[3] He was put into connection with her in some of her magnetic sleeps, and asked her many questions. Mrs. S. told me one anecdote, about which I wish you would ask Augusta. Some famous magnetizer (I believe it was Poyon, whose name I don't know how to spell) exhibited in Salem. The lad whom he magnetized was easily put into a sleep; but from that time appeared not to be influenced in the slightest degree by the magnetizer. Everything he was expected to do, he did *not* do. The audience chuckled over "the humbug," and the magnetizer was in a blue maze. Another subject was tried, with the same result. The audience chuckled more audibly, and the magnetizer was deeply mortified. He said it was contrary to all his former experience, and that he knew not what to

1 *American Notes for General Circulation* (London, 1841; New York, 1842).
2 Child probably refers to Samuel Stillman Osgood (1808–85), a painter.
3 Anna Cora (Ogden) Mowatt (1819–70) was a writer and later an actress.

make of it; whereat the audience laughed. At last, a gentleman expressed a wish to try some experiments on the sleeper with a magnet he had with him. As soon as the magnet was held over the sleeper, all the hairs of his head stood upright toward it, and other parts of his frame were visibly affected. When the magnet was taken away, it was found to have derived a great increase of magnetic power. It was again applied, with similar result; and again there was a great increase of magnetic power. The third time it was applied; but the magnet had now more electricity than the boy; the excess passed into him, and threw him into convulsions. The gentleman then acknowledged that his attention had been for some time drawn to the relation between electricity and animal magnetism; that he had stood close beside the subject being magnetized; every time Dr. P. willed him to do anything, he applied a magnet which he carried in the cuff of his coat; and, as he expected, every time he applied it, all power over the subject was taken away from Dr. P.   This particularly interests *me;* for I have long settled it in my own mind that what *electricity* is in the natural world, the *will* is in the spiritual. At which you, graceless materialist that you are, will jeer.

My best love to Louise and Anna. I did mean to send back Jean Paul; but I don't think I *can;* it is such a perpetual well-spring of refreshment. I want you to write my name and the date of your visit, on a little slip of paper, with any saucy appendage you please, to paste into the volumes. I want *two* slips.

Yrs most affectionately,
L. M. C.

I wish Mrs Chapman would turn magnetizer. I believe *she* could magnetize the Devil; the consequences of which must be right curious, especially on N. Org.

ALS; Manuscript Division, New York Public Library (microfiche 15/422).

To Ellis Gray Loring

New York Nov 23d 1842

Dearest Friend,

I hope you will read the article on Hydropathy in this week's paper, every word of it; and with less of a prejudiced determination to be killed after "the good *old* way," than you usually evince. I always have been amazed at the amount of drugs they have made you pay for. Seriously, though, do give hydropathy a candid consideration. The cures in Northampton are really wonderful.

I received Anna's little letter, for which I am much obliged. It was quite entertaining, though not as full of information about your dear selves as I could have wished. She seems quite taken up with animal magnetism.

You remember, perhaps, that it was generally supposed that four or five rowdies were concerned in the murder of Mary Rogers; and that the testimony of the doctors was strong to that effect?   Well—now for animal magnetism. Some time last Spring, *five or six months ago,* Mr. Page told me that the blind girl, who has been magnetized here, was casually inquired of by some of the family where she staid, "Who murdered Mary Rogers?" In her magnetic sleep she answered, "It was not several men, as folks say. Only one ⟨knew anything about⟩ had anything to do with the murder." When asked if no one else knew anything about it, she replied, "There is a young man over at Hoboken, who helped about the body." She described the complexion and appearance of the murderer, and said he had now gone a great way off. I repeated this to different members of the family, at the time; but thought no more of it, until ten days ago, an old woman died at Hoboken; and on her death-bed confessed that a young physician brought Mary Rogers to her house, to procure premature delivery; that she died under the process; that he was terrified, and pledged her to secresy, and persuaded her son to help him carry the body to the river. The clothes were afterward scattered in the thicket, as a decoy.

This came out, you will observe, *months after* the girl in magnetic sleep gave her answers.

Verily, this being of ours is a mysterious thing.

Cant you stir up Wendell Phillips, and Edmund Quincy, and F Jackson, &c. to do something about the abolition of capital punishment in Massachusetts? O'Sullivan is *very* desirous to have a simultaneous movement in Mass.[,] Penn. and N. York Legislatures.[1] He *ought* to be supported; for he is working like a brave true-hearted fellow. Petitions might be signed at the same time as with the anti-slavery petitions; and it *ought* to be done. We are verily guilty for our indifference in this matter.

If you want copies of O Sullivan's speech to scatter, I will see that you are furnished; I have printed a hundred petitions at my own expense, and have already set 40 people to work with them. Curse the Presbyterians! I'll match'em for energy, *this* session.

If you please, you may send me Wood's note. I can't get along without it. Look at the poetry next paper after this. Harry Franco is Briggs, Page's friend.[2]

Best love to Louise and Anna. Ever Yrs truly, Maria.

ALS; Manuscript Division, New York Public Library (microfiche 15/425).

In September 1841 the body of a New York printer, Samuel Adams, was found packed in salt in a wooden box, waiting shipment to New Orleans. Tried and convicted of Adams's murder was John C. Colt (1810–42), the brother of Samuel Colt (1814–62), inventor of the revolver. John Colt was sentenced to hang. On the day of his execution, 18 November 1842, he married his mistress in his jail

1 O'Sullivan was then urging the New York legislature to end capital punishment.
2 Samuel S. and William Wood published Child's *The American Frugal Housewife*. Charles F. Briggs (1804–77) was a writer and later a magazine editor in New York.

cell in the Tombs; a fire broke out after she left; and when the fire was extinguished, he was found in the cell with a fatal knife wound. The death was called a suicide.

Child wrote about John Colt's death in her "Letters from New-York" column, seeing it as a horrible example of the cruelty of capital punishment; she noted that the gallows had been erected right outside the cell window. Samuel Colt then came to see if Child would help his brother's widow and infant son. Child agreed and wrote to John Dwight at Brook Farm. Two years later Child was once again seeking help for the young woman.

Whether Child knew the real facts of the situation is not known. The so-called widow, Caroline Henshaw, had apparently been married to Samuel Colt, the surviving brother, for several years, and the baby was theirs. For reasons not clear, Samuel Colt was determined to keep the marriage secret, and a few years later he married someone else. Caroline Henshaw eventually moved to Germany, took a new name, and married one of Colt's wealthy sales agents. Samuel Colt maintained support of the boy, leaving him a bequest of more than two million dollars in stocks.

To John S. Dwight

New York Dec 1st 1842

Dear Friend,

Again and again, since I parted from you at Northampton, has it been in my heart to write to you; and if I have not done so, it has not been for want of grateful recollections of the many pleasant hours, and pure thoughts, and beautiful images, which I owe you; but in good truth, I live in perpetual hurry; and my friends will never know how many letters I write them, till some sort of spiritual daguerrotype is discovered, to take down thoughts as they rise. I will confess the plain truth, that I should not write to you now, if I had not *business* on hand, in which I need your assistance.

My heart is very full of a project, in which I need you as a kind of *mediator*. You know the painful tragedy of John C. Colt, and have doubtless heard of Caroline Henshaw, the woman to whom he was married a few hours before his death. Her history is this. She was an ignorant, worthy, affectionate German girl, apprentice to a corset-maker in Philadelphia. In some way, I know not how, she was about the premises, either as domestic or boarder, at the boarding house where John C. Colt was. ⟨boarding⟩ He befriended her in sickness, for she was poor and friendless. She became extremely attached to him, and when he came to N. York followed him, without his knowledge. Her strong affection awakened a kindred feeling in him; but judging like a man of the world, he thought it would not do to offend his genteel family by marrying her. They lived together without legal marriage, in a very secluded way, till the murder of Adams brought it all to light. She was then pregnant; and not long after gave birth to a son. Her love for Colt was of the strongest and most disinterested stamp; as is shown by her willingness to take his name under such awful circumstances. Mr. Colt's brother has been to see me, and consult with me about her. He says he believes her to be a modest, worthy girl; that she never formed any other connexion than that with his unfortunate brother; and that this had the palliation of most devoted love, and of friendless poverty. He says he feels it a duty to do more for her than feed and clothe her; that he ought, as far as possible, to throw a protecting influence around her and the child, ⟨which⟩ whom he shall in all respects treat as if he were his own son. "I want to educate her," says he; "to put her under influences that will make her a judicious mother for my brother's son. But where shall I find a suitable place? I have thought of a country clergyman's family; but she would be pointed at in a country village, and she would have little chance to improve intellectually; and in most cases there would not be that entire forgetfulness of her peculiar situation, which is desirable."   I at once thought of the West Roxbury Community, and mentioned it; at the same time telling him that you were so much crowded, that I thought it not very likely you could take her. I had *other* fears than those of your being crowded. I thought you might perhaps fear the "speech of people." But, my dear friend, this is a real case of a fellow creature fallen among thieves, wounded and bleeding by the wayside. If she were a loose woman, I would be the last to propose such a thing. But I think she is not. She is, as I believe, an honest confiding young creature, the victim of a false state of society. She is almost heart-broken, and longs for seclusion, soothing influences, and instruction how to do her duty. If you, with your large and liberal views, and your clear perception of human brotherhood, if *you*, at West Roxbury, reject her, where, in the name of our common Father, *can* I find a shelter for her poor storm-pelted heart? And the family of Colt, is it not *noble* in them to *wish* to deal thus with a poor ignorant German peasant? And will you throw them back on the worldly, the selfish, and the bigotted, and thus repress the noble impulse? Is it not enough to say to cavillers, "She wants to learn to be good, and who should help her, if *we* would not? These men desire to do a noble deed, and we *dare* not take the guilt of crushing their kindly feelings."   My soul is on its knees before you, to receive this poor shorn lamb of our Father's flock. I am in agony, lest you should not listen to my supplications; for somehow or other, though a stranger to me, God has laid her upon my heart.

Mr. Colt seemed to leave the arrangements to *me;* but I thought his idea was to have her board with you for a year, doing what she conveniently could, consistently with the care of her child; and you to make such deductions from the price of board as her labors were worth; and if you found her a useful and pleasant inmate, to make such after arrangements about the education of the child, &c as should seem proper.

I believe you would find the brother disposed to be honorable, and liberal. He is not a *rich* man, but a prosperous one.   Oh here is a rare chance to teach the world a noble lesson! Will you forego the opportunity?

Write to me soon, directed to 143 Nassau St. care of Isaac T. Hopper. Oh, *how* disappointed I shall feel if you say me nay. Mr. Page is very earnest, too, that you should do it.

I wish I could say more. If I could *talk* with you, I believe I should so hang about the necks of your hearts, that you *could* not refuse me. This poor young creature *must* be saved.   Yrs. most truly, L. M. Child.

ALS; Anti-Slavery Collection, Rare Books and Manuscripts, Boston Public Library (microfiche 15/428).

To Francis Shaw

New York Jan 15th 1843

Dear Friend,

For the first time in my life, I *believe*, I am going to ask a pecuniary favor of you; and I pray you copy my freedom, and refuse the request, if you see fit. I sadly want the money for the enclosed note, and the booksellers are, as Mr. Loring will tell you, as good as the bank. But I don't know anybody here, whom I could ask to advance money on it. James S. Gibbons, treasurer of the American Society, is connected with a bank, and I dare say would manage it for me, if I asked him. But his credit has been so drawn upon, to keep our printers from starving, and our paper-maker from siezing the types, that I do not like to ask him. Will *you* lend me the money, deducting interest up to the date? If you can do it, it will be a great convenience to me. Mr. Loring told me to get it done in N. York, and so I don't like to plague *him;* especially as I have always been plaguing him.

And now another favor. I have long been wanting to revise, correct, and enlarge the best portions of the Juvenile Miscellany, for republication, with a few very neat plates; but I have always been afraid that the paper and binding would become due, before enough books sold to meet the bills. That it will more than cover the expense, eventually, I have no doubt; but it is torture to me, to have the bill for anything presented before I can pay it; for instead of scorning prudence, as you suppose, I am *over*-anxious about such matters. Are you willing to have the edition made over entirely to you, on condition of meeting the bills? Are you willing to do the same for an edition of the best of the New York Letters?

Mr. Child is now going through the bankrupt process. It will not make the slightest difference with him about paying his debts, as fast as he is able; but he will be more free; and to me, it will be an inexpressible relief to be relieved from his entanglements. If God spares my life the coming year, I intend to start afresh in the race, and rebuild my literary reputation. If I can have a little helping-hand at the outset, I think I can soon go *alone*. You see I have spoken as freely as to a brother; but you will not like me less for it, I know.

Mr. Page is more cheerful than I have ever seen him, since I knew him. His Ecce Homo seems to me a very admirable thing; though to my eye, it has lost somewhat of the divine expression it had in the first drawing. He showed me your letter, wherein you complain of his calling it an embodiment of Non-Resistance. Take care, my dear friend, that you do not let the vulgar fanaticism of a few disagreeable individuals blind you to principles of the greatest universality, and the highest holiness. The non-resistance *society* is as distasteful to me as it possibly can be to you, and most of their writings offend me greatly; but I every day become more and more enamored of the *principles*, and see in them, more and more clearly, a sovereign cure for all the ills that flesh and spirit are heirs to. The idea of overcoming evil *always* with good, is to my mind the *one* idea which stamps the Christian religion as divine, above other religions. Well might the angels proclaim, in joyful prophecy, the advent of this idea.

I have not time to write to Sarah by this package. Tell her I am *very* much obliged to her for her kind letter, and New Year's gift. Since she was seeking for a *useless* gift, I think she made a remarkable failure. I wanted a thermometer badly, to regulate the heat of my room. Moreover, (she will think me more truthful than polite) I regard its usefulness as its *only* recommendation. Mr. Page, and everybody else, consider it very handsome and rich-looking; but I am not in love with that *mosaic* dispensation of squares and angles. They have a *Calvinistic* look to me, and I am strongly inclined to think they *are* Andover in "scientific ooltimates," as Mr. Graeter used to say.[1] Then, bird's-eye maple, or rose-wood, or mahogany, seem so much more beautiful than such checkering. It reminds me of the old women, who cut up handsome copperplate to make square patchwork. And now that I have abused Sarah's present, in good set terms, I will add that I thank her for it, very heartily, nevertheless. Do you see how I leave out words? My eyes pain me badly, and I am hurrying to get done, yet I keep thinking of a thousand things that I want to say. I rejoice to hear John S. Dwight is coming here to lecture on music. With best love to Sarah and yourself, farewell.

Yrs most truly, L. M. Child.

. . .

ALS; Houghton Library, Harvard University (microfiche 16/441).

In January 1843, Child began preparing to resign. Divisiveness in the movement had spread beyond the split between the Garrisonian and political abolitionists to a split over the issue of nonresistance. While many abolitionists, including Child herself, sympathized with nonresistance ideas, a minority demanded that abolitionists *must* be nonresistants. Child objected to this demand as she did to the related doctrine of "come-out-ism," the insistence that people resign from all organizations, political or religious, that were not actively antislavery. "Come-

[1] The German-born artist Francis Graeter had boarded with the Childs in Boston in the early 1830s. He made engravings and translated stories for the *Juvenile Miscellany* in 1831–32, and taught drawing at Bronson Alcott's Temple School in 1835.

out-ism" was supported by Thomas Parnell Beach (1808–46), an abolitionist Congregational minister, whom Child mentions in the following letters. "Come-out-ism" was also supported by Garrison; it became a significant principle of his wing of the movement in the mid-1840s.

To Ellis Gray Loring

New York Jan 24'th 1843

Dear Friend,

Many thanks for your kind letter. But you mistook when you wrote, "I know you are harrassed and vexed." I have n't for many years been so happy as I am this winter; and perhaps never have known a time when vexations have passed over me so very lightly. The reason probably is, that after many fluctuations, and being influenced by a wish to please others, I have at last settled down upon a deliberate conviction of what course is best for my own soul.

You reason with me about Beach, as if I had any hostility to the man. I have never spoken of him otherwise than very respectfully and kindly. He has scarcely interested me enough to feel any dislike for him. I feel toward him very much as I do toward Miller and his proselytes; i.e. simply as if there were no use in our attempting to argue together, because it would be impossible for us to look at any object from the same point of view. As for my state of mind, it is hardly worth while to write a syllable about it, or for anybody except myself to expend a thought upon it. I have endeavored to *edit the Standard* conscientiously, according to *my* views of the good of the Society; and thus I shall continue most carefully to do, during the short time it remains in my hands. Mrs. Chapman thinks I have not been sufficiently willing to follow counsel. Perhaps it is so; but the fact is so many different kinds of counsel have been urged upon me, that I have found the absolute necessity of relying only upon my own judgment. Had I done otherwise, I should have shifted about without rudder or compass.

. . . I believe *my* line of policy will carry abolition more generally among the *people*, and make a great many more half-abolitionists, and three-quarters abolitionists; but I decidedly think *his* [Collins's] course is best calculated to resuscitate the energies of the *Society*, and keep it from expiring. I thank you for your kind invitation to come to the meeting; but I disagree with you altogether in thinking I could either do good, or receive good. I am not made for such scenes. Mrs. Chapman can say appropriately,

> "We Arteveldes are *made* for times like these
> The Deacon of the Mariners said well,
> That we are of such canvass as they use
> To make *storm* stay-sails."

If I came, I should probably say something, which would do mischief, without intending to do so. James S. Gibbons is in great anxiety of mind. Mrs. Chapman has written to him as if the salvation of the cause depended upon his going to Boston; and it is not possible for him to find any one to supply his place at the Bank. In these days, when there are so many applicants for office, he will be in great danger of losing his situation by being absent. I do not see what good he can do by going; for his views are as well-known, as if he were to express them there; and we have no *constituents* to represent. However, I think he would go, if within the range of possibility. I am glad you liked Friend Hopper better than ever. He is a good old man. He enjoyed his visit very highly, and is always talking of your kindness.   Tell Anna I thank her heartily for her kind little letter, as well as for her N. Year's keepsake. With best love to dear Louise, and thanks for her New Year's gift. Augusta's wreath charms everybody. Even Page, who always finds some fault with everything, thought it perfect.

I hope you will not think me in a fidget; because I am as cool and philosophic as possible. The conviction that the paper needs a *man* at the helm in these days of Liberty Party, and clashing with sects, is too strong to be mistaken.

Yrs. most truly,
L. M. Child.

ALS; Manuscript Division, New York Public Library (microfiche 16/447).

To Ellis Gray Loring

New York Feb. 21'st 1843

Dearly Beloved Friend,

I enclose a communication, which I wish you would read, and then read to the Massachusetts Board, unless you see good reasons for not doing so. I am sorry to trouble you with it; but it *must* be settled what we are to do, and what we are to do it *with*.

While I am upon business, I will ask you to obtain a copy of Philothea at the bookstore, tell them it is for *me*, and send me the price. I should like to have it *by next package*, and I will send pay by return. Can you let Robert Morris copy the story I wrote for Anna, called the Remembered Home? He might copy it on common paper, and take no especial care. I only want it to be *plain*, which Augusta's hand is not, always. I am hesitating whether or not to print it in the volume of my N. York Letters, to give a little novelty and variety to it. Would you? I shall not print *all* the letters; only the best ones. Would you omit the last two about Women's Rights, or not? I think it best to omit them. Would you publish the one about the execution of Colt, and against Capital Punishment? I should like to have you give me a little advice about this; even if you have but time to say a few words. I think I shall print them this Spring. The Langleys here seem disposed to undertake it; and I have a great many requests to do it, from various quarters. I *think* enough will surely sell, to cover the expense. Page has *promised* to draw a vignette for it; but he may forget it.

Last Sunday evening Emerson, and J. R. Lowell, and Page were here. Emerson has been very cordial and hearty—gave me tickets for the course, and sent word he wanted to come and see me. I should never have thought of asking him, if he had n't proposed it himself; for I supposed he would consider it a bore. John and I go to the lectures, and find them refreshing as a glass of soda-water; but, as usual, not *satisfactory*. He gave, in one of the lectures, such a glowing and graceful picture of Southern manners and character, that I might have supposed he considered arbitrary power one of the most beneficial influences on man. I should not have quarrelled with this, had he made the least allusion to any *bad* effects. Speaking of the discrepancies between our professions and our practice, as a people, he did not *allude* to slavery. I cannot think that this is manly and true; for the subject *must* occur to him. However, the lectures are a prodigious treat to me, though they are evidently adapted more to the *popular* taste, than those he delivered in Cambridge and Boston. I was struck with one of his peculiar phrases: "The man of *will* makes his jacket invisible." Even Page did not understand this as merely saying, "When a man's *character* produces a decided impression, we do not observe his *clothes*." He called Commerce "a varioloid of cannibalism—every prosperous merchant had eaten up five or six unlucky ones." I wish Theodore Parker would come here, and give the Calvinists a tussle.

It makes me sad to attend Emerson's lectures. All the faces around me are strange. I think of the pleasant times when you and I and Louisa and Caroline S. rode out to Cambridge, merry-making as we went. If I could only have you and yours near me, I would'nt care ever to see Boston again; but at times my heart does yearn after you, inexpressibly. Do not understand that I am discontented. On the contrary, N. York seems to me more and more like home, and my affections have taken deep root here. Unless God overrules my will with a *very* strong hand, I shall remain here, till I pass into the invisible. I never *wish* to move, until I am carried. I think I can enter into literary arrangements here, at once profitable and safe. At all events, I am bent upon trying the experiment, and putting my utmost energy upon it; and if the devil ever draws me into reform, of any kind, again, he is a smarter fellow than I take him to be.

. . .

John is the same good son. The stay and staff of my life, as if he were *indeed* my son. On my last birth day (a week ago) he scattered new coppers among the poor children from Grand St. to 26th St. and gave me a beautiful astral lamp, which makes moonlight equal to the heavens. But *gifts* are the smallest causes of my gratitude. The fountain of his *sympathy* and *kindness* is never dry. The good old gentleman has been on an anti-slavery tour to Chester Co. Penn. and has done much good, and received much honor.

I know not when I shall see you; for you cannot spare time to come to N. York much, and my disinclination to travelling grows stronger and stronger.

Best love to dearest Louise and Anna, and believe me Yrs Most affectionately,

Maria.

ALS; Manuscript Division, New York Public Library (microfiche 16/455).

To the Board of the Massachusetts Anti-Slavery Society

New York Feb. 21st 1843

To the Board of the Massachusetts Anti Slavery Society

James S Gibbons has replied to a letter from Mr. Philbrick; but it seems to me necessary to enter into a little more full explanation of our condition, and of our relation to you.[1]

When I took the Standard, it was deeply involved in debt; I *think* more so than it now is; at any event, the embarrassment was great. My own views of doing business are always to choose *safe* ground, however narrow. This policy I urged upon the committee, and their own experience made them well disposed to adopt it. I knew there would be an outcry that we were *doing* nothing; but I did not think we had a right to violate principles of honesty, in order to make a great display; a thing which associations, in their unthinking zeal, are very apt to do.

We arranged everything on a safe and economical scale. Our receipts exceeded our expenditures. Every month we paid all our current expenses, and considerable of our old debts. Each month the debt dwindled more and more, until we owed of the old load only $800, and all present expenses were promptly met. In this prosperous state of things, we received an urgent request from the *Massachusetts Board* to appoint John A. Collins General Agent, with a view to enlarging our sphere of operations. I dreaded this, because I knew we had not the *means* of extending our circle of agitation, and I had not faith that we could *obtain* the means, in the present state of the anti-slavery cause. James S. Gibbons had the same feeling; but much as he had been embarrassed and perplexed by the pecuniary condition of the society, he, like myself, felt an extreme reluctance to oppose our judgment to that of the good friends of the cause in Massachusetts. We acquiesced, with foreboding hearts; and from that day to this, we have been getting deeper and deeper into debt. We are now over $2,000 in debt, and our monthly receipts about *half* meet our expenses.

This pecuniary result cannot be owing to management of the Standard, either editorially, or financially. We have made no increase in wages or salaries. An addition of $300 (making our salary $1,500 per annum) was voted to Mr. Child and myself; but we declined to accept it; and when I see Mr. Child, I presume that he will agree not to take more than $1,000. The *subscription* to the Standard is larger, now than it was the year we were so rapidly freeing ourselves from embarrassments; larger than it has been at any period; being now about 5000. If we had gone on the *cautious* system, we should by this time have been out of debt, and had a little stock in trade, whereby we could gradually enlarge our operations. But this was too slow a process to meet *your* approbation. Merely getting out of debt, and *preparing* to do something, seemed to you to be doing

---

[1] Samuel Philbrick was treasurer of the Massachusetts Anti-Slavery Society.

nothing. You urged us to a different policy. We find ourselves over head and ears in difficulty; scarcely able to pay our printers a weekly allowance to save their children from hunger; buying paper of one man, till we are so deeply in debt that he will let us have no more, and then getting more of another man, with the same result; dunned by our landlord for rent; sniffed at by S. W. Benedict, the new organizationist, because we cannot pay him what we owe. Of our own discouraged, mortified, and insulted feelings, I say nothing—because we neither of us deem them of sufficient consequence to talk about. In this distress, we are promised money from Massachusetts; week after week, the promise comes, but the money does *not* come. We repeat the promise to the landlord, printer, and paper-maker, till we blush to repeat it again, and are obliged to confess that the American Society has no credit, and her word is not worth a farthing. In all this, we care more for the effect on the *cause*, than we do on ourselves. At last, in desperate extremity, we renew our appeals to you; and instead of the promised $2,000, receive a letter from Mr. Philbrick in the coolest style of finance, inquiring how much we owe, and what we owe it for; and advising us to call upon Pennsylvania for help, and to recall our agents. We might as well call upon a dead dog, as upon Pennsylvania, so far as *money* is concerned. As for our agents, there is no use in recalling them, for they *have* eaten up our yearly resources. *They* are not to blame, poor fellows! They have been diligent, economical, and self-sacrificing. But they *must* eat, and they must be conveyed about from place to place; and *subscriptions* to the Standard constituted nearly the whole they received to defray expenses. That they have aroused a great deal of anti slavery feeling, where it was heretofore dormant, I doubt not; but we have no right to starve our printers and press men, even to do good. Moreover, two thirds of the anti slavery zeal, thus awakened, goes to the benefit of Liberty Party; and is therefore suicidal to the American Society, instead of benefiting it. Conventions have been held in rapid succession; they are expensive machinery; and our farmers and mechanics, who give a certain annual sum for the advancement of anti-slavery, if they give it in one way, do not give it in another.

In all this, do not understand me as blaming John A. Collins. The cause has not a more disinterested laborer; and I believe he has done zealously, what his sanguine temperament considered for the best. But he was a great trader, without capital. The American Society cannot possibly do more than to sustain a paper, and keep an office open, without perpetually incurring debt. It is not *honest* for us to attempt to do more.

I attach blame to no one. All have done what they thought was for the best. But *you* advised us into this scheme of large adventure, against our own judgment; and I now put it to your consciences, whether you *ought* to leave us in the lurch, and turn a starving horse into the stony stubble-field of Pennsylvanian generosity. Either the American Society is worth supporting, or it is *not* worth supporting. If *not* worth supporting, you should have been more sparing of promises.

I write with perfect freedom in this matter, because *I* have nothing at stake.

Personally, it is of no consequence to me, whether the Standard exists another week. If I looked at it in a selfish point of view, I should rejoice at its downfall, as a means of ridding myself more speedily of a disagreeable burden. Whether things can be so arranged, as to still continue it a useful instrumentality to the cause, it is for the Society to determine. But it is not fair for any association to place a Committee in the situation in which we have been placed for the last year; and no person of principle, or the least pride of character, can consent to remain in it.

If I have spoken bluntly, my excuse must be, that our emergencies are pressing, and our burden of debt grows absolutely intolerable.

Respectfully,
L. Maria Child.

P.S. It may be well to remark, that of the receipts acknowledged in the Standard, a large proportion are never *received* by us, but used by the agents, and credited to them. The *apparent* amount of our receipts has deceived many of our friends.

ALS; Anti-Slavery Collection, Rare Books and Manuscripts, Boston Public Library (microfiche 16/456).

To Ellis Gray Loring

New York. March 6'th 1843.

Dear Friend,

I have taken a large sheet of paper, and begun up high, because I foresee that I shall have a great deal to say. In the first place, I hope my not being here at the anniversary will make no difference about *your* coming. If I were here, it would not be a friendly time, you know, for cozy conversation. On many accounts, I wish to be away. I am about to leave the Standard, and I do not wish to hear the talking pro and con about it, which I should be obliged to hear. If you ascribe this decision of mine to pettishness, or personal feeling, you do me injustice. My pets are always a mere flash in the pan, and do not last an hour. You seem to have made the mistake that many others do, that I am peculiarly sensitive to the opinion of others. I *am* very sensitive to the opinion of those I *love*; but I believe it would be hard to find another in the U. States more completely indifferent to the general opinion. With regard to N. P. Rogers, Beach, &c to whom you allude, I have the greatest respect for them as sincere, well-meaning men; but their minds are too one-sided, ill-balanced, and incomprehensive, for me to attach any weight to their opinion of the course of the Standard. I confess that Rogers's literary praise *would* annoy me; for one who has any appreciation of literature does not like to hear it crackled at, by a man who talks of "Dr. Channings *gorgeous* style", "Francis Jackson's *princely* mansion," and Mr. "Pierpont's *mellifluous* poetry." He has a spontaneous, brilliant way of his own, which I often enjoy extremely;

but as for his *judgment,* · Let me explain to you, once for all, that I am not disturbed by what he, *et id genus omne,* think of *me;* the difficulty is, what I think of *them.* I do not allude to personal feeling; for I have none but the kindest. But neither my taste, my judgment, my reason, nor my conscience approves the course they are pursuing. My feelings are completely and forever alienated from the anti-slavery *organization.* I cannot go with them, without fighting with my own best instincts. This has been growing upon me, ever since the split in the Female Anti slavery society. I felt afraid it was my distaste to *disagreeable scenes,* and so struggled against it. But it comes more and more forcibly and clearly to my mind, that we are fighting in the spirit of *sect;* a spirit which I abhor, in all its manifestations. Edmund Quincy's attack upon Arthur Tappan took the last scales from my eyes, and made it manifest that we care too much for our own particular *organization.*[1] The feeling that will not allow us to express a word of sympathy for the misfortunes of a man, who has done and sacrificed so much for anti-slavery as Arthur Tappan has, merely because his bigotry led him into *one* mistake, *cannot* be a right feeling. I know it is justified on the plea that the New organizationists might get some money and countenance from young converts, which ought to come to *our* side; but *all* sectarian attacks and wrangling are justified in the same way. It *always* seems necessary to be narrow and one-sided.   Mrs. Chapman has written to me three several times, to get me to say *editorially* that *I* considered Joshua Leavitt a knave. She urged the necessity and importance of my doing it, in a style which, as you say, "might draw wine out of a turnip." The shortest paragraph would answer, and I might choose my own language, provided I would make it clear to all the people that I considered him a *knave.* I replied that I consented to take the Standard expressly on conditions that I would have nothing to do with fighting and controversy. I wrote in reply to Abby Kelly, when she first urged me to come to New York, that I should edit like Ellis Gray Loring, and confine myself to appeals to reason and good feeling; that I should aim more at *reaching the people* than at pleasing abolitionists. She replied, "You are just the editor we want. We need oil upon the waves. The general feeling is that we have had too much of fighting; there is now an opening for something better." I came accordingly; and I have most conscientiously endeavored to do my duty. I threw myself *wholly* into the paper, with but a single eye to its prosperity. What Mrs. Chapman considered a love of popularity, and an over anxious desire to please *my* public, was in fact nothing but a desire to gain the ear of intelligent and judicious people in behalf of anti-slavery. My views with regard to the best means of advancing the cause are the same now, that they were when Abby Kelly urged me to take the paper; but in a letter from Abby, which James S. Gibbons received to day, she says, "L. Maria Child has disgraced and degraded the Standard to the level of new-organization." John A. Collins

---

[1] In *The Liberator,* 23 Dec. 1842, Quincy charged Tappan with illicitly transferring the *Emancipator,* organ of the American Anti-Slavery Society, into the hands of the anti-Garrison faction in 1840.

says the reason that he cannot raise money, is that "abolitionists do not like the Standard, and will not give anything toward it." I do not mention these things as *worth* mentioning, for any other purpose than to show you that I *am* really in a false position, as editor of the Society's organ; and that I do not give it up from mere caprice, or restlessness. The society has an undoubted right to decide what sort of paper they want, and having settled that point, they should employ an editor who can, in freedom of conscience, do the work they want done. But they ought to have sense enough to be aware; that they cannot have a paper to fight with abolitionists of all stamps but their own, and at the same time to find its way *generally* among the people. If they make the Standard like the Liberator, it will, like the Lib——, repel all but a limited number. Some seem to think that a *little* attacking might be done, without injury; but if you put in a little, the other side claims to put in a little in reply, and so on, like a shuttle-cock. In Mrs. Chapman's letter attacking Leavitt, I struck out three tomahawk sentences, and left but one severe allusion to him, which I thought she might consider necessary to the history of the scene she was describing. Yet I have had three replies to it, and am much blamed for not inserting them; though if I should do it, it would completely open the flood-gates of the old quarrel.

These *personal* affairs have nothing to do with my alienation from the anti-slavery organization It is the bad *spirit* which I see everywhere manifested, and the increasing tendency to *co-erce* individual freedom. Abby Kelly is employing all her energies to make everybody sign what she calls "the tee-total pledge"; and she says the American anti slavery Society *must* take that as their basis. This pledge requires every abolitionist not to vote for any but an out-spoken, &c and not to belong to *any* religious association, or help support *any* religious teacher, who is not publicly acting with the anti-slavery society. I have no sectarian ties whatever; but I resist this innovation upon my freedom. If I see fit to contribute toward the hire of a Catholic Cathedral, or a Mahometon mosque, I have an undoubted right to do so. As if anti-slavery were the *only* idea in the universe! This, let alone Beach and Foster's mad movement, shows me plainly enough that the parting hour has come between me and the anti-slavery organization. I shall be careful, however, not to let this appear, in the interim between now and the anniversary. When I said I would have nothing to do with reforms, I merely meant with the organized machinery. I will work in my own way, according to the light that is in me. They have tried very hard to make me join an association here for the abolition of Capital Punishment; but I have constantly refused. William H. Channing is *very* desirous that I should join his association for Christian Union; but I tell him I never again will join *any* association, for any purpose.[2]

The letter I wrote to the Massachusetts Board was extorted from me by the

[2] William Henry Channing (1810–84), nephew of William Ellery Channing, became a Unitarian minister and later a Christian socialist. He was at this time forming the Christian Union, devoted to redefining Christian values; the society lasted until 1845, when Channing moved to Brook Farm. From Sept. 1843 to Apr. 1844 he published *The Present*, a journal of his ideas.

sufferings of Mr. Eastman, a printer to whom we owed a good deal, and who had a little suffering family, without means to get them bread or clothing, and creditors dogging him at every step. We have put him off, week after week, with the story that $2,000 was coming from Massachusetts; and when we were obliged to tell him that we were not likely to receive that, at present, he seemed so utterly desperate and woe-begone, that I could not help writing, to stir somebody up. Since that, we have received $500 from Philadelphia, beside the $600 from you. This has renewed the spirits of our workmen, and prevented our landlord from giving up in despair of our *ever* keeping our word.

I wish you would again send me Nony's little book about the Swallows. I think the little picture at the end will make a pretty vignette for the Letters from N. York. I do not agree with you about inserting *all* of them. Some are of a merely temporary and transient interest, and a few were merely written to fill up. The doubt I had about the letter on Colt's execution was that it described a scene of local and temporary interest, and painful withal. As for the letters on Women's Rights, they did not seem to me to amount to much. I am much obliged to you for your offer of overlooking them, and will send them, as soon as I get them ready. If any apt quotations or mottoes occur to you, as you read them, I will thank you much to help me to them. You mistook, if you supposed I was going to have *pictures* engraved for the volume. I merely meant that Page was going to draw a *vignette* for the title page, and perhaps a *very* little tail piece at the end. I am as afraid of expense, as you can desire me to be. I am more than half afraid of publishing it at all, for fear of getting into debt. I hardly care what happens to me, if I can only manage not to be separated from John. I have come to be *afraid* to lean upon David in all matters connected with a *home* and *support;* I am weary of moving about; and John is such a good hand to lean upon, and manages all my affairs so well. Having no children of my own, he supplies to me the place of a real son, and my affections have got so entwined around him, that it would almost kill me to have to leave him. I do hope things will so happen that David and he and I can live together, and bless each other. It is my wish to do them both "good and not evil all the days of my life."

As Mr. Page makes me his *confidante*, I have no right to tell you much more than you probably already know from James Russell Lowell. The affair commenced about three months ago. The young lady is the sister of his friend Dogherty; just seventeen; a good deal of fresh, youthful beauty, and apparently very child-like, docile, and innocent.[3] She is extravagantly attached to him. This is a fortunate circumstance; for he *requires* to be loved a great deal. I see him but once a week now; during which time he tells me everything Sarah has said in the interim. They are a very infatuated couple; but I love to see it, and wish all the world were so infatuated. He will probably remove to Boston before he is married.

[3] William Page married Sarah Dougherty on 29 Apr. 1843.

I thank you very much for the Sleepwaker.[4] It completely chained me, till I had finished it. Nobody knows so well as you do, how to choose books that charm *me*. There was Sartor Resartus, which I kept under my pillow for weeks, and shouted over with joy. Then there was that blessed book Jean Paul.   Did you observe how the sleep-waker talked Swedenborgianism. Would to Heaven *they* would'nt be a *sect!* But a sect they are, and a very pinched one, too.

Have you seen the Pathfinder, by Godwin, Bryant's son-in-law? I like it *extremely*. Since the days of Leggett's Plain-Dealer, I have seen no newspaper to be compared to it.[5] I do not mean that it is much like that, either, except in its general spirit and aim.

. . .

I know not when I shall have a chance to talk with you, so I have written seven pages, and am still obliged "to leave out the pith and the marrow, for want of room". My heart is drawn closer and closer toward you every day. I wish there was not so much material space between us.

You need not be afraid of my turning *against* the anti-slavery organization. Those who leave old associates, from personal or selfish feelings, are prone to *attack* those they leave; not so with those who withdraw from the honest dictates of conscience or reason. Henceforth, the whole anti-slavery agitation is to me as the forgotten storm of last year; but this I shall not say to the world.

It is strange to me that people of good sense do not perceive that this "tee-total pledge" is as narrow and co-ercive in its character, as the test that all men must vote, or all must belong to the Liberty Party. Shall Sam J. May, and Mr. Stearns of Hingham, and John Parkman, &c be driven off the anti-slavery plat-form, because they believe they can do good by continuing connected with the Unitarian association? Shall Lucretia Mott, and Isaac T. Hopper, and James Canning Fuller, &c be excluded, because they believe it a duty to remain con-nected with the Quaker Society?[6]

Manifestly, the principle is a wrong one. Men might with more propriety be called upon to quit their domestic and social relations, their commercial, and manufacturing, and literary relations. Anti slavery does not, and cannot, supply the *religious* wants of our nature. By enforcing this test, we shall drive the *best* spirits from among us. It is the same principle in the *church*, that the formation of the Liberty Party is in the *state*. It seems to me such a needless injury to the

---

[4] *The Sleepwaker: A Tale from the German of Heinrich Tschokke* (Boston, 1842) con-cerned the effects of mesmerism.

[5] Parke Godwin (1816–1904), who had married William Cullen Bryant's daughter Fanny in 1842, published the *Pathfinder* from Feb. to June 1843 and worked with Bryant at the *New York Evening Post*. William Leggett (1801–39), a radical and Jacksonian, published the *Plaindealer* in New York City, 3 Dec. 1836–30 Sept. 1837. Both men were abolitionists.

[6] Samuel J. May, Oliver Stearns (1807–85), and John Parkman (1813–83) were pacifist Unitarian ministers. Fuller (1793–1847) was an abolitionist Quaker in Skaneateles, N.Y.; in 1842 he had been mobbed in Utica, N.Y., for expressing his antislavery views.

cause, that I hardly feel justified before God and my own conscience, for not coming out strongly against it. But the paper belongs to the *Society*, and I can see that the tendency of the powers that be is madly radical. They ought to call themselves Destructionists, rather than abolitionists. I am weary, weary of this everlasting pulling down, and no building up.

Best love to dear Louise and Anna.

Yours with stedfast affection,
L. M. C.

ALS; Manuscript Division, New York Public Library (microfiche 16/463).

Child published her last issue of the *Standard* on 4 May 1843, just before the annual meeting of the American Anti-Slavery Society. In her farewell editorial she wrote, "I have repeatedly said that I did not *intend* to edit the paper for abolitionists. It seemed to me that the Liberator, the Herald of Freedom, and various 'Liberty Party' papers, were sufficient to meet their wants; and that the cause needed a medium of communication with the *people*. My aim, therefore, was to make a good *family* newspaper. . . . I am too distinctly and decidedly an individual, to edit the organ of any association." Garrison responded in *The Liberator*, 19 May 1843, that the organ of the American Anti-Slavery Society "should not shrink from controversy." The difference over tactics could not be resolved.

The following note to Maria (Weston) Chapman about the annual fund-raising fair conveys the coldness of Child's mood. Chapman endorsed the letter with equal coldness: "A revelation of character."

To Maria (Weston) Chapman

New York May 19'th. [1843]

I have just received your note about the Fair, and will attend to it as requested. Please take off my name from the list; as I have retired from the anti-slavery cause altogether. I write promptly, because I would rather it should be quietly left off, than to have it inserted, and then taken off. Mr. Child will probably be detained in Northampton two or three weeks longer, by the bankrupt process, auction, &c.

Yrs respectfully,
L. Maria Child.

ALS; Anti-Slavery Collection, Rare Books and Manuscripts, Boston Public Library (microfiche 17/494).

5

August 1843-May 1850

After Child resigned from the *National Anti-Slavery Standard*, she continued living in New York City. Antislavery became a minor theme in her life, a matter of strictly personal rather than group action. Although her husband took over as editor of the *Standard*, she withdrew from all abolitionist organizations and turned instead to the New York world of the arts.

In these years the United States was expanding. "Manifest destiny" became the keynote phrase. Politicians struggled with the question of admitting pro-slavery Texas to the Union; and then, in 1846, came the war with Mexico. Migration westward was steady, intensifying in 1848 with the discovery of gold in California. The city of New York was also expanding rapidly in the 1840s, though Forty-second Street still bordered farm land. But farther downtown, building boomed, and New York became a cultural center. Charles Dickens visited the city, and a stream of European musicians and actors came to perform in New York's concert halls and theaters.

Child took an intense interest in these changes around her, but the years were difficult ones for her. Depression characterizes many of her letters of this time and tends to flatten the tone of the consciously cheerful ones. Her husband resigned just one year after becoming editor of the *Standard*, because Garrison objected to his enthusiasm for Whig politics. David went back to Northampton, to Maria's dismay, trying to farm and doing odd jobs, including carting stone for the railroad. He wrote an important pamphlet in 1845, *The Taking of Naboth's Vineyard* (New York), exposing the Democrats' maneuvers to acquire Texas, but he never made any money. To protect her own income Maria legally separated her financial affairs from David's. No formal separation took place in the marriage, but they lived apart a great deal of the time, and for a while there seems to have been an estrangement in her feelings for him.

She went on living with the Hoppers in New York, taking part in their work with prisoners and prison reform. She was still attached to her "son," John Hopper, but his attention was shifting to women of his own age. In March 1847, when she was forty-five, he thirty-two, he unexpectedly married, and the news came as a shock to her. She felt that she had to leave. Moving to an isolated farm belonging to her old friend Joseph Carpenter in New Rochelle, New York, she spent nearly two years there, working on a lengthy history of the world's religions. She became even more depressed. The isolation seemed not to clarify her life but only to reinforce her sense that nothing would change for her. She came back to the city in March 1849, once again staying with the Hoppers. David joined her there in the fall, after a year working with a brother in Tennessee.

Before the move out to New Rochelle, however, Child kept up a hectic pace of writing. After the success of her first series of *Letters from New-York* (1843), a publisher immediately issued a collection of her tales, entitled *Flowers for Children* (1844), reissued some of her previous works, and in 1845 published a second series of *Letters from New-York*. She became a frequent contributor to newspapers, writing reviews and articles about New York life—its neighborhoods, institutions, social reforms—and the arts. In 1845 she contracted with the *Columbian Ladies' and Gentlemen's Magazine* to do a story a month for them, and these she published in *Fact and Fiction* in 1846. Her writing provided modest support and allowed her to go to the concerts she loved to review. Artists and performers came to her for friendship and help. The music of the Norwegian violinist Ole Bull inspired her to write articles on his behalf, and a poverty-stricken Bohemian composer, Antony Philip Heinrich, turned to her for encouragement and publicity. She also wrote on behalf of sculptor Horace Kneeland and actress Jeannie Barrett. Margaret Fuller was working in New York from December 1844 to August 1846, and the two renewed their friendship.

Child's success as a writer at this time is remarkable in view of her reputation as an abolitionist. The Langley brothers, who at first wanted to publish her *Letters from New-York*, later backed out for fear the book would offend their Southern customers. Child decided to publish the book at her own expense. The following letter to an abolitionist Boston bookseller, written right after the edition was finally printed and bound, shows her back in the book business. Her long familiarity with the enterprise, along with her experience on the *Standard*, stood her in good stead. As it turned out, *Letters from New-York* sold out its first printing, and with the second a distant cousin, Charles S. Francis, took on the book for his own publishing firm.

To Henry W. Williams

New York Aug 29th 1843

I send you 25 copies of the N. York Letters, on the same terms that I have sent them to the N. York and Philadelphia anti slavery offices: viz: I will pay you 33 1/3 commission on the retail price. The retail price is 75 cts per vol, and the price to the trade is 60 cts. I expect you to pay me 50 cts a vol. for all you sell; ⟨as fast as you send for fresh supplies.⟩ at the end of three months, at the latest.

I do not wish you to vary the prices under any circumstances; those who want them cheaper may leave them. I want you to sell for cash only, unless *you* choose to be responsible for any sold on credit. I shall look to *you* for the pay.

I am thus particular, beca[use]¹ I have published the book on my own risk, and of course feel anxious to have returns in season to pay printer, binder, &c.

If you wish for more, pleas[e] write me an order, when they are wanted.

Yrs. Respectfully,

L. M. Child.

ALS; Williamsiana Collection, Williams College (microfiche 18/509).

Although David Lee Child was supposed to take over as the *National Anti-Slavery Standard*'s editor as soon as Maria resigned in early May 1843, he in fact did not leave Northampton until mid-July. Whether Maria continued to manage the paper in his absence is unclear. Garrison hoped that she would go on contributing to the literary department, and her "Letters from New-York" went on being published there. A letter to Lucretia Mott suggests her continued influence on the paper, as well as conveying something of her style as editor.

To Lucretia Mott

New York Sep 3d [1843]

Dear Friend,

Edward handed me the two extracts from Irish letters, which you had the kindness to send, but he seemed to have no definite idea of the purpose for which they were sent.¹ The message was "to do what I thought best with them." Therefore, I tore up the extract relating to myself, as soon as I had read it; being desirous that it should neither be published; nor handed about. I have an exceeding aversion to personal remarks about myself; especially of the laudatory kind. While I was editor, I always drew my pen heavily through all compliments to myself, and all criticisms upon my own, or other people's style of editing.

All I then cared for, and all I now care for, is to have my own conscience, and my own judgment satisfied concerning my own course. No individual is of much consequence, and the fewer remarks that are made about individuals the better.

¹ The edge of the letter is worn away.
¹ Edward Morris Davis (1811–87), a Philadelphia abolitionist and nonresistant, was Mott's son-in-law.

The extract relating to Father Mathew, I gave to David for the Standard thinking it might interest some of the readers.[2] I am much obliged to you for sending it.

I am glad the reception of the New York Letters afforded you any pleasure. It was a testimony of sincere respect for the pure excellence of your preaching, both in word and life.

Believe me very affectionately Yr friend, L. Maria Child.

P.S. David desires a most cordial remembrance to you and your household.

ALS; Clifton Waller Barrett Library, University of Virginia (microfiche 18/510).

Child had a lifelong distrust of utopian groups and a fun-loving eye for the ridiculous. Two letters describe her encounter with Bronson Alcott and Charles Lane, who in June 1843 founded the community of Fruitlands in Harvard, Massachusetts. Lane (1800–70) had come over from England, where he was a journalist, to organize the very strictly vegetarian Con-Sociate Family. Alcott brought his wife and four small daughters, Lane his son William; but the group disbanded at the end of the year. Alcott's daughter, Louisa May, who was eleven at the time, later drew upon her diary to write a satirical account of Fruitlands, *Transcendental Wild Oats* (*Independent*, 18 December 1873; repr. Harvard, Mass., 1975).

To Augusta G. King

N. York. Sep. 19th 1843

Dear Augusta,

. . . Theodore Parker spent a long evening here. I dont wonder you like him so much. I was extremely pleased with him. We held much fair discourse together, I believe to mutual edification; for I had some new facts to tell him, and he much to tell me. Harriet Sturgis has a rare chance.[1]

Alcott and Charles Lane have likewise been here. Perhaps Lane is one of the best and greatest of men; but his countenance pleases me not. In the first place, it looks as if the washwomen had caught it and scrubbed it on a washboard; and in the second place there is an expression, which would make me slow to put myself in his power. The day after they called, W. H. Channing came to tell me that he and they would hold a sort of social "palaver" together,

---

[2] Father Theobald Mathew (1790–1856), a Franciscan priest, crusaded for the temperance movement in Ireland and supported abolitionism in the United States.
[1] Harriet Sturgis may be one of the five daughters of William Sturgis, a Boston China trade merchant. What Child means by her "chance" with Theodore Parker is not clear; Parker had married Lydia Cabot in 1837.

that evening, at a room in Medical Hall. Not to slight the kind invitation, I went; but the air of the small room was so very stifling, that I turned and went off, knowing I should pay the penalty of a severe head-ache, if I remained half an hour. David and John tried it, for awhile, and then *they* left; David's patience giving way first. When he came home, I said, "Well, how did the conversation impress your mind"? He replied, "After I had been there a few minutes, I'll be cursed if I knew whether I *had* any mind at all." "What did they say?" "I dont know." "What was it *about*"? "I cant tell." Being much urged to remember *something*, he at last said that "Charles Lane divided man into three states; the disconscious, the conscious, and the unconscious. The *dis*conscious was the state of a pig; the conscious was the baptism by water; and the the [*sic*] *un*conscious the baptism by fire."

In a few minutes, John came home, with a violent head-ache. "Well, John," said I, "have they done you any good?" "They've put my body and mind both in a devil of a muss," [[a N. York phrase for utter confusion]] said he, "and I wanted to kick 'em all." "What did they say?" "They did'nt know themselves— how should *I*?" "What was it *about*"? "Mind and body." "Well, what did they *say* of them"? said I, for I felt too mischievous to leave him in peace. For some time, I could learn nothing more, than that they said "a snarl of things;" but being urged unmercifully, he at last stated that W. H. Channing held a discussion with C. Lane; that "Channing seemed to think there *was* some connection between soul and body; but them Boston chaps, so far as he could understand 'em, seemed to consider the body all a damned sham."   So ended Lane and Alcott's visit to enlighten Babylon. When I first saw them, I said "What brought you to N. York?" "I dont know," said Mr. Alcott; "it seems a miracle that we are here." "What was your object in coming"? "I don't know," replied he; and I believe he left the citizens as little enlightened as himself. I would have given a trifle, just for pure mischief, to have smuggled in the reporter of the N.Y. Herald, to take, or *make,* notes of the conversation.   Seriously, I grow less and less inclined to seek aid from any of these wandering prophets. Not a morsel of spiritual food did I ever gain from any of them. All the real progress that I make is in the quietude of my own spirit. More and more do I seek to be *alone.* All this whirl of reforms are but shifting shapes of the evil and the false; but they indicate the approach of the good and the true.
. . .

ALS; Lydia Maria Child Papers, Anti-Slavery Collection, Cornell University (microfiche 18/511).

To Ellis Gray Loring

Sep. 26'th 1843

Dear Friend,
    I intended to have sent a letter with the volumes of N. York Letters, but had so much business on hand that I was obliged to postpone it. However, you

lost little; for my monotonous life gives me little to say, except that I love you both from the very depths of my heart.

No "strangers of distinction" have crossed my path, except Theodore Parker, Alcott and Charles Lane. My last letter to Augusta describes the "whereabout and whatabout" of the two last; or rather it shows that neither they nor others know where to find it. Lane was dressed in linen throughout—having scruples concerning all other materials for wearing apparel. I felt some fear lest linen should come under ban before his next call, and so leave no reserve but the primitive fig-leaf. Even *this*, David thought might be cast aside before his visit was concluded, should it happen to occur to him that it was used for purposes of hiding, and that hiding, being all a sham, could have no place in the divinely unconscious state. In fact, there is no prank so mad, that it would surprise me in these insane, well-meaning egotists. W'm H. Channing's zeal for innovation is tempered by more discretion and practical good sense; but some of *his* hobbies will throw him, I think. I admire him exceedingly—he is so beautiful in character and person! The great deficiency of his mind seems to me to be that he makes no *points*, has no *centres* whence to radiate his lines. I believe this is the reason why he takes so little hold of other minds, beautiful and true as he is. He is at present in a state to sympathize with all reform—or rather with the *spirit* of all reforms; for he would not work in their *machinery* a week.

This puts me in mind that, in your last letter, you argued that organizations for reform were as necessary as ever. It may be so. I was always a poor hand to calculate the effect of things; and I certainly feel too little interest in this point, to argue it. For five years I have felt an increasing inability to work in organizations with conscientious freedom. Things deemed necessary for the support of the cause seem to me to be *wrong*. If this feeling is mistaken, even by my friends, for personal pique, or petty resentment, I cannot help it. I shall not defend myself. My conscientious objections to the narrow bigotry of the Swedenborgians is, by them, termed my "excessive pride of self-derived intelligence." Let them have their say. They verily think it is so; but in humility of soul, before my God, I know that this is *not* the reason why I feel repelled from their circle. Sects and organizations never forgive those who leave them. I have no word of discouragement to offer to those who *can* labor in freedom, in either sects or organizations for reform. On the contrary, I rejoice in all the good done by such instrumentality. I make no effort to influence David's mind. I never inquire what his editorials are to be, and never read them till the paper is issued. I can see, however, that he kicks occasionally in the fetters of an organization. My own belief is, that no free soul can fill such an office; but perhaps I am mistaken. I wish you not to read this, or any of my letters, out of your own family connexion. When I write to *you* I want to feel free; and I do not, if I have the idea that my letters will be shown about. . . .

ALS; Manuscript Division, New York Public Library (microfiche 18/515).

Although *Letters from New-York* sold well in America and was also published in England, Child found herself toward the end of November 1843 having to pay the paper manufacturer, the printer, and the binder before the booksellers had paid her. She borrowed one hundred dollars from Frank Shaw to tide her over. By December she was running out of books to send to the booksellers, as this letter to a Boston bookseller and publisher indicates. She at this time once again began writing regular "Letters from New-York" columns for the *Boston Courier*.

To James Munroe and Co.

New York Dec 20'th, 1843

Messrs. Munroe & Co.

It is not in my power to supply you with any more Letters from New York. Of the 1500 I published I have but about 40 on hand, and I have orders for four times that number, which were received earlier than yours. Francis has sold between 500 and 600. He has but about 25 on hand, and called for more, three weeks ago. I could not then furnish him with any, because the few remaining in my hands were not bound. I cannot now furnish him with more than 20. So small a number would hardly be worth dividing between you.

The book has sold exceedingly well; much better than I expected. I would publish another edition myself, were I not straitened for means. I think another edition would sell, but of course more slowly than the first. Five or six letters were omitted in the first edition, because I feared to make the book too expensive. I know not whether it would be best to dress these up and add them to another edition.

If you are disposed to publish another edition, what will you offer me a thousand, for all *sold*, with the understanding that you do not pay me unless they sell?

I am much obliged to you for selling my English copy.

Yrs Respectfully,
L. M. Child.

P.S. Francis Geo. Shaw will probably soon present you with an order from me, for $100 which I borrowed of him to pay my printer. Please to pay the money as soon as suits your convenience.

ALS; Anti-Slavery Collection, Rare Books and Manuscripts, Boston Public Library (microfiche 18/524).

Anna Loring, the only child of Ellis Gray and Louisa Loring, was thirteen years old when Child wrote her the following letter about an orphan. Child eventually found the boy a home.

To Anna Loring

New York Dec. 26'th. [1843]

Dear Anna,

I send you a necklace of satin spar, as a slight love token for the New Year. I hope you will like it. I remember when I was of your age, I had a great passion for necklaces.

I had a very happy Christmas, and I will tell you how it happened. The watchmen picked up a little vagabond in the street, who said he had neither father nor mother, and had lost his way. He said his mother used to get drunk and sleep in the streets; but that he had not seen her for five years. They put him in the tombs, not because he had committed any crime, but because he had nowhere to go. He was about 10 years old. I applied to the orphan asylum, but he was older than their rules allowed them to admit. The poor child worried my mind greatly. On Christmas morning the asylum ladies sent me $5 and a pair of nice boots for him. Mr. Child went to the Tombs for him, and after a good deal of difficulty found him and brought him home. He was in a situation too dirty and disgusting to describe. I cut off his hair, put him in a tub of water, scrubbed him from head to foot, bought a suit of clothes, and dressed him up. You never saw any little fellow so changed, and so happy in the change! But above all things his boots delighted him. I could hardly keep his eyes off them long enough to wash his face. "Are them boots for *me*?" he asked; and when I told him yes, it seemed as if the sun had shone out all over his face. "I never expected to have such a boot to my foot," said he: "I shall remember *this* Christmas the longest day I live.["] As he sits before me now, making pictures on his slate, he every now and then thrusts out his foot, and examines the boot from toe to heel. He is nearly white, quite good looking, remarkably bright, and very docile and affectionate. I do not yet know what I shall do with him, but I hope to get him a good place in the country. When I asked him what he used to do, "I don't know exactly," said he; "sometimes I sat down on a stone, let the sun shine on me and cried." Poor little fellow! His joy and gratitude have given me a happy Christmas. Farewell.

Your affectionate Aunt Maria.

. . .

ALS; Child Papers, Clements Library, University of Michigan (microfiche 18/527).

On 5 May 1844 the American Anti-Slavery Society opened its annual meeting in New York, one which Child avoided by going out to Long Island for a few days. Still, she followed the proceedings closely. In a letter to Loring she attacks the "come-outer" rejection of all nonabolitionist churches and political parties. David Lee Child, who had just resigned from the *National Anti-Slavery*

Standard, urged in an enclosed letter of the same date that they form a new antislavery organization. The new organization would advocate compensation to slaveholders for freed slaves and "a conciliatory as well as compromising spirit and love towards the church, clergy, and the state." Maria, however, gives no indication of supporting her husband's idea, and his proposal apparently found no response.

To Ellis Gray Loring

Confidential.   New York, May 16'th 1844
Dearly Beloved Friend,

    . . .

. . . I am thankful that you have entered a protest against the wild spirit of ultraism, which is driving one of the best of causes to its ruin. I have long felt that the judicious and moderately conservative among us gave up the reins too much to these Jehus. The effect is, to make our money and abilities serve to advance things which we do not in our consciences approve. If they go on with their favorite work of sifting out all but the Simon Pures, they will soon sift down the society to N. P. Rogers, Abigail Folsom, and S. S. Foster.[1] It must be a strong cause indeed that can bear such repeated repulsion of sincere and devoted friends.

I cannot express the degree of my dislike, of my utter abhorrence, of this come-out-ism. It seems to me irrational, unphilosophic, impracticable, mischievous in its effects, and excessively tyrannical in its operation. It was this that drove me from the Standard. It was not satisfied with being treated kindly and respectfully, and left in peace to do its own work; it *insisted* that the Standard should endorse it. This, neither my reason or my conscience would allow me to do. Between you and I, Mrs. Chapman was *determined* that the popularity of the Standard should be *forced* to sustain the come-outisms of church and state. She probably thought that rather than lose the salary, I would consent to be so used; and that by and bye I might come into it myself. But from the first, I looked upon the whole thing as another form of sectarianism, on the altar of which individual freedom must be sacrificed.

It has pained me to suppose that you might consider me capricious and impatient. I preferred to appear so, rather than start a new controversy, and bring new accusations into the anti-slavery ranks. But, my dear friend, I was *not* impetuous and over-sensitive. I bore and forbore, and tried to do my best, until this ultraist pressure, on all sides, almost drove me mad. It no longer depended on my will. Such a night-mare was on me, that I *could* not write, either one thing or another. I have not yet recovered from the effects of it. It will yet take

---

[1] Folsom (ca. 1792–1867), like Rogers and Foster, was regarded by many as a fanatic. She often interrupted antislavery meetings and had to be carried out.

great quantities of music, and blossoms, and serene engravings, to restore me to my former self. Mr. Spear, the man who made a book on Capital Punishment, confessed a similar experience to me.[2] He said these come-outers talked to him, till the tower of Babel seemed falling about his ears, and his brain was all on fire. One told him to come out of one thing, and another out of another, till the whole earth seemed slipping away under his feet, and the heavens rolling off overhead. He said he found some strength and consolation in attending meeting, and that he thought his occasional testimony there was not without use; but they told him this was a deception of the devil, and that he was recreant to his duty to God and man in holding any communion with a sect. He asked me if I thought so. I told him certainly not, if he thought otherwise; for his own soul could alone judge of his duties and his needs. He seemed to me a very conscientious, tender-spirited man. I advised him to stroll in the green fields, to hear music and prayer, to *worship*, wheresoever and with-whomsoever he could. His health was evidently wearing away under excitement and conscientious conflict.

We are all well, and in pretty good spirits, though not without anxiety. *My prospects are very good. I have a good deal of profitable work on my hands, if I can only find time to do it, and have a mind free from perplexity for others.*

. . .

ALS; Manuscript Division, New York Public Library (microfiche 19/555).

Although Child had left the antislavery organization, she still continued helping slaves when she could. In the spring of 1844, John Gorham Palfrey sought advice in this regard. Palfrey (1796–1881) was a Unitarian minister in Boston, a professor of sacred literature at Harvard, owner and editor of the *North American Review* from 1835 to 1843, and a Massachusetts state legislator. His father and brother owned slaves in Louisiana, and when he came to Child, she informed him that she had once helped one of his brother's slaves to freedom.

To Henrietta Sargent

New York June 23d 1844

Dear Henrietta,

. . .

. . . Dr. Palfrey called on me, on his way to N. Orleans. I agreed to find places for five of his slaves, and have done so. He behaved nobly. His brothers offered to let him take his share in real estate; and that would have satisfied the conscience of most people; but he at once answered that he should consider

---

[2] Charles Spear wrote *Essays on the Punishment of Death* (Boston, 1844).

such an arrangement equivalent to selling the slaves; and begged that as many slaves as *possible* might be put into his share. He told me that he had some fears as to how Mrs. Palfrey would approve of his resolution; since it would alienate considerable property from her children, when his own pecuniary affairs were considerably embarrassed; but, to his surprise and delight, she promptly replied, "I want no child of mine to inherit a dollar from the sale of slaves." We have not labored in vain—have we dear Henrietta? Here is some of the fruits of your purses and baskets. Luckily no true principle can be smothered by the worst possible management of its supporters. Give my respects to good Dr. Adam, when you see him. Tell him I liked his protest extremely.[1] It seemed to me to be written with the best sense, the best temper, and the best taste.

David is at Northampton, attending to a little business. He has seemed like his own cheerful and buoyant self, ever since he got rid of the burden of the Standard. He kept hold of it longer than I thought he would. He has not quite settled his mind between two or three plans for the coming year; but the way opens pleasantly for him in two or three directions. With best love to Catherine I am Yrs most gratefully & affectionately, L. M. C.

. . .

ALS; Lydia Maria Child Papers, Anti-Slavery Collection, Cornell University (microfiche 19/563).

To Francis Shaw

New York July 18'th, 1844.

Dear Friend,

I thank you for your kind letter. It was really refreshing, it was so long since I had heard from you. I am glad to give you pleasure in any way, by Philothea, or anything else that I can write or do. There is another edition of Philothea in press now. Francis had so many calls for it, that he thought he might venture to print. I doubt, however, whether the sale will be great. The second edition of N. York Letters is nearly gone. The great popularity of that volume surprises me; for it is full of ultraisms. However, there is always a sort of fascination about whatever gives out *itself* freely. I mean to devote the remainder of my life to the attainment of literary excellence. Perhaps you will think from this, that I am smitten with what Milton calls "the last infirmity of noble minds." But the feeling rather is, that my life has hitherto been too

[1] In a letter published in the *National Anti-Slavery Standard* on 13 June 1844, William Adam (1797–1881) declared his objection to being called on by "come-outers" to leave the church and support disunion. A native of Scotland, Adam had been a professor of Oriental languages at Harvard until 1839; he subsequently moved to Northampton, Massachusetts, where he helped found the Northampton Association of Education and Industry, the Fourieristic experiment in cooperation.

fragmentary, and therefore without important result. I have turned aside from my true mission to help Mr. Child in various emergencies; or rather to *try* to help what did not admit of help. I have allowed my thoughts to be frittered away on pecuniary calculations how to meet current expenses, when there were always elements at work, which upset my calculations. Now I intend to live for one individual object. Formed as my character now is, I cannot do otherwise than make literature the honest agent of my conscience and my heart; and if I do this, the more glowingly and gracefully I can write, the better.

You ask whether Mr. Child has inoculated me *again* with politics. Your memory is better than mine if you can recollect any period of my life when I regarded politics otherwise than with extreme aversion. Perhaps I see through the miserable sham a little clearer now, than I did when younger; but conversation on the subject was always as discordant to me as the clashing of tongs and brass pans. As for Henry Clay, I have no confidence whatever in him. There is a cold superciliousness in his reply to honest Mr. Mendenhall, which betrays a nature capable of being very mean and unprincipled. Mr. Child, who is the most honest and unselfish man I ever knew, is carried away with the idea that Texas is *the* question on which the extension of American slavery depends, and that Henry Clay is the only man that can save the country from annexation.[1] I smile; for ever since I can remember men have been expending their energies in *saving the country;* and what comes of it? I did [give] your message; in answer to which he admits that Clay was shuffling in that transaction; but then he is certainly going to save the country from annexation. I do not want to annoy him on the subject. He leaves me to be a very free individual, and I wish to do the same by him. In Frederika Bremer's Home, I was charmed with the recognition of a higher harmonizing principle than unity of opinions, tastes, or pursuits; viz: a sincere desire to lead each other into all good.[2]   I have had a most unexpected and pleasant visit from my dear brother, who will bring you this. It was a joy to me to see him. As for *smoking*, I did cure my adopted son of the bad habit. He did not touch a cigar for a year. But at the end of that time, he went to N. England, and certain persons, among whom I think was one Francis G. Shaw, persuaded him that people did not feel any better for leaving off smoking. He resumed his habit, which has been still more confirmed by Mr. Child, so that I

[1] Mr. Mendenhall, a Quaker from Indiana, had petitioned Henry Clay, then running for president, to free his own slaves. Clay in turn said that he opposed slavery but was against immediate emancipation, and asked if Mendenhall were willing to raise fifteen thousand dollars to take care of the slaves if they were freed. Clay lost the 1844 election because of his noncommittal stand on Texas; he later sponsored the Compromise of 1850.
[2] *The Home; or, Family Cares and Family Joys,* by Swedish writer Frederika Bremer (1801–65), had been translated and published in New York the previous year.

despair of breaking it up. Indeed I say nothing; for if one cannot convince a friend, it is not worth while to tease him.

. . .

ALS; Houghton Library, Harvard University (microfiche 20/565).

When *Letters from New-York* came out in 1843, Child sent a copy to her friend Margaret Fuller. Fuller published a review of it in the *Dial*, which she and Emerson were then editing, and the following year sent Child a copy of *Summer on the Lakes* (Boston, 1844), her reflections on the new America of the Midwest. She and Child had been out of touch for several years, and Fuller wrote that she hoped they might renew their friendship: "In former days, you used to tell me much which I have stored in memory as I have in my heart the picture of your affectionate, generous, and resolute life."*

To Margaret Fuller

New York, August 23d, 1844

Dear Miss Fuller,

It has doubtless been your experience, as it has mine, to have the heart and mind full of some favorite purpose—to neglect it at the auspicious moment, on account of petty obstacles—and then to give it the go-by for uncounted days and weeks.

Such has been the history of my not writing to you. My heart was very much touched and gratified by your kind note; and when your book came, I read it with the constantly gushing feeling, "I will write immediately to Miss Fuller, and tell her how much I thank her." But with the morrow, came relatives unexpectedly from a distance; then illness in the family; then hurried orders from the printer; then illness for myself. And so time passed on, and I did *not* write to Miss Fuller; though she was ever in my heart.

Now let me thank you most cordially for your kind remembrance of me. It has been a most pleasant gleam in a life somewhat monotonous and sombre. The book is a highly agreeable book, full of touches of beauty, and original piquant sayings. I was struck, as I am in all you write, with the vigor and acuteness of intellect. Shall I tell you what always, more or less, mars my pleasure? I have no critical skill, and you have much; but the impression on my mind may be taken for just what it is worth. In a word then, you always seem to me to write with too much *effort*. It may now be the mere *habit* of elaborateness; but it has the appearance of effort. The stream is abundant and beautiful; but it always seems to be *pumped*, rather than to *flow*. In other words I might say, your

---

* 13 Mar. 1844, Fruitlands Museum, Harvard, Mass.

house is too full; there is too much furniture for your rooms. This is the result of a higher education than popular writers usually have; but it stands much in the way of extensive popularity.

I live so much out of the world, that I do not know what has been the general popularity of your book. Those whom I have seen have liked it very much. My brother, in particular, thought it delightful. He thinks that you have done so much for his daughter's intellectual and moral culture, that you are a ⟨very⟩ prime favorite of his.[1]   I am often tempted to envy those who have had the advantages of a thorough education. For myself, I have done nothing but "hear the grass grow," as Bettine says. If I were now to attempt to be something other than I am, I should be neither one thing nor the other.

Shall you ever translate the remainder of Gunderode?[2] Surely, it might be done by subscription, if not otherwise. Bettina has been such a full and flowing fountain of inspiration to me, that I cannot bear to lose a word she has uttered. No writer has ever made me so wild with joy, as Bettina.

Farewell. May the blessing of God be with you.

Gratefully and respectfully Yrs,
L. M. Child.

ALS; Fuller Papers, Houghton Library, Harvard University (microfiche 20/570).

Robert Cassie Waterston (1812–93), a Unitarian minister in Boston, sent Child some pamphlets on social reform, titles unknown.

To Robert Cassie Waterston

New York, Aug. 27th 1844.

Dear Sir,

. . .

. . . I am strongly inclined to think that the re-construction of society on a new basis is the *only* thing that can arrest the frightful increase of pauperism and crime. If it be true that you cannot change the outward structure of society till men are morally and intellectually improved, on the other hand, the masses *cannot* be morally and intellectually raised, until they are placed in a more com-

[1] Abby Bradford Francis (d. 1886), probably then in her late teens, was the daughter of Convers Francis.
[2] Fuller had published her translation of *Günderode*, by Bettina von Arnim (1785–1859), in 1842. The author, known as Bettine, was a leading figure in the intellectual life of Berlin and was involved in struggles for working-class relief, emancipation of the Jews, and the abolition of capital punishment. *Günderode*, first published in 1840, is a series of letters to a poet who had died in 1806, Karoline von Günderode. Three more numbers of these letters were announced, but never appeared.

---

fortable physical condition. I know an excellent Quaker lady who went to England, to preach to the poor. "When I gathered them into my meetings," said she, "I found that I could not gain their attention, because they were hungry. At last I came to the place of meeting provided with a store of comfortable food. I fed them well, and after that, they listened to me, many of them with their hearts."

This preaching about Christian brotherhood to men who *see* no practical brotherhood, has slight effect; and he who from childhood has felt the hard grip of poverty, listens quite skeptically to accounts of the overflowing goodness of God, and his equal love to the human race. Our religion and our institutions are so horribly discordant, that one or the other must vanish.

On this question of reconstruction, I think and speak with diffidence, because I do not see my way clear. But the sum cannot be rightly stated, which yields such a product as now lies before us.

I thank you and all others, who are helping to disentangle the snarl. All kinds of work, that are done with a sincere heart, must and will leave an impression on all coming time.

I thank you most cordially for your kind estimate of the influence I exert. I will show my gratitude by trying to deserve it better. Please remember me in the most friendly manner to Mrs. Waterston. May the blessing of our Heavenly Father be with you, and may you be strengthened to go on in your works of love and mercy.

With the highest respect,
L. M. Child.

ALS; New-York Historical Society (microfiche 20/571).

Child had first heard the Norwegian violinist Ole Bull (1810–80) in December 1843 and written an enthusiastic review of his concert for the *Boston Courier*, 23 December. Ole Bull began a new series of New York concerts in October 1844. Child's response was even more intense than in the year before. Although her descriptions of him and his music tend to hyperbole, her passion was plainly genuine and revitalizing. The man "has opened unknown depths in my soul," she wrote Anna Loring after one of his concerts. "My nerves were so excited, that I came home and wept that the time must come, sooner or later, when I could hear Ole Bul no more."* Bull's playing and personal charm captivated others as well. He made a number of tours in the United States and founded a colony for Norwegian immigrants called Oleana, near Coudersport, Pennsylvania. In the next letter, she asks her old friend from Northampton, John S. Dwight, to write an article on Bull. Dwight in 1851 would start *Dwight's Journal of Music*, which was to be influential in shaping American musical taste.

* 13–14 Oct. 1844, Child Papers, Clements Library, University of Michigan.

To John S. Dwight

[[Please not read this letter to strangers. I have written with too much *abandon* for the public eye.]]

New York Oct. 23d 1844

Dear Friend,

How soon you went silent again, after writing me that beautiful letter about Vieux Temps![1] And I wanted so to have you write me what you thought of Ole Bul! I will not be like the man who urged Stuart, the artist, to come and give his opinion of some old pictures he was exhibiting. "Some people say they are copies," said he; "but I swear I'll knock down the first person that intimates they are not by the old masters."

I will not *thus* ask your opinion of Ole Bul; but I *shall* be grieved if you do not deeply feel the beauty and the power of his music. It has awakened in me a new sense—it has so stirred the depths of my soul, and kindled my whole being, that my heart bounds forth to meet one that sympathizes with me. Old as I am, it is the strongest enthusiasm of my life. I could have thrown my arms round Susan Lyman's neck, when she told me that her experience had been like mine; that from him she dated the birth of a new sense.[2] It may seem presumptuous in poor ignorant me, to say it; but against a million learned critics, I do say I would venture to assert that nothing but genius, and transcendant genius, too, could take such possession of my soul.

There has been a French clique here, that have tried from the beginning to underrate him. Partly on account of Vieux Temps, and partly because he and his music are both too spontaneous and inartificial to please the French. They have done a great many mean things, and tried hard to set a fashion of criticising and depreciating him, as they did Shakespeare before him. What's the use of comparing him and Vieux Temps, or Shakespeare and Racine? The things are too different in character to be compared.

Concerning the alleged "false notes" of Ole Bul, I, of course, do not presume to judge. But I don't believe the assertion. Simply because I do not believe that an organization so exquisitely attuned to music as his, could itself endure false notes. Certainly he has reasons for departures from established rules; wild and wayward they may be; but it surely is not want of ear, or want of knowledge. You know the critics complained much of Beethoven's aberrations. They alleged that he did certain things which distinguished masters of the science had forbidden. "Do they forbid it?" said Beethoven. "Well, then, *I* permit it."

One of the oldest musicians here, says: "I am a cool and candid observer. I have heard Vieux Temps, and admired his perfect skill and finish. I have heard

---

[1] Henri Vieuxtemps (1820–81) was a French violinist then on tour in the United States.
[2] Susan Lyman (1823–1904), the then twenty-one-year-old daughter of Judge Joseph and Anna Jean Lyman of Northampton, Mass., often visited Child in New York. She married Peter Lesley in 1848.

all that the French and Italian critics here have to urge; I have heard Paganini again and again. But there is no mistake about it; no man has done such wonders on the violin as Ole Bul. No man living or that has lived, equalled him in tone and power. Paganinni himself fell short of him in these attributes."

You would be charmed with the personal character of Ole Bul. He is just like a child. Diffident of himself, and sensitive, oh *so* sensitive, that a rude breath hurts him. The extreme and beautiful simplicity of his character is not appreciated by the worldlings. To them it seems like weakness. Then all nature breathes through his soul with such free joy! The other day he was playing on the violin, and a bird in the room mocked him exactly. He cried, he laughed, he jumped. He was like a child to whom an absent mother had returned and spoken suddenly. *He* make false notes! If he does, so does nature herself.

Now my object in writing this is to ask you, if you admire his genius, as I hope you do, to write one of those eloquent articles of yours for the Democratic. Don't let any one know that I asked you, though; for should he hear of it, I think it would both give him pain, and offend him. He pursues a very dignified and manly course about such things. He leaves his reputation to take care of itself, without any such efforts on the part of himself or his friends.

Does he impress you enough to make you *wish* to write about him? If not, I need not charge you not to undertake it. If you wish to hear him frequently, with a view to understand and describe his characteristics, I can easily have matters arranged, so that it will be pecuniarily easy for you to do so. Tell me frankly, whether you would like to do it. And I pray you, answer *this* letter before the end of the world.

Susan Lyman spent a week in N. York a short time ago, and I got more acquainted with her than I ever was before. She is a lovely and a gentle creature. We talked much of you. I have been studying a great deal about music for the last few months; and I have *so* wanted you near to answer questions. There are so many things that books cannot tell me.

By the way, Ole Bul says that what I write and talk is to him like the study of counter-point. What does that mean? It must be *florid* counter-point I think.

Now please do write before a great while. If I do not sign any name, you will know that this bubbling effusion comes from your affectionate friend, L. Maria Child.

. . .

John Hopper, my good adopted son, desires the most cordial remembrance to you. *Will* you answer me? *Will* you?

ALS; Anti-Slavery Collection, Rare Books and Manuscripts, Boston Public Library (microfiche 20/582).

Ralph Waldo Emerson sent Child a copy of his *Essays, Second Series* (Boston, 1844).

To Augusta G. King

New York Oct. 30th, 1844.

Dear Augusta,

. . . Emerson has sent me his new volume. As usual, it is full of deep and original sayings, and touches of exceeding beauty. But, as usual, it takes away my strength, and makes me uncertain whether to hang myself or my gown over a chair. What is the use of telling us that everything is "scene-painting and counterfeit"; that nothing is real; that everything eludes us? That no single thing in life keeps the promise it makes? Or if they keep it, keep it like the witches to Macbeth? Enough of this conviction is forced upon us by experience, without having it echoed in literature. My being is so alive and earnest, that it resists and abhors these ghastly eluding spectres. It abhors them, and says "Be ye ghosts, and dwell among ghosts. But though all the world be dead, and resolved into vapory elements, *I* will live!" Emerson would smile at this; because it shows how deeply I *feel* the fact I quarrel with. But after all, if we extend our vision into the regions of faith, all this mocking and unreality vanishes; and in the highest sense, all things *keep* the promises they make. Love, marriage, ambition, sorrow, nay even strong religious impressions, may, and will, fall short of the early promise they made, if we look to this life only. But they are all means, not ends. In that higher life, we shall find that no deep feelings, no true experience, has slid over the surface of our being, and left no impression.

But I am preaching, dear Augusta, instead of giving the light careless touches that belong to letter-writing. What have you seen and heard of Theodore Parker, since his return? John requested him to buy a few engravings in Italy; and I think he chose admirably. One of them was intended for me; and if my spirit had been with him (as perhaps it was) he could not have chosen to my more complete satisfaction. It is the Cumæan Sibyl, by Domenichino. She holds a scroll of music in her hand, and seems listening intently to the voices of the universe. It is the likeness of my soul, in some of its moods. Oh *how* I have listened! I am trying to know something of the science of music too, as well as its significance and expression. You would smile to see my table piled up with History of Music, Music Explained, Musical Dictionary, &c. But all these books, though they tell me somethings [*sic*], do not tell me half as much as music itsel[f.][1] I begin to be content with the old-fashioned heaven, of hear[ing] music through all eternity. Oh dear, I do so want John [S.] Dwight's help. He has the feeling and the science, to[o.] It is curious, but standing as I am on the verge of declin[ing] life, my senses are all growing more acute and clear. So acute, that my sources of pain and pleasure are increased tenfold. I am a great deal more *alive* than I used to be.

. . .

I am very much contented with my situation. I can keep off all intruding

1 The paper is torn here, cutting off the ends of five lines of writing.

strangers, I can earn enough to pay my board, and I have a superb silk gown, and the prettiest shawl that I have seen this long time. Then I have certain other sources of internal satisfaction, deeper and holier, of which I do not care to *talk*. If you want to be *alive*, give your sympathies freely to all God's creatures. "The prayers of the heart are always answered, if the *hand* prays with them."
. . .

ALS; Lydia Maria Child Papers, Anti-Slavery Collection, Cornell University (microfiche 20/584).

Margaret Fuller arrived in New York from Boston in December 1844, to take on a job with Horace Greeley's *New York Tribune*. She lived with Greeley and his wife in the house described in the following letter. *Woman in the Nineteenth Century*, Fuller's treatise on the limitations imposed on women, appeared early in 1845 in New York. In it she took up sex and prostitution, urging sympathy for prostitutes and action to help them, and specifically mentioning Child's assistance to a prostitute, Amelia Norman, early in 1844. Child was impressed with the book and wrote a strong review for the *Boston Courier* of 12 February 1845, noting Fuller's courage in speaking out plainly on matters generally avoided. Most reviewers, however, castigated the book.

To Anna Loring

New York Feb. 6th, 1845.
Dear Anna,
You always say you like to receive letters from me, and so it makes me happy to write, because I think I may give you some pleasure.
A little while ago, I set forth to make our friend Margaret Fuller a visit. It was an undertaking for *me*, I assure you; for we live three miles apart, and the roads were one mass of mud. I went out in the Harlem omnibus to *forty ninth street,* where she told me she lived. But instead of a street, I found a winding zigzag cart-track. It was as rural as you can imagine, with moss-covered rocks, scraggly bushes, and a brook that came tumbling over a little dam, and run [*sic*] under the lane. After passing through three great swing-gates, I came to the house, which stands all alone by itself, and is as inaccessible, as if *I* had chosen it, to keep people off. It is a very old house, with a very old porch, and very old vines, and a very old garden, and very old summer-houses dropping to pieces, and a very old piazza at the back, overgrown with very old rose-bushes, which at that season were covered with red berries. The piazza is almost *on* the East river, with Blackwell's Island in full view before it. Margaret's chamber looks out upon a little woody knoll, that runs down into the water, and boats and ships are passing her window all the time. How anything so old

and picturesque has been allowed to remain standing near New York so long, I cannot imagine. I spent three or four delightful hours with Margaret, and then trudged home in the mud, afoot and alone. I carried out your likeness, and she seemed so extremely pleased with it, and so glad to see it, that I left it with her. It was so plain that she grudged it to me, that I should have given it to her, if I could have brought my mind to part with your dear father and mother's present. I like Margaret *very* much. We had many pleasant little anecdotes to tell each other about you.

. . .

My good John is lying here beside my light-stand, on three chairs and a pillow, reading a novel. Mr. Child is in the next room writing a letter, but sings out that I must give his love to all your household, and Nony especially. The good old gentleman is well and cheerful, and we all jog on comfortably, with the usual proportion of sunshine and shadow. All of us think of you all with heartfelt, unabating love. What *has* become of Augusta? Is she dead, or married? Give my love to her. Please ask dear father whether it is Wordsworth who says, "All gifts of noblest origin are breathed upon by Hope's perpetual breath." "A cheerful heart is what the Muses love, a soaring spirit is their prime delight."

Farewell, dear child. Don't forget to love

Aunt Maria

ALS; Child Papers, Clements Library, University of Michigan (microfiche 21/604).

To Louisa Loring

New York, Feb. 8'th 1845.

Dearest Louise,

Mr. Hudson[1] made a flying call half an hour ago, and left your dear affectionate letter. I was a good deal depressed in spirits, feeling as if I were good for nothing, and as if nobody cared for me; and your kind words did my heart a great deal of good. God knows I would dearly like to fly right into your "cozy back parlour," and have a skirmish with Ellis and all his cyclos. But I don't see how I can at present. Philothea is going through the press, and I have proofs every night. The second volume of N. York Letters is going through, and I have several more new letters to write, beside attending to the proofs. They want another volume of Flowers for Children, and I stand pledged to write a story a month for the Columbian Magazine, whether there is any grist in my mill, or not. All this I *must* do to meet the expenses of my little nest.

I am very much obliged to you for putting my name to the present for Harriet Martineau. I honor her character highly, and would be glad to show her any mark of respect that my humble means and influence would allow. I have no objection whatever to my name's being used with the anti-slavery ladies,

[1] Erasmus Darwin Hudson.

in anything that does not involve me in their narrow partizanship, and their disposition to tear down rudely all that differs from them in opinion.

I have read Margaret's book, Woman in the Nineteenth Century, and I like it much. I procured it in proof-sheet, and sent a brief notice of it to the Boston Courier, thinking it might possibly help the sale a little. It is a *bold* book, I assure you. I should not have dared to have written some things in it, though it would have been safer for me, being married. But they need to be said, and she is brave to do it. She bears a noble testimony to anti slavery principles in several places. She is a great woman, and no mistake. I like her extremely; and I especially like her, because she feels what has so strongly impressed my more untutored soul, that Ole Bul is a *poet*-musician, that his conceptions are *romantic* and full of *genius*.

You need not apologize for mentioning another lecturer alongside with Emerson. He always excites my mind strongly; but I never was so mad about *him*, as to allow no other genius to be mentioned with him. I do maintain, though, that he is the best *poet* in the country, by all odds, and I am ready to do battle with anybody that maintains to the contrary.

. . .

ALS; Lydia Maria Child Papers, A/C 536, 1, Schlesinger Library, Radcliffe College (microfiche 21/605).

The composer Antony Philip Heinrich (1781–1861) came to the United States from Bohemia in 1805; lived in a variety of places around the country, including a log cabin in Kentucky; and in 1842 helped found the Philharmonic Society in New York. Among his many works using American themes was "The Wild Wood's Spirits Chant, or the Pilgrims of the New World," which Child reviewed in the *Boston Courier*. Heinrich, who was known as the "mad musician," replied to the following letter with a detailed description of how he lived in a room with no furniture, boxes of music his only table, his piano missing a leg, his only chair borrowed from the black woman who was his landlady. He supported himself by giving piano lessons to little girls. Child characteristically befriended him, but his fortunes never improved and he died in poverty.

To Antony Philip Heinrich

                                        Third St. April 29th, 1845.
To Anthony Phillip Heinrich.
Dear Sir,

. . .

You greatly misunderstood my character, when you suggested that your not being in "court dress" was the reason I did not see you. I did not know who you were, or what you were, when I said, "I am too much engaged to see strangers." But certainly had it been John Jacob Astor's son, the reply would have been the same. I never in my life asked any questions concerning a man's coat; but should I accidentally learn that his coat was thread-bare, it would be an *inducement* for me to set aside engagements to see him. You would forgive my apparent rudeness, if you knew how numerous are the demands on my time and attention. I am absolutely obliged, in self-defence, in a city like this, to refuse to see strangers; though in so doing, I am oftentimes apparently un-courteous to those whom I would *wish* to treat with the utmost courtesy. All artists are to me as brothers, and to musicians, in particular, I would be most kind and respectful; for my reverence for their divine art amounts almost to worship. But my situation compels me to lead a secluded and industrious life. All my means of helping myself, or others, must be of my own earning. I would gladly see everybody, sympathize with everybody, help everybody, and be enter-tained and instructed by everybody. But, as the Spanish proverb says, "No man can carry three water-melons under one arm." One comes to me, as you did, merely to express kindness and respect; another comes to ask my opinion about the rights of women; another, to ascertain my views about the Trinity or the atonement; another, to get me to help him in establishing a community; another, to look at his first picture, and decide whether he can make an artist; another to revise and correct an unpublished poem; another, to find a suitable situation for some outcast; another, to persuade me to take charge of a crazy mother. In short, there is no end to the catalogue. I found myself under the necessity of adopting the invariable rule of never seeing strangers, & you came under this rule, without my having the least idea whether you were prince or peasant. But when I received your letter, I was grieved, because I thought you were offended; and still more was I grieved, when my husband said, "I remem-ber him well. A child-like, honest, kindly soul, full of enthusiasm for music."

Your request concerning adapting poetry to your music, I would gladly have complied with, if I had had the ability to do so; but it is a thing I never attempted, and I am sure my ear is too inaccurate to enable me to do it well. Mus[ic] is with me a *feeling*, an absorbing *passion*. In early life, I had no op-portunity even to *hear* good music; and during the last ten years, it has opened upon me with such overwhelming and ever-increasing power, that natures less susceptible and earnest than my own may well deem it an insanity. But slowly, slowly, and through infinite difficulties, come the practised ear and the scientific knowledge. Perhaps I shall lose more than I can gain, in trying to learn *why* my whole soul melts and flows onward with the stream of sound. In fact, my eager labored efforts are almost entirely in vain to understand the why and wherefore of the effects I feel. Yet I will patiently learn what I can, and wait for that other world of light and music, for fuller revelations.

Your composition is of course far above my comprehension; but I will not "transfer it to some practical votary of the art", because I would like to keep it, as a memorial of your talent, and of your kind and flattering attention to one whose love and reverence for the Art so immeasurably transcends her knowledge.

. . .

ALS; Harris Collection, John Hay Library, Brown University (microfiche 22/613).

Typical of many letters Child wrote on behalf of artists is one to John Jay (1817–94), son of the abolitionist William Jay and grandson of Chief Justice John Jay. A lawyer himself, and one who defended many fugitive slaves, Jay also had a deep interest in history. Child's efforts for sculptor Horace Kneeland (ca. 1808–ca. 1860) were successful; within a month, he had received enough subscriptions to go abroad and cast his statue of George Washington.

To John Jay

Third St. May 24th 1845

Dear Sir,

I think I need not apologize to *you* for seeking to interest you in a man of genius, who is struggling with discouraging circumstances. He is neither relative nor friend of mine, and my interest has been excited solely by the very uncommon talent indicated in his works, and by the knowledge that he was very poor.

I refer to Horace Kneeland, the sculptor. If you will closely observe his bust of Mapes, in the Gallery of Design, I think you will at once perceive that it has merit of a very high order.[1] He is making another bust of Ericsson, the steam propeller, which I think will be superior to Mapes's, though now injured by being cast in bad plaster.[2] I confess myself a convert to an opinion I have often heard expressed by my friend William Page the artist; that "Kneeland has the ability fully to equal Powers, if he can only have a fair chance to develope himself."   This Spring, I discovered accidentally that he was very poor, and in a very discouraged and harrassed state of mind. I gave him a letter to Edward L. Carey, of Philadelphia, whose generous patronage of artists is so well known, and advised him to take with him some specimen of his workmanship.[3] He took a small equestrian statue of Washington, in plaster. Mr. Carey, who is perhaps as good a judge of *Art* as any in the country, was so much pleased with the horse, that he proposed to have an improved and enlarged model made and cast

[1] James Jay Mapes (1806–66), a chemistry professor and inventor of a number of manufacturing processes, taught at the National Academy of Design between 1835 and 1838.
[2] John Ericsson (1803–89) was a Swedish engineer; he designed the steam-powered screw propeller for ships.
[3] Carey, art patron and son of publisher Matthew Carey, carried on his father's business in Philadelphia.

in bronze. For that purpose he agreed to take one cast himself, and be responsible for two others; and promised to contribute liberally toward sending the artist to Berlin to cast the statue. If ten subscribers can be obtained, it will enable the sculptor to carry this plan through successfully. The casts will probably be three or four hundred dollars each. Mr. Cozzens of this city has subscribed for one. Do you think you could induce your father-in-law, or some other man of wealth, to subscribe for another? Kneeland's soul is so on fire with love of his art, and he has struggled so long and so hard with adverse circumstances, that I really wish he could have a fair chance to show the world what he *can* do.

I have already assured you that I have no other motive but sympathy with genius. I respectfully offer the subject for your consideration. The bust you can see for yourself, and the particulars concerning the equestrian statue, you can, if you think proper, learn of the artist himself, at his room, opposite the Granite Building, corner of Chamber St and Broadway.

Yours very respectfully,
L. Maria Child.

P.S. I cannot forbear saying that I have been disgusted with the attacks on you, by abolitionists. They appear to me to be neither just nor kind. Very few connected with the transfer of the Emancipator *intended* anything dishonorable or treacherous. Arthur Tappan, for instance, though his judgment is at times a little blinded by bigotry, I have always believed to be one of the most upright and conscientious, as well as the kindest of men.

I have always had the highest respect for yourself, for your manly independence in vindicating anti slavery principles, in a city where they are unpopular, and in a social position that would have tempted ninety nine young men out of a hundred to forsake them.

I have no sympathy whatever, and never have had, with the bitter, partisan attacks of abolitionists upon each other. Let him that is guiltless of any error of judgment cast the first stone.

ALS; Lydia Maria Child Papers, A/C 536, 1, Schlesinger Library, Radcliffe Library (microfiche 22/615).

While Margaret Fuller was in New York, she led a hectic life, falling in love with the German businessman James Nathan and writing for the *New York Tribune*. To what extent Child was involved with Fuller is not clear; though Child's letters make no mention of the love affair, the couple may have met at Child's place. The two women shared a common interest in the insane asylums, prisons, and refuge house for discharged female convicts on Blackwell's (now Roosevelt) Island. Child refers in the next letter to Fuller's 10 June 1845 *Tribune* review of the *Narrative of the Life of Frederick Douglass, an American Slave*, published that year in Boston. Douglass (1817–95) escaped from slavery in 1838 and worked as a laborer in New Bedford, Massachusetts. From 1841 to 1845 he was an agent for the Massachusetts Anti-Slavery Society. His autobiographical *Narrative* became a bestseller in the United States and abroad.

To Louisa Loring

New York, June 22d 1845

. . .

I have always loved Margaret Fuller ever since she expressed such impatience with all who did not perceive the *genius* which gives so much expression to his music.[1] I do not see her *very* often. We live too far apart, and her health is too poor. Once in a while, when she goes to theatre or concert, she stops here, and sleeps with me; and twice I have been out to see her. She seems to delight in the picturesque old house, with its ruined arbours, and garden flowers running wild among the grass. She says she never wants to quit it. It has remarkable attractions, it is true; but I should be afraid to live there, it has such a bad name for fever and ague. She has given up Dr Leger, the magnetiser, and it has seemed to me that she was not quite so well this spring as she was in the winter.[2] She has written some most admirable things for the Tribune. I liked her notice of the life of Frederic Douglass, which is I think the best thing ever written by a colored man. It has, what our colored friends are very apt to lack, (and so are *females*) and that is *ballast* enough for the sails. I think it is a pity Garrison wrote a preface. It will create a prejudice in many minds, at the outset. They had better have let him tell his own story, in his own simple manly way. As for Edmund Quincey, he is one of the many examples of a mind losing its balance completely, by looking everlastingly not only on one *subject*, but on one *side* of one subject. I am more and more convinced of the bad effect of reforms on the character, where they are not balanced by other and more genial influences.

I am glad you like my second series of Letters.[3] I am agreeably disappointed to hear that the Swedenborgians are much pleased with them. I thought they would be offended.

I did not need your poetic description of the waving grass to make me want to be with you. As for my finding "N. York so very delightful in June," I do not find it delightful at *any* season. But that terrible year of toil and discord at Northampton made *any* life seem pleasant by comparison; and I am convinced that N. York is the best place for me to fulfil my appointed mission. I live henceforth for one undivided object; viz: to build up my literary reputation, and make it the vehicle of as much good to the world as I know how. For this purpose, N. York affords advantages that no other place does. It has acknowledged

---

[1] I.e., Ole Bull's.

[2] Fuller went for treatment of spinal problems to Théodore Léger, author of *Animal Magnetism; or, Psycodunamy* (New York, 1846).

[3] *Letters from New-York, Second Series.*

me far more cordially than Boston ever did; and books published here have twice the sale. Moreover, I like it, because it is not loaded with mortifying remembrances, and painful associations, like Boston. David is at Northampton, superintending the carting of stone. He verily believes that he shall realize $2000 of the rail road, for stone that will cost an outlay of only $150. I might try to convince him that the contractors must be crazy to make such a bargain; but it is of no use to argufy.

. . .

ALS; Lydia Maria Child Papers, A/C 536, 1, Schlesinger Library, Radcliffe College (microfiche 22/623).

Child's life in 1845 and 1846 was a fairly steady, quiet routine of writing and occasional outings to concerts or art exhibits. This letter to Anna Loring, age fifteen, shows Child about to have a party, a rare event for her. Most of the guests were musicians. William Wetmore Story (1819–95) and his wife Emeline (Eldredge) Story (1813–92) were not: the son of Joseph Story, an antislavery Supreme Court judge, W. W. Story trained as a lawyer and then became a sculptor. Christopher P. Cranch (1813–92) was a painter. Child refers to two pianists, Henry Christian Timm (1811–92), who came from Germany in 1835, and Wilhelm Scharfenberg (1819–95), a leading member of the Philharmonic Society. The pianist Edward L. Walker ultimately went into manufacturing pianos. Ole Bull had sailed for Europe on 5 December 1845.

To Anna Loring

New York, March 23d, 1846

Dear Anna,

William Story and his agreeable wife, and her pretty little Dot of a sister are coming here this evening. So I asked Mr. Cranch to come with his flute and tuning key, and invited John S. Dwight. I am still in the *musical* dispensation, you see. Indeed, you would laugh to see how the sheer force of untutored enthusiasm, of unaffected feeling, has carried me on in this matter. Timm, our best pianist, (that is *I* think so, though some of the scientific prefer Schaffenberg) Timm, whose exquisitely delicate and graceful style of playing rejuvenates my blood every time I hear him—what do you think he has done? Sent to ask it as a *favor* that I will *allow* him to come and play to me, on my piano! Walker, the inventor of the Harmonic Attachment, has done the same. It is really *too* funny. What will happen next, I know not. Perhaps Franz Liszt will beg of me to *condescend* to listen to him, while he extemporizes fantasias of his own, or transposes some of Beethoven sonatas, for my edification. Really, it is the oddest thing, how such a little dot of a magnet draws the big musicians! I cannot make them believe that "I don't know nothing at all." They only answer, meekly, "Neither do I." Old Father Heinrich insists upon calling me "Queen of Song." Heaven help my subjects, if they are as ignorant as their queen.   I seize every opportunity of hearing good music, and the time and expense is re-warded by slow gradual improvement of ear and taste; and that is the most that the "Queen of Song" can say for herself. But music possesses me, like a spirit. Nothing else interests me. I cannot *make* anything else interest me, any way I can fix it.

I have been enchanted with John Dwight's lectures. I have not been so taken off my feet with delight, since the first evening I heard Ole's violin; and when *I* say that, you know that imagination can no farther go. Dear Ole! God bless him! His romantic music, and his fresh character, have taken ten years off my weary life, and carried my soul back to the season of blossom-fragrance and bird-singing. I did not think anything would ever excite me much again; but John Dwight's two last lectures charmed me so much, that I wanted to catch him up and kiss him. But as such a proceeding might have seemed singular to a N. York audience, I had to content myself with sending out and buying him a bouquet, in the midst of his lecture. He told us any quantity of things, that your father cannot find in the lexicon; such as that Handel corresponded to the note C, in the natural scale; and Mozart to E; and Haydn to G; and Beethoven to B. The best of it was, I jumped before the lecturer all the time. I saw, or rather I *felt*, where each composer would come in the scale; only I was doubtful whether Haydn were F or G.

He had no sooner said that Handel was Do, than I wanted to cry out aloud, "You will tell us that Beethoven is the Seventh—the dissonant Seventh, clamor-ing for the perfect octave, and within a semi-tone of it, too." But a N. York audience would have thought *that* strange; so I contented myself with whisper-ing it in John's ear. Dont *you* hear Beethoven's music scream aloud for some-thing, with desperate earnestness? and clear as a bell far up in the heavens, dont you hear the promise that the something is near, and will shortly come?

But I am going to get down from my high-flying Pegasus. I am not alto-gether clear in my own mind whether I am not a little insane on the subject of music. I rather think I am.

. . .

AL; Lydia Maria Child Papers, A/C 536, 1, Schlesinger Library, Radcliffe College (microfiche 23/655).

The daughter of the Unitarian minister in Medford, Massachusetts, Lucy Os-good (1791–1873) became a regular correspondent of Child's. She lived with her sister Mary in Medford and maintained a steady, somewhat conservative interest in the ideas of the time, especially those to do with religion.

To Lucy Osgood

My Dear Friend,

I thank you cordially for your kind letter, and for your attention to my childish request about the engravings. I received them safely, when I returned from my visit to the Quaker farmer, in whose rustic abode I annually seek refuge from the din of the anniversaries.[1] . . .

But when you speak of the church as "the place which I no longer frequent," I trust you do not confound me with those who think there is no need of social worship. On the contrary, my spirit craves it above all things. If I could only *find* a church, most gladly would I worship there. My soul is like a hungry raven, with its mouth wide open for the food which no man offers.

The Unitarian meetings here chill me with their cold intellectual respectability. Mr. Barrett, the Swedenborgian, has only transferred the padlock of his chain from St. Paul to Swedenborg. He is so narrow and bigotted, that when I come within his spiritual sphere, I feel like a bird under an exhausted receiver. At the Calvinistic meeting in the next street, the preacher, in his prayer, says, "We thank thee, O Lord, that there is a hell of despair!" I quote his very words. At the Episcopal churches, the minister, with perfumed handkerchief, addresses ladies in silks and satins, with prayer-books richly gilded, and exhorts them to contribute something toward building a chapel for the poor; it being *very* important that the poor should be taught sufficient religion to keep them from burning the houses and breaking open the stores of the rich.

Now what can a poor sinner, like me, with such an intense abhorrence of shams, do in such places? When I find myself in such situations, I assure you that it is hard work to keep from rushing out of the nearest window, through the painted glass, at the risk of demolishing the image of St Paul, or breaking Peter's sword, in my exit.

Friend Hopper has been so alarmingly ill, that for a week we felt that we were liable to lose him any day. But his iron constitution resisted the severe attack, and he is now rapidly recovering. I relieved the tediousness of long hours of watching in his room, by reading Consuelo again in the translation. It is very faithfully rendered, but, as Mr. Shaw himself says, I think it has lost *something* of the grace and beauty of the original.[2] I cannot quite sympathize with the Boston wholesale enthusiasm about this book. Portions of it are radiant with poetic beauty, and all alive with that vitality which characterizes George Sand. But it seems to me there is too much of the French striving for *effect;* too

[1] Child refers to the many annual meetings of societies customarily held in New York in May, and particularly to the annual meeting of the American Anti-Slavery Society.
[2] Child's friend Francis Shaw had just published a translation of George Sand's *Consuelo*. Child was fascinated by the life and novels of George Sand (1804–76), who was nearly Child's own age.

much artificial management to bring about out-of-the-way adventures. Count Albert, with his subterranean grottoes, resuscitated Hussites, masked invisibles, and dead-and-alive relations, was not only intolerably tedious to me, but excited my positive aversion. It was all so cold, severe, and spectral, that to my bird-like nature it was like going down into caves, among owls and bats. Consuelo's marriage with Albert made me shudder, as if she had been buried alive. I wanted her to find a bright, joyous, unobstructed love, such as is congenial to the sunny artist-temperament. The close of the story does not disturb me, as it did you. Genius and virtue rarely do anchor safely in the harbour of worldly prosperity, and books teach falsely in representing it so. It is time that this *outward* reward for goodness should cease to be held up as an allurement.   And if Consuelo was left in poverty, as such characters as hers and Albert's certainly *would* be in real life, they must either be gipsies or wandering musicians, in order to be invested with any poetry. It suits *my* taste extremely well. I had much rather tramp through forests to the sound of a tambourine, with my baby strapped on my strong shoulders, than to live amid the constrained elegance of Beacon St. At first, it puzzled me that a book of such severe morality could be written by one that had led the life George Sand is reputed to have done; but then I reflected that Tom Moore wrote the highly spiritual Epicurean, and Robert Burns wrote Mary in Heaven. Why should not a *woman* likewise pass through strange fires, and come out with her inmost nature unscathed? Is the question too bold?

I have the pleasantest recollections of your transit across N. York. I don't know what the reason is, but I have always had a great affection for you, and it makes me happy to think you have any regard for me.

Margaret Fuller is to sail for Europe on the first of August.   Your letters are always *very* pleasant to me.

Remember me respectfully to your brother and sister, and believe me ever your truly attached friend,

L. M. Child.

I was disappointed in Leutze's picture of the Landing of the Northmen.[3] It did not equal the expectations I had formed from what I had heard of it.

ALS; Lydia Maria Child Papers, Anti-Slavery Collection, Cornell University (microfiche 23/660).

In July 1846 Child made a brief visit to her father in Wayland, Massachusetts, and then returned to New York to see both Christopher Cranch and Margaret Fuller off for Europe. The Lorings, too, were planning a trip abroad; David was in Northampton; and John Hopper was going on trips to the country with

---

[3] The German-born Emmanuel Leutze (1816–68) grew up in Philadelphia and became noted for his historical paintings, especially *Washington Crossing the Delaware*.

young women his own age. Subdued by her loneliness, Child wrote with extraordinary candor to Frank Shaw, then living near Brook Farm. Perhaps his recent translation of George Sand's *Consuelo* encouraged her to write so openly; Shaw's notation on the letter, however, indicates that he did not reply until nearly two months later. His letters to her have not survived.

To Francis Shaw

New York, Aug. 2d, 1846.

Dear Friend,

Since I received your very kind and most welcome letter, I have been to Massachusetts, to see my good old father, whom I have not visited for a long time, and who is now eighty years old. I looked wistfully toward Boston and Roxbury, only sixteen miles from me; but I could not visit you and my dearly-beloved friends the Lorings, without likewise visiting a great many relatives and friends, and being introduced to many strangers. I had neither time nor money for this, and you can hardly imagine my extreme aversion to mixing with the world. They tell me it is a diseased state of mind, and perhaps it is; but at present, seclusion seems to be an absolute necessity of my being. I feel the discords of the present condition of society, without seeing clearly how they can be harmonized. I am passing through a spiritual transition, and like the lobster, when a new shell is forming, I protect my thin skin by hiding away in the crevices of rocks.   When I spoke of being more and more convinced of the truth of Swedenborg's views with regard to *individual uses,* I did not mean that I had the least degree of increased liking for the narrow, number-one notions of his disciples. I agree with you entirely in thinking that man's paramount duty is toward his race; but *how* best to perform that duty? that is the question. Some, for instance, would convince me that I am doing very wrong not to attend reformatory meetings, to be on their committees, to draw up reports, help settle disputes, visit prisons, &c. But when I try to do these things, I feel that I am going out of my own life, into something which is to *me* artificial, and therefore false. My own appropriate mission is obviously that of a writer; and I am convinced that I can do more good to my race by working in that way; infusing, as I must necessarily do, *principles* in favor of peace, universal freedom, &c into all I write.

What I meant to say was, that these extra and excessive efforts indicated a very diseased state of things. I confess, too, that I am more doubtful than I used to be, whether much is really accomplished by them.

As for my more than usual tendency to low-spirits, it is not of that superficial kind which can be remedied by change of objects. It is never worth while to trouble friends with what they cannot help. I will, therefore, briefly say that for the last six or seven years my conviction has been constantly growing stronger that my husband's deficiences in business matters are *incurable;* that he inherits the causes in his organization, and can no more help having them than he can help the color of his eyes, or the inches of his stature. For the last three years, I have, in self-defence, withdrawn my earnings entirely from his plans, and pursued my own avocations without any reference to his whereabout or whatabout. He cordially assented to it, as a measure equally necessary and just; but still he *will* go on, always getting into new tangles. This leaves me isolated, and I am naturally very affectionate and domestic. Moreover, he has such a noble kind heart, and such perfect integrity of purpose, that I cannot help feeling sad to see *him* always pumping into a sieve, though I have resolutely ceased to do so myself. In addition to this, he is living in the woods, with animals and coarse men, while I am growing more refined and poetic every day, under the influences of music, pictures, and mystical contemplation. Of course, strongly as we love each other, our growth is more and more divergent; and this above all things makes me sad.

In answer to your question, I must say that I think the *real* situation of the world *cannot* be revealed to young women, and that it would not benefit them, if it could. I do not wonder that so many men are libertines; I had *almost* said, I do not *blame* them. Nature is so outrageously dammed up, her strongest instincts are so repressed, her plainest laws are so violated, in the present structure of society, that nature *will* revenge herself, in spite of all we can do. I think the mere knowledge of facts would only lead women to tolerate and conform to the evils existing. You *cannot* make men and women have a horror of each other; the impulses of nature are too strong. But this is a subject on which I *dare* not speak, though I have thought more busily upon it, than upon any other, for the last ten years. I am, in fact, unqualified to speak, because here lies the weak side of my own nature. "The strong necessity of loving" has been the great temptation and conflict of my life; yet I sincerely believe that few women are more pure-minded than myself.   The state of society is frightful, and plainly enough proves that the laws of nature are dreadfully obstructed, or such universally bad results could not take place. I confess myself completely bewildered in my attempts to decide what *are* the genuine laws of pure, rational nature.

It would give me the greatest pleasure to see and talk with you, in New York or elsewhere; but I have nothing to impart that is worth coming for. I have a sort of undefined faith that I am making progress, as I feel that I am moving on toward the light, when I am travelling through dark tunnels of the rail-road, unable to see my hand before me.

I am glad Margaret Fuller has gone to Europe. I think it will refresh both mind and body. She is a woman of the most remarkable intellect I ever met with.

Remember me most affectionately to Sarah. Whether you hear from me often or seldom, there is no diminution in the strong attachment I have for you both. Good night. Yrs truly, L. M. Child

Speaking of agriculture, hens, &c. Do you know that if hens are fed on oats, and have occasionally chopped meat, without salt, and pounded oyster-shells or clam-shells, mixed with their food, they will lay eggs all winter long?

What I say of feeling occasionally sad about the hopelessness of remedying Mr. C.'s business defects, is of course for the ear of a *friend* only. The good, noble, kind man has no other defect.

ALS; Houghton Library, Harvard University (microfiche 23/664).

To Francis Shaw

[October 1846]

[. . .]¹ I probably shall never do so. I do not think I shall ever again be able to feel the necessary degree of confidence in my fellow beings. Men come into organizations with so many prejudices of sect and party, so many abominable traditions, and one-sided opinions, that it would be impossible for me ever to act with them, in any form of combination. But I think my writings indicate that I work to the same *end* as organized reformers; only I belong to the group of *sappers* and *miners*, instead of laying rails on the open direct road.

My distrust of human nature again comes in with regard to the Manual Labor School.² *Government* always spoils everything of the kind, with their theorems of chaplain-religion, and drill-service of every kind. Nothing has a chance to *grow* from within outward. The children's souls will all be fashioned, like clay, from outward pressure. Everywhere, everywhere, God's creatures are suffering for larger space, and freer growth. I would I were *out* of this world, into some corner of the universe more in harmony with my inward perceptions.

But, to speak less impatiently, I would suggest that the entire management of the institution be based on the idea of *attracting* to improvement, by increase of privileges; not on the usual theory of deterring from wrong by prohibition and penalty. Corporeal punishment ought not to be allowed in any form, under any circumstances. Seclusion, and the loss of customary privileges should, in *my* humble judgment, be the only consequences of improper conduct. But above all, have the system of *reward*, reward for every bad habit broken, for every deficiency overcome. If I had *my* will, I would have access to a pleasant library (not an accursed theological one) one of the privileges granted for certain improvements and performances. I would have the privilege of witnessing curious experiments in Natural Philosophy, with simple explanations, another reward for good conduct. I would have a singing school, and teaching on instruments; and have the Concert room open once or twice a week to those who had done as well as they could. But of course all this would seem Utopian to respectable aldermen, and matter-of-fact representatives.

---

¹ The first two pages of this letter are lost.
² The Manual Labor School was a reform school in Westboro, Mass.

Brigg's squibs on Margaret Fuller are, I think, very ungentlemanly.[3] Not because she is a *woman*—but ungentlemanly from one human being toward another. This rabid desire for *personalities* seems to increase. I abhor it altogether. I do not think that a mind which has anything *real* to offer, will ever cater to such a diseased appetite. Briggs, though a man of considerable smartness, knows no more how to judge of Margaret Fuller, than I do of Goethe's theory of colors, which I never read. His ideas of women are at least a century behind the age. They are to him merely bread-and-butter, or pieces of nicely polished parlor furniture. By the way, I do not know that it *is* Briggs who writes them. I only know that report says so.

Margaret's egotism is a fault much to be regretted. It mars the nobleness of her views, and of her expression. But it is the consequence of her father's early injudicious culture, never *allowed* to forget *herself*.

. . .

ALS, incomplete; Houghton Library, Harvard University (microfiche 24/676).

Rufus Wilmot Griswold (1815–57), the prominent literary critic, in 1847 published an anthology, *Prose Writers of America* (Philadelphia), that included work by Child. In the following account of her work many of the dates she cites are wrong; the correct ones are supplied in brackets.

To Rufus Wilmot Griswold

[October? 1846?]

To Mr. Griswold.
Dear Sir,
    The following is a list of the books, which you requested. In 1828 [1826], I began to edit the Juvenile Miscellany for children, and edited eight years. It makes 16 bound volumes, and about one third of the articles were written by myself. But this is not worth mentioning. I merely state it to show that my time was occupied, and the writing of larger works prevented. I had rather you would *not* mention the Miscellany. In 1831, '2 and '3 I edited the Family Library, for Carter & Hendee, of Boston. When they failed, I had prepared for them Vol 1 Lives of Madame de Stael & Roland; Vol 2 Lives of Lady Russell and Madame Guyon; Vol 3 Good Wives; and Vol 4 and 5 Condition of Women. But as these are all compilations woven together with remarks of my own, I do not include them in the list. In 1832 [1831] I wrote The Girl's own Book

[3] Presumably she refers to author Charles F. Briggs; the "squibs" have not been identified.

for children. In 1831 [1829] The Frugal Housewife, an economical cookery book; but these I think, had better not be in the list; though you may put in the Girl's Own Book, if you choose.

Hobomok, an Indian Tale.	1826	[1824]
The Rebels, a Tale of the Revolution	1827	[1825]
The Mother's Book	1831	
Appeal for that Class of Americans called Africans	1833	
Philothea, a Grecian Romance	1836	
Letters from N. York Vol 1	1843	
Flowers for Children	1844	
Letters from N. York 2d series	1844	[1845]

Hobomok was the first thing I ever attempted to write for print. I had for several years, until then, lived in the interior of Maine, almost entirely removed from literary influences. I ⟨came⟩ went to Watertown, Mass. where my brother, Dr. Francis, of Harvard University, was then settled as Unitarian clergyman. Soon after I arrived there, one Sunday noon, I took up the N. American Review, and read Mr. Palfrey's review of Yamoyden, in which he eloquently describes the adaptation of early N. England history to the purposes of fiction. I know not what impelled me; I had never dreamed of such a thing as turning author; but I siezed a pen, and before the bell rang for afternoon meeting I had written the first chapter, exactly as it now stands. When I showed it to my brother, my young ambition was flattered by the exclamation, "But Maria did you *really* write this? Do you *mean* what you say, that it is entirely your own?"   There were at that time scarcely any American books. Cooper's and Mrs. Sedgwick's had not appeared. I finished Hobomok in six weeks. Hasty, imperfect, and crude as it was, it excited a good deal of interest, under the then existing circumstances. Upon the strength of it, the Boston fashionables took me up, and made a "little wee bit" of a lion of me. But I did not stay among them long enough to have much life suffocated out of me. In such company, I am like a butterfly under a gilded glass tumbler; I can do nothing but pant despairingly, or beat all the feathers off my wings, thumping against the glittering wall of limitations.
The Rebels was not as good as Hobomok. With my present views of war, I regret very much that I ever wrote it, and I hope it will never be republished. In fact, its literary merits do not deserve it. It is rather odd that the speech of James Otis, which occurs in it, is often quoted in school-books, as having been made by James Otis; though in fact I coined it for him. Likewise Whitfield's Sermon. The Appeal for Africans was the first anti-slavery volume published in this country. I mean the first in favor of *immediate* emancipation. It was the occasion of my first introduction to Dr. Channing. He walked up to Roxbury Neck, a mile and a half, and introduced himself, to thank me for writing it.
    I have written a great variety of articles for different publications, and tracts for temporary purposes.   I can think of nothing more likely to interest

you. I thank you very cordially for the high appreciation of my works, which you have been pleased to express. I have very little ambition or literary vanity; but cordial discriminating praise is cheering to me.

To myself, my productions seem so fragmentary and imperfect, that I believe I should never take pen in hand for the public again, if it were not for the necessity of earning my bread.

With sincere respect and gratitude, yr friend,

L. Maria Child.

ALS; Frank H. Stewart Collection, Glassboro (N.J.) State College (microfiche 23/646).

The sadness and uncertainty Child had expressed to Frank Shaw did not pass. She wrote frantically to her husband in Northampton, begging him to come to New York, afraid he was seriously ill. He did not come. Even though she saw two of her books published that December—*Fact and Fiction* and a third series of her *Flowers for Children*—her depression continued.

To David Lee Child

New York, Nov. 2d 1846

Dear Husband,

I am dreadfully anxious about you. Do come to me; and come *soon*. Do you feel well enough to undertake the journey? or shall I come to accompany you? Do write as soon as you receive this. I imagine a thousand horrible things. Oh do come to me. Come to good nursing, to cheerful influences, to hearty love; for you shall have all these. Come *soon*, and let the farm go to the devil. I feel sanguine that patient care will restore your precious health, if you do not wait there *too long*. Don't procrastinate, dear husband, from any idea that you can save a little money by staying. Let the money go to the dogs, only let me have *you*. Don't keep me in suspense by not writing soon. I would set right off, if it were not that my two books are going through the press, and I am very desirous to have them out ready for sale at New Year's time. If you feel able to undertake the journey, it will be better to save the expense of my coming; but if you do not feel fully able, say so at once, and I will come. Any little household matters, books, or anything you value, Mrs. Lyman[1] will take care of for you. Dont lose time. Come to "little danny." I don't doubt it will cure you. If you are not well enough to write, cause somebody to write to me, as soon as this is received. Don't, out of kindness to me, represent yourself as better than you are. I wish you would follow my advice to come *soon* to my nursing. You are really out of your element there, my dearest friend; and I believe the

[1] Child's friend in Northampton, Anna Jean Lyman.

depressing influences on your *mind* have a vast deal to do with the health of your *body*. Everybody needs to be prosperous sometimes; and you never will be prosperous there. Everybody needs sympathy, and intercourse with congenial minds. *That* you shall have here. I will walk you out, and nurse you, and talk my prettiest. Only don't repeat your old error of *procrastination*. If your wood contract is still unfinished, your brother John will devise some way to help you out of that. Only tell him how important I think it is, that you should come here to be nursed.

AL; Lydia Maria Child Papers, Anti-Slavery Collection, Cornell University (microfiche 24/677).

A letter from Caroline Gilman, Louisa Loring's antiabolitionist sister-in-law in Charleston, South Carolina, seeking help for the mulatto grandchild of the Marquis de Lafayette, provoked Child's disgust with good works. No more information on the child has been found. The compassionate comments on the failed marriage of Louisa's cousin John King and his wife, Jane, suggest Child's concern with her own marital problems. The description of marriage as "legalized prostitution" is noteworthy in an era immersed in the ideology of the "woman's sphere" and the sanctity of marriage.

To Louisa Loring

New York Jan 15th 1847

Dearest Louise,

. . .

I enclose you a letter from Mrs. Gilman, which you will perceive she asks me to send to you. I shall not answer it; therefore I wish you would say to her, the next time you write, that I did not consider best to take any steps about the Bloomingdale school. Three times, since I have lived in New York, I have exerted myself to get boarding places, or schools, for people of doubtful connexions or character; and in *every* instance I have made trouble for myself and others. In one instance the board has not been paid for a child's board, for a year; and though the people do not express one word of blame to me, or of me, still I cannot help feeling as if I was in some sort responsible, because the place was procured through my influence. In the other cases, the conduct of the boarders brought trouble and disrespectability on those who took them. Between you and I, I am almost sick of amateur philanthropy. The causes of the world's sickness lie too deep for *this* kind of cure.

I have not mentioned the subject of Mrs. Gilman's letter to Friend Hopper; for the good old man has already more responsibilities than his broad shoulders can bear.   Mrs. G. seems to think it is a *very* hard case that the grand child of Lafayette should be a slave; and *white*, too! But for my part I should feel just as much sympathy for the grand child of Pompey, the wood-sawyer, and black as the ace of spades. That Washington, Lafayette, and *all* the heroes of the Revolution, left descendants among the slaves, is a matter of course. The *wise* construction of society makes such results inevitable. This is a precious world we live in. Above all things, do I long to get out of it.

I *hope* you do not make yourself unhappy about the separation of John and Jane. As for ⟨which⟩ the question which is the most blame, nobody *can* explain it, and it seems to me the wisest thing is perfect silence. You may rely upon it, that when people *are* incongruous and mutually *feel* that they are, it is the wisest and best thing to separate, let society say what it may. Nay *I* go so far as to consider it positively *wrong*, under such circumstances, to live together in the married relation. Look around you and see what fitty ricketty children, what miserable organizations, mind and body, are the consequences of wide-spread legalized prostitution! I know it is a dangerous subject to speculate upon; but experience and observation have *forced* upon me a close attention to it; and though I am bewildered when I try to harmonize the discordant elements of nature and law, thus far I *can* see clearly—that it is wrong to have children unless people love each other.

I would try not to concern myself about any injustice that may be done to John. Of course, people will ingeniously contrive to make out that there *must* be something dreadful bad, on one side or the other. But it is enough that they and their friends know there *is* nothing bad. Those who do not understand the simple words, "We are unhappy because we are incongruous," can never be *made* to understand by all the arguments and explanations in the world.

They can neither of them help their temperaments, any more than they can help the color of their eyes, or the height of their persons. They made a mistake in supposing their temperaments *could* harmonize; that's all; and I do not see why either must necessarily be to blame. Mrs. Jameson, you know, does not and cannot live with her husband; Yet he is a gentlemanly, worthy, and fine-looking man.[1] She is impulsive, warm, and poetic; he is cold, sluggish, and legal. Heaven help her! She *could* not feel herself freezing to death by inches, and so she went to Europe again, and left him in Canada.

If you yourself had felt this painful incongruity, you would pity John and Jane from the depths of your heart.

Give my best love to Ellis and Anna. I am sorry my book made him feel sad. I must try to cure myself of my Bellini tendency to sad minor cadences. But life has been a battle, not a game, with me. Much of my time, I am sad. Oh, my God what fierce conflicts I have had under my sober exterior of practical common sense! How I *have* suffered! how I *have* wept!   But no more of

[1] Anna Brownell (Murphy) Jameson (1794–1860), an English writer popular in the United States, was married to Robert Jameson, who lived apart from her in Canada.

that. I am strong, and many friendly waves bear me up. The All Kind Father will carry me through, even to the end.

John desires to be very affectionately remembered. Good night, thou precious and beloved friend. Always thy affectionate

Maria.

ALS; Lydia Maria Child Papers, A/C 536, 1, Schlesinger Library, Radcliffe College (microfiche 24/691).

Early in 1847 Child temporarily stopped writing for magazines and newspapers. Her final "Letter from New-York" appeared in the *Boston Courier* on 23 February 1847. In March John Hopper eloped with a young woman from Rhode Island named Rosa D'Wolf. Child told young Susan Lyman that the news "came upon me like a thunderclap."* She decided at once to move out of the Hopper home.

To Louisa Loring

New York April 29th 1847

Dear Louise,

The streets are full of moving-furniture on the go everywhere. It recalls to me how much I have had of it, in my fugitive skulking life; and it makes me feel sad. That brings back Cottage Place, and Nony, and the great grey cat, and my little garden; and so the spirit moves me uncommonly strongly to sit down and chat with you. John and his bride are here, and all his relations seem extremely pleased with her. She is a very loveable young creature, with very unassuming manners, and obliging ways. So far as I can judge of one whom I only know as a pleasant visiter, I should think she had a good disposition and temper. They are very happy now, of course. God grant that it may prove a happy union, when years have tried it. I see no reason why it should not. They take my warmest blessings with them, on their adventurous voyage.

Mr. Child has not yet arrived, but *promises* that he certainly will in 12 or 15 days. On the 10'th of May, I retire to my little bed-room in the old farm-house at New Rochelle; and I shall probably remain there all the summer. It does not at present seem very likely that I shall ever return to the city to reside. A baggage wagon passes the farm-house three times a week, and through this medium I can communicate with printers and engravers in N. York. With slight expense, I can come to the city by rail road, whenever it is necessary. I think the country air will be better for David, than the hot atmosphere of summer in the city; and his affairs being again in a tangle, I shall probably have

* 9 Apr. [1847], Lesley Collection, American Philosophical Society.

to meet his personal expenses; which I can do more economically up there, than with my present *large* arrangements. For six or eight months past, the state of David's "pecunary" affairs, and his decreasing health, have made me anxious to curtail my expenses by going into the country. But I could never see my way clear about leaving my impulsive and ardent friend John without some companion who would make a home for him. Now he *has* such a companion, and I can at once study economy and their convenience by transferring my apartments to them.   How long David will stay with me, I know not; but I hope all summer; that I may make a business of recruiting his health, and cheering him up. He promises that he certainly will not carry on the farm another year; but *that* he has promised these three successive years.

I had a letter from gentle Susie Lyman, the other day. She describes a sleigh-ride which she took three weeks ago with Mr. Child. It amused me; it was *so* characteristic of him. She says they struck off into unknown paths, through the depths of a wood, and went tumbling over stumps and rocks, and tearing down perpendicular hills, till she began to think it would be a miracle if they ever reached home with unbroken bones. At last they met two surveyors, and Mr. Child asked, "Can you tell us where we are?" "Where do you wish to go?" inquired one of the men. "Nowhere in particular," replied Mr. Child. "Very well," rejoined the man, "you are on the straight road there."

Susan adds, "So we kept on, and arrived there, and found no one at home."

Poor David! He drives on at much the same result in *all* the affairs of life. He constantly reminds me of Emerson's remark that "Some men expend infinite effort to arrive nowhere."

Did you see in the paper an anecdote of a poor vagabond, who was picked up very ill, and carried to a Hospital to die? A minister was sent to talk and pray with him. By way of *consolation*, he asked if he were not afraid to die, and meet his God. "Why no," replied the vagabond; "I am more *afraid* of t'other chap."   I write that to make Ellis laugh.

Is it true you have leased your house? And are you really going to Europe at last?

Tell Ellis they are stirring the legislature here to get a law passed similar to that in Massachusetts, Pennsylvania, and New Hampshire—that no officer of the State shall be allowed to aid or assist in any way, in the arrest or detention of fugitive slaves. I do hope the Empire State will come up to the work.

Give my best love to dear Anna and to Ellis. Remember me mostly kindly to Augusta King and to John, and to Mr and Mrs. King. I have her backgammon board yet. It has remained long unopened, but I dare say David and I shall find use for it this summer.   Good night. Yours affectionately, Maria.

John and Rosa often speak gratefully of your kind attentions. They desire cordial remembrance.

ALS; Lydia Maria Child Papers, A/C 536, 1, Schlesinger Library, Radcliffe College (microfiche 25/708).

From May 1847 to March 1849 Child lived in the farmhouse of Joseph Carpenter in New Rochelle, New York, making occasional extended visits to New York City. She was working on her history of the world's religions, *The Progress of Religious Ideas*, in an effort to counter the accepted view that Christianity was the only true religion. She had a new correspondent at this time, Marianne (Devereux) Silsbee (1812–99), the wife of the wealthy mayor of Salem, Massachusetts, Nathaniel Silsbee (1804–81). Although Marianne followed her husband's political conservatism, the two women shared interests in art, music, and literature.

To Marianne Silsbee

New York April 17th 1848

Dear Friend,

    . . .

    I had read Jane Eyre before you had the kindness to send a copy. I was perfectly carried away with it. I sat up all night long to finish it. So much for the irresistable attraction of naturalness and truth! I do not at all agree with the critics who pronounce Rochester unloveable. *I* could have loved him with my whole heart. His very imperfections brought him more within the range of warm human sympathies. *Ought* Jane to have left him at that dreadful crisis? She was all alone in the world, and could do no harm to mother, sister, child, or friend, by taking her freedom. The tyrannical law, which bound him to a mad and wicked wife, seems such a mere figment! I wanted much, however, to make *one* change in the story. I liked Rochester all the better for the impetuous feeling and passion which carried him away; but I wanted conscience to come in and check him, like a fiery horse reined in at full gallop. At the *last* moment, when they were ready to go to church to be married, I wish he had thrown himself on her generosity. I wish he had said, "Jane, I *cannot* deceive you"! and so told her the painful story he afterward revealed. There might have been the same struggle, and the same result; and it would have saved the nobleness of Rochester's love for Jane, which has only this one blot of deception.   I am glad the book represents Jane as refusing to trust him; for in the present disorderly state of the world, it would not be well for public morality to represent it otherwise. But my *private* opinion is, that a real living Jane Eyre, placed in similar circumstances, would have obeyed an *inward* law, higher and better than outward conventional scruples.

    I have been to the opera only once since I came to the city. The house is very light and elegant. The opera was Lucia, but not so well performed as I have heard it at Palmo's. There had been some dispute, the company were out of temper, and out of spirits. Benedetti was superior to everybody else, but not equal to himself.   Rosa has some of the Steyermarckers' (I don't know how to spell it) Polkas, which throw my favorite Azalea quite into the shade. I

238

bought for her the other day two pieces by Wolff; "La Melancholie" and "L'Espoir." They are perfect gems, and she plays them very charmingly. There has been a good deal of the Steyermarcker's music published. It is admirable for parlor music; it is so full of variety and life.   Rosa has given me a likeness of Mendelssohn, in Berlin transparency. I have kissed it again and again. He has none of the gush of genius, but he was a most beautiful and highly cultivated artist, and had withal great moral excellence. Perhaps this last was because he was *not* a genius; for that element of fire is a very disturbing one. What *makes* me be so perverse as to worship it?

The Gallery of Design is better than usual this year. There are two *very* admirable landscapes by Durand.[1] One of them an exquisite moonlight scene; *not* the one you saw half finished; but simply a cottage, a country-road, and two lovers walking in the light of the moon. It is extremely beautiful. There is a glorious landscape there by Doughty, the best I ever saw from his hand.[2]

I suppose you have seen by the papers that Jeannie Barrett has been most graciously received by John Bull.[3] Called out, showered with bouquets, praised by critics, diamond rings given, &c. I do not suppose she will make much money; but this London trip will be beneficial to her health, spirits and professional reputation. I am *so* glad she is doing well! Her life has been full of remarkable contrasts and reverses.

Mr. Sloane says the mistake in the figure of the carpet was his fault, and he will change it whenever you will send it, with an exact description of what you do want.

John and Rosa seem very happy in each other, and his excitable temperament becomes more quiet and equable under her gentle influence. They both desire to be cordially remembered to you and yours.   I thank you for the books. Mary Howitt I will send tomorrow in a package to John King. Jane Eyre is lent and on the rounds somewhere. Remember me very kindly and respectfully to Mr. Silsbee. I thank him for his friendly toast on Feb. 11.

Please give my love to Mary, and believe me very affectionately and gratefully your friend,

L. M. Child.

. . .

ALS; Lydia Maria Child Letters, American Antiquarian Society (microfiche 26/729).

[1] Asher Brown Durand (1796–1886) was an American landscape painter of the Hudson River school and president of the National Academy of Design, 1845–61.
[2] Thomas Doughty (1793–1856) was an American landscape painter.
[3] Barrett (1801–53) was an American actress befriended by Child.

To Marianne Silsbee

New Rochelle, Nov 9th. 1848

Dear Mrs. Silsbee,

From my hidden nest here in the fields, I send you an affectionate greeting. Taylor is president, so I suppose you will make the anticipated visit to N. York.[1] Will you write and inform me *when* you expect to make your descent? Please direct to the "care of Joseph Carpenter, New Rochelle, N. York"; and write on it "please send this soon." I will right gladly obey the summons, and come down to the city to meet you. I don't think my company will exhilerate you much, though; for *now* I am really growing old; growing so in my *feelings*, which I never before have done. But perhaps your magnetism will renew my youth. At all events, whether I am grave or gay, it will give me heartfelt pleasure to meet you. As for your enthusiasm about General Taylor, we can none of us sympathize with *that*; for we all dislike the character of the man, and disapprove of the reasons that made him a candidate for the presidency; but friends can easily be silent on subjects whereon they do not agree.

I staid eight weeks in New York, and did not go to *one* public place! I seem to have got out of the dispensation, somehow. If I asked anybody but my good John to go with me, he might think it strange, and I do not often like to ask *him*, for fear it may not be exactly the time and place to suit both of them, or that it might not agree with Rosa's health. So, being, to a remarkable degree, the creature of habit, I have ceased altogether to care about going.

I often ran into the Art Union, and found more good pictures there, than I ever before saw in one season. Leutze's picture of Queen Isabella and the Jews has tempted many hundreds of people to subscribe, in hopes of obtaining the prize. The chance is small, but each one hopes to win it.

I have not yet seen Jeannie Barrett, but I hope to meet her early in December. I want very much to hear about her English experience.

Margaret Fuller it seems is so much in love with Italy, that she will not return until she has expended her last dollar. Dr. Loring, who has recently returned from there, says she has in her rooms extremely pleasant reunions of artists, American and Italian. Have you seen Harriet Martineau's "Eastern Lands, Past and Present"?[2] It interested me extremely; particularly the portions relating to *ancient* affairs in Egypt and Palestine. If the pious *see* the drift of it, they will be down upon it, "like a thousand bricks" of Babel. She says very coolly that most of the laws and institutions of Moses "he obtained from the Egyptians, from what source he received the remainder is unknown"; or something to that effect. Now if that be the fact, how *awful* it has been to reverence

1 Zachary Taylor (1784–1850) was a Whig like Mrs. Silsbee's husband.
2 Martineau's book was published that year in London and Philadelphia.

them so long! Of *course*, God never inspired an Egyptian! Oh no indeed! He confined himself to his "peculiar["] people, the Jews; and a very peculiar people they were, it must be confessed.

. . .

In the fall of 1848, David Lee Child took a job with his brother John building a railroad in Tennessee, and Maria's reclusive, depressed mood continued.

To Lydia (Bigelow) Child

New Rochelle, Feb 16th, 1849.

Dear Mother,

Mr. Haskin's letter arrived this evening, and I opened it.[1] I was not at all aware that you were ignorant of David's movements, or I would have written to inform you all that I knew, that you need not be anxious. I have not seen him since last August, when he left me with a new fitting out of shirts and vests, which I scrambled to make for him as fast as I could. He *said* he should certainly come again before winter. But David, like his poor father, you know is not remarkably prompt, and punctual to his engagements. It has been one great cause of his want of success, poor fellow.   Some time after he left me, I received a letter informing me that he was going West and South, as far as Mobile, on rail-road business; and that he would come to see me on his route. In December, or the last week in November, he went through New York city in great haste; called at Friend Hopper's office, and told him that he had deferred starting so *late* that he had not half a day to spare; and wished him to inform me that he should lose his engagement on the rail-road if he stopped to come and see me. After that, I heard nothing from him till about a fortnight ago. I was anxious, and would have written if I had had the least idea *where* to write. At last, I had a letter from him, dated in the woods at Tennessee. He intimates that his job is a pretty hard one, and his pay small; but that everybody has to serve such an apprenticeship before they can get at more profitable employment. He says: "I find that my health is improved by change of climate, and that I get along with considerable ease and satisfaction. I am thrown with fourteen young men, engineers, in different stages of their education as such; all from the Northern states. They are all friendly, obliging, and harmonious. I could not have expected to find my situation and duties more pleasant, or my views of acquiring practical knowledge more kindly and zealously promoted. I have become some acquainted with the inhabitants, and find them kind and

[1] Robert Haskins was the husband of David's sister Lucretia, who died in 1848.

hospitable. A Mississippi slaveholder asked my advice about emancipating three of his slaves. I wrote a deed of manumission, which he presented to the mother and two children in my presence, and carried them into Illinois. When he got there, some men from New York and Connecticut tried hard to dissuade him from his purpose, and even threatened to mob him. I find some of the farmers in this region earnestly opposed to slavery; but they don't see how to get freed from it, without leaving the state. I never introduce the subject, but express myself plainly when my opinion is asked."—So you see, dear mother, David is at his old business, doing good to everybody but himself. He is a good soul; but I have no hope that he will ever change in those points which stand in the way of his success in business. I do not think he *can* change, if he tries ever so hard.

I had a letter from my poor old father last week. He will be eighty three years old in a few weeks, and still has his faculties bright and his health pretty comfortable.

I do not expect David will come this way till pretty late in the spring. As he is continually moving about, I do not know how to direct you to write to him. If I hear anything of importance from him, I will let you know.

. . .

AL; Child Letters, MC 305, Schlesinger Library, Radcliffe College (microfiche 26/747).

Child's account in this letter of her wholesale burning of past correspondence, for all its self-reproach and perhaps self-pity, also reveals Child's extraordinary ability to express her sorrow with a plain-spoken eloquence. Even the humor that characteristically flashes through only heightens the poignancy of her evident struggle to stay afloat. Many years later she herself looked back on this period of her life with a bemused dismay.

To Louisa Loring

New Rochelle, March 8th 1849

Dearest Louise,

It has been a good deal impressed on my mind, within the last year, that people grow old, and are wont to die. Certainly the fact was not new to me; but for some reason or other, it has of late been often and very distinctly present with me. It is probably owing to the fact that nearly all of the last year has been spent literally in *complete* solitude, reading much about God and the soul. Whatever may have been the *cause*, the *result* has been that I set my small pecuniary affairs in very *clear* order, and devoted a week to examining old letters. I knew I had some confidential epistles, which might do injury to others, in case of being seen by other eyes than my own. I resolved to destroy all letters, which told any *secrets* or made any allusions to *persons,* that might by any accident give pain. Dear me, how imprudent people have been in writing to me! I burned 339 letters. In the old box was one thick bundle, marked "Nony," containing her very first effort in the epistolary way, down to the last letter from *Miss Loring*. Another bundle was marked "Ellis and Louisa." I dreaded to open them; for I knew I should have a good crying-spell; and of late years I do not think so much of "the luxury of tears," as I used to when I was 16. They leave me with the head-ache *now*. However, I went resolutely to work, and read them all; and I was astonished to find how many *you* had written; considering that you are a person who "never does anything, but sit in a rocking-chair and look happy," as Miss Eldridge once said.[1] And what delightful letters they were! Such a friendly heart-warmth! Such a genial, sunny, dimpling *humour* went mantling all through them! I kept smiling, smiling; but when I came to your attendance upon Margaret Fuller's conversations, and the prolonged discussion upon love and marriage, between Elizabeth Peabody and Miss Haliburton, I shouted with laughter, here all alone by myself.[2] Miss Peabody thought the perfection of love was to love the object so well, that it was perfectly immaterial whether you ever saw him or not. What a comfortable, cozy idea! I advise all such high spiritualists to fall in love with the *idea* of Plato. I say the *idea* of Plato, two thousand years off; because the man himself I apprehend was made of other metal. At all events, history records that he left a legacy to his son. Miss Peabody's shadowy sentiment amused me, and your real indignation amused me much more.

Dear Louise, it was well worth all the trouble of writing those letters to have done my poor weary heart so much good. They let in a whole world full of sunshine. It was a fortnight ago I read those letters; and every hour in the day since, I have had tender recollections what angels of blessing you and Ellis have always been to me.

Dearest and best of friends, I have been much and often in the wrong. I have been of late years in a discouraged, reckless, unhealthy state of mind. I have struggled with it, and tried to hide it that it might not cast a shadow over others; but it *has* peeped out in little caprices and abrupt ways, which were not a true index of my real heart. Of the severity of my trials, in one way and another, you could not judge, even if I were to try to make it clear to you; for one human soul never *can*, by any possibility, understand the trials of another. But I will not try to make any defence or apology for myself. I *could* have done better, and I *ought* to have done better. All I have to say is, forgive my many sins of omission and commission, and believe that I am not in reality capricious, or ungrateful for the love that you have bestowed on me. I have made strong resolutions to keep out of the shadows, and be good and genial; and one favor-

[1] Probably Emmeline Eldredge, who married William Wetmore Story in 1843.
[2] Elizabeth Palmer Peabody (1804–94) was the Boston educator and Transcendentalist; Miss Haliburton is unidentified.

able sign is that I feel a humble distrust of myself; I doubt whether I shall be *able* to do it. But I will *try*, and that earnestly.

I am obliged to quit my homely retreat, on account of the increasing size of the family. They have so many laborers, that they cannot spare my sunny little old room. The sunshine, the pure air, and glimpses of the green fields are all the place *has* to recommend it; for my guileless honest friend Joseph[3] is yoked to a most unpropitious mate. But with my feline propensity to cling to accustomed places I have become attached to it, and am reluctant to leave it. When I came here, I calculated to remain until the death of my poor old father enabled me to judge what I *had* to provide some humble corner, where I could take care of David in his old age. If I died myself, meanwhile, Joseph has on his farm a burial-place for the colored people, (excluded by prejudice from other burying-grounds) and it was satisfactory to me to think of "bearing the testimony," as Quakers say, of being buried there, among my human brethren, of a despised race. But my plans are frustrated again. I am packing up, as I have been most of the time, for the last fifteen years. It is my destiny to be always boxed up, but *not* directed. I am going back to F[rie]nd Isaac's, to take a small garret room. I can use Rosa's parlor wh[en] I have occasion to see anybody. But that is not often; for nobody comes to see me, except Page and Frank Shaw and his wife; and they come but seldom. I shall miss my dandelion-carpet and my bird; but I must fall back on the consolation of music. In your letters, you run me a little, in a good humored way, about my childish fancy for *useless* things. Dear Louise, the poetic in my *nature* more than balances the practical; I cannot help it, if I would; and being *always*, from my birth to the present hour, dammed up by mean and meagre external circumstances, the sparkling stream finds vent in these little follies. There is very little of this childishness left in me now. The only traces of it I have had here in my rustic retreat are the tasteful little fifty cent vase Anna sent me four years ago and a chandelier drop hanging in my window; to throw rainbows over my paper. I have at times some floating visions, though, of dressing up my little garret with evergreens and some medallions sent me by artists. "*Natur*" is mighty strong.

. . .

A poor way-worn slave came along here, a month or six weeks ago. I paid his fare to Hartford, in the cars, and gave him a letter to Mr. Jackson, asking him to let me know whether it arrived safely. I felt anxious, because they were in pursuit of him, and he took the cars by *my* advice. Another fugitive came along the week after. I gave him a dollar and a letter to Ellis, with directions to John King to open it, in case of his absence.[4] I have never heard from either

[3] That is, Joseph Carpenter.
[4] On 28 Jan. 1849, Child had written Ellis Gray Loring as follows: "I hereby introduce you to a young man, for whom I should like very much to have you obtain a situation as steward in some vessel. 'For further particulars inquire within'" (Loring Papers, Schlesinger Library, Radcliffe College). Francis Jackson's account on the back of the letter reveals the day-to-day work done by the Massachusetts Anti-Slavery Society with fugitive slaves (Jackson was then president of the society):

of them. I should feel dreadfully, if I thought the poor fellows were captured on the way. My letters were *very* cautiously worded. . . .

ALS; Loring Family Papers, Schlesinger Library, Radcliffe College (microfiche 26/ 750).

At the end of March 1849, Child moved back to New York, where she witnessed the Astor Place riot on 10 May 1849. The riot was an outgrowth of a rivalry between the American actor Edwin Forrest and the English actor William C. Macready and was an expression of both anti-British and antiaristocratic hatred. The pro-Forrest mob formed outside the Astor Place Opera House, where Macready was appearing in *Macbeth;* the police failed to disperse them, the militia arrived, and thirty-six people were left wounded and twenty-two killed.

To Ellis Gray and Louisa Loring

New York, May 14th, 1849

Dear Friends,

. . .

The next day after you left, Henrietta Sargent came, on her way from Washington, with Mrs. John Parker.[1] I called at the hotel, and met the wealthy widow, for the first time during many years. I was struck with the different

Feb 1849 Got him a birth in Wm T. Welds vessel for Hayti

Paid out fit viz	
vest	1.25
Thick Jacket	2.50
3 pr socks	.75
4 shirts	2.50
pr thick shoes	1.25
mattrass	1.75
Comforter & blankets	3.
Trousers & Flannel	2.
making up protection &	
Sundries &c	2.50
	17.50
Cr by Cash in Feb	5.
May 1 Rec^d of the Capt	12.50
in full	4.50
due	8.00

F. J.

[1] Ann (Sargent) Parker was possibly a sister or cousin of Henrietta Sargent.

points of view from which we were looking at society. The imminent peril of the rich seemed to occupy all her thoughts. I gathered from her conversation that there was no security for life or property in Massachusetts. Nine hundred boys made it the only business of their lives to burn barns, and judges and juries pronounced it merely a phrenological fancy for fire, a misdirected development of a sparkling faculty. Dwelling-houses were safe for the time being, on account of capital punishment for burning them; but there were so many philanthropists about, unwilling to have anybody punished for *any*thing, that there was no telling how long *that* security would last. I pocketed the neat compliment, without saying so, and perhaps she thinks the cut direct was lost on an obtuse victim.

I am sorry I cannot secure your safety, by inviting you and your barns to N. York; but in sober earnest, our own position is a little unsteady just now. The beautiful opera-house is half dismantled, and the paving-stones all round it are torn up by the mob. That ruffianly Forest, how much he has to answer for! His coarse, wicked appeals to bad, petty, national prejudices have brought about this awful result. Two years ago, I was in a state of indignation against an article in the Democratic Review, concerning his visit to England. It was in the style of the worst Fourth-of-July slang.

We went to bid Mrs. Silsbee good bye at the N.Y. Hotel, and found both doors besieged by an infuriated mob, yelling for Macready, who boarded there. Volleys of musketry were being discharged in quick succession, in the opera-house street near by. We found afterward that a bullet had whizzed across the street we were passing. Deeming it necessary to inquire concerning the safety of Mrs. Silsbee, we pressed on, thro *such* yells! When she exclaimed, "Oh what a frightful city N. York is!" I replied, "I witnessed a very similar scene in Milk St. Boston, when the mob were yelling for George Thompson; and we slept rather insecurely in our beds, when the Convent was burned, and the city under military protection."[2]

When we had seen Mrs. Silsbee safely in a friend's carriage, we returned home by a round-about route to avoid the excited multitude; but we were obliged to take shelter on a door step, to make room for the military, passing with drawn swords and loaded cannon. When we reached home, Rosa and I found ourselves a little pale. There is outward quiet now, but a raging volcano underneath. That jacobin demon, who guides the destinies of Tammany Hall, is striving to make political capital of it—doing his best to kindle a war between the rich and poor, by attacks on "the white-kid gentry who frequent the opera." Sooner or later, I am afraid the elegant building will be demolished by the blind rage they thus excite. God knows my sympathies are with the ignorant million. There are *instants*, when the sight of rags and starvation make *me* almost ready

[2] Mobs threatened the life of English abolitionist George Thompson on his American tour in 1834–35. The Ursuline Convent, Charlestown, Mass., was burned by anti-Catholic arsonists on 11 Aug. 1834.

to smash thro' the plate-glass of the rich, and sieze their treasures of silver and gold. But alas for such outbreaks as these! They right no wrongs. Such things make me very sad for human nature. I wish there were virtue enough in the community to let Forrest see himself deserted as an actor, by all but rowdies. His conduct seems to me to have been extremely culpable, from beginning to end. I should call it murderous, if I supposed he was aware to what a terrible result his influence was tending. But I apprehend he is a base, blind, bad *animal.* But it will be wise to turn to a pleasanter subject. Mrs. Silsbee was here several weeks, and I did any amount of shopping with her; thus getting a peep at rich goods, I should otherwise have no chance to see. As I wore my new bonnet and shawl, the clerks treated me with marked respect, and I might have made quite a speculation by purchasing goods on credit. I was sorry to delude them into the idea that I was a person of property, but the shawl was circumstantial evidence not to be doubted. Mrs. S. and I went often to the Dusseldorf Gallery. I am *so* sorry it was not opened until after you left! It is much the best gallery I ever visited. Some of the landscapes are admirable, and there is a lovely little gem representing fairies bringing offerings to childhood. I came home very unhappy that I had not a son at Dusseldorf. Gradually my unhappiness enlarged itself, as I thought how pleasant it would be to have *four* sons; two musical composers, one painter, and one sculptor, and *all* poets. Then our practical common-sense Anna might take her choice among them. Hurra for artists! Do you remember the tipsy man, who bobbed up and down at the table, every moment, to defend society from Socialism? And his companion, who hiccuped a "Hurra" for everything?

I like Mrs. Silsbee more, the more I am acquainted with her. Aristocratic education comes in with its limiting influence, and sometimes perverts her judgment. But her natural impulses are noble, and when a right principle is suggested to her active mind, she receives it kindly, and thinks earnestly about it. It is queer she should take such a liking to me. She thought my gown was not good enough for my shawl, so sent me a silk dress. I am now caparisoned for the street for four years to come. I am almost afraid to wear my shawl for fear The Empire Club will mob me as an aristocrat.

I have not heard from Mr. Child since I saw you; and I feel anxious.

. . .

ALS; Child Papers, Clements Library, University of Michigan (microfiche 27/751).

David returned from Tennessee in August 1849, had a brief reunion with Maria, and went on to visit his mother and sister in West Boylston, Massachusetts.

To David Lee Child

New York Aug. 31. 1849

Dear Husband,

I was rejoiced to hear that you found your good old mother living, and in her right mind. Poor Lydia! Her religious extasy would annoy me exceedingly if I was near its influence; but I should be sorry to disturb it by any of the suggestions of right reason. Life has been a dreary monotone to her. She has had little chance to judge of any of the pleasures of this world, or any of its excitements, except those founded on aspirations after a better existence. Let her shout! since, as the Irishman said, "it is her only recreation."

I saw Paul Duggan last night. He says Professor Mapes has been analyzing some peat in his own neighborhood, and that he doubtless will do yours, if you will bring him a piece.[1] He resides in N. Jersey, and Paul will I think willingly take the trouble to carry a specimen to him, when he goes on one of his usual visits. I want you to avoid expending money upon it; and if I were you, I would not talk much about it with any one. Whether the peat proves valuable or not, it is the better way to *say* little about it. So much for my old habit of *advising*.   I have ripped open your carpet bag, in want of the key, and hired a strong woman, and had all your blankets and old rags washed clean. What a mess they *are*, to be sure!

I have had grateful and affectionate thoughts concerning your last brief visit. It was a little glimpse of the good old times. Thank God even for that *little* glimpse!

What time you have for rest, do try to spend with *me*. I will try to make everything as pleasant as I can, and not to recall any pictures of our bad luck. I wish I could manage to prevent the necessity of your enduring another western campaign. At your period of life with all the hardships you have undergone, I fear it is too toilsome for your strength. I have many anxious thoughts about it. Oh if we only *could* have ever so small a home, where you could be contented, and have no dreams about Congress!

I love you dearly. I see no one who seems to me to have such a large, noble, generous, kind heart as you have. God bless you, dear husband! I do hope we shall yet have a chance to comfort each other, and enjoy each other's society, without anything remaining of all our troubles and all our errors, except the improvement we derive from such severe experience.

Little Dolores was mightily pleased with the message you sent to her.[2] She wants to see the husband of her "dear little sistita" again, and chatters away in

---

[1] If David had a scheme involving peat, nothing came of it. Peter Paul Duggan (d. 1861), an artist in New York, frequently exhibited at the National Academy of Design, where James Jay Mapes, inventor and agriculturalist, had taught.
[2] Dolores was a young orphaned Spanish woman brought to the United States by an uncle and unofficially adopted by Child.

excessive compliments, in extremely pretty English. She is a very pleasant little creature, but I should probably never have been drawn into companionship with her, were it not for her peculiarly lonely situation. Poor little thing! she has suffered dreadfully; the more so, because, like me, she *cannot* be careless about the future.

Everybody seems to me to have a great deal of trouble, to quote an original remark of my poor father's, "the world is *full* of trouble."

Cranch the artist called to see me yesterday. He is just returned from 3 years in Italy. Two children born there; and so poor, that he was obliged to borrow money to get home to her mother's. He has not a dollar to hire either painting room or lodgings; and is at a loss what to do. He says Margaret Fuller is *very* poor in Italy. He doubts whether she can raise funds to get home.

Come to your little old partridge as soon as you can. She is not in a state to drum much with quills or otherwise now; but she is capable of making a warm nest yet.

We are all well here. John and Rosa are expected next Tuesday.   Good bye, and blessings be with you.

Your affectionate
Maria.

P.S. You *say* you shall come in the course of a fortnight from the time you left. Don't tempt me to twit you about the old habit of *procrastination;* for I don't want to make myself disagreeable.

ALS; Lydia Maria Child Papers, Anti-Slavery Collection, Cornell University (microfiche 27/758).

Child continued writing *The Progress of Religious Ideas* in New York, and when David returned from Northampton in September 1849, he joined her there at the Hopper house. In October the Swedish writer Frederika Bremer came to the United States for a two-year tour. In 1853 she published her letters on her trip to America, *The Homes of the New World* (New York), and there recorded her first impression of Child—"a beautiful soul, but too angular to be happy" (p. 14).

To Louisa Loring

New York, October 21'st, 1849.

Dearest Louise,

A few minutes ago, I opened Mary Howitt's "Birds and Flowers," and when I read the affectionate inscription in your hand-writing the tears rose to my eyes, as they often do when I meet with traces of your dear self. David was sitting by me, and the book led to reading your last letter aloud. He was exceedingly amused at your statement, "I have nothing in the world to do; but I am in such a prodigious hurry, that I must draw to a close." "That is just like Louisa!" said he, "She always had a witty way of saying things." He has been with me about four weeks; an unusually long visit for him. I have not seen him in such good health and spirits for several years. His *"pecunary"* situation is certainly not very brilliant; having worked very hard and suffered a good deal in his engineering expedition, for forty dollars a month, out of which his travelling expenses must be paid. However, the understanding is that the pay is to be gradually increased, and the labor less arduous, after he gets out of his apprenticeship. He does not yet know whether the route will be carried on by the Company, so as to afford him employment this winter. Since he has been here, I have done nothing but make and mend, to get his garments into comfortable and respectable condition. When he visited me at N. Rochelle a year ago last summer, I made him four new shirts, of very strong cloth, very strongly sewed. One of them he left at West Boylston, by accident; the other three were stolen from him before he reached Cincinnati. So he had no good from them during his hardships in the woods. It is curious how much of my life has been spent pumping into sieves. But he is such a good and noble soul, that one ought to be willing to put up with many inconveniences for his sake. We have had quite a second honey-moon; a little flowery oasis in the desert of our domestic life.

What think you of Margaret Fuller's marriage and motherhood? Cranch, who called upon me on his return from Italy two months ago, knew nothing of it. Eliza Robbins, who you know has a quaint satirical way of saying things, says, "She *bought* the boy, I *know* she did! Never tell me again that Aaron's rod did not blossom, or the dry bones live!" For my own part, I approve of Margaret's taste in having a private marriage all to herself, and thus keeping a little of the *romance* of the tender sentiment.[1]

Have you any wish to see Frederika Bremer? I did not intend to call; first because I have a phobia of all lionhunting, and secondly because I am so inconveniently situated, that I have it not in my power to pay her any attention. But she sent up a messenger, to say that she was told I had an aversion to making calls, and therefore, if I pleased, she would call upon *me*, if I would specify convenient time and place.

Of course, even *I* could not be sufficiently rude to repel the kindness of such an advance. So two hours after, I put on my white crape shawl, and my ten-dollar bonnet, and took my new parasol, and my laced handkerchief with Maria embroidered in the corner, and thus attired like a woman "of property

[1] Margaret Fuller's marriage to Giovanni Angelo, Marchese d'Ossoli, took place in the summer of 1849; their son, Angelo Eugene, had been born 5 Sept. 1848. All three drowned off Long Island on 19 July 1850 when their ship sank as it neared port in New York. Eliza Robbins is not identified.

and standing," I proceeded to the Astor house. I did not tell her that all my finery was given to me by a munificent friend in Boston; but I probably *shall* do so, if I see her again. In her *person* Frederika is insignificant and rather unprepossessing; but her manners are unaffected and simple, the natural language of a kind sincere soul. She speaks English tolerably well, but with so much effort, that it stops the easy flow of conversation.

. . .

ALS; Lydia Maria Child Papers, A/C 536, 1, Schlesinger Library, Radcliffe College (microfiche 27/761).

To Ellis Gray Loring

New York, Nov 7'th 1849

Dear Friend,

. . .

I spent most of last Sunday with Frederika Bremer; four or five hours entirely alone with her. Mrs. Spring very kindly invited me to meet her there, and still *more* kindly invited all her other friends to come the next day.[1] By this trick, a quiet and cozy time was secured for me. What a refreshment it was! She is so artless and unaffected! Such a *reality*. I took a wonderful liking to her, though she is *very* plain in her person, and I am a fool about beauty. We talked about Swedenborg, and Thorwaldsen, and Jenny Lind, and Andersen.[2] She had many pleasant anecdotes to tell of Jenny, with whom she is intimately acquainted. Among other things, she mentioned having once seen her called out in Stockholm, after having successfully performed in a favorite opera. She was greeted not only with thundering claps, but with vociferous hurras. In the midst of the din, she began to warble merely the *tones* of an air in which she was very popular. The retournelle was, "How shall I describe what my heart is feeling?" She uttered no *words*, she merely warbled the *notes*, clear as a lark, strong as an organ. Every other sound was instantly hushed. Graceful—was it not? Frederika plays the piano with a light and delicate touch, and in a style indicative of musical feeling. She played to me a charming quaint old Swedish melody, the Song of Necken, the ancient Spirit of the Rivers, as he sat on the waters, singing to the accompaniment of his harp. She sketches admirable likenesses with colored crayons. She showed me one she had made of Andersen, a whole gallery of celebrated Danes, and a few Americans, whom she has sketched since her arrival. I particularly liked her for *one* thing; she did

[1] Rebecca (Buffum) Spring (1811–1911), a Quaker living in Brooklyn, N.Y., was a long-time friend of Child's. She and her husband, Marcus, had accompanied Margaret Fuller to Europe in 1846.
[2] Her references are to Emanuel Swedenborg, the Swedish Christian mystic; Bertel Thorwaldsen (1770–1844), the Danish sculptor; Jenny Lind (1820–87), the Swedish singer; and Hans Christian Andersen (1805–75), the Danish storyteller.

not attempt to *compliment* me, either directly or indirectly. She never heard of J. R. Lowell till she came here. His poetry has inspired her with strong enthusiasm. She said to me, "He is the poet-prophet of America." Emerson seems to have made on her the same vivid impression that he makes on all original and thinking minds. What a fuss they *will* make with Frederika in Boston! She will have no peace of her life. I hope they will not be ambitious of burying her by the side of Dr. Spurzheim.[3]

Will you ask Theodore Parker what are the most *distinct* allusions to the immortality of the soul in the Old Testament? and whether *he* considers that there is *any* recognition of the doctrine in the *books* of *Moses,* so called?

From the sacred books of other religions I am going to give extracts, to show both their *beauties* and their weaknesses. I want to treat our Bible exactly in the same way, without showing the slightest preference for one over another, either by any remarks, or by my manner of selecting. What shall I select as the best specimen of sublimity and beauty in the Old Testament? What to illustrate its obscurity, puerility, and superstition? What shall I select from the N. Testament, to illustrate the same things?   I do not know what effect my book will have on *others,* if I am ever permitted to finish it; but for *myself* I am growing worse than Theodore Parker a great deal; and David is more wicked than I am. I was reading to him the other day a poetical account of Chrishna's flute-playing, from the sacred Pouranas of the Hindoos. He remarked, with the utmost gravity, "I always thought *Jesus* would have been much more interesting, if he had taken an interest in the fine arts." Shade of the Rev. Dr. Dwight! what a remark was that, for one living in the light of the Gospel.

  . . .

ALS; Lydia Maria Child Papers, A/C 536, 1, Schlesinger Library, Radcliffe College (microfiche 27/763).

To Ellis Gray Loring

New York, Feb. 1st, 1850.

Dearly Beloved Friend,

  . . .

It is now settled that Mr. Child will remain with me till Spring. What will then open for him, I know not. He is as good as he can *be*—a nobler, better heart man never had—but it seems to me "his fingers are all thumbs" more than ever; so mal-adroit is he in all practical matters. In resigning myself to this inevitable destiny, and conforming my own tastes and inclinations to his, I find peace of mind; but it takes all the electricity out of me. However, I am in excellent health, have enough for our daily wants, and am serenely indifferent

---

[3] Dr. Johann Kaspar Spurzheim (1776–1832), German-born founder of phrenology, was buried in Boston.

to anything the world can give or take; and those are blessings to be thankful for.

I suppose you saw a copy of the letter which Mrs. Story wrote to J. R. Lowell about Margaret Fuller's marriage? I was very glad to see it; not on my own account; for I was perfectly satisfied to allow her to manage her own affairs in her own way, without remark of mine; but I was rejoiced to find that she had not imprudently put herself in the power of small female minds, of both sexes.[1] I am sorry to hear she is so very poor. In a letter to Mrs. Spring, she expresses anxiety concerning her daily bread, and "milk and pearl-barley for her boy." I was in hopes the child would resemble his handsome father, with his "large, dark, melancholy eyes"; but Quincy Shaw, who called upon them in Florence, writes that he is the image of his mother.[2] The love and tenderness induced by these new relations I think will greatly soften and beautify Margaret's character.   Give my best love to our good precious Louise, and to dear Anna, who seems to be as good as you both.

Yours with ever warm affection,
L. Maria Child.

. . .

ALS; Child Papers, Clements Library, University of Michigan (microfiche 27/776).

To Ellis Gray Loring

New York March 24th 1850

Dear Friend,

I now write to make a proposition, which I beg you will refuse, without reluctance, if your judgment or your feelings incline you to do so. I did not intend to make the proposition until next summer, and then with a view to its being carried into effect next fall, or next spring. But circumstances compel me to anticipate my plans. When Mr. Child came here last fall, he expected not to remain more than six weeks, at farthest; and ever since that time, we have every week been expecting a letter from his brother John, summoning him to rail-road duties in the West. But now, I am *convinced* that John does not intend to have him on the rail-road. Circumstances, which I could explain to you, make me suppose that he considers David's abolition likely to be injurious to his own interests in that quarter. Perhaps David may not always have been as prompt as he ought to have been; though I have no reason to *think* so, except from my knowledge of his character.   When I supposed that David was likely to be gone all summer, I thought it best to be in no hurry about making a permanent arrangement; especially as I had an idea that I *might* die in the course of the year myself. But dreams are very fallacious, and I am now con-

---

[1] The reference is not known.
[2] Quincy Adams Shaw (1825–1908), younger brother of Francis Shaw, later became the wealthy owner of copper mines.

vinced that John is not inclined to employ his brother. The farm at Northampton is let. What had I better do?

If there was any humble little place, with three or four acres of ground, would you be willing to buy or hire it, and let me pay you rent? If my father should leave me anything, I might by the help of my own earnings finally buy it. In the mean time, if my health is spared, I can certainly pay the rent. I am willing to leave it *entirely* to your judgment where and what the place shall be. I am very indifferent about it myself. I only want some quiet obscure corner, where I can die in peace, and meanwhile see you and Louisa occasionally.

If you know of such a place, Mr. Child might go early in May to plant some vegetables in the garden, and I would follow two or three weeks after.

The reason I do not *come* to consult with you, instead of *writing* is that I am just in the most perplexing part of my troublesome book, which I wish from my soul I had never undertaken. I hope by the middle of May to get at least all of the rough draught completed. My books and papers are now all round me, and I have easy access to all I want in libraries. To pack up and move now, would put me back *very* much. And I have been so *dreadfully* hindered ever since I began the confounded job! Obliged to toat *up* to N. Rochelle with all my books and papers; to go back and forth 36 miles to libraries; then obliged to toat *down* from N. Rochelle with all my books and papers; ill accommodated through the scorching hot summer; and Jeannie Barrett here over three months, ill most of the time. I am now scratching as fast as ever I can write, and I hate to break off if I can help it. Beside, there is no need; for I had rather than not, you should choose the place, if you think well of my proposition. If you do *not* think well of it; advise me *what* to do; will you.

I have scraped and scrimped *every* way, this year. I have $300 of my own laid by to get furniture; and that will be more than enough for my humble plans. Edmund,[1] the generous soul! deposited $500 for me, the day before he left for Europe; but *that* I shall not touch, unless driven by sickness, or some extraordinary emergency.

Give my best love to dear Louise and Anna. I shall wait patiently to hear what you think is my wisest course under existing circumstances. I want to act with reference to David's good, more than my own.

Gratefully and affectionately yours,
L. Maria Child.

ALS; Lydia Maria Child Papers, A/C 536, 2, Schlesinger Library, Radcliffe College (microfiche 28/778).

[1] Edmund Benzon.

6

July 1850-February 1859

In 1850 the Childs, reunited permanently after long years of intermittent separation, moved from New York to Massachusetts. They would live out their years in their native state. Their first home was a farm in the Boston suburb of West Newton owned by Ellis Gray Loring. They and Dolores, the young Spanish woman they befriended, stayed there for two and a half years. The time was an unhappy one. The farm's soil was poor, and the Childs, unable to pay their rent, were dependent upon Loring's generosity. Late in 1853, however, they made their last move, to live with Maria's father in Wayland, and Dolores moved away.

Though the Childs' personal fortunes were depressing, the world outside was explosively exciting. In the early months of 1850 the country was gripped by a political crisis. Slavery had become entwined with every public question. The United States, with a population of 23 million, had nearly doubled in territory—by treaty and by conquest—in the recent term of President Polk. A congressional debate on slavery in the new territories taken from Mexico held center stage: should slavery be allowed to spread into newly won lands? The forty-niners, mostly from the free states, had demanded that California come into the Union without slavery. Whichever way Congress voted on California, it would upset the Union's balance of fifteen free and fifteen slave states. The slaveholders warned that the South would regard California as a test case. They threatened disunion if Congress executed the power to ban slavery.

A showdown seemed near when Senator Henry Clay offered what would become known as the Compromise of 1850. After great debate, Congress enacted Clay's proposals into law. Texas was brought into the Union as a slave state, California as a free state. The slave trade was abolished in the District of Columbia, and a new and harsher fugitive slave law was passed to force Northerners to return runaways to their owners. Central to the compromise was a "popular sovereignty" provision which said that when a territory came into the Union as a state, it would enter with or without slavery as its constitution prescribed at the time of admission.

Most Americans hailed the compromise as a final settlement of the slavery question, hoping that it would mean peace in their time. But Clay himself admitted that it was more a Southern victory than a compromise. The abolitionists condemned the Fugitive Slave Act and almost at once began to violate the law by helping to rescue runaways.

Child's letters are fewer in the first part of the 1850s, when she felt isolated by small-town life and her political energy seemed to have faded. Entering her fifties, she writes of encroaching old age, her interest in spiritualism, and theories of history. Although there was much anxiety and suffering in those first years back in her home state, she thought she came out the better for it, "like iron that has been heated and hammered" (20 January 1856). She finished years of labor on her three-volume history, *The Progress of Religious Ideas*, again challenging conventional views as she had done with her *Appeal* in 1833. While the work's sale was painfully small, it won high praise from independent minds.

In 1854, with the onset of the troubles in Kansas, she felt a resurgence of strength and with David gave all her energy to helping the Free-Soilers, writing a song and a serialized story, organizing sewing projects, and sending clothing and money west. The 1856 election, with Frémont the candidate of the new Republican party, infected her with political excitement. After twenty-five years of unpopular agitation, the abolition principles seemed at last "to sway the masses" (14 September 1856). With the Dred Scott decision, she feared the nation might be driven to deeds of blood as all hope of justice for the blacks was denied. In the nation's future she read disunion and civil war.

In the summer of 1850 Child accompanied the Lorings on a brief vacation to Lake George, N.Y. It was a rare event for her: for lack of money she took few holidays. When her well-to-do friends invited her to spend time at their homes or to travel with them, she usually refused; unable to reciprocate in their style, she preferred not to be under obligation. She describes the opulent scene at Saratoga, N.Y., to Lucy Searle (1794–after 1862), a schoolteacher and daughter of a Newburyport, Mass., banker.

To Lucy Searle

Lake George, July 18'th 1850.

Dear Friend,

   . . .

Were you ever at Saratoga? It is a curious place to examine human fossils. I only wish they were relics of antediluvian species no longer in existence.

There are consumptive young beaux panting in tight stays, and wrinkled old beaux with wigs, torturing their poor uncertain feet with tight boots. Among the ladies, she who made the greatest dash was a pupil of yours, I understand. Mrs. Wetmore of New York, the three times millionaire, arrived in yellow satin turned out with black velvet, as if in full mourning for Talma, whom the French thus honored with funeral weeds, in style à la papillon. Eighteen travelling trunks, following in Mrs. Wetmore's train, cast before them the shadows of coming ball-dresses, of silks and velvets, jewels and blonde. The lady herself I saw floating up and down the piazzas, draped in Honiton or Valenciennes, like a disembodied "ame de dentelles." . . .

ALS; Lydia Maria Child Papers, Anti-Slavery Collection, Cornell University (microfiche 28/786).

Slave catching became a profitable business under the new Fugitive Slave Law of 1850. Each captured slave meant a fee for the federal officer who rounded him up, and the law obliged citizens to aid the officers. In her defiant hatred of the law, Child was typical of many Northerners. Southern slaveholders hunting the runaways in free states risked being mobbed, sued for false imprisonment, or prosecuted for kidnapping.

To Marianne Silsbee

West Newton, March 27th 1851

My Dear Friend,

. . .

I *was* in a towering indignation against Mr. Silsbee, as I *first* heard the story of the fugitive slave.[1] I walked the room as vehemently as Miss Betsy Trotwood, when her mind was unusually agitated. I said, "Well! I don't suppose I should have gone to Mrs. Silsbee's oftener than once a year, under *any* circumstances; but now I will *never* go; and if she invites me, I will tell her so." Mr. Child reminded me how unwilling I should feel to hurt *your* feelings, or to seem ungrateful for all your kindness. Thereupon, I burst out crying, and said, "I know it; but so help me God, I will bury every friendship on earth, rather than shake hands with a man that has assisted in restoring a fugitive slave." This was for the private satisfaction of my own conscience, you understand, not because I supposed it would be a matter of any importance to Mr. Silsbee. On this subject, my convictions are so strong, and my moral sense so clear, that I am absolutely *unable* to make any compromise with principle.

I see the difficulties of the case, as affairs now stand. I can excuse a man for not *resisting* the unrighteous law of the land; but I *cannot* excuse him for not *evading* it, and passively refusing to be an *instrument* of it. If he does not act as honest lovers of freedom always find a *way* to act, when called upon to abet tyrannical laws, which their inmost hearts abhor,—why then I can hold no

---

[1] In Boston on 15 Feb. 1851, blacks had forcibly rescued the runaway, Shadrach, from the courthouse and sent him off to Canada and freedom.

communication with that man. Afterward, Augusta King told me the circumstances, as you have explained them; and I was glad I did not write to you while the fire-heat of indignation was on me; though I have no doubt I should have been eloquent. The coals of my free nature are burning yet, though the ashes of many disappointments cover them. Touch a hair of a slave's head, and a tongue of flame shoots up from the suppressed volcano!

. . .

ALS; Lydia Maria Child Letters, American Antiquarian Society (microfiche 28/803).

To Ellis Gray Loring

West Newton, April 13th, 1851.

Dear Friend,

I sit down to a task, which I greatly dislike; and that is to write a letter about "pecunary" affairs. Notwithstanding my strong efforts to prevent it, I am afraid I shall be obliged to be, in some degree, a pensioner on your bounty, this year.

I had laid by a little more than $400, in New York, with a view to settling down on some little place, after David had earned some money, by three year's work on the rail road. He received only $400 for his first year's labor, which barely sufficed to pay the expenses of food and clothing, and a few small debts at Northampton. At the end of that year, when I was expecting a doubling of his salary, he was thrown up entirely on the beach by his brother John's unbrotherly conduct.[1] Then I had his expenses for board, washing, and et ceteras, during eight months in N. York; the expenses of getting here; the eternal annual interest of $60 to father, for money lost twenty years ago; and about $300 for furniture, and out of door tools and fixtures, since we came here.

In some things my expenses prove heavier than I calculated upon. Wood has cost more than I expected; for what little David had time to get from our own premises was necessarily green. I have been obliged to pay $38 dollars for food for cow, pig, and hens, because we came here too late to raise anything for them. The soil is good, they all say, but it is very hard to work, being remarkably full of rocks, stones, and stumps. I have agreed to pay an Irishman twenty dollars, for grubbing the stones and stumps out of one quarter of an acre, near the house, which we greatly need for vegetables. He considers it a hard bargain, at that price, for there are stones enough in it to make a ⟨ladder⟩ path to Olympus, for the Titans. It is clearly good policy to subdue the land immediately round the house, for nothing will so much increase the value of the property. *That* is a subject I have much at heart, that you may not eventually lose money

[1] Child had hoped for several years that John Childe would assure his brother David of steady employment. When he failed to do so, she felt that he had "not acted well," and she decided that John's dislike of abolitionism had a good deal to do with it.

by helping us at this pinch. However, with my customary caution, I limited David to only one quarter of an acre of the rough land this year. He labors very industriously, and sticks to his promise of not expending one dollar, without consulting me.[2] But between you and me (don't tell it to anybody) he owes something at Northampton. Father said I might have the rent of the farm there. I expected to receive $100 from it on the 1'st of Jan. last; but I was obliged to deduct $25 of it to pay a debt he had contracted there. He says he owes only $150 in all, since he took advantage of the Bankrupt Law. He thinks there is not the least danger of anybody's calling upon me for it, and that he shall soon pay it by sale of a wood lot up there, which belongs to *him,* and not to my father; part of the aforesaid debt having been contracted to purchase the wood lot. But sometimes *I* think it would be safest to quietly transfer all my little goods and chattels to you, by some legal form, without saying anything to him about it. He feels badly, poor fellow; and he is *so* good! He is doing his very best *now* to keep out of expense, and and [*sic*] I don't want to do anything to discourage him.

Some expenses I have had I am going to ask permission to transfer to you, and have them all added to the expense of purchasing the house and land. The drain to the sink plagued us very much last winter. When Mr. Child dug it open, he found it was a regular cheat. It was made of old rotten boards, all falling to pieces. Iron pipe is the only thing that will last, except bricks laid with Roman cement. He found the first was no more expensive than the last. Accordingly I bought pipe enough to answer the purpose, for which I paid $9..75 cts. David will lay it himself. It is a hard job, but he thinks he can do it. I am going to ask you to pay this, and $7..45 cts for paper I purchased for the rooms, and $2 dollars which I paid for fastenings to the windows; and charge all in the account for the house. What *more* I shall have to ask this year, I know not. I had rather be dependent on *you* than on any person in the wide world; but still it is so disagreeable, that I shall avoid it as far as possible. After *this* year, I hope we shall contrive to *begin* to get out of your debt.

Ever with grateful love yours,
Maria.

9.75
7.45
2.
___
$19.20

Please destroy this letter.

ALS; Lydia Maria Child Papers, A/C 536, 2, Schlesinger Library, Radcliffe College (microfiche 28/804).

___

[2] She had already separated her financial affairs from David's. This promise does not seem to have been kept.

During 1851, popular opposition to the Fugitive Slave Law increased, and many moderates joined the abolitionists in open disobedience. In April, a large crowd had besieged the Boston courthouse clamoring for release of Thomas Sims, a runaway from Georgia. But Sims, guarded by hundreds of armed constables, was sent back south with his master. Rescues which succeeded that year were Jerry McHenry's in Syracuse, New York, and William Parker's in Christiana, Pennsylvania.

To Joseph Carpenter

West Newton, August 24, 1851.

There seems to be a lull just now in fugitive slave matters. What experiment our masters will try next, remains to be shown. The commercial and moneyed portion of the community will doubtless obey their orders to any extent. But in the heart of the people I think a better and braver sentiment is gradually being formed. A friend of mine in Medford sheltered a fugitive a short time ago. When the firemen of the town heard of it, they sent for the man chattel, elected him a member of their company, and promised, at a given signal, to rally for his defence in case he was pursued, and to stand by him to the death, one and all.

L, extract; *Letters of Lydia Maria Child*, 1882 (microfiche 29/810).

To Ellis Gray Loring

West Newton, Oct 27th, 1851.

Dear Friend,

I come to you again with fresh demands, and I am afraid it will not be the last time, either. I never was so terrified and discouraged about pecuniary affairs, as I am now. I toil incessantly, but I toil without the least ray of hope. I was not aware how much my spirits had been kept up by the idea that John Child would find some profitable employment for his brother. His strange, unfeeling conduct leaves me utterly disheartened about the future. In endeavoring to provide a home for David's old age I was trying to do what I thought was my duty. Whether I made a mistake or not, God knows; I do not. I don't know what *is* judicious to be done. It is evident we cannot remain long here, unless some means of raising an income from other sources can be found.

Everything has gone against David, as usual. The season has been remarkably untoward; for two months he was very ill and weak; he has had a bad fall; and divers others smaller misadventures. The outgoes have been much more than I expected, the income will be less. I work hard and practise a degree of economy which pinches my soul till I despise its smallness. Even if I had *time* to write, all power of thinking, and still more of imagining, is pressed out of me by this perpetual load of anxiety.

I *will* not live dependent upon friends. For myself I could provide amply, and have something to spare for others. But I cannot see what course it is wise for me to pursue with regard to David. The more I ponder upon it, the more I get bewildered.

He has kept his promises, and really tried to do his very best, this past year; but it is my firm conviction that let him do what he will, his hard labor will always cost more than it comes to.

Mr. Francis writes that the sale of my books has stopped, because I neglect to keep up an acquaintance with the public. I am very sorry now that I listened to the advice of friends, who told me I ought to try to write a large book, and not fritter myself away in stories for common-place Magazines. I thought I was *safe* in trying the experiment, because I clearly saw the way of paying my own small expenses for three years. Had I foreseen how John Child was going to act, I never would have undertaken anything that did not bring immediate payment. Now I must get out of the dilemma as well as I can. May God help me to keep my wits, and turn them to some account! Till I can do this, I must rely upon you, my dear friend, to help me through the dark hours. If I die without getting my bark afloat again, you must take your pay out of the farm at Northampton. I will try my best to keep from sinking utterly.

We have put up the cooking stove, and it works admirably. By using some old pipe that came from Northampton we avoided involving you in any additional expense. I am sorry you did not get a small second-hand stove, instead of such a superior article. It will prove a warm friend in the winter hours, as the giver has proved in the winter of our fortunes. The only fault of *that* metaphor is that we never had any summer; only I had a brief Indian summer in New York.

Speaking of New York, I judge from what I hear that Hicks is rather in a bad way.[1] He says of Anna, "Oh if I had only met her before she was engaged, and if she only had been without the prospect of a dollar in the world, how I would have toiled to win her!" But he says he deemed it dishonorable under the circumstances to let her know the state of his feelings. I think you mistake somewhat in your estimate of artists, as a class. Puplic [*sic*] performers of all sorts, as a general rule, are doubtless more unprincipled than other men, because they are flattered so much, and form the habit of requiring perpetual excitement. But the *quiet* pursuit of art, in sculpture, painting, and musical *composition* does not produce the same effects. I am inclined to think such artists are, as a *class* more noble and honorable than other classes of men.

With best love to the dear good Louise, I am affectionately & gratefully yours,

Maria.

ALS; Lydia Maria Child Papers, A/C 536, 2, Schlesinger Library, Radcliffe College (microfiche 29/815).

[1] Thomas Hicks (1823–90) was a popular American portrait painter whose subjects included Lincoln, Longfellow, Bryant, and Stephen Foster.

Apparently the Lorings proposed that the Childs move near the Loring summer place at Beverly, Massachusetts.

To Ellis Gray Loring

West Newton, Feb. 6th 1852

[[Please consider this entirely *confidential*]]

Dear Friend,

I have reflected much on the hint you dropped concerning plans for my future. How deeply grateful I am to you no language can express. But the more I reflect upon it, the more I am confirmed in my first feeling that it would be *impossible* for me to endure such a life. On the *land* very few things could be raised. Milk, eggs, pork, and butter, would all have to be bought. In such a place, Mr. Child could of course get nothing to do that would bring even ten dollars a year. All the income we could be certain of, must come from my writing. The dull monotonous life of the country kills my mind so stone dead, that I cannot write. Anxiety about money matters, and a sense of dependence makes the matter still worse, so that all my faculties go from me. The tendency to sadness, which I inherit from my father, increases under such circumstances; and I think it would nowhere take such strong hold of me, as near the sea-shore, to which I have a peculiar aversion, except during a few hot days in mid-summer. In spring, fall, and winter, it seems to me almost insupportably gloomy. I should be far from Mary Stearns,[1] and find it about as difficult to get to father, in case of any emergency, as I should if I were in New York. There is only *one* advantage to balance these objections—that is being near you and dear Louise. *That* would be to me a privilege of inestimable price. But the longest and gloomiest part of the year, you would be away; and during the summer months, you would have a continual run of company. However, all these draw-backs are minor considerations. I should not mind disliking the place; for it is a matter of great indifference to me where or how I spend the remainder of life, provided I can pay for daily bread. But *that* is precisely what I shall *not* be able to do in such a position. The inevitable result would be that we should be more than half supported by you. I had rather be dependent on you than on any other person in the world; but I prefer death by Prussic acid to being dependent on *any*body. What I have suffered since I came to West Newton has burned that feeling into my soul with a deeper brand than ever. There is no use in arguing about it. Such a situation is torture to my temperament; and I cannot help it. I thought I would say all this *in good season*, for fear you might lay some plans, or incur some expense, with reference to the project of which you spoke.

I am exceedingly sorry that I have given you so much trouble. The fact

1 Mary (Preston) Stearns (1821–1901) was Child's niece in Medford, Mass.

is, John Child's unexpected conduct so frustrated all my plans, and drove me to such extremity, that I did not know *what* to do, or which way to turn. Nothing has worked as I hoped it would when I thought of returning to Massachusetts. I expected to be near you, and near the Shaws. They have gone to Europe, and you are going to Beverly, which is about as bad. I hoped we should raise from the land what would be worth one hundred dollars to us. What we have raised has cost more than it would bring in the market. I thought Dolores would get scholars, and David would get something to do by which he could earn 2 or 300 a year. None of these things have come to pass; and we have all found ourselves recipients of bounty for which we felt deeply grateful, though it cut us to the soul.

I think there is *now* really a prospect opening to sell the Northampton farm. If I get any money I shall place it in your hands. This place I think had better be advertised next Fall, and sold as soon as there is a good chance. I am more than ever convinced that David can never "make buckle and strap meet" by working for *himself* in any way. Marcus Spring, Mr. Shaw, and Horace Greely all say that the North American Phalanx is on a much more *safe* business foundation than any association that has ever been formed in this country.[2] It is not in the hands of spiritual loafers, as was Brook Farm, but of practical men, enterprising mechanics and farmers. I have heard that they need teachers. If David could teach a certain number of hours in the day, and agree to keep a certain number of acres weeded, or hens fed, and be *paid* for it, it would be the *safest* situation for a man of his peculiarities. I might board there, and write for publishers and editors in New York, where such talent as I have is more recognized than it ever was, or ever will be in Boston. The situation would not be agreeable to me, in many respects; but I *cannot* be agreeably situated while I am involved in David's destiny. He is good and kind, and I have made up my mind that "I never *will* desert Mr. Macawber." I want to go to New York and make minute inquiries about the Phalanx, without intimating to any one that *we* have any interest in the inquiries. If I find there is a reasonable prospect that we can *earn* our way there, I shall feel strongly inclined to go. David's nephew, who comes here often, is going to California in 3 or 4 weeks. David wants to go with him to dig. But I think he is too old, and his constitution too much broken, to try such an experiment. However, the nephew, who is a practical managing Yankee, is going to report to us whether there is any kind of opening suitable for his uncle, and in the course of the year we can decide between that and the Phalanx. If he goes to California, I shall go to New York, dive into the thickest of the fight, allow myself to be lionized, sell comfort, repose, taste, everything but conscience.

[2] The most long-lived of Fourierist colonies, the North American Phalanx, was founded near Red Bank, N.J., in 1843. It expired in 1854. The Childs did not join the colony.

The substance of this long yarn is that we *must* earn our bread, not receive it.

AL; Lydia Maria Child Papers, A/C 536, 3, Schlesinger Library, Radcliffe College (microfiche 29/820).

J. Peter Lesley (1819–1903), minister and geologist, married Child's friend Susan Lyman in 1849. He gave up the ministry in 1852 to devote himself to geology, publishing scientific work and also fiction and poetry. Child corresponded frequently with both husband and wife.

To Susan (Lyman) Lesley

West Newton, March 29'th [1852]

Darling Susie,

. . .

Have you read "Uncle Tom's Cabin, or Life among the Lowly"?[1] The story is told with great pathos and power. I think Mrs. Stow has a larger dash of *genius* in her talent than any of the Beechers. I am glad she has written such a book, and I am also glad that it has a moderate sprinkling of Calvinism in it. Not that *I* like that fiery medicine, even in homeopathic doses; but it will make it acceptable to a much larger class of readers, who are not in the habit of taking in much humanity, unless stirred up with a portion of theology; like brimstone and molasses.

All these side-hits are on purpose for Peter—God bless him!

. . .

ALS; J. Peter Lesley Collection, American Philosophical Society (microfiche 29/822).

Harriet Hosmer (1830–1908), the daughter of a physician, took up sculpture at the instigation of Fanny Kemble. Hosmer studied in Boston and Saint Louis and went to Rome in 1852 to continue study with the English sculptor John Gibson. She was to become Child's close friend.

In a letter to Frank Shaw, then in Europe, Child mentions her biography of Isaac Hopper, who had died on 7 May 1852. Her book, in part a defense of his

[1] *Uncle Tom's Cabin*, by Harriet (Beecher) Stowe (1811–96), ran serially in the abolitionist paper the *National Era* from 5 June 1851 to Mar. 1852, when it appeared in book form. The first printing of five thousand copies sold in two days. Within a year, three hundred thousand copies had been sold in the United States alone. By the time the Civil War began, the American and British sales ran into the millions and people all over the world were reading it in forty translations.

radical Quaker views, was full of anecdotes from his long and rich life of social service, gathered during her nine years with the Hoppers and adapted from articles he had written for the *Standard*. The biography's popularity was immediate, and it remained in print for over thirty years.

To Francis Shaw

West Newton, Sep. 5th, 1852.

Dearly beloved friend,

. . .

. . . Harriet Hosmer, daughter of a physician in Watertown, has produced a remarkably good piece of statuary. It is a bust of Hesper, the Evening Star. I never saw a tender, happy drowsiness so well expressed. A star shines on her forehead, and beneath her breast lies the crescent moon. Her graceful ⟨head⟩ hair is intertwined with capsules of the poppy. It is cut with great delicacy and precision, and the flesh seems to me very flesh-like. The poetic conception is her own, and the workmanship is *all* her own. A man worked upon it a day and a half, to chop large bits of marble; but she did not venture to have him go within several inches of the surface she intended to work. Miss Hosmer is going to Rome in October, accompanied by her father, a plain, sensible man, of competent property. She expects to remain in Italy three years, with the view of becoming a *sculptor by profession*. I have not mentioned you to her; but if you happen to meet her pray speak encouraging words. If she keeps on as she has begun she will do much for the cause of womanhood. When I first met her, I did not like her; because her voice seemed unmodulated and her manners brusque. But upon further acquaintance, I found her very earnest, true, and unaffected. The external roughness is merely owing to the free out-of-door life she has led, skating, rowing, riding on horseback, &c. Her father having lost all his other children, sacrificed everything to making her physically strong and lo, the result!   Mrs. Stowe's truly great work, "Uncle Tom's Cabin," has also done much to command respect for faculties of woman. Whittier has poured forth verses upon it; Horace Mann has eulogized it in Congress; Lord Morpeth was carried away with it; the music ⟨stories⟩ stores are full of pieces of music suggested by its different scenes; somebody is going to dramatize it; and ⟨50,⟩ 100,000 copies sold in little more than six months! Never did any American work have such success! The passage of the fugitive slave law roused her up to write it. Behold how "God makes the wrath of man to praise *Him!*"

Charles Sumner has made a *magnificent* speech in Congress against the Fugitive Law.

. . .

ALS; Houghton Library, Harvard University (microfiche 29/828).

To Francis Shaw

Dearly Beloved Friend,

. . .

I have no news to write about myself except that Friend Hopper's Biography is almost finished, and that I have had a legacy. Do you recollect the maiden ladies, by the name of Sargent? The eldest of them[1] died a few months since, and left me $200 and Dolores $100. I was very much surprised at my own legacy, and still more so at the one for Dolores; for she had never seen her but two or three times. This unexpected kindness from the good old soul made me cry like a baby. Mrs. Loring said to me, ["]Of *course*, Maria, you will send the money back." And perhaps I should, if I could contrive any method of doing so. Perhaps the Knockers may invent some spiritual Express Trains, for such purposes. Apro-pos of knockers, your brother Quincy told Anna Loring "a merry toy" the other day. He says your father, in some of his recent visits to "the mediums" had a conversation with the spirit of Dr. Webster, who assured him that he was "very happy"; as they all do, much to the edification of the Universalists. Your father inquired, "Do you ever see Dr. Parkman, now?" He answered, "Oh yes. He and I are in the same sphere". "What occupations do you have in the other world?" "Various occupations. *I* keep a boarding house; and at present, Dr. Parkman is with me, taking out the old debt."[2]

When I first heard this, I was distressed at the thought that *debts* followed us into the other world. But upon second thought, I was charmed with the prospect; for on *that* ground, I shall have you and Sarah, and Mr. and Mrs. Loring, and Anna Loring, boarding with me through all eternity. How long do you suppose *Daniel* Webster will have to keep a boarding-house, to work out *his* debts?

Have you seen that Marcus Spring, Wm. H. Channing, Theodore Weld and others, are about forming a new Phalanx, called the Raritan Bay Association? I felt rather sorry, because all the strength of property and talent would concentrate in the N. American, and thus make *one* Phalanx capable of carrying out Fourier's idea. . . .[3] I am rejoiced to hear that your children are de-

---

1 Catherine Sargent.

2 John White Webster (b. 1793), a Harvard professor and physician, was convicted of murdering George Parkman (b. 1790), his colleague, in 1849. Parkman's dismembered body was found in one of the college buildings about a week after he had been killed; he had been trying to collect on a loan to Webster. After a sensational trial in Boston, Webster was hanged on 23 Nov. 1850. Parkman was the uncle of the historian Francis Parkman and of Francis George Shaw.

3 Marcus Spring (1810–74), the philanthropic New York businessman, took the lead in establishing a cooperative society in New Jersey called the Raritan Bay Union; dissidents from the North American Phalanx were among its founders. Child's friends the Grimké sisters and Theodore Weld committed themselves to the union in Dec. 1852.

veloping their faculties so well. How is it with Robert? So far as I have had opportunity to observe, I have not much liked the effect of European education on boys. The fact is, in a foreign land, young people are floating on the *surface* of things; they do not form an *integral portion* of society, as they do at home. In their own country they are unavoidably *mixed* more or less with those among whom they reside. They cannot pursue ambition, business, or even amusement, *without* becoming so; and this I apprehend has its use, in the stimulus, the responsibilities, and the restraints it brings.

I believe I wrote you some time ago about the School of Design for women. Several of the pupils have since entered on a successful career. One of Miss Searle's nieces obtains a good living by making patterns for a calico and chintz manufactory. I wish Anna Page could be fitted to make first-rate drawings for wood-engravers. The demand for such is almost unlimited. How *is* Page? Does he get more orders? Please remember me very affectionately to him. . . . Thus far, we have had a very mild winter. We had our first snow on the 13th of this month, and it fell as gently on the earth as kind words upon the soul. Our hens are comfortably housed at last. Your original six have increased to forty four. They sometimes amuse me by their resemblance to humans. When Mr. Child is digging, if he throws them a worm, it is curious to see how unhappy it makes the individual that receives it. He runs round and round, everywhere, trying to eat it in peace; but his good luck soon becomes known, and the whole tribe are after him, pell-mell, just as a rich man is hunted in this world of greedy unfortunates. Thus I *philosophize;* but in truth, I wish Providence would throw *me* a sizeable mouthful of worldly prosperity. I hope I shall not be *left,* in my old age, to consider money the greatest good; but the devil tempts me *dreadfully* in that way.

. . .

ALS; Houghton Library, Harvard University (microfiche 29/835).

To Louisa Loring

Wayland, March, 16th [1853]

Dearest Louise,

. . .

Mr. Richard Fuller seated himself next to me in the cars, and spent his time in urging me to go to revival meetings.[1] You would have been amused, if not edified, if you had heard the anathemas I poured out upon Calvinism. He said it was particularly impressive and interesting to attend "the business-men's meetings, to hear men who had been devoted to lucre singing and praying so de-

[1] This was possibly Richard Frederic Fuller (1821–69), brother of Margaret Fuller and a lawyer then living in Wayland.

voutly." I told him I was afraid most of them were but taking out a new lease to cheat with impunity.

He, very condescendingly, informed me that God did not make *me* to have *opinions;* that God made *me* for the *affections;* that he intended *me* to write about children and flowers; implying, all the while, that it was for *him,* and such as *he,* to decide upon matters high profound. Well, he fulfils *his* intended mission; for, as David says, God, plainly enough, made *him* for an egotistical fool. He is greatly distressed about the wickedness of Emerson, and he has discontinued the Atlantic Monthly, because "it contains so much offensive to the pious."

I was greatly relieved when I got into the stage, and saw him mount on his horse. But, alas, my happiness was of short duration; for a woman, in the stage was fresh from the Boston revival-meetings, and *she* pounced upon me. Her voice was as hard and as sharp as her theology, and she had with her a very pert disagreeable little girl, whom she set to reciting verses about the "Lord Jesus," in a manner as mechanical as the Buddhist praying-machines. Alas for religion! What absurdities are everywhere enacted in its holy name!

I send you Mr. Sears' book on Immortality, with which I am inclined to think you will be pleased.[2] I love and reverence Mr. Sears, though I cannot quite agree with all his conclusions.

. . .

ALS; Loring Family Papers, Schlesinger Library, Radcliffe College (microfiche 30/840).

In December 1853 the Childs moved into the home of her father, David Convers Francis. It was a small house near the Sudbury River in Wayland, a town of fifteen hundred people about fifteen miles west of Boston. Not long after, Congress began a bitter debate on the Kansas-Nebraska Bill, introduced by Senator Stephen A. Douglas. Becoming law in May 1854, it extended a provision of the Compromise of 1850, permitting the new territories to come into the Union with or without slavery. This "squatter sovereignty" was an open invitation to fierce battles between the free-labor forces and slaveholders in the territories. The law erased the Missouri Compromise line, wrecked the Compromise of 1850, and opened the western lands to slavery.

Near home, in Boston, a Virginia runaway slave named Anthony Burns was captured on 24 May and held prisoner in the courthouse. An attempt by the abolitionists to storm the courthouse and free him failed. The sensational case described here by Child, writing to Frank Shaw in Europe, caused thousands more to feel that the Union would break apart over the slavery issue.

[2] Edmund Sears (1810–76) was pastor of the Unitarian Church in Wayland. He and his wife, Ellen, were close friends of Child's. The book may be *Regeneration* (Boston, 1853) or an earlier edition of his *Athanasia, or Gleams of Immortality* (Boston, 1857).

To Francis Shaw

Friend always Beloved,

. . .

With regard to the Present, here in our own country, my dear friend, it is
gloomy enough. My soul is by turns sorrowful and indignant; and I feel
habitually as if I should be willing to pour out my blood, like water, if I could
do anything to arrest the downward course of things. The only hope seems to
be, that the South, in her swift career of pride and success, will become out-
and-out insane, as conquerors are wont to do, and so blindly rush upon her own
destruction, dragging us after her, of course. Of all our servile senates, none
have been so completely servile to the slave-interest, as the present one. They
have passed the Nebraska Bill, in open defiance of the people; they will soon
have Cuba, either by war, or by immense bribes to the Spanish government;
and similar designs on Hayti, which I have suspected for these five years, are
now beginning to manifest themselves. These measures have been followed up
by the most outrageous insults and aggressions upon the North. Only three
days ago, another poor slave was hunted in Boston, and though a pretty general
indignation was excited, he was given up by Boston magistrates, and triumphantly carried back to bondage, guarded by a strong escort of U.S. troops.
The court-house was nearly *filled* with troops and hired ruffians, armed with
cutlasses and bowie knives. No *citizen* was allowed to enter without a *pass,* as
is the custom with *slaves;* and these passes were obtained with great difficulty;
none being given to any one suspected of being friendly to the slave. The Rev.
Samuel May had his pass taken from him, and he was thrust out rudely by the
soldiers. Men were even arrested and imprisoned for merely making *observations* to each other, which the ruling powers considered dangerous. My dear
friend, my very soul is sick, in view of these things. They tell me "The Lord
will surely arise for the sighing of the poor and the needy," as he has promised.
I *think* to myself, "Oh yes, that promise was made some 3000 years ago, and
the fulfilment seems as far off as ever." But I suppress the impatient blasphemy,
and only *say,* as poor Aunt Chloe does in Uncle Tom, "Yes, missis; but the
Lord lets dreadful things happen."

Whether there is *any* limit to the servile submission of the North, I know
not. The South seems resolved to try to the utmost how much kicking and
cuffing she *will* bear. The Richmond Enquirer compares the connexion between
North and South to the relation between Greece and her Roman masters. "The
dignity and energy of the Roman character, conspicuous in war and politics,
were not easily tamed and adjusted to the arts of industry and literature. The
degenerate and pliant Greeks, on the contrary, obsequious, dexterous, and
ready, monopolized the business of teaching and manufacturing in the Roman
empire, allowing their masters ample leisure for the service of the state, in the

Senate, or the field. We learn from Juvenal that they were the most useful and capable servants, whether as pimps, or professors of rhetoric."

Now do you know that my inmost soul *rejoices* in all these manifestations of contempt? The North richly deserves them, and I have a *faint* hope that they *may* be heaped on, till some of the old spirit is roused.   There was a large meeting at Faneuil Hall when the slave was arrested. Mr. Russell presided, and the speeches and resolutions were uncommonly spirited and eloquent.[1] But they *talked* boldly of a rescue the next *morning* and so did more harm than good, by forewarning the Southerners and giving them time to summon a great array of U.S. troops. If they had *only* struck when the iron was hot, and used very slight precautions, I think the poor slave might have been rescued without shedding blood. But it was *not* done, and "*order* reigns in Warsaw," as the Russian officials declared after the knout had driven all the Polish heroes into Siberia. My soul is just now in a stormy state, and it curses "law and order," seeing them all arrayed on the wrong side. This fierce mood will soon give place to a milder one. But oh, my friend, these continually baffled efforts for human freedom, they are agonizing to the sympathizing soul.

. . .

ALS; Houghton Library, Harvard University (microfiche 30/866).

To Ellis Gray Loring

Wayland Sep. 26th [1854]

Dear Friend,
I called at your office again to say to you that I feared my brother Convers would be seriously hurt and offended, if I should place my M.S.[1] in Theodore Parkers hands. When I arrived home, I found that Mr. Child held the same opinion very strongly. I moreover think it *would* get rumored round, and the *inference* would be that Theodore Parker assisted in writing it. I should be sorry to have such an idea prevail; first, because it would be untrue, and secondly because it would give many an unnecessary prejudice, to begin with. So I think, upon the whole, I had better stand or fall on my own poor merits. I cannot be grievously disappointed, because my expectations are very small.

Mr. Francis objected to the word Glance in the title, and wished it to be Progress of Religious Ideas through Successive Ages.

I long to get the boat launched, that it may be off my hands. I have labored utterly without sympathy, half *afraid* to trust the plain truth to take care of itself; and I am *so* weary!

---

[1] George R. Russell (1800–66), active in the antislavery movement, was head of the Boston firm of Russell and Sturgis. He was married to Sarah Shaw, sister of Francis Shaw.
[1] *The Progress of Religious Ideas.*

I long to refresh my spirit with a little visit to you and dear Louise; but I know not when I shall be able to compass it. God bless you all.

Yours with grateful love,

L. M. Child.

ALS; Lydia Maria Child Papers, Schlesinger Library, Radcliffe College (microfiche 30/869).

To J. Peter Lesley

Wayland, Jan. 1st, 1855.

. . .

It was much, *very* much, that a man of your learning and kindliness should approve of the manner in which I had executed the book, and be so entirely satisfied with its spirit.[1] He who knoweth the heart knows that I performed the task most *conscientiously;* keeping my mind stedfastly fixed on the *one* object of speaking the truth in love. *Some*body *must* clear away the theological rubbish, which lies piled up in the way of man's progress; and who could better *afford* to do it, than I, who care little for popularity, and who am also passing off the stage? I expected almost universal censure, and scarcely any sympathy; but I have been agreeably disappointed. I have received several very cordial letters, and four or five highly commendatory newspaper-notices; among which was the conservative Daily Advertiser! Stranger still, I am *told* that the New York Observer praised the learning, candour, and spirit of the book, though it added some disclaimer. I can hardly believe it, till I *see* it. The N. York Evangelist is severe upon it. The Christian Register, of Boston, contains a very narrow, sneering and unfair notice, said to have been written by the *Rev* Mr. Holland.[2] I expected all the Reverends out against me and I was aware that Theodore Parker would bring them down in *greater* force, by his Thanksgiving Sermon; in which I am told that he pronounced, in his *deep* tones, that the Progress of Ideas was "*the* book of the age; and written by a *woman!*"

You say that a jury of critics could not decide whether it was written by a man or a woman. It is a curious coincidence with your remark, that *three* people, in magnetic sleep, who have had some of my M.S. letters placed in their hands, have begun by saying, "I cannot clearly make out whether this was written by a man, or a woman." Now I have been such a fool, such a slave, of my *affections*, all my life long, that *I* know very well that I am very *much* of a woman. I am more doubtful whether I partake much of the manly nature. I admire a *manly* woman, though I dislike a *masculine* one.

I am collecting all the letters, notices, and remarks about my book, intending to place them in a Scrap-Book, as a measurement of the spiritual stature of

---

[1] Although the copyright date of *The Progress of Religious Ideas* is 1855, the book, judging by the reviews Child cites, must have appeared late in 1854.
[2] Frederick W. Holland (1811–95) was a Unitarian minister.

the time. With the exception of the Christian Register, all the notices I have seen preserve a tone of courtesy and respect, even when expressing disapprobation. The world has certainly made some progress since the learned and good Dr. Priestly had his house, library, manuscripts, and scientific apparatus burned by a theological mob, and was obliged to expatriate himself on account of his views of the Trinity.[3] Truth is mighty, and will at *last* prevail.

You say I seem to *believe* in the supernatural, and yet to *ridicule* it. That expresses precisely my state of mind. I have no sympathy whatever with the *general* form of belief in miracles. I do not believe the laws of the universe were *ever* set aside, to serve *any* temporary purpose. I believe the stars would fall, if a *single* curve of the spiral ladder between the finite and the Infinite were moved out of its course. As for your *test* miracle, about the she-bears and the forty two children, I will only say that the bears must have had miraculous *appetites*, and that both they and the Prophet ought to have been ashamed of themselves; especially the Prophet.

From another point of view, I have exceeding *reverence* for the super-natural, and strong belief in supernatural influences, always and everywhere acting on the human soul. The creation of this world—what a *mass* of stupen-dous miracles! The formation and birth of a child—the mysterious union of soul and body—the whole oak enclosed in the acorn—the unswerving march of the squadron of stars—the strange Orphic utterance of music, forever chant-ing the secret of creation, in language incomprehensible to finite ears—before all *these* miracles, my soul bows down, awe-struck, with its forehead in the dust. With regard to *influences* continually acting on us from a superior orders [*sic*] of beings, I am *more* than reverential; I am positively superstitious. My own experience has repeatedly confirmed Bettina's[4] remark: "There were thoughts shaped within me. I did not *perpend* them, I *believed* in them. They had this peculiarity, that I felt them not as self-thought, but as *imparted*." My reason for avoiding expressing any *opinion* concerning miracles, and other matters, was that I *could* not do it, without impairing the perfect impartiality I had deter-mined to observe. Of course you jest when you say it is dubious whether or not I consider Christ and Crishna identical. I show, *plainly* enough, that I regard Jesus as a very real benefactor to the human race, and to my own soul; but I show only *indirectly* that I believe much that was originally said of Crishna became *transferred* to the history of Christ. The weight of evidence seems to me decidedly against the authenticity of the two first chapters of Matthew. But it is not a point I *care* about. I have no *objection* to their being proved genuine. I find that the greatest difficulty, with most readers, is that Christianity is looked at from the same point of view as other religions. It is natural that this should give them a shock; but in what *other* way could I have observed

---

[3] Joseph Priestly (1733–1804), the English chemist who discovered oxygen, was a clergyman and a political radical; in 1794 he emigrated to the United States.
[4] Bettina von Arnim, German author.

perfect impartiality? Mankind have been kept separated by high partition-walls simply because the defenders of each and every religion maintain that there *can* be but one true religion, and that all other *must* be false. There can be no Universal Church on earth, till this feeling gives way. My book is one of many signs that it is beginning to yield. Have you noticed that the Arab, Abd-El-Kader, now in Paris, has written a book to prove that Judaism, Christianity, and Mohammedanism are in reality only one religion, varying merely in details? and that the professors of all those systems ought to regard each other as brethren? He complains that Christians are not so *reverential* toward the Divine Author of all things, as they ought to be. This rebuke from a Mohammedan is a sign of the times.   With regard to music, I affirm that it *does* not, and *can* not express sin. It is the veritable *Voice of God*, by which creation was evolved from the Divine Essence. All perfumes, all colors, all forms, as well as all sounds, are modulations and variations of the primeval tones. On *that* point, I am dogmatic; as people always are about what they can neither prove nor understand. Mr. Furness could not *help* associating the *words* with the tones in his mind; though he might be unconscious of it. Even the *name* Don Giovanni would give the music a wicked sound. Perhaps also he cannot free himself entirely from the prevailing notion that sexual attraction is in itself impure. We may thank theology, in a great measure, for trailing the slime of the *Serpent* over the rose of life. The *passion* of love (as it is in *nature*, not as it is in this perverted state of *society*) is altogether respectable in my eyes. Music also finds nothing unworthy in it. All music where *thirds* abound, as they do in Mozart, sound like two gliding into one. The waltz, which moves in *thirds*, expresses the same thing in *motion*.   But I *must* stop! for now that I have mounted my favorite hobby, I must dismount, or I shall be off to the extremest ring of Saturn. I wish you and I could correspond; about anything and everything; just as it bubbles up—gas, steam, or diamond water-drops. It would refresh my soul mightily. I have published a new book for children,[5] which I want you to see. I enclose an order, which you can send to New York, if you find a convenient opportunity.

. . .

ALS; J. Peter Lesley Collection, American Philosophical Society (microfiche 31/877).

To Ellis Gray Loring

Wayland Nov. 4th 1855.

My dear, ever kind friend,

. . .

You don't know how odd human nature appears to me, when I get an occasional glimpse of it, in the stage and cars. Coming home, after I left you, I

[5] *A New Flower for Children* (New York, 1856).

encountered a woman **from** Boston, who talked a great deal about the education of children; how desirable it was for them to have a happy home, and see *beautiful things.* The chance for the *latter* was the reason why she greatly preferred the *city.* "Such beautiful droves of oxen and pigs as went by our house last week, to the Agricultural Fair! Really *beautiful* oxen! *fat and all ready for cooking! That's* what *I* call *rational* amusement; don't *you?*"

I, (God forgive me!) not knowing *what* to say, said "Yes"; though I make it a *general* rule, in such dubious cases, to say, No.

Going *down* to Boston, I encountered a women [*sic*] who made a violent attack upon the poor—"There was no need of *any*body's being poor. They ought to *work;* and if they asked for assistance, it was better to *flog* them, than to *help* them." She had a low, narrow forehead, a thin, shrill voice, and other symptoms of the most malignant type of *femality.* I tried to reason a little with her; but finding she had no *heart* to admit a *feeling,* and no *mind* to perceive a *principle,* I soon desisted. But *she* went on a long time afterward, defending *capital* against *labor.*

When we arrived at the Depot, I asked a gentleman who she was. He had been seated next to her in the stage, and occasionally spoken to her. "I don't know," he replied. "I *guess* she's an abolitionist." "An abolitionist!" exclaimed I; "nothing could be more opposite to *their* sentiments, than *her* conversation has been." "Ah?" said he. "Well, I dont know. I thought she seemed to be some *kind* of a radical; and she was so fond of hearing herself talk, I concluded she was an abolitionist."

I thought to myself that I had met with a couple of *rare* specimens of stupidity.

My best love to dear Louisa & Anna. I long to see them. Your affectionate Maria.

ALS; Child Papers, Clements Library, University of Michigan (microfiche 31/889).

To Parke Godwin

Wayland, Jan 20th, 1856.

It was a genuine pleasure to me to hear from you again; for I have always cherished a grateful and most agreeable recollection of your friendly attentions, and the pleasant snatches of intellectual communion, which I occasionally enjoyed in your company. Since I left New York, I have met you but once; and that was in the pages of your poetic and interesting fantasy about Jenny Lind. I supposed you were continually writing witty and wise things, for newspapers and magazines; and I have often wished that I knew where to find them.

With regard to myself, you may imagine me as looking very much older; partly because I have arrived at that period of life when people change fast; but still more because I have had a great deal of anxiety, toil, chagrin, and suffering, since I returned to New England. I have lived through troubles that would have broken down most women; but if the soul can only *live* through fierce struggles, it comes out the stronger; like iron that has been heated and hammered. . . .

You ask, "how many miles I have penetrated into Swedenborg's illuminated cave"? *That* part of my spiritual travelling was performed 28 years ago. I was young then; and all he said seemed to me a direct revelation to his soul, from the angels. His doctrine of Correspondences seemed a golden key to unlock the massive gate between the external and the spiritual worlds. I then *"experienced religion"*; and for a long time lived in a mansion of glories. I thought Correspondences would unlock a store-house of jewels, when applied to *Scripture*. By degrees, I was constrained to admit that the golden key opened the way to *nothing;* though it turned smoothly in the lock, and was beautiful to look upon.

I became enamored of Plato; and his poetic doctrine of *archetypes* seemed to me essentially the same as Swedenborg's *correspondences*. As my knowledge increased, it dawned upon me, more and more fully, that what had most charmed me in Swedenborg had been drawn from very ancient sources; and those sources neither Jewish nor Christian; but thoroughly oriental. I still regard the learned Baron as a great benefactor to my soul; but it is long since he ceased to appear to me in the light of an inspired guide. It is rather singular that in some of his writings he intimates very much such a state of things as now exists with regard to Spirit-rappings. He says they are an *inferior* order of Spirits, near this earth, and continually drawn toward mortals, by their affinities; that they can pass themselves off for Spirits of the great and good departed; but that it is all a sham &c   I confess this modern "spiritualism," which in some of its aspects seems so very *un*-spiritual, puzzles me exceedingly. Tables *do* move, without help of human hands; for I have *seen* it. Things which apparently *could* not be in the minds of any persons present, *are* rapped out by the alphabet. But these communications are more disappointing than the golden key which unlocked *nothing;* for they are the merest mass of old rags, saw-dust, and clam-shells. The subject is well worth looking into, if one could only find out *how* to look into it. . . .

With regard to my big book, I am doubtful whether you will like it. But after you have read it, I should like to have you write and tell me frankly whether you do or not. So far, the reception has been more favorable than I expected. I looked for anathemas *only;* but the condemnatory notices I have seen have, (with exception of the Christian Register,) been respectful and courteous; and warm commendation has come from various quarters, public and private. The public seems to have been more prepared for such a work than I was aware of. I enclose an order for you to obtain one. And that recalls to my mind that you did not send me the *second* vol of Goethe's Autobiography. You gave me the first, and promised the second, when it came out. I cannot *purchase* one vol separate from the other. I suppose the bivalve of my red shell is lying lonesome *somewhere*. If it happens to be on *your shelf*, I wish you would give it to Charles S. Francis, 252 Broadway. His brother in Boston will receive it, and keep it for me. But dont *break* a set, or take any *trouble* about it; I charge you.

I can scarcely realize that you are the Patriarch of so large a family. Alas, I wish I had *half* as many children; but they would bind me to the world, which I am now ready to leave. It is better so. It would give me very great pleasure to look in upon you and Mrs. Godwin, and your "six babies;" to "eat a little, and talk a good deal." But it is very doubtful whether I ever see New York again. If *your* life in that city seems spectral in the halls of memory, you may well suppose that mine seems much *more* so. *Some* figures remain very much alive; and yours is one.

I thank Minna for her nice little note, and send her a kiss. Ever truly your friend L. Maria Child.

ALS; Manuscript Division, New York Public Library (microfiche 32/899).

To Lucy Osgood

[11?–19? February 1856]

. . . With regard to the Demon Penalty and the Angel Attraction, I suppose the expression grew out of my acquaintance with some of the writings of Fourier. The nucleus of *his* system is that men are to be attracted toward goodness instead of being driven away from evil. The holy teacher of Nazareth tells us to *attract* a man toward goodness by giving him a coat, if he needs it, instead of going to law to *punish* him for taking a cloak. This is what I mean by the Demon Penalty and the Angel Attraction—I believe whips and prisons are the discipline of the Devil, and make society worse, instead of better. You will ask the common question, How can we do without them? We cannot *now;* but we ought all to be working toward *producing* a state of things when it *can* be done. One thing is certain; whenever it is *practicable*, it will be *safe*. So all the old fogies may sleep comfortably in their beds, meanwhile, and dream of profitable investments. I am afraid their lease is a *long* one, yet. You speak of some *expression*, at which you cavilled. I live in *hopes* it was a mis-print, of which there are several. Thus, Vol 2. page 178, 19th line from the top, they have printed "*practical* allegories" instead of *poetical*.

You are right in supposing that while engaged on that work I "felt like an inhabitant of the second and third centuries." Everything around me seemed *foreign;* as it did when I came out of Athens into Boston, after writing Philothea. *That* was a pleasant ramble into classic lands; but this Progress of Ideas was a real pilgrimage of penance, with peas in my shoes, walking over rubble-stones most of the way. You have no *idea* of the labor! It was greatly increased by my distance from libraries, nearly all the time, which rendered copious *extracts* necessary. I have on hand old M.S.S. enough to heat all the baths of ancient Alexandria, six months.

You ask how I have employed myself since I completed the task. In the first place, I have written and published a "New Flower for Children"; and I was surprised to find how easily I came back into a juvenile atmosphere. In the next place, I wrote a story for the Liberty Bell, which Professor Palfrey[1] likes, and that is all I have heard about it. My father had a severe illness early in January, and has ever since required such *frequent* attention, that I can never be secure of two uninterrupted hours, day or evening. I had a great accumulation of sewing on hand, which I take this opportunity to do up. This, with the daily routine of sweeping, making beds, filling lamps, preparing meals, and washing dishes, leaves very little time for recreation, this savagely cold weather. The few moments I *can* spare, I have spent in reading some of my old favorite books; and none of them have pleased me so much as Mrs. Lee's (né Buckminster) Life of Jean Paul. What a perfectly delightful book it is!   I looked in upon my friends at the Anti Slavery Fair at Christmas time; but since then, I have *literally* not stepped out of the *door*. Last winter I used to run in my very small garden to breathe the fresh air; but *now*, the snow is up to my throat, and blows back as fast as it is shovelled away.

I am glad you like what I say about *slavery*. I think the pro-slavery and the anti slavery advocates have *both* tried to twist the Bible to sustain their respective theories. I tried to follow the plain truth *only*, wheresoever it might lead. I thought to *myself* that I deserved some *credit* for this, considering how *very* strong a bias I have upon that subject. How absurdly the Old Testament is treated by Christians! used for all *convenient* purposes, neglected whenever it is *in*convenient! Moses is good authority for holding slaves, but *not* for the healthy practice of abstaining from pork.   As for miracles, in one sense I do *not* believe in them, and in another sense I *do*. I do not believe that the laws of the universe are ever changed, or suspended, for any temporary purpose; for if they *were* the sky would certainly fall. On the other hand, I believe there is a constant, and at present a very mysterious relation between the spiritual world and the natural world. In certain states of the *nerves*, and in certain states of the *soul*, Spirit can see through Matter, and can control it, in a way that seems miraculous, because we do not understand it. A holy state of the *soul* I believe gives this insight and this power to a degree far superior to any of the phenomona of diseased nerves, and the consequently slight adhesion between the soul and the body. Those who live near to God, I believe really do attain, in various degrees, to real spiritual insight into truth on many subjects. Did you ever read George Fox's description of how the medicinal properties of all the shrubs and plants he passed were suddenly *revealed* to him, as he walked in the fields?[2]

I confess to you that one side of my mind tends to the extremest rationality, and the other to a reverential faith, that sometimes borders on superstition. Most devoutly do I believe in the pervasive and ever-guiding Spirit of God; but I do

[1] John G. Palfrey.
[2] George Fox was the founder of the Society of Friends.

not believe it was ever **shut up** within the covers of any *book,* or that it ever *can* be. Portions of it, **or rather** *breathings* of it, are in *many* books. The words of Christ seem to me *full* of it, as no other words are. But if *we* want truth, we must listen to the voice of God in the silence of our *own* souls, as *he* did. Protestants, in their blind hereditary worship of the Bible, worship an *image* as truly as the Catholics do, when they pray to an image of Mary, around which they have fastened holy **rags** of tin-foil or shining wire, which cannot in reality light any pilgrim on his path. Thoughtful souls are becoming more and more convinced of this.

My good brother C. is not *altogether* pleased with what I say about *theology;* and he told me that you also demurred to *that;* asking whether the "science of God" is not the highest and best of all sciences? Undoubtedly it is; but *is* there any such science, within the ken of our finite vision? Is not faith and aspiration *all* that we have, or *can* have, in this state of being? And must not faith and aspiration vary, according to the state of culture in the age, and in the individual soul? If so, how can any man, or any class of men, teach others concerning God with any of the certainty of basis that belongs to a *science?*

Perhaps I am too much prejudiced against theology. It seems to me to have done such an evil work in dividing nations, neighbors, and friends. I perceive that an immense good has been done to the human race by *religion;* by which I understand practical love and truth toward our fellow-beings, and humble reverence with regard to the infinite and incomprehensible, which we call God. But what good has been done by *doctrines* concerning God and the soul, I am yet to learn. So it seems to me; but Brother Convers views it differently. With this exception, he seems to rejoice in my book. He wrote me a most excellent and cheering letter about it.

Have you read Ida May, and Caste?[3] I found them both highly interesting; though some of the incidents seem to me exaggerated; especially in Caste. Still, the pictures are true, with slight exceptions of unimportant details; and the stories are managed with much talent.   I want *very* much to have a talk with you; but I cannot leave my feeble old father while the weather is so cold. He was much gratified by your message, and desired me to thank you. I have not been in Medford since last August; and then he was with me.

Mr. Child sends his best respects. He says, "Thank them for their sensible and learned letter. I think no one has formed such a just and complete estimate of the merits of the work, as their letter evinces."

God bless you! Yours with affectionate respect, L. Maria Child.

ALS, incomplete; Lydia Maria Child Papers, Anti-Slavery Collection, Cornell University (microfiche 32/906).

[3] Mary (Green) Pike (1824–1908), of Calais, Maine, was the author of *Ida May* (Boston, 1854) and *Caste* (Boston, 1856), both antislavery novels. She used the pseudonym Mary Langdon for the first book and Sidney A. Story, Jr., for the second. In 1858 she published her final novel, *Agnes* (Boston), about an Indian in revolutionary times.

That a husband had to sign the wife's will to make it a legal document symbolized for Child women's inferior legal status. She never published the broadside she refers to in this letter.

To Ellis Gray Loring

Wayland, February 24, 1856.

David has signed my will and I have sealed it up and put it away. It excited my towering indignation to think it was necessary for him to sign it, and if you had been by, you would have made the matter worse by repeating your old manly "fling and twit" about married women being dead in the law. I was not indignant on my own account, for David respects the freedom of all women upon principle, and mine in particular by reason of affection superadded. But I was indignant for womankind made chattels personal from the beginning of time, perpetually insulted by literature, law, and custom. The very phrases used with regard to us are abominable. "Dead in the law," "Femme couverte." How I detest such language! I must come out with a broadside on that subject before I die. If I don't, I shall walk and rap afterward.

L, extract; *Letters of Lydia Maria Child*, 1882 (microfiche 32/908).

To Sarah Shaw

Wayland, March 23d, 1856.

Dearly Beloved Friend,

. . .

I am glad you rejoice in your new son.[1] Thank you for wishing that I knew him; though I never *shall*, in *this* world. What I have read of his writings impress me with the idea that he has a brilliant mind, and, what is better, a free and manly one. Always I observe a leaning toward the *progressive* side of everything. Mr. Child heard one of his lectures in Boston, this winter, and liked it much. I was delighted to hear of his eulogy upon Dickens, in comparison with Bulwer.[2] Bulwer seems to me undoubtedly a man of genius; but artificial, and world-worn; a superior genus of the species Willis.[3] I have *admired* several of Bulwer's heroines, but I never *loved one* of them, and hugged them to my heart as I do Little Nell, and Esther, and Little Dorrit. Dickens is the great Apostle of Humanity. God bless him. I am a little *suspicious* of the disposition there is to disparage him, in comparison with Thackery. I believe that it originates, in part, at least, in the fact that the *aristocracy* are *nettled* by his witty

[1] George William Curtis (1824–92), writer and editor, married the Shaws' daughter Anna in 1856.
[2] Edward George Bulwer-Lytton (1803–73), English novelist and dramatist.
[3] Nathaniel P. Willis, American editor and writer.

thrusts at the existing abuses in English society; and by his unfailing sympathy for the neglected and abused masses. Of course, the aristocracy *here*, especially in *Boston*, sympathize with such a feeling as *that!* Bachelor Appleton says: "When the *good* people of Boston die, they go to *Paris*."[4] You don't know how happy I am to hear it. Their company would be a dreadful bore to me, in heaven, if I should ever get there; yet I'm not hard enough to wish to have them consigned to "tother place." Paris is an *appropriate* Limbo for them; where they make artificial flowers, pronounced "superior to natural ones, because they are more like what flowers *ought* to be"; where they plant them in *artificial earth,* and surround them with *artificial poudrette,* to make them *appear* to grow. O, yes, decidedly, *that* is the Limbo for Boston respectables! What a relief it must be to the angels, to have them go there!

. . . I don't know what it *is*, that draws me so toward those ancient Grecians! Rather guess I *lived* among them once; and, for my sins, have been sent back into this practical country, in the *form of a woman.* That form, you know, was Plato's conception of worst punishment; and I'm thinking he was n't far from right.   I suppose this same attraction toward Grecian forms of art, is what made me in love with Mendelssohn's music; because I *felt* (without *understanding*) its harmonious proportions, its Doric simplicity, its finished beauty. I recognize the superior *originality* and *power* of Beethoven; but he does not minister to my soul as he does to yours. He overpowers me—fills me with awe. His music makes me feel as if I were among huge, black mountains, looking at a narrow strip of brillant stars, ⟨seen through clefts,⟩ in the far-off heaven, seen thro' narrow clefts in the frowning rocks. I *love* best to hear the *Pastoral* Symphony, which is the least Beethovenish of all. The fact is, my nature has less affinity for grandeur and sublimity, than it has for grace and beauty. I never looked twice at engravings from Michal Angelo; while I dream away hours and hours over copies from Raphael. I delight in Milton's Comus, but I never *could* get through his Paradise Lost. I always liked the flowing sunflecked Connecticut, better than misty-headed Mt. Holyoke.

. . .

ALS; Houghton Library, Harvard University (microfiche 32/911).

To Lucy and Mary Osgood

Wayland, May 11'th, 1856.

Dear and Honored Friends,

. . .

In the low state of my finances, I seldom allow myself to buy a book. I believe I have bought but five, during the last nine years. But I did purchase Olmstead's View of the Southern States; partly because I wanted some of the

---

[4] Thomas Gold Appleton (1812–84) was a Boston writer and wit.

information it contained; and partly because I was much pleased with its candid good-natured tone toward the masters, and its obvious sympathy with the slave.[1] I think it is calculated to do a great deal of good; especially to Southerners, if they would only *read* it! When I went to the Anti Slavery Office to inquire for it (preferring to put the commission-money into *their* hands) I encountered Miss Holley, niece of the eloquent Holley, of Hollis St.[2] I hear continually of her great success as a lecturer; and as a woman, she pleases me much. She has a quiet, lady-like manner, and tones of voice that indicate earnestness and sincerity of character. She made me smile, by telling me that the little daughter of Abby Kelly and Stephen Foster was much disturbed because "prayers always ended with A*men*." "Ought they not to say A*woman*, sometimes?" said she. That comes of sucking her mother's milk! I should like to come back to this world, table-tipping, a hundred years hence, to see what all these things have come to.

As for modern spiritualism, I do not know enough about it to give an opinion. Of one thing only am I certain; and that is the impossibility of accounting for *all* its phenomona by any process of jugglery or deception. *Some* laws are at work, beyond what "our philosophy has dreamed of"; but what they *are*, I cannot explain satisfactorily to myself. I am aware that *some* of the⟨m⟩ spiritualists have adopted the Free Love theories, as *one* of the inferences from their doctrines concerning spiritual *attraction*. But it does not seem to me quite fair to describe it as a necessary part of their system. The Free Love movement begun [*sic*] in New York, and with people who had nothing to do with modern Spiritualism. The fact is, there is a wide spread restlessness on the subject of love and marriage; a restlessness not confined to the profligate, but troubling many honest and reflecting minds. The *present* state of things is very *bad;* of *that* all are convinced who *know* anything about it; and daring spirits maintain that *no* change can make it *worse*. I see the immensity of the evil, but I do not see the safe remedy. I stand still, puzzled and frightened. If I cannot see a way opened to do any *good*, I trust God and good angels will keep me from saying any word that can do *harm*.

Is it not strange that the removal of old *theological* landmarks is always accompanied by controversies concerning the boundaries on *that* subject? Love and Religion anchor together, and get unmoored together. The Roman Catholic church makes marriage a *sacrament;* the Protestant makes it a *contract*. The rabid infidels of the French Revolution scouted both sacrament and contract. For myself, I am so well aware that society stands over a heaving volcano, from

---

[1] Frederick Law Olmsted's *Journey in the Seaboard Slave States* (New York, 1856) was the first of three influential volumes on his travels in the South. The next year he began an eminent career as a landscape architect.

[2] Sallie Holley (1818–93), daughter of Myron Holley, a founder of the Liberty party, and niece of Horace Holley, minister at the Hollis Street Church in Boston, 1809–18, was an agent for the American Anti-Slavery Society.

which it is separated by the thinnest possible crust of appearances, that I am afraid to speak or to think on the subject. I confine myself to *pitying* the unwary victims who get entangled in the snares lying about everywhere, and generally concealed with roses. On *many* subjects you have seemed to me singularly large-minded, for women brought up in such seclusion; but the few words you spoke concerning such victims inspired me with more respect than I had ever before felt for you. George Stearns told me of your kind efforts in behalf of the poor girl accused of infanticide. God bless you!

. . .

AL; Lydia Maria Child Papers, Anti-Slavery Collection, Cornell University (microfiche 33/915).

To Ellis Gray Loring

Wayland July 3d, 1856

Dear Friend,

I have come to try your patience again about "pecunary" matters. I am in a state of high indignation, because the assessors here have taxed us the enormous sum of $26..10cts for the Northampton farm, under the head of "personal estate." The town got themselves into a foolish law-suit, which proved unfortunate and expensive. They also built a house for a High School, at the useless expense of $6000; and the building is now shut up, for want of scholars, and of means to pay a teacher. There were three or four vacant buildings in town, which would have answered every purpose for a High School; but vanity led them to do something more showy than richer towns had done. I was not permitted to *vote* about the extravagant building, or the needless law-suit; yet here am I called upon to *pay* for them, out of my small means. I mean to petition the Legislature to exempt me from *taxes,* or grant me the privilege of *voting.* Oh *what* a sex you are! It's time you were turned out of office. *High* time. You've been captains long enough. It's *our* turn now.

However, I did not sit down to blow you up on the subject of women's wrongs; but merely to ask whether this tax is *legal?* Ought they to tax us for any more than the $600 we have *received* toward the payment of the farm? David is doubtful about it, and said he would like to have me ask *your* opinion.

. . .

ALS; Child Papers, Clements Library, University of Michigan (microfiche 33/923).

Civil war between proslavery and antislavery settlers erupted in Kansas in 1855 as a result of the popular sovereignty formula. In May 1856, Senator Charles Sumner's fiery speech in the Senate denouncing the "slave oligarchy" for "the crime against Kansas" infuriated Southerners, and Representative Preston Brooks of South Carolina took revenge by beating Sumner savagely on the head with a heavy cane. The abolitionists feared that Sumner might die or be crippled for life. That month proslavery Missourians sacked Lawrence, Kansas, the center of Free-Soil strength, and killed two men. In retaliation, John Brown with seven men attacked proslavery settlers on Pottawatomie Creek, killing five people.

To Charles Sumner

Wayland, July 7th, 1856.

To the Honorable and Honored Charles Sumner.

. . .

I had begun to write to you, to thank you for the flower-seed you were so kind as to send me, when I received news of the [. . .]age,[1] which so nearly [ter]minated your precious life. I have never [. . . ov]erpowered by any public event. I was rendered physically ill, [. . .] of painful excitement; which never before happened to my strong constitution. It seemed as if the necessity of remaining inactive at such an eventful crisis would kill me. My first impulse was to rush directly to Washington, to ascertain whether I could not supply to you, in some small degree, the absence of a mother's or sister's care. Had I not been tied to the bedside of my aged father, I verily believe I *should* have done it; for I thought I might trust to my venerable years to sanction the proceeding. Doubtless Mr. Douglass[2] would have been shocked; but you know it is difficult to *avoid* shocking a person of such fastidious delicacy of sentiment, as he manifests.   I am always eager to read your speeches, and you may judge whether, under such circumstances, I omitted a single line of your last and greatest speech. My heart has bled so freely for suffering Kansas! I have felt such burning indignation at the ever-increasing insults and outrages of the South, and the cold, selfish indifference of the North! I have so longed to sieze a signal-torch, and rush over all the mountains, and through all the vallies, summoning the friends of freedom to the rescue! If they only *would* forget all minor differences, and form a solid phalanx to resist this gigantic evil, how soon the blustering despots would cower before them! At times, my old heart swells almost to bursting, in view of all these things; for it is the heart of a man imprisoned within a woman's destiny.

My chief motive in writing is to thank you for your magnificent speech, which met the requirements of the time with so much intellectual strength and moral heroism. Some "patriots" called it Un-Americ[an . . .] to my mind the words of Aristophanes: "Sparta shall fin[. . .]

[1] The edges of this nine-page letter are worn away in many places, omitting a word or two out of a line.
[2] Sen. Stephen A. Douglas, presumably.

An *honest* chronicler, though fear may try
The prize with truth. Yes, I have fears; and those
In no small brood. I know the people well,
Their temper's edge and humor. Does some tongue
Link cunning *commendation* with their own
And country's name? Their joy o'erflows the measure!
It matters not the praise be *wrong*, nor that
Their *freedom* pays the tickling of their ears."

Your political adversaries made such an outcry about your imprudent severity and unjustifiable personalities, that I cautiously examined whether there was any ground for such an allegation. Few persons have stronger aversion to harsh epithets and personal vituperation, than I have; but I confess I could find nothing in your Kansas Speech, which offended either my taste or my judgment. You rebuked States and individuals merely as the representatives of that ever-encroaching Slave-Power, whose characteristic artifice, arrogance, and despotism, it was necessary for your [*sic*] to portray, in connection with the subject under debate.

In your reply to the mean and insolent personalities of Mr. Douglass, I did find one distasteful comparison. I acknowledge its appropriateness; and I agree with Wendell Phillips, that the *animal* is the one insulted by being compared with that unscrupulous agent of despotism, of heart and mouth unclean. It was not that I felt any injustice was done to *him;* but it seemed a slight departure from the characteristic refinement of your taste. But the wonder is that [. . .]d so *little* from your usual politeness, considering the very [. . .] and provoking manner in which you were personally [as]sailed. *Much* might be excused under such provocations, and I rejoice over your forbearance. I do earnestly hope that the cruel gauntlet, which the public friends of freedom are now compelled to run, will never tempt them to give the adversary advantage, by turning aside to fight their *own* battles, when all their energies are needed in the great battle for the *truth*. I felt extremely anxious when Mr. Wilson was challenged.[3] Again and again, I said, "I do hope the fear of being called a coward will not mislead him into sanctioning that absurd and bloody barbarism; but I would rather have him dead, much as he is needed, than to have him retract or extenuate one single word he has uttered." My heart jumped with joy, when I saw how wisely and bravely he had steered between the two. I smiled at the declaration that he *"religiously"* believed in the right of self-defence. The word was so peculiarly well adapted to *take* with the popular mind of N. England, that I queried whether or not he had chosen it with diplomatic skill, as politicians are prone to do. I confess that *I* am totally unable to deduce any such doctrine from

[3] Sen. Henry Wilson (1812–75) was a Free-Soiler elected U.S. senator from Massachusetts in 1855. When he denounced the attack upon Sumner as "brutal, murderous and cowardly" in the Senate, he was challenged to a duel by Preston Brooks. It never took place.

the words of Jesus. The injunction *never* to return injury for injury seems to me the one prominent point of superiority over all other moral teachers of mankind. When I hear of cruel outrages against unoffending citizens in Kansas, and attempted assassination of a senator, who defended their cause, in words "that were *severe* merely because they were *true*," I confess that my peace-principles are sorely tried; insomuch, that nothing suits my mood so well, as Jeanne d'Arc's floating banner and consecrated sword. But I find myself compelled to resist such states of mind, or else to admit that infidels speak truly, when they say, "The teachings of Jesus are contrary to human nature, and not adapted to its needs." I would frankly adopt their conclusion, if it seemed to me true; but it does not. I believe in a holiness much higher than heroism, in the usual acceptation of that word. But I have never been one of the intolerant ones on the subject of war. I can never call those men murderers, who forsake home and kindred, and all that renders life agreeable, and with noble self-sacrifice go forth to suffer and to die in the cause of freedom. Yet there is a higher standard than theirs, to which the human soul will gradually rise, until there remains no trace of the old ideas of overcoming evil by brute force. It is well to hold up this standard, meanwhile, whether any among us consistently act up to it, or not; for "they who *aim* at the stars will at least *hit higher*, than if they aimed at a pine tree." But I cannot arraign as criminals those who aim at a tall hemlock, instead of the stars, which seem to them beyond human reach. I honor those who conscientiously fight for justice, truth, or freedom; but I revere those who will *die* to advance great principles, though they will not *kill*. I classify them into the greater and the lesser heroes.

On this subject, and on the subject of political action, the American Anti-Slavery Society appears to me narrow and intolerant. There seems to me something sectarian in their inability to acknowledge any one as a helper who d[oe]s not work for the cause in their way. I was delighted with the tribute paid to you by those great moral heroes, Garrison and Wendell Phillips, at the late Anniversary. I did not *hear* it; for when I proposed to attend the meeting, Mr. Child checked the wish, by saying, "Do you want to hear Stephen Foster abuse Charles Sumner?" I replied, "He *cannot* be such a monomaniac, as to attack Mr. Sumner *now*." But he did; and I am glad I was not among the audience; for I am afraid I could not have restrained my disapprobation within judicious bound[s.] Such comets *must* always be coursing about among moon and stars. Doubtless they have their use, though God alone knows what it *is*. How often have I contrasted a remark in your letter to me, three years ago, with his fierce denunciations of all who seek to abolish slavery in any other way than his own! You say: "Ours is a great battle, destined to be prolonged many years. It has a place for *every* nature. I believe that every man does good, who is earnest against slavery; whatever name of party, sect, or society, he may assume, I welcome him as a brother." In that letter, you describe yourself as sitting in the Senate-Chamber, between Mr. Butler of S. Carolina, and Mr. Mason of Virginia; and you speak of the constant and courteous intercourse between yourself and them.[4] They did not *then* know, for a certainty, whether you were incapable of being either blindfolded [. . .] bought. As Northern statesmen generally proved themselves ready to do their bidding, for "a *consideration*," they doubtless had hopes that there was *some* weak place in your citadel also. You, on your part, had not *then* learned that no degree of candour or courtesy can induce slave-holders to tolerate any expression of dislike to the despotic system they have built up so artfully and so strongly.

That letter of yours has always been preserved among my choicest treasures; but *now*, money could not buy it from me. You therein give me the delightful assurance that your public course had been influenced by the effect my anti-slavery writings had on your mind, when you were a younger man. What a well-spring of joy has that assurance proved to my soul! How often has it cheered me, when I felt as if I *had* done nothing, a[n]d *could* do nothing, to arrest the course of violence and wrong! I have never, for one moment, regretted that youthful enthusiasm led me into the front ranks of Anti Slavery, in its day of small beginnings; but it has sometimes caused transient sadness to think of many pleasant and influential friends I lost thereby, and the literary unpopularity, which I could never outgrow. But if such moods of despondency could be measured by years, instead of moments, they would be amply repaid by the consciousness of having had ever so little share in inducing you to consecrate your abilities to the cause of truth and freedom. Mr. Wilson has recently made a similar statement to Mr. Child concerning the influence of my writings on *his* mind; and he has thereby greatly refreshed my soul. Soon after The Appeal for Africans was published, Dr. Channing called upon me, for the first time, and thanked me for rousing *him* to the conviction that he ought not to remain silent on a subject of such vast importance. Some years afterward, Dr. Palfrey told me the emancipation of his slaves grew out of the impulse which that book gave to his mind. It is certainly *something* for one small mouse to do, to gnaw open the nets of prejudice or custom, which might have obstructed the action of such great lions; and no wonder the little mouse rejoices over her work, with infinite satisfaction. But I do not allude to these things for the purpose of self-gratulation. I mention them to suggest encouragement to you. Perhaps you and your companions in arms may not live to witness the downfall of the giant with which you are so vigorously contesting. But if *my* poor agency has thus modified the career of some who followed me, who can estimate the influence on future citizens and statesmen, from the many brave, strong words *you* have spoken for truth and freedom? Great and glorious is the mission whereunto you have been called, and nobly are you fulfilling it.

Your letter declining the testimonial proffered by your native Commonwealth pleased me more than anything you ever did. I had previously said, "I

4 Andrew P. Butler (1796–1857) was the senator from South Carolina whose denunciation by Sumner so angered Preston Brooks, Butler's nephew, that Brooks caned Sumner. James M. Mason (1798–1871) was U.S. senator from Virginia and author of the Fugitive Slave Law of 1850.

hope Massachusetts will express her gratitude toward him with princely munificence; and I hope *he* will transfer the gift to Kansas; that would be morally grand on *both* sides." And Mr. Child answered, "Depend upon it, he *will* do it. Nothing could be more characteristic of the man." That letter, and Mr. Wilson's answer to the challenge, have revived my early faith in human nature. It is impossible to calculate the salutary influence of such examples. Do you think any of your little namesakes will dare to do a mean thing, after hearing of that letter? You counted them by hundreds after the Nebraska Speech, but now I think you and Mr. Wilson will count them by thousands. If one of them should be inclined to become a Northern Doe-face,[5] he will, for very shame, change his name before he takes the first step. The Senate of Athens forbade any slave to bear the name of Harmodius or Aristogiton; and the tyranny *you* are so manfully seeking to destroy is a thousand times stronger and more despotic than that of Hipparchus.

Excuse me for writing so much. I did not intend to do it; but the fountain of feeling was so full, the waters *would* run over abundantly. The flowers you sent me have all prospered. The sight of them has often brought tears to my eyes, of late. You are present to my mind every hour in the day, and all my thoughts of you are baptized with blessings.

May God and good angels guard you, and restore your precious health!

Yours with affectionate respect,

L. Maria Child.

ALS; Houghton Library, Harvard University (microfiche 33/925).

To Lucy and Mary Osgood

Wayland, July 9'th, 1856.

Dear Friends,

. . . I have always dreaded civil war and prayed that it might be averted; but if there is no *other* alternative than the endurance of such insults and outrages, I am resigned to its approach. In fact, I have become accustomed to the thought that it is inevitable. One would think that the shallowest statesman might have foreseen that two such antagonistic elements as freedom and slavery could not long co-exist in the same government. When Lord Byron was in Greece, years before the Anti-Slavery agitation began in this country, he declared that those two principles in the government of the United States were destructive of each other; and that the question *which* must be destroyed would sooner or later produce civil war. The statements of Mr. Sumner's physicians at the present time fill me with anguish. Ah, would that "fair senatorial head" had been crushed beneath those brutal blows, rather than live for *such* a fate! But under these exciting circumstances, it is natural that the fears of his physicians should be exaggerated. Let us hope that it *is* so.

[5] "Dough-face" was the derogatory term for Northerners with Southern sympathies.

. . . I can readily understand the *serene* state of mind produced by faith in the Catholic church. The time *has* been when I should have envied Mrs. Ripley; but I have outgrown that.[1] Better the restless search after truth, than the quiet acceptance of error! Disappointed reformers are very *apt* to swing to the extreme opposite to their early enthusiasm. No wonder at it; for it takes fish very *much* alive, to be able to continuing [*sic*] swimming *up* stream always.

. . . For my own part, I do not believe there *is* such a thing as an atheist. People are called atheists, and think themselves atheists, because they disbelieve in some established *representation* of God. You make an admirable remark, when you say that Pantheism and the idea of a personal God are merely centrifugal and centripetal aspects of the same thing. It is merely different reflections and refractions of the same central Light, which we all discern through the thick darkness. Even the most sceptical "worships when he knows it not." For myself, reverence restrains me from arguing much, or thinking much about the manner of God's existence. The squirrel for whom I daily place corn in the garden, has become accustomed to me, as a sort of Providence; but what does he know of the manner in which I raised the corn? or if [*sic*] the feeling that led me to place it there for him? Yet that squirrel might as well puzzle his brain with Kant's philosophy, as for me to strive to comprehend the Divine Mind, and His action on the universe. On this subject, my humility is profound.

. . .

ALS; Lydia Maria Child Papers, Anti-Slavery Collection, Cornell University (microfiche 33/928).

For the next several months, Child was absorbed by the developing presidential campaign. John Charles Frémont (1813–90) headed the ticket of the new Republican party. As explorer of the West and leader of the conquest of California he had won national attention and had been elected U.S. senator from California. The Republican platform upheld congressional authority to control slavery in the territories; the chief campaign issue was "Bleeding Kansas."

To Lucy and Mary Osgood

Wayland, July 20th, 1856

Dear Friends,

. . .

I feel no very lively interest about Miss Bremer's new work. Her thoughtless gossiping about people who, in all confidence, had admitted her to the privacy of their homes, somewhat diminished my respect for her; though I am

---

[1] Sophia Ripley (1803–61), a Transcendentalist, was with her husband, George Ripley (1802–80), a leader of the Brook Farm experiment. Shortly after the community collapsed in 1847 she became a Catholic convert.

well aware that circumstances connected with the publication of her Travels rendered the oversight in some degree excusable.[1]

Have you read the first Chapter of Mrs. Stowe's new Novel,[2] published in the Tribune? It bears the same marks of superior genius and dramatic power, that characterized Uncle Tom. I was charmed with it, and am hungry to get at the succeeding Chapters. Goëthe said, "If a man has done *one* good thing, the world takes care to prevent his ever doing another." I was afraid Mrs. Stowe would add another to many proofs of the truth of that statement; but I verily believe that the balloon that went up with such extraordinary velocity will sustain itself at its high elevation. It delights me to see an ugly, crooked old negro, like Tiff, made so interesting by the mere force of goodness. Dickens has transfigured humanity in the same way in several characters placed amid the meanest surroundings. Witness dear Little Dorrit! How miserably trashy, in comparison, seems N. P. Willis's twaddle about the "porcelain clay of humanity;" meaning those who dance with dukes, and speak in the "subdued tone indicative of social refinement." Bah! ugly old Tiff is worth a hundred such. *His* tones are modulated by inward *feeling. He* wears the star of *God's* order of nobility. . . .

For the first time in my life, I am a *little* infected with *political* excitement. For the sake of suffering Kansas, and future freedom in peril, I *do* long to have Fremont elected. Dont *you?* Let's *vote!* Good night. God bless you!

Yours affectionately,
L. M. Child.

ALS; Lydia Maria Child Papers, Anti-Slavery Collection, Cornell University (microfiche 33/932).

To Sarah Shaw

Wayland, Aug. 3d, 1856.

My very Dear Friend,

. . .

The recent public events have also greatly discouraged me. To have labored so *long* against slavery, and yet to see it always triumphant! The outrage upon Charles Sumner made me literally ill for several days. It brought on nervous head-ache, and painful suffocations about the heart. If I could only have *done* something, it would have loosened that tight ligature that seemed to stop the flowing of my blood. But I *never* was one of those who knew how to serve the Lord by standing and waiting; and to stand and wait *then!* It almost drove me mad. And that miserable Faneuil Hall Meeting! The time-serving Geo. Hillard

[1] The new work was Frederika Bremer's *Hertha* (New York, 1856).
[2] *Dred: A Tale of the Great Dismal Swamp* (Boston, 1856), based upon the life of Nat Turner, leader of the Virginia slave revolt of 1831. The novel sold 100,000 copies in the first month.

talking about his *friend* Sumner's being a man that "hit hard"![1] Making the people *laugh* at his own witticisms, when a volcano was seething beneath their feet! Poisoning the well-spring of popular indignation, which was rising in its might! And then that miserable tool of a Governor Gardiner, proposing that the State should pay Mr. Sumner's *board!*[2] God forgive me, that I wanted to take Boston by the throat, and stop the sluggish blood that feeds its servile life. I wish Mr. Russell *was* dictator, and hemp *already* risen in the market.[3] Those Boston respectables, I tell you they are *criminals.* Greater criminals than those who merely destroy *physical* life; for they systematically blind the *minds* of the people, and stagnate their *moral energies.*   Mr. Apthorpe, on the eve of departing for Europe, wrote to me, "The North will not really *do* anything to maintain their own dignity. See if they do! I am willing to go abroad, to find some relief from the mental pain that the course of public affairs in this country, has for many years caused me."[4] But I am more hopeful. *Such* a man as Charles Sumner *will* not bleed and suffer in vain! Those noble martyrs of liberty in Kansas will prove missionary ghosts, walking through the land, rousing the nation from its guilty slumbers.   Our hopes, like yours, rest on Fremont. I would almost lay down my life to have him elected. There never has been such a crisis since we were a nation. If the Slave-Power is checked *now*, it will *never* regain its strength. If it is *not* checked, civil war is inevitable; and, with all my horror of bloodshed, I could be better resigned to that great calamity, than to endure the tyranny that has so long trampled on us. I do believe the North will not, *this* time, fall asleep again, after shaking her mane and growling a little. If Buchanan *is* elected, I believe there will be such an army of ironsides in the field, as have not been seen since the days of Cromwell. The Puritan blood is like Lehigh coal; slow to be ignited, but when once it is a-glow, it is hard to cool it down. I see that Garrison charges Sam. J. May with being unfaithful to his peace-principles, in wishing to have Fremont elected. To *me*, it seems otherwise. Because I would *avert* war, I desire to have Fremont victorious. And "our Jessie," bless her noble soul![5] Is n't it pleasant to have a *woman* spontaneously recognized as a moral influence in public affairs? There's *meaning* in that fact.

1 George Stillman Hillard (1808–79) was at one time a law partner of Charles Sumner. A Cotton Whig, he had pro-South sympathies that separated him from Sumner and the abolitionists.
2 Henry J. Gardner (1818–92) of the Know-Nothing party was governor of Massachusetts. In 1855 he vetoed the Personal Liberty Bill.
3 George R. Russell, a partner in Russell and Sturgis, merchants, was active in the antislavery movement.
4 This was probably Robert E. Apthorp (1811–82), Boston philanthropist and abolition supporter, who moved to Europe in 1856.
5 Jessie (Benton) Frémont (1824–1902), a writer and the daughter of Senator Thomas Hart Benton, married Frémont in 1841 and helped write and edit the popular reports of his western expeditions. "Frémont and our Jessie" was a standard campaign-song refrain.

I saw by the papers that Mr. Curtis was in the field, and I rejoiced to know he was devoting his brillant talents and generous sympathies to so noble a purpose.[6] I envy him, I want to mount the rostrum myself. I have such a fire burning in my soul, that it seems to me I could pour forth a stream of lava, that would bury all the *respectable* servilities, and all the *mob* servilities, as deep as Pompeii; so that it would be an enormous labor ever to dig up the skeletons of their memories.

I sent to your brother, Mr. John Parkman, a Sermon about Kansas, by our minister Mr. Sears. It seemed to me a very admirable document. If you have not read it, I wish you would. I purchased 25 for distribution, and I should have sent you one, but I thought you would see Mr. Parkman's copy, and I deemed it best to give my copies to those who had greater *need* of being waked on the subject. What I have said expresses Mr. Child's state of mind, as well as my own.

We also talk of little else but Kansas and Fremont. Mr. Child thinks his chance of success is great, *provided* fraud can be kept away from the ballot-boxes. Our elections, for some time past, have been systematically managed by bribery and trickery. The idea of *glass* ballot-boxes seems to me a good one. What a shame that *women* can't vote! We'd carry "our Jessie" into the White House on our shoulders; *would* n't we? Never mind! Wait a while! Women-stock's rising in the market. I shall not live to see women vote; but I'll come and *rap* at the ballot-box. Wont *you?* I never was bitten by politics before; but such mighty issues are depending on *this* election, that I cannot be indifferent. Backward or forward the car of human freedom *must* roll. It cannot stand still.

　• • •

ALS; Houghton Library, Harvard University (microfiche 33/933).

To Sarah Shaw

Wayland, Sep. 14th 1856

Dear Sarah,

I am thinking how you and Frank are rejoicing over Vermont, Maine, &c. David is certain *sure* of victory; but *I* rejoice with trembling. I have seen so *many* political elections, that I have become accustoming [*sic*] to hearing *both* sides express themselves confident of success. Even at this present moment, the democratic party either *are* or *pretend* to be very sure of gaining the victory. They are unscrupulous as to *means*, and they are guided by the astute politicians of the South.[1] At the *last* moment, they bear down on the issue, with all the force of falsehood, fraud, and flattery. They bribe with offices, they bribe with

[6] Curtis was using his skills as orator and political journalist to serve Frémont, the anti-slavery candidate.

[1] James Buchanan (1791–1868) was the Democratic nominee for president on a platform affirming the Compromise of 1850 and supporting the Kansas-Nebraska Act.

money, they stuff the ballot-boxes, then turn round and say, "Lo! the *people* have chosen *our* candidate! Did we not *tell* you it would be so?" The blinded people respond, "We have done our best, and we must be resigned. The voice of the majority *must* be obeyed." Old Fogy pats Towzer on the head, and says "Good dog! Good dog!" And Towzer goes to crunching his bone, and winks his eyes with satisfaction and the cheers and the pats that are accorded to him on all sides. *Order* reigns in State St! And for *such* result; the people have expended their time, their talent, their money, and their energy! Oh, I have seen this game so *often*, that I am weary of it.

However, one thing seems pretty clear—Fremont will in *reality* have a majority of the people's votes; whatever hugger-muggery they may practise to defeat the legitimate result. *That* is a great step gained. For it cannot be denied that an *Abolition* Principle is the big wave which has taken Fremont on its back, and is floating onward in the open light of day. Certainly, it is far enough from being such thorough-going anti-slavery, as you and I would like to see triumphant. But the few must always toil long and vigorously before they can even *start* the many. We old abolitionists may well feel repaid for twenty five years of labor, discouragement, unpopularity, and persecution, since our principles, at *last* begin visibly to sway the masses. I, for one, thank God that I live to see it. It shows that the lump is *leavened*.

But in view of the circumstances, to which I have alluded, I dare not crow till we are fairly out of the wood. Meanwhile, I am constantly trembling for those poor Kansas emigrants. If they can *only* keep the hounds at bay, till we *know* whether Fremont is to ride into the field and call off the bloody pack! I am not satisfied. I want to see emigrants pouring in by thousands. Not to fight for what has already been done; but to stand shoulder to shoulder, in solid phalanx, saying, with one voice, "not another Border Ruffian[2] shall enter the territory! let the President *say* what he will; let the army *do* what they will. In the name of Freedom we defy them both."   Oh, that Army Bill! I never *can* forgive Burlingame for being absent from his seat when the vote was taken.[3] I feel *sure* how Charles Sumner would act in any given emergency. I do *not* feel quite so sure about Burlinghame. Several little things in his course have excited distrust in my mind. How came he ever to admit, in *private* conversation, that the assassin Brooks was a man of "courage and honor?" How came he to be absent when that important vote was taken? his apology for it seems to me shuffling and unsatisfactory. I shall never be able to remove the impression

[2] This was the term applied to the proslavery Missourians who crossed the border for raids into Kansas, using fraud and violence in the elections to the territorial legislature.
[3] Anson Burlingame (1820–70) was a Massachusetts congressman who helped form the Republican party. After Preston Brooks's assault on Sumner, Burlingame had challenged Brooks to a duel, choosing Niagara Falls as the site. As Brooks could not travel safely through the North, the duel did not take place. In August 1856 House Republicans unsuccessfully tried to prohibit the use of federal troops in Kansas by attaching a rider to an Army appropriations bill.

from *my* mind that he was quite willing thus to avoid meeting Brooks at Washington, though he did crow so loudly, standing here on Northern ground, with a bulwark of friends. Then, what a miserable mistake it was to accept the challenge at all! And how much it is in the Southern vein for the Fremont papers to be boasting of his "pluck"! The moral effect is every way bad. How majestically does Wilson's example loom up in comparison.[4]

How does your patience hold out with the Filmore men you meet?[5] I encountered your relative W'm Sturgess the other day.[6] He informed me, with much self-complacency, that he was not prepared to go *quite* so far as Mr. Choate;[7] that *he* should vote for Filmore. I told him the moral distinction between the two was so small, I did n't wonder he plumed himself upon his sagacity in perceiving it. He answered, "You are a very independent woman, Mrs. Child; but *I* am as independent as *you* are. I take counsel of no one". He put his gloved middle finger to his *heart* in a most touching manner, and said, "I seek my monitor *here*"; then he added, with a significant *emphasis*, intended to be very sarcastic, ⟨"And touching his *forehead* with the forefinger of his other hand,⟩ "And *I*, madam am accustomed to place the monitor *here*, under the control of the guide *here*";—touching his *forehead*, with the forefinger of his other hand.

Did you ever chance to hear a respectable appeal to his *heart?* It is inexpressibly comic. In comparison with it, there is epic dignity in a thief swearing by his *honor.*

. . .

To return to the old subject, I cannot say that I feel any enthusiasm about Fremont, as a man. I would not whisper a word to abate Nelly's and Effie's enthusiasm about their "first hero."[8] But I confess, to your private ear, that I don't like the expression of his countenance; and I dislike some of his antecedents. He did much to stir up that most unjust war with Mexico. But I have lived too long to expect perfection, even in private characters, much less in public ones. He has pledged himself to oppose the extension of slavery, and it is for his interest to *keep* the pledge. *That* is enough for *me.* . . .

. . .

ALS; Houghton Library, Harvard University (microfiche 34/941).

[4] See n. 3, letter of 7 July 1856, on p. 284, and the letter itself.
[5] Millard Fillmore (1800–1874) was the presidential candidate of the Know-Nothings. Though they leaned towards Republicanism, the Know-Nothings disliked Frémont because it was widely if mistakenly believed that he was Catholic. By nominating Fillmore, the Know-Nothings split the anti-Democratic vote.
[6] William Sturgis, of Russell and Sturgis, served in the Massachusetts legislature for many years.
[7] Rufus Choate.
[8] Nelly and Effie were Ellen and Josephine Shaw, daughters of Sarah and Francis Shaw.

To Louisa Loring

[26? October? 1856]

[. . .][1] Stowe's civility to President Pierce? Out of respect for his *office* forsooth! I wonder whether he would treat a "minister of the *Gos* pel" with respect, on account of his *office*, when he knew him to be an accomplice with murderers and robbers? I *always* suspected there was a streak of the Jesuit in Professor Stowe. If I were his wife, I'd sue for divorce, and *take* it, if I could'nt *get* it by petitioning.

When I read of his doing honor to that wretch, I wanted to burn him up, and sweep up his ashes.[2]

I understand the Boston Post is down upon me, for lines I wrote about the President, in the Tribune. I could'nt *help* it. His name would'nt *rhyme* to anything but *curse*.[3]

. . .

ALS; Loring Family Papers, Schlesinger Library, Radcliffe College (microfiche 34/950).

Maria spent much of the summer of 1856 writing "The Kansas Emigrants," a long story she sent to Horace Greeley in the fall. He decided to run it at once as a serial in his *New York Tribune*, interrupting Dickens's *Little Dorrit* to make room for it. David Lee Child was in the Berkshire hills of western Massachusetts during October 1856, helping the New England Emigrant Aid Society to recruit Free State settlers and raise money and buy guns for the antislavery settlers in the disputed territory. Organized in 1854, the Emigrant Aid Society was active until 1857. It brought some two thousand settlers to Kansas.

To David Lee Child

Monday Morning, Oct. 27th 1856

Darling David has n't begun to think Mariquita has forgotten him; *has* he? I should n't wonder. The fact is, I have *thought* enough about my dear absent

---

[1] The first page or pages of this letter are lost. Franklin Pierce (1804-69), then completing his single term as president, was a New Hampshire Democrat scorned by Child for his devotion to proslavery interests. Calvin Stowe (1802-86), theologian and husband of Harriet Beecher Stowe, had been Pierce's classmate at Bowdoin College. While president, Pierce once said that he got good marks at Bowdoin because he sat next to Stowe.

[2] The editors have been unable to identify what "honor" Stowe did Pierce.

[3] In Child's "Free Soil Song" (*New York Tribune*, 22 Oct. 1856) are these two lines: "New Hampshire has sent us a bloody curse / In that servile tool, their Franklin Pierce."

mate, but I have found it nearly impossible to get an hour's time to *tell* him so. In the first place, there was the press waiting for that Kansas story, which I got so fretted over, because it seemed as if I should *never* be able to get it done. Then father had one of his poorly turns, and for three nights I was obliged to be up frequently with him, and it was also necessary to keep close watch over him during the day. He is better now, but more feeble than when you left. Then I felt bound to stir up the women here to do something for Kansas; and, in order to set the example I wrote to Mr. Hovey, begging for a piece of cheap calico, and a piece of unbleached factory cotton.[1] He sent them; but said he did it out of courtesy to *me;* he himself deeming that money and energy had better be expended on the immediate abolition of slavery, and dissolution of the union, if that could not be soon brought about. I did not think it best to wait for either of those events to take place; before I made up the cloth. Cold weather was coming on, the emigrants would be down with fever-and-ague, and the roads would soon be in a bad state for baggage-wagons. So I hurried night and day; sitting up here all alone till eleven at night, stitching as fast as my fingers could go. It was a heavy job to cut and make more than 60 yds of cloth into garments; but, with a little help from Mrs. Rutter and the children, I completed it in eight days.[2] The women in town, both orthodox and Unitarian came up to the work cordially, and sent about $60 dollars worth of clothing. Nobody acted refractory, except a few of the democrats, who were not willing their wives and daughters should do anything; saying all the *money* raised for Kansas was used for electioneering purposes; that the hue and cry about clothing and provisions was a part of the same game; and moreover, the clothing would never *get* there. I had a mind to ask them whether they had received private information to that effect, from their friends the Border Ruffians.   I think you will gather from this account of my doings that I have had little leisure since you left. Oh dear! How I *have* missed you! We poor, ungrateful mortals never know the value of blessings till they are taken from us. My nest seems so dreary without my kind mate! I have nobody to plague, nobody to scold at, nobody to talk loving nonsense to. I do long to have you get back. *Voting* day will bring you, of course. If you *dont* come, I shall put on your old hat and coat, and vote *for* you. Alas, I am afraid that it is no matter what New England does; since Pennsylvania and Illinois seem likely to go so wrong. However, there is still *hope,* and the Free Soil men must be all the more vigilant and active, because there is danger that the battle is going against them.   My anxiety on the subject has been intense. It seemed as if my heart would burst, if I could n't *do* something to help on the election. But all I could do was to write a Song for the Free Soil Men, and scatter a dozen copies of it about.[3] . . .

Henry Ward Beecher made a capital speech in Faneiul Hall, excepting the

[1] Charles F. Hovey (1807–59) was a Boston merchant and abolitionist.
[2] Mrs. Rutter rented rooms in the house for herself and her children.
[3] Child's song was published broadside about the country.

value he sets upon preserving the Union.[4] What does he and others *mean* by solemn assurances that they have no idea of attempting to abolish slavery where it already *is*, by any *political* action, but should use only *moral* influence for that purpose. In the first place, nobody *can* act *politically* on the institutions of the South, unless they are Southern citizens; and, in the next place, neither Garrison nor any other person, ever *proposed* to act in any other way, than by the exertion of *moral* influence. The *pious* folks are getting very uneasy about Henry Ward Beecher. They warn him solemnly that *wolves* may get in among his flock, while their pastor is going about lecturing on politics. If I were he, I would tell them I'd run the risk of the *wolves*, if such *foxes* as they would keep out of the fold.

The scenery up in that hilly region must indeed be beautiful this sunny autumn. I should mightily enjoy rambling about with you; but then I think the pleasure would be more than balanced by the liability of being called upon by such highly respectable people. I should demur about heaven itself, on *such* terms. If you happen to be visiting at any house where they have a fine flower-garden, I wish you would ask the lady if she could give me one or two bulbs of the low early Snow-Drop; or of a later kind of Snow Drop, which grows *taller*, and bears the same kind of blossom, only a little *larger* than the early kind.

Your Uncle Tyler came here last week, and spent a couple of hours.[5] I was really glad to see him, and urged him much to stay to tea; but he came to Weston, to bring his housekeeper on a visit to her old friend Mrs. Alpheus Bigelow;[6] and he had promised to be there in season for tea. He was much disappointed to find you absent. He seemed *hot* about Free Soil, and says all his sons are Free Soil Men. Oh dear! If we lose the battle *this* time, I am afraid it will put back the cause of freedom in this country, for half a century at least.

I shall be looking out for somebody next Saturday night; and I shan't hail him with the exclamation, "What did you come back for?" Dear soul! How I do long to see you, and to have one of our old cozy chats, and say over the old prayer, before we go to sleep. Father is groaning to have you come back; not merely because he has divers things to be attended to; but because he "misses David." Good night. God bless you, dear.

Your affectionate old Mariquita.

ALS; Lydia Maria Child Papers, Anti-Slavery Collection, Cornell University (micro-fiche 34/951).

[4] Beecher (1813–87) was the popular antislavery pastor of Brooklyn's Plymouth Church.
[5] David's uncle Tyler Bigelow (1778–1865), a lawyer in Watertown, Mass., was to leave David a legacy of a thousand dollars.
[6] Mary Ann Bigelow (1792–1870) was the wife of a lawyer in Weston, Mass., a distant relative of David's.

To Lucy and Mary Osgood

Wayland, Oct. 28th 1856

Dear Friends,

. . .

Did you take note of T. W. Higginson's sermon to the people of Lawrence, in Kansas?[1] His text was from the Prophet Nehemiah, commanding the people to "fight for their wives, their children, and their homes." What a convenient book that Old Testament is, whenever there is any *fighting* to be done. Many people seem to be greatly shocked by Higginson's course; but if they admit that war is *ever* justifiable, I think they are inconsistent to blame him. If the heroes of '76 were praiseworthy, the heroes of Kansas will be *more* praiseworthy for maintaining their rights, even unto death. But, It is treason, It is revolution, they exclaim. They seem to forget that the war of '76 was precisely that. It was a contest with our own government; not with a foreign foe; and the wrongs to be redressed were not worthy of a thought, in comparison with the accumulation of outrages upon the free settlers in Kansas. So far, the emigrants have manifested a most wonderful forbearance, and have gained nothing by it, either from the Missourians, or the U.S. government. The present neutrality is merely a sham, to be kept up till the election is over. Some simple souls are blinded by it, and indulge hopes that Kansas will be protected, even if Fremont is not elected. But the dogs of war will be let loose again, as soon as it can be done without injuring the interests of the South. What the result will be is known only to Him who guides the destinies of nations. But we are on the verge of an awful crisis. For twenty-five years, the abolitionists have been calling out in vain, to cotton-stuffed ears that the slavery of colored men must be abolished, or there would be left no vestige of freedom for white men. Well, the fulfilment of the prophecy is coming upon us rapidly. We have all been involved in the national wickedness, and perhaps the laws of God require that we should all sink to the bottom together. Still a hope survives in my mind that a strong boat may be got out and manned from the sinking wreck. Alas for the hopes of freedom for the world, if *we* have not virtue enough left for *that!*

How did you like Dred? Our minister, Mr. Sears, remarked, "Mrs. Stowe wrote Uncle Tom because she could'nt help it; and she wrote Dred because she had written Uncle Tom." Perhaps *some*thing of such an an impression was left on my own mind, when I closed the volumes. But though it is less exciting than Uncle Tom, and though the end does not quite fulfil the promise of the

[1] Thomas Wentworth Higginson (1823–1911), pastor of a Free Church at Worcester, Mass. at this time, was a militant abolitionist. In 1854 he was a leader of the attempt to rescue the runaway slave Anthony Burns. In the fall of 1856 he went to Kansas carrying rifles for the emigrants, and in Lawrence he preached upon the text, "Be ye not afraid of them; remember the Lord, which is great and terrible, and fight for your brethren, your sons, and your daughters, your wives, and your houses." It was the text used by the Reverend John Martin the Sunday after he had fought at Bunker Hill.

beginning, it is a great book, and a wise book, and a *very* witty book, and will exercise an immense power over the public mind for good. Old Tiff was the *real* hero of the book. I delighted in Old Tiff, from beginning to end. His earnestness to get those "chillen into Canan," without thinking anything about himself was charming. But after they inherited a *fortune*, he manifested much less anxiety about their getting into Canaan. That's the natural effect of riches; and old Tiff had a deal of "human *natur*" in him. The book seemed to me to hit *orthodoxy* almost as hard as it hit *slavery*. What *sort* of Calvinism is it that Young Beecherdom swears by?

I also luxuriated in the reading of Emerson's book on the English.[2] It seemed to me wise, discriminating, and eloquent. Have you read Geo. Curtis's (Howadji Curtis) Address to Scholars on their duties to their country?[3] It is a glorious production. I *was* afraid that Curtis would waste his brilliant talents on mere external things; as Willis had done before him. But this crisis has brought out the manhood in his soul; as it has in many others. Partly also I attribute his rapid growth to the healthy influence of Frank Shaw and his wife, whose daughter he is soon to marry.

. . .

AL; Lydia Maria Child Papers, Anti-Slavery Collection, Cornell University (microfiche 34/953).

The Democrats won the presidency, with Buchanan taking fourteen slave and five free states. Frémont won eleven free states, and Fillmore one slave state. But the new Republican party, electing 195 representatives and 15 senators to the Thirty-fourth Congress, showed strength enough to alarm the South.

To Sarah Shaw

Wayland, Nov. 9'th, 1856.

Friend always precious and dearly beloved, your letter came duly to hand, and the sight of the well-known writing, as usual, played round my heart "like a kiss-glow." I have never loved any woman so well as I love thee, except my little Doloresita; and I loved her, not only because she was of singularly *true* and *earnest* nature, like thee, but because she was also alone in the world, and consequently no husband and children came *between* us. It is a selfish, but a very natural feeling, to desire to be more important than *any* one else can be to those we love. I cannot say that "Many love me;" but oh, how often, and how keenly do I feel, "But by none am I *enough* beloved." Well, Doloresita does

---

[2] *English Traits* (Boston, 1856).
[3] *The Duty of the American Scholar to Politics and the Times. An Oration Delivered on Tuesday, Aug. 5, 1856* . . . (New York, 1856).

not *need* me now. Her uncle will come before me in her affection, and in all probability others also.[1] In your situation, you could not possibly have such an *exclusive* feeling toward me as she had; but you have always been a most constant and kind friend, and while a pulse of the warm old heart beats, it will always throb with love for you. The coolness of expression in my last letter (it *seemed* cool to you because I have accustomed you to such tropical heat) was entirely oweing to the deep dejection of mind under which I wrote. During this autumn, I have seen the darkest hours of my clouded life. I have been considered unpatriotic, because I have written and said so much concerning our national sins; but this crisis [h]as made me realize, as I never *before* realized, that I have a very strong love for my country. The news of the October elections in Pennsylvania made me feel as if I had just buried my mother. I could think of nothing but Kansas; and everything else in the world seemed like "*Mr. Shaw*"; as much like Mr. Howl—and Shaw, as anything.[2] I never was at all sanguine about Fremont's election, and he was not *the* candidate that I wished to have nominated. Mr. Child's familiarity with politics, for many years past, made me too familiar with the frauds and tricks of all sorts resorted to at the *last* moment, for me to be easily elated by signs of success at the outset. The South plays with us, like the cat with a mouse. We are permitted to amuse ourselves with the idea that we are going to obtain our freedom; but the tiger is watching us closely all the while, and is sure to grip us at last. For many years, it has been a settled conviction in my mind that there is no remedy for this, except Dissolution of the Union. But *how* can it be dissolved? *That* is the question. The South will never do it. She understands her own safety and interests too well. And there is not *virtue* enough in the North to secede. The noble ship of Freedom is sinking fast. We have lost our *last* chance to stop the leak. Would to God there were *men* enough on board of her to man a new Life-Boat, the Northern Republic! But there *are* not men enough for that; and whether there ever *will* be seems to me very doubtful. Greely thinks the Fremont party did wonders, considering it was "born of yesterday"; and he prophesies success for it in the future. I cannot view the subject in that light. If the Kansas outrages, and the assault on Charles Sumner could not arouse the Free States to *unanimous* resistance to Southern tyranny, we have no reason to suppose that any event which may hereafter happen will sufficiently arouse them. Probably such an exciting combination of circumstances will *never* occur again. We shall go sl:d'ng down unconsciously to utter ruin, on a gently inclined plane of political compromises. But though we have proved ourselves utterly unworthy of the glorious mission of guiding the World onward to Freedom, I have still faith in God, and do not believe in the Devil. All is working wisely for great ultimate results; perhaps through the very defeats which seem to us so dis-

[1] Dolores had returned to Madrid to live with her uncle.
[2] Gardiner Howland Shaw (1819–67) was a rich, conservative brother of Francis Shaw.

couraging. The motto on *my* banner shall always be, "Onward! Straight Onward! God and Victory!" Whether the ship I sail in sinks rapidly, or floats tremulously for a long time, with this dreadful leak at the bow, I will still wave this banner to the last, to cheer the kindred souls who are sadly watching our experiment. With my latest breath, I will shout aloud to them, "It is not *Freedom* that has failed, my friends. *She* faileth never. We are sinking because we have Despotism on board. Throw her over from *your* ships, my friends! Throw her over, whatever form she takes!"

. . .

My old father has been full of interest about Fremont's election. After the attack I mentioned, he gave up for a time his cherished idea of going to vote. One day, when he was considerably better, I said, "If your heart is set upon it, perhaps you will be able to go, in an easy carriage." He answered impatiently, "I don't care who is President. It will make no difference to *me*. *I* shall be out of the way." "But don't you care anything about posterity?" said I. "No" replied he. "Posterity acts like the Devil."   However, when the eventful day came, he said, "I *must* go. My *first* vote was given for Washington, and my *last* shall be given for Fremont." So we lifted him carefully into the carriage, and drove him very slowly to the polls, where he deposited his vote with trembling hands. He is much dejected at the result. Good bye, dearest.   Always your loving and grateful Mariechen.

. . .

ALS; Houghton Library, Harvard University (microfiche 34/956).

Child's father, David Convers Francis, died on 27 November 1856, at ninety years of age.

To Sarah Shaw

Wayland, Dec. 8th, 1856.

Yes, my beloved friend, the old man has gone home; and unless you had had a similar charge for three years, you could not imagine how lonely and desolate I feel. Night and day, he was on my mind, and now the occupation of my life seems gone. I have much work to do, both mental and manual; but as yet, I cannot settle down to work. Always that dreary void! I went to Boston and spent four days; but the dreariness went with me. The old man loved me; and you know how foolishly my nature craves love. Never again can I be so important to any human being as I was to him. Always, when I came back from Boston, there was a bright fire-light in his room for me, and his hand was eagerly stretched out, and the old face lighted up, as he said, "You're welcome back, Maria." *This* time, when I came home, it was all dark and silent. I almost cried myself blind; and I thought I would willingly be fettered to his bedside for years, if I could only hear that voice again. This is weakness, I know. The poor old man dreaded the long cold winter, and he *wanted* to be released. He passed away entirely without pain, with no disease but old age. His feebleness increased so rapidly in the last weeks, that it was necessary to lift him a great deal; and I suppose that *something* of the stifled feeling I have about my heart, and the continual tendency to weep, may be attributed to *nervousness*, induced by fatigue and anxiety. My spirits will doubtless rebound from the pressure, as soon as I can fairly get to *work*. Work! Work! *that* is my unfailing cure for all troubles.

. . .

I am greatly delighted with Mrs. Browning's Aurora Leigh.[1] It is full of strong things, and brilliant things, and beautiful things. And how glad I am, to see modern literature tending so much toward the breaking down of social distinctions!

. . .

ALS; Houghton Library, Harvard University (microfiche 34/964).

To John Greenleaf Whittier

Wayland, Jan. 2d. 1857

Dear and Honored Friend,

. . .

I have often wanted to propose a subject to you, for a tragic poem, or a poetic tragedy. Did you ever examine into the history of that noble chieftain, who bore the musical name of Oceola?[1] You know the bloody war with the Indians in Florida in *reality* grew out of the fact that our runaway slaves took refuge there. Oceola married a beautiful runaway slave. She and her children were torn from him, under circumstances of peculiar cruelty. He instigated his tribe to resist the aggressions of the white men. He performed deeds braver than any recorded of any Douglass or Bruce. He was at last treacherously entrapped by a flag of truce (the basest of civilized crimes) and died in prison, of a broken heart. It has always seemed to me an exceedingly romantic and poetic history, which could not be told without conveying a salutary moral rebuke to this guilty nation. Alas, volumes might be written, without unfolding a thousandth part of our cruel injustice, especially of our *treachery*, toward the red men.

When I was in Boston, last week, Charles Sumner called to see me, and I

[1] (London, 1857).
[1] Osceola led Indian resistance in the southeastern United States to the federal government's removal policy. He was captured by treachery in the Seminole War (1835–42) and died in prison.

had two or three hours conversation with him. He seemed to me absolutely *holy;* so gentle is he in his manner of speaking of Brooks, and of others, who have injured and and insulted him. His health has improved considerably since his return to Boston; but his nerves are still very excitable, and the muscles of the back are so much injured, that it is painful to see him attempt to rise from a chair. His intellect seemed bright and strong, and he looks so well in the face, that his political enemies will accuse him of *shamming* illness, if he persists in his unwise resolution of going to Washington this month. Alas, it is no sham! His restless mind is but too eager to overcome the hindrances of its shattered envelope. He told me of letters from the South, which stated that the *only* regret in S. Carolina was that Seward had not been the victim. "And he *would* have been, if Seward had not been backed by a powerful party in New York, while Sumner was known to be unpopular in Massachusetts." So said the *chivalry* of the South. Complimentary to our native Commonwealth—was it not?

. . .

ALS; Manuscript Division, Library of Congress (microfiche 35/975).

To David Lee Child

Wayland, Jan. 7th, 1857.

. . .

Henry Wilson came into the Anti Slavery Fair, and I talked with him an hour or so. He seemed very much depressed in spirits. He told me I could form no idea of the state of things in Washington. As he passes thro the streets in the evening, he says the air is filled with yells and curses from the oyster-shops and the saloons for gambling, the burden of which is all manner of threatened violence to Seward, and Sumner, and Wilson, and Burlingame. While he was making his last speech the Southern members tried to insult him in every way. One of them actually brandished his cane as if about to strike him; but he ignored the presence of him and his cane, and went on with his speech. The speech gave great offence, and he was informed that a desperado was dogging his steps, who had promised to do the same job for him that Brooks did for Sumner. Wilson says he never leaves his room to go into the Senate, without thinking whether he has left everything arranged as he should wish if he were never to return to it alive.

What a state of things! I believe in my soul that Garrison's prophecy will be fulfilled. He says it will not be long before there will be a band of hired ruffians to control the speeches and the votes in Washington, as they did in Kansas.

What do you think Edmund Benzon sent me for a Christmas present? An order for $100 to be used for Kansas! I sent it to Mr. Nute with a request that the women and children of Kansas might have the benefit of it.[1]

. . .

ALS; Lydia Maria Child Papers, Anti-Slavery Collection, Cornell University (microfiche 35/980).

To Convers Francis

Wayland, January 9, 1857.

As for the rank which the world assigns to one avocation over another, I can hardly find words significant enough to express the low estimate I put upon it. The lawyer who feels above the bookseller seems to me just as ridiculous as the orange-woman who objected to selling Hannah More's[1] tracts. "I sell *ballads!*" she exclaimed. "Why, I don't even sell apples!" How absurdly we poor blundering mortals lose sight of the reality of things, under the veil of appearances! In choosing an employment, it seems to me the only question to be asked is, What are we best fitted for? and What do we most enjoy doing?

L, extract; *Letters of Lydia Maria Child*, 1882 (microfiche 35/981).

To Marianne Silsbee

Wayland, Feb. 1st 1857

My dear Mrs. Silsbee,

I will not answer your letter in detail, because you have particularly requested me *not* to do so; and because I could hardly do so, with my natural frankness, without interrupting, by many vexatious snags, your smooth sailing through my epistle. I will, therefore, merely say, in *general* terms, that the pervading *tone* of your letter, though very kind in its spirit, and carefully restrained in expression, made me feel, more distinctly than I had previously felt, how very difficult it is to throw even a plank bridge over the chasm that separates *my* habits of thought and feeling from those who trace the outrages in Kansas to the Emigrant Aid Society, who ascribe the reckless violence of slaveholders to the provocations of abolitionists, and impute the misery and degradation of the European peasantry to the bad influence of the radicals.

The different points of view, from which we habitually look at things, is [*sic*] manifested by the fact that I have seldom been with you, for more than an hour, without hearing some hit at my especial favorites; and I dare say that *I*, without thinking of it, run against *your* predilections in the same way. Theodore Parker, Samuel Johnson, O. B Frothingham, T. W. Higginson, &c. are the

---

[1] Ephraim Nute (d. 1897) was active in the Emigrant Aid Society and served as pastor in Lawrence, Kans.
[1] Hannah More (1745–1833), English author.

chosen sons and brothers of my soul.[1] You dislike them all exceedingly. I agree with you in not being partial to *satirical* speaking, or writing. But with some men, satire is a *natural* talent. I do not quarrel with T. Parker, or Garrison, for using it, though it is not according to *my* taste; first, because it is a weapon born in *their* hands, and secondly, because they never use it from *personal* spite, but always against the practice, or the advocacy, of *principles* and *institutions*, which they deem bad. You say you "like Garrison, and detest Parker." Yet Garrison is a *great* deal more severe and satirical than Parker. The thunderbolts *he* hurls are often *hissing* hot. *I* have but *little* natural turn to satire, and that little I often restrain. If I *did* indulge in it, I should certainly turn its sharpest edge on those ministers who preach according to the prescription of their parishioners. But if they consider it an object *worth* living for, to manifest in their own persons what a beautiful relation may exist between *kind masters* and ⟨a⟩ *contented slaves*, I am very willing to leave them to the enjoyment of their lot.

With regard to Charles Sumner's being "chief architect of the wall," I think you forget, that difficulties on this subject drove us apart a few days after you returned from Europe; though we had met a few hours before with the strongest personal affection. Mainly by the agency of a man drunk with Southern wine, and bribed by promises of Southern votes for the presidency, a diabolical law was passed, by which the citizens of Massachusetts were converted into slave-catchers; and when my soul was boiling over with shame and indignation, that my native Commonwealth should, by tyrants and their base tools, be converted into a slave hunting-ground, you called it "making a ridiculous fuss about one nigger." How *hard* I tried not to enter into a pitched battle, then and there, up to the hilt of the knife, you will never know, or imagine; because you have never realized how very strongly I feel on all subjects connected with human freedom and equality. When the next 11'th of February came round, you did not write a letter of good wishes, as had been your custom for several years; though you afterward wrote to me that you were "thinking of me all day." I knew very well what snag ⟨is⟩ was in the way; and I took no offence. I was sorry for "the wall" between us; but I saw that neither you nor I could help it. It is possible for strong personal attachment to exist without the possibility of mutual pleasure in intimate intercourse. This is one of the saddest experiences, as we drift down the stream of life, to see how many boats are parted from our side by counter currents; boats into which we would gladly throw all the flowers we *have*, though it is out of our power to keep them company.

And now let us turn to more pleasant themes. Have you read Zaidee?[2] It

---

[1] Samuel Johnson (1822–82) was the abolitionist minister of a Free Church in Lynn, Mass. Octavius Brooks Frothingham (1822–95), Unitarian pastor in Salem, Mass., had broken with his congregation over the slavery issue and moved to Jersey City, N.J., in 1855.

[2] Margaret Oliphant, *Zaidee: A Romance* (Boston, 1856).

is a very cleverly written book, wholly occupied with aristocratic life in England, somewhat improbable in plot, but very interesting. It is astonishing what a great number of highly interesting novels are produced in these days. Every year, half a hundred are turned out, any one of which would have made a glorious reputation for an author a century ago. It is a trying time for us authors; the market is so glutted with superior specimens of our commodities. I am so overwhelmed with this conviction that I feel no heart to touch pen to paper again. Aurora Leigh, especially, withered me all up with its scorching superiority.

. . .

ALS; Lydia Maria Child Letters, American Antiquarian Society (microfiche 35/987).

To Anna Loring

Wayland, Feb. 12'th, 1857
My Darling Child,
. . .

Uncle David . . . has been, for a fortnight past, over head and ears in law-papers and M.S.S. preparing a Memorial to the Legislature concerning the constant overflow of the meadows here. The Cochituate Company pour upon us *18,000,000 of gallons* of water *a day!* This destroys thousands and thousands of dollars worth of produce, produces rheumatism by continual dampness, and fevers by the malaria of soaked and decaying vegetation. If the Legislature does not grant redress, I believe the towns all along on the river will unite to pull down the dams, law or no law; for the farmers are full of wrath against aristocratic corporations; and when the slow Yankee blood *is* once fairly roused, the tea goes overboard.

You will find nothing in George Sand's biography worse than you have already found; unless it be the tacitly *implied* admission that her relations with Chopin were too intimate. If they had seemed to me impure, I should not have sent the volumes to you. I may be mistaken; but from the evidence of her writings, I find it *impossible* to believe her such a woman as many represent her. Under the bewildering influences of French society, and an unfortunate marriage, acting on a temperament extremely susceptible and affectionate, she has undoubtedly lost her way sometimes. But those who deem one or two aberrations in *her unpardonable* ought not to write poetry for the Burns' Festival, or praise it after it is written.

"Gently scan your brother man,
Still gentler sister woman."

I enclose some lines which Mrs. Browning wrote upon Geo Sand, years ago. You may keep them in your desk till I come, if you please; for I have no other copy.

. . .

ALS; Lydia Maria Child Papers, A/C 536, 5, Schlesinger Library, Radcliffe College, (microfiche 35/991).

A decision on the Dred Scott case, which had been pending before the Supreme Court for years, was handed down on 6 March 1857. Scott, a slave, claimed that he was free because of temporary residence on free soil. Chief Justice Roger B. Taney's ruling held that Scott was not a citizen, and that no *free* Negro had ever been one. Negroes, he went on, were "so far inferior that they had no rights which the white man was bound to respect." Going still deeper, Taney ruled that "Congress had no power to abolish or prevent slavery in any of the Territories." The Taney decision outraged the Republicans and made the slaveholders jubilant. The doctrine would remain law until adoption of the Fourteenth Amendment in 1867.

In the next letter, Child mentions Martha (Mattie) Griffith (ca. 1838–1906), with whom she began corresponding in 1857 when Griffith published *Autobiography of a Female Slave* (New York). Born in Louisville, Kentucky, to an aristocratic family, Griffith freed the slaves she inherited from her father.

To Sarah Shaw

Wayland, March, 20th, 1857.

Darling Sarah,

You are right. God doubtless does intend that we should fight our battles *alone*. Oh, how often have I put out my trembling feelers after some kindred sympathizing soul, that I could draw *into* my own; but, alas, they come back empty, and for the most part wounded. We think if we could only be *externally* near those we love, the craving for companionship, and for the confessional, would be surely gratified. We try it, and lo! a thousand barriers rise up to separate the souls that long to mingle; barriers impalpable as mist, but insuperable as granite. If I lived in the same house with you a year, would you know what had been my keenest griefs, my fiercest struggles? Should I be able to do more than dimly conjecture yours? I trow not.

> "*Alone*, since God so wills it, we must die;
> For not the dearest heart, and next our own,
> Knows half the reasons why we smile or sigh."

I have inexpressible yearnings for you. No friendship has ever gone out of my life, that I *missed* so much. By *nature*, we have much in common, though many differences have been occasioned by the dissimilarity of our social position. We both see through shams very quickly, and are uncomfortably impatient with shams. We both have a rabid love for freedom in general, and more especially for freedom in particular. I don't feel any necessity of being *respectable* when I am with you; and that is *such* a comfort!

. . . I read Thackeray's Newcomes, according to your request.[1] I recognized the genius of the author; but every one of the characters, except the old Colonel, made me uncomfortable. I was in society's masked ball, and was in a hurry to get away from the company. He describes well—wonderfully well; but he describes *artificial* life. Then I had rather not be *confirmed* in my bad opinion of human nature, which the advancing years have forced upon me. I need help to look on the brighter side. Altogether, Thackery always makes me uncomfortable. I feel what the matter is. He used to have ten-thousand a year, and he spent it in sowing wild oats. He is *blasé*, and cannot see the world through a fresh, natural medium. It is said some one asked him why he never described loving and constant women. He replied, "Because I never *knew* of any."

. . .

Mattie Griffith continues to write to me. Her slave-holding relatives and friends are doing their worst to induce her to deny publicly that she wrote the Autobiography. This excites her youthful indignation. "What a mean *thing* they would make of me!" she exclaims. "I will *die* first." She is true metal, and rings clear under their blows. Yet she has a loving womanly heart, made desolate and sad by separation from early friends. Angelina Grimké Weld has invited me to come there to spend May with Mattie. But if I got so near N. York as *that*, Staten Island would pull me away from Raritan Bay.

Yes, there is no doubt that my heroic Mattie *will* experience disappointment, and some disgust, at the bigotry and harshness of some of the abolitionists. But she will learn to do, as I have learned to do; to pass by their sharp corners without hurting myself more than can't be helped; and if they jostle me rudely, to bid God bless them, because they are earnestly walking straightforward. They *do* try me, by abusing Sumner and Wilson, as they do. If those men had no faith in the *Constitution*, they could not possibly *be* in Congress. If they *professed* to believe in it, for the *sake* of being there, I should despise them. But their words and deeds bear the stamp of sincerity. *They* believe that the Constitution has vital force enough to throw off the internal disease. *I* think they are mistaken. I think that the Constitution must be either amended, or thrown overboard, to save the sinking ship. But when they are acting honestly and courageously, according to their *own* conviction, in the face of obloquy and danger, why should I accuse them of being spurious abolitionists because they do not come out for Disunion? As representatives to Congress they *cannot* come out against the Union; but under the banner of the Constitution they

[1] (London, 1854–55).

307

can fight against the *Fugitive Slave Law*, because the U.S. had no constitutional right to pass it; they can fight against the *extension* of slavery, because the U.S. has no constitutional right to govern the territories in a manner detrimental to *freedom*—in a manner that *must* counteract the original object of the government, as expressed both in the Declaration of Independence, and in the Constitution. Now, ought we not to be thankful that there *are* men who can conscientiously go to Congress, and there fight *one* part of the great battle? In the early days of the Anti Slavery enterprise, it was a common thing for our speakers to say that *eventually* the work must be completed by *politicians*. How we should have *then* rejoiced over any man that would have stood up on the floor of Congress, with even *half* the courage of Giddings, Sumner, and Wilson! But *we*, in the mean time, have been marching ahead; and the van of the long army has the folly to despise the rear. As if there could be a van *without* a rear! As if *all* the forces were not *needed*, to attack the enemy at *all* his weak points! *I* say, God speed the van, and God bless the rear! And for my own part, I am willing to ride about, here and there, "promiscuous like," as I see occasion.

I drew, from the decision of the U.S. Supreme Court, the same consolation that *you* did. They have got rope enough, and they will hang themselves. Bless God also for *this* way of helping on the work! I have a relative who is very fond of quoting the Classics; not being aware that he thereby displays a "vast amount of mis-information." He often pompously announces, "First get the gods mad, and then they'll destroy *themselves*." Well, we've got the gods mad, and may the remainder be a swift conclusion.

. . .

ALS; Houghton Library, Harvard University (microfiche 36/998).

To David Lee Child

Chauncey St. Wednesday
[25 March 1857]

My Dearly Beloved David,

I am getting homesick already, and meditating how I can get through all my affairs to wend homeward at the earliest. I found a gentleman and lady from Philadelphia staying here, and the house is rather crowded. The Midsummer's Dream proved rather a failure to *me;* for we had seats so high up, and so far off, that I could only now and then catch some very loud tone of Fanny Kemble; and hearing screams by snatches, without knowing what they were about, was rather tedious and ludicrous. The music I could hear well, and it gave me much pleasure; but it was not brought out so well, as I had heard it in New York, two or three times. I missed several things, and that marred the pleasure somewhat; then Mrs. Kemble's part kept coming to interrupt.

. . .

Tuesday night (no, Monday) I went to hear Fanny Kemble read Othello.

Her powers of voice are wonderful—from the deepest and strongest tones to the clearest silvery threads. But it seemed to me like perfect *drilling*, not like inspiration. Once or twice, she absolutely ranted—tore a passion into tatters; but that was *rare;* and with other readers and actors on the stage, it is the *prevailing* character. She brings *out* Shakespeare, in all his shadings of meaning wonderfully. But the play is painful, and she did *not* excite me.

Edmund Quincy dined here yesterday, and inquired after you, expressed his regret not to meet you, and wished me to convey his cordial greetings and respects. This afternoon, I am going, with Mrs. Follen and H. Sargent, to the Museum to see a piece called Farmer Jackwood.[1] It represents slave-catchers outwitted by Vermont farmers, and the fugitives getting off safely through many perils. *That*'s a sign of the times; is n't it?

Peter Leslie says Joseph Lyman has had letters from Iowa and Kansas which state that the Free Soil emigration is very great; never been equalled since 1841.[2]

One thousand men were already on their way, from the states north & west of Kansas. One hundred stout Kentuckians, swearing to defend Free Soil to the death, ⟨were⟩ had also started for Kansas. He said Mr. Lyman's source of information was *authentic*. He desired a heap of love to you; and so does Deborah Weston, who has just left for Weymouth.[3] Your loving,

Mariquita

"I want to go *home*."

ALS; Lydia Maria Child Papers, Anti-Slavery Collection, Cornell University (microfiche 36/999).

To Sarah Shaw

Wayland July 7'th, 1857

Dearly Beloved,

. . .

. . . I have read the Professor, and I think those were judicious who advised Miss Bronte not to publish it.[1] It has good points, as *any* emanation from such a mind *must* have; but it seems to me by no means calculated to sustain the fame of Jane Eyre, or of Vilette. I dont wonder her biographer[2] has been threatened with a law-suit. When I read the volumes, I said that a brief *general*

---

[1] A play by John Townsend Trowbridge (1827–1916), adapted from his novel, *Neighbor Jackwood* (Boston, 1856).
[2] Joseph Lyman (1812–71), a civil engineer, travelled extensively for railroad construction and was opposed to slavery.
[3] Deborah Weston (b. 1814) was a teacher and one of the prominent antislavery Weston sisters.
[1] Charlotte Brontë, *The Professor* (London, 1857).
[2] Elizabeth Gaskell, who wrote *The Life of Charlotte Brontë* (London, 1857).

statement of the brother's dissipated course would have been more kind and more judicious; especially as the woman had children living. Even if the woman were as culpable as she was represented to be, I don't like the hard severe manner of treating her.   The pamphlet about a Medical College had already been sent to me, and I admired it much. It is very sensible, and contains no offence against good taste. I was glad to see your name among those interested in the project. I think it is the very best step ever yet taken for the advancement of woman. I understand that the elder Miss Blackwell wrote the Appeal.[3] What I know of her sayings and doing inspires me with great respect. I am always *so* rejoiced to find a woman that does not carry more sail than she does ballast!

We were invited to the Anti Slavery celebration of the 4th of July at Framingham. I would have gladly gone to hear Wendell[4] and Garrison, if Stephen Foster's name had not been appended to the list. The Traveller of yesterday says he called Sumner and Wilson both villains. Garrison, in answer to "Gregory," maintains that if they criticise Republicans, "it is always with seriousness and dignity"; that they "never sneer at them."

Certainly, the beam in his eye *has*, "by its long lodging, become a sleeper." In Sumner, I have the most implicit reliance. Wilson[5] has, in the main, behaved nobly, I think, and I believe that his motives are honest and honorable; but I feel a *little* fear about his future course. He has too much of the politician's tendency to *compromise*. God keep him straight, for his own sake, as well as the country's!   An orthodox minister preached here last Sunday, who said "The *English* abolitionists prevailed, because they were believers in the Trinity; but what have Garrison and Parker, and Phillips accomplished by all their infidel bawling?" If anybody asks the best method to educate donkies, tell them to stable them in a pulpit, and feed them on thistles of doctrine.

. . .

With hearty love to your good Frank, and affectionate remembrance to Page, I am always your loving Maria.

Is'nt that "Helper" from N. Carolina a thoroughly grand good fellow?[6] God bless him!

ALS; Houghton Library, Harvard University (microfiche 36/1011).

[3] Elizabeth Blackwell, *Address on the Medical Education of Women* (New York, 1856). Dr. Blackwell (1821–1910) received her medical degree in 1849, the first woman in modern times to accomplish this step. She founded the New York Infirmary for Women and Children in 1857.
[4] Wendell Phillips.
[5] Henry Wilson.
[6] This was Hinton Rowan Helper (1829–1909) of North Carolina, whose book, *The Impending Crisis* (New York, 1857), was an appeal to the South's poor whites to unite against the slaveholders. A racist, Helper opposed slavery not for what it had done to blacks, but because it harmed nonslaveholding whites. The abolitionists circulated his book widely.

To Maria (Weston) Chapman

Wayland, July 26th [1857?]

Dear Mrs. Chapman,

I like the Call to the Fair extremely, and return it with my signature. I have erased the s at the end of Mattie Griffith's name, because she told me it was a mistake to spell it with an s. I was *very* much pleased with Mattie, and the more I saw of her, the better I liked her. She is strong as a young lion, wherever her sense of *right* is concerned. Yet how girlish she seems! How youthfulness effervesces in her. Her cousin, partner of Prentiss, in the editorship of the Louisville Journal, took her away from me, for a ride; and so we parted somewhat hurriedly.[1] He was *determined* to coax her to take a journey with him and a fashionable party from Kentucky, including the Governor and his daughter. She said the Governor's daughter was a fashionable flirt, and she did not want to go. But he would not take No for an answer. She urged that knowing her sentiments, they would not *like* to have her join the party; to which he replied, in the true South Western style, "I should like to see the person who dares to object to your company, in *my* presence."

They have tried to frighten her by cutting her dead, and finding *that* does no good, I am inclined to think they mean to try what coaxing and flattery will do. She is *worth* trying for. If they have many such girls in Kentucky, it is a lucky State. I am glad you like her so much. The "smitation" is mutual.

Angelina Weld's resuscitation cannot justly be ascribed to her influence. Angelina wrote to me last winter, before she saw Mattie, that the Spirit often impelled her to go to work in the Anti-Slavery field again. I should have added *my* voice to that of the *spirit*, had I not been withheld by fear of the influence of her Bloomer dress, which Mrs. Follen says "looks as if it was made of all the old dusting-cloths she could muster."[2] I think the long interregnum in her anti-slavery action is mainly to be attributed to her strong feeling that it was her duty to devote herself wholly to her children. They are now old enough to be trusted alone, and I suppose she feels free again. I never heard her say a word about Abby Foster, so cannot judge of her opinions.

But of one thing I am sure; that, to the day of my death, *Stephen* Foster will be as good as an unleashed bull-dog to keep *me* away from Anti Slavery meetings. I could scarcely find words to express my extreme disapprobation of that man's way of doing things. All the gold of California could'nt pay for the mischief he and Henry C. Wright have done to the cause. They effectually

---

[1] George D. Prentice (1802–70) was editor of the *Louisville Journal*.
[2] The Bloomer costume—tunic, short skirt, and pantaloons—designed to free women from the uncomfortable and unhealthy garments fashion dictated, was a step forward in simplicity in dress and a symbol of revolt against senseless restrictions imposed upon women.

repel even as earnest an abolitionist as *I* am; and I would lay down my *life* to abolish slavery.

. . .

ALS; Anti-Slavery Collection, Rare Books and Manuscripts, Boston Public Library (microfiche 36/1014).

To Marianne Silsbee

Wayland, Sep. 11th, 1857.

Dear Friend,

. . .

You behave so magnanimously about my anti-slavery scolding, that you compel me to love you better than I ever did before. *Very* few people, in the relative social position which you bear to me, would have done anything toward picking up the dropped stitches of our friendship. It shows a large nature, and a kind heart. I appreciate it, and I thank you for it.

If I have in aught done you any injustice, or done Mr. Silsbee any injustice, I pray you pardon me.

I feel keenly and deeply on the subject of slavery, not merely from motives of justice and humanity toward the colored race, but because I see so clearly that *all* the fair prospects of this broad and beautiful land have for years been driving toward an inevitable wreck on that rock so carefully concealed beneath a smooth surface.

Feeling thus, and seeing so *many* drawn aside from their duty on the subject, by the fear of offending those who are influential in society, or by an amiable desire to keep on good terms with friends who were looking at the subject from a more distant point of view, I have watched over myself with great jealousy. Again and again, I have said to myself, "Take care! Maria Child! Take care! Dont allow this pleasant friendship, and these kind attentions, to draw you away from the advocacy of an unpopular cause. Let no one mistake, for a moment, your willingness to lay upon *that* altar anything and everything that renders life agreeable."

Such has been my normal state of mind for twenty five years. But the capture of Burns, the outrages in Kansas, and the attack upon Charles Sumner, roused from the depths of my nature feelings, of whose existence I was not aware. The Puritan metal within me was struck, and rung a loud tocsin through my soul. For the first time in my life, I understood Charlotte Corday.[1] For the first time in my life, I felt that I *might* be driven to deeds of blood, when all hopes of justice from the laws, and aid from public sympathy was [*sic*] denied to the fugitive slave.

[1] Charlotte Corday (1768–93) worked for the Girondin cause in the French Revolution. Blaming Marat for the fall of that party and for inciting the people to violence, she stabbed him to death and was executed for it.

You could not understand this state of mind, dear friend; for, in the first place, the subject had not been kept so *near* to your large kind heart, by frequent interviews with fugitives, during twenty-five years; and you had been long abroad among sunny vineyards, and galleries of beauty.

I did not remember this, as I ought, and I pray your forgiveness, if I seemed to strike against you with a sharp collision, in return for your many proofs of love. I love you truly, and that is a fact.

. . .

ALS; Lydia Maria Child Letters, American Antiquarian Society (microfiche 37/1023)

A bank failure in August 1857 precipitated a financial panic. During the depression that followed, thousands of businesses failed.

To Marianne Silsbee

Wayland, Oct. 25th 1857.

Dear Friend,

. . .

I am glad that you have taken in your sails till the storm blows over. It is the wisest course for any ship to take, however strong her timbers may be. *My* fortunes lie too low to be endangered. I shall probably be somewhat *better* off for the crisis; that is, what little money I have will, for a short time, purchase more conveniences. But it will be for a short time only. The monopolisers and speculators will soon be in full career again.

I made my visit to Miss Hosmer, and went with her to look at the statue, which seemed to me *very* far superior to anything she has yet done. I was greatly attracted toward Harriet. She seems to be so strong, so true, and so much in earnest. I was charmed with the entire absence of pretension, which really was remarkable in a young person who has received so many flattering attentions in Europe. I think she is really great by nature. She seemed much gratified by the message you sent. "I wish I could *see* Mrs. Silsbee," she said. "If I were not in such a desperate hurry, I *would* run down to Salem for a few minutes, just to look on her pleasant countenance again. I cottoned to Mrs. Silsbee greatly."

The Ticknors have been making much of her, during her visit; giving her rings, bracelets, &c. It made me think of the time when they used to follow me up with similar attentions; but I can't say I had the slightest wish for a return of their patronage.

Harriet expected to sail for Havre yesterday. She was to have been met there by a wealthy American family, who had invited her to take a seat in their carriage to Rome. But when I saw her, she had just received word that, on account of the pecuniary crisis, they must hasten home. She is, however, quite competent to travel alone; being fully able to manage both horses and pistols. She must go, in order to finish the Monument, which she has moulded in clay, for the church of Sant' Andrea della Frata; and since she *must* go, her father wished her to be on her way before the autumn was farther advanced. For that monument, which gives great satisfaction to the parents of the deceased, she is to receive $2,500.

Her next statue is to be of Zenobia in Chains, the captive of Aurelian. A noble subject, I think.

Did you go to hear Vieux Temps? From Dwight's Journal, I judge that his second visit to this country will not be anymore successful than the first. The pecuniary crisis is unfortunate for him, as well as for others.   Mr. Child is still suffering acutely from rheumatism. He is very patient, but almost discouraged about being cured. He unites with me in cordial remembrance to you and all your house; especially Mary.

Good night. Blessings be with you!

Your grateful and affectionate friend,

L. M. Child.

ALS; Lydia Maria Child Letters, American Antiquarian Society (microfiche 37/1027).

Ellis Gray Loring, Child's confidante and legal adviser, died suddenly on 24 May 1857 at the age of fifty-five.

To Lucy and Mary Osgood

Wayland, June 12th, 1858.

My Dear & Honored Friends,

I was just about answering your welcome letter of May 4th, when that overwhelming blow came suddenly, and for a time seemed to crush all life and hope out of me. Nothing but the death of my kind husband could have caused me such bitter grief. Then came your precious letter of sympathy and condolence. I thanked you for it, from the depths of my suffering heart; but I did not feel as if I *could* summon energy to write to any but the bereaved ones of his own household. You knew that he was a valuable friend to me, but no one but myself could know *how* valuable. For thirty years, he has been my chief reliance. In moral perplexities, I always went to him for counsel, and he never failed to clear away every cloud. In all worldly troubles, I went to him, and always found a judicious adviser, a sympathizing friend, a generous helper. He was only two months younger than myself, but I had so long been accustomed to lean upon him, that the thought never occurred to me, that it was possible I might be left in the world without him. All my plans for old age were based upon him; all my little property was in his hands; and if I had ever so small a sum, even ten dollars, for which I had no immediate use, he put it on interest, though it were but for a single month. No other person in the world would have taken so much trouble with my petty affairs. But the loss, in this point of view, seems trifling compared to the desolation his death has made in my affections. If I could only hear his gentle voice again, I would be willing to throw all the dollars into the sea. Oh, this dreadful silence! How heavily the dark veil drops down between us and that unknown world! The patient resignation of Mrs. Loring and Anna is the most beautiful and touching sight I ever witnessed. With Louisa, I think it is partly, as you suggest, that she is "stunned by the suddenness of the blow"; and partly it is owing to her natural temperament, which takes all things easily, and also to her habitual trust in the Heavenly Father. Anna, I think is mainly sustained by the earnest wish to bear her mother up. But she has always had, from early childhood, a remarkable degree of self-control, and the religious sentiment is very strong within her. She wears her Spring-like dress of violet silk, which she wore last year, and keeps the house garlanded with the numerous flowers sent in by sympathizing friends. I have never seen her shed a tear; and often, when talking over reminiscences of her father, she smiles, as if he were only away on a short journey. Yet the bond between them was the strongest I ever witnessed between parent and child. Louisa once broke into sobs in my presence, but only for a moment. She talks of him continually, with only the gentlest tinge of sadness. She told me her most trying season was when she first woke in the morning, when memories came over her in a flood, before reason and religion had time to check the impetuous impulse of grief. The two first mornings after the funeral, she woke with passionate sobs. The third morning, when she opened her eyes, Anna (who never leaves her) was bending over her, looking into her face with anxious love. Meeting that tender gaze, the first thing as she emerged from the realms of sleep, the mother smiled upon her child; and Anna exclaimed, "Oh, dear mother, how *glad* I am to see you wake so! I have been praying this half hour that you might waken peacefully." What a treasure such a daughter is! . . .

I don't think your theory about people's dying in the manner they *wish* to die is sustained by facts. We *notice* the rare coincidences between the wish and the event, but we do *not* notice how generally the fulfilment fails. Henrietta Sargent's mother had a most passionate desire to be removed before her faculties failed her, and she had the greatest dread of being a care to others. She was *always* talking about it. Yet she lived five years in a state of complete dotage, and was ministered to, in every respect, like an infant. The case was a good deal the same with my poor old father. When I carried him some punch and cake on his last birth-day, he drank, uttering this toast, with affectionate solemnity: "May neither of you live to be as old as I am."

It is curious how you have found me out. I have always known that George Sand was my twin sister; but I never mentioned it to anybody but Mr. Child. When I say that she is my twin sister, I mean with allowance for the difference occasioned by one of us being born in France, and the other in New England;

and I, by no means, presume to claim such close affinity with her remarkable *genius*. But the grain of the wood is certainly the same in both of us. This consciousness of her being my double has given her works an irresistable fascination for me. They often provoke me; sometimes shock me; but I am constrained to acknowledge, "Thus in all probability, should *I* have written, had I been brought up in France." I never read a book of hers without continually stumbling on things that seem to have been written by myself. You are perfectly right. She *is* my double; and if the external influences of our lives had been the same, I should doubtless have been like her, faults and all. That she has fallen into great errors seems undeniable; but I don't believe those who pronounce her to have been a wanton woman. The affections in her nature are too strong for her intellect, and they have befooled her. Don't I know how to sympathize with *that?* She has lived in a very artificial and corrupt state of society; while I, thank God, was born in New England. There are very few of her writings that I would willingly put in the way of being read by young people. But I do not think their dangerous tendency is owing to the corrupt nature of the woman. On the contrary, judging of her by the internal evidence of those writings, her aspirations are pure and noble. But her sincerity is *exceeding* great. She is under the *necessity* of speaking the *truth*. She sees society promenading and waltzing over an infernal pit, from which ⟨they are⟩ it is separated by the thinnest coating of conventional respectability. Others may put finger on lip, if they please, but *she* knows, and *they* know, that the pit is there, and thousands are continually tumbling into it; and God has made *her* so sincere and direct, that she *must* describe the pit, in all its horrible and disgusting details. With a kind of moral desperation, she says, In God's name, let the truth come out, be the consequences what they may, to myself, or others. That is *my* version of George Sand. Did you ever see Elizabeth Browing's lines to her?[1]

. . .

ALS; Lydia Maria Child Papers, Anti-Slavery Collection, Cornell University (microfiche 38/1062).

To Convers Francis

Wayland, August 8th, 1858.

My Very Dear Brother— It is somewhat difficult to answer your letter, because you start with the determination not to believe me, unless I endorse your own estimate of yourself. You declare that you "have been nothing and done nothing to excuse you for living," and you add: "You know this is true,

---

[1] Two sonnets to George Sand are in Elizabeth Barrett Browning's *Poems* (London, 1844).

and you know that *you* think so." Now the simple fact is, I do *not* think so. But how to make you believe it,—that is the question. I think you have done a vast amount of good in many ways. Your conversation always tends to enlarge and liberalize the minds with which you come in contact; many times I have heard people speak of the good your sympathizing words have done them in times of affliction; and for myself I can say most truly, before God, that I consider such intellectual culture, as I have, mainly attributable to your influence; and most sincerely can I say, moreover, that up to this present hour, I prize a chance for communion with your mind more than I do with any other person I know.

I am not what I aspired to be in my days of young ambition; but I have become humble enough to be satisfied with the conviction that what I have written has always been written conscientiously; that I have always spoken with sincerity if not with power. In every direction I see young giants rushing past me, and I am glad to see such strong laborers to plough the land and sow the seed for coming years.

As I have before said, I, as well as yourself, inherit a tendency to despondency, and we ought to doctor it as we would any other disease. I have thought it likely in your case, the hereditary tendency might be increased by the physical effects of tobacco. To break off suddenly from the habit I fear might be injurious; therefore, I have wanted to supply some agreeable substitute for the powerful narcotic . . .[1]

I have tried of late years to adapt myself to the world as it is. I try to cheer, rather than to be cheered. If I have whereof to impart of inward or outward good, I do it with all my heart. To make people feel happy without violating the truth or compromising my own sincerity is the moral arithmetic of my life, and each time I work out a sum of this kind I find the product is my own happiness. So there is selfishness again! But if I must be, by reason of imperfect human nature, I gain something if I can form the habit of being influenced by an enlarged and enlightened kind of selfishness.

. . .

Good night, dear brother. I love and respect you very deeply and truly and am always

Your sympathizing sister,
Maria.

L, extract; Maria S. Porter, "Lydia Maria Child," *National Magazine: An Illustrated American Monthly* 14 (May 1901): 165–66 (microfiche 96/2541).

---

[1] These ellipses are in the source.

To Sarah Shaw

Wayland, Dec. 1st, 1858.

Dear Sarah,

. . .

You ask me to tell you what I think of Sarah Page's letter.[1] I really don't know what to think. I am in a perfect miz-maze about it. That Page's Philadelphia experience, and his thoughtless neglect in Italy, should have thrown the young creature into the arms of another love, I could readily imagine, and as readily forgive. But to live with the Italian and *not* love him, is more difficult to comprehend, and *far* more difficult to excuse. If she hypocritically *assumes* to have loved Page through the whole of it, she is an incredible fool; for it makes the case much worse for her.

I can easily conceive that her husband's indifference might have made life very insupportable to her, especially after those troublesome girls were added to the burden. But why did she not return to her relatives in America? Why go and live with another man, if she loved Page all the while? Yet there seems to be no room to doubt that she *did* live with the Italian. It is a bewildering statement. Her sister, in her letters, has all along taken the same ground that Sarah does; viz: that she is a victim, and has been most unjustly dealt by. Certainly, I did not think that Page has acted either conscientiously or kindly by the young creature. Since the imperiousness of passion made him *insist* upon taking one so unsuited to him, he ought to have been tender and careful of her youth and beauty. The affair has decidedly diminished my respect for *him*. With regard to *her*, I halt between two opinions. In my letter to her, I confined myself to affectionate allusions to former years, and expressions of sympathy for the *suffering* she had passed through. When I answer her letter, I intend to ask plainly how it is possible to love one man, and live with another. Since she has opened the subject herself, I think I have a right to ask that explanation.

. . . How did you like Miles Standish' Courtship?[2] For my own part I can find no poetry either in the measure, or the thoughts. The *one* poetic image, comparing aged men to snow-capped mountains nearest heaven, was borrowed from Robinson. It is wonderful what may be accomplished by prestige for a *name!* If David had written that book nobody would have dreamed of calling it a poem. The *measure* I should always dislike, however skilfully managed; because it seems to me to take away the freedom of prose without impart-

[1] Sarah Page had become William Page's second wife in 1843. She accompanied the artist and his young daughters to Italy but left him for another man, Count Cerelli. Abandoned by Cerelli, she returned to the United States.
[2] Henry Wadsworth Longfellow, *The Courtship of Miles Standish* (Boston, 1858).

ing the gracefulness of poetry. But this Miles Standish is a lamentable falling off from Evangeline, both in the beauty of the thoughts, and the *manufacture* of the verse.

. . .

ALS; Houghton Library, Harvard University (microfiche 39/1087).

To Sarah Shaw

Wayland, Jan. 12th, 1859

My precious friend,

. . .

I have buckled to Buckle.[1] It is so remarkable a book, and the spirit of man is so large and free, that I foresee I shall be obliged to read it through. His theories make me uncomfortable; the more so, because I have, for the last ten years, been struggling hard against a tendency to believe in Fate. When I look back upon my own experience, when I set to thinking how I can extricate myself from a situation extremely uncongenial to me, and which I feel is killing my soul, I find that I have been, and am, so overborne and trampled upon by external circumstances, that I really feel as if I had no volition. Then that idea that *material* influences form and fashion the *soul!* It seems to me so inside out, that it keeps my poor brain all of a twist. But it is a great book, and will have prodigious influence on all future historians. I think he forces his facts a little, sometimes, to sustain his theories; but the book is an invaluable store-house of facts and suggestions. He's an original thinker, any how; and a candid and free one also. Did you read the lines in the Liberator, two or three weeks ago, entitled "Buckle's Belief"? They were in the National Era, also. Speaking of newspapers, are you not vexed and disgusted with the Tribune? That any republican, while Charles Sumner is alive, or remembered, should allow himself, for one moment, to think of supporting that damnable Douglass for the Presidency![2] There is nothing I abhor like politics. I believe the Devil has no other snare to be compared to it, for drawing honest souls out of a straight-forward line into all manner of serpent-like sinuosities.

. . .

. . . [T]he phenomona of spiritualism can *not* be accounted for by the supposition of imposture, or self-delusion. "There are more things 'twixt heaven and earth, than are dreamt of in our philosophy." Yet the whole thing is extremely tantalizing and unsatisfactory. It *cannot* be trusted, and it is *well* that it cannot. We should become mere passive machines, if spirits told us just what

---

[1] Henry Thomas Buckle, *History of the Civilization of England*, vol. 1 (London, 1857).
[2] Sen. Stephen A. Douglas, unsuccessful contender for the Democratic presidential nomination in 1852 and 1856, was now working for the 1860 nomination.

to do and what to believe. We were sent here on purpose to work in the dark; by faith, and not by sight. Our education for eternity would be marred if Superior Intelligence did our work *for* us. When I see some people so ready to regulate their daily affairs, and their religious opinions, by the tipping of tables, I see how well it is that falsehoods and tricks should throw doubt over the whole subject. Have you seen the book of 'Communications from J. Q. Adams.' J. Q. Adams, Gen. Washington, Napoleon, &c. all write in the same florid style, like the very ambitious composition of a smart school girl.

The first thing that troubled my implicit faith in Swedenborg was that all the spirits he met talked on the same *subjects* and in the same *manner*. The manner was *his own,* and the subjects were those which engrossed his own mind. I have perfect reliance on the honesty of Swedenborg. I believe he really saw and heard all that he *says* he saw and heard. But I feel sure that in many cases he simply *saw* his own mind. In transcendental phrase, the *sub*jective became *ob*jective, by the abstraction and extreme tension of his thought.

. . .

AL; Houghton Library, Harvard University (microfiche 40/1092).

To Sarah Shaw

Wayland, Feb. 11th, 1859.

My Darling Sarah,

. . .

I have finished Buckle; and, contrary to my usual practice, I have read every line of it. I was delighted with it. I never read a book that so much extended my mental vision. The simplicity and directness of the style is refreshing in these days of inverted sentences, obsolete words, and parentheses within parentheses. How I do hate their "peacock trains, and swell of ostentation"! Buckle seems to have but one object, ⟨and that is⟩ in *his* choice of expressions, and that is, how most clearly to convey his idea to the mind of the reader. I resisted continually the theory that gives *all* the credit of human progress to the developement of the *intellect*. Intellect and the moral sense continually go hand in hand. It is as difficult to separate them, as to separate light and heat. It was *moral feeling* which excited Howard to examine into the condition of prisons; and it was to the *moral feeling* of others that he appealed; then *statistics* were brought in, to sustain his appeal. Slavery was abolished in England by rousing the *moral feelings* of the people; and under that stimulus, they collected *facts* to convince the *intellect*. Nations that have subsequently abolished it have done it more from *policy*, being convinced by the facts and arguments arrayed in the British struggle; but those weapons would never have been ready for general use, if they had not been heated in the fire of the British *heart*.

Buckle says truly that intellect grows continually, while moral principles are precisely the same they were thousands of years ago. True the *principles* are the same, but the *application* of those principles is continually growing wider. At one period, intellect applies them to the treatment of prisoners, at another to the treatment of the insane, of slaves, sailors, women. But in all these cases intellect is excited to action by *moral feeling*. Probably Buckle embraces more than the *general* significance in his understanding of the word *intellect;* if he does not, there is a strange fallacy in his theory, for such a large deep thinker. It seems to me that Hegel, in his Philosophy of History uses a better word. He calls the motive-power of the universe *spirit.*

David has been, for this fortnight past, immersed in a Memorial to the Legislature about our meadows, drowned by the effects of the Cochituate Reservoirs, which pour 18,000,000 gallons of water a day upon us, destroying the valuable produce of the acres, causing rheumatism, fevers, &c. The meadows look beautifully now; a great expanse of unsoiled snow, with lakelets of ice, which gleam silver bright in the moonlight, and glow like wine under the farewell glances of the sun. But oh, how I do long to see *Southern* scenery! If I were a man, I would take my valise in hand, ⟨and⟩ go to Savannah next week, and, for a few days change snow and ice for Jessamines and orange-blossoms. It seems a shame to go out of the world without seeing any more of it than the head of a pin. But being a woman, I must submit to imprisonment. Luckily, I can *read* about all the universe; and that is a great thing to be thankful for. . . .

. . .

ALS; Houghton Library, Harvard University (microfiche 40/1102).

7

October 1859-1861

When John Brown's band of twenty-two men attacked Harpers Ferry on 16 October 1859, attempting to seize the federal arsenal and free slaves, the news stunned the nation. Taken prisoner by government troops, the wounded Brown was asked, "Upon what principle do you justify your acts?" He replied, "Upon the golden rule; I pity the poor in bondage that have none to help them; that is why I am here; not to gratify any personal animosity, revenge or vindictive spirit. It is my sympathy with the oppressed and wronged, that are as good as you and as precious in the sight of God. . . . You all have a heavy responsibility, and it behooves you to prepare more than it does me. . . . You may dispose of me easily, but this question is still to be settled—this Negro question—the end of that is not yet."*

The South was appalled and infuriated by Brown's deed. Did it mean that the North was now ready to take arms against slavery? Child opposed the raid for its violence and folly but honored Brown for his disinterested and courageous sacrifice to free others. For decades the abolitionists had fought against slavery by peaceful, constitutional means. But with the passage of the Fugitive Slave Law of 1850, many moved to defy the law and used force to free captured runaways. In Kansas thousands had fired guns to ensure that the territory should come into the Union free. And now Brown, the best-known freedom fighter in Kansas, who had long been convinced that moral appeals to the South were futile, had chosen the path of armed insurrection to liberate the slaves.

Harpers Ferry hurled Child into action. She did all she could to aid Brown, his family, and the men captured with him. "Before this affair," she said, "I thought I was growing old and drowsy; but now I am as strong as an eagle" (27 November 1859). And reaching out to rally public opinion, she published four pamphlets within the year.

When Congress met a few days after Brown went to the scaffold on 2 December, it was clear that public opinion had been revolutionized. Antislavery and proslavery men came to their legislative desks armed. As the 1860 presi-

---

* Louis Ruchames, ed., *A John Brown Reader* (New York, 1959), pp. 121, 124.

dential campaign began, the line dividing the country burned deeper. While some Northerners tried to be conciliatory, voices from the slave states cried secession. If an antislavery Republican were elected, said prominent Southerners, it would be cause for breaking up the Union. Lincoln became the Republican choice. He appealed for sectional understanding but warned that there could be no compromise with principle on the issue of stopping the spread of slavery. Both the candidate and the party were sharply criticized by many abolitionists because neither was for the immediate and total abolition of slavery. When Lincoln won, every state in the deep South took steps toward secession, and in April 1861 the Civil War began.

For Child, fifty-seven years old at the time of Brown's martyrdom, the next bloody years, while full of grief and pain, would be a time of renewal. "I feel as if every day were lost, in which I do not try to do *something* to hasten emancipation" (26 October 1860).

In the months that followed John Brown's raid, Child's thoughts were given to the fate of the prisoners and to an assessment of how the event might affect the struggle over slavery. Although Brown had seized federal property, the Virginia governor, Henry A. Wise, took state jurisdiction on the ground that the raiders had violated Virginia's soil and killed her citizens. Brown and the other captives, held in prison in Charlestown, were swiftly indicted for murder, conspiracy with slaves to rebel, and treason against the state of Virginia. Brown's trial began 27 October, the day after Child wrote both to him and to Governor Wise.

To John Brown

Mass'ts, Wayland, Oct 26th, 1859.

Dear Capt Brown,

Though personally unknown to you, you will recognize in my name an earnest friend of Kansas, when circumstances made that Territory the battle-ground between the antagonistic principles of slavery and freedom, which politicians so vainly strive to reconcile in the government of the U.S.

Believing in peace principles, I cannot sympathize with the method you chose to advance the cause of freedom. But I honor your generous intentions, I admire your courage, moral and physical, I reverence you for the humanity which tempered your zeal, I sympathize with your cruel bereavements, your sufferings, and your wrongs.[1] In brief, I love you and bless you.

Thousands of hearts are throbbing with sympathy as warm as mine. I think of you night and day, bleeding in prison, surrounded by hostile faces, sustained only by trust in God, and your own strong heart. I long to nurse you, to speak to you sisterly words of sympathy and consolation. I have asked permission of

---

[1] Two of Brown's sons, Oliver and Watson, died in the raid. A third, Owen, escaped.

Gov. Wise to do so. If the request is not granted, I cherish the hope that these few words may, at least, reach your hands, and afford you some little solace. May you be strengthened by the conviction that no honest man ever sheds his blood for freedom in vain, however much he may be mistaken in his efforts. May God sustain you, and carry you through whatsoever may be in store for you!

Yours with heartfelt respect, sympathy, and affection,

L. Maria Child.

ALS; John Brown Collection, Manuscript Division, Kansas State Historical Society (microfiche 41/1123).

To Henry Alexander Wise

Wayland, Mass., Oct. 26th, 1859.

Governor Wise:

I have heard that you were a man of chivalrous sentiments,[1] and I know you were opposed to the iniquitous attempt to force upon Kansas a constitution abhorrent to the moral sense of her people. Relying upon these indications of honor and justice in your character, I venture to ask a favor of you. Enclosed is a letter to Capt. John Brown. Will you have the kindness, after reading it yourself, to transmit it to the prisoner?

I and all my large circle of abolition acquaintances were taken by surprise when news came of Capt. Brown's recent attempt; nor do I know of a single person who would have approved of it had they been apprised of his intention. But I and thousands of others feel a natural impulse of sympathy for the brave and suffering man. Perhaps God, who sees the inmost of our souls, perceives some such sentiment in your heart also. He needs a mother or sister to dress his wounds, and speak soothingly to him. Will you allow me to perform that mission of humanity? If you will, may God bless you for the generous deed!

I have been for years an uncompromising abolitionist, and I should scorn to deny it or apologize for it as much as John Brown himself would do. Believing in peace principles, I deeply regret the step that the old veteran has taken, while I honor his humanity towards those who became his prisoners. But because it is my habit to be as open as the daylight, I will also say that if I believed our religion justified men in fighting for freedom, I should consider the enslaved everywhere as best entitled to that right. Such an avowal is a simple, frank expression of my sense of natural justice.

But I should despise myself utterly if any circumstances could tempt me to seek to advance these opinions in any way, directly or indirectly, after your

[1] Wise, after talking with Brown, had expressed respect for him, calling him "a man of clear head, of courage, fortitude. . . . He is a fanatic . . . but firm and truthful and intelligent." Speech of 21 October 1859, quoted in Oswald Garrison Villard, *John Brown* (New York, 1943), p. 455.

permission to visit **Virginia** has been obtained on the plea of sisterly sympathy with a brave and suffering man. I give you my word of honor, which was never broken, that I would use such permission solely and singly for the purpose of nursing your prisoner, and for no other purpose whatsoever.[2]

Yours respectfully,
L. Maria Child.

L; *Correspondence between Lydia Maria Child, Gov. Wise and Mrs. Mason, of Virginia* (Boston, 1860), pp. 3–4 (microfiche 41/1125).

To William Lloyd Garrison

Wayland Oct. 28th, 1859.

Dear Friend Garrison,

. . .

My thoughts are so much with Capt. John Brown, that I can scarcely take comfort in anything. I would expend all I have, to save his life. Brave old man! Brave and generous, though sadly mistaken in his mode of operation. Whether they put him to death, or he escapes from their hands, I think this will prove the "Concord *Fight*" of an impending revolution, and that "Bunker Hill *Battle*" will surely follow. May God make us strong for freedom! I would say that evil days were near, were it not that *no* days are evil, which lead to good.

What do you think of the policy of continually pasting something on Webster's statue, calculated to rouse the moral sense of the people?[1] Or perhaps it might be better to hang printed placards about his neck, and renew them soon after the authorities took them away. . . .

. . .

I should like to see some such caustic rebukes hung on his hollow breast every week, till the abomination is taken down.

Give my most affectionate greetings to your wife and daughter, in which David cordially unites.

Yours with affectionate respect,
L. M. Child.

ALS; Sophia Smith Collection, Smith College (microfiche 41/1126).

[2] When Governor Wise replied, on 29 Oct. 1859, he said that he could not prevent her coming, but warned that community feeling made it unsafe. He blamed her and the abolitionists for Brown's raid, calling it "a natural consequence of your sympathy, and the errors of that sympathy ought to make you doubt its virtue from the effect on his conduct" (Massachusetts Historical Society).

[1] The statue, placed in front of the Massachusetts State House in Boston, was an affront to the abolitionists, who had detested Webster ever since his speech in support of the Fugitive Slave Law. Webster died in 1852.

To John Brown

Dear Capt. Brown,

I received your friendly letter, and its contents touched me deeply.[1] If you had wanted me, I would have come to you; but since you think I can serve you better here, I thankfully accept the mission you propose. Feel no anxiety about your family. They will be abundantly cared for. I have no need to ask any one to contribute for that purpose. Those who read your letter to me offer before I have a chance to ask. I have lying by me six letters, from strangers, by this evening's mail, all desirous to contribute. A Mr. Bullard of Waterford, N.Y. pledges $100 a year, for five years, to educate your children. It made the tears come to my eyes, that you should make such a very modest request to me personally. Be assured that I will give annually, during my life, much more than the small sum you ask of me. Effectual measures are being taken, by the friends of the enslaved, to form a fund for the comfortable support of your family. [. . .]self,[2] such ability and influence [as I?] have shall be cordially devoted to [your?] service.

An orthodox clergyman, named Hudson, called to see me the other day. He said his mother was your cousin. He had some very interesting anecdotes to tell concerning your sober, thoughtful boyhood, and the sympathy you early manifested for the poor and the abused. Verily, God gave you a great heart!

My friend Mrs. Spring, has written me a highly interesting account [of?] the solemn pleasure she felt in her interview with you.[3] I am glad they allowed you to see her; for a friendly face within the walls of a prison must be as pleasant as the sunshine.

I suppose "the humane gentleman," whose family do for you "all that your situation requires," is the jailer.[4] Give him my thanks, and tell him should hours of adversity come to him or his, I trust they will never want for a friend.   Alas! would that the plague-spot were removed from this fair land, so that North and South, black and white, could serve each other with mutual good will! What is in store for us I know not. But we are indeed a guilty nation. Guilty toward the Indians, toward the negroes, toward all that are weak and within our power.

I trust God will enable me to do my whole duty on the subject of this great wrong existing among us. In these sad days, I consecrate myself with renewed earnestness to this service. I care not who frowns, or who smiles upon me, if power is given me to be faithful to my own conscience.

---

[1] Brown's reply said that he was recovering and being well cared for. He asked her to help raise funds to aid his wife and children, and the families of the men taken with him.
[2] The writing is faded; one or two words are missing.
[3] Rebecca Spring, wife of Marcus Spring, the philanthropist, visited Brown in jail.
[4] John Avis, the jailer, a Charlestown native, admired Brown's courage and gave him kindly care.

How I rejoice in you, because you remain so calm and stedfast in the midst of your great tribulations! A moral influence goes forth from this, better than anything the world calls success.

Please give my respectful, heart-felt sympathy to Mr. Stevens.[5] I should have sent this message in my former letter, if I had known that he occupied the same cell with you. I think of you and your companions in misfortune almost continually; and in the silent watches of the night, I often pray that the Heavenly Father may send his angels to comfort and sustain you. Your sufferings are not in vain, either for yourselves, or for the age in which you live. From your prison a mighty influence is going forth, throughout the length and breadth of the land. God works in a mysterious way, and blessed are they, who put their trust in Him.

My husband, David Lee Child, who was introduced to you in 1857, sends to you his most respectful sympathy.[6] Farewell, brave and generous man!

Your true and sympathizing friend, L. Maria Child.

ALS; Charles Aldrich Papers, Historical Museum and Archives, Iowa State Historical Department (microfiche 42/1135).

Thaddeus Hyatt of New York, who had been president of the National Kansas Committee, would later serve three months in a District of Columbia jail for refusing to testify before a Senate committee investigating Harpers Ferry.

To Thaddeus Hyatt

Wayland, Nov. 17, 1859

Mr. Hyatt:—Dear Sir:—I think your plan of raising a fund (for the relief of the family of John Brown) by photographs is excellent, and I have no doubt it will be very successful. I enclose $2.00. I should like to have every form of his likeness that can be devised, and have no corner of my dwelling without a memorial of him. The brave, self-sacrificing, noble old man.

Yours respectfully,
L. Maria Child.

L, transcript; Simison Papers, Beinecke Rare Book and Manuscript Library, Yale University (microfiche 42/1137).

[5] Aaron Dwight Stevens (1831–60), then twenty-eight years old, had joined Brown in Kansas. He was wounded in the raid on Harpers Ferry.
[6] In 1857 Brown had visited Boston to gain more support for the struggle in Kansas. He met with many members of the Massachusetts Kansas Committee, for which David Lee Child had done much work. On Brown's return to Kansas he had written to David Child.

To J. Peter and Susan (Lyman) Lesley

Medford, Nov. 20th, 1859

Dearly Beloved Peter and Susie,

I meant to have written sooner to thank you for remembering the picture I wanted; but I have been so taken up with receiving letters and answering letters connected with the present exciting state of things, that I have been unable to find time.   You know Miss Lucy Osgood has lost the sister who had been the companion of her whole life. I have been here for the last eight days, hoping to make the old homestead a little less desolate for her.   But here or elsewhere, I can think and talk of nothing but Capt. John Brown. How unexpected this developement was, and how singularly it is being over-ruled for great good! In no possible way could *moral* influence on the subject have been so widely disseminated thro the whole length and breadth of the land. That short speech of Brown to the Court is a most effective anti-slavery document; and all the slave-holders will read it, and not a few of the slaves.[1] Whether they hang the noble old man, or keep him shut up in prison, he will continue to be a dangerous agitator. No peace and quietness for Slavery after this! In vain will politicians turn and twist every way to avoid being identified with the ever-increasing tide of public opinion! In vain will the clergy cry Peace! Peace! Henceforth, there is no peace.

I am astonished at the extent and degree of sympathy manifested for the brave old martyr. It is a remarkable example of the power of a great moral principle to overcome the worst disadvantages of external circumstances. To all outward appearance, all is defeat and ruin. Yet in reality what a glorious success! He is cursed, and scoffed at, and spit upon. Yet how the best intellects, and the largest hearts of the land, delight to do him honor! How will his name be reverenced in all coming time!   Mattie Griffith, writing to me about him, says: "What a splendid martyrdom it is! That scaffold will be as glorious as the Cross of Calvary. Never afterward let the gallows be regarded with odium; for by it a great soul goes to immortal glory."

My time and thoughts are now all taken up with helping to raise a fund for his family, and those of his companions in misfortune. It is taken up with great enthusiasm. I have no need to *ask*, everybody who takes any interest in

---

[1] After Brown was convicted he was allowed to make a statement before sentencing. On 2 Nov., he stood up in court and spoke for five minutes, saying, among other things, ". . . the New Testament . . . teaches me that all things whatsoever I would that men should do to me, I should do to them. It teaches me further to remember them that are in bonds, as bound with them. I endeavored to act up to that instruction. I say I am yet too young to understand that God is any respecter of persons. I believe that to have interfered as I have done in behalf of His despised poor, is no wrong, but right. Now, if it is deemed necessary that I should forfeit my life for the furtherance of the ends of justice, and mingle my blood with the blood of millions in this slave country whose rights are disregarded by wicked, cruel, and unjust enactments, I say let it be done" (Ruchames, *John Brown Reader*, p. 125).

free principles, hastens to *offer*. Hyatt's plan of raising $8000 by means of Photograph likenesses is an admirable one, and no doubt will prove highly successful.

. . .

I did contemplate writing a Biography of John Brown forthwith for the benefit of his family; but Redpath is going to do the same thing, so I withdraw.[2]

. . .

ALS; J. Peter Lesley Collection, American Philosophical Society (microfiche 42/1138).

To Parke Godwin

Wayland, Nov. 27th, 1859

Dear Friend,

I have a short Biography of Harriet Hosmer, containing many anecdotes, which I received from her father. I should think it would make about twenty magazine pages. I want to print it in some periodical that will pay me for it, upon the same terms that they pay their other well-known writers. Can you tell me of any in New York, that you think would like to have it?[1] I dont want anything to do with the Harpers, because they are pro-slavery.

I suppose you are feeling the same excitement that we all feel about old Capt. Brown. He is my last thought at night, my first in the morning. How futile are all their attempts to degrade him! If they execute him, they will merely render the gallows glorious. But *will* they execute him? *Nous verrons.*

What a wonderful instance it is of moral power conquering the most adverse circumstances! His failure is a most signal success; and all owing to the simple greatness of his own character! He speaks from an eminence none of us have reached, and he has the whole United States for an audience. Whether he lives or dies, he will shake that rotten institution to its foundation. If one believed in the transmigration of souls, it would really seem as if Cromwell had come back again. Didn't you laugh at the grim Puritan humour of his making those Border Ruffians pray, at the point of the rifle?

I am overwhelmed with letters of laudation from people in the Free States, and of the most *inconceivable* scurrility and abuse from the Slave States. I cannot understand what I have done to deserve either the one or the other. The publicity I have so unexpectedly acquired is no fault of mine. If Gov. Wise had not published the correspondence it would never have seen the light. I have to thank *him* for having gained for me a Southern audience.

Before this affair, I thought I was growing old and drowsy; but now I am as strong as an eagle.

[2] James Redpath (1833–91), a journalist, published in Boston, 1860, two works on his friend John Brown, *Echoes of Harpers Ferry* and *Public Life of Captain John Brown.*
[1] The *National Anti-Slavery Standard* of 6 Apr. 1861 reprinted Child's sketch of Hosmer from the *Cincinnati Ladies' Repository.*

I was delighted with your Resolutions at the Convention of the Republican Party.[2] They had the genuine ring of unadulterated metal. I was as proud as a peacock that the author was one of my friends.

Charles Sumner called to see me when I was in Boston, last week. I was rejoiced to see him looking so well and strong. He had not heard anything about John Brown until he arrived at Halifax, and was quite surprised when I told him he was an accomplice, and was about to be arrested. Greely met those threats in the best manner, by offering to go to Virginia at his own expense, in consideration of the low state of their treasury.

After all, I compassionate the people in Virginia; especially the women. If they could *only* see that their insecurity ⟨was⟩ is owing to the hateful institution they cherish so blindly! Slavery or Freedom *must* die; and the death-grapple is close at hand. God speed the right!

With cordial greetings to your family, I remain always your affectionate friend, L. Maria Child.

ALS; Manuscript Division, New York Public Library (microfiche 42/1140).

On 2 December 1859, the day of John Brown's execution, Northerners gathered in many cities to pay tribute. At the hour of his hanging, church bells tolled. Garrison, long an uncompromising believer in nonviolence, spoke at Boston's meeting in Tremont Temple. His words showed that Brown had converted him: "As a peace man, I am prepared to say, 'Success to every slave insurrection at the South and in every slave country.' . . . Rather than see men wearing their chains in a cowardly and servile spirit, I would, as an advocate of peace, much rather see them breaking the head of the tyrant with their chains."*

To Maria (Weston) Chapman

Wayland, Nov. 28th 1859.

Dear Friend,

. . .

. . . If it does not storm, I expect to go to Boston on Thursday, to help Garrison a little about the meeting he is getting up on Friday Evening, to commemorate Capt. Brown's execution. But *will* he be executed? Emerson writes to

[2] The Republican party's moderate and conservative leaders, including Abraham Lincoln, dissociated themselves from John Brown. Nominally antislavery, the party was officially opposed only to the extension of slavery into the new territories; it did not propose to act against slavery where it already existed. But to Southern planters, Lincoln was no different—after John Brown—from a Wendell Phillips.
* Villard, *John Brown*, p. 560.

me: "I have hopes for his brave life. He is one for whom miracles wait." And I confess I have a *little* of the same hope. Yet his death would be a magnificent martyrdom. What a success he has made of failure, by the moral grandeur of his own character! Whether he lives or dies, he has struck a blow at slavery, from the effects of which it will never recover.

Shall you not come to Boston, to attend the meeting on Friday? I wish it might be so. Then I should have an opportunity to see you, and have a talk. How *much* may happen between now and then! I long to be at the Telegraph Office every ten minutes. Sometimes I think the poor prisoners will all be lynched *before* the time. Sometimes I think they will be rescued, though I cannot imagine *how* it can be done. . . .[1]

ALS; Anti-Slavery Collection, Rare Books and Manuscripts, Boston Public Library (microfiche 42/1141).

Child's exchange of letters with Governor Wise was published in the *New York Tribune* on 12 November, to her surprise. Apparently Wise had released the correspondence to the press. Now made public, the letters evoked great response from both North and South. Among the replies was a furious letter from Margaretta Mason, wife of Virginia's senator James M. Mason, who had fathered the Fugitive Slave Law of 1850 and who joined Governor Wise in questioning Brown after his capture. Labelling Brown a murderer, Mrs. Mason called Child a hypocrite for wishing to give him sisterly care. She added that no Southerner should read a line of Child's writing or touch a magazine to which she had contributed, nor should any Northerner who deserved the name of woman.

Child's reply to Mason urged her to examine slavery dispassionately for the sake of the state's own prosperity and the welfare of both whites and blacks. Those in the North, she wrote, "as a portion of the Union, involved in the expense, the degeneracy, the danger, and the disgrace of this iniquitous and fatal system, have a right to speak about it and a right to be *heard* also." She noted that while the North freely published proslavery opinion, the South blotted out the other side. Would its press print her reply? That it would not proved "how little reliance you have on the strength of your cause. In this enlightened age, all despotisms ought to come to an end by the agency of moral and rational means. But if they resist such agencies, it is in the order of Providence that they must come to an end by violence. History is full of such lessons." Child laughed at Mrs. Mason's threat of boycott, for the South had largely

---

[1] There were schemes to rescue Brown from jail, one of them plotted by T. W. Higginson. But Brown rejected the plans, writing on 12 Nov. 1859, to "Dear Brother Jeremiah," "I am worth inconceivably more to *hang* than for any other purpose" (Ruchames, *John Brown Reader*, p. 134).

stopped reading her twenty-seven years before, after the *Appeal* was published.

When Mason's letter appeared in Virginia papers, Child sent the full correspondence to Greeley and other Northern editors. *The Liberator* printed the exchange on 31 December 1859. Early in 1860, the American Anti-Slavery Society published the Wise-Mason-Child letters in a pamphlet that achieved a sale of three hundred thousand copies, an enormous readership for that time and the greatest audience Child ever reached.

To Horace Greeley

Not to be published.

Wayland, Dec. 18th, 1859.

Mr. Greely,

I send you a letter from Mrs. Mason, first sent to me, and soon after published in the Virginia papers; also my reply to it.   I want you to publish them both together if you can; if not, to send it to the Evening Post, with the enclosed note to the Evening Post. But if you *do* publish it, destroy the note to the Post. I would not ask you to take the trouble if it were *my own* affair. But I am extremely anxious for the success of the Republican party; and I think such facts spread before the people are entering wedges for their arguments. The facts I quote are very familiar to you and I; but the people need "line upon line, and precept upon precept." Many do not *know* the facts, others need to be *reminded* of them.

I find many people curious to know the real *facts* about the Kansas struggle. Their minds are confused about it. Could I serve the Republican cause by making a Tract for distribution, giving the *prominent* facts in a very concise form?

Would it serve the cause, to make a similar Tract about the successive Aggressions of the South, going farther back than those I quoted in my Reply to Gov. Wise?

The crisis is so important that I feel a desire to call upon everybody, "[Those?][1] that have pens, prepare to use them now"!

Respectfully,
L. Maria Child.

. . .

ALS; Manuscript Division, New York Public Library (microfiche 42/1149).

[1] The writing is faint.

To Aaron Dwight Stevens

Wayland, Mass'ts, Dec. 19th, 1859

Dear Mr. Stevens,

Though you are personally a stranger to me, I address you thus, because you *are* dear to my soul, in common with all those who sacrifice themselves from a disinterested love of freedom. You are not left alone, though your companions in misfortune have gone to the spirit-world. God and his angels are with you; and thousands and thousands of hearts in the Free States are earnestly praying for you, that you may be sustained and strengthened to bear whatever may be in store for you. My principal object in writing now is to ask whether you have wife, or children, or mother, for whom you wish us to do anything; and whether those who have gone left families that need assistance; especially the *colored* men.[1] Poor victims of their generous zeal for their persecuted and down-trodden race! Also, I should like to know if anything can be done for you, to render your situation more comfortable, in any respect. If you answer, perhaps it will be better to enclose it to Mrs. Spring, to whom you have already written. *My* name might perhaps be the occasion of stopping the letter; for though I am by nature very averse to conflict with my fellow beings, God has given me the strength of ten, wherever questions of oppression are concerned. With respectful sympathy, your friend

L. Maria Child.

. . .

ALS; Stevens Family Papers, Massachusetts Historical Society (microfiche 42/1152).

To Oliver Johnson

Private.

Wayland, Dec. 20th, 1859

Friend Oliver,

. . .

As soon as you get reliable information about the murder of Doyle, I hope you will lay it before the readers of the Standard.[1] The statement of the enemy about it checks admiration and sympathy in many minds.

[1] Of the five blacks in Brown's band, one escaped, two were killed in action, and two were hanged by Virginia.

[1] James P. Doyle was one of five proslavery men killed at Pottawatomie Creek in Kansas on 23 May 1856, immediately after Missourians had sacked and burned Lawrence. Brown, with four of his sons, his son-in-law, and two others, was responsible for the killings. Although he justified the murders as avenging the deaths of Free-Soilers, he kept his role secret from the public and from his New England supporters. The South was now levelling the charge of murder in Kansas against Brown, in an attempt to destroy his image as a martyr. Not knowing the facts, Child and other abolitionists hoped to prove his innocence. Johnson was at this time editing the *National Anti-Slavery Standard.*

With regard to the Fund for Brown's family, I earnestly hope the *other* sufferers will not be overlooked; especially the *colored* men. Perhaps some of them have left wives, children, or mothers, destitute.

How mean in the Virginians to make a difference in the *coffins* of their white and colored victims! If I were John Brown's widow, I would send back his coffin, with word that his noble spirit would not rest while his body was better housed than his colored associates.[2]

Very cordially your friend, L. Maria Child.

ALS; Child Papers, Clements Library, University of Michigan (microfiche 42/1153).

At the time of this letter to him, Sydney Howard Gay (1814–88) was on the staff of the *New York Tribune*. He had edited the *National Anti-Slavery Standard* from 1844 to 1857.

To Sydney Howard Gay

Wayland, Dec. 21st, 1859.

Mr. Gay,
    Dear Friend,
        In the first place, I never write for a periodical that restricts my liberty on *any* subject. I have never been put into harness, and I never will, while there's a Poor House in the land to resort to, in my old age.

In the second place, the thing I detest most, next to Slavery, is Calvinism. I consider its moral influence most decidedly pernicious. On *that* subject, and I believe it is the *only* one, I am intolerant. But from regard to principles of freedom, I never *publish* my intolerance. I consider that I deserve great credit [. . .][1] effort; for their doctrines are as disagreeable to me as the smoke of brimstone in my eyes.   In the third place, I do not altogether like the course of the Independent. It has a strange amalgamation of editors. And what does Henry Ward Beecher himself mean by treating W. L. Garrison as he has done? and superciliously wishing that Theodore Parker was a Christian? And sending rifles to Kansas, and then denying that the *slaves* have a right to insurrection? I should like to know who *has* a right to fight, if the *slaves* have not?

There you have, in brief, my reasons for not wishing to write for the Independent. To Mr. Tilton you may give the enclosed.

With a cordial greeting to Mrs. Gay, [. . .]

[2] Brown's body had been placed in a coffin and shipped to his widow, who buried him at North Elba, N.Y., on 8 Dec. The bodies of some of the others executed may have been placed in packing cases and buried in the woods.
[1] A line of writing is missing where the page was cut off for the signature on the verso.

[. . .] I have merely declined to write on the ground of the injustice of the Independent toward Mr. Garrison. He has fought the battle of freedom too long to be treated contemptuously by new recruits, coming in when the battle is half won.

AL; Special Manuscript Collection, Columbia University (microfiche 42/1154).

To William Lloyd Garrison

[Before 23 December 1859]

Who would not rather be John Brown, and have his memory cherished with such tender gratitude by the poor and the oppressed, than to have his brazen statue[1] set up in front of the State House, a reward for hunting slaves?

I agree with the colored man, in thinking that John Brown was a 'misguided philanthropist.'[2] But no one who believes war to be right under *any* circumstances, is authorized so to judge him. If we justify *any* men in fighting against oppression, how can we deny that right to men whose wives are constantly at the disposal of their master, or his sons, and whose children are torn from them and sold on the auction block, while they have no redress at law, and are shot down like dogs, if they dare to resist? It is very inconsistent to eulogise Lafayette for volunteering to aid in *our* fight for freedom, while we blame John Brown for going to the rescue of those who are a thousand times more oppressed than we ever were, and who have none to help them. Let us understand our principles well in this matter, and deal even-handed justice in our estimate of actions.

We who believe that all fighting with carnal weapons is contrary to the teachings of Jesus, do think that John Brown made a grievous mistake; but while we deeply regret the means he employed to advance righteous principles, we cannot withhold a heartfelt tribute of respect to the generous motives and self-sacrificing spirit of the brave old martyr.

Instead of blaming him for carrying out his own convictions by means we cannot sanction, it would be more profitable for us to inquire of ourselves whether we, who believe in a 'more excellent way,' have carried our convictions into practice, as faithfully as he did *his*. *We* believe in *moral influence* as a cure for the diseases of society. Have we exerted it as constantly and as strenuously as we ought against the giant wrong, that is making wreck of all the free institutions our fathers handed down to us as a sacred legacy? Do we bear our testimony against it in the parlor and the store, the caucus and the conference, on the highway and in the cars? Do we stamp upon the impressible minds of our children a deep conviction of its inherent wickedness and consequent danger?

[1] The statue was of Daniel Webster.
[2] Child was commenting on a letter from Samuel Jackson, identified in *The Liberator* as a "colored man from Ohio."

Do we exclude the ravening monster from our churches, as we ought to do? Do we withhold respect from ministers, who are silent concerning this mighty iniquity? Do we brand with ignominy the statesmen, who make compromises with the foul sin, for their own emolument? Nay, verily! We erect statues to them. And because *we* have thus failed to perform our duty in the 'more excellent way,' the end cometh by violence; because come it *must*.

Let him who is without sin in this matter cast the first stone at the gray head of that honest old Puritan, John Brown!

He believed, more earnestly than most of us do, that it was a religious duty to 'remember those in bonds as bound with them;' and he verily thought it was serving God to fight in a righteous cause. Therefore, shall his memory be forever enshrined in the grateful hearts of a down-trodden race, and command the respect of all true friends of justice and freedom.

In the midst of awful tribulations, his sublime faith in God lifted him above all need of our compassion. Leaning on the Almighty arm, he passed triumphantly through the valley of the shadow of death, smiling serenely, as he said, 'I don't know as I can better serve the cause I love so well, than to die for it.'

Farewell to thee, faithful old hero and martyr! The Recording Angel will blot out thy error with a tear, because it was committed with an honest heart.

L. M. C.

L; *The Liberator*, 23 Dec. 1859 (microfiche 43/1158).

Mary Ann Day (1816–84), at the age of sixteen, married John Brown after the death of his first wife. She bore him thirteen children; seven died in childhood and two were killed at Harpers Ferry. She was allowed a visit with Brown in jail the day before his execution.

To Mary Ann Brown

Wayland, Dec. 23d, 1859

Mrs. Brown,

My dear Friend,

Among the many eloquent things that have been said concerning the great and good man, who has gone from us, nothing has touched my feelings more than the letters I have received from colored people in various parts of the country. You will see, in this week's Liberator one from a colored man in Ohio. A fortnight ago, there was one in the Tribune, from a colored man in Canada, saying that all the Fugitives there wanted to give their "mite" toward a fund for John Brown's family. At the meeting-house in Southac St. Boston, I heard an old black man pour forth his soul in prayer to God, on the solemn 2d of Dec.

about half past 11 o'clock.[1] His speech was rude; for the pride and oppression of his white brethren had given him no chance for mental culture, but there was touching eloquence in the manner in which he prayed for *you;* that the Lord would comfort you, and hold you up, and make clear to you the mysterious ways of his Providence. He told the ⟨the⟩ Lord that he had "been a slave, and knew how *bitter* it was"; and he ejaculated, in fervent tones, "Since it has pleased Thee to take away our Moses, Oh, Lord God, raise us up a Joshua!" to which all the audience responded with a loud "Amen!"

Miss Frances Ellen Watkins, a colored woman of great intelligence, who has lectured, and written some very clever poetry, wrote to me last November: "I thank you for your sympathy with that dear old man, who reached out his brave and generous hand to the crushed and blighted of my race. I thank him in the name of bleeding humanity, of injured childhood, of young girls sold from mothers' arms to the clutches of libertines. Thank God! that in an age, which bears such a prolific crop of cowards, a few men have been found brave enough to die for a principle. Will you please to send me a lock of the dear old man's hair, that I may preserve it as the most precious souvenir of my life?"[2]

I replied to Miss Watkins that if I ever *procured* a lock of his hair, she should have half of it. I have tried to procure some, but have not succeeded. Could you, my dear Mrs. Brown, without robbing relatives and friends, who have nearer claims, send me a little?

It would be extremely precious to me; for apart from my respect for your noble husband, as the brave advocate of freedom, and the self-sacrificing friend of the oppressed, I owe him personal gratitude for what his example has done for my own soul. Since he was offered up, I have consecrated myself with renewed zeal to the righteous cause he loved so well; and I see indications of the same influence on multitudes of minds in all parts of the Free States. Letters to that effect come pouring in upon me from all quarters; from Minnesota to Maine. He will prove the greatest benefactor the colored race have ever had.

Eight or ten days ago, I transmitted in a letter to you, $10 from one of your husband's friends. Did you receive it?

Yours with affectionate respect and heartfelt sympathy,

L. Maria Child.

ALS; Baker Library, Dartmouth College (microfiche 43/1159).

[1] Child attended a prayer meeting in a black church.
[2] Frances Ellen (Watkins) Harper (1825–1911), the daughter of free black parents in Baltimore, began publishing her poetry in 1845. In 1854 she became a lecturer, combining antislavery talks with readings from her poems. By the late 1850s, she was the best-known black poet since Phillis Wheatley. She gave much of her income to aiding fugitive slaves.

Sarah Maria (Preston) Parsons (1822–98), Child's niece, was the daughter of Warren and Mary (Francis) Preston. Married to Henry Parsons, she resided mainly in Brooklyn, New York.

To Sarah Parsons

Wayland, Dec. 25th, 1859.

My dear Niece,

I thank you very cordially for your affectionate letter, and I am right glad you and your husband were so much pleased with my doings. Recent events have renewed my youth and strength. I am full of electricity; and any proslavery hand that touches me receives a torpedo shock.

What a sublime martyrdom was that of old John Brown! There was nothing wanting in the *details* of his conduct. There was a grand simplicity and harmony throughout. I reverenced him for refusing to be prayed over by slave-holding priests; and how my heart jumped toward him, when I read of his kissing the little colored child, on his way to the gallows![1]

. . .

The 16th of December was more *painful* to me, than the 2d.[2] Those other victims were young, and wanted to live; and they had not so many manifestations of sympathy to sustain them, as their grand old leader had. If Brown had not taken the Arsenal, but had simply taken off such slaves as wanted to go, as he did in Missouri, and had died for *that*, I should be more completely satisfied with his martyrdom. But he liked Old Testament heroes better than I do. He had his mind filled with the idea of founding "A City of Refuge"; and since he acted according to his own conscientious convictions, I have no disposition to blame him, though I wish it had been otherwise. . . .

I had a note from Mary last night. She was just recovering from one of her bad neuralgic head-aches. Her sympathy with these sufferers has almost worried her down. George was at home, in excellent health.[3]

---

[1] This legend sprang up overnight and was perpetuated by a popular lithograph. But no child was held up for Brown's kiss: the street was blocked off by soldiers.
[2] On 16 Dec. four other raiders were hanged: John E. Cook, Edwin Coppoc, Shields Green, and John Copeland, Jr.
[3] The references are to Child's niece, Mary (Preston) Stearns, and her husband, George Luther Stearns (1809–67). Stearns was one of the "Secret Six" who gave money to finance Brown's raid (the others were T. W. Higginson, Samuel Gridley Howe, Theodore Parker, Frank Sanborn, and Gerrit Smith). Worried by the discovery of papers which implicated them as accessories, and desiring to avoid arrest, Stearns, Howe, and Sanborn fled to Canada, returning home after Brown's execution. Later in February, Stearns would testify before a Senate committee headed by Mason of Virginia and proclaim, "I believe John Brown to be the representative man of this century, as Washington was of the last" (Villard, *John Brown*, p. 534). None of the six was indicted.

Uncle David unites with me in cordial greeting to you and your husband.
Your affectionate Aunt Maria.

ALS; Lydia Maria Child Papers, Anti-Slavery Collection, Cornell University (microfiche 43/1165).

To Charles Sumner

Wayland, Dec. 26th 1859.

Dear Mr. Sumner,
God bless you! and preserve you in strong health. Of all *other* kinds of strength, I feel sure. And you never will know what a blessing it is to my soul to have *somebody* to swear by.

I am vexed, vexed at heart, by the timidity of the Republican Party.[1] When *will* they learn that success depends upon bravery? Upon sinking all minor considerations, personal and sectional, and standing *firmly* in one *united* phalanx, against the monster that is sucking our life-blood? Will they *never* learn that the more the North cringes, the more the South will trample on her?

All the moral power is on our side; and we could not fail to conquer, if we only used it manfully. The slave holders have nothing but audacity to rely upon. I have had several epistles from them of late; and though many of them are inconceivably violent and filthy, even those characteristics are less conspicuous than their utter *weakness*. They are like men who, having no *weapons* to fight with, try to scare well-armed adversaries, by making up awful faces, and fierce gesticulations. They do not even succeed in frightening one old woman; and how they keep Members of Congress so effectually under their thumb, I cannot understand. Mr. Cobden said very wisely, "All that the Republicans lack for success, is *pluck*."[2]

Yours with affectionate respect, and never-failing gratitude,
L. Maria Child.

. . .

ALS; Houghton Library, Harvard University (microfiche 43/1167).

Fanny Kemble, the British actress who lived on her husband's plantation in 1838–39, kept a journal of her observations of slave life which Child had urged her to publish in 1841. After a delay motivated by strong personal reasons, Kemble had the text published in England and the United States in 1863. It

[1] When Congress met a few days after Brown's death, Southern Democrats blamed Republicans for Harpers Ferry. The abolitionists scorned politicians who temporized on the issue.
[2] Richard Cobden (1804–65), British statesman and reformer, visited the United States in 1859 and supported the North's cause.

came too late to influence public opinion, but *Journal of a Residence on a Georgian Plantation* proved one of the most penetrating accounts of slavery in America ever written. The missing Kemble letter Child responds to here apparently criticized Brown for inciting insurrection that might have cost the lives of many whites.

To Fanny Kemble

Wayland, Jan. 1860.

Mrs. Kemble,

I do not write again with the wish to induce you to give anything to the bereaved family of John Brown, or to do anything for them in any way. I do not even wish you to take the trouble of answering this letter. All I ask of you is that you will give it a dispassionate reading.

I reply to your brief note because I think you have a large, kind heart, and I judge from the contents of that note that your associations may have led you to ignore the fact that slaves and slaveholders are *both* objects of compassion; and that the class most *wronged* has the *strongest* claims on the sympathy of the just and humane.   In the comparison you make between John Brown's movement and the setting fire to a house whose inhabitants are infected with the plague, you treat Slavery as if it were merely a *misfortune*, not a *wickedness*. You entirely set aside the moral and religious view of the subject. *I* would compare that abominable institution to a house where a few strong men and women are violating and torturing a large class of helpless men, women and children.

But accepting your metaphor of "the plague," what would say of people who insisted upon sending *out* the plague, and infecting the *whole* country therewith?

I would not set fire to a house where they had the plague, or even where they were torturing helpless victims; because I think there is a more safe and rational way of proceeding. You cannot have a greater horror of insurrections than I have. But I believe John Brown was an honest, heroic, generous and great soul, though somewhat blinded, perhaps, by that trust in God, and the sure victory of Truth, which men call fanaticism. In view of so many sins and errors growing out of selfishness and skepticism, I do not find it difficult to excuse a mistake growing out of exceeding love to man, and unwavering trust in God.

My pity flows like a fountain for those widows and children who have for years worked hard and lived in destitution, for the sake of sustaining husbands and fathers in the terrible struggle for freedom, in Kansas, and in their noble efforts to help poor hunted slaves.

Having thus briefly explained my reasons for compassionating the destitute

family of John Brown, I leave you to exert your great social influence in whatever way you deem most satisfactory to your own heart and conscience.

Yrs respectfully,
L. Maria Child.

ALS; Boyd Stutler Collection, Archives and History Division, West Virginia Depart-
partment of Culture and History (microfiche 44/1195).

To Samuel May, Jr.

Wayland, Feb. 26, 1860

Mr. May,
Dear Sir,

I send you the copy for my Tract.[1] Please take *very* good care of it, as I
have no other complete copy. I calculate that it will make about 72 pages.
I have tried to make it as *concise* as was consistent with doing justice to the
subject. I have often taken things scattered about on different pages in the
works I consulted and packed them into one sentence.   You will perhaps
wonder that I leave out the question of *justice* and *humanity*. But you must
remember that I wrote it especially for the *South*. It is strongly impressed upon
my mind that there are *reflecting* people at the South, who might be influenced
by those statements, if we could only contrive to place them before them. I
have thought it might perhaps be well to omit the fact that it is printed by the
Anti Slavery Society; lest the *word* anti-slavery should stop it in the Post Office.
Please consult with Mr. Garrison and Mr. Phillips about it.

I want to have it printed as *soon* as you can, so as to send one to each
member of Congress, before that Assembly dissolves. I have thought it would
also be a good plan to send one to the Governor of *every* state; and to the
editors of all the Southern newspapers. And for each of us to send to such
individuals in the Southern States as we happen to know, or whose residence
we know; always *paid*. I cannot think such an effort would be *wholly* lost. But
to be efficacious, it ought to be done *quietly*; no sounding of the trumpet *before*
it, in any of the newspapers. The Standard ought to be cautioned about that,
when the pamphlets are sent there. I mean about saying anything of *an intent
to circulate them in the South.*

My plan is to attack them with a "troop of horse shod with felt." I should
be glad to omit *my name*; but as I happen to be notorious at this time, it seems
to be necessary to help its extension. Please be careful to attend to the direction

---

[1] As general agent of the American Anti-Slavery Society, May handled its publications.
The tract was probably *The Right Way, the Safe Way, Proved by Emancipation in
the British West Indies, and Elsewhere* (1860).

on the other page; and if you are to be absent, give the direction to whoever is responsible.   Yours cordially,

L. M. Child.

ALS; Anti-Slavery Collection, Rare Books and Manuscripts, Boston Public Library (microfiche 44/1200).

To Aaron Dwight Stevens

Wayland, March 6th, 1860.

Dear Friend Stevens,

I write to you from the depths of a sympathizing heart; but what can I offer you, *except* my sincere and affectionate sympathy? During your long imprisonment, you have doubtless thought of all the worldly, and all the religious, aspects of your painful situation.[1] That there is compensation hereafter for what seems mysterious and unjust in God's dealings with us here, I doubt not. And even here, there is some compensation for your sufferings, in the fact that your own conscience does not accuse you of the crime for which you are condemned. You know that your own intentions were kind and generous; and *that* is a satisfaction which no earthly tribunal can take away. We know, also, that *that* record is the one which angels enter in the Book of Life; not the record of human courts, whose decisions are based upon laws, sometimes wicked, and very often erroneous. Law is, in fact, only the exponent of the aggregate public sentiment of the community; and consequently its purity depends on the favorable or unfavorable condition of that community, for a clear perception of eternal principles of truth and justice. So, as the centuries pass on, one age canonizes a man for what a preceding age condemned him to the flames. And even at the *present* time, one part of the world glorifies a man for what another part of the world condemns him. But a small part of the civilized world regard you and your companions as guilty of the crime for which you have been condemned. They may not be able to dispute the *legality* of the sentence, but heart and head pronounce a verdict against its *justice*. But it matters not much to you, I suppose, what the world now think, or what impartial posterity will think. But it *is* important to you, that your own conscience does not convict you of any intention to commit the crime for which you are condemned. When the wife of Socrates murmured because he was to die *innocent*, "What!["] exclaimed Socrates, "would you have me die *guilty?*"

I wrote to you some three or four weeks since, perhaps five weeks, enclosing $5 for you, from my friend Henrietta Sargent, accompanied by some sympathizing expressions from her pen. I hope you received it safely. I would

---

[1] Stevens was in jail awaiting execution for his part in the raid on Harpers Ferry.

not mention so small a matter at this solemn time, if it were not that I wish you to know you have not been forgotten.

I thank you for your account of the women in Kansas. I hold them in the same degree of respect that I do the heroic, self-sacrificing women of the Revolution of '76. How I wish I could have a talk with you about your reminiscences there! Every little incident you could remember, would be precious to me. I thank you for your efforts there in the cause of human freedom. The situation of unborn generations will be the better for those efforts. Let that be a consolation to you in these trying hours!

My heart is very heavy while I write; for I have the greatest desire to console you, and I feel powerless to do it. There is but One, who *can* lead you safely through this dark passage; but He is a Being of infinite mercy and goodness.

May God and good angels console, and strengthen, and sustain you!

In all this, I include your companion in misfortune.[2] I know not whether you are near each other, or whether you have any opportunity to communicate with him.

There is wide-spread sympathy for you both; and here, as elsewhere, it has been manifested in the form of Petitions.

Farewell, my brethren! *All* farewells in this world, are for a short time only. Whether your time be long or short in this troubled scene, the pilgrimage will be brief for all of us, and leads to a better world. There, at least, if not here, I hope to meet you.

Yours with affectionate respect and sympathy,
L. Maria Child.

ALS; Eldridge Collection, Huntington Library (microfiche 44/1203).

To vindicate John Brown's purpose, and prove to skeptics that blacks would fight for their freedom, Thomas Wentworth Higginson decided to study the history of slave revolts in the Americas. He asked Child for information and wrote a series of articles about revolts that appeared in the *Atlantic Monthly* between 1860 and 1862.

To Thomas Wentworth Higginson

Wayland, March 17th, 1860

Dear Friend,

Such information as David or I have is most heartily at your service. But if you ever speak again of paying us for anything we can do in the Anti Slavery cause, or anything we can do for *you*, I shan't forgive it in a hurry.

[2] Albert Hazlett, age twenty-three, a Pennsylvanian who had fought in Kansas, escaped from Harpers Ferry but was captured and executed with Stevens on 16 Mar. 1860.

In Philadelphia, some years ago, David became acquainted with Thomas C. Brown, a free colored man, who was born in Charleston S.C. in 1800, and left the South in 1832. He was there at the time of Vesey's Insurrection;[1] and we have a journal in which is written down some of his statements about it, as follows:

"In 1822, a ⟨colored man⟩ slave, brother of Mr Devany, now in Liberia, told of the projected insurrection to another colored man named Pensil and he communicated it to a white man. Pensil received a thousand dollars; and Devany had his freedom, and was set up in business with two or three drays and horses. Six slaves were executed first, afterward 22; and still later 13. I cannot recollect how many in the whole; but I do not think these were all. I was a young man then, and owing to the policy of preventing communication between free colored people and slaves, I had little opportunity for ascertaining how the slaves felt about it. I know several of them were abused in the street, and some put in prison, for appearing in sackcloth. There was an ordinance of the city that any slave who wore a badge of mourning should be imprisoned and flogged. They generally got the law, which is 39 lashes; but sometimes it was according to the decision of the court.   Denmark Vesey, sometimes called Telemachus, was a Corromantee negro. He was brought from the coast by Capt Vesey, and bought himself for a low price, on account of his good conduct. He was a large, stout man. He was called the leader of the insurrection, and it was said arms were collected in his house. I was a carpenter, and worked with Vesey, who was also a carpenter; and I knew of his plan. I knew that several persons were in the habit of meeting at his house, who were afterward convicted and executed. I heard, at the time, of arms being buried in coffins, at Sullivan's Island. But that is not the negro burying ground. The slaves are buried in a place called the Potter's Field, and the colored people have a ground of their own. In the time of the insurrection, the the [sic] slaves were tried in a small room, in the jail where they were confined. No colored person was allowed to go within two squares of the prison. Those two squares were filled with troops, 5000 of whom were on duty day and night. I was told Vesey said, to those that tried him, that *the work of insurrection would go on;* but as none but white people were permitted to be present, I cannot tell whether he said it."   The Thomas C. Brown, from whom the above is quoted, went to Liberia in 1832, but returned to Philadelphia. I don't know whether he is now living.

You will recollect that in Mrs. Stowe's Dred, there is something about Vesey. See Vol. 1st—from page 248 to 254.

A gentleman (I cannot remember whom) told me that he had talked with a

---

[1] Denmark Vesey, a slave carpenter of Charleston, S.C., bought his own freedom and plotted a slave revolt in 1822. It was betrayed, and he and thirty-six other blacks were executed.

South Carolinian about Dred, and that *he* said Mr. [*sic*] Stowe ought to have chosen Peter Poyes as the hero of the Insurrection; for his character was much stronger and sterner than Vesey's. He said that Peter was remarkable for a kind of magnetic power in his eye, which gave him great control over the colored people. If he fixed his eye upon one of them, he was sure to subdue him to his purpose. After his arrest, he was chained to the floor, in a cell with another of the conspirators. White men came and by promises and threats tried hard to ascertain the names of their accomplices. His companion, wearied out with fear and suffering, and stimulated by the hope of saving his life, at last began to confess. Peter rose up from the floor, leaned on his elbow, and fixing his powerful eye on the poor fellow's face, said "Die like a *man!*" and immediately laid down again. The scene was brief as a flash of lightening, but no promises, and no threats could extort another word from the prisoner. What *tortures* were applied we shall never know.

Mrs. Loring was with her brother Dr. Gilman, in Charleston, when the executions were going on.[2] Perhaps she could tell you something about it. Joshua Coffin has written a Tract on Insurrections, recently published.[3]

In New York, David and I were acquainted with a very interesting old colored woman, who had been a slave in Edenton N.C. on the borders of Virginia. Her name was Charity Bowery, and I told her story in one of my N. York Letters.[4] She had a vivid recollection of the excitement at the time of Nat Turner's insurrection.[5] She sang to us some portions of a Methodist Hymn.

> "I have some friends has gone before me;
> And I must try and go to meet them;
> There's a better day a coming!
> O, Glory! Hallelujah!"

Charity gave us a roguish look, as she said: "The whites wouldn't let us sing *that*. They said, 'You want to kill your masters.' They thought we was going to *rise*, cause we sang 'A better day is coming.' At the time of the old Prophet Nat, the colored folks was afraid to pray loud; for the whites threatened to punish 'em dreadfully, if the least noise was heard. The patrols was low drunken whites; and in Nat's time, if they heard any of the colored folks praying or singing a hymn, they would fall upon em, and abuse 'em, and sometimes kill em, afore massa or missis could get to 'em. The brightest and best was killed in Nat's time. The whites always suspect such ones. They killed a great many at a place called Duplon. They killed Antonio, a slave of Mr. J. Stanley, an eminent lawyer, and a great friend of the colored people. Antonio was chained

---

[2] Louisa Loring had been visiting Samuel Gilman, Unitarian pastor in Charleston, S.C.
[3] Joshua Coffin (1792–1864), abolitionist and agent of *The Liberator,* was the author of *An Account of Some of the Principal Slave Insurrections* (New York, 1860).
[4] *Letters from New-York, Second Series,* pp. 48–56.
[5] Nat Turner's Virginia slave revolt took place in 1831.

with another, whom they shot; then they pointed their guns at him, and told him to confess about the insurrection. He told 'em he did'nt know anything about any insurrection. They shot several balls through him, quartered him and put his head on a pole, at the fork of the road leading to the Court. It was there but a short time. He had no trial. They never do. In Nat's time, the patrols would tie up the colored people, flog 'em, and try to make them be against one another, and often killed them before anybody could interfere. Mr. James Cole, High Sheriff, said if any of the patrols come on his plantation, he would lose his life in defence of his people. One day, he heard a patroller boasting how many niggers he had killed. Mr. Cole said, 'If you don't pack up, as quick as God Almighty will let you, and get out of this town, and never be seen in it again, I'll put you where dogs won't bark at you.' He went off, and was'nt seen in them parts again."   "If Polly M'c Niel was here, she could tell you about a great deal of shooting in Wilmington, (N.C) just before the Prophet Nat's time. The reason of it was this. A colored Baptist preacher, named Spaulding had one of Walker's books.[6] He lent it to another, and his master saw him reading it. The white folks got together and read the book, and they had the colored folks up in no time. The slave that was found reading the book said Brother Spaulding lent it to him. John Spaulding was a cooper, and was busy at his work when a crowd of people took him prisoner and put him aboard a vessel in chains. He never see his home again. He lives in New York now, and gets a living by blacking boots. I believe they shot eight slaves in Wilmington at that time. They shot Polly Mc Niel's husband; and she has been a poor broken hearted woman ever since. She has been here in New York; but I believe she is in Canada now. Her husband was the best carpenter in Wilmington. His name was Billy M'c Niel."

In the Liberator Vol 2. 1832 there are some accounts of the Southampton Insurrection.[7] In the Richmond Whig (Va) there is also a narrative by the editor, who was on duty, in the militia. In one or the other of those papers, there is the following statement: "A party of horsemen started from Richmond with the intention of killing every colored person they saw in Southampton County. They stopped opposite the cabin of a free colored man, who was hoeing in his little field. They called out, 'Is this Southampton County?' He replied, [']Yes, sir; you have just crossed the line, by yonder tree.' They shot him dead, and rode on."

I think you would do well to consult with colored people, who have lived at the South. I heard Rev. Stella Martin say, in a public address, that when he was a slave in Georgia, scarcely a month passed without *some* attempt at

---

[6] David Walker (1785–1830) was a free black and the author of the pamphlet *Walker's Appeal*, an open call for slave insurrection, which was published in Boston in 1830 and secretly circulated in the South.
[7] The Nat Turner revolt took place in Southampton County.

planning an insurrection; but the newspapers were very *silent* about it.[8] He told of one case within his knowledge, where I think he said *nine* slaves were hung. He had learned to read, previous to that time, and he watched for the papers, to see if any account was given of the affair; but there was not the slightest allusion to it.

The only authentic account of Nat Turner's Insurrection, that I know of, is in Abdy's "Residence and Tour in the U. States" Vol 3. page 391.

A strike for freedom occurred in the jail or workhouse, Charleston, S.C. which is described by a Mr. Adams, an exile from S. Carolina. It was in the Tribune about 4 years ago.

There were, as you recollect, attempts at insurrection during the Fremont campaign, owing to the Southerners railing against the Republican Party as enemies of their "peculiar institution." I wish the charge were true. There were many slaves executed at that time. But, according to their usual policy, everything was kept from the public as much as possible.

Mrs. Adams, in her letter to John Adams, in Congress, says that the slaves in Massachusetts (in 1775) threatened to join the British unless they had their freedom.

There was a conspiracy of slaves in the city of Lima for a general rising throughout the Vice-Royalty in 1809.

Insurrection in Jamaica 1795. See "History of Maroons." Another in Jamaica 1832; alluded to by Bleby, with some interesting details, in his First of Aug. Address.[9]

There was an insurrection in Barbadoes in 1816, and I think one in Antigua, not far from the same date.

See "Stedman's Narrative of a five Year's Expedition against the Revolted Negroes of Surinam."[10]

See the Oasis,[11] page 113, for an account of Three Colored Republics formed of slaves.

. . .

I felt exceedingly heavy of heart, yesterday. Poor Stevens![12] what a sad reward for the rash generosity of his noble young heart! And he had not the sympathy and the glory to sustain him, that John Brown had. I had written to him often, and so felt somewhat as if I were acquainted with him.

---

[8] J. Sella Martin (1828–76), born a Louisiana slave, became a Baptist preacher and abolitionist in Boston.
[9] *The History of the Maroons* (London, 1803) was by R. C. Dallas. Henry Bleby was a British missionary in the West Indies. The reference is probably to his *Death Struggles of Slavery* (London 1853).
[10] J. G. Stedman's *Narrative* was first published in 1796.
[11] Edited by Child in 1834.
[12] Aaron Stevens had been executed the previous day.

I do not see the Atlantic Monthly, and have had no chance to read the articles to which you refer.

Yours cordially,

L. M. Child.

ALS; William Palmer Collection, Western Reserve Historical Society (microfiche 45/ 1209).

To Lucy Osgood

Wayland, April 6th, 1860.

My very dear friend,

. . .

. . . I did not take Seward's Speech quite so philosophically as you did.[1] Of course, I did not expect him to come out anti Slavery; and I was glad to have him temperate, and even conciliating, in his tone. Neither had I anything to say against his clearing his skirts effectually of John Brown and the abolitionists. All I wanted of him was to stand on his *own* platform, in a manly way. But he travelled *beyond* the record, and said more than there was any *need* of saying; and obviously on purpose to fish for a nomination. What else could have induced him to put that reprobate Daniel Webster into "an *honored* grave"? He had just come from old England, where the highest are controlled by law, and where the meanest are protected by law; he had before him the history of Missouri, paying hordes of ruffians for robbery and carnage; of S. Carolina striking down the right of free speech, and apotheosizing an assassin; of Arkansas driving out her free colored population, for no offence whatever; and yet he stood up in Congress, and said the lowest State in this Union was superior to the best country in Europe! It would be an insult to his understanding, to suppose that he did n't *know* he lied, when he said it. But what excited my indignation the *most* of anything was his making "the African in bondage" chime in with hurras for this Union, which is crushing the blood out of his veins, and the soul out of his body. There seemed to be a diabolical kind of mockery about such an assumption. However, the Republican Party is an agency, and a powerful one, in the good work. I say of it, as witty Mrs. Chapman did of something else, years ago. "The *Lord* sometimes makes use of instruments, that *I* would n't touch with a pair of tongs."

. . .

ALS; Lydia Maria Child Papers, Anti-Slavery Collection, Cornell University (microfiche 45/1212).

[1] Senator Seward had been an unsuccessful candidate for the Republican presidential nomination in 1856 and was again campaigning for it in the 1860 race.

To Lucy Searle

My dear and honored friend,

. . .

My feelings with regard to "Spiritualism" are the same as your own. I am convinced that its phenomona are not all impositions, or self-delusions; but they do not satisfy the wants of *my* soul. *I* do not need to be convinced that the spiritual world is all around us, and that our vision of it is obstructed only by the bodily senses. I believe most fully in a future, conscious state of individual existence. It seems to me that only a malignant Being could have placed us here, so walled in by mysteries, with such an intense desire to penetrate beyond them, with such agonizing yearnings for reunion with those we have loved and lost, if there were no *reality* in our aspirations and hopes. If there is no other existence than *this*, it is a cruel mockery to endow us with the power and the tendency to *form* such ideas. But I think there are many *proofs* of existences out of the body. Dark and heavy is the veil between us and the unknown; but splendid gleams of light along the *edges* indicate interior effulgence behind the veil. There have been times, when I have been half wild to know *how* and *where* we should exist, when the body returned to the elements that formed it. But the older I grow, the more humility I have on these subjects. I know it is wisely ordered that we must walk by faith, and not by sight. We could not perform our duties here, if future modes of existence were tangible to our senses; and our spiritual freedom would be utterly destroyed, if we could always lean on unseen, infallible guides. But that superior orders of beings *are* in constant connexion with us, that they sustain us, and help us, I have no doubt. If you pass out of the body before I do, who can tell how many conflicts you may help me through, how many ideas of usefulness you may suggest? I have a very strong feeling that Ellis Gray Loring indited my letter to Mrs. Mason. What may I not do with Mrs. Follen's impetus, and his restraining grace, to aid me in my combats with inward and outward evils? If you pass behind the veil first, dear friend, do help me with your clearer light!

How it is there beyond, I know not; but I think there is truth in Plato's idea of heavenly archetypes, of which all forms here are but dim reflections. It seems to me as if everything there must be of a more *etherial* character; as if the common air were ether; and as if the flowers were luminous from a light *within* them, not *on* them. It seems to me as if the *souls* of *other* things were there, as well as the souls of our former bodies. It would be happiness enough, without anything else, to come face to face with the *realities* of things. What sort of Spirit I shall make, I cannot conjecture; but I know enough for my good; for I know that the more humble and the more useful I try to be here, the wiser I shall be there. These words of Swedenborg are always present with me: "The *wiser* the angels are, the more *innocent* they are; and the more innocent they are, the more they appear to themselves as *infants*."

You have so conscientiously performed your duties here, that your soul must needs enter into a state of child-like wisdom, when externals are removed. May I so follow the Heavenly guidance, as to be fitted for more companionship with you *there*, than has been granted to us here! . . .

ALS; Lydia Maria Child Papers, Anti-Slavery Collection, Cornell University (microfiche 45/1219).

The charge that Child had a daughter abandoned in the South was a slander fabricated in early 1860. Ironically, she regretted having no children.

To the Editor, *New York Bee*

Wayland, May 25, 1860.

To the Editor of the New York Bee:

I am very much obliged to you for the friendly remarks in your paper of the 19th, prefacing the story you copied from a Georgia paper, concerning a destitute daughter of mine. In reply, it will be conclusive to say that I never had either son or daughter. Moreover, I never heard of any one connected with me, or bearing my name, who was ill, or in suffering circumstances, in any of the slaveholding States.

The story made its first appearance last January, in the New Orleans *Picayune*, written by a correspondent, who pretended to have heard it from some Southern lady. As the editor sent it to me marked, I supposed he wished to ascertain whether it was true; accordingly I wrote to him the same statement I have now written to you. I seldom see that paper, but I have been recently told that my answer was published in it. Two other requests from editors of newspapers I also answered, but in all cases very briefly. I make it a rule never to talk to the public about myself. First, because I suppose they have, or ought to have, something more interesting to occupy their attention. Secondly, I consider it a better employment of my time and energies to defend principles of truth and freedom, than to defend myself. I always admired Lamartine's saying: 'Let our *names* perish, so that our *principles* remain.'

In addition to my own statement, the story has been contradicted by several editors. But it still continues to be copied by Southern papers, and by Democratic papers of the North. I presume many of the editors know it to be untrue. But falsehood diligently circulated often serves the purposes of politicians. Those who defend a system so bad as slavery have no great choice of weapons at their command. They betray the weakness of their cause by answering to facts and arguments with noisy threatenings and indiscriminate personal abuse.

> Yours, respectfully,
> L. Maria Child.

L; *Liberator*, 29 June 1860 (microfiche 45/1221).

At the presidential nominating convention in spring 1860, the Democratic party split; the Southern Democrats went one way and the Douglas Democrats the other, making it certain that the Republicans would choose the next president. At Chicago on 16–18 May, the Republicans nominated Abraham Lincoln for president on the third ballot (Seward had led on the first two ballots). In the Republican program there was only one antislavery plank—exclusion of slavery from the territories—and even this was subordinated to many other planks, which, as with all parties, promised something for everyone. The platform appealed to both East and West, to conservatives as well as radicals.

To Henrietta Sargent

> Wayland, May 27th, 1860.

My beloved friend,

. . .

. . . I don't place much reliance on any political party; but I am inclined to think this Mr. Lincoln, whom the Republicans have nominated, is an honest, independent man, and sincerely a friend to freedom. *One* thing makes me strongly inclined to like him and trust him. At a public meeting in Illinois, two years ago, in discussion with Stephen A. Douglass, he said, "A negro is my equal; as good as I am." Considering that Lincoln came from Kentucky, and that his adopted state, Illinois, is *very* pro-slavery, I think he was a brave man to entertain such a sentiment and announce it.[1]

The Republican leaders in Congress have tried my patience wofully during the past winter. I am glad it was not in my power to give them a good shaking and pounding; for I fear I *should* have done it. I had a letter from Charles

---

[1] While Lincoln was plainly against slavery, he did not favor its immediate, total, and universal abolition. Despite the remark Child quotes, Lincoln had declared, in his fourth debate with Douglas in 1858, that he did not believe in social and political equality of the races, nor was he in favor of letting blacks vote, hold office, sit on juries, or intermarry with whites. Nevertheless, most white abolitionists and most Northern blacks did work for Lincoln's election. No matter how far the Republican platform and candidate fell short of their own goals, Lincoln's election, they hoped, would be the first step toward the eventual abolition of slavery.

Sumner, about a fortnight ago, in which he says: "I am, at times, disheartened, even to unhappiness, by the indifference my associates manifest toward the cause. I am deemed impracticable and incorrigible." Of *course* he is. *Honest* men are always so deemed by politicians. How I did want to read to you Lovejoy's Speech in Congress![2] He came down upon the slave holders "like a thousand of brick." He is the brother of the martyred Lovejoy; and the mantle of Elijah has fallen on a prophet worthy to follow him.

. . .

ALS; Lydia Maria Child Papers, Anti-Slavery Collection, Cornell University (microfiche 45/1222).

On 4 June 1860, Sumner delivered a four-hour speech in the Senate, published as "The Barbarism of Slavery." This, his first Senate speech since the time of the Kansas debate, relied on the recital of facts drawn from Southern sources. It closed the discussion of slavery in Congress, which adjourned as the presidential campaign began.

To Charles Sumner

Wayland, June 17th, 1860.

Dear Mr. Sumner,

. . .

I have never sympathized fully with those who ignore or depreciate the importance of the political element in our Anti-Slavery cause. I have always wished God-speed to the Republican Party; but I *have* been somewhat impatient with the *excessive prudence* they have manifested. Mr. Wilson would doubtless smile to hear *me* presume to judge of *policy*.[1] But I believe in my soul their timidity has been bad policy. Do what they will, they cannot do *enough* to satisfy the South, or even to abate their enmity; and in *trying* to do it, they chill what honest enthusiasm there is at the North. Mr. Seward's Speech made me wretched. I exclaimed, "Oh what a mistake he has made! What a glorious opportunity is thrown away! The *hour* has come, but not the *man*." Mr. Child, though the habits of his mind are very political, shared my disappointment. He answered, sadly, "Yes. That Speech very obviously was worked out in *chains*."

Feeling thus, you may partly conjecture how your whole-souled utterance warmed and cheered our hearts. Mr. Child at once pronounced it, "The most thorough analysis of Slavery that has yet been made; the bravest and ablest

[2] Owen Lovejoy (1811–64), an Illinois congressman, proposed the bill which abolished slavery in the territories.
[1] Senator Henry Wilson of Massachusetts.

Speech ever uttered in Congress." I responded to his remark with a hearty, "God bless Charles Sumner! Nothing ever tempts *him* to throw a sop to Cerberus."

. . .

What I particularly enjoyed in your Speech was your exposé of the *meanness* of Slave-holding. It has always excited my indignation to have those dissipated despots boast of their *chivalry;* claiming to be the only real *gentlemen* in the country; yet all the while living on the unpaid toil of the poor, whipped out of their bones and muscles! Still more indignant have I been that the North are so generally willing to *allow* the impudent claim.

. . .

I presume you were not disappointed that so many Republican editors pronounced your Speech injudicious, ill-timed, &c. I was not surprised; though I confess I did expect something better from the N.Y. Evening Post. Honest utterance generally frightens, or offends, the wise and prudent; but it gains the *popular heart;* and thus renders political parties the *greatest* service, though it is one they least know how to appreciate. They themselves are also carried onward by such agencies, as certainly as cars follow the engine. Mr. Wilson has borne brave and able testimonies to the truth; but he is too much of a politician to trust her *entirely.* Always he is looking to the immediate effect on some party, or some measure, not to the ultimate and universal effect on the character and motives of the country. He spent an hour, some weeks ago, trying to convince me that the people were not *ready* for the truth on the subject of slavery. Grant that it *is* so; the question arises how are they ever to *become* ready, if the leaders of public opinion systematically keep back the truth from them? . . .

I have always felt thankful that I was born and educated in the midst of New England influences; and I have always loved Massachusetts, with all her sins of omission and commission, even to the setting up of Webster's brazen image; but I never felt such respect and gratitude for the old Commonwealth, as I have since her Legislature passed Resolutions heartily endorsing your Speech. By they [*sic*] way, those two titles, "Old *Commonwealth*" and "*Old Dominion,*" are significant; are they not?

. . .

That noble girl, Mattie Griffith, spent two days with me last week. She is going to rusticate in Wales, with some friends, this summer. I am very glad of it, for her health is a good deal impaired. I have never met with *any* person, who so *completely* identifies herself with the slaves, as she does. The most sensitive of the colored people is not more sensitive to any *shade* of insult or wrong toward themselves, than she is *for* them. She seems to me very great, in her uprightness, directness, and earnestness of soul. I wish Helper was as free from prejudice; but at present, his sympathies are not large enough to embrace more than the *white* people.

. . .

Yours with affectionate respect, and never-ending gratitude.

L. Maria Child.

P.S. Please give my respects to Mr. Wilson, and ask him to have the goodness to return the M.S. of my Tract,[2] if he thinks the Republican Committee will not want to make use of it.

ALS; Houghton Library, Harvard University (microfiche 45/1227).

To Wendell Phillips

Wayland, July 22d 1860

My dear Friend,

. . .

Mr. Garrison wrote to me about making a sort of very concise Anti Slavery Register. I decidedly think it had better be defered till another year. There is not time now to do it *well;* especially as I should have to make various journeys to the city to examine newspapers, pamphlets, &c

But there is a Tract which I have planned out, which seems to *my* mind calculated to do much good; and if the powers that be think so likewise, I should be gratified to have it published and circulated by the Hovey Fund.[1] I want to act on the next Legislature, concerning the Fugitive Slave Bill. There are some thrilling *Stories* concerning Fugitives, showing how we at the North are made legal instruments of cruelty. There are eloquent *Speeches* before the N. York and Massachusetts Legislatures, from which very effective extracts might be taken. In a Chapter by itself the *Unconstitutionality of the Law,* might be concisely and very clearly stated. And finally perhaps I might sum up with some urgent appeal of my own. This Tract, I want to send to every member of our Legislature, *as soon as they are elected,* that they may have time to read it in the quiet of their homes, undisturbed by the distractions of the city. What think you of my plan? If you think well of it, please indicate what extracts I had better make from your own Speeches; and remind me also of any *story* peculiarly illustrating the cruelty of the Law. I remember one several years ago, called "The Famished Hand," which affected me deeply.

I have a small Tract now on hand, which the Society may publish or not,

[2] One of the pamphlets she wrote for the Republican campaign.
[1] The tract was *The Duty of Disobedience to the Fugitive Slave Act: An Appeal to the Legislators of Massachusetts* (1860). Charles F. Hovey (1807–59) was a wealthy Boston businessman who left a bequest to support antislavery, woman's rights and other reforms.

according to their pleasure.[2] It is all taken from *Southern* sources, and is so arranged as to be very sarcastic. I planned it so that *some* might distribute it, as a Political Campaign Document; being desirous to make use of the political excitement of the present year, to spread Anti Slavery Ideas. I shall take the M.S. into Boston with me, and leave it at the Anti Slavery Office, with Mr. Walcutt.[3] If the Society publishes it, it ought to be done *soon*.

There is a request, that I have long wished to make of you, but it is so difficult to catch you, that I have not succeeded in doing it.

If you survive me, please see to it, that I am not buried at Mr. Auburn, or in any such place, and that no monument of any kind whatever is erected to my memory, in any such place. Please see to it that I am buried in some ground belonging to the *colored people*. Let the stone placed over my remains be very unexpensive; and for epitaph inscribe on it the following: Buried in this place, at her own request, among her brethren and sisters of dark complexion, as the *last* testimony it is in her power to bear against the wicked, cruel, and absurd prejudice, which so grievously oppresses them in a country that boasts loudly of its free institutions.[4]

My dear friend, I have this matter much at heart. Don't allow the vanity or pride of relatives or friends to cheat me out of this post mortem testimony.

With affectionate remembrance to Mrs. Phillips, I remain always your very grateful and truly attached friend

L. Maria Child.

. . .

Dont touch a hair of Charles Sumner's head, in your speeches. No politician has ever served our cause so honestly and faithfully as *he* has. It sticks a dagger in my heart to hear him found fault with.

Mr. Francis, my bookseller, has failed;[5] and the *plates* of all my books, except The Girl's Book, will be sold at the Boston Trade Sale, early in August; subject to my small per-centage on what may be *sold* of the books. I presume they will be sold very low; for the market is now glutted with plates sold by booksellers that have failed.

. . .

ALS; Wendell Phillips Collection, Houghton Library, Harvard University (microfiche 96/2545).

[2] *The Patriarchal Institution, as Described by Members of Its Own Family* (1860).
[3] Robert Folger Walcutt (1797–1884) was a Unitarian minister who became manager for *The Liberator* from 1846 to its cessation in 1866.
[4] She would be buried in the cemetery at Wayland, next to her husband's grave. Nearby were the graves of two slaves. The epitaph she requests here was not used.
[5] Probably as a victim of the protracted depression which began in 1857.

Harriet (Brent) Jacobs (1814?–97) escaped from slavery probably in 1842 and, on reaching the North, worked as nurse-housekeeper in the family of Nathaniel Parker Willis. When the Fugitive Slave Law of 1850 endangered Jacobs's safety, Willis bought her freedom. Jacobs wrote a memoir of her life in slavery, which Child edited for publication as *Incidents in the Life of a Slave Girl* (Boston, 1861). Although some critics of slave narratives had questioned the book's authenticity, research by Dorothy Sterling for *A Woman and Black* (New York: W. W. Norton, in press) verifies the accuracy of its details.

To Harriet (Brent) Jacobs

Wayland, Aug. 13th 1860

Dear Mrs. Jacobs,

I have been busy with your M.S. ever since I saw you; and have only done one third of it. I have very little occasion to alter the language, which is wonderfully good, for one whose opportunities for education have been so limited. The events are interesting, and well told; the remarks are also good, and to the purpose. But I am copying a great deal of it, for the purpose of transposing sentences and pages, so as to bring the story into continuous *order*, and the remarks into *appropriate* places. I think you will see that this renders the story much more clear and entertaining.

I should not take so much pains, if I did not consider the book unusually interesting, and likely to do much service to the Anti-Slavery cause. So you need not feel under great personal obligations. You know I would go through fire and water to help give a blow to Slavery. I suppose you will want to see the M.S. after I have exercised my bump of mental order upon it; and I will send it wherever you direct, a fortnight hence.

My object in writing at this time is to ask you to write what you can recollect of the outrages committed on the colored people, in Nat Turner's time. You say the reader would not believe what you saw "inflicted on men, women, and children, without the slightest ground of suspicion against them." What *were* those inflictions? Were any tortured to make them confess? and how? Where [*sic*] any killed? Please write down some of the most striking particulars, and let me have them to insert.

I think the last Chapter, about John Brown, had better be omitted. It does not naturally come into your story, and the M.S. is already too long. Nothing can be so appropriate to end with, as the death of your grandmother.

Mr. Child desires to be respectfully remembered to you.

Very cordially your friend,
L. Maria Child.

ALS; Post Family Papers, University of Rochester (microfiche 46/1243).

———

357

In September 1860, Child visited John Greenleaf Whittier in Newburyport, Massachusetts.

To Sarah Shaw

Wayland, Sep. 16th, 1860

Darling Friend,

. . .

. . . Friend Whittier and his gentle, Quakerly sister seemed delighted to see me; or rather *he* seemed delighted, and *she* seemed pleased. There was a Republican Meeting that evening, at which he felt obliged to show himself; but he came back before long, having indiscreetly excused himself by stating that I was at his house. The result was, that a posse of Republicans came, after the meeting was over, to look at the woman, who fired hot shot at Gov. Wise. In the interim, however, I had some cozy chat with Friend Whittier, and it was right pleasant going over our Anti Slavery reminiscencies, before there was division in the ranks. Oh those were glorious times! working shoulder to shoulder, in such a glow of faith! Too eager, working for humanity, to care a fig whether our helpers were priests or infidels. *That*'s the service that is pleasing in the sight of God.

Whittier made piteous complaints of time wasted and strength exhausted, by the numerous loafers who came to see him out of mere idle curiosity, or to put up with him to save a penny. I was amused to hear his sister describe some of these irruptions, in her slow, Quakerly fashion. "Thee has no idea," said she, "how much time Greenleaf spends in trying to *lose* these people in the streets. Sometimes he comes home, and says, "Well, sister, I had hard *work* to lose him; but I've lost him." "But I can never lose a *her*," said Whittier. "The women are more pertinacious than the men. Don't thee find 'em so, Maria?"

I told him I did. "How does thee manage to get time to do anything?" said he. I told him I took care to live away from the rail-road, and kept a bull-dog and a pitchfork; and I advised him to do the same.

. . .

ALS; Houghton Library, Harvard University (microfiche 46/1252).

To Harriet (Brent) Jacobs

Wayland, Sep 27th, 1860

Dear Mrs. Jacobs,

I have signed and sealed the contract with Thayer & Eldridge, in my name, and told them to take out the copyright in my name. Under the circumstances *your* name could not be used, you know.[1] I inquired of other booksellers, and could find none that were willing to undertake it, except Thayer & Eldridge. I have never heard a word to the disparagement of either of them, and I do not think you could do better than to let them have it. They *ought* to have the monopoly of it for some time, if they *stereotype* it, because that process involves considerable expense, and if you changed publishers, their plates would be worth nothing to them. When I spoke of limiting them to an edition of 2000, I did not suppose they intended to stereotype it. They have agreed to pay you ten per cent on the retail price of all sold, and to let you have as many as you want, at the lowest wholesale price. On your part, I have agreed that they may publish it for five years on those terms, and that you will not print any abridgement, or altered copy, meanwhile.

I have no reason whatever to think that Thayer & Eldridge are likely to fail.[2] I merely made the suggestion because they were *beginners*.   However, several of the *oldest* bookselling firms have failed within the last three years; mine among the rest. We must run for luck in these matters.

I have promised to correct the proof-sheets, and I don't think it would be of any use to the book to have you here at this time. They say they shall get it out by the 1'st of Nov.

. . .

I want you to sign the following paper, and send it back to me. It will make Thayer and Eldridge safe about the contract in *my* name, and in case of my death, will prove that the book is *your* property, not *mine*.

Cordially your friend,

L. Maria Child.

. . .

ALS; Post Family Papers, University of Rochester (microfiche 46/1255).

Thomas Sims, the fugitive slave shipped back to bondage from Boston in 1851, wrote to his sister in Boston and stated that his owner was asking eighteen hundred dollars for his purchase. Child saw the letter and, vowing to raise the money to free Sims, began writing anyone who might help.

[1] Probably because it would risk injury to others, still in the South, who figured in the memoir. Use of Jacobs's own name might help identify them.
[2] Thayer and Eldridge, a Boston firm, did in fact fail by the end of the year.

To Samuel E. Sewall

Wayland, Sep. 27th 1860

Mr. Sewall,

Dear Friend,

I am going to write to several wealthy gentlemen about contributing to the purchase of Thomas Sims; and knowing they will feel implicit confidence in you, both on account of integrity and property, I am going to refer them to *you;* asking them to subscribe at your office, and leave the money with you, if they prefer doing so, to sending it to me; also promising them that I will deposit *all* I receive in *your* hands, there to be kept till Thomas Sims makes his appearance; the master being duly informed that the money awaits his order.   If you have any objection to aiding me in this way, please inform me.

. . .

Cordially & gratefully Yr friend,

L. Maria Child.

Sim's master charges $1800 for him, on account of his intelligence and mechanical skill. It will be a weary long while before the aged mother could make up that sum.

Besides, Boston *ought* to do it.

. . .

ALS; Robie-Sewall Papers, Massachusetts Historical Society (microfiche 46/1256).

To Henrietta Sargent

Wayland, Oct. 13'th, 1860.

Dear Henrietta,

After I left you, it occurred to me that my remarks about my stereotype plates, might convey a wrong impression to your mind. They could be of no value to me, unless I had capital enough to publish my books at my own expense; which I never *shall* have. When they were for sale, it floated through my mind, (a mere castle in the air) how I should like to have control over them, and publish for myself. Anti Slavery has put me at disadvantage always, with regard to a *choice* of publishers; and my John Brown manifestation made the matter rather worse. But that is no matter. *Live* fish can swim *up* stream. Let the dead ones float on the current. What I wish to say to you is, that the time has gone by for securing my plates.[1]

. . .

[1] Child's publisher, Charles S. Francis, who failed in July 1860, had to sell the plates for ten of her books. All were bought, and new printings of a few books were undertaken by other publishers.

Did you read, in the Standard, Mrs. Staunton's wide-awake Speech to the Wide-Awakes?[2] It seems to me a very great speech; one of the noblest that ever came from the lips of a woman. How absurd it seems, that any tipsy, ignorant fool, with a *hat* on, can vote, while *such* a woman is disfranchised. Oh dear! what a labor it is, to get this world right side up!

. . .

To Francis Jackson

Wayland, Oct. 14'th, 1860.

Dear & Honored Friend,

. . .

There are a few old-fashioned remedies, of which I think very highly. If you feel rather weak and faint at the stomach, and have not much appetite, I would advise you, by all means, to take wormwood, early in the morning, on an empty stomach; and continue as long as you need it. You can buy the *herb*, as it is prepared by the Shakers, steep it in boiling hot water over night, and take half a wine glass of the *very strong* decoction, cold, the next morning. Or you can buy the *Essence* of Wormwood, and drop 20 or 30 drops on a lump of loaf-sugar, and take it early in the morning. It used to strengthen my poor old father wonderfully, when his appetite failed him; and Mr. Child, also experiences very beneficial results from it.

When you take a cold, that affects the throat, or lungs, there is nothing so good as Hoarhound Tea, drank very *strong*, several times in the day, whenever you feel thirsty, and especially at night, before you go to bed. I have broken up several severe colds in that way; and I learned to do it from my father's experience of many years. The Shakers prepare it for sale. Wormwood and Hoarhound I believe to be the two very best articles in the whole range of vegetable medicines.

I had very unexpected good luck in my efforts for poor Sims.[1] I supposed it would take me most of the winter to raise the funds; but all that will be needed was placed at my disposal in a few weeks; and not one cent of it aboli-

[2] The *National Anti-Slavery Standard* of 13 Oct. 1860 carried Elizabeth Cady Stanton's address to the Wide-Awake Club of Seneca Falls, N.Y., a Republican political group of men opposed to the extension of slavery. She asked them to work instead for the total abolition of slavery.

[1] After writing eighteen letters on behalf of Sims, Child heard from Charles Devens that he would put up the eighteen hundred dollars if his name would be kept secret. Devens, as U.S. marshall in Boston, had felt obliged to carry out the Fugitive Slave Law and had helped send Sims back to his master in Georgia. His conscience had troubled him ever since, and this was his chance to atone. Later Devens became a major general in the Union army.

tion money. But you and your family must be *very* careful not to give publicity to this fact. Sims's sister is in great trepidation, for fear it will get into the *papers;* in which case, she fears there will be great trouble in negotiating with the master.

. . .

ALS; Nathaniel Bowditch Collection, Phillips Library, Essex Institute (microfiche 46/ 1260).

John Curtis Underwood (1809–73) was a Northern lawyer who had settled in Virginia. He supported Frémont in the 1856 election and was at this time backing Lincoln.

To John Curtis Underwood

Wayland Oct. 26th, 1860.

Mr. Underwood,
Dear Sir,

I was extremely glad to receive your letter, this evening. I was troubled at not hearing from you. My zeal is exceeding great to convince the South that immediate, unconditional emancipation would be conducive to their safety and their prosperity. I compiled the evidence expressly for the *South*.[1] For that reason, I forbore to make any allusion to slavery in the United States. I thought the evidence might make more *impression* upon them, if nothing was said to irritate them, or excite their prejudices. I was very desirous that you should think well of my effort, and give me such aid in the circulation of the pamphlet, as was consistent with your own convenience. Not hearing from you, I concluded that you did not think the Tract likely to do good. I sent to Mr. Helper,[2] for a list of names in N. Carolina, of persons to whom I could send it; but he declined, on the ground that "the *negro* was too prominent" for the Tract to be acceptable in his native State.

I presume the copy I sent you was lost during your absence. I enclose an order, which you can use or not, as you please. If you choose to send copies into Virginia, and elsewhere, yourself, you can do so. If you prefer that I should do it, I will attend to it, as soon as I receive a list of names from you. At all events, I should be obliged to you for as many names as you can conveniently furnish; for I may write some other Tract, suitable to send to them. I have exercised my ingenuity, in all possible ways, to find out the Post Office address of

[1] In her pamphlet *The Right Way, the Safe Way.*
[2] Hinton R. Helper.

individuals in Slave-holding States. I have sealed up and superscribed, with my own hand, over a thousand; and I have lately found out about a hundred more, to whom I shall send immediately. Oh, if I could only live to see *one* State fairly try emancipation, I should feel that I had not lived and labored in vain!

The Tract called "The Patriarchal Institution," I compiled for circulation at the *North.* I have not sent it South, except to Gov. Wise, and Mrs. Mason, and a few editors, who have been particularly *attentive* to me. I hope you will not think me *very* unamiable, if I confess that I a little enjoyed annoying them by the presentation of a mass of *Southern* evidence, so little to their liking.

. . .

I will thank you, at any time, for any suggestion of ways and means, by which I can help in this good work. I feel as if a day was lost, in which I have not tried to do *something* to hasten emancipation. Let us not be disheartened by the pride and prejudice of some, and the icy indifference of others. No particle of scattered truth is ever wasted. The harvest will come in time.

Yours with great respect,

L. Maria Child.

P.S. If the New York Anti Slavery Office cannot furnish you with as many West India Tracts as you want, please let me know. You will observe there is no imprint of Anti Slavery on the title-page. I avoided that, lest it should excite prejudice at the outset.

ALS; John C. Underwood Papers, Manuscript Division, Library of Congress (micro-fiche 46/1263).

To Wendell Phillips

[October? 1860]

Dear Friend,

I have written an Appeal to the Legislature, after my own fashion.[1] But I thought it best to add to the Tract some other testimonies, of more weight than mine; also something about the *Constitutionality* of the Fugitive Slave Act. *I* don't care a button about that; and I presume *you* care as little; but I thought it was best to besiege the legislators in *all* directions. Some honest men really think we are bound to assist in robbing, because our fathers made an agreement for us to that effect. For such, it seems well to open a loop-hole of escape. The testimony of old Mr. Quincy seems to me very important to go in.[2]   I have added some stirring poetry, thinking it would have a more *rousing* effect than argument. The lines will be familiar to many, but not to all; and even those who know them will not be harmed by having their memories refreshed. But

[1] *The Duty of Disobedience to the Fugitive Slave Act.*
[2] Josiah Quincy (1772–1864), in a public letter of 14 Oct. 1850, had impugned the constitutionality of the fugitive slave laws of both 1793 and 1850.

I am willing to leave out anything, or to add anything, which you or the Committee may think proper. My sole desire is to produce the greatest *effect* I can on the question.

When the legislators for the ensuing winter are elected, I want to have a *list* of them all, at the Anti-Slavery Office; and I will come down and send a copy of the Patriarchal Tract[3] and the Fugitive Bill Tract to each one of them.

In Peter Lesley's book on Iron and Coal, I have unexpectedly come upon a rich mine for *me* to work.[4] There are in the volume nearly *500 Southern names,* with Post Office address.

If *you* can think of any Southern names of men or women, with their address, I wish you would note them down for me. I am getting the West India Tract into the South, through every crack I can find. The effects will not be obvious at once; but that evidence *must* take hold of *some* minds, and have *some* effect on the final result of this long struggle. I work in *faith*, without much encouragement. Yours cordially,

L. Maria Child.

I should like to have the Fugitive Tract published *soon.*

In taking books of Eldridge & Thayer, please contrive to pay Mrs. Jacobs, out of what you owe.[5]

Please ask Edmund Quincy whether he knows the address of any Southerners.

ALS; Wendell Phillips Collection, Houghton Library, Harvard University (microfiche 96/2548).

To John Curtis Underwood

Wayland, Nov. 15th, 1860.

Mr. Underwood,
Dear Sir,

I thank you for the new list of names. I sent to thirty of them this morning, and shall continue to do so by every mail. Previous to writing to you, I had sent to all the Members of Congress, and to all the names I could find in the American Almanac; Governors, Judges, &c.

There is no occasion for your advancing any money. All I ask of you is to keep on doing just what you *are* doing; advancing the good cause according to you own judgment.   I give the time and the labor, but the expense of printing and postage is paid out of a fund left by a Boston merchant for the dissemination of Anti Slavery truth, "not of a political character."[1] I knew

---

[3] Child's *Patriarchal Institution.*
[4] This was one of Lesley's numerous works on geology.
[5] The reference is to Jacobs's *Incidents in the Life of a Slave Girl.*
[1] The Hovey Fund (see note to letter of 22 July 1860, p. 355).

364

him well, and knew that these West India facts were what he would especially like to have widely spread. As for the trouble I take, I would willingly take a thousand times more to see Virginia a Free State. I believe I would willingly be hung, if that would accomplish it; so sincerely do I wish well to every portion of my country. You would be surprised, or perhaps you would not, be surprised to see the abominable letters I have received from Va. in the time of the John Brown excitement.

I have tried to procure the Tribune containing your Speech, but have not succeeded as yet.

God bless you.

Yours with much respect,
L. Maria Child.

ALS; John C. Underwood Papers, Manuscript Division, Library of Congress (microfiche 46/1266).

To John Curtis Underwood

Medford, Dec. 6th, 1860

Mr. Underwood,
Dear Sir,

I have left Wayland for the winter, to stay with a friend who is afflicted and lonely.[1] If you have occasion to write again, please address me at Medford, Mass'ts. I send 25 of my West India Tract into Virginia every day; and am delighted to be assured that *all* the seed does not fall into stony ground. No native Virginian can feel a more sincere and friendly interest in her welfare, than I do; and that is true of the abolitionists in general. It is the *system*, and not the men, with which we are at variance.

With regard to taking up the waste lands of Virginia, I believe there would be a rush of emigration, *if slavery were abolished.*[2] I have myself always supposed the scenery of that State to be more beautiful, the climate more desirable, and the resources for acquiring wealth more abundant, than in any other State of this Union. Years and years ago, I had a great desire to remove thither; and this feeling I have often heard expressed by intelligent farmers and enterprising mechanics; but always it is accompanied with the remark, "But there can be no feeling of security in a Slave State." In the first place, let slaveholders *say* what they will, there is always an interior *consciousness*

[1] Between Nov. 1860 and Apr. 1861, Child spent most of her time living in Medford with elderly Lucy Osgood.

[2] The mountainous part of western Virginia would refuse to recognize secession. Its people organized a Union government in June 1861, and two years later West Virginia was admitted into the Union with a constitution providing for the gradual emancipation of slaves.

that human beings forcibly deprived of freedom are *very* liable to attempt to regain it forcibly. The friend in whose house I am now staying, was for years an intimate friend of Thomas Clay, of Georgia, and his sister Ann. More thoroughly religious, conscientious, and kind slaveholders, probably never lived. Their slaves were as comfortable & happy, as it is *possible* for human beings to be *in slavery*. My friend once said to Ann Clay, "You say your servants are happy and strongly attached to you. In case of insurrection, do you suppose they would join the insurgents"? "Undoubtedly they would, if there was any prospect of success," she replied; "for all human beings want to be free."

While Virginia continues to be a Slave State, only mean and servile Yankees will take up their abode there. The *better* portion of our population will prefer cold, distant, uninhabited Minnesota, because it is Free Soil. In addition to the mine of gunpowder, on which slaveholders are always standing, our emigrants dread and abhor the Lynch Law, which is the violent product of a system of violence. Virginia must become *free*, before the best class of emigrants will be attracted to her soil. Emancipation would effectually wet the dangerous mine of gunpowder, and attract free laborers and capitalists, like a powerful magnet acting upon metals.

In thinking over the prospects of Virginia, I have often thought that emancipation ought to be accompanied with the introduction of *new staples*. For instance, I should suppose Virginia admirably adapted to the culture of mulberries, and the manufacture of silk. Grapes, to *any* extent, could be raised. I presume the olive, and even the Tea plant, could be domesticated. I do hope that wise precautions will be taken, whenever the change takes place; for some *temporary* inconveniences must necessarily always be the result of changing the relations of labor and capital, even if it be infinitely for the better. It is of immense importance to the cause of freedom, that the *first* State which sets the example of emancipation should proceed wisely, as well as justly. Did you read the account of Mr. M'cDonough's slaves in Louisiana, some twenty years ago? What magical power the offer of wages had over them? That immediate, unconditional emancipation is the best *policy* seems to me so *very* plain, that I marvel men of sense and reflection can have the least doubt upon the subject. It is the only course adapted to the laws which govern human nature. *Half* measures, *gradual* measures, only excite, without *satisfying*. For instance, if it be enacted that all born after a *certain* date shall be free, that excites great discontent among those who were born a year, or a month, or a week, too soon. The only safe and sure way is to stimulate *all* by wages, increasing according to their industry and skill; and to enact laws that judiciously restrain, while at the same time they justly and carefully protect the laborers. I feel *so* earnest to have such an example set in our favored country, that I feel sometimes as if I could storm Heaven with prayers for Virginia; which seems to me the most favorable place for trying an experiment so *sure* to be blessed.

Yours with great respect, & cordial good wishes for yourself and your cause,

L. Maria Child.

ALS; John C. Underwood Papers, Manuscript Division, Library of Congress (microfiche 47/1273).

Within a few weeks of Lincoln's election, the states of the deep South had taken steps toward secession. South Carolina was the first to break away, seceding on 20 December 1860. Agonized Republicans in Congress offered concessions and compromises to appease the South and save the Union. As Congress debated the proposals that winter of 1860–61, it seemed, ironically, that Lincoln's victory might give the South everything it wanted. But the abolitionists stood firm against any concessions on the issue of slavery.

As for the crisis over secession, while President Buchanan regretted the disruption of the Union, he declared the federal government impotent to prevent it by force. To hold the South, he even suggested a constitutional amendment guaranteeing the protection of slavery.

Most of the abolitionists said, Let the South go. For a generation Garrison and others had argued that the free states should break away from the slave states; with the South leaving the North, the result would be the same. Disunion would destroy slavery. The slaves would rise in mass revolt, and the South would not have the strength to put them down.

But a minority of the abolitionists disagreed. To permit the South to go peaceably would be to desert the slaves and leave them helpless, they argued. By January 1861, they were making a case for the government's right to abolish slavery under the war power. By seizing federal property the South had begun war, and this made her liable to all the laws of war—including liberation of the slaves to help put down the rebellion.

To Lemuel Shaw

Medford, Jan. 3d, 1861.

To the Hon. Lemuel Shaw.

By this mail, I send you three pamphlets, for which I ask a candid perusal. With deep sadness, I saw your respected and influential name signed to an address in favor of repealing the Personal Liberty Bill.[1] I trust you will not

---

[1] Lemuel Shaw, chief justice of the Massachusetts Supreme Court, was the judge who had ruled in the Med case of 1836. With many other leaders of the Massachusetts bar, he was advocating repeal of the state's Personal Liberty Law, which denied federal authorities any state assistance when recapturing fugitive slaves. The abolitionists considered this a mistaken move to conciliate the South.

deem me disrespectful, if I ask whether you have reflected well on all the bearings of this important subject.

Perhaps you may consider me, and those with whom I labor, as persons prone to look only on one side. Grant that it *is* so—is it not the *neglected* side? it is not the *right* side? And are not you, yours[elf][1] in common with all human beings, liable to look upon things too much from one point of view. I presume that your social environment is almost entirely conservative; and conservative of *habits* and stereotyped *sayings*, rather than of the original *principles*, on which the government of this country was founded. Have you carefully examined, and duly considered, the *other* side?

This mutual agreement between North and South to keep millions of fellow beings in abject degradation and misery cannot possibly be right. No sophistry can make it *appear* so, to hearts and minds not frozen or blinded by the influence of trade or politics.

If the common plea of the inferiority of the African race be true, that only adds *meanness* to our guilt; the magnanimous strong are ashamed not to protect the weak. But then everybody knows that an immense proportion of American slaves are *not* black. Thousands upon thousands of them are lighter than Italians, Spanish, Portuguese, Greeks, &c. They are the sons and daughters of our Presidents, Governors, Judges, Senators, and Generals. The much-vaunted Anglo Saxon blood is coursing in their veins, through generations after generations.

If you set aside heart and conscience, as appropriate guides for *women* only, and assume pure, cold intellect for a standard of action, what answer will enlightened *reason* give, if you ask whether free institutions in one part of the country can possibly survive continual compromises with despotism in another part? If the lowest person in the community is legally oppressed is not the highest endangered thereby? And does not the process inevitably demoralize the people, by taking away from Law that which renders it sacred—viz: equal and impartial Justice?

I again ask you, respectfully and earnestly, to read my pamphlets with candid attention. If the request seems to you obtrusive or presumptuous, my apology is that I believe you to be an upright and kind man, and therefore infer that your heart and conscience are not in fault, but only the blinding influences of your social environment.

Yours respectfully, L. Maria Child.

ALS; Charles Aldrich Papers, Iowa State Historical Department (microfiche 47/1277).

[1] A blot obscures part of this word.

To Francis Shaw

Medford Jan. 8, 1861.

Dear Friend,

My state of mind at this time is not so serene as I wish it was. My fear that the Republican Party will compromise their principles fills me with a degree of anxiety, that makes me easily despondent and easily irritated. Mr. Child is very sanguine that they will stand firm, because thus far they *have* stood firm. But I, who am prone to be a Cassandra, remind him of the time of the old Missouri Compromise when the Northern Representatives fought a brave battle session after session; but at last, all of a sudden, news came that the South had carried her point, by the treachery of one Massachusetts member. At this crisis, the pressure is much stronger that it was then. Seward, when he had the Presidency in view, showed that his back-bone was of India-Rubber. What a pity it will be if from motives of personal ambition, or temporary expediency, they throw away the glorious vantage-ground they have gained! Alas, I am sorry to say I have more hope in Southern arrogance and rashness, than I have in Northern courage and conscientiousness. My hope is that the South will scorn to accept *any* compromise, that the North will get on her knees to offer. The crisis *must* come; and it seems to me there can never be a time more favorable than the present. Certainly, I shudder at the *possible* consequences; but if we seek to avoid them, at the expense of principle, we shall only prepare a worse crisis for our posterity. The demands of despotism are insatiable and can never be satisfied, short of the entire annihilation of our free institutions. My own belief is, that if the North would only show a bold, united front *now*, despotism would quail before it, and be compelled to become subordinate to freedom; and if once subordinated, it must ere long cease to be.

Ever your affectionate, and grateful Mariqita

L, transcription in unidentified hand; Lydia Maria Child Papers, Anti-Slavery Collection, Cornell University (microfiche 47/1278).

That winter the compromisers used mob violence against the abolitionists. The business class, fearing the loss of vast sums from secession, and blaming the abolitionists for their troubles, joined with workers ridden by antiblack prejudice to disrupt antislavery meetings. Wendell Phillips was their prime target; he carried a revolver in those months and was protected by bodyguards.

To Sarah Shaw

Medford, Jan 25th, 1861.

My precious friend, tired in mind and body, I sit down to write to you, and tell you all about it. On Wednesday Evening, I went to Mrs. Chapman's Reception, which was better ordered than it was last year. The Hall was beautiful with light and banners, and outside, the street was beautiful with moonlight and prismatic icicles. All went on quietly. People walked about and talked; occasionally enlivened by music of the Germania Band. They seemed to enjoy themselves; and I, (being released from the care of unruly boys, demolishing cake, and spilling slops, as they did last year) did my best to help them have a good time. But what with being introduced to strangers, and chatting with old acquaintances half forgotten, I went home to Derne St. very weary. Yet it was impossible for me to sleep. I knew there were very formidable preparations to mob the Anti Slavery Meeting the next day, and that the Mayor was avowedly on the side of the mob.[1] I would rather have given $50 than attend the meeting; but conscience told me it was a duty. I was excited and anxious; not for myself, but for Wendell Phillips. Hour after hour of the night, I heard the clock strike, while visions were passing through my mind, of that noble head assailed by murderous hands, and I obliged to stand by, without the power to save him.

I went very early in the morning, and entered the Tremont Hall by a private labyrinthine passage. There I found a company of young men, a portion of the self-constituted body-guard of Mr. Phillips. They looked calm, but resolute and stern. I knew they were all armed, as well as hundreds of others; but their weapons were not visible. The women-friends came in gradually, by the same private passage. It was a solemn gathering, I assure you; for though there was a pledge not to use ⟨their⟩ weapons unless Mr. Phillips, or some other Anti Slavery speaker, was *personally in danger*, still, nobody could foresee what *might* happen. The meeting opened well. The Anti Slavery sentiment was there in strong force. But soon the mob began to yell from the galleries. They came tumbling in by hundreds. The papers will tell you of their goings on. Such yelling, schreeching [*sic*], stamping, and bellowing, I never heard. It was a full realization of the old phrase, "all hell broke loose." Mr. Phillips stood on the front of the platform for a full hour, trying to be heard, whenever the storm lulled a little. They cried "Throw him out"! "Throw a brick-bat at him!" "Your house is a fire. Dont you know your house is a fire? Go put out your house!" Then they'd sing, with various bellowing and shrieking accompaniments, "Tell John Andrew, Tell John Andrew, John Brown's dead."[2] I should

[1] The annual meeting of the Massachusetts Anti-Slavery Society was held at Tremont Temple on 24 Jan. 1861. Boston's mayor was a Democrat; his followers were expected to try to break up the meeting while the police stood by.
[2] John A. Andrew (1818–67), the new Republican governor, had presided over a meeting in aid of John Brown's family.

think there were four or five hundred of them. At one time, they all rose up, many clattered down stairs, and there was a surging forward toward the platform. My heart beat so, that I could hear it; for I did not *then* know how Mr. Phillips's armed friends were posted at every door, and in the middle of every aisle. They formed a firm wall, which the mob could not pass. At last, it was announced that the police were coming. I saw and heard nothing of them; but there was a lull. Mr. Phillips tried to speak, but his voice was again drowned. Then by a clever stroke of management, he stooped forward and addressed his speech to the reporters stationed immediately below him. This tantalized the mob, and they began to call out, "Speak louder! We want to hear what you're saying!" Whereupon, he raised his voice, and for half an hour seemed to hold them in the hollow of his hand. But as soon as he sat down, they began to yell and sing again, to prevent any more speaking. But Higginson made himself heard, through the storm, and spoke in very manly and effective style; the purport of which was that to-day he would set aside the subject of slavery, and take his stand upon the right of free speech, which the members of this society were determined to maintain, at every hazard. I forgot to mention that Wendell Phillips was *preceded* by James Freeman Clarke, whom the mob treated with such boisterous insults, that he was often obliged to pause in his remarks. After Mr. Phillips, R. W. Emerson tried to address the people, but his voice was completely drowned. After the meeting adjourned, a large mob outside waited for Mr. Phillips; but he went out by the private entrance, and arrived home in safety.

In the afternoon meeting, the uproar was greater than it had been in the forenoon. The mob cheered and hurraed for the Union, and for Edward Everett, and for Mayor Whiteman, and for *Charles F. Adams*.[3] (I want Frank to take note of that last significant fact. I do not change my opinion, upon mature reflection. I still think Adams has done *wickedly*.) The Mayor came at last, and mounting the platform, informed his "fellow citizens in the galleries," that the Trustees of the building had requested him to disperse the meeting, and clear the Hall. Whereupon the mob gave three cheers for Mayor Whiteman. Turning the meeting out of doors was precisely what they *wanted* him to do. The President of the Meeting demanded that the letter of the Trustees should be read. It turned out, as they had supposed. The Mayor had made a[4]

I agree with you that S. Carolina still governs us; and I have now very little doubt that her whip will effectually frighten our merchants, and by their influence, combined with the South, the Republican leaders will be subdued into one miserable mush of concession. Charles Sumner is said to be very sad. No wonder. An honest man, standing alone among traitors and cowards may

[3] Adams was one of those who offered concessions to the South.
[4] The following page or pages are lost; the passage following appears on the first page. The mayor lied: the Trustees had asked him to quell the rioters and protect the meeting. Instead, he ordered the hall closed, preventing the scheduled evening session.

will [*sic*] be sad. So, all the fight has to be done again! If I wanted *any*body hung, it would be W'm H. Seward. But God forgive them all!

Good bye, with a blessing from your loving old Mariquita.

ALS; Houghton Library, Harvard University (microfiche 47/1280).

Senator William Seward offered a number of compromises to the South. In a speech of 12 January—which Sumner had pleaded with him not to make— Seward recognized a constitutional obligation to return fugitive slaves and supported a constitutional amendment to deny Congress any power to deal with slavery in the states.

To Charles Sumner

Medford, Jan. 28'th, 1861.

Dear and honored Mr. Sumner,

I thank you for the [pam]phlet[1] you sent me last week, because any attention from you is always pleasant; but deem me not ungracious, if I ask you never again to send me anything bearing the name of William H. Seward. *Mr.* Child may like to receive his Speeches, because he makes it his business to preserve a record of the degeneracy of the times. But to me, it is unmitigated pain to be reminded of Mr. Seward, and it cannot be of any use to endure that pain. It is an immeasurable crime for a public man to chill the moral enthusiasm of his countrymen, to lower the standard of the public conscience, to make it impossible for honest minds to trust in political leaders. No one can calculate the mischiefs of such a course; they go down through the centuries, making it more and more difficult to retard the degeneracy of national character, and to save our free institutions from utter corruption and ruin. Of Webster and Seward, I *try* to say, "Father forgive them! for they *know* not what they do."   What wholesale swindling of the people, to cheat them of their votes on the pledge of non-extension of slavery, and then to offer territory, that despots may cease to clamor! If all this excitement does not settle down into a miserable mush of concession, leaving [the?] country in a worse state than it found it, we shall owe it less to the stedfastness of Republican leaders, than to the utter impossibility of satisfying the demands of the South, however patiently we may crawl in the dust, or whatsoever quantity of dirt we may consent to eat. That was my hope when I read Mr. Adams's proposition to give up New Mexico to the chances of slavery, and to grant to that amiable institution the *monopoly* of proposing amendments to the Constitution; and I see, by his explanation, that he recants because our masters will not condescend to

[1] The edge of the page is worn away.

372

accept the liberal offer. The mob at Tremont Hall, last week, gave three rounds of cheers for Charles F. Adams; and I thought to myself he had earned his laurels. It is to be hoped that the spirits of his father and grandfather were not there to listen.

. . .

Alas, what a lamentable deficiency of conscience and of courage does the present crisis make manifest! Yancey can be invited to Faneiul Hall to *eulogize* slavery, and men applaud it, on the ground that free speech is sacred; but when those *opposed* to slavery hire a hall to hold the Annual Meeting they have held for more than thirty years, they are mobbed out by rowdies, paid from a Bell-Everett fund, and with scarcely an *appearance* of restraint from the Democratic Mayor.[2] "How much did you get by to-day's job?" said one of the mob to a comrade. "I got $5," was the answer. "How much did *you* get?" They are evidently drilled and organized carefully, to do no *more* than is necessary to effectually break up the meetings; because anything *beyond* that might excite popular sympathy for abolitionists. As soon as the Police *try* to disperse them, they do it very easily; but they take care not to try, till the meetings are broken up. The fools! They might as well think of extinguishing fire with alcohol. I have been in the midst of two of these mobs; and judging by the effect on my own soul, I think they will not *gain* much by their mad efforts. Time will show. My prayer is for patience and strength. Heaven's best blessings be with you, whose brave example helps us all to be strong for freedom!

Please give my respect & cordial greetings to Mr. Wilson. . . .

P.S. Mr. Child sends his gratitude and his blessing to you, and Mr. Wilson, and all who stand on their feet at this important crisis.

I feel the more sad to be so disappointed in Mr. Seward, because I honored him so much for his noble course concerning the Virginia Fugitives, and the poor crazy negro, Freeman.[3] I wish the Presidency was a disease men could have but once.

ALS; Houghton Library, Harvard University (microfiche 47/1281).

[2] William L. Yancey (1814–63) was an Alabama secessionist. John Bell (Tennessee) and Edward Everett (Massachusetts) had been the candidates for president and vice-president on the antiabolitionist Constitutional Union party ticket.
[3] Seward had defended Bill Freeman (1823–47), a black who killed four white people in Auburn, N.Y., in 1846. Freeman, though deaf from earlier beatings and insane, was nearly lynched. Seward helped obtain a reversal of his conviction, but Freeman died in jail; an autopsy revealed extensive brain damage.

To Henrietta Sargent

Medford, Feb. 9'th, 1861

Dear Henrietta,

. . .

I agree with you in thinking that the City of Washington is in danger. I believe that there is an extensive and powerful league at the *North* in confederacy with the South to place Breckenridge in the chair and compel the Republicans to submit.[1] What will be the result, God alone knows. *I* am resigned to *any*thing, except compromises of *principle* on the part of the Republican leaders; but that is precisely the thing which I think is the most likely of all to happen. I think the Republican *party*, if they could be fairly appealed to, would be pretty generally disposed to stand on their platform; for the majority of them doubtless *do* detest slavery. But the trouble is, their *leaders*,— partly from cowardice, partly from a sincere attachment to the Union, and partly from lures of personal ambition, which will be artfully held out to them, and partly from the selfish appeals of merchants and office-holders,—from all these motives, the *leaders* will be in great danger of hugger-muggering up compromises, to which the *party* would never consent, if their votes could be taken. The Peace Convention now in session at Washington sit with closed doors.[2] I don't like these *secret* doings. It is only despotisms that need secresy. The people ought to *know* what their rulers are about, before the mischief is accomplished. My fear is that the slaveholders will get all they want *before* the 4th of March, and then if Lincoln is allowed to come into power, it will be too late for him to undo what has been done.

If the Republicans do *not* yield up all they have gained, I suppose the alternative is civil war. It is a horrid alternative; and God knows I have no desire that a single Southern head should be harmed. But here lies the alarming fact; we must *always* keep on compromising our principles, or else civil war will be threatened; and if we go on in the shameful path we have so long travelled, our free institutions must be everywhere and entirely crushed. Freedom must come up manfully to the struggle, or die by a slow but certain poison. Therefore, much as I deprecate civil war, I deliberately say even *that* is better than compromises of principle, at this momentous crisis. Such epochs come in the history of individuals and of nations, when we are solemnly called upon to decide whether we will serve God or the Devil; and if we choose the latter, ruin is inevitable.

. . .

I think Linda is a remarkable book, and that its circulation will be much

---

[1] John C. Breckinridge (1821–75) of Kentucky, presidential candidate of the seceding southern Democrats, had carried eleven slave states in the 1860 election.
[2] In February, men from Southern, border, and Northern states met privately in Washington in an unsuccessful attempt to work out a compromise plan to save the Union.

calculated to help the anti-slavery cause. I am sorry the Liberator and the Standard manifest so little interest in it.[3] I am grieved to hear of Mr. Garrison's ill health. May God long spare him to us!

. . .

. . . Your affectionate old friend,

L. M. C.

P.S. I hardly think Mr. Phillips is personally in danger. Our adversaries are too *cunning* to give the abolitionists such an advantage. They hate him; but they know "the *people* regard him as a prophet."[4]

ALS; Lydia Maria Child Papers, Anti-Slavery Collection, Cornell University (microfiche 47/1285).

To Charles Sumner

Medford, Feb. 9th, 1861.

Dear and honored Mr. Sumner,

In these times, you doubtless have all manner of rumors written to you; and I have felt some hesitation in writing to you certain remarks, addressed to me; but, as it is very desirable that the Republicans should *know*, as far as possible what is being said & done at this time, I have concluded to repeat to you what I heard, and let it go for what it is worth.

A fortnight ago, or more, I called on my friend Mrs. Silsbee, wife of Nathaniel Silsbee, ex Mayor of Salem. They were at the Winthrop House, Boston. I knew Mr. Silsbee was a ferocious Bell-Everett, and did not mean to introduce either anti-slavery or politics, during my call. But S. Carolina came in, with sound of trumpet, as she does everywhere, now a days. The conversation became very earnest. Neither of us went beyond the bounds of politeness; but Mr. Silsbee grew red in the face, and his lips were occasionally tightly compressed.   He maintained that the slaves were much better off than the poor in Massachusetts; that the moral character of Southerners was much better than that of Northerners; that the South had been abominably abused by the North; that the *North* passed the Missouri Compromise, for her own selfish purposes; that the *North* passed the Nebrask [*sic*] Bill; &c &c. In a word that all his sympathies went with the South. That there would be more fighting *here* than there would be at the South. That *he* was not going to fight, but there was a powerful organization that *would*, and plenty of money would be contributed by the friends of "law and order" to put down the Republican agitation. His greatest wrath was poured upon John A. Andrew, and others, who proposed

[3] Harriet Jacobs's *Incidents in the Life of a Slave Girl* was published under the pseudonym Linda Brent. Probably the imminent threat of civil war explains the lack of interest in still another slave narrative.
[4] Every speech of Phillips's was being spread nationally by the press. After decades of denunciation he was at this time viewed with respect.

by force of arms to resist secession. He did not blame the South for forming a Confederacy to protect their rights, he said. He upheld them in it. &c He said the Bell-Everett party had become an organization under *another name*.[1]

A few days ago, riding out here in the cars, Rev. Mr. Nute, of Kansas notoriety, sat beside me.[2] He told me his father had always been a "Democrat died in the wool;" was formerly an officer in the Custom House, but had left it; though he was sorry to say he had not left his pro-slavery behind him. He was now a Breckenridge Democrat, of the fiercest kind. During his call upon his father, the Boston Post was brought in from the Post Office. When his father opened it, a few small sticks knotted together dropped out. His father said these sticks were a secret mode of communication adopted by a very large organization. The messages thus conveyed throughout the organization were modified by the number and arrangement of the sticks. The organization consisted of Democrats and Bell-Everetts. Some of the richest gentlemen in Boston and some eminent lawyers were in league with it. Fifty millions of dollars would be forthcoming, if needed, to accomplish their object.   Mr. Nute inquired, "What *is* the object?"

His father replied, "That is *our secret*."

My own idea is that these arrangements point to the taking of Washington, and the placing of Breckenridge in the chair. But of that you can judge better than I.

Yours with the deepest respect & gratitude,

L. Maria Child.

ALS; Houghton Library, Harvard University (microfiche 47/1286).

To Lucretia Mott

Medford, Feb. 26'th 1861.

Dear Friend Lucretia,

I have had much comfort with your pleasant grandchildren this winter, and now that they are going to Philadelphia, I am moved to write to you, to say how warmly I cherish you in my heart. When I remember my first and only visit to Philadelphia, and have a vision of your pretty daughter just then beginning to yield to the attraction of early love, and then look upon your winning grandchild, with her smiling, vivacious baby, I feel very old.

But when there is anti slavery work to be done, I feel as young as twenty. There *was* a time when I grew tired of incessant strife, and of the distasteful

---

[1] Child was reporting early signs and rumors of what soon became the "Copperhead" movement, composed mainly of Northern Democrats who opposed the war. One of their organizations was the secret Order of Knights of the Golden Circle.
[2] This was Ephraim Nute, the antislavery pastor who would soon become a Union army chaplain.

labor of reform. I wanted to repose on the serene height⟨hs⟩ of mysticism, to quit rocky and rugged paths, and sleep among flowers, lulled by the tones of music. But those audacious oppressors will not *let* us sleep. Consciences far ⟨less⟩ more drowsy than mine find themselves unable to slumber in the presence of such rampant wickedness. When Anthony Burns was carried from Boston, and when Charles Sumner was stricken down in the Senate, I swore a solemn oath, in the depths of my soul, that, so long as God spared my life, I would hunt the Demon Slavery with all the energy and all the activity I possessed. Conscience twinges me now and then, that I ever turned aside from this duty, to dally in primrose paths; but I make the best atonement that can be made, by working *now* with redoubled diligence. I consider a day lost when I have not made *some* effort to abridge the term of Slavery.   The spirit has moved me to try to act upon minds at the South. I have written many letters, and sent over a thousand copies of my West India Tract to slaveholders. I get a few encouraging responses, and I cherish the hope that much of the seed, which now seems to fall on barren soil, will produce fruit in the future. It is our duty to work & wait.

I think the aspect of the times is encouraging. If the Republicans had been braver, much more *might* have been gained for freedom, than *will* be gained. But we abolitionists have created, or aroused, so strong a sentiment against slavery, that politicians, for the sake of their own interest, will not venture to compromise by *wholesale,* as they have formerly done.[1] The North has become a political power, as well as the South. What aspect public affairs will assume, it is impossible to foresee. But I think we shall get rid of *some* of the Slave States, at all events. If we could only get rid of *all!* But whatever turn affairs may take, the term of slavery is *sure* to be abridged by the present agitation. The blind fury of the Secessionists have converted them into the most valuable Anti Slavery Agents.

How sublime in his moral heroism does Charles Sumner stand! A noble column standing erect and strong in the midst of so much leaning and sliding!   Immense efforts have been made to persuade him to compromise. One compromiser, after laboring with him in vain, said, "Well, Mr. Sumner, if you *persist* in standing so stiffly against the intreaties of your party, you will find yourself standing *alone.*"   "Very well," replied the brave soul; "I *can* stand alone. Better to stand alone on *principle,* than *compromise* with a multitude." God bless him!

With respects to your good mate, and cordial greetings to your children and their households, I am ever your friend, with affection and respect, L. M. Child.

ALS; Collection of American Literature, Beinecke Rare Book and Manuscript Library, Yale University (microfiche 47/1290).

---

[1] Child was anticipating what would soon become clear: the great role abolitionists would play in molding Union sentiment.

To John Greenleaf Whittier

Medford, April 4'th 1861

Dear Friend Whittier,

I thank you for your friendly letter, and your gentle sister also for her kindly greeting.

I am glad you liked "Linda". I have taken a good deal of pains to publish it, and circulate it, because it seemed to me well calculated to take hold of many minds, that will not attend to *arguments* against slavery. The author is a quick-witted, intelligent woman, with great refinement and propriety of manner. Her daughter, now a young woman grown, is a stylish-looking, attractive young person, white as an Italian lady, and very much *like* an Italian of refined education. If she were the daughter of any of the Beacon St. gentry, she would produce a sensation in the fashionable world. The Mrs. *Bruce*, with whom the mother is described as living in New York, is in fact Mrs. *Willis*; for ⟨in fact⟩ my protegée has for many years been the factotum in the family of N. P. Willis, the distinguished poet. He has mentioned her incidentally in "Letters from Idlewild," in the Home Journal, as "our intelligent housekeeper," our "household oracle," &c. He would not have *dared* to mention that she had ever been a fugitive slave. The Home Journal is not *violently* pro-slavery, but it is very *insidiously* and *systematically* so. The N.Y. Herald, the Day Book, and the Home Journal, are announced by the Jeff. Davis organs to be the *only* Northern papers that the South can securely *trust*. Mr. Willis entertains many Southerners at Idlewild, and is a favorite with them; for that reason, the author of "Linda" did not ask *him* to help her about her M.S. though he has always been very friendly to her, and would have far more influence than I have. *Mrs.* Willis is decidedly *Anti* Slavery in her feelings. The advent of *any* truth into society is always a Messiah, which divides families, and brings "not peace, but a sword." These things ought not to be mentioned in the *papers*. I use fictitious names in the book; first, lest the Southern family, who secreted Linda some months, should be brought into difficulty; secondly, lest some of her surviving relatives at the South should be persecuted; and thirdly, out of delicacy to Mrs. Willis, who would not like to have her name bandied about in the newspapers, perhaps to the injury of her husband's *interests*, and certainly to the injury of his *feelings*.

The publishers of "Linda," failed, before a copy had been sold. The author succeeded in buying the plates, paying half the money down. The Boston booksellers are dreadfully afraid of soiling their hands with an Anti-Slavery book; so we have a good deal of trouble in getting the book into the market. Do you think any bookseller, or other *responsible* person in Newburyport, would be answerable for a few? They sell here, at retail, $1 a volume. Whoever would take one or two dozen of them might have them at 68 cts per vol. If you think it worth while to send any to Newburyport or Amesbury, please inform me to whom to send.

378

With regard to the present crisis of affairs, I think the *wisest* can hardly foresee what turn events will take; but *whatever* way they may develope, I have faith that the present agitation will shorten the existence of slavery; and we ought to be willing to suffer *any*thing to bring about *that* result. The ancient proverb declares that "whom the gods would destroy, they first make mad"; and surely the South are mad enough to secure destruction. My *own* soul utters but *one* prayer; and that is, that we may be effectually separated from *all* the Slave-States. My reasons are, first, that we can in no *other* way present to the world a fair experiment of a free Republic; second, that if the Border-States remain with us, we shall be just as much bound to deliver up fugitives as we now are; third those Border-States will form a line of armed sentinels between us and the New Confederacy of "Slave-own-ia", (as *Punch* wittily calls it) preventing the escape of slaves from the far south, just as they now do; lastly, we shall continue to be demoralized, politically and socially, by a *few* slave-states, as much as we should by *all* of them; they will always be demanding concessions of principle, and our politicians will always be finding reasons for compromise. There is no *health* for us, unless we can get *rid* of the accursed thing. My prayer is, "Deliver us, O Lord, from this body of Death! ["]

This does not arise from any sectional or partisan feeling; but simply because my reason, my heart, and my conscience, *all* pronounce this Union to be *wicked*. The original compact is *wrong;* and the attempt to obey the laws of *man*, when they are in open conflict with the laws of *God*, must *inevitably* demoralize a nation, and ultimately undermine all true prosperity, even in a material point of view.

. . .

ALS; Manuscript Division, Library of Congress (microfiche 48/1300).

Few Northerners thought that war would come. They expected that, if the Southern states seceded, they would eventually come back into the Union. Even the abolitionists did not anticipate war. Lincoln, in his inaugural address on 4 March 1861, assured the South that he would protect her rights but stressed that he would not permit secession. On 12 April the shore batteries in Charleston fired on Fort Sumter, beginning the Civil War. The attack revolutionized public feeling in the North, and people were galvanized into resistance. On 15 April, Lincoln declared that "insurrection" existed and called for seventy-five thousand troups.

In calling for troops Lincoln promised "to avoid any destruction of, or interference with, property"—by which he meant slavery. Greeley's *Tribune* likewise assured readers, ". . . this war is in truth a war for the preservation of the Union, not for the destruction of slavery. . . . Slavery has nothing to fear from a Union triumph."

Child, like all abolitionists, worried about the war's objectives.

379

To Lucy Osgood

Wayland, April 26th, 1861

My very dear friend, here it is ten days since we returned from your cozy, hospitable mansion! I can hardly muster any good reasons for so long delaying to write. I found the house damp and chilly, and the weather has been so cloudy most of the time, that I had little energy to hunt for things and set them to rights for Spring arrangements; and so the necessary jobs have dragged on longer than usual; and after doing a little, I have crouched over the fire, tired and sleepy. The reading of Adam Bede has been a great satisfaction. If I had read it before I read the Mill of the Floss, I dare say I might have liked it better than the Mill; but as it is, my first love does not suffer by the comparison.[1] They are both remarkable books.

. . .

The excitement reaches us here only in very faint echoes. Now and then, a cart-horse goes by with a small U.S. flag at his ears. I am surprised at the unanimity of all parties in supporting the government; and I thank God that I live to see the day when it is risky to talk in praise of the South. Nevertheless, I do not think there is much of either right principle, or good feeling, at the foundation of this unanimous Union sentiment. Our merchants are alarmed about dangers to commerce; our national vanity is piqued by insults to the U.S. flag, likely to render it contemptible in the eyes of the world; great numbers of the people think there is an imperious necessity of defending the government *now*, lest there should soon *be* no government to protect us from utter anarchy; and still greater numbers are ready to rush into whatever is the fashion. Two thirds would be as ready as ever to throw *away* sop to Cerberus, if he would only be content to spare the passengers in *our* boat, and eat everybody else. But thank God, Cerberus is ferocious to eat up *every*thing. May he continue so, till the work of complete separation is accomplished!

Rumor says that 30 Florida slaves, who escaped to Fort Pickens and offered their services in defence of the U.S. were sent back to their masters, in chains; and that our Mass'ts General Butler proposes to employ the soldiers under his command in putting down a projected insurrection of slaves in Maryland. God knows I *want* to love and honor the flag of my country; but how *can* I, when it is used for *such* purposes? When men strive to enslave others, the spirit of justice within me cries out, "May God do so unto them, and more also"!

Did you read, in the Standard, the mournful exodus of the colored people from Chicago? Helpless and defenceless victims flying from the tyranny of the U.S.! In view of these things, the Union-shouts, and hurras for the U.S. flag, sound like fiendish mockery in my ears. Well may Fernando Wood, and the editors of the Boston Courier, and Rev. Nehemiah Adams join hands to uphold

---

[1] The references are to George Eliot's novels *Adam Bede* (Edinburgh, 1859) and *The Mill on the Floss* (Edinburgh, 1860).

such a Union!² But I believe God is in the whirlwind, tho' men do not recognize his presence.

. . .

ALS; Lydia Maria Child Papers, Anti-Slavery Collection, Cornell University (microfiche 48/1302).

To Lucy Osgood

Wayland May 7'th, 1861

My very Dear Friend,

When I received your letter saying, "Not a booby is to be found so stupid as not to know that this war is on account of slavery, and nothing else," I had just finished reading a long and elaborate editorial in the Boston Advertiser, to prove that slavery had nothing whatsoever to do with this war, and that it was altogether absurd to suggest that it had; it was a war to put down *treason*, not to meddle with *slavery*, and that everybody ought to remember that, and inculcate it carefully.   Here in the little drowsy village of Wayland, last week, David attended one of the fashionable meetings for furnishing aid to the U.S. He was very violently treated, and almost mobbed, for saying something about the duty of the U.S. toward slaves that might offer to fight on its side. He was told the war had "nothing to do with the damned niggers"; the war was to preserve the *Union*, that's what they were fighting for, and they would n't hear a word about the niggers. Our neighbor Baldwin is quite zealous for the stars and stripes; but then he expects the worst part of the fighting will be "putting down the niggers." Our Mass'ts Gen. Butler has publicly announced that if any slaves desert to him, he shall send them back to their masters.¹ Thirty Florida slaves escaped to Fort Pickens, through great perils & sufferings, and asked to serve for the U.S. They were chained & sent back, and their masters whipped them nigh unto death.

. . .

Sunday before last, Mr. Sears preached an excellent discourse on the times.² I went to meeting rather tearful, having just bid goodbye to a neighbor's son, going to the war. He is the son of a widow, and he looked so handsome in his new uniform, that I could hardly help folding him to my heart. I looked after

² Wood, a proslavery Democrat, was the notoriously corrupt mayor of New York. He proposed that if disunion came, New York should secede from the United States and establish itself as a free and independent city. Adams (1806–78) was a Congregational minister and author so proslavery he was called "Southside Adams."

¹ Gen. Benjamin Butler, who had offered in April to use his Massachusetts troops to put down a rumored slave rising in Maryland, here showed his readiness to carry out the Fugitive Slave Law. Governor Andrew of Massachusetts soon rebuked him, and Butler quickly shifted position.

² Rev. Edmund Sears was the Unitarian pastor in Wayland.

him with moistened eyes, thinking how soon the new uniform might be draggled in blood and dust. "To die is not the worst thing that can happen," said I to myself. "If I could only be *sure* that if he dies, he will die for *freedom!*"

I went to meeting with my heart full of him, and on the way I thought to myself what a support and consolation Mr. Sear's preaching would be in these troubled times. But lo! he announced that it was the last sermon he should preach as our pastor. I had a good cry when I got home. I didn't know I was so much attached to him.   Bronchitis makes it difficult for him to preach more than *one* sermon a week, and his people think they must have two, for fear "the Philistines will hear of it." I am told that a few weeks ago he spoke of Slavery as the great demoralizer and troubler of the nation, and one of his principal parishioners, a Bell Everett, rose and went out. Mr. Sears is very sensitive; and I suppose he neither chooses to be muzzled nor to live in a turmoil. I walked thro' the woods last week to make him a visit, and I found him ploughing. He gave me a most affectionate reception, and we had much edifying discourse together. I have been to see six of my nearest neighbors, including the orthodox deacon's wife, who is a right friendly old body, and always very cozy with me. I have been to [. . .]³ twice, and said not a word about the times, concerning which he is enlightened to his own satisfaction by the lying columns of the Boston Post, which joins in the hurra for the U.S. flag, while it does its utmost to sustain slavery.

I have also been a mile, to a brook in the woods, to see the miller, who constructed a telescope for himself. I sat on a log by the mill-wheel and settled the affairs of the nation with him, much to our mutual satisfaction. To *him* the war means emancipation.

Now I think I have done pretty well, for one who don't love her "fellow critters." I told Bro. C. that you said I loved the human race, but took no interest in John & Sam. He said he thought just the contrary. He thought I was *too* apt to be interested in individuals, and to expend my energies in their service. You are both right. I do not often take much interest in individuals I meet with; but when I do take an interest in them, I devote myself to them very zealously; or rather I *have* heretofore done so. I do not warm up so easily now.   And *never* can I warm, in the slightest degree, toward anybody who defends slavery, or apologizes for it, or is indifferent about its abolition. It is not a difference of *opinion*, which excites my opposition; the *moral tendency* of the whole man is indicated thereby. I detest the confusion of moral principles which induces men to set up statues of Daniel Webster and Horace Mann, side by side.

I suppose you saw that Prof. Ticknor⁴ gave $500 to carry on the war. Do you suppose *that* "booby" knew the war was "on account of slavery, and nothing else"? . . .

        . . .

³ A name crossed out here is unrecovered.
⁴ George Ticknor.

But you are nevertheless right in supposing that the crisis is educating men to higher views of justice and humanity. I see the guiding hand of God and reverence it; but my respect for Bell-Everetts and Breckenride [*sic*] men is not increased one whit; on the contrary their jumping on the popular wave, to save themselves, makes them more contemptible in my eyes.

. . .

AL, part cut away; Lydia Maria Child Papers, Anti-Slavery Collection, Cornell University (microfiche 48/1306).

To Lucy Searle

Wayland, June 5, 1861.

I return "Silas Marner" with cordial thanks.[1] It entertained me greatly. His honest attempts at education were extremely amusing. What a genuine touch of nature was "Eppie in the tole hole!" What a significant fact it is in modern literature, that the working class are so generally the heroes. No princes in disguise are necessary now to excite an interest in the reader. The popular mind is educated up to the point of perceiving that carpenters, weavers, etc., are often real princes in disguise. The longer I live, the more entirely and intensely do my sympathies go with the masses.

I am glad to see some amendment with regard to sending back fugitive slaves.[2] Those at Fort Monroe are to be protected so long as Virginia continues in rebellion. God grant that all the slave-holders may rebel, and remain in rebellion, till the emancipation of their slaves is accomplished! Success to Jeff. Davis, till he goads the free States into doing, from policy and revenge, what they have not manhood to do from justice and humanity! It is a dreadful thing, a most demoralizing thing, to have the laws of one's country at such variance with the laws of God. I never realized it so fully as when I heard your good, conscientious, intelligent friend say that he would send back a fugitive slave because the Constitution required it. When our fathers joined hands with slave-holders to form the Constitution, with their feet on the prostrate and helpless slaves, they did sad work for their descendants. If my father had made a compact with a rich neighbor that I would help him rob a poor one, I should break the compact. Law is not law, if it violates principles of eternal justice. If drunken foreigners are hired to vote for a member of Congress, and the vote of that member causes the enactment of the Fugitive Slave Law, probably because he wishes to obtain some still higher office, am I bound to sell my soul to perdition

---

[1] George Eliot, *Silas Marner* (Edinburgh, 1861).

[2] On 23 May Butler had begun labelling fugitive slaves entering Union lines at Fortress Monroe, Va., "contraband" of war. He refused to return them to their masters and instead put them to work. Soon thousands of contrabands were sheltering behind Union lines.

because the iniquity has been framed into a law? The dictionary does not contain words enough to express my detestation of all laws framed for the support of tyranny. To keep that unrighteous compact with fellow-citizens was bad enough, but to keep it with rebels, who have over and over again violated all their part of the compact, is adding imbecility and absurdity to wickedness.

L, extract; *Letters of Lydia Maria Child*, 1882 (microfiche 48/1311).

To Lucy Searle

Wayland, June 9'th, 1861.

Dear Lucy,

You misunderstood the import of my note; at least of what I *intended* should be its import. I presume I expressed myself carelessly. It was not my intention to impute anything wrong to George, for whom I have a very high respect and a most friendly regard. What I *meant* to say was this: that incalculable mischiefs result from the fact that the laws of a country are at variance with the laws of God; that under such circumstances even the intelligent and conscientious are sorely puzzled how to reconcile what seem to be conflicting *duties;* how to be true to their *civil oaths*, without violating their *religious convictions.* On the mass of the people, such conflict has a very demoralizing effect; tending to do away belief in any such thing as *fixed principles* by placing *laws* on the same sacred level, though often passed by bad men, for bad purposes. And not only are the mass demoralized, but even the good, the intelligent, and the strictly conscientious, sometimes become effectually bewildered, when some emergency compels them either to violate their *civil oaths*, or to violate the most obvious and generally admitted *commands of God.* A government which places its citizens in such a dilemma does them a grievous wrong, the consequences of which extend too far to be calculated. That is what I *meant* to say.

The fact is, I identify myself so completely with the slaves, that I am kept in alternating states of anxiety and wrath, concerning their rendition by the officers of the U.S. If I wake up in the middle of the night, it is the first thing I think of. I long to get at the poor creatures, to tell them to run away to Canada or Hayti, and not trust to the promises of the U.S. always perfidious and cruel to the colored man.

I am waiting with great anxiety to see what will be the results of this war; for if things are patched up on the old foundation, I will quit the country, and lay my bones on a foreign soil; *any* soil not cursed by a Fugitive Slave Law. Under that law I will not live.

It is a beautiful peaceful Sabbath. Cloud-shadows are flitting over the broad green meadows, in front of my window; and all is so still that one might "hear the grass grow," if the ear were fine enough. It seems difficult to realize the fierce passions that are raging a few hundred miles from us. You will think it strange, and perhaps wrong, that I do not wish them to be less fierce, at present. I want the "irrepressible conflict" to intensify to a focus, that will kindle a fire powerful enough to sweep over and effectually destroy the *cause* of the conflict. This does not arise from partisan feelings on my part, from any hatred to slaveholders, or any want of love for my country; but because it is my deliberate and firm conviction that in no other way can our free institutions be saved. It will be better for *all* parties to have the question completely settled *now;* and it does seem as if Divine Providence were wonderously over-ruling things for that result.

   . . .

ALS; Lydia Maria Child Papers, Anti-Slavery Collection, Cornell University (microfiche 48/1312).

To Sarah Shaw

Wayland, June 14'th, 1861

   . . .

I suppose Robert belonged to the 7'th Regiment, and consequently that he is at home now; and that must be a relief to your mind.[1] This civil war is an awful thing; and we cannot possibly foresee what is to be the end of it. I suppose no sane person doubts that the North must eventually beat. But after we have conquered them, what are we to *do* with subjects whose character is so incongruous to ours, and who hate us, our institutions and our manners, with such an irreconcilable hatred? The worst of it is, a large number of them, probably a majority, if we could fairly ascertain the sentiments in many of the States, wish to remain under the U.S. government; and it becomes a duty to protect such citizens from the lawless violence of their own oligarchy. My prevailing wish is that they might *all* want to go out of the Union, and that they might *all* go out, and stay out. But God knows best, and his hand is obviously in this work. We are on the top of a giant wave, and it must drift us whithersoever He wills.

I am sorry the English press has maintained such a tone on the subject.[2] It has a bad moral influence on people *here.* They seem to speak of the contest, as if it were six of one and half a dozen of the other. They say the North has no *cause* to fight for. Good Heavens! when we are fighting to have *any* government preserved to us! to be saved from utter anarchy!   They tell us these

[1] Robert Gould Shaw (1837–63), whom Child had known from infancy as the son of Sarah and Francis Shaw, was a captain in the Second Massachusetts Volunteers.
[2] With strong economic ties to the South and fears of rising competition from the North, British merchants and industrialists showed sympathy for the Confederacy, or at best neutrality. A major problem for the Lincoln administration was how to swing British opinion to the Union side. The abolitionists believed that only a firm commitment to the destruction of slavery would do it.

States are like partners in business, and if a portion of the firm want to dissolve the partnership, why not let them go? The comparison is not correct. We are a *consolidated government*, not mere partners, as long as suits ⟨all parties.⟩ any party.   But granting that we *are* mere partners, how does the case stand? A. and B. form a partnership. A. is the most industrious partner, pays much the largest share of the expenses, and increases the business in every direction. Years pass on, and the firm grows rich. Then B. says to A. I want to quit you, and set up in business for myself. I shall take as much of the property as I please, and if you make any objection, I'll burn your house and your manufactories to the ground, and rob all your ships.

Even Harriet Martineau writes as if the Pennsylvania Tariff were just as wicked as Southern Slavery. I am a believer in Free Trade, and have been for many years. The Divine government leaves water to find its own level; and *human* governments are wise and salutary in proportion as they aim at the same thing. But what an absurd confounding of moral distinctions to place restrictions on trade on the same moral level as Slavery! She is eloquent against "class legislation," forsooth! As if every department of life in England were not based upon class legislation! This mother of ours is greatly given to self-sufficiency and dictation; and the worst of it is, she does not take the trouble to *understand* our affairs, before she gives us advice and pronounces her decisions.

Russell's Letter to the London Times is a precious developement of Southern feeling.[3] Their boasting to him of having been Tories in the Revolution, and their desire to have an English Prince to rule over them, are lures thrown out to obtain the friendship of England; but the *spirit* of their statement is true. They *do* dislike governments based on ideas of freedom and equality. They *like* despotism, and they *believe* in despotic principles. The forces are gathering together for the great battle of Armageddon, all the world over. We Americans are divided, and seem destined to help both sides about equally. The Southerners are for despotism, and the Bell-Everetts among *us* are just as truly aristocrats at heart. They would like a demarcation of classes so strong, that the common people should be allowed to know only just enough to serve the aristocracy faithfully.

. . .

Ah, the poor slaves have so few friends, and so many enemies! In all this war, there seems to be no feeling for *them*. As "contraband" articles of *property*, a few may escape, friendless wanderers, to find a home where they can. But any master, who swears he is a Union-man, can have the chattels back again, to scourge at pleasure; and it is so *easy* for the chivalry to swear![4]

Good bye, my precious friend. Do ask Frank to inform me how you are,

[3] William H. Russell arrived in New York in Mar. 1861 and covered both the Northern and Southern fronts for the *London Times*. He published his American impressions in *My Diary North and South* (Boston, 1863).

[4] The contrabands' legal status was vague; they were not actually free, and as Child asserts, they could be returned to slavery.

if you don't feel like writing yourself. David has been alarmingly ill, but is getting to be himself again.   Yours with warmest love, Mariquita.

ALS; Houghton Library, Harvard University (microfiche 48/1313).

To Charles Sumner

Wayland, July 16th, 1861.

Dear Mr. Sumner,

In the Boston Traveller of the 13th, mention is made of a soldier of the New York Second Regiment, who refused to obey orders to stop fugitive slaves; saying he was willing to take the consequences, but he did not enlist to arrest fugitive slaves, and he would not do it. I am very desirous to learn the name of that soldier, and to ascertain how I can address a letter to him.[1] Mrs. Stowe also wishes to write to him, and I promised to inform her of his address, if I could obtain it. Will you help us in this matter, as *soon* as you conveniently can? I should like also, if convenient, to ascertain the address of the picket guard, or sentinel, who let the slave pass as "all right," and refused to let his master follow on his track; not needing any information to convince him that *he* was *not* "all right." . . .

The very last drop of my patience is exhausted. Whoever stands in the way of the slave's freedom, at this crisis, may he be swept from the face of the earth! The steam of popular feeling is up pretty high. If the conductors don't take care, the boilers will burst. If there is much more delay in rightly reading God's lesson of the hour, I hope they *will* burst. *How* I thanked Ow[en] Lovejoy for his manly resolution![2] How I rejoiced over the vote of the House! The spirit of our fathers is not quite dead, as I have sometimes feared.

. . .

ALS; Houghton Library, Harvard University (microfiche 48/1318).

On 21 July, the day Child wrote the next two letters, Union forces were routed in the battle of Bull Run. The North had been confident of success in the move toward Richmond. News of the defeat (it had not yet reached Child in that day of slower communications) was a stunning surprise, and made many despair. But the abolitionists expected that the disaster would shock the North out of its easy optimism and help it see the slavery issue in another light.

[1] This soldier is unidentified.
[2] A congressional resolution affirming that "it is no part of the duty of soldiers of the United States to capture and return fugitive slaves" had just been passed by the House. But simply as an expression of opinion it had small effect upon army officers, who continued to return fugitive slaves.

To Sarah Shaw

Wayland, July 21'st, 1861.

Darling Friend,

. . . [L]ast week I performed the extraordinary feat of going, in out-spread fashionable garments, to a stylish party in Weston, where over a hundred people were assembled. Mrs. Stowe was there, and she and I got into a corner, and, with few interruptions, succeeded in ignoring the party. I paid no attention to any of the strangers, except one Bell-Everett malignant, who came with prancing horses, and chariot lined with white, making the air resound with orders to his coachman. He had a thin, hard face, and skinny clutching hands, like a beast of prey. He looked so much like a slave-holder, that I could not help drawing down my lip-corners every time he passed near me. It was a great triumph of politeness that I did not accompany the gesture with a movement of my foot.

Mrs. Stowe's habitual stiffness of manner vanished the moment we spoke together. We dived at once into public affairs, and I found faith and hope stronger than anxiety in her mind. She has no more faith in politicians than I have; and most especially does she distrust that selfish diplomat, William H. Seward, who exerts so much ingenuity to say what he does *not* mean. It is a pity the Delphic Oracle has fallen into disuse. He would be invaluable to the priests in writing responses that might be turned *any* way, according as circumstances required. Sarah, let nobody ever induce you ⟨ever⟩ to trust that man! If he does not do the cause of freedom an irreparble [*sic*] mischief, it will merely be because the spirit of the people holds him upright, so that he has no *temptation* to lean or crawl. I do not say this because I am rabid, or entirely one-sided. I recognize the usefulness of expediency; but its legitimate province is to choose between wise and unwise *modes of advancing principles.* To *compromise principles* is *never* expediency, however *appearances* may, for a time, indicate the contrary; and the politician who is willing to compromise *principle* is never a statesman, in any true and large sense of the word. Such men as Seward are capable of doing great mischief to noble young souls. Distinctions between right and wrong get all enveloped in fog by such diplomatic influence. Mrs. Stowe agreed with me in thinking that the spirit of the people would render it *politic* for him to walk straight. God and the people we *can* rely upon; the people, because God is now moving them. Thus far, events have been wonderfully over-ruled. They so plainly indicate the Divine *intention*, that I cannot be otherwise than hopeful about the result. If God *has* determined to deliver these people from the house of bondage, William H. Seward will be no more than a fly on his chariot wheels. So let him go!

I was extremely pleased with Mrs. Stowe, and also with Professor Stowe. I noticed in her continual indications of *Puritan* education. She said she had been convinced that slavery would be overthrown, ever since our Chief Justice passed *under the chain,* to enter the Court House; it was one of those *signs,* such as God inspired the old *Prophets* to enact, to reveal to the people the depth of their degradation; and, from that time to the present, she thought the hand of God had been very remarkably and peculiarly manifest in the ordering of events.[1] The conviction that all this could not be for *nothing*, she said, was the foundation of her faith that Pharaoh would be swamped and Israel was to go free. I am surprised to find how indifferent I am to the drowning of Pharaoh's hosts, provided the Israelites get on dry, firm ground. The fact is my Christian patience and forbearance ⟨is⟩ are utterly exhausted. Every now and then, I sincerely *try* to get a fresh stock; but then comes along some Col. Cowden, or Col. Jones, and fills me with such wrath, that I want to behead half the world.[2]

. . .

ALS; Houghton Library, Harvard University (microfiche 48/1319).

To Theodore Tilton

Wayland, July 21st, 1861.

Dear Mr. Tilton,

I am very sorry you were obliged to apply to Mr. Francis for a copy of Fact and Fiction.[1] If I could have procured a copy here, I should have sent you one; but it is out of the market, and I tried in vain at all the Boston bookstores to procure a copy for myself, a short time ago. I agree with Mrs. Stowe that the publication of ⟨the⟩ the story at this time will help the formation of public opinion in the right direction. For the same reason, I sent you, the other day, a few verses extracted from Whittier. It seems to me very desirable to manufacture public opinion *fast* now, that it may be in readiness to make suitable use of the crisis, which the madness of the South, under the guiding hand of Divine Providence, is bringing upon itself.

I have no personal knowledge of Mrs. Browning, for I have never been abroad.[2] In the grandeur of her intellect, ⟨and⟩ the nobleness of her aspirations, and the generous outflow of her sympathies, I think she is unsurpassed among women. Aurora Leigh is a great book; intellectually very great, morally still greater. It kindled in me a glowing enthusiasm while I read it. Still, I will confess to you that my favorite author, *par excellence*, is Mrs. Stowe. I have a more lively pleasure in her works, than I have in those of any other writer, man or women [*sic*].

When Aurora Leigh appeared, it was generally voted to be Mrs. Browning's best production; and some said, "Her soul has expanded and improved

[1] During the Sims case of 1851, Chief Justice Shaw, entering the courthouse, had to duck under iron chains strung across its doors to keep angry abolitionists from effecting a rescue.
[2] Probably these were army officers who returned fugitive slaves.
[1] Child's *Fact and Fiction* (1846).
[2] Elizabeth (Barrett) Browning had died on 29 June 1861.

under the influence of *Mr.* Browning." I never assented to such remarks, because *all* her writings, from the beginning, seemed to me to indicate that *hers* was the superior soul. Harriet Hosmer, who has been intimately acquainted with Mrs. Browning, during her long residence in Italy, told me a fact, which shows that Mr. Browning's influence had no share in the excellence of Aurora Leigh.[3] She said Mrs. Browning told her she was surprised at the success of the book; that she had written nearly the whole of it *seven years before*, but had felt so very doubtful whether it were worthy of publication, that she had laid it aside, with the idea that she should never publish it. If I mistake not, she was unacquainted with Mr. Browning at the time she says Aurora Leigh was mostly written; at all events, she was not married to him, till some time after.

Mrs. Frank G. Shaw of Staten Island, with whom I believe you are acquainted, was intimate with Mrs. Browning in Italy. Perhaps she could tell you something interesting about her. If you wish to make use of anything in this note you are welcome so to do.

I thank you for the number of the Independent containing the obituary notice of Mrs. Browning. (I have put the n in her name *this* time. I don't know what possessed me to leave it out. Do you ever have days when your [*sic*] are under a spell, that renders you unable to spell? I do.)

I am very cordially yours,

L. Maria Child.

ALS; James Fraser Gluck Collection, Buffalo and Erie County Public Library (microfiche 48/1320).

To Sarah Shaw

Wayland, Aug. 11'th, 1861

Darling friend,

. . .

The question you ask is of course one that has occupied my own mind not a little. I made up my mind some weeks ago; and from Wendell Phillips' First of August Speech I infer that he takes a similar view, though he does not go into the details that have taken form in my mind.[1]   Amid the complicated relations in which we stand at this crisis, I do *not* think it would be politic for government to proclaim freedom to the slaves. Events may ripen public opinion for such a measure, but it is not *yet* ripened.   But according to my ideas, no proclamation from government, and no official action of any sort, is *needed*. There are but two horns to the dilemma. If the runaway slaves who come to our camps and forts say their masters are avowed secessionists, why then the

[3] Hosmer enjoyed a long friendship with the Brownings during her many years in Italy. They were the models for her cast *Clasped Hands*.
[1] Wendell Phillips's "First of August" speech celebrated the emancipation of slaves in the West Indies, which had taken place in 1838.

veriest pro-slavery hunker would not contend that we were under any constitutional obligation to send back their fugitive slaves. By their treason, they have
obviously forfeited the protection of the Constitution. In such a case then, the
slave should be told that he is free, and that he may work for the U.S. at the
same wages other men receive.

If, on the other hand, the slave says his master is a Union man, the answer
should be, "If your master comes here to claim you, we have no legal power
to protect you; but then we have no legal power to stop your going wherever
you choose. You can go to Hayti, or to Canada, or wherever you like."

The *reason* I would have them say this, is that military officers really have
no legal power to act in such cases. When a slave is claimed, a *civil process* is
required to prove his identity, and to prove that the man who claims him did
legally own him in the State he ran from. In forts and camps there is no proper
tribunal to examine and decide in such cases, and military officers have no
shadow of right to proceed without due process of law. The consequence is,
that our army is not bound, in *any* case, to send back a fugitive; and if, wherever
our soldiers went, their uniform practice showed that slaves seeking protection
under the banner of the U.S. *never were* sent back, the instinct for freedom
would settle the matter for itself, and the government would have no *need* to
issue a proclamation. It might all be done quietly, without violating any existing
legal obligation, and without exciting any disunity of parties. At least, so it
seems to *me*. I have just written a brief paragraph for the Tribune to that
effect, and I hope they will publish it. It may help a little to disentangle the subject in some minds.

Didn't you like Mrs. Stowe's letter to Lord Shaftsbury?[2] I did, *amazingly*.
I thank God for Mrs. Stowe.

. . .

I cannot decide in my mind whether the defeat at Mannassas will do most
harm or good.[3] We *needed* such experience, to make us more careful about
suitable officers, and more vigilant about spies and traitors. I think, too it will
invigorate the patriotism of strong characters; but it obviously has an unfavorable effect on the numerous class of timid and undecided ones; and there are
plenty of secret enemies among us to use such minds as tools in their project of
disuniting the North.

We are on the top of a huge wave, in a stormy sea, and where we shall be
drifted no mortal can foresee. I recognize the hand of God in the tempest. All
we can do is to fulfil whatever seems to be our duty, and try to trust in *Him*.
Sometimes my patience fails, at other times, faith and hope are re-assured.

The nurse of a sick child repeatedly told the mother she saw evident signs

---

[2] Stowe had begun contributing a column to the *Independent* in 1852. Lord Shaftesbury,
the English reformer, who had opposed slavery, made statements sympathetic to the
South, and Stowe reproached him for it in her column.
[3] The Battle of Bull Run was fought near Manassas, Va.

---

of recovery. "But," said the anxious mother, "the medicine don't seem to produce the effects we expected." "Trust in God," was the reply. "He's *tedious*, ma'am, but He's *sure*."

. . .

ALS; Houghton Library, Harvard University (microfiche 49/1324).

To Lucy Osgood

Wayland, Sep. 1'st, 1861.

My very dear friend,

. . . Silas Marner impressed me very deeply. It seems to me that no writer since Shakespeare has had such insight into human nature, as this Miss Evans; and she *uses* her insight to far better purpose, so thoroughly is her soul pervaded by loving sympathy for the *common people*. My instincts point *that* way, "true as the needle to the pole"; nay truer; for no brilliant Aurora can make it fluctuate from its point of attraction. Aristocracy is *always* my aversion, whether in the form of English noble, Southern planter, or Boston respectable. Adam Bede the carpenter, Silas Marner the weaver, Uncle Tom, and Old Tiff[1] interest me more than the elegant artificiality of all the high-bred classes. I honestly *believe* in the dignity of labor. I say truly, with Eppie, in Silas Marner, "I *like* the working-people; I like their ways."

I am rejoicing now in reading Buckle's 2d vol.[2] His slight estimation of the importance of kings and nobles, and his constantly recurring hard hits at superstition, do my soul good. He wields the sledge-hammer of truth even more boldly than Theodore Parker did; tho' not more boldly than he *would* have done, if he had lived to write the great work, the History of Religions, which he had planned.

I hope Count Gasparin's book cheered you as much as it did me.[3] Theologically, he is somewhat narrow. He *condescends* to be thankful for such reformers as Dr. Channing and Theodore Parker, *notwithstanding* their theological errors. He ignores the *pioneers* of the Anti-Slavery cause, having probably derived his information from sources which represented them as infidels. I smiled at his regret that American women were so masculine. To *me*, the manly women among us seem very rare exceptions. As a general thing, they seem to me as twining female vines, as any reasonable lord of creation could desire. But Count Gasparin is a true friend of freedom, and has manifested a

---

1 Tiff was a slave character in Stowe's novel *Dred*.
2 Henry Thomas Buckle's *History of Civilization in England*, vol. 2 (London, 1861).
3 Agénor de Gasparin (1810–71), a Frenchman who supported the Union cause, wrote *The Uprising of a Great People: The United States in 1861* (New York, 1861).

remarkable knowledge of American affairs. His just appreciation of the U.S. cause, and his hearty sympathy ⟨is⟩ are very cheering amid the gloom of the present crisis.

But the news that came last night made my heart leap up, for the *first* time since Lincoln was chosen. It is rumored that Gen. Fremont has invited the slaves of Missouri to fight under the flag of the U.S. If he *has* taken a step so bold and so wise, the hour has struck at *last*. The contagion will spread like fire on the prairies. But I rejoice with trembling, for I am afraid the next news-paper will contradict the report.[4] It is the *only* step that can save the country, and bring this horrid conflict to a speedy close. I have long ceased to have any hope, except in a sagacious use of the war-power by some bold and able military commander. As soon as I heard that Fremont was to be a general in the U.S. army, the hope arose in my heart that God had sent us the man for the hour. I drew this conclusion from what I had previously known of his character and opinions. From Gen. Lyon, also, I hoped much. The news of his death agonized me.[5] He seemed such a brave man, no *sham* about him, no "fuss and feathers." Since his death, ⟨Mr. [. . .]⟩[6] writes to me that he was an avowed anti-slavery man, and under the domination of our Southern masters, that fact had always hindered his rise in the army. He was also a warm friend of Theodore Parker's, and had imbibed his large and liberal views.

. . .

ALS; Lydia Maria Child Papers, Anti-Slavery Collection, Cornell University (micro-fiche 49/1330).

By September, prominent Massachusetts abolitionists, including Garrison, Phil-lips, Stearns, and Quincy, were organizing quietly to promote emancipation through articles for the press, lectures, and petitions. They called themselves the Emancipation League, and their primary goal was to educate the public to grasp the magnitude of the war and the bearing of slavery on its outcome. Both Child and her husband contributed their energies to the league's work that sum-mer. David wrote *The Rights and Duties of the United States Relative to Slavery under the Laws of War* (Boston, 1861), a major pamphlet designed to prove the constitutionality of wartime emancipation. In the next letter Maria urges Whittier to write war songs and ballads.

[4] On 30 Aug. 1861, General Frémont, commander in the West, proclaimed martial law in Missouri and declared all property of the enemy confiscated and their slaves free. Although an unauthorized act, it was applauded by the abolitionists. Lincoln revoked the order and then removed Frémont.

[5] Gen. Nathaniel Lyon, antislavery Union officer, was killed at the Battle of Wilson's Creek, Mo., on 10 Aug. 1861.

[6] The name was cancelled, probably by the editor of the 1882 edition of Child's letters.

To John Greenleaf Whittier

Wayland, Sep. 10th 1861

Dear Friend Whittier,

I suppose you have been informed that the warmest of the Republicans, and the most unprejudiced of the Abolitionists, are laying their heads together, with no more *publicity* than is necessary, to influence popular opinion, through the press, and help on the turning-tide in the right direction. Of course, *you* are one of the writers on whom they most rely; and I have the object so much at heart, that I cannot help being so impertinent as to make some suggestions to you.

Nothing on earth has such effect on the popular heart as Songs, which the soldiers would take up with enthusiasm, and which it would thereby become the fashion to whistle and sing at the street-corners. "Old John Brown, Hallelujah!" is performing a wonderful mission now. Where the words came from, nobody knows, and the tune is an exciting, spirit-stirring thing, hitherto unknown outside of Methodist Conventicles. But it warms up soldiers and boys, and the air is full of it; just as France was of the Marseillese, whose author was for years unknown.

If the soldiers only *had* a Song, to some spirit-stirring tune, proclaiming what they went to fight for, or *thought* they went to fight for,—for home, country, and liberty; and indignantly announcing that they did *not* go to hunt slaves, to send back to their tyrants poor lacerated workmen, who for years had been toiling for the rich without wages; if they *had* such a song, to a tune that excited them, how rapidly it would educate them!

Ballads, too, told in your pictorial fascinating style, would do a great work at this crisis. If you see returned soldiers, you will have plenty of subjects suggested. Dr. Furness wrote me that a young friend of his was a volunteer in a wealthy aristocratic company, that went from Philadelphia. They returned much worked up about slavery. The young man told Dr. F. that he one day met a rude, rough man, a corporal, crying right out, blubbering like a schoolboy. When asked what was the matter, he replied, "They've just sent a poor fellow back into slavery. I did n't leave my home to do such work as *this*; and I won't do it. I come here to fight for the country and the flag; not to hunt slaves; and if the Col. orders any more such work, I'm afraid I shall shoot him."

Another who was ordered on picket-duty, of course at *unusual* risk of his life, was told that while he was sentinel, if any *slave* attempted to pass the lines, he must turn him back. He replied, "*That* is an order I will not obey." Being reminded of his duty to obey orders,   ,[1] he replied, ["]I know the penalty I incur, and am ready to submit to it. But I did not enlist to do *such* work, and I *will* not do it."   The officers being aware that his feeling would easily become contagious, *modified* the order thus: "If anybody tries to pass, ascer-

---

[1] There is a blank space in the original letter.

tain that *all's right* before you allow them pass."   That night, the moon shone brightly, and the sentinel on duty saw a moving in the bushes before him. "Who goes there? Answer quickly!" Up rose a tall ebony man. "Who are you? ["] "A Fugitive." "⟨Is⟩ Are you *all right?*" "Yes, massa." "Then run quick." ⟨before I've time to fire."⟩

Another time, a lordly Virginian rode up to the U.S. lines, with a pass to the other side. He curled his lip contemptuously, when a U.S. sentinel barred the course of his stylish chariot. "Where's your pass"? The Virginian scorning to acknowledge authority from a "greasy mechanic" of the North, did not deign to make any reply, but motioned to the slave, who was driving his barouche, to deliver the paper to the soldier. The slave dismounted and gave the sentinel the required pass. The sentinel siezed him, and by a quick motion set him twirling down the hill, at the bottom of which were marshalled the U.S. forces.   "Now *you* can turn back," said the sentinel. "But I obtained an order allowing me to pass. How dare you hinder me?" "Where *is* your order?" "My servant just gave it to you."   "Oh, that was an order to pass only *one*, and he has already gone with it."

The Virginian swore roundly, and called vociferously to his slave to come back. The bewildered slave attempted to do so, but the mischievous sentinel put his musket across the path. "Show the paper!" shouted the master. The slave did so. The sentinel read it, and coolly replied, ["]This is a pass *from* Norfolk. You must obtain another pass to go *to* Norfolk." And so the haughty Southerner was obliged to guide his own horses back again, whence he came.

Friend Whittier, it is impossible to exaggerate the good effect of such things as these, if put into the form of popular ballads.

I write in haste, because the bearer to the P. Office is waiting, but I *will* take time to say, beware how you endorse W'm H. Seward! He is no more to be trusted than Daniel Webster was. He is thoroughly unprincipled and selfish. I do not speak rashly. I *know* whereof I affirm.

I was very sorry not to meet you and your sister at Sam. E. Sewall's, as Mrs. Sewall encouraged me to hope.

With affectionate greetings to her, I am most cordially your friend,

L. M. Child.

ALS; Manuscript Division, Library of Congress (microfiche 49/1333).

To Lucy Searle

Wayland, Oct. 11'th, 1861

Dear Lucy,

. . .

. . . Really, it becomes a serious question how much longer patience with our short-sighted, fluctuating government will be a virtue. We could not have been punished for our national sins in a more mortifying manner than by having *such* rulers at such a crisis. Only one thing they seem to be persistent in; and that is in carrying out ⟨Buchanan's⟩ Pierce's hateful theory of "a subject race", in their treatment of the colored people. Only to think of official orders that the "contrabands" at Fort Munroe should not be allowed to wear any article of military dress! Officers and soldiers frequently want to give them some cast-off garment, but it is contrary to *orders;* so the poor fellows are suffering for clothing. Is it not *shameful?* I see that two of them have been recently given back to their masters by a subordinate officer, without authority, and without examination. How long will the people suffer these things?   I did not mean to talk so much about public affairs; but this imbecile, pro-slavery government does try me so, that it seems as if I *must* shoot somebody. Willis is out again with a florid description of Mrs. Lincoln's autumn bonnet, called "The Princess."[1] "Rose-colored velvet, with guipure medallions, trimmed with black thread lace, put on full, and this again trimmed on the edge with a deeper fringe of minute black marabout and ostrich feathers. &c &c. At the same establishment were purchased elegant garnitures for the evening dress of this *representative lady in the American world of fashion.* Pompadour set, of wreath, chatelaine, and bouquet of mixed flowers. Complete garniture for white moire antique dress, of white narcissus and black fruits. Another of violets and roses; the wreath being composed wholly of violets, with a single large rose over the forehead, and clusters of rose-buds behind."

So *this* is what the people are taxed for! to deck out this vulgar doll with foreign frippery! And oppressed millions must groan on, lest her "noble native State" should take offence, if Government made use of the beneficent power God has so miraculously placed in its hands. To *see* these things, and have no power to *change* them, to see the glorious opportunity so *near,* yet slipping away, leaving the nation to sink deeper and deeper into the abyss of degradation—this is really the torment of Tantalus.

. . .

ALS; Lydia Maria Child Papers, Anti-Slavery Collection, Cornell University (microfiche 49/1340).

When the *American Missionary* reported that slaves fleeing into the Union lines would lack clothing and bedding for the winter ahead and appealed for help, Child at once made her home a relay station for aid to the contrabands. Hers was the first package to reach them at Fortress Monroe. She writes here to Helen Frances Garrison (1844–1928), fourth child of William Lloyd Garrison, who married Henry Villard in 1866.

[1] Nathaniel P. Willis edited the popular family periodical the *Home Journal.* Stories about Mrs. Lincoln's extravagances infuriated the abolitionists.

To Helen Frances Garrison

Dear Fanny,

My big box was sent off to the "contrabands" on Monday morning, and your letter arrived Monday Evening.   I did see the statement in the papers that Gov. *intended* to give each of the fugitives a "plantation suit." But there seemed to be no *official* authority for the statement; moreover, a "plantation suit" does not sound very comfortable, in view of approaching winter. It is also stated in the papers that the Gov. have *recently* resolved to pay the "contrabands" in their employ; but I find that their friend, Edward L. Pierce, doubts whether there is official ground for this;[1] and even if there *is*, the Gov. will pay wages only to those they *employ*, and many of them are *not* employed by the U.S. but scramble for a living as they best can. Rev. L. C. Lockwood, the missionary among them, gives a very interesting account of them in the American Missionary.[2] He describes them as generally a sober, industrious, religious people, and many of them very intelligent. I have had three letters from him. He says they *do* need assistance, and will suffer for clothing and bedding this winter unless the charitable extend a helping hand. He wrote that mine was the *first* contribution offered in answer to his Appeal in their behalf, in the American Missionary. People are so busy giving and working for the soldiers that few think of the poor fugitives. In answer to my questions, he informed me that some of the women could cut and make garments, and that many of them were good knitters. So I sent thread, tape, buttons, needles & knitting-needles &c with the new cloth. I bought $15 dollars worth of flannel and calico, and for a fortnight worked as hard as I could drive, repairing second-hand garments, (which the Missionary wrote would be gratefully received) and making hoods for the women, and woollen caps for the men, out of such pieces as I could muster. Mrs. Stevenson, of W. Newton gave me various second-hand articles of clothing for children, One pair of woollen socks, and 20 picture books, and Primary School books. Mrs. Sears of this town made a similar contribution. I re-stitched many of the books, and enclosed them in good strong covers. I gathered up all the Biographies of ⟨the⟩ runaway slaves, that I could find. I bound them anew, and pasted on the covers the Liberator heading of horses and men sold at auction. I sent 6 of my West India Tract, and cut from duplicate Liberators the Christ coming to rescue the oppressed, and the happy Emancipation scene of the children with their lambs &c; these I pasted on the

---

[1] Edward L. Pierce (1829–97), Boston abolitionist and a private in the Union army, had supervised the work of the contrabands at Fortress Monroe, providing them with the same wages, hours, and rations as white labor. His article in the *Atlantic Monthly* on the contrabands informed the public how well the blacks worked when treated fairly and decently.

[2] The Reverend Lewis C. Lockwood, a missionary, helped start schools and churches for the contrabands at Fortress Monroe.

covers, as nicely as if I were doing it for Queen Victoria. These, and a copy of Uncle Tom's Cabin, which Mrs. Sears sent, I did up in separate parcels, directed to two of the most intelligent "contrabands," who, according to Mr. Lockwood's statement, could read easily. I sent with them a short letter to Mr. Carey, a preacher who is one of the "contrabands," and I enclosed the letter in that funny envelope, of slaves running to Fort Munroe, with their master after them.   My good Henrietta[3] gave me $10 in money, which, according to her directions, I sent to the Missionary, to be expended for whatever the "contrabands" most needed. She also sent 5 books, 7 pair of woollen socks, and two woollen shirts. A friend in Weston sent me 30 yds of white cotton flannel and 21 skeins of yarn. I left it to the Missionary to distribute the clothing & schoolbooks according to his judgment.   It cost me 50 cts to get the box to Boston, and $3.. 60 cts by Adam's Express, to its destination. The Express agreed to send it at the same reduced rate that they send to the soldiers; but the box was large, and it was *heavy,* having four large woollen blankets, and a fear-nought great coat, beside 30 books. If the poor creatures have *half* as much satisfaction in receiving the contents, as I had in buying, making, and repairing, I shall be glad.

I think you had better put your articles, and some Henrietta Sargent writes me are in readiness at her room, into another box, of size adapted to the articles. The Express must be *pre*-paid, through. The direction is: Revd L. C. Lockwood, care of Capt. Burleigh, Seminary near Fortress Munroe, Virginia. Paid through.

Excuse my bad writing. I write in haste to send to Post Office. Yours with true love, L. Maria Child.

. . .

ALS; Houghton Library, Harvard University (microfiche 50/1344).

On 7 November 1861, Union troops captured Port Royal in South Carolina and occupied the neighboring Sea Islands between Charleston and Savannah. The slaveholders fled the islands before the Union invasion, leaving about ten thousand slaves to work the rich Sea Island cotton plantations. What would the Lincoln administration do about the blacks—neither slave nor free in this moment? What was called the Port Royal Experiment became a dress rehearsal for Reconstruction of the South. The most drastic social changes ever tried in U.S. history were begun in the microcosm of the Sea Islands, only seven months after the fall of Fort Sumter, and far behind the Confederate lines. "Here," writes Willie Lee Rose, historian of Port Royal, "the first troops were recruited among the late slaves and put to the test of battle; the first extensive schools for slaves got under way and the assault on illiteracy began; abandoned land was

[3] Henrietta Sargent.

confiscated and freedmen took precarious title; the wage system received fresh trials and freedmen experimented with strikes and bargaining; political rallies and local politics first opened up an exciting range of experience."*

The Port Royal slaves were among the most isolated in the South. If they could lead productive lives in freedom, this would wreck the arguments of those who claimed that emancipation would not work because black people were primitive and shiftless. With the North watching the experiment closely, abolitionists did all they could to nurse the infant freedom into full maturity and strength.

To Mary Stearns

Wayland, Dec. 15'th, 1861.

Dear Mary,

I have been knitting a pair of suspenders for Col. Montgomery.[1] It needs a buckle and a leather strap, with a *button hole at each end*, for each of the suspenders. I cannot procure such an article in this enterprising town. Will you buy a pair of straps and fasten them on the suspenders, after I send them to you. I would not get *dandy* straps but real strong, stout ones. There ought to be a little strip of leather sewed across, to prevent the strap from slipping out of the buckle; otherwise he will be liable to lose them in the hurry of camp life. Some straps are sold with this piece to fasten them in the buckle, others are sold without it. I saw in the paper a rumor that Col. Montgomery was taken prisoner. I trust in God it is not true. If the rebels should get possession of *him*, they would treat him most cruelly.

I am much disappointed that nothing more comes of the Port Royal affair.[2] If they had welcomed the contrabands, set them to work, and stimulated them by payment, they might have gathered and sent to New York these millions of dollars worth of cotton, which the rebels have burned so diligently. It seems as if some wizard paralyzed our government and commanders by an evil spell. Lincoln says, "We must let things *drift*." What else could we expect from King *Log?*

Frank Shaw says Lincoln is *Providential;* for if we had a more energetic man at the helm he would rouse all the pro-slavery in the country to violent activity, whereas now they are lulled by his slow and timid course, and will

---

* Willie Lee Rose, *Rehearsal for Reconstruction* (Indianapolis, 1964).
[1] Col. James Montgomery (1814–71) had fought with the Free-Soilers in Kansas and was at this time leading Union troops there, encouraging fugitive slaves from Missouri to seek sanctuary with him and sending expeditions into Missouri to liberate its slaves.
[2] The commanding officer at Port Royal was authorized to employ fugitive slaves for whatever service they were fitted for. Abolitionists hoped he would interpret this directive to mean that he should recruit the blacks as Union soldiers, a step he was reluctant to take.

not fairly wake up till the current of events has carried them too far out to sea to steer for the port they *intended* to make, and supposed they *were* making. That idea had previously occurred to me, and I found a crumb of comfort in it.

Mrs. Shaw writes: "We went to see Gen. Fremont, when he was in New York; and if that face belongs to a man who is anything but a good, high-principled, energetic, and "up-to-the occasion" man, then I am very much mistaken. I wish in my heart *he* were President."

She enclosed a photograph of Mrs. Lincoln, which I herewith transmit to you. I suppose you will frame it, and carefully train vines around it, in some place of honor. I reckon the presence of "our Jessie" in Washington will make her a little uncomfortable.

Have you seen The Song of the Contrabands? The words & music, as sung by themselves, have been published by Lockwood the Missionary at Fortress Munroe, and he sent me a copy. How glad I am that what the poor creatures have been singing in corners is, at last, getting proclaimed upon the house-tops!

I don't want you to *do* anything about the Anti Slavery Reception, but if you are well enough to be there, I hope we shall see you. If it amounts to nothing more, it will be a pleasant meeting with some whom it is always agreeable to meet.

When is your Kansas box to be closed?[3] My finger-tips fairly ache with knitting. I want to get as much done as *possible*. *Perhaps* I should not have spared time to write this, though it *is* "Sabber Day," had I not wanted you to procure the leather straps, in season.

With cordial love to your good George, in which Uncle David unites, I am ever

Your affectionate

Aunt Maria.

I enclose an article which I sent to the Springfield Republican. The Boston Traveller is out with *another* description of Mrs. Lincoln's new bonnet; her *winter* one, I presume. She looks more like a dowdy washerwoman, in the photograph, than like the "representative of fashion" that Willis describes. The countenance seems to me mean and vulgar; but perhaps I am prejudiced.

. . .

ALS; Walter G. Perry Collection, Westfield, N.J. (microfiche 50/1357).

[3] This is probably a reference to material gathered for contrabands in Kansas.

8

1862–April 1865

By the winter of 1861–62 abolitionists both in and out of Congress were trying to influence public opinion toward immediate emancipation. They gave lectures; made speeches; held rallies; and wrote pamphlets, editorials, and articles, reaching everywhere for support for their policy. Child's letters demonstrate an impatience with Lincoln. She thought that the Union had a glorious chance to redeem the country from the sin of slavery, but the president, shackled by political expediency, was moving with agonizing slowness. Public pressure built to great height as she and many others urged the issue daily. Following Lincoln's Emancipation Proclamation on 1 January 1863, Child by mid-year began to feel that the war would end in a great victory for freedom and progress; still, she was gravely concerned about what would come after emancipation. Her letters discuss long-term policy concerning the blacks, and she gave all her energy to mustering aid to meet their needs. During the war she wrote many pieces for the press; she also wrote two books, setting aside their proceeds for the freedmen.

To Francis Shaw

Wayland, Jan. 28'th, 1862.

Dear Friend,

I enclose $20, which I wish you to use for the "contrabands," in any way you think best. I did think⟨ing⟩ of purchasing shoes, of which I understand they are much in need; but I concluded it was best to send to you to appropriate it as you choose. In November I expended $18 for clothing, mostly for women and children, and picked up all the garments, blankets, &c that I could spare. I sent them to Fortress Munroe. Last week I gave Anna Loring $20 toward a great box she is filling for Port Royal. My interest in the "contrabands," everywhere, is exceedingly great; and at this crisis, I feel that every one ought to be willing to do their utmost. I still have $40 left of a fund I have set apart for the "contrabands."[1] I

---

[1] Child received a one-hundred-dollar bequest from Francis Jackson, who had died 14 Nov. 1861; she reserved it for the contrabands.

keep it for *future* contingencies; but if you think it is more needed *now*, say the word and you shall have it.   Oh, if slavery could *only* be abolished, there is no *limit* to the sacrifices I would be willing to make!

I am glad Mr. Olmsted is interested.[2] He knows, better than any other man, how necessary is a healthy *stimulus* to the production of labor. The "contrabands" ought to be employed on such terms that the more they *do* the more *money* they get. I wish white people could get rid of the idea that they must manage *for* them. I think it is a bad system at Fortress Munroe to keep back so large a proportion of their wages to support the sick and the aged. *White* laborers would not work with much heart under such circumstances. They ought to pay them *wages* in proportion to their *work*, and let *them* form Relief Societies among themselves, so that they might feel that *they* did the benevolent work themselves.   I think a great deal depends upon the application of proper *stimulus* to their industry. Mr. Olmsted's writings show that his eyes are open to this fact, and I hope, he will bring his influence to bear in quarters where it is needed.   How I *do* wish he would take up a large tract of land in Illinois, and employ 2 or 3000 "contrabands" in the culture of cotton, on such terms that the more cotton they *raised* the more they would *earn!* It would be a blessed thing for *them*, and for our manufacturers also. When you see Mr. Olmsted, why wont you suggest it to him? With his great agricultural knowledge, and his enlightened views about labor, I am sure he could make it a profitable thing for all parties.[3]

Sam. Colt made a fortune from a great growth of willows in the moist portion of the place he bought near Hartford.[4] He wanted to cut down many of the willows, to improve his grounds, and he was too much of a Yankee to throw them away. So he imported Swiss basket-workers who converted them into tasteful baskets, chairs, rustic tables &c. A great many of the "contrabands" have doubtless been used to making baskets. I have two very pretty ones manufactured by Tom. Clay's slaves in Georgia. Projects for employing these poor creatures, so that they can have a share of profits proportioned to their labor, occupy my thoughts more than half the time. In the future that is close upon us, this question will become very important to the welfare of *all* parties.

Where we are drifting I cannot see; but we are drifting *some*where; and, our fate, whatever it may be, is bound up with these same despised "contrabands." Oh, if the country could be saved, *all* free, by jumping into a great gulf, as Quintus Cartius did, I would hurry to the sacrifice!

With best love to dear Sarah, I am always most cordially and truly your friend,

L. Maria Child.

ALS; Manuscript Division, New York Public Library (microfiche 51/1372).

2 Frederick Law Olmsted was the author of three books about the slave states.
3 Nothing came of Child's suggestion. In June, Olmsted became executive secretary of the Sanitary Commission, established to look after the health and other needs of Union soldiers.
4 Samuel Colt's firearms factory was at Hartford, Conn.

George Washington Julian (1817–99) was an Indiana abolitionist and congress-man.

To George W. Julian

Wayland Jan. 30'th, 1862.
Mr. Julian,
Dear Sir,

I thank you very much for your Speech, which seems to me admirably cal-culated to help on the good work, at the present all-important crisis.[1] I feel per-sonal obligations to you for bringing so much sound good sense and high moral courage to the aid of Freedom, in its hour of peril. I was glad you ventured to say that our fathers made a mistake at the beginning, in admitting compromises into the Constitution. It is a true word. Wholesale lauding of the Constitution has made it an object of idol-worship. It is undoubtedly a valuable document, wise in nearly all its parts. But the best feature of a Republican Government is the power to modify it, according to the needs of the people. I suppose our fathers did really believe that slavery would be short-lived in this country; yet when my reverence for them leads me to make this excuse, I never can forget the ugly fact that they legislated for the continuance of the African Slave Trade twenty years. The fact is, they were determined to have a *Union*, on *any* terms; and the South then, as now, were imperious and unprincipled in their demands. The wise and good men of that time adopted a great fallacy, when they supposed that *any* compromise of moral principles *could* be transitory in its effects. Our politicians, with few exceptions, have gone on ever since in the same path; and whether our crooked ways will ever be made straight, God alone knows. Only seven generations have passed away since that noble band of Puritans in the May-Flower made their memorable Covenant with God: "As the Lord's free people, we will walk in all his ways made known, or to be known to us, accord-ing to our best endeavors, *whatever it may cost us.*" Only seven generations! and now how difficult it is to find a man who really *believes* in principles; in other words, who *really* believes in God! If there had been anything like a general state of moral healthfulness in the Free States, they would have long ago insisted upon calling a Convention of the people to modify the Constitution. But Alas! the same year that witnessed the landing of those sturdy freemen of the Lord in the May Flower, witnessed the landing of negro slaves to wait upon the "vaga-bond gentlemen," who settled Virginia.[2] It was a mysterious Providence, that brought these two antagonistic elements in juxta position in this grand new field of human progress. If we could only get *rid* of the ⟨poisonous⟩ virus infused

[1] This was probably Julian's speech in the House attacking General Henry W. Halleck for restoring to her master a slave girl who had fled to the camp of an Indiana regiment and whose colonel had refused to give her up.
[2] The Mayflower landing was in 1620; the blacks reached Virginia in 1619.

throughout the blood of our body politic! But it is not an excrescence to be cut off; it has infected the whole system with disease. If *all* the Slaves States had seceded, the prospects for freedom would be hopeful; but I fear the *Union* Slave-holders are dragging us all down to ruin.

As for the government, I had better say nothing; for on *that* theme, I find it difficult to keep within bounds. Never had men such a glorious opportunity to redeem a country and immortalize themselves! Never did men show themselves so miserably deficient in all the qualities, which the crisis demanded! When I see the great swelling tide of popular enthusiasm ooze away through the slimy mud of shallow diplomacy, it seems as if my heart would break.

Thanks, thanks, to you, and Mr. Conway, and Mr. Lovejoy, Mr. Stevens, and others, who try to keep the sacred fire of freedom alive on our national altar![3] We are not *worthy* of becoming an *example* to the nations; and perhaps the best use God can put us to is to make us a *warning*.

But I still hope; especially as you, Mr. Sumner, Mr. Greely, and others, in whose judgment I place confidence, agree in thinking that the new Secretary of War is "the right man in the right place."[4]

With cordial thanks for your kind expressions to me personally, I am, with truest respect and gratitude,

L. Maria Child.

P.S. I will do all I can to extend the circulation of your excellent Speech.

ALS; Manuscript Division, Library of Congress (microfiche 51/1373).

To Mary Stearns

Wayland, Jan. 30'th, 1862.

Dear Mary,

. . .

Did n't you enjoy Whittier's Boat Song for the Negroes at Port Royal?[1] I was so taken with it, that I waked up in the night to repeat it. Your young friend must find some music for it, and learn to sing it. Indeed, it almost sings *itself*.

Oh nebber you fear, if nebber you hear
De driver blow his horn!

It would amuse you to hear David anathematize Old Abe. He exhausts the vocabulary of contempt. A fortnight ago there was one of the sensation rumors

---

[3] The references are to Moncure D. Conway (1832–1907), a descendant of Virginia slaveholders who became an abolitionist; Owen Lovejoy; and Thaddeus Stevens (1792–1868), Pennsylvania abolitionist and congressman.
[4] On 15 Jan. 1861, Lincoln replaced the corrupt secretary of war Owen Cameron with Edwin M. Stanton (1814–69), an Ohio lawyer.
[1] Whittier's "Song of the Negro Boatmen" (1862).

that there had been "treason discovered in high places, that ought to be above suspicion; and that a *woman* was connected with it." I suggested that it might be Mrs. Lincoln. David siezed the idea with delight. "I hope it is," said he; "I'd wear out my best boots walking to Washington to see her hanged, and old Abe made a *widder*." I never see old Abe's *pictur* without thinking that his lanky neck looks as if *he* was made to be hanged. I wonder whether Conway's eloquent letter to him in the Rejected Stone stirred his stagnant soul at all. I should think it would make a door-post tingle; but I doubt whether the faintest idea of its mighty import got into his wooden skull.   I thank him for one thing, however; for giving Jim Lane a long rope.[2] There'll be *some*thing smashed when *he* gets under way. Jim Lane *was* the one who showed himself so hostile to Fremont. He is a strange mixture, and I don't altogether trust him. I doubt whether he has any fixed *principles*. But he is brave and energetic, and I think he will *do* something.

I hope Col. Montgomery will receive his big barrel safely, and have comfort in the articles it contains. The papers have lately stated that Missouri Ruffians, in the John Brown Kansas times, tied him to a tree, and violated his wife before his eyes. Is that true?

I have received several letters from Missouri lately, asking for "The Right Way the Safe Way." That's a good sign, so far as it goes. But dear me, how *much* leaven it will take to leaven the cold dough of this nation! Good night. Blessings be with you. Your affectionate Aunt Maria.

. . .

ALS; Walter G. Perry Collection, Westfield, N.J. (microfiche 51/1375).

To Lucy Searle

Wayland, Feb. 10'th, 1862

Dear Lucy,

. . .

So you dispute Gerrit Smith's testimony about my being "wise and candid"? I cannot say I have much respect for my wisdom. I think less and less of it, every year I live. But when I *write for the public*, I think I *am* generally candid. I do not profess to be so in my *talk*, because that bubbles up, and I do not take time to examine its spirit.

We all present different phases of character, according to circumstances; and I think I do more than most people. It is natural enough that Gerrit Smith should deem me "wise". When I approach *him*, I don't go dancing on a slack rope, decorated with spangles and Pschyche-wings [*sic*]. I walk on solid ground, as demurely as if I was going to meeting, with Psalm Book in hand. If I happen

---

[2] General James H. Lane, of the Kansas Brigades, had been saying publicly that it would give him no pain "to see a Negro handling a gun."

to catch a glimpse of a fairy by the way, she and I wink at each other, but I never "let on". *He* supposes the chosen teachers of my mind to be profound statesmen, and pious Christian Fathers. I never introduce to *him* any of my acquaintances of light character. I have a consciousness that fairies are not the most respectable company for a woman of my venerable years; (I shall be sixty tomorrow;) and it is only to a few that I manifest my predilection for such volatile visiters. Dear Sarah Shaw likes to see fanciful dancing on moon-beams; and when I write to *her*, I sometimes caracole in a fashion that would make good, sensible Gerrit Smith wonder what had become of the "wisdom" of his sage friend. *You* seem also to be amused with my lofty vaulting and whirling with garlanded pole and tinselled shoe-sparkles. That encourages me to appear before you in that trim. It is not a very frequent mood with me, now. Here in my lonely little den, away from all the world, I have many solemn thoughts, and not a few sad ones. But I do not choose such states of mind to write to my invalid friend, shut up in her room, day after day. . . .

AL, Lydia Maria Child Papers, Anti-Slavery Collection, Cornell University (microfiche 51/1384).

At the time of this letter to Horace Greeley, Lord Lyons, Britain's minister to the United States between 1858 and 1865, was involved in negotiations over the *Trent* affair. A Union vessel had stopped the British steamer *Trent* in November 1861 and removed James M. Mason and John Slidell, Confederate commissioners bound for England. War with Britain threatened until State Secretary Seward ordered the release of Mason and Slidell in late December. Child discusses what offers the Confederates might have been prepared to make Britain and France in order to get their support in the war.

To Horace Greeley

Private

Wayland, March 9'th, 1862.

Friend Greely,

. . .

I *have* felt exceedingly despondent about public affairs. From the very beginning I have felt afraid of the evils that the Democratic Party might weave about us. I always supposed the loyalty of many of them might be assumed, the better to cover their plans. I have dreaded *them* much more than I have the rebels, because insidious enemies are more dangerous than open ones.

But when I read Lord Lyon's letter to Lord John Russell, ten days ago, I began to be of good cheer. I took it for granted that he would not have written it, if he had not been *instructed* to do so; ⟨and⟩ at least the British cabinet would not have *published* it, unless they had designed that an effect should be produced; and as governments never mention moral principles without they expect to serve some turn by it, I began to inquire into the *motive* for this diplomatic parade of morality on the question of slavery. I had previously seen letters from Europe, which stated that Mason & Slidell were offering to abolish slavery, as the price of a league with France and England. I did not dare to trust to this report, until I read Lord Lyon's Letter; but I at once concluded that letter was sent forth as a note of preparation. Bitter as the pill of emancipation would be to the South, I have no doubt they would swallow it, rather than acknowledge themselves conquered by the U.S. And really there is no way in which they could so effectually humiliate us, and revenge themselves upon us. We should be the scorn and laughing-stock of the world; while England, by serving her own interest, would be covered with laurels for her justice and humanity. How she would boast of doing for freedom what the republic of the U.S. *refused* to do! The *tories* would effect *their* object of splitting the Union; and a measure that abolished American slavery, at the same time that it opened the cotton ports, would be prodigiously popular with the English *people*. England and France would secure a monopoly of Southern commerce, and we should be shut out. It is a transaction that *everybody*, except our blind, foolish selves would gain by.[1] The poetical justice of such a retribution would strike everybody. W'm H. Seward would make a remarkably foolish appearance, under such circumstances. I guess he would feel like hiding himself in a knot-hole, and having his "wittles" sent to him.

Perhaps Lincoln may have had trains of thought similar to those that have occupied my mind of late; and his recent Message may be the result.[2] The papers I have read do not seem to appreciate its *full* import. It certainly says plainly enough, ["]If the rebels continue to resist, the U.S. gov. must and will resort to emancipation; and, gentlemen of the Border States, I ask you to reflect how much *your* slaves will be worth under those circumstances. Had n't you better accept of compensation from the U.S. before their market value is gone?"

It seems to me that all will soon be resolved into *one* question: Which party shall emancipate *first?* Really "this is the Lord's doing, and it is marvellous in our eyes"! That two selfish parties should be forced by events into competition for doing what neither wanted to do! It is wonderful! Be of good cheer, God reigns, let the earth rejoice!

Yours respectfully, L. Maria Child.

ALS; Manuscript Division, New York Public Library (microfiche 51/1394).

[1] Child would make the same point to Sen. Charles Sumner in a letter of 22 June 1862.
[2] Lincoln's 6 Mar. 1862 message to Congress proposed a joint resolution offering federal compensation to any state which would adopt gradual abolition of slavery. As the president's first recommendation on emancipation, it encouraged the abolitionists.

To Theodore Tilton

Wayland, April 11'th 1862.

Dear Mr. Tilton,

I cannot sufficiently thank you for your kindness in sending me Mrs. Browning's Poems,[1] and her photograph. The latter pains me, but still I like to have it. There is so much experience of suffering written in that face! It hardly seems possible that so frail an envelope could have held such a mighty soul. How strong she was, yet how full of all womanly sympathy and gentleness! She seems to have approached, nearer than any other person I know of, the ideal standard of perfection in a human being; that is, a harmonious apportionment of the masculine and the feminine elements in character.   I have not had time yet to read all the poems in the vol. you sent; but in those I have read I find her characteristic wealth of poetic imagery, and her broad range of thought forever floating toward the infinite.

Your Memorial is exceedingly interesting; worthy of its lofty theme.

I thank you very cordially for sending it to me. It will be precious to me, both on account of the profound reverence I feel for her memory, and the lively interest I take in you and your noble doings.

That makes me think of telling you how glad I was that The Independent rebuked the artist, who represented a negro boy stealing while the white boys were listening to music.[2] In the first place, the colored boy, as you say, would have been more likely to have been occupied by the music, than would any of the white boys; and even if there were probability in the representation, it would still be very *mean* to minister to prejudice against an oppressed class of people. Few are wise enough to estimate the immense influence of such indirect modes of educating the popular mind. I always rebuke a child when I hear him call an Irishman a "Paddy," or a colored person a "nigger." The terms are harmless enough in themselves, but they have become stereotyped forms of contempt, and therefore ought to be suppressed. I remember astonishing some boys, whom I met in Chatham Square. They were following a man with a long black beard, and calling after him, "I say, old Jew, got any ole clo's?" I stopped them, and said, "Why do you insult a man because he is a Jew? Don't you know that Moses, and Solomon, and St. Peter, and St. Paul were Jews?"

The idea seemed new to them. I know not whether the seed I threw ripened to future fruit; but, at the time, they ceased to persecute the man with the beard.

This links itself to something I wrote to you a long time ago, when you were so kind and complimentary as to ask me to write for The Independent. I have often thought since that I answered in too brusque a manner. I did not *intend*

[1] Elizabeth (Barrett) Browning, *Last Poems* (London, 1862).
[2] Stereotypes of America's racial and ethnic groups, commonplace in the nineteenth century and long after, were disseminated in literature, journalism and on the stage. Cartoonists used the crudest means of ridicule.

to be uncourteous. When I am writing to a person whom I like, I am apt to indulge in fun or straightforwardness, without thinking what effect it may have. You apologized for The Independent's having spoken against my *"friends." That* was not the point. My intercourse with Mr. Garrison has been so slight, and my mind is interested in so many things with which he would have no sympathy, that I should hardly think of calling him a personal friend. I respect him very highly; and every year that I live, my respect and admiration for him increases. He is a truly great and good man; but the feelings I entertain for him partake very little of a *personal* character. The same is true of Theodore Parker, with whom I never talked more than two hours in my life. What annoyed me in The Independent, was its intolerance of other men's opinions. As if a man could not be good, unless he believed in the Trinity, or the Atonement! Perhaps I have not so much patience with such assumptions, as I *ought* to have. But I know, by experience, that we cannot *choose* our belief. It is literally *impossible* for me to believe *now* what I believed *thirty years ago*. It is neither a fault nor a merit in me. The simple fact is, I have outgrown my old spiritual garments, and now they will not go on. And not only difference of *years*, but diversity of *temperaments* necessarily modifies belief. A doctrine that is essential to one person is non-essential to another, and to a third may prove a positive hindrance to religion. God *intended* this diversity in *spiritual* structure and growth, as He intended diversity in *natural* structure and growth. Henry Ward Beecher accepts Calvinistic ideas of God, and finds strength and comfort in them. In me, they excite abhorrence, detestation, fierce revolt. Shall I pronounce *him* a bad man, because the God he worships seems to *me* very much in the likeness of the Devil? Has he a right to pronounce *me* bad, because the God I worship seems to *him* like a "shadowy abstraction"? It is enough that his God is *not* a Devil to *him*, and that mine is *not* an abstraction to me. This passing of judgment upon each other on account of opinions concerning abstract subjects, is both absurd and wrong; and *that* was the fault I had to find with The Independent. It would have displeased me all the same if the persons attacked had been Baptists, or Methodists, or Roman Catholics.

The Independent is a good paper, an able paper, a highly interesting paper; and I feel deeply grateful for its efficient advocacy of so many forms of truth and freedom.[3] I must confess, also, that it is difficult to find *any* paper that is not intolerant about *some*thing. If I was brusque, forgive me.

I thank you for copying Mattie's letter about her slaves.[4] I had serious thoughts of sending it to you, in the beginning. I hope its publication will do something to help on public opinion. Do you ever put *pictures* in the Independent? Oliver Johnson will show you, in the Anti Slavery Almanac for 1843, Slave

[3] The *Independent* was the largest and most influential political-religious weekly paper in the country. In 1862 its circulation was seventy thousand. Beecher became nominal editor in December 1861, but Tilton had been running the paper since 1856. When Beecher resigned in 1863, Tilton became chief editor and made the weekly less a religious and more a political organ of abolition.
[4] Griffith's letter appeared in the *Independent* on 27 Mar. 1862.

Labor and Free Labor illustrated by the different modes of influencing two donkeys. I wish it could be circulated in the Border States.

Good night. Blessings be with you! Ever cordially your friend, L. Maria Child.

ALS; James Fraser Gluck Collection, Buffalo and Erie County Public Library (microfiche 52/1401).

On 16 April 1862, Lincoln signed the act providing compensated emancipation of all slaves in the District of Columbia.

To Lucy Osgood

Wayland, April 20'th, 1862

My dear and honored friend,

What a pleasant little visit we had to your right comfortable and cheerful domicil! It did my heart good, and is refreshing to look back upon.   Well! slavery is abolished, at *last*, in the District of Columbia! Ten miles square is not much, but it is *some*thing gained, and its effects on the future are very important. I have hoped that thirty years of arguing, remonstrating and petitioning, would have borne *bigger* fruit than this; yet even *this* would not have been done, if the slave-holders had not kicked the Republican Party, when it sought to kneel at their feet, with kisses and protestations. Thank God for the pride and passion of the South! May it not diminish suddenly! And I think it will *not* diminish, because the Lord has work for them to do, which there was not *righteousness* enough in the land to accomplish. . . .

. . . ·We went into Boston by the horse-cars. A Medford man, finding out who I was, wanted to read to me the concluding sentences of a lecture on The Crisis, which he had agreed to deliver. It was an eloquent appeal to the North to forgive and forget as soon as this "*fratricidal* war" was over; never to say a word to remind our Southern brothers that they had been rebels, but to receive them with open arms; &c   Of course, I "opened my mouth, and spake." I told him I was very willing to welcome our Southern brethren, provided *Sambo* was acknowledged as a Southern brother. He said he thought the best way was to let slavery entirely alone. David answered, "I'd kill it first, and *then* let it alone." A reply which seemed greatly to delight an intelligent mechanic at his side. I don't know who the lecturer was, but I have no doubt of his having been a Buchanan Democrat. That set are very busy about peace, and forgiveness of our "Southern brethren." Oh, those Northern hypocrites, that go about preaching a spurious Gospel of Freedom, how I do dislike them! I like much better the rebel who frankly blasphemes freedom.

. . .

ALS; General MSS, Princeton University (microfiche 52/1403).

To Sarah Shaw

Wayland, May 18'th, 1862

Dearest Friend,

. . .

. . . I am greatly interested in the Educational Commission for the "contra-bands," which they have started in Boston.[1] I shall do all I can for it. It is refresh-ing to find *some* green spots in our blood-red landscape. Oh, how heartsick I am of the war! Almost every day my heart receives some stab, which makes it writhe with anguish. It is not merely our own soldiers that excite my pity. I can not help compassionating the "poor whites" of the South, led into wickedness and danger by men who care no more for their souls or bodies, than they would for so many blind dogs. I was glad to see that several hundreds of them deserted from Georgia to the U.S. giving as a reason that they were "tired of fighting the *rich men*'s war." Through this terrible process, *they* will come up to the light, as well as the negroes; and they have been scarcely less wronged. I was powerfully drawn to be a teacher among the "contrabands"; but my good David would get sick if he went with me, or if he staid at home alone. The *nearest* duty must not be neglected.

. . .

ALS; Manuscript Division, New York Public Library (microfiche 52/1410).

To Charles Sumner

Wayland, June 22d, 1862.

Dear and Honored Mr. Sumner,

. . .

I do not marvel that so *few* men preserve their moral integrity entire amid the temptations of political life. It requires an immense amount of rectitude to persevere in walking straight in such slippery, crooked paths, jostled by so many tipsy and befogged companions. The continual supremacy of *policy* over *right*, in the whole course of this war, has been the principal source of my despon-dency. The enthusiasm of the people and of the army has been constantly checked. The moment a tongue of flame glimmered, an extinguisher has been immediately clapped upon it. I know the position of things has been exceedingly tangled and difficult, and that great caution and prudence has been necessary. But I look upon it as a settled law of our being that men cannot fight in such a

[1] On leaving the army, Edward L. Pierce had been appointed special agent of the U.S. Treasury to select superintendents and teachers for the contrabands (private philan-thropic societies would have to pay their salaries). On 7 Feb. 1862 the Boston Educa-tional Commission was organized to send supplies, teachers, and labor superintendents to the contrabands. Thus began the freedmen's aid movement, which swiftly took na-tional form.

way as to make victory *swift and certain,* unless they are warmed up, to a degree approaching fanaticism, by some *idea* of religion, justice, or freedom. This idea of "restoring the union," (to say nothing of its moral turpitude, if it means restoring it with slavery) has not *vital force* enough to kindle the souls of men. We shall never fully prove what the North can do, till the God-given instinct for freedom has full play. I do not belief [*sic*] the Southern leaders could have kept *their* armies together, if the mass had not been deluded with the idea that they were fighting for their *invaded homes.*

You will doubtless think that I am a poor judge of *policy;* and so I am. When I hear politicians talk, I always feel as if I were looking at a basket of slippery, squirming snakes. But I am very far from despising that wise expediency, which seeks to advance right *principles* by the best *means.* I do not believe this suppression of enthusiasm is *good policy.* It is *politician's* policy, which, according to my thinking, is very apt to be short-sighted in its views and low in its aims. I do not blame the President. I believe he is, as you think, honest and right-minded. I sometimes wish he were a man *strong* enough to *lead* popular opinion, instead of *following* it so conscientiously. Unless the moral sense of the community can be raised above its present level; I do not see how a God of Justice *can* save us from ruin. Events have a continual tendency to raise it; but will it rise fast enough? I think the policy of the U.S. has been so inconsistent, and so bewildering to the poor slaves, who trusted us so implicitly, that much vantage-ground has been lost, never to be regained. . . .

But why do I dwell so much on the ugly side of the picture? Instead of fretting about what has *not* been done, let me rather thank God, and the true, brave men who have been His agents, that so much *has* been accomplished. Slavery has been abolished in the District, an event which I had long given up the expectation of living to see. Liberia and Hayti are recognized as States among the sisterhood of nations. Military officers are forbidden to return fugitive slaves. . . . The last, best work of this Congress is the passage of the emancipation bill.[1] Of course, it is not what either you or I wish it was; *that* was not to be expected; but it recognizes the right of Congress to abolish slavery in the States. Thank God for that visible step of progress! I am infinitely cheered and encouraged by it. . . .

ALS; Houghton Library, Harvard University (microfiche 52/1415).

William P. Cutler (1812–89), to whom the next letter is addressed, was an Ohio congressman.

---

[1] On 19 June 1862 an act of Congress abolished slavery in the territories of the United States.

To William P. Cutler

Wayland, July 10th, 1862

Hon. Mr. Cutler,
Dear Sir,

. . .

. . . I see much in the present Congress to inspire me with hope that there is vitality enough left among us to save our free institutions. I have a genuine, practical *belief* in *Freedom;* and it grieves me to see what a mere abstraction, what "a glittering generality," it is in many minds. I also believe in *labor,* and prove my faith by my works. Few women, who pass for "respectable," have done so large a share of manual labor; and I shall continue to do it while my strength lasts; because I reverence usefulness far more than I do gentility. Nothing Senator Wilson has said has inspired me with so much respect for him, as his Speech, "Are Working Men Slaves?"[1] Think of those lordly aristocrats of the South declaring that the position of Northern workingmen was no higher than that of their slaves, when they had before them in Congress those two specimens of Northern working men, Wilson and Banks![2] A South Carolinian told me, in a sneering tone, some years ago, "I pity you Northern women. You are mere beasts of burden." I replied, "For my own part, I had rather be a beast of *burden,* than a beast of *prey.*"

It is a true word you have spoken, and I thank you for uttering it, that Slavery has done incalculable injury to this country by its "systematic degradation of laborers." Unless we can get rid of this poisonous system, there will be no health left in us. Sometimes, I fear that this great and glorious structure of free government must go down to ruin, with its epitaph, Done to death by efforts to help the Border States in sustaining Slavery. But then I think over the manly utterances, and righteous votes, in *Congress,* and my courage is renewed. . . .

What can we do with the *slaves?* is a foolish question. "Take them away from Mr. Lash and place them with Mr. Cash" settles that imaginary difficulty. But what we can do with their *masters* is a much more difficult problem to solve. Of course, the substitution of free institutions for slave labor would change the moral and intellectual condition of the whole Southern people, in a few generations. But in their transition state, what a troublesome and dangerous set they will be to deal with! They talk about *slaves* being unfit to be trusted with legislation; doubtless it is true; but it seems to me that slave*holders,* by the inevitable necessity of their position, are rendered even *more* unfit to legislate for free men.

---

[1] On 20 Mar. 1858, Henry Wilson made a lengthy speech in reply to South Carolina Congressman James Henry Hammond. Hammond had said, "Cotton is king"; he also said that Northern workingmen were "essentially slaves."
[2] Nathaniel Banks (1818–94), a Massachusetts congressman, like Wilson was of working-class background.

The horror that many people have of future social equality, and inter-marriage of the races, makes me smile. The argument is so shallow! the fear is so contradictory of itself! If there *is* an "instinctive antipathy," as many assert, surely that antipathy may be trusted to prevent amalgamation. If there is *no* instinctive antipathy, what reason is there for the horror? If the colored people are *really* an "inferior race," what danger is there of their attaining to an "equality" with us? If they are *not* inferior, what reason is there for excluding them from equality? *My* belief is, that when generations of colored people have had a fair chance for education and the acquisition of wealth, the prejudice against them, originating in their degraded position, will pass away, and our moral and intellectual estimate of a man will be no more affected by the color of his skin, than it now is by the color of his hair. But it must necessarily be a long time before such a revolution is completed, and meanwhile society will become prepared for it. The change will be so gradual that it will be unper-ceived, and consequently it will cause no shock. We may safely leave that ques-tion to take care of itself. Carlyle says, very wisely: "The old skin never falls off till a new one has formed under it."

For myself, I have no prejudice against color. I do not claim it as any merit, or apologize for it as any defect. I was simply born without it. I naturally and habitually forget it, just as I unconsciously ignore all conventional distinctions of rank. I have a few colored acquaintance, who rank very high in my estima-tion for intelligence, culture, and fine manners. What they *are* I believe that multitudes of them *might be*, under favorable influences. I know one dark brown girl, whose handsome face absolutely *flashes* light when the inferiority of her race is alluded to.[3] I have sometimes watched her, when her nostrils ex-panded proudly, and her well-shaped mouth expressed a beautiful disdain of such insults, and she seemed to me queenly enough for a model of Cleopatra. And such vulgar, shallow fools as some of them are, who consider it a degrada-tion to be seated by her side! Really, the contrast is sometimes ludicrously to their disadvantage; but they, encased in a seven-fold armor of prejudice and self-conceit, are all unconscious of their inferiority. The superiority of this girl is to be ascribed to the fact that she was never a slave, that her parents were never slaves, and that her grandfather amassed sufficient property to enable his descendants to overcome the formidable obstacles in the way of their intel-lectual culture. Looking at that girl, and reading the intelligent productions of her pen, I recognize the possibilities of improvement now damned up in the souls of her oppressed people, and our long-contined [*sic*] guilt, as a nation of oppressors and accomplices, seems to me so immeasurable, that I hardly dare to hope that God will save our national existence. The worst part of it is the perpetual *lie* we have been enacting before God and the world. Mohammedans

[3] This was probably Charlotte Forten (1837–1914) of Salem, Mass., whose grandfather, James Forten, had been owner of a large sailmaking business in Philadelphia and a prin-cipal backer of *The Liberator*. She became a teacher of the freedmen.

say there are seven hells, each deeper than the other, and that the *lowest* is for *hypocrites.* Other nations have been bad enough. It ill becomes England to profess to be shocked by "American barbarities," considering how many heads of English rebels have been stuck upon poles for birds to peck at, the skulls remaining a ghostly spectacle to the passers by; proclaiming, Thus England deals with rebels! If they say *that* was in olden time, what excuse have they for *Hindoo* rebels shot from the mouths of cannon, a mangled mass? It is a very observable fact that it is only the necessary results of war in the action of the *Free* States, that affects English nerves so unpleasantly. The barbarities of *slaveholders,* unknown in any *civilized* warfare, are ignored by them. The fact is, they want to split this nation asunder. They are *encouraging* the rebels to hold out, by proclaiming, through their press, that if they only keep on fighting a while longer, it will become a duty to recognize them.

But mean and selfish as England has shown herself at this crisis, candor compels me to admit that *we* deserve a place in that seventh pit *rather* more than *she* does. We have made such loud and large *professions!* We have so vaunted ourselves as the guardians of *freedom!* And, alas! behind our president's chair, behind the seats of Congress, in the pulpits with our preachers, on the platform with our Fourth-of-July orators, stood the ghost of the slave, saying by his mute presence, more emphatically than words could utter it, "Oh, ye *hypocrites!*["] For more than thirty years, I have seen that ghost *everywhere;* and what a mockery it made of our grandiloquent boastings!

Yours with true respect & gratitude, L. Maria Child

ALS; Child Papers, Clements Library, University of Michigan (microfiche 52/1417).

From the sounding of the first guns, blacks had volunteered to fight in the Union cause. But deep-rooted Northern prejudice opposed using them in "a white man's war." Frederick Douglass warned, "This is no time to fight only with your white hand, and to allow your black hand to remain tied."* Blacks had fought in the American Revolution and the War of 1812; why not now, for their own freedom? Early in 1862 a Thaddeus Stevens bill to enlist 150,000 black troops had passed the House but had been killed in the Senate. In July, Congress authorized the president to use blacks in military labor and to recruit free blacks and freedmen as soldiers. But Lincoln did not believe that public opinion was ready for such action, nor did he believe the blacks would make good fighters. Despite his opposition, some Union generals recruited black men. On the Sea Islands, in Kansas, in Missouri, and in Louisiana black regiments were formed of fugitive slaves and free blacks. Their valor in action and a series of military defeats for the Union began to change Lincoln's mind. In late August, with the terrible losses in the defeat of the Second Battle of Bull

* Philip S. Foner, *Life and Writings of Frederick Douglass* (New York, 1952), 3:153.

Run, the trickle of volunteers for the Union army almost dried up. Men were badly needed.

Lincoln issued the preliminary Emancipation Proclamation on 22 September 1862. It said that on 1 January 1863 all slaves in rebellious states would be declared "forever free," but loyal states and rebellious states who returned to the Union before that date would be exempt from the terms of the edict. It was a conservative and conditional, not an immediate and complete emancipation. While it disappointed some abolitionists, Garrison called it "an important step in the right direction, and an act of immense historic consequence."† On 6 September 1862, in the *National Anti-Slavery Standard*, Child had published an open letter to Lincoln, urging emancipation.

To Charles Sumner

Wayland, Oct 3d, 1862.

Dear and Honored Mr. Sumner,

I received your copy of the President's Proclamation, for which accept my thanks. It is a great step onward, and as such I welcome it. But it excites no glow of enthusiam, because I cannot get rid of misgivings concerning contingences that *may* occur before the edict goes into effect. It is of no great consequence to me to wait three months longer, after having waited more than thirty years for this event; but I cannot conceal from myself that between now and the 1'st of Jan. there is ample time for rebels at the South and traitors among ourselves to mature their plans. I have for months past been more apprehensive about those plans than most people seem to be. Mr. Child thinks my fears on the subject are excessive though he is also anxious. I do not believe, [eith?]er,[1] that even *now* the war is being carried on *in earnest*. Five months ago I became strongly impressed with the idea that Mc'Lellan was playing a political game; amusing the country with promises, and reconnaissances, but avoiding battles, because his object was to prolong the war till the next presidential election, and then sell the country to slaveholders. My opinion is still the same. When pushed to extremity by the pressure of public opinion and the increasing audacity of the rebels, he has done some fighting, and his small successes are hailed as "splendid victories." But, after all, the rebels were allowed to make a good thing of it. They siezed our money, destroyed our rail-roads, got plenty of forage, and went back into Virginia. Why was that army *allowed* to go back into Virginia? Why were they not intercepted? I believe they would have

† *The Liberator*, 26 Sept. 1862.
[1] The word is partially covered by opaque tape.
[2] George Brinton McClellan (1826–85), appointed general-in-chief of Union forces in Nov. 1861, was widely criticized for his procrastination in battle.

been, if General Mc'Lellan had not been playing false, for political purposes, as he has been from the beginning.[2] Then in the civil department we have another snake. In the few conversations I have had with you, I have betrayed my aversion to W'm H. Seward. But language affords no terms adequate to express the *extent* of my distrust and aversion. People praised his "magnanimity" in supporting Lincoln. I believed it to be all a sham. It was done to get into a high position, where he could embarrass the movements of the man who superseded him. I have had no confidence, and little hope about the management of public affairs, since that crooked and selfish hypocrite was made Sec. of State. I believe he has always owed a grudge to the Republican Party, for not nominating him, and that he has been willing to make it a failure. That he would be willing to throw his influence in favor of *any* party likely to be successful in overthrowing it, I have no doubt; nay, I believe he has all along been pulling strings for that purpose.   If my suspicions are correct, what a horrid crime it is before high Heaven, to lead hundreds of thousands of our young men to slaughter, merely to keep up a sham!

Before the 1'st of Jan. I believe the rebels will proclaim emancipation, if not to *all*, at least to all the able-bodied slaves who will fight for them; and so those who might have been fighting *for* us, during the whole of the past year, will be fighting *against* us.[3] It will be a righteous retribution for our blind, suicidal pro-slavery prejudice.

The step of emancipation has been so long delayed, and such a long time has been given to the rebels to make their arrangements to meet it, that I do not believe the step will now save the country. We are again sacrificed to the Border States. The advantages that might have been gained by emancipation must be lost, that Kentucky may have time to secure compensation. I wish the Border States had *all* seceded in the beginning. They have been a mill stone about our necks.

The Kentuckian, Mr. Candee, seems to me to have devised a plan that *will* save the country; that of attracting the poor whites to us by a distribution of lands.[4] His letter seems to me extremely acute and well reasoned. The general features of his plan were familiar to our thoughts, having often talked them over.

God bless you for your able and unceasing efforts in the cause of freedom! He *does* bless you, in giving you the ability to do so great a work.

Yours with profound respect, and the warmest gratitude, L. M. Child.

ALS; Houghton Library, Harvard University (microfiche 53/1433).

[3] The Confederacy did not move to offer emancipation until close to the war's end.
[4] George Candee, a Kentuckian living in Green Springs, Ohio, published a letter to President Lincoln calling for confiscation of the property of rebels and its redistribution to Southern men who fought against the rebellion. The *National Anti-Slavery Standard* published his letter on 27 Sept. 1862.

To Sarah Shaw

Wayland, Oct. 30'th, 1862

I don t wonder my darling thought something extraordinary was the matter with her old friend. You were right in your conjecture. Despondency concerning public affairs has been the *principal* reason of my long silence. But then there have been many subordinate ones. One week I was too ill to do anything. At another time, David was very ill for some days. No other hands except my two, to do *every*thing. Winter coming on. Garments to be made and repaired. A carpet to be made and put down, because the old one was ragged beyond even *my* powers of darning, turning and piecing. Seed to be gathered and labelled. Plants to be moved. Currant wine to be made. Barberry & currant jelly to be made for the Hospitals. Flannels to be made for the Sanitary Commission. Apples to be cut and dried. All this and more, in addition to the every-day routine of cooking, washing dishes, &c. Mrs. Rutter's absence, while it greatly contributes to my comfort, also increases the number of rooms I have to keep in order. . . .

. . .

In the military department, there is one whom I dread as much as I do Seward. You asked me, months ago, what I thought of Mc'Lellan, and I answered guardedly; for I felt diffident of judging military affairs, and did not want to be *always* "Mrs. Croaker." But ever since this year came in, I have watched him with increasing suspicion; and his Proclamation professing to sustain the President's Proclamation by no means diminished my distrust. I believe he has all along been playing a dark and cruel game.[1] His Staff Officer, Major Key, has doubtless given us the key to his policy, in his brasen-faced statement: "It is not our *game* to conquer the rebels, but to *worry out* both sections of the country, so that a compromise with Slavery can be effected." *Game!* Think of the thousands slaughtered, and the thousands more that dug their own graves in the Swamps of Chickahominy! It makes me wild to get thinking about it. And now, the same *game* seems to be going on, as there was *last* fall. The rebel army allowed to go back into Virginia. "All quiet on the Potomac"; and the people lulled to sleep by promises of what Gen. Mc'Lellan is *going* to do, when he gets clothing for his troops, means of transportation, &c. The man has somehow acquired a strange degree of power. It is difficult to say *how*. Certainly not from anything great or dazzling that he has accomplished. I suppose the secret is that a powerful party have all along been making use of him, to "worry out" the enthusiasm and energies of the people, for the benefit of Slavery. Our *greatest* peril is a military dictatorship. Did you observe that the new mammoth steam boat is named "The Dictator"? "Straws

---

[1] McClellan, who was proving ineffective against Confederate forces, was perceived by the abolitionists as proslavery in his political views. He would become the Democratic candidate for president in 1864, running on a peace-at-any-price platform.

show which way the wind blows." However, there are many gleams of light between the dark clouds. I have not lost all hope that our free institutions will yet be saved; and if they *are* saved, they will be purer, and therefore stronger, than they have ever been. Gen. Mitchell was pro-slavery, and sent back fugitives, a few months ago. Now, what a noble, heart-cheering letter he has written to Secretary Chase![2] I hated Gen. Prentiss, he was so cruel in sending back the poor slaves that sought his protection. When the rebels put him in prison, and horse whipped him for turning his back on a Secesh woman who was insulting him, I chuckled exceedingly.[3] Now, he out Garrisons Garrison in his hatred of slavery. He has *learned* something from the *stripes,* and Gen. Mitchell has learned something from the *stars.* So, by all sorts of instrumentalities, the work of the good Lord goes on. Let us hope.

As for the President's Proclamation, I was thankful for it, but it excited no enthusiasm in my mind. With my gratitude to God was mixed an under-tone of sadness that the moral sense of the people was so low, that the thing could not be done nobly. However we may inflate the emancipation balloon, it will never ascend among the constellations. The ugly fact cannot be concealed from history that it was done reluctantly and stintedly, and that even the degree that *was* accomplished was done selfishly; was merely a war-measure, to which we were forced by our own perils and necessities; and that no recognition of principles of justice or humanity surrounded the politic act with a halo of moral glory. This war has furnished many instances of *individual* nobility, but our *national* record is mean.   Another reason why my joy at the Proclamation was not exulting and exuberant was that it was not to go into effect immediately. It was nothing to wait three months longer, after waiting more than thirty years, but I had misgivings about what might *occur* between now and the 1'st of Jan. It gives ample time for our town traitors and their blinded tools to cooperate with the slaveholders, aided by Seward and McLellan. Everywhere I see signs that the subtle poison is working. The educated are saying, "A republican government has proved weak for times of war; better have a Dictator, and done with it." The ignorant masses are saying, "Let us have peace on *any* terms." This is the "worrying out" which Mc Lellan has aimed at. . . .

. . .

ALS; Houghton Library, Harvard University (microfiche 53/1434).

[2] Gen. Ormsby M. Mitchel (1809–62), commanding the Department of the South, was urging the wider use of blacks as military auxiliaries; he died on the day Child wrote this letter. Salmon Portland Chase (1808–73) was secretary of the Treasury.
[3] Benjamin Mayberry Prentiss (1819–1901), commander of the army in Tennessee, was captured at Shiloh in Apr. 1862 and exchanged in October.

To Sarah Shaw

Wayland, Nov. 11'th, 1862.

O, joy! joy! M'c Lellan is removed, and Seward is going to resign![1] What a night-mare it takes from my soul! I have restrained myself from telling you how I have suffered. If these men, as I more and more suspected, were really playing into the hands of the South, reckless of the expenditure of blood and treasure, in pursuance of their vile political game, I was more than willing that *you* should not be convinced of it; for was not the precious life of your son one of the pawns they were playing with? I mix very little with the world, and have little opportunity to learn the opinions of other people. It was merely a careful observation of *events*, as reported in the newspapers, which convinced me that a dark, insidious game was going on behind the scenes, while the people were quieted with promises of what was *going* to be done. I can scarcely mourn over the elections in the West, and in New York, for they have driven "old Abe" to the wall. *Now*, the Republican Party must "*do* or *die*." Thank God for putting them in that fix! At last, I really believe "old Abe" has got his back up. Like the old man in the fable, he has "pleased nobody"; but he is at least determined that he won't "lose his Ass into the bargain.["] I have not felt so hopeful since this horrid war began. I think we shall now go ahead in earnest; and, having tried everything else without success, we shall at last rely upon principle. Did you read Epes Sargent [*sic*] Speech in Boston, during the recent political canvass?[2] It is capital. Everywhere proofs multiply that the righteous cause is gaining ground, and I begin to have faith that "the gates of hell will not prevail against it."

Massachusetts did *not* disgrace herself. Andrew and Sumner were sustained by handsome majorities. No public men have proved themselves purer and firmer than they. They will go down to history with a glorious moral halo round their brows. I never thoroughly like anybody who disparages Charles Sumner. He is one of the "Touchstone" men. The disposition to depreciate him indicates some moral disease; at least, I have always found it so.

. . .

. . . Mrs. Jacobs wrote to me about her visit to you, and the generous contribution you gave in aid of her plans. I was glad; for I think she is doing a really good work. When she was here, she harrowed up my soul with accounts of the suffering she had witnessed.[3]

Oh, dear Sarah, what terrible tearing and rending is caused by the going out of this big devil of Slavery! But it is going out. It *is* going! and when it is gone, the nation will get well, and have no more fits. Then you and I will have a good time, somewhere; won't we? I'll buy a fashionable bonnet and go on "a

---

[1] McClellan was removed from command on 7 Nov. and replaced by Gen. Ambrose E. Burnside; Seward did not resign.
[2] Epes Sargent (1813–80) was editor of the *Boston Transcript*.
[3] Harriet Jacobs was a nurse to the contrabands.

spree." This news makes me feel as if I had been drinking champaigne. If we only *can* bring this war to an end, without endangering our free institutions, I shall feel re-juvenated.

Winter made an early call upon us, before the house was banked, or roots protected. We have retreated suddenly into the one little warm room, which is our winter den, and we do not expect to look out upon the world again till Spring opens. What changes may have taken place ere then!

In the course of your reading have you ever met with anything peculiarly wise, or genial, written *for* old folks, or *about* old folks? If you have seen anything of the kind, either in the form of sermons, essays, stories, or poetry, I wish you would tell me where you found it. I am collecting such articles in a scrap book.[4] If you meet with any charming engraving of happy old folks, I wish you would mention it to me.

. . .

ALS; Houghton Library, Harvard University (microfiche 53/1437).

To Mattie Griffith

Wayland, Dec. 21st, 1862.

My Darling Mattie,

I have just been reading your story about "Little Pratie," and I was charmed with it.[1] It is a delightful story and delightfully told. The constant maturing of your fine powers of mind is very obvious in what you write. I wish you would illustrate in a story, the kindness, devotion and religious trust of some old slave you have known. The great variety of new openings for pleading the cause of our poor oppressed slaves, and the many proofs that the people are really beginning to understand the subject at last, go far toward reconciling me to all the horrors of this war. It needed an earthquake to shake down the walls of prejudice and let in the light into dark places. If the war should last ten years we should not be punished more than we deserve; and I sometimes fear that God cannot complete the education that is necessary for our salvation in less time than that. Our obduracy and hardness of heart are wonderful, and yet they are less wonderful than the rapid progress that the public mind is making in the right direction. In view of the moral victories I try to forget Bull Runs,

---

[4] Child had begun collecting material for her book to be called *Looking Toward Sunset;* she published it in 1865.
[1] Mattie Griffith's story, "Ratie: A True Story of a Little Hunchback," appeared in the *National Anti-Slavery Standard* on 20 Dec. 1862. The story tells of a hunchbacked slave girl with a beautiful singing voice who is sold to a man charmed by her voice; despite his kindness, she dies of homesickness.

and the retreat from Fredericksburg.[2] The slaughter at Fredericksburg made me feel sad and despondent, but my firm conviction is that nothing happens to us that is not necessary for the progress of freedom. Oh this great work of individualizing the masses! What a struggle it is! How the pride and prejudice of men all over the world fight against it! What utter perversion of moral sentiment is manifested by the English aristocracy!

The working classes of England behave well. In several of the manufacturing districts, in the midst of extreme destitution, they have manfully resisted the influence of those who sought to induce them to uphold the Southern Confederacy. Their instincts are true against slavery.[3] I am glad to see such a disposition to send them relief from this country. If my means equalled my wishes I would send them one thousand dollars.

I hope you are going to write more about "The negro as he is." I was peculiarly interested, because I knew it was about your own slaves that you were writing. . . .

. . .

L; Maria S. Porter, "Lydia Maria Child," *National Magazine: An Illustrated American Monthly* 14 (May 1901): 165 (microfiche 96/2554).

To Mary Stearns

Wayland, Dec. 22d, 1862

. . .

Did you read Mattie Griffith's story of The Little Hunchback, in The Standard, last week? I thought it was a charming little story. How Sambo figures on the historical canvass, now! Nobody can overlook him, whether they wish it or not; for he is *every*where. This is one of the principal advantages gained by this war; if not *the* principal; and it is a vantage ground which never can be lost. When I reflect how impossible it was, a few years ago, to get a word in Sambo's favor into any paper or periodical, except a few of the out-and-out abolition papers, from which nobody copied anything; and when I look round now, and see how the pro-slavery Harper pitches its tune; how new Magazines start with the best talent of the country singing in chorus for freedom; how proslavery Generals lecture in favor of arming the negroes; and when I write emancipation articles, and find them readily accepted by the Wheeling, Virginia, Intelligencer, and the St. Louis Democrat; when I take a view of all this, I cannot but thank God and take courage. . . .

ALS; Walter G. Perry Collection, Westfield, N.J. (microfiche 54/1444).

[2] On 13 Dec. 1862 the Union forces were shattered by the Confederates in the Battle of Fredericksburg.
[3] The Union blockade of Confederate ports kept cotton from reaching English textile mills. It caused British textile workers great hardship. Nevertheless, they supported the Union cause.

To William Lloyd Garrison Haskins

Dear Willie,

A letter from your good Aunt Lydia, last night, informed me of your whereabout; and my heart prompts me to write to you, though I do not know that I have anything to say, that can either cheer or strengthen you. I can only say, May God bless you, and all other noble young souls, who, from a sense of duty, devote themselves to their country, in its hour of utmost need![1]

I reverence you for the unselfish step you have taken; and I trust you will live to see a great and good work accomplished, with the delightful consciousness of having helped on the glorious result.

I look forward with great anxiety to the first months of the approaching New Year. If emancipation had been proclaimed in the beginning, I have no doubt that the war would have been ended ere this. The distinguished French Liberal, Emile Girardin expressed exactly my opinion, when he said, "President Lincoln should have *begun* where he has *ended*." But, after all, it would not be fair to blame the President for moving so slowly. The *people* were not prepared to sustain him in any such measure; they had become too generally demoralized by long subservience to the Slave Power. Apologizing for despotism, and yielding inch by inch to its aggressions, had caused a great decline in the spirit of Liberty among us; and had not our downward course been arrested by this war, I think our free institutions would have been effectually undermined, and completely destroyed. The two antagonistic elements of Slavery and Freedom cannot, in the eternal nature of things, co-exist long under one government. If the white working-men of the North want to be secure of their *own* freedom, they must see to it that the black working-men of the South have *theirs*. From the time the very first gun was fired, I have seen plainly that there was but *one* way to put down the rebellion. Posterity, in reading the history of these times, will be amazed that this nation was so long blinded, not only to the plainest principles of justice and humanity, but also to the most obvious dictates of enlightened policy. But it is wonderful how the wise Providence of God has so managed events, as to push us continually forward in the right direction, against the most stubborn resistance of our will. In view of this, I cannot otherwise than trust that all is coming out right, at last. We shall continue to suffer much from treachery in our midst; we may have many more retreats and defeats; but whatever battles may be lost in detail, I feel confident that the *great* Battle of *Freedom* will surely be won. It is worth living for, worth dying for, my dear young friend. Your good uncle David has all along been anxious to go to the war, and the desire has increased greatly since he heard

[1] Haskins (1840–1919), the son of Lucretia Child and Robert Haskins, enlisted in August 1862 for a year, then served again from August 1864 to the end of the war.

that you and George[2] had enlisted. But his health is so very precarious that one day's march would break him down. If it were not that he needs so much care, I should myself be serving in some of the Hospitals, or teaching at Port Royal. As it is, I do all that I can, in my small way, making lint, bandages, garments, &c; and patching my old clothes, so as to contribute all the money I can save, to help the many who are suffering.   I wish I could do something for *you*, dear Willie. Is there anything I *can* do? If there is, tell me frankly. I can think of many things I would *like* to do; but they would not be suitable for a soldier, who is all the time on the move, and cannot be encumbered with more than his knapsack will hold.

I am glad the S.C. Volunteers have Col. Higginson for a leader. He seems to be "the right man in the right place";—and we have not been blessed with *many* such in this war.[3] Our greatest misfortune has been that too many of our own officers have been full of sympathy with slaveholders. I have, for many years, considered the Military Academy at West Point as a hot-bed of aristocracy and pro-slavery, of the haughtiest kind. I believe the influences of that institution tended more than anything else to pervert the natural good qualities of your Uncle John's character, and to make him a proud, hard man.[4] However, there are some glorious exceptions, such as Gen. Mitchell, Gen. Hunter, and Gen. Phelps.[5] God bless them! The men who could come out of *West Point* unperverted, must have had good and great natures.

Your Uncle David sends you his love and blessing. We should like very much to have you write to us, if you can get time. If you should meet with any little incident likely to be interesting, or to do good, by helping along public opinion, the Boston newspapers would be glad enough to publish, and I would send it to them, either with or without your name, just as you choose. If you write to us, don't take any pains, but scribble off your thoughts just as they come. However blotted, or dirty, or helter-skelter they may be, your letters will be extremely interesting to us; and we know very well that a soldier cannot stop to be particular.

[2] George Thompson Haskins (1835–63) was William's brother.
[3] Thomas Wentworth Higginson, veteran abolitionist and captain of a company in the Fifty-first Massachusetts Infantry, was chosen by General Rufus Saxton in November 1862 to command the First South Carolina Volunteers, the first black regiment mustered into the Union army. His 1864–65 *Atlantic Monthly* articles on the experiences of the regiment, later formed into the memoir *Army Life in a Black Regiment* (Boston, 1870), are a classic of the Civil War.
[4] David's brother John, an engineer, was educated at West Point.
[5] Gen. David Hunter (1802–86) assumed command of the Department of the South in March 1862 and liberated all the slaves in that territory. President Lincoln annulled the order. In April Hunter also organized a troop regiment made up of former slaves from Georgia, Florida, and South Carolina, but a few months later the War Department dismissed the soldiers without pay. Gen. John W. Phelps (1813–85) was forced to resign for organizing black troops in Louisiana prematurely in 1862; he was also outlawed by the Confederacy for inciting slaves to revolt.

Your uncle keeps up a brave heart. A dozen times a day I hear him singing at his work:

"And conquer we *must;*
For our cause it is *just.*"

I hope that the same spirit sustains you amid the difficulties and dangers of your position. May God protect you, and return you safely to your friends, to be happy under the free government you have helped to save! Again and again I say, God bless you! With true affection and respect,

L. Maria Child.

If you write about the "contrabands," or the spirit of the army, write out the *details* of anecdotes & incidents.

Don't fail to express freely any wish you have that I can gratify.

When Lydia wrote she said that she and Maria had had severe colds, but were both recovering

ALS; Child Letters, MC 305, Schlesinger Library, Radcliffe College (microfiche 54/1446).

Convers Francis, Child's brother, died on 7 April 1863. His colleague, the Reverend John Weiss (1818–79), author and abolitionist, wrote a memorial address and sought Child's recollections.

To John Weiss

Wayland, April 15'th, 1863.

Mr. Weiss,
Dear Sir,

Looking back thro' the long vista of memory, I do not recall anything concerning my dear brother, which would be likely to interest the public.

My earliest recollections of him are all manner of indications of a passion for books. Whatever work he was set about, he always had a book in his pocket; and he was poring over it, at every moment of leisure. This must have been purely from *nature;* for my parents were hard-working people, who had had small opportunity for culture, and there was, at that time, nothing like literary influences in the family, or its surroundings. He very early manifested an earnest desire to go to college. My father was not inclined to favor his wishes; for he was a great believer in manual labor, and considered a college-education something out of the line of himself or his family. But Gov. Brooks, who was our family physician, said: "Mr. Francis, you will do very wrong to thwart the inclinations of that boy. He has remarkable powers of mind; and his passion for books is so strong, that he will be sure to distinguish himself in learning; whereas, if you try to make anything else of him, he will prove a total failure." This advice decided my brother's destiny. He fitted himself for college very thoroughly and rapidly; and I remember seeing him throw himself on the bed and sob, because some difficulty about a room or a boarding place made him apprehensive that he might not be able to enter that year.

I owe my own literary tendencies entirely to his early influence. When I came from school, I always hurried to his bed-room, and threw myself down among his piles of books. As I devoured everything that came in my way, I, of course, read much that was beyond my childish comprehension. I was constantly calling upon him to explain: "Convers, what does Shakespeare mean by this? What does Milton mean by that?" He almost always gave me a clue out of my mental labyrinths; but he was roguish, and sometimes tried to bamboozle me; in which he usually suceeded. Thus he made me believe that the "raven down of darkness," which was made to smile, was the fur of a black cat, that sparkled because it was stroked the wrong way; though why the word *down* should be used, instead of *fur*, puzzled me greatly. It would be very curious to recall those juvenile conversations, in a little world of our own, into which no one about us entered. But I cannot remember them, while I am in *this* world. When I go hence, they will come back to me. I anticipate much from the gallery of Old Pictures I shall have there, with the smoke and dust all cleaned off. The indistinct recollection I now have is sufficient to fill me with gratitude to God for the gift of such a brother. ⟨for⟩ Such developement as my mind has attained, ⟨to⟩, I attribute to the impulse thus early given by his example and sympathy. Being seven years my senior, he was qualified to be my leader; but, as my mother had no other children between us, he was my companion also.

I think few appreciate duly the liberal influence of my brother in his teachings at the University. He never sought to impress his own opinions, or the doctrines of any sect, upon the minds of his pupils; but presented questions from various points of view, and left their minds free to decide which aspect was the true one. Sectarians complained of this, and he had many difficulties to encounter in consequence of their opposition; but he had his reward in the liberalizing effect of his system.

Yours very respectfully & cordially,
L. Maria Child.

The last day of his consciousness, he was in a very serene state of mind. "I have not a want in the world," said he. I replied, "That is a blessed state, dear brother." "Yes it *is* blessed," said he; "and I thank God for it." Afterward, when he was dozing, I heard him murmur: "Blessings upon blessings!"

ALS; Special Manuscript Collection, Columbia University (microfiche 55/1476).

To William Lloyd Garrison Haskins

Wayland, April 30'th, 1863.

Dear Willie,

I hope you have received the illustrated newspapers, (four, I think) which I ordered to be sent to you from Boston. If we did not live in such an out-of-the-way place, we could often be picking up something entertaining to send you. But there is nothing here; and we are getting old and rheumatic, and very seldom travel to the city. I herewith send you a leathern drinking-cup, which your uncle had when he was a soldier in Spain, in his young, enthusiastic days.[1] It will take scarcely any room in your knapsack, and may be convenient to dip into a brook, when you are tired and thirsty.   We think and talk about you a great deal, and keep a close look out for news of the 51st Regiment. *No* news of you is *good* news; and so we feel happier when we have looked in vain for your name.

I try not to be anxious about public affairs, and I am tolerably successful in the effort, because I have a prevailing belief that we are coming out right, *at last*. Our insane prejudice against color is very gradually, but surely, giving way before the emergencies of the time, and the laudable conduct of the colored people. Colonel Shaw, of the Mass'ts 54th is a friend of mine; a noble-hearted young gentlemen, who left wealth and luxury, and a most happy home, to serve his country in her hour of need.[2] His mother writes me that he is delighted with his regiment; he finds so many of them more intelligent than he expected, and all of them orderly, full of pluck, and quick at acquiring military skill. From the very outset of this war, I said we should never effectually put down the rebellion till we emancipated the slaves, treated them in a manner to gain their confidence, and made the fullest use of their knowledge of the rebel country, and of their natural antipathy to their masters. We have been wofully, but I trust not *fatally*, blind to our own *interest*, to say nothing of the great principles of *justice* and *humanity*. I wish the North had been great and good enough to have met this crisis in a spirit as devoted to freedom, as the South is to slavery. But long subservience to an unprincipled oligarchy had too far demoralized the people to admit of their being worthy champions of a great universal idea of human rights; and so they are compelled to suffer and fight for their *own* rights. For, say what we will, this is a war to decide whether this is to be a free country, where working-men elect their own rulers, and where

[1] David Lee Child fought in Spain against the occupation of the French.
[2] Early in 1863, Governor Andrew had been authorized by Secretary Stanton to raise black troops in Massachusetts, and the Fifty-fourth Massachusetts Infantry would be the first black outfit in the North. Andrew chose Robert Gould Shaw, then twenty-five and a combat veteran, to be the regiment's colonel. The son of the wealthy Francis and Sarah Shaw, Robert, too, was an ardent abolitionist. George Stearns headed a committee to raise men and money for the Fifty-fourth. Frederick Douglass, one of its leading recruiters, signed up his own two sons, Charles and Lewis.

---

free schools give all an equal chance for education, or whether we are to live under despotic institutions, which will divide society into two classes, rulers and servants, and ordain ignorance as the convenient, nay, even *necessary* condition of all who labor. These are Southern ideas; and unless the rebels are conquered, they will assuredly invade *us*, and force their institutions upon the whole country. It is, therefore, a great cause, involving the freedom and progress of the human race, in all parts of the world. Your noble-hearted brother did not sacrifice his young life, for any sectional or small idea.[3] Our army stand before God the champions of human freedom, which includes their own. May they prove true to their trust, and may their long-deferred hopes be crowned with victory!   The Spring is opening pleasantly here. Meadows and fields are green, and the farmers are busy with their oxen. How glad we shall be when you are safely restored to these peaceful pursuits! Good night. The blessing of God be with you!

Your affectionate aunt,
L. Maria Child.

Col. Shaw and his 54th (colored) regiment leave for N. Carolina soon; so you will see what kind of soldiers they make.

Uncle David sends you his warm love and blessing. I hope his letter reached you safely.

ALS; Child Letters, MC 305, Schlesinger Library, Radcliffe College (microfiche 55/1477).

To Sarah Shaw

Wayland, May 1'st 1863.

Darling Sarah,

If there ever was an inspired friend, you are one! You always know what will give me the most pleasure, and go and do it. I have longed for Mendelssohn's Letters, and resolved that the buying of it should be the first selfish luxury I indulged in. Liszt is also a great favorite with me as a writer, and I coveted his Life of Chopin, as soon as I saw it.[1] Judging by the lady's Dedication, I should think she might make rather an *inflated* translator.   Do you know, dearest, that you are a most *flattering* friend? In the kind attentions you pay me, you *think* enough about me to *remember* my tastes; and that is what other people do *not*. I notice it, as a measure of how much they really care for me; but I do not *expect* to be cared for, and so am not disappointed. But when a friend remembers my tastes, and ministers to them with such thoughtful delicacy and kindness as you do, I feel it, to my heart's core. Thank God that you continue

[3] George Thompson Haskins died under unknown circumstances.
[1] *Letters of Felix Mendelssohn Bartholdy from 1833 to 1847* (London, 1863); Franz Liszt, *Life of Chopin* (Boston, 1863).

in this world, and that you find time, among your many excitements and cares, to think of your lonely old friend! When the stage-driver left the package, I kissed the dear hand-writing, and then I said aloud, to myself, "I hope she has not sent anything about the war."

Don't suspect me of inclining to be a copperhead. I am far enough from that. But I had been very sad all day, and I wanted something poetic or cheering; something that would make me forget sorrow and strife, and lull my perturbed feelings, like the sound of music from across the water. I opened the package, and lo! there was Mendelssohn, whose whole existence, inward and outward ⟨seemed⟩ was a golden chain of harmonies. I never could understand what it is that has always attracted me so powerfully toward him; for I do not *begin* to comprehend his music. But the *effect* it has upon me is invariably charming. It draws me toward him with a strong feeling of affection. Beethoven generally makes me afraid. I listen to his music with such a feeling as I imagine I should have if I were alone among the shadows of high black mountains, crowned far up with a rim of golden sunshine. It is grand, but it oppresses me. Mendelssohn's music affects me like a noble river flowing through pleasant scenery. His countenance charms me in the same way. How beautiful he is! I shall never forget a dream I had about him, soon after his death. It was one of those *vivid* dreams, that seem at the time, and afterward in the memory, like something that really happened. I was in the spiritual world, in a large Hall, where the angels were going to give a Concert. There were music-stands on a large platform, with music lying open upon them, as in this world, on such occasions. Then I began perplexing myself, as usual, about the mystery of music, and wondering whether the angels would help me to understand it. There were very few people in the Hall, and I sat there waiting for the performers, and lost in reverie. I raised my eyes, and there, opposite to me, at the other end of the Hall, sat Felix Mendelssohn! He was looking at me, as if reading my thoughts. I was all in a flutter of joy and love. He seemed to know that also; for he smiled and came toward me. He took me by the hand, and led me up on the platform. He opened a box on one of the stands. It seemed to be full of jewels. He took from it several golden violins, not bigger than beetles, and a golden heart. He placed them in my hand, with a smile, and then took from inside his vest a small golden key. He showed me a key-hole in the heart, and said, "There is the key. You will open it." He moved away, and I followed, as if attracted by a spell. He went from the Hall, through a long, narrow passage. At the end, he opened a door, and a shower of soft golden light flooded him, as he looked back and smiled upon me. He was far more beautiful than any artistic dream of an angel, but so like his portraits, that I should have known him anywhere. The door closed and shut him in, with all that glorious atmosphere of transfigured light, and I was left in the darkness. But I had in my hand, the golden heart with its golden key, and he had said "You will open it."[2]

[2] Child's letters make mention of this dream several times over the years.

David has been unusually well for several months. He sends cordial greetings.

I wrote to you, at Staten Island, a few days before I received the precious books.

May Heavens best blessings be with Robert & his bride.[3] How hard it must be to leave a honeymoon to go and fight! Bless his noble young soul!

I have read ten or twelve of the Letters, and am delighted with them. What a *genuine*, earnest man he was! That letter of advice about his father, which you marked, is full of good sense and kindly feeling. The book is a real blessing to me in my sadness.

Your ever grateful and loving old Mariquita.

ALS; Manuscript Division, New York Public Library (microfiche 55/1479).

In March 1863 Elizabeth Cady Stanton and Susan B. Anthony issued a call for a national convention in New York to take place on 14 May 1863, at which the Women's National Loyal League would be organized. Because Lincoln's emancipation proclamation applied only to slaves of certain Confederate states (Tennessee and parts of Virginia and Louisiana excluded), the Loyal League launched a mass petition campaign to extend emancipation nationwide by a constitutional amendment.

To Elizabeth Cady Stanton

Wayland, May 24'th, 1863.

Dear Mrs. Stanton,

I am sincerely grieved that I should have seemed neglectful of a request of yours; for there are very few people in the world, whom I should be so unwilling to neglect as your honored self. You are interesting to me for your husband's sake, who came boldly and frankly to the aid of the slave in all the freshness and strength of his early manhood. How I used to delight in his spontaneous eloquence, in those dear old days when our little band of moral enthusiasts paid the American people the compliment of believing that the accursed system of slavery could be upheaved and overthrown by moral influence!   Then you are especially interesting to me, by reason of the true and earnest utterances of your soul, which have reached me, from time to time through the press. Yet I have seemed to treat you uncourteously! That is a misfortune. Let me explain how it happened. I did not answer you *personally*, because I intended to send a letter to your Convention, and wished to enclose

[3] Colonel Shaw married Annie Haggerty of New York a few weeks before his regiment was to sail south.

it in the one to you. But immediately after I received yours, I began to be uneasy about the health of my dear brother Dr. Francis. He lived sixteen miles from me, and I went back and forth frequently, which hurried me with avocations when I returned home; because I keep no domestic. Moreover, my mind was anxious and disturbed, on *his* account; and I never can write unless my mind is *free*. He failed rapidly, and died. I was fatigued and worn down with watching, with attending the funeral, and all the wear and tear of mind and body consequent upon a great sorrow. He was in florid health but a few months ago, and his death came upon me so suddenly, that it had a stunning effect. Will it seem very strange to you that I forgot all about the Convention? His sick-chamber, death-bed, and funeral, were present with me all the time, calling up a thousand tender memories of our childhood and youth. I was stunned, bewildered, oblivious of other things. When one is past sixty, the heart does not rebound from the pressure of such heavy weights so easily as it does in more elastic years.

At last, I remembered the Convention, and the letter I had intended to write; but when I looked for the date, I found it was to meet the very next morning!

I was right heartily vexed at myself. "That I should have treated Elizabeth Cady Stanton so, of all women in the world!" I exclaimed, indignantly. How many times, when I have seen articles from your pen, have I said to my husband, "There is a woman after my own heart!" and he has responded, "Amen"! Of the additional claim of your relationship to Gerrit Smith I was unconscious, until you enclosed his letter. He is a man whom I regard with feelings of affectionate reverence. He has been a benefactor to my soul; for again and again, have I been stimulated, encouraged, and strengthened, by his fearless pursuit of truth, and his unflinching loyalty to conscience.

I have just read, in the Standard, an account of the proceedings in your Convention. I sympathize with them cordially and entirely. Next week, I will send a trifle to the Treasurer.

As for the aspect of the times, I trust in God, and have little other trust. Always I say to myself, "He did not bring the Mayflower here for nothing. The spiritual cargo it brought was leaven for a Continent, and these swords are stirring it in, though the work is done unconsciously."   I respond to Mr. Bright's sentiment that, "God is carrying on the Revolution in America very *slowly*, that He may make emancipation sure."[1]

Certainly, if the Lord wanted *slow* work to be done, He could nt have employed a better hand than "old Abe."

Mr. Child unites with me in most respectful and friendly greetings to you and Mr. Stanton. Yours very cordially,

L. Maria Child.

ALS; Elizabeth Cady Stanton Papers, Manuscript Division, Library of Congress (microfiche 55/1481).

[1] John Bright, an English statesman, favored the North in the Civil War.

Early in June a fire burned down the ell of the Child home but not the main part of the house. It took most of the summer to clean the house and repair the damage.

To Sarah Shaw

Wayland, June 16th, 1863.

Darling Friend,

While I was yet rejoicing over your visit, and thinking how pleasant it was to have had you see how comfortable & cozy my little home looked, after years of gradual improvements, brought about by much hard labor, a sudden change came over everything. The very day after you left, my house took fire about 2 P.M. The cause is a mystery to us. The conjecture is that fire was communicated to the interior wood-work by some concealed fault in the kitchen chimney. I do not lie down in the day-time twice in a year, but that day I had become weary transplanting in the garden, and I went to my chamber to sleep a little. David *always* takes a nap after dinner; but that day he said he *must* finish some transplanting while it was rainy. How thankful I am that he did not go up stairs to sleep as usual,! for he always takes his nap in a little chamber over the kitchen. He could not have come to his senses, in the dense smoke; the whole house must have been burned if we had *both* been asleep, and we burned in it. He discovered some smoke which alarmed him, when he was working in the garden, and when he opened the back-door the *whole* kitchen was in a light blaze. He judged it was an hour or hour and a half, after I went to lie down. Yet when I left the kitchen, one moment before I went up stairs, all was calm and cool; no smoke, no fire. We had eaten a cold dinner, and so had not been cooking. My poor mate was in *such* agony! For I was asleep up stairs, and the front-door was fastened. When his terrified screams wakened me, I attempted to pass down the back-stairs, not knowing *where* the fire was; but the heat of my chamber-door burned my hand badly, and the next room was so full of dark smoke, that I could literally see nothing, and was at the same time choked and bewildered by inhaling it. By instinct, I thrust the door to, and ran down the front-stairs; but the smoke darkened everything so that I could not find the latch of the door. Oh, it was a horrid scene! There is no engine in town, but the neighbors brought garden-hose. Such an old pine tinder box as it is, and the ell-part so completely on fire, it is marvellous how any portion of the house was saved. The interior of the ell-part, upper and lower, is entirely consumed, but the roof and clapboards are left. The front parlor and chamber over it are uninjured, except some breaking of windows. The little sitting-room, which looked so cozy when you were here, is black as the chimney back; walls, and ceiling both; the paper in some places so scorched as to be hanging in tatters; looking-glass cracked and shivered by the heat; clock blackened, broken, & stopped; everything looked utterly funereal. By the blessing of God, I had

432

presence of mind as soon as I got into the open air. I secured my pocket-book and silver-spoons, and then the first thing I took care of was your photograph Album, and the little shell-basket; then the photograph of your house and cottage; then all the pictures on the walls, and all my little "playthings." ⟨on the walls.⟩ I passed them to my good, kind neighbors, who took them home carefully. It is wonderful how quick the neighbors gathered, and how efficiently they worked. It is a perfect miracle how they quenched the flames. We, and everybody else, thought the *whole must* go. But I had no other feeling than that of gratitude to the good God, that my dear, kind mate was not smotherd, and that I was enabled to find my way into the open air. If such a calamity *must* happen, it could not have been attended with more favorable circumstances. It rained; it was calm; being Saturday afternoon the farmers were near[1]
. . .

ALS; Houghton Library, Harvard University (microfiche 55/1483).

On 18 July 1863, Col. Robert Gould Shaw's regiment of black troops, along with other regiments, stormed Fort Wagner, guarding Charleston Harbor, and was driven back with very heavy losses. Shaw was shot dead through the heart. It was the first major test of the black troops, and it proved their courage and soldiership. Colonel Shaw and the Fifty-fourth became symbols of the best that soldiers in a good cause—black or white—could do. Fort Wagner ended all doubts about using black troops to crush the rebellion. The next letter is Child's message of condolence to the colonel's mother.

To Sarah Shaw

Wayland, July 25th, 1863.

My precious Sarah,

Oh, darling! darling! if the newspaper rumour be true, what I have so long dreaded has come upon you. But rumour very often exaggerates, and sometimes invents; so I still hope, though with a heart that bleeds for you. If the report be true, may our Heavenly Father sustain you under this heavy sorrow. Severe as the blow must be, it is not altogether without consolations. If your beautiful and brave boy has died, he died nobly in the defence of great principles, and has gone to join the glorious army of martyrs; and how much more sacred and dear to memory is such a life and such a death, than a life spent in self-indulgence, gradually impairing the health, and weakening the mental powers. Your darling Robert made the most of the powers and advantages God had given him, by consecrating them to the defence of freedom and humanity. Such a son in the spirit-world is worth ten living here for themselves only.

[1] The rest of the letter is missing, except for postscripts and signature on the margin, here omitted.

Besides, dear, the separation is only for a little while. You parted from him a *young* man, but rendered thoughtful and anxious beyond his years, by reason of the heavy responsibility that devolved upon him. You will meet him a serene angel, endowed with larger vision, and better understanding why it is that we are doomed to suffer here. Ah, darling, my words fall coldly upon your bereaved heart. God comfort you! He alone can carry you through this dark passage. He has given you beautiful little grandchildren to love, and I trust their soft arms will help to bear you up. Most sincerely do I wish that my old life could have been sacrificed to save your brave and beautiful boy. But the Heavenly Father ordereth all things in wisdom, and in mercy too; as we should acknowledge, if we could only see the end from the beginning.

In your last but one, you wrote as if I might think you did not pity *me* enough. I was going to answer that you pitied me *more* than enough; more than I pitied myself. I was going to ask you what was *my* misfortune, compared with that of the poor wretches driven from their desolated homes by a murderous mob; or what it was compared with the anxiety of a mother, whose only son was leading a colored regiment into S. Carolina. But *now*, in view of this terrible rumour, how utterly insignificant and contemptible seem all *my* troubles! I thank Mrs. Gay very much for her hearty sympathy; but tell her that, at a crisis like *this*, it is merely as if a musquito had stung me.

Ought I not to be taking care of the sick & wounded soldiers? Sometimes that thought worries me.

Yours with a heart brim full of love and sympathy,

Old Mariquita.

It greatly relieved my mind to be assured that *your* side of the Island was considered safe.

ALS; Wayland (Mass.) Historical Society (microfiche 56/1491).

In the next letter, Child refers to the draft riots in New York and to Fanny Kemble's *Journal of a Residence on a Georgia Plantation*. The book was published in England and the United States in May 1863. By the time it appeared, British opinion had already turned against the South. In March 1863 a conscription act made all men aged twenty to forty-five liable to military service, except for the rich, who could buy their way out. In New York City a four-day draft riot erupted in mid-July. Homes and offices of abolitionists and Republicans were sacked, the Colored Orphan Asylum was burned, and many blacks were lynched on the streets. Police and federal troops finally put down the mob. Many of the rioters were Irish immigrant laborers who feared that with emancipation blacks would come North, lowering wages and taking jobs from whites. Reacting against the violence, prosperous New Yorkers fired Irish servants and hired blacks. A campaign succeeded in abolishing Jim Crow on the city's streetcars. Child's prejudice against the Irish was part of the antiforeign fever taking hold in the United States.

To Oliver Johnson, Editor, *National Anti-Slavery Standard*

[Before 22 August 1863]

It is long since I have read anything with so much interest as Mrs. Kemble's Journal on a Georgia plantation. Mrs. Sedgwick told me about it, years ago, and wished to have it inserted in *The Anti-Slavery Standard,* which I then edited;[1] but this was prevented by the peculiar state of Mrs. Kemble's domestic affairs. I was disappointed at the time, but I am very glad it did *not* appear then; for it will do a hundred-fold more good now. It came out in the very nick of time. I think it will prove one of the most powerful of the agencies now at work for the overthrow of slavery.

I saw Mrs. Kemble personate various characters in Shakspeare, at a time when Bostonians were crazy about her, and everybody called her by the pet name of Fanny Kemble. In later years, I heard her readings several times. Always, I recognized in her a woman of remarkable genius, and always I derived great intellectual pleasure from her performances. But I never fairly did homage to her until now. For a woman of her transcendent powers, accustomed to ease, elegance, and the excitement of perpetual adulation, to sympathize with those poor loathsome slaves as she did, and persist in rendering them such personal services as were in her power, indicates great nobility of soul. Then she saw through all the apologies for slavery with such clear, practical good sense! Only once her good sense failed her, I think; when she states that she had not been an Abolitionist, because she thought "the emancipation of the slaves was exclusively the business and duty of the owners." This was a very general fallacy, as we Abolitionists well know. Yet people who urged that plea would have deemed it very absurd to say that no efforts ought to be made against theft and murder, because it was exclusively the business of thieves and murderers to decide when and how their vocation should cease. It seemed very harsh and unjust to call such elegant men as the Southerners by such names; but if we had been their slaves, how should we have deemed it? Have they not in this rebellion fully earned the titles we bestowed upon them?

. . .

Knowing, as we do, that the work-houses and penitentiaries of Europe are continually emptying themselves into our cities, we have no reason to wonder at any amount of depravity that may be manifested by the rabble of such a place as New York, which is a sort of common sewer for the filth of nations; but I must confess I *was* surprised at the degree of wanton wickedness and

[1] It was to Elizabeth D. Sedgwick of Lenox, Mass., one of Kemble's closest friends, that the journal entries, all written in 1839, were addressed, as though they were personal letters.

cruelty exhibited by the recent rioters. But the political instigators are more guilty than the reckless and ignorant mob.

I have real anguish of soul about the fate of those of the 54th regiment who were taken prisoners.[2] I feel as if I wanted to stir heaven and earth to get them out of slavery. The Order issued by the President does not seem to me strong enough to ensure their being sent back. Rebel prisoners of rank and influence ought to work in chains, as hostages for them. It will be of little use to put the common soldiers of the rebel army to hard labor; for the haughty slaveholders have no more respect or pity for *them* than they have for slaves; they would not care how long the "low whites" were kept to work in our trenches or our prisons.

In common with all who have any feeling, I have suffered much in the course of this war; but nothing has caused me so severe a pang as the death of the noble-hearted and brave young Col. Shaw, and the fate of a portion of his regiment. The conduct of the rebels with regard to his burial was characteristic, and altogether worthy of their slaveholding education.[3] His father wrote to me of it thus: "Our darling son, our hero, has received at the hands of the rebels the most fitting burial possible. They buried him with his brave, devoted followers, who fell dead over him and around him. The poor benighted wretches thought they were heaping indignities on his dead body, but the act recoils on themselves, and proves them absolutely incapable of appreciating noble qualities. They thought to give an additional pang to the bruised hearts of his friends; but we would not have him buried elsewhere, if we could. If a wish of ours would do it, we would not have his body taken away from those who loved him so devotedly, with whom and for whom he gave up his life."

Now is not that sublime? History has recorded few things more grand than the self-sacrifice of that young hero, and the elevation of soul with which his parents have consented thereto. I was glad Gen. Saxton proposed to the freedmen to erect a monument to Col. Shaw, but the colored soldiers who fell ought to have a monument also.[4]

L, extracts; *National Anti-Slavery Standard*, 22 Aug. 1863 (microfiche 56/1499).

[2] Nearly a hundred of the Fifty-fourth's men were missing or taken prisoner. Child voiced the common fear that the South would not regard the black soldiers as prisoners of war but would execute them as felons. That summer there were persistent reports of captured black soldiers being murdered after fighting at Port Hudson and Milliken's Bend. Lincoln proclaimed a policy of retaliation for violation of the laws of war. As a result, the prisoners from the Fifty-fourth were not enslaved or killed but held captive until the war's end.

[3] Shaw was buried with his men. The North believed that it was as a gesture of contempt that the Confederates threw him into a ditch "with his niggers." Proposals were made to recover his body, but Francis Shaw stopped them, saying "We hold that a soldier's most appropriate burial place is in the field where he has fallen."

[4] A monument to Shaw, sculpted by Augustus Saint Gaudens, was erected on the Boston Common in 1897.

Child's relationship with the prominent Boston publisher James T. Fields (1817–81) of Ticknor and Fields had begun back in the 1850s. Publication of *Looking Toward Sunset*, the book in question here, was postponed until 1864 (the copyright date was 1865).

To James T. Fields

Wayland, Dec. 10'th, 1863.

Mr. Fields,

    Dear Sir,

    I thank you very much for your kind offer, but I have no need of accepting it. My disappointment at the non-appearance of the book is more a matter of feeling, than anything else. I wanted to send it to several friends of former years, from whom I have long been separated, without the power of paying them kindly attentions. They fall around me like autumn leaves now. Three have died since the book was in press. How many will survive till the close of another year, God alone knows.

    Another reason for regret is that the book was *announced*, and to fail in the promise looks as if I had grown old and lazy. Old I am, but lazy I am not.

    I doubt whether it would be advisable to make a very elegant book. The old care less about elegance, than the young. It is not a book to put on the centre-table for show, but intended to be a quiet, sober, every-day friend. And, though I have put in something for all sorts of tastes, I have *mainly* endeavored to make it useful and acceptable to what are called the common people.

    My sympathies tend as inevitably toward the masses, as Willis's[1] do toward the "upper ten." I have not the slightest talent for respectability.

    . . .

    I see that "Rainbows for Children," and "the Magician's Show-Box" are advertised under my name. I did not write them. They were written by Mrs. Tappan, who was Caroline Sturgis, daughter of the late W'm Sturgis.[2]

Yours very cordially,

L. Maria Child.

ALS; James Thomas Fields Collection, Huntington Library (microfiche 57/1519).

To Henrietta Sargent

Wayland, Feb. 11'th, 1864.

Dearest Henrietta

    Sixty two years old this very day! How *long* ago it seems since I first went

[1] N. P. Willis.

[2] Caroline Sturgis's *Rainbows for Children* (Boston, 1848) and *The Magician's Show Box* (Boston, 1856) had been edited by Child.

into your cozy little parlor in Poplar St. and was introduced to Dr. Howe, then a handsome, romantic-looking young man, just returned from Greece, with Byron's helmet![1] How many pleasant hours I afterward spent with you and dear good Catherine![2] How she cared for me, and nursed me up, and made me comfortable! What lively chats we had together in the old days, when the little band of abolitionists were a sort of apostolic church, fervent and united! If we could have foreseen all the difficulties in the way of the mission we undertook, few of us would perhaps have ventured to put their hands to the plough. But it was the Lord's work we were doing, Henrietta; and *He* kindled our hearts, to produce the glow that was needed to loosen the ice-berg of popular feeling, and send it drifting toward warmer seas, gradually melting by the way. How fast it is steering toward the tropics *now*, melting as it goes! *Have* you read the Speech of Gen. Gantt, of Arkansas, delivered at Concord, N.H.?[3] His frank, downright, Western way of saying things charmed me. I shouted over it with delight. The spirit moved me to write him a long letter, which I hope *may* produce some good results for the emancipated slaves of Arkansas. I sow a great deal of such seed in silence, and *some* of it, I trust, falls into good ground.

I send you some needle-books and bivouac-caps. I made the caps rather differently from your pattern, because I was told the soldiers like to have them come down in the neck, to keep the cold winds out. I had no thimbles, and could obtain none in this town. I have furnished the needle-books with the other articles. I have put in each four needles and a darning-needle, which I suppose will make the freedwomen who receive them feel very rich. I was told, by one who had been among them, that they said to each other, "How rich the Yankees must be, and how generous they are! They have sent us all *three* needles a piece! and ole missus never giv us but *one*."

I wanted to make more needle-books, and more caps; but the fact is, I have raked and scraped the house for all sorts of scraps that could be used for soldiers, or hospitals, or for colored refugees; and I now have scarcely anything left.

The bits of calico were remains of the gowns of former years. How *many* recollections they conjured up! nearly all of them sad. I have a great quantity of little bags, for thread, tape, buttons, different colored sewing-silks, &c. They are all made of the gowns of friends. Ah, what bags full of memories, they

[1] Dr. Samuel Gridley Howe, abolitionist and social reformer, served with the Greek revolutionary forces from 1823 to 1830.
[2] Catherine Sargent.
[3] Gen. Edward W. Gantt had made a speech recanting his secessionism and returning his allegiance to the United States. On 7 Feb. Child had written to him a commendatory letter that was later published in the *National Anti-Slavery Standard* (22 Apr. 1865).

are! Sometimes I get crying over them, and always they make me very thoughtful.

. . .

ALS; Lydia Maria Child Papers, Anti-Slavery Collection, Cornell University (microfiche 57/1536).

To George W. Julian

Wayland, March 27'th, 1864.

Dear Mr. Julian,

I thank you heartily for your Speech concerning the public lands.[1] I have
almost as strong an aversion to Land-Monopoly, as I have to Slavery. It is, in
fact, only another phase of Slavery; another form of the absorption of Labor by
Capital, which has tormented and degraded the world from the beginning.

I have observed with anxiety that large tracts of Southern confiscated lands
were being bought by Northern capitalists. They ought to be mainly distributed
among the emancipated slaves, and the poor whites who will consent to become
loyal citizens of the U.S.; for the poor whites have been *almost* as much wronged
by slave holding aristocrats, as the enslaved blacks have been. I was much
pleased with a letter written to President Lincoln, some time ago, by a Kentuckian then residing in Ohio. I think his name was Candy. His plan of con-
fiscating the lands of rebels, and *offering* them to such poor whites as would
espouse the cause of the U.S. seemed to be both just and *politic*. His plan
also embraced such colored men as worked in any way in the employ of the
U.S. The letter seemed to me singularly wise in its suggestion and I wondered
that so little attention was paid to it.

One of the pleasantest features in British emancipation was the cutting up
of large plantations into little lots. I rejoiced to read that the emancipated
laborers were in many villages combining together to build small sugar-mills
for their mutual convenience. I hope these mills will become as common as
cider-mills in New England, and that every cultivator will carry his load of
cane to be manufactured into sugar, as our farmers carry apples to the cider-mill.
It is all a mistake that the manufacture of sugar cannot be carried on without rich
capitalists. *Combined* capital of the laborers is far better, every way, than the
monopolizing of the mills by a few men of overgrown wealth.

The individualizing of the masses is the ultimate end of *all* reforms; but

---

[1] Julian, chairman of the House Committee on Public Lands, had proposed extending
the Homestead Act of 1862 to the forfeited and confiscated lands of the Rebels. His
intent, he said, was "to deal with these lands as public lands, and parcel them out into
small homesteads among the poor of the South, black and white." The bill narrowly
passed in the House but was dropped by the Republican leadership during its national
convention that June.

so strong is the spirit of monopoly, that the work goes on with extreme slowness, in all parts of the world.

But, though I fully and earnestly sympathize with the spirit of your Speech, I have some doubts concerning the method by which you propose to advance the interest of cultivators. Experience and observation have taught me that men are generally injured by having property *given* to them. They don't prize it so highly, keep it so carefully, or improve it so diligently, as they do when they take some pains to obtain it. In various ways, it impairs the strength and dignity of character to receive *gifts*. Whosoever would be a *man* must *earn*.

Labor is now in such demand, and wages are so high, that a thrifty emigrant from Europe, or elsewhere, could earn enough on his way to the public lands, to buy himself a farm in a short time, by stopping to do agricultural or mechanical jobs, of which there is urgent need in all parts of the country. The sort of men who would proceed in this way are the kind of emigrants we *need*. The outright *gift* of lands would attract a swarm of idlers and vagabonds to our shores. As a general thing, the chief [thing?] *they* would care about the land would be to secure a title to it for the purpose of selling it; a circumstance of which land-monopolists would speedily take advantage.

The *political* mischiefs which would result from an inundation of idle, dissipated loafers are incalculable. We have had bitter experience, in the use which Southern slaveholders and Northern democrats have made of the ignorant Irish.

The *sale* of the public lands would not, as you say, *begin* to pay the national debt; yet, other things being equal, it would be of *some* importance as a help toward liquidating it. You truly remark that the wealth arising from the *cultivation* of the soil is what we must rely upon. But the sort of men who would *earn* their way to the possession of farms from the public lands would be the men most likely to *cultivate* them well, to keep them in their own hands, and gradually to increase their acres by new earnings. And, in the present state of things, the jobs they would do to obtain the small sums of money requisite for such purchases, would be no inconsiderable benefit to the country.

You recollect that the settlers of Georgia, to whom the English crown *gave* fertile lands, and liberal donations, were always in debt and difficulty, and always petitioning for more and more assistance from the home-government; while the settlers of New England, who worked their *own* passage, were always self-sustaining, notwithstanding the hardness of the climate and the poverty of the soil.

. . .

ALS; Joshua Giddings Papers, Manuscript Division, Library of Congress (microfiche 58/1553).

To Gerrit Smith

Wayland, Mass'ts, April 4'th, 1864

Dear and Honored Friend Smith,

I have a project in my head, and I want to advise with you about it. The Freed men and women are fast learning to read, and are much taken up with the new acquisition. There seem to be very few books *suitable* to their condition. I have had thoughts of compiling one, consisting of the best *biographies* of colored people, *stories* about slaves, good *hymns,* and the best pieces of *poetry* by colored people, &c. &c.[1] The whole to be carefully adapted to their condition, and especially to have a *good moral* effect, and an *encouraging* effect. The miscellaneous contents might be introduced to them by an Address written especially for them. I would have it sold at the lowest possible price, and the money it brought used to purchase libraries for their schools. I should, of course, take nothing for my services, and if I could possibly afford it, I would print it at my own expense. But our house was half burned last summer; and though in repairing the damage done to house and furniture, we confined ourselves strictly to what was necessary, and did a large portion of the work with our own ⟨slands⟩ hands, still, the prices are so enormously high, that we could not avoid expending considerable more than the small insurance. I mention this merely as a reason why I cannot pay for publishing the book; and I despair of finding any bookseller to do it gratis.

Does the idea seem to you a good one? Is it of sufficient importance to be attended to, in the midst of so many *other* claims upon time and money? Do you think it worth while to do anything about it yourself?

I meant to have written to you some time ago, to thank you for your letter to the Rev. Thomas Worcester, of the New Jerusalem Church.[2] I had the same thoughts about his letter myself, and could scarcely refrain from telling him that I had small respect for any church, which forbore to rebuke wickedness, till political economy brought proof that it was *safe* and *profitable* for the sinner to repent. But I restrained the strong temptation to satire, because, for the poor negro's sake, I was glad to have people come over to the right side from *any* motive. Still, I was inconsistent enough to be glad that you gave him a rap over the knuckles. It may set him to thinking. In my youth, I "experienced religion" in the form of Swedenborgianism; but the church and pastor were so bitterly pro-slavery, and so intensely bigotted, that I doubted whether *such* a church could have come down from heaven. Much of the influence of some portion of the doctrines will probably always remain impressed on my interior life. But I have had no connexion with the church, or its members, for twenty years; during which I have spiritually wandered far and wide, and with a free step.

[1] The collection Child proposes here was published in 1865 as *The Freedmen's Book.*
[2] Thomas Worcester (1795–1878), a Swedenborgian minister, was pastor of the New Church Society in Massachusetts.

You are a marvellous man! Farmer, lecturer, member of Congress, preacher, and now play-actor! What *next*, I wonder? Perhaps I shall yet see you Col. of a regiment, or General of a brigade, in full uniform, feather in cap; though you have feathers enough in your cap already.

I think your daughter must make a charming Desdemona.[3] I was so vexed that I sat at table with her, without knowing she was your daughter! She interested me as a stranger; but I should have made much of her, if I had known she was Gerrit Smith's daughter. Please give her my love and a cordial greeting to her husband and children. Also best respects to Mrs. Smith.

God bless you!

Yours with affectionate respect,
L. Maria Child.

Are you not glad that Gen. Grant has the control of military affairs?[4]

ALS; Gerrit Smith Collection, George Arents Research Library, Syracuse University (microfiche 58/1555).

To Lucy Osgood

Wayland, April 5'th, 1864.

My very dear friend,

. . . The sunshine does not come out, as you prognosticated. The weather is lowering and dreary, just as it was a year ago at this time, when I was travelling back and forth between here and Cambridge, with a heavy heart.[1] It all comes back to me with painful vividness; and especially the dismal obliteration of that noble mind by laudanum. I *do* hope I shall have nobody near me in my last illness, who will dose me with opium, in any form. Better let the body suffer, than to lay rash hands upon the sacred altar of the mind. The account of Starr King's last hours thrilled me through and through; and, with a gush of tears, I prayed that I might be enabled to depart thus calmly and clearly.[2] I was struck with the grand simplicity and naturalness of his exit. No stereotyped phrases, no thought of dying as it was becoming in a clergyman to die; but simply and sweetly saying, "Good Night," and falling asleep like a child on the bosom of its mother. I never saw Starr King; but his address at the funeral of Charles F.

---

[3] Elizabeth (Smith) Miller (1822–1911), daughter of Gerrit Smith, was noted in the 1850s for promoting the Bloomer costume. The allusion to Desdemona is unexplained.
[4] Gen. Ulysses S. Grant (1822–85) took supreme command of the Union armies on 9 Mar. 1864.
[1] Child's brother Convers Francis had died in Cambridge the previous year.
[2] Thomas Starr King (1824–64) was a Unitarian clergyman and author; he had helped keep California loyal to the Union in the early war years.

Hovey gave me the impression that he was a large and beautiful soul. I have also been very much attracted toward his writings. His style is far from perfect; but it is natural and all alive. . . .

. . .

You express the hope that I shall not find myself so isolated as you are. My dear friend, you know not *how* isolated I am. I have had so many removals, in the course of my married life, that my friendships and my social relations have been sadly disturbed thereby; and during the last ten years, my small remaining circle has been constantly diminished by death. Every New Year's day, I think, "Who will be taken *this* year? Will more dear ones go from *me*, or shall I go from *them?*["] I have literally but *four* friends; Louisa Loring, Henrietta Sargent, Sarah Shaw, and yourself. Since Ellis's death, Louisa has felt an utter indifference toward me, and everybody else. She is very kind, when she thinks of it, but she would never notice if she did not see me from the beginning of the year to the end of it. Henrietta seems to be greatly cheered and enlivened by my presence; but owing to her sister Parker's dislike of me, for electing Lincoln, my visits to her have to be unfrequent and brief. Sarah Shaw has been assiduous in kindness and pleasant attentions, beyond any friend I ever had; but since the death of Robert, a pall of sadness has fallen over her. It is three months since I have heard from her, and when she last wrote, it was to say that her heart was too heavy to write.

. . .

ALS; Lydia Maria Child Papers, Anti-Slavery Collection, Cornell University (microfiche 58/1556).

Eliza Scudder (1821–96) was an antislavery advocate from Boston and the author of hymns.

To Eliza Scudder

Wayland, Friday, April 22d '64

Dearest Eliza,

. . .

The state of the country has never weighed so heavily upon *me*, as it does this Spring.[1] I get more and more sensitive about the cruelties and the sufferings; and the mean conduct of the government toward the negroes fills me with shame. I think we shall ultimately be saved as a nation; but I have painful doubts whether we are *worth* saving. Then this long, long "waiting for something to

---

[1] After the Battle of Chattanooga in late Nov. 1863, there had been a stalemate for several months.

turn up" is so tedious, and so trying! It seems as if I *could* not hold out much longer, unless we soon obtain some great, *decisive* victories.

But on the other hand, there is much to encourage us. Grant, who seems to be what we have so long wished for and waited for,—a real military genius,— is at the head of military affairs; and if he dont break *something somewhere*, I am much mistaken in my estimate of him. He reminds me very much of Garibaldi, in many ways; in his courage, promptness, energy, and presence of mind; in the brevity and good sense of his letters; in the simplicity of his manners, his aversion to being lionized; &c.

Another encouraging thing is the marvellous and constantly increasing change in public opinion on the subject of Slavery. Only think of George Thomson's speaking in the Halls of Congress,[2] and of John Brown's Hallelujah being performed there!   Capt. Wade, of the U.S. Navy, who bought a house for his wife in this town, has been a bitter pro-slavery man, violent and vulgar in his talk against abolitionists and "niggers." Two years ago, he was for having us mobbed because we advocated emancipating and arming the slaves. He has been serving in the vicinity of N. Orleans, and has come home on a furlough, an out-spoken abolitionist. He not only says it in private; but has delivered three lectures in town, in which he has publicly announced the total change in his sentiments since he has had "an opportunity to *know* something on the subject." A few days ago, he was going in the cars from Boston to Roxbury, when a colored soldier entered the car. Attempting to seat himself, he was repulsed by a white man, who rudely exclaimed, "I'm not going to ride with niggers." Capt. Wade, who sat a few seats further forward, rose up, in all the gilded glory of his naval uniform, and called out, "Come here, my good fellow! I've been fighting along side of people of your color, and glad enough I was to *have* 'em by my side. Come and sit by *me*."

Two years ago, I would not have believed such a thing possible of him. So the work goes on, in all directions. There are two sides to the shield; one dark as midnight, the other bright with the Rising Sun. God is great; and He has taken this matter in hand. So keep up a good heart.

Always Yours with true affection, L. Maria Child.

. . .

ALS; Lydia Maria Child Papers, Anti-Slavery Collection, Cornell University (microfiche 58/1561).

[2] George Thompson, the English abolitionist, was at this time in the United States making speeches to large audiences in many cities. The climax was a lecture he gave in the House of Representatives, which Lincoln and many notables attended.

To Gerrit Smith

My Honored Friend,

I herewith return to you, with my thanks, the order for thirty dollars, which you were so kind as to send me.   I find, upon inquiry, that it will be necessary to postpone my Freedman's Book indefinitely.[1] At the present prices of things, I cannot print two thousand copies, in the cheapest manner, consistent with durability, under an expense of $1000; and if stereotyped, it will cost $150 more. I shall prepare the copy at my leisure, and wait for a more favorable time to publish it. It is extremely uncertain how long that may be, and I have no right to detain your money, which you use so generously for all good purposes.

I thank you for your volume on Rational Religion.[2] It is calculated to do much good, as all your efforts are. I do not agree with all you say; on the indissolubility of marriage, for instance. I see so *much* matrimonial unhappiness all round me, and I know so many families of children morally and intellectually blighted, by growing in a household where the domestic atmosphere is made dark and cold, by the aversion of the parents for each other, that I cannot but think it would be well for *all* parties to have the right to separate without loss of reputation. It is a difficult question, however, and a dangerous one to meddle with. How far *individuals*, especially in great numbers, ought to be sacrificed for the safety of *society* is a knotty problem. Your recipe for marriage is undoubtedly the best one; that the parties should be involuntarily and desperately in love, to begin with. But it is comparatively a rare thing for people to fall in love. *I* doubt whether more than one in a thousand experiences that enchantment; certainly there are not more than one in a hundred. A powerful natural instinct, accidental propinquity, and selfish advantages of one kind or another, produce the greater part of marriages. They are formed in the early, unreflecting, and inexperienced period of life, and once formed they are irremediable. Viewing society as it is, it sometimes seems to me almost as frightful as the immolation of human victims in Dahomy.

In your letter to Mrs. Stanton, you say that either Lincoln or Fremont would make a good President. I doubt that proposition. Lincoln is a man of slow mind, apparently incapable of large, comprehensive views. It is his nature to potter about details; in the doing of which he wastes valuable time and golden opportunities. But he is an honest man, and conscientiously hates Slavery.

Fremont, I am afraid, is a selfish unprincipled adventurer. That pretended *scientific* Exploration of Oregon was a humbug. It was sent by the Slave Power to do mischief in Mexico. They scarcely touched on the borders of Oregon.

---

[1] It was put off until 1865.

[2] Smith had been publishing his *Discourses on the Religion of Reason* periodically since 1859.

All their time was spent in California, which the slaveholders were anxious to grab. Instead of scientific men, the party was composed of Missouri Ruffians and low Southern whites, who had been sent into that region on *purpose* to excite war. By their own showing, this party, headed by Fremont, shot down Indians, wherever they saw them, without waiting for a *pretext* of provocation. Finally they got to fighting with the Mexicans, by whom they had been treated with confidence and hospitality. It was all so obviously in the service of the Slave Power, that we always felt misgivings about Fremont's being nominated for President; Mr. Child voted for him, however, because the choice was between him and Buchanen. When he made the Proclamation of Freedom, I, for the first time, began to have some enthusiasm for him. But since he was removed from the command in Missouri, his course seems to me every way petty, selfish, and ignoble. I have no confidence in him.

I had no thoughts of writing so long a letter; but it wrote itself.   Yours with affectionate respect,

L. Maria Child.

ALS; Gerrit Smith Collection, George Arents Research Library, Syracuse University (microfiche 59/1574).

To Sarah Shaw

Wayland, Nov. 3d, 1864.

Precious Friend,

. . .

When I was in Boston, a fortnight ago, I went to the room of Edmonia Lewis to see the bust of Robert.[1] I was agreeably surprised. It really seems to me very good, without "making allowance for circumstances." I felt sorry when she wrote to me of her intention, for I feared she would not do it well; and for *your* sake, as well as *her own*, I felt very unwilling to have her make a failure. I gave her no encouragement to undertake it, and I fear she thought me somewhat cool. But, whether the little lady has *genius*, or not, she certainly is largely endowed with *one* element of success; for her *perseverance* is unconquerable. What she *undertakes* to do that she *will* do, though she has to cut through the heart of mountains with a penknife. She evidently put her whole soul into this bust. She told me she thought and thought of Col Shaw till it seemed as if he were in the room. "If I were a Spiritualist," said she, "I should believe he *did* help me make this bust; for while I was moulding it, I had such a strong feeling that he was *near*."

[1] The black sculptor Edmonia Lewis (1845–after 1909) modelled Robert Gould Shaw's bust from photographs. The sale of a hundred copies provided the funds for her to go to Rome to work in 1865. The bust, lost until recently, is now in the Boston Athenaeum.

The same day, I went to spend a little money at the Fair for Colored Soldiers. There I saw a full length likeness of Robert, painted by Bannister, a colored artist.[2] Over it was the touching and appropriate motto, *"Our Martyr."* My eyes moistened as I looked upon it. To me there is something very beautiful and pathetic in these efforts of a humble and oppressed people to canonize the memory of the young hero who died for them.

I saw your sister Mrs. Greene there, and I was surprised to find her in favor of Mc Lellan. That comes from the influence of her perverse husband, fed on the Boston Post while he was growing.[3] Such aliment is enough to make anything gnarled and crooked.   I long to have Tuesday come and go. I almost hold my breath with anxiety. The indications are certainly strong that Lincoln will be re-elected; but there is so much management and fraud, that one can never tell what will happen at the last moment. Still my faith remains that God is guiding us to universal freedom. How my heart exults over Maryland! I wish I could be there to see the banners wave, and hear the bells ring for the birth of a Free State.

I cannot and will not believe that your two sons have been martyred for anything less than the salvation of the whole country.[4] Did you hear what Mr. Bates replied, when your brother Russell said he never approved of Robert's taking command of that regiment?[5] "That young hero will be remembered long after you and I are forgotten," rejoined Mr. Bates.

Good night, darling! With hearty love to Frank, Your affectionate old Mariquita.

. . .

ALS; Houghton Library, Harvard University (microfiche 60/1585).

John Fraser (or Frazier) was married to Ruth Child, a daughter of David's brother Levi; they had moved to Australia.

[2] Edward M. Bannister (1828–1901) was a painter who lived in Boston from 1858 to 1871 and thereafter in Providence, R.I.

[3] Anna (Shaw) Greene (b. 1817), Francis Shaw's sister, was married to William Batchelder Greene, a minister in Brookfield, Mass., and a Civil War general.

[4] Besides the Shaws' only son, Robert, their son-in-law, Charles Russell Lowell, died 20 Oct. 1864 from war wounds; he had married Josephine Shaw (1843–1905) the previous year.

[5] Mr. Bates may be the Boston financier and philanthropist Joshua Bates (1788–1864), who was married to Lucretia Augusta Sturgis. Russell Sturgis, Sarah's brother, also had a son who served in the Civil War.

To John Fraser

Dear Mr. Fraser,

We were much gratified to hear that you and Ruth had arrived safely, and that the voyage and change of climate appeared to affect Ruth's health favorably. I hope she practises drawing in long breaths, with the mouth shut, and when the lungs have been distended a while letting it pass out slowly, with the mouth still shut. I believe the daily practice of this to be very strengthening to weak lungs.

We are still in the midst of civil war, and prices have gone up enormously within the last year. Butter has been 58 cts a pound all summer, potatoes 12 dollars a barrel, cotton shirting 75 cts a yard, and other things in proportion.

The U.S. have had many brilliant successes, and the Rebels are more hardly pushed than they ever were. Gen. Sherman took Atlanta in Georgia, which was considered even more important than Richmond, on account of its being the focus of their railroad supplies. The latest news is that he has burned Atlanta, where he has been for some time garrisoned, because he is marching to Charleston S.C. to attack it by land. Gen. Sheridan has had a succession of marvellous victories in the Shenandoah Valley. Gen Grant has been slowly, but steadily pushing on toward Richmond, taking fortification after fortification. His immense army is now within a few miles of it. He appears to prefer cutting off their supplies and hemming them in closer, rather than to make an onset, which would involve a much greater sacrifice of life. All his plans have been successful, and competent judges think the desired result is near.

The Rebel army suffers greatly by desertion. The "poor whites" have in many places resisted the power of the Confederate government. They have taken to the mountains in formidable numbers, refuse to fight, receive and arm all runaway slaves that go to them, and intrench themselves so strongly, that the Rebel officers think best to let them alone. Still Jeff Davis and other leaders talk and act as if they felt as strong as ever. They are now about to arm 300,000 slaves, with the promise of freedom and fifty acres of land a piece, if they fight well for the Confederacy. This shows their desperation, for it is certainly a great risk for them to run. If these armed slaves are faithful to the cause of their masters, it must protract the war, which otherwise would seem to be drawing to a close. But how wonderfully Divine Providence is helping on the poor negroes, *every* way. If the slave holders resort to the desperate experiment of arming so many able-bodied slaves, they certainly will be obliged to give up the wicked institution for which they begun the war. Really, the whole course of events has been the most marvellous manifestation of Providence compelling men to do His work, against their own wills.

Another sign of desperation in the Rebels is that they have emissaries in Canada, and in all the Northern cities, especially on the frontier, plotting with the Copperheads to burn cities, rob banks, murder leading men of the Republican

Party, &c. St Albans in Vermont was attacked by a company of these raiders, the banks robbed, and several citizens killed. The Canadian authorities seem to be acting very justly and vigorously, and several of the raiders have been arrested and brought to trial. There was a plan to rob and burn Chicago, but secret information was given to the magistrate in time to prevent it. Great quantities of arms were found in the possession of certain Copperhead leaders. Buffalo is watched by an armed force, in consequence of discovered plans for the destruction of that city.[1]

Very extensive and formidable secret societies have been discovered, for the overthrow of the government, and the establishment of a North Western Confederacy, to act in league with the Southern Confederacy. Some of the arrested traitors have turned State's evidence, and their confessions are truly startling. Extensive plans of conflagration, robbery, and murder, were so cautiously arranged, that it is marvellous how the Northern cities have escaped from them.

But through all this wickedness, confusion, alarm, and suffering, the good work goes steadily on. Maryland has voted to adopt a new constitution which excludes slavery forever; and they do it without claiming compensation! The contest was a hard one, but the vote of the *soldiers* turned the scale in favor of freedom. Maryland is a Free State! She wheeled into the circle of Free States with ringing of bells and waving of banners. Glory to God! Tennessee seems to be following closely in the footsteps of Maryland. Andy Johnson has been delivering spirit-stirring addresses to the colored people of Nashville, in which he told them, "They who would be *free, themselves* must strike the blow"; and they responded "Amen!" He said, "I trust the Lord will raise up a Moses for your leader;" and they cried out "*You* are our Moses." "I *will* be your Moses," said he, ["]until the Lord sends you a better one."[2] The colored people passed through the streets of Nashville in procession, to be addressed by him, and people watching them from the windows of the houses they passed, waved hats and handkerchiefs, and saluted them with hurras. *This* in Nashville, where thirty years ago Amos Dresser was publicly flogged for having a small abolition tract in his carpet-bag! Verily, "it is the Lord's doings, and it is marvellous in our eyes."

Day before yesterday was the great day of the Presidential Election. The only candidates were Lincoln and Gen. McLellan. There was an attempt made

---

[1] The Copperhead movement had grown rapidly in the summer of 1864, with the Union armies stalemated and casualties mounting. The Frémont candidacy was suspected of links with Copperheads, who worked to split the Republicans so as to elect McClellan. Mob actions disrupting the North were thought to be inspired by Copperheads.

[2] These and other actions of Andrew Johnson (1808–75) made some abolitionists believe that he was bitterly hostile to the slaveholders and would side with the Radical Republicans. Johnson, a Union Democrat from Tennessee and Lincoln's running mate, was the only Southern senator to support the Union in the war. His origins and his ties to the poor whites of the South commended him to Child.

to get up a Fremont Party, but it proved a fizzle. His conduct since he left Missouri had inspired the people with distrust, and his name had lost its power. Copperheadism put forth its utmost strength, and resorted to all manner of frauds to elect McLellan. But, luckily, the Rebels could not conceal their joy at his nomination. Their papers exulted over it, and their armies hurraed for McClellan. This opened the eyes of *our* troops, and made some Democrats at home ashamed of their candidate. The result is that honest old Abe is re-elected President, and Andy Johnson, the Moses of the colored people is Vice President.[3] Glory to God! I breathe freely now that this great danger is passed. If McLellan had been elected, the slave holders would have had it all their own way.

I think I have told you a great batch of public news. Deprived of newspapers, as you are, I thought you would be glad of this small private Gazette.

. . .

Hoping to welcome you here again one of these days, I am yours with true respect & affection, L. M. Child.

David has been very much hurried with work this summer; having to repair damages by the fire in addition to his usual labors. He is unusually well, and very hopeful about the country. He sends you both much love.

. . .

L, transcript; Simison Papers, Beinecke Rare Book and Manuscript Library, Yale University (microfiche 60/1590).

To Samuel J. May

Wayland, Jan. 5'th, 1865.

Dear Friend May,

. . . I cordially reciprocate your wish that we were not so far apart. It would be an inexpressible satisfaction to me to have you within walking distance. I am glad you have had such a host of goodly women among your friends. I judge it is because you have a peculiar affinity with goodly women. I also owe much to the elevating influence of several women; among whom Miss Osgood of Medford is pre-eminent. But *my* best friendships have generally been with men. No woman has ever been to me what Ellis Gray Loring was. I should hardly venture to call Charles Sumner a personal friend, but the influence of his character has been very powerful in helping me to walk in a straight line on great moral questions; and so has the influence of W. L. Garrison, with whom my personal acquaintance has, however, been far from intimate. Affection has

---

[3] Lincoln was reelected on 8 Nov. by 212–21 electoral votes but with a small popular majority.

mingled largely with my respect for yourself. You have always been a moral sunshine to me; and I thank my God for every remembrance of you.

. . .

ALS; General MSS, Princeton University (microfiche 61/1611).

To Lydia B. Child

Wayland, Feb. 11'th 1865.

Dear Lydia,

. . .

I have been in luck this year. My book sold with wonderful rapidity.[1] The whole edition of 4000 were gone before New Year's Day, and they might have sold 2000 more if they had been in readiness. I had vowed the proceeds of the book to the Freedmen, whether more or less. I received $450 on New Year's Day, and immediately sent every dollar to the poor suffering creatures, in different departments. *That* is something worth living for; to comfort thousands of old people with the book, and pay over the proceeds to those whom the nation has so long wronged. It made me very happy, and I am humbly thankful to God, who had given me the power to do it. As soon as the poor creatures can have a little land to cultivate, or can get regular employment, they will take care of themselves; but *now* there is imperious need of help. Nor will it do to diminish our care for the wounded soldiers. I remembered them, too, on New Year's Day. . . .

. . .

ALS; Child Papers, MC 305, Schlesinger Library, Radcliffe College (microfiche 61/1633).

Lee surrendered to Grant on 9 April 1865.

To Lucy Osgood

Wayland, April 13'th, 1865.

My Dear Friend,

. . .

I am rejoicing over the good news, which promises cessation of slaughter; but I rejoice with trembling. I am *so* afraid that, in our zeal to get the rebel states back into the Union, we shall reconstruct on a basis that will make future

---

[1] The success of *Looking toward Sunset* was greater than anticipated. Child donated all its income to aid for the freedmen.

---

trouble. The lands of the leading rebels ought to be confiscated. I do not desire this from any feelings of revenge, but because it is unsafe to trust these haughty oligarchs with a monopoly of land. If they have any power left, they will certainly use it to keep down the poor whites and the emancipated blacks. The large plantations ought to be confiscated by the U.S. government, divided into small farms, a certain number of acres given to the soldiers, white and black, and the remainder sold on easy terms to the poor whites and the emancipated slaves.[1] I am much afraid that Lincoln's good-nature may mislead him in this matter.

I do not feel blood-thirsty toward *any* of the rebels. I even hope that Jeff Davis will succeed in slipping away to some place of safety. But I do not feel any especial tenderness for Lee; and I have three reasons for it. In the first place, he wrote to his sister that he thought the rebellion was wrong; that there was no cause of complaint against the U.S. government; but that, as Virginia thought otherwise, he should stand by his State. I think a man could not have a very enlightened conscience, who made such a decision. In the second place, he kept up a show of intimate friendship with Gen. Scott almost up to the day when he joined the rebel army, and consequently carried with him a detailed knowledge of all our plans and resources. In the third place, his wife's father, Mr. Custis, emancipated all his slaves by will; to take effect five years after his decease. Gen. Lee kept as many as he wanted to carry on business at Arlington House & the White House, and the remainder he sold to the far South. None of them obtained their freedom till they secured it by this war. It is stated, I know not how truly, that the slaves who have left him represent him as a very hard, severe master.[2]

However, I wish him nothing worse than to get a good living by his own honest industry. If Forrest, of Fort Pillow memory, should be sentenced to be hung, it would, I confess, require some effort on my part to sign a petition for commutation of punishment.[3] Yet the poor wretch was morally blasted by that malignant institution which we all helped to uphold. The fact that we were so long accomplices in the guilt ought to modify the harshness of our judgment. If we can only preserve a just *medium*, I shall be thankful. If we can use success with magnanimity, and at the same time be strict and uncompromising in all that regards the future welfare of the country, the war will prove a prodigious blessing! . . .

---

[1] A Freedmen's Bureau with many liberal features was established on 3 Mar. One section called for assigning not more than forty acres of abandoned or confiscated land to freedmen at rental for three years with option to buy. The act was too vaguely defined to suit the abolitionists, but they hoped that new bills would guarantee the freedmen land in the reconstructed South.

[2] Child's marshalling of the facts about Lee gave no ground to the mythmakers who would soon begin canonizing the general.

[3] After the surrender of Fort Pillow on 12 Apr. 1864, scores of Union soldiers, particularly blacks, had been slaughtered by Gen. Nathan Bedford Forrest's men.

I am surprised that you like your tintype better than Mrs. Sewall's photographs.[4] I felt greatly indebted to her for making my plain old phiz present such a good appearance to posterity. The one reading is positively handsome & lady-like. That is not much in favor of the *likeness* you will say.

. . .

ALS; Lydia Maria Child Papers, Anti-Slavery Collection, Cornell University (microfiche 62/1653).

Lincoln was shot on the evening of 14 April and died the next morning; Andrew Johnson took the oath of office.

To Sarah Shaw

[After 15 April] 1865

Darling Sarah,

Your kind letter was joyously received last evening. I was not very exultant over Lee's surrender. I did not like the *terms* that Gen. Grant made with him. I am weary of seeing the U.S. bow before those arrogant rebels. To be so very careful not to offend them, only makes them *more* arrogant. The tone assumed by Lee is more befitting a conqueror in a righteous cause, than a defeated traitor. Already he begins to threaten that the South will make *another* war, if any severe measures are taken with those who needlessly and recklessly caused all this bloodshed. They think such bravado will intimidate the North; and I am afraid it *will* have that effect. It seems as if we could never unlearn our old habit of standing cap in hand before those aristocratic slaveholders. As for those delegates of the Christian Commission, they disgraced themselves, and their country. The assassination of our good President, shocked and distressed me. Yet I have been so deeply impressed by the wonderful guidance of Providence during this war, that five minutes after I heard the sad news, I said, "Dreadful as this is perhaps it is only another of the wonderful manifestations of Providence. The kind-hearted Abraham, was certainly in danger of making too easy terms with the rebels. Perhaps he has been removed, that he might not defeat his own work, and that another, better calculated to carry it to a safe and *sure end*, might come into his place." I have all along said, that nothing could happen which would shake my faith, that God was not going to *destroy* this nation, but only to mould it *anew* for the performance of a great work in the world. The murder of the President did not shake that faith for an instant; and I thought *nothing* could shake it. But I found that I was like the woman who

---

[4] Early in 1865, at the insistence of her friend Harriet Sewall, Child sat in three poses for John Whipple, the Boston photographer.

"trusted in Providence till the breeching broke," when the horse was running away. The news of Sherman's negotiations with Johnson filled me with dismay, and indignation.[1] It looks like downright treachery to the U.S. I suppose they will "hugger-mugger" it up; but it will take a *good deal* to convince *me*, that it was not something worse than an error of judgement. I think nothing since the war commenced has excited me so much. It made me use language quite too muscular for polite circles. When Frederika Bremer was reminded that certain strong words were not deemed proper by well-bred people, she replied, "When I am very much incensed I *must swear*."   Our new President in some respects resembles Andrew Jackson. He has impressed me quite favorably. He *seems* to have honesty, and sincerity. His being Southern born is a favorable circumstance, and the fact that he belonged to the class of "poor whites" will, I think, have quite an important influence in bringing over that class. Andrew Johnson could not have been *elected* President, but Providence has placed that responsible trust in his hands, and perhaps he will better finish the work, his upright, and careful predecessor began, and carried forward so well. Yet[2]

L; Lydia Maria Child Papers, Anti-Slavery Collection, Cornell University (microfiche 62/1657).

[1] Lee had surrendered his army on 9 Apr., but other Confederate armies were still in the field. Child may refer to the Confederate General Albert S. Johnston's surrender to William T. Sherman on 18 Apr.; in return Sherman granted liberal, unauthorized political concessions. Resistance did not end until 26 May.
[2] The rest of the letter is missing.

9

July 1865-1874

With the surrender of the last Confederate army, American slavery came to an end. By the close of 1865 the Thirteenth Amendment, abolishing slavery, became part of the Constitution. The problem of Reconstruction gripped the mind of every politician and reformer. How would the freed slaves live and where would they work? How would their ex-masters take the enormous change forced on them by their defeat? Would the South adopt the North's politics and principles or would it hold fast to its own and try to nourish old roots back to life? Child's letters during the next decade trace the development of her ideas about Reconstruction and reveal her responses to the shifts and turns of a tumultuous time.

Before the Civil War ended Child had begun collecting and editing material for two volumes. *The Freedmen's Book* (Boston, 1865), an anthology of short poems, biographical sketches, and essays, dealt with aspects of black life. Her plan was to distribute it among the ex-slaves, in the hope that they would "derive fresh strength and courage from this true record of what colored men have accomplished, under great disadvantages" (p. [iii]). Many of the fifty-five pieces were by blacks; sixteen of them were her own.

With a sensitivity to the interests and needs of the elderly, Child compiled another anthology, *Looking Toward Sunset* (Boston, 1865). This time, nine of the seventy-five selections were by her; the others ranged from Burns and Wordsworth to Tennyson, Whittier, Stowe, and Dickens. A large book of 450 pages, it ran through several editions. In these years Child also published her fourth and final novel, *A Romance of the Republic* (Boston, 1867), a story of slavery days whose plot and characters were designed to show the reader how slavery had influenced national life in all its aspects. She was disappointed in the response of the public, which was indifferent perhaps because of the book's own weaknesses, and because slavery had died too recently for summoning it up again in fiction. Her last publication of the period was *An Appeal for the Indians* (Boston, 1868), an attempt to rouse the nation's conscience to the gross wrongs done another racial minority.

To William Lloyd Garrison

Wayland, July 7'th, 1865.

Friend Garrison,

I want some help, which perhaps you can render me. I know you will, if you can. I am writing an account of William & Ellen Crafts, and I cannot obtain all the information I wish.[1] I applied to Mr. Nell, some time ago, but he could only procure newspaper scraps about what occurred while they were in Boston.[2] I have also Theodore Parker's Life, wherein they are mentioned; and Conway's Letters to the Commonwealth.[3] But what I want most, and cannot get, is something about them before they came North. Did they belong to the same master? How old were they? When did they first begin to think about freedom, and *how* was it? Did William then know a trade, and what trade was it? Were their masters kind or severe? *Had* William a *young* master, for whom Ellen passed herself off? &c. &c. *When* did they arrive in Boston?

Was there any pamphlet about them published at the time? Or was there a full account in the Liberator? If there was, I wish you would take it off file, if you can without injury, and send it to me. I will send it back carefully very soon. If you cannot get it off file, I will come to the office and consult it, if the account is a copious one.

Perhaps Mr. Louis Hayden can give some information, or tell where it can be obtained.[4]

I am writing it for the Freedmen's Book which is nearly completed. I am writing over nearly every prose article I extract, so as to give them as *much* as possible in the *smallest space*, and to give it in a very clear and simple form.

I am a great lover of mental order, and in this case it is peculiarly necessary for the class of readers I address. I am taking more pains with it than I should if it were intended for young princes, or sprigs of what men call nobility. In the first place, my theory is that whatever is done *at all* ought to be *well* done; and in the next place, I have a more and more tender feeling toward what are called "the lower classes." If I live to be ninety years old, and go on at this rate, I shall be the rabidest radical that ever pelted a throne, or upset an image.

How refreshing it is to live in days, when Senators and Governors, and

---

[1] William Craft (ca. 1826–1900) and his wife Ellen (1828–ca. 1897) fled slavery in Georgia in 1848, disguised as a white mistress and slave manservant. After the passage of the Fugitive Slave Law in 1850, they left Boston for England and did not return to the United States until 1868. Both died in Charleston, S.C. Their story is told by Child in *The Freedmen's Book*.
[2] William C. Nell (1816–74) was a black historian and abolitionist who lived in Boston.
[3] Theodore Parker performed a second marriage ceremony for the Crafts after they arrived in Boston. Moncure D. Conway sent Child a report on the Crafts' activities in England.
[4] Lewis Hayden (1816–89), an escaped slave, sheltered the Crafts when they reached Boston.

Presidential Candidates address colored men as "Gentlemen"! Thank God we live to see it! I want to live a while to see the glorious work go on. Don't you? Perhaps, however, we should see it better from yonder; and perhaps be enabled to *help* better, too.

Remember me with true affection to Mrs. Garrison, and the younger members of your household, and believe me always very truly and cordially your friend

L. Maria Child.

P.S. Mr. Child is very well, and would send greetings if he knew of my writing.

Please reply as soon as you can conveniently. I have written this nearly in the dark; so please excuse the scrawling.

ALS; Anti-Slavery Collection, Rare Books and Manuscripts, Boston Public Library (microfiche 63/1670).

To Sarah Shaw

Wayland, Aug. 11'th 1865

. . . I have been exceedingly occupied this summer making "The Freedman's Book." It is intended to encourage, stimulate, and instruct them, and I hope it will perform its mission. I have taken pains to re-write all the biographies of colored people, that I made use of; in order to have everything very simple, clear, and condensed for them. I shall not take a cent of the proceeds myself, and shall furnish it to them at the cost of paper and printing, which will be immediately used as a fund to print more, if the freedmen manifest a disposition to have the book.

Perhaps you will be pleased to hear that I made $1000 by my Sunset Book. I have paid $750 of it over to the Freedmen, in different sections, for books, clothes, tools, &c; and the remaining $250 will be used for their benefit as soon as I have settled in my mind what is the best way to use it. I vowed the proceeds to the Freedmen, and the popularity of the book has been a prodigious satisfaction to me, on that account.

The poor freedmen! I feel so anxious about them! I don't know what to make of Andy Johnson's course; and yet my confidence in him is too strong to be easily shaken.[1] The slaveholders manifest the same diabolical disposition that they did in Jamaica; and it is very plain that the strong arm of the U.S. government will be required to make them behave themselves.   If I had been told, thirty years ago, that Slavery would be abolished in my day, I should have

---

[1] President Johnson had been issuing Reconstruction proclamations for the Southern states, permitting them to return to the Union on the basis of white suffrage. The abolitionists feared that, if blacks were excluded from the franchise, they would be doomed to serfdom.

anticipated such enthusiastic joy as would set me half crazy. But in reality I have felt no enthusiasm, no exhileration. I have been thankful to God for the wondrous change; but, what with the frightful expenditure of blood; and emancipation's being forced upon us by *necessity*, instead of proceeding from the repentance of the nation; and the shameful want of protection to the freed-men since they have been emancipated;[2] there has been no opportunity for any out-gushing of joy and exultation.

Are we not the best *taxed* people in the world at this time? My brother's death added $200 to my annual income, otherwise, I should not have have been able to "make the ends meet." This year, on an income of $720, I pay $152 dollars tax; and $50 more to the U.S. for income from the Sunset Book. But I do not grudge anything to resuscitate the country.   The other day, I read in the commercial papers, "Cotton is easy." I thought to myself I was glad it was easy at last; for it has made uneasiness enough for the last thirty five years. What a lesson God is teaching the world by our example! When I get thinking about our future, I am bewildered, lost in the immensity of the view. Those great States west of the Missisippi, growing up like mushrooms, large enough to make "fourteen holy Roman empires"! settled by Germans, and French, and Swiss, and Mormons, &c—with the freedmen flocking into them, on account of the scarcity of labor—What will it all result in? I don't try to foresee. It is alto-gether too vast for me. I don't even know the *geography* of my own country, now-a days.

. . .

ALS; Houghton Library, Harvard University (microfiche 63/1676).

To James T. Fields

Wayland, Aug. 27'th, 1865

Dear Mr. Fields,

Many, many thanks for the kind interest you take in the project I have so much at heart.[1] I herewith send you the M.S. about half of which is paged for the press; the other half I have left unpaged for the present, as alterations in the arrangement may become desirable. In printing it, my idea is to get as much into every page as is consistent with sizable type; no spaces left at top or bottom. Where spaces occur, I shall fill them up with short extracts, as in the Sunset Book. I want economy rather than beauty consulted in the whole getting up; but I want the materials to be *strong*. The utmost limit I allow my-self is 312 pages. If my M.S. overruns that, I must take something out, but ac-cording to my estimate, it will not overrun.   The reason my name appears

---

[2] Reports of whippings, shootings, and lynchings of the ex-slaves had begun appearing in Northern papers.
[1] *The Freedmen's Book.*

so often in the Index is that I re-wrote all the Biographies. They are not only interspersed with remarks of my own, but are so completely and entirely told in my own way, that I cannot, with any propriety ascribe them to any one else. This I shall explain in the Preface. My object in doing this was to *condense* as much into small space as possible, and to give the *most interesting* facts only, and those in very *clear* and *simple* language.

You will find William and Ellen Crafts the most interesting. I collected it from various sources; some of it verbal information. James Madison Washington is also very romantic, and every word of it true.[2]

The book has a continuous plan. It begins with Ignatius Sancho, because he was the *first* intelligent black of whom we have a record.[3] It passes along through the groans and aspirations of slaves, the prayers and prophecies of their friends, till Toussaint L'Ouverture makes an *opening* for them. Then Emancipation in the West Indies. Then fugitive slaves hunted in the U.S. Then Emancipation in District of Columbia. Then Lincoln's Proclamation. Then jollification and jubilee.

I have written four short pieces of Advice. One about Animals, one about Children, one about Health, and one concerning things in general.

At the present prices of things, I calculate that it would cost $1,200 to print & stereotype an edition of 2,000. I have laid up $600 to use in the publication, and I suppose I could contrive some way to get $600 more. But I have a very strong aversion to asking for money, and it would moreover be very difficult for me to make judicious contracts with printers, binders, &c. My idea now is, if I can get it published, to buy $600 dollars worth, and get them into the hands of the Freedman, through the agency of teachers. If they sell, I shall expend the money in buying *more* copies; and so on; keeping the $600 as a kind of floating capital, as long as the book continues to sell; and then use it in some other way for the Freedmen.

I enclose you a note from Mrs. Cheney, of the Freedmen's Aid Association.[4] I do not agree with her in thinking "the book will have a rapid sale at the North." But I do think it would have an important bearing on the Suffrage Question, if issued *soon*.[5] I wrote it *solely* for the Freedmen, and aimed continually to bring myself down near to their state of cultivation. But, *just at this time*, the negro is invested with paramount interest, and I think that we might with certainty calculate upon the sale of more than 500 copies among the white people.

I thought you had better look at the copy, and talk with me afterward, if,

[2] Washington was a Virginia slave who led a successful revolt aboard the *Creole* in 1841. The slaves sailed to freedom in the British West Indies.
[3] Sancho, an African born aboard a slave ship in 1729, was freed in England. His writings made him widely known.
[4] Ednah D. Cheney (1824–1904) was a Boston writer and reformer.
[5] Child and many abolitionists favored male and female suffrage for both black and white, unrestricted except for age and residence requirements.

upon reflection, you were disposed to do so. I will come whenever you appoint a time, unless prevented by some unforeseen emergency.

Don't let my M.S. get lost or burned, for I have been two years preparing it.

Yours gratefully & cordially,
L. Maria Child.

ALS; Alma Lutz Collection, Schlesinger Library, Radcliffe College (microfiche 63/1679).

To Theodore Tilton

Wayland, May 27'th, 1866

Friend Tilton,

I should n't wonder if you had begun to think I was huffy with you anent that rocket of a letter which you sent up from Washington. Such, however, was not the fact. It amused me, and the spirit moved me to send up an answering rocket. But there was a tornado in our house, of Spring cleaning, accompanied with a general painting, varnishing, and papering; a large proportion of which I did with my own hands. I am not so young as I once was. I over-exerted myself, and had to take to my bed. Company came in the midst, and one of my dearest old friends became ill, nigh unto death. Among all these confusing claims, the witticisms I had in store for you got extinguished, and I now poke the ashes in vain to find a few sparks. ⟨in vain.⟩ Suffice it, therefore, to say, that some associations of childhood make the name of Lydia unpleasant to me. I added the name of Maria when I was baptized at twenty years of age.[1] I was then "in search of a religion," and wanted to try "the ordinances" to ascertain whether they would help my spiritual growth. They did *not*. They never seemed *alive*. I believe the name of Maria was all the benefit I derived from baptism. If you call me "Hebrew-hater" on account of my aversion to the name of Lydia, you mistake. The name is Grecian, and so far would commend itself to my heathenish propensities. I am, moreover, no Hebrew hater in *any* sense of the term. I greatly admire the legislation of Moses, in most of its prominent features, and have great veneration for the sublime utterances of the grand old prophets. Men who speak from the depths of their own consciousness speak for *all* time.

If you dislike my "one armed" name, cut off *both* arms, and print it L. M. Child. Margaret Fuller had the same dislike to her first name, Sarah, and often signed S. M. Fuller.[2]

With regard to the article from "Every Saturday," it seems to me to have

[1] This would place her adoption of *Maria* in 1822. However, despite her aversion to *Lydia*, she sometimes used it. In 1841–43, editing the *National Anti-Slavery Standard*, she printed her name below the masthead as *Lydia Maria Child*.
[2] Fuller thought *Sarah* an old-fashioned name. By the age of thirteen she had persuaded her family to call her *Margaret*.

a sub-stratum of truth with a tall superstructure of exaggeration. The *spirit* is offensive to me, because the whole article is pervaded with the idea that woman was made *for* man, whereas I believe that men and women were made for each other. I am not of those who maintain there is "no sex in souls." The material is always the form of something spiritual. I believe there *is* a sex in souls. I don't think there is inherent *superiority* on either side; I simply think there is a *difference*. That difference is indicated by their voices. Woman's floats higher, and is more pervasive, but less powerful. Her whole organization is finer, keener, less strong. That women, as a class, do think a great deal more about love than men in general do, is undoubtedly true; but I think the reason is to be sought not so much in their *natures*, as in the constant *education* they receive from the influences of their position in society. They have vanity and ambition, and so have men. Men can gratify theirs in a thousand ways. Every avenue of business, politics, art, and science is open to them. Until quite recently, *all* these have been closed to woman. The law regards marriage as her "promotion," and so does the general tone of society. Consequently, in addition to the natural instincts, (which, in a healthy state of things, would be merely incidental on either side) woman seeks in marriage a better position in society, and a respectable mode of securing a good living. Under these circumstances, how can the subject otherwise than occupy her thoughts above all others?   As for the friendships of women, it seems to me to amount to this. Frivolous people will form frivolous friendships; and there are *more* frivolous women than there are frivolous men, because society shuts them out from business, politics, art, and literature. Sensible people form sensible friendships, and when they meet naturally talk on sensible subjects. Four friendships with women have lasted through many years, up to this time.[3] When we have met we have always talked about the books we have read, the scientific discoveries we have heard of, and the state of public affairs; occasionally interlarded with some new stitch in knitting, or some new recipe for cooking. *My* female friends have been more stedfast than my gentlemen friends. Still, as a general rule I think the friendships of men with each other are more enduring than those of women with each other. The customs of society give men more solid and enduring subjects of interest in common. It is in vain to speculate about the *nature* of woman, so long as her nature is every way repressed by false customs, which men perpetuate for their own convenience, and then quarrel with the consequences.

Yrs Cordially,
L. M. Child.

    This letter is not for public.

ALS; James Fraser Gluck Collection, Buffalo and Erie County Public Library (microfiche 65/1722).

----

[3] The four friends were Louisa Loring, Sarah Shaw, Henrietta Sargent, and Lucy Osgood.

To Sarah Shaw

Wayland, June 17'th 1866

My Darling Sarah,

. . .

Mrs. Loring has been very ill. I supposed I was going to lose her; but homeopathy has done wonders for her, and if she has no relapse, from imprudence, I think she will doubtless recover. It took a load from my heart when I found the crisis had past. So few links remain in the chain of old friendships, that their value increases as they diminish. You never saw such a little darling as Anna's daughter; si petite, si jolie![1] A visible little fairy. I should get foolishly fond of her, if I saw her much; for my old heart will not unlearn its trick of loving. I feel latterly, more than I ever did, what a misfortune it is not to have had children. I should doat on grand-children.

I am glad Congress has put a stop to rebels being elected to office.[2] It is n't *all* I would have liked, but it will cramp the rebels in their mischievous designs; and, in process of time, I hope they will learn that their best *policy* is to grant suffrage to the blacks. If we can only keep out of a foreign war, we may steer safely through the breakers. Do you and Frank read the letters Gerritt Smith is always publishing?[3] It seems to me as if he really *had* a crack in his skull. In his last, he proposes that the South should pay no direct taxes, because she is poor, and has been laid waste by the North. Whose *fault* was that? The North was reluctant enough to go to war, but the South *would* have it. They have loaded *our* necks with a mill-stone of taxation, and Gerritt would have us pay them a premium for it. But "they are poor," says he, "and the North are rich." If they chose to impoverish themselves in mad attempts to destroy the Republic, shall we reward them for it? Shall we make it an object for them to try it again? Besides, they won't be taxed for the property they have n't got. Every hundred dollars I earn I have to pay five of it to the U.S.; and if ten dollars is due to me, the U.S. clutches at fifty cents of it; and all owing to the madness of those haughty, lazy slaveholders. *I* am to be taxed for everything I eat, and drink, and wear, and look at, and even for what I *do;* and they, forsooth, are to go scot-free because they have grabbed at other people's earnings and spent them all in efforts to destroy the country, and are too poor to begin the game again so soon as they would like. I am out of all patience with this spurious magnanimity.

. . .

ALS; Houghton Library, Harvard University (microfiche 65/1724).

[1] Anna Loring married Otto Dresel, a concert pianist, in 1863. They had a daughter, Louisa, and a son, Ellis.
[2] As part of the Fourteenth Amendment, Congress had voted to disqualify from political office certain classes of leading Confederates.
[3] Smith published letters urging moderation in treatment of the Confederates.

To Sarah Shaw

Wayland, Sep. 7'th, 1866.

Darling Sarah,

. . .

You ask me what I would have Congress do. In the first place, I think they ought to have done something to diminish the inflated currency of the country, which is having such an unsettling and demoralizing influence. In the next place, I was vexed and grieved, beyond measure, that they voted *themselves* such a large additional salary. They could n't have put a worse weapon into the hands of Johnson's party; besides, I hold it to be wrong in itself, and dangerous as a precedent, for men to vote how much they themselves shall take out of the public treasury. Thirdly, they ought to have *repealed* the power to grant amnesty, with which they endowed Abraham Lincoln.[1] *Lincoln* had a *good* motive for offering amnesty; for he wanted to use it as a means of *winning over* rebels. But when the war was ended, by their defeat, there was no longer any *good* use to be made of amnesty. Andy Johnson has made use of it, not to lure rebels back to loyalty, but to encourage traitors in persistent treason; and Congress have done nothing to stop his doing it. They ought to have confiscated the lands of rich rebels and opened the way for freedmen to procure portions of the land on easy terms.[2] Under Johnson policy, the old slave holding nabobs hold their thousands of acres, and will not let the freedmen have an acre. If the lands had been confiscated, and sold at low prices, it would also have done more than anything else to gain over the poor whites to the side of the U.S; and the sale would have helped considerably toward paying the national debt, while it would at the same time have done justice to two much wronged classes. However, I stand by Congress, because they have done a great deal that is good, and because there is nothing else to stand by.

Was there ever such a braying Ass as Johnson? I think that wily fox, Seward encourages him to bray, on purpose to disgust the people, and so give himself a chance to saddle and ride the new party. To think of a man like H. W. Beecher lending himself to the unprincipled schemes of that tippling traitor, that boozy boaster, that devilish demagogue![3] What *can* be his motive? I dont think he is "one of the *devils* unaccountables," but he is certainly one of the *Lord's* unaccountables.   I take it you mean to compare the extract from

[1] Both Lincoln and Johnson had offered full pardon to all but a few Confederates. Early in 1866 Congress adopted a Reconstruction program that took away Johnson's emergency powers and made Congress supreme in this matter.
[2] The abolitionists urged a land confiscation policy, but Congress, the president, and the army would all fail to develop a sound land policy for the blacks. By the end of 1867 the chance to put through land reform in the South had faded.
[3] Radical abolitionists by now were squarely opposed to Johnson's Reconstruction policies, but some moderate Republicans who feared risking a split in their party still tagged along with the president.

Parson Brownlow with "a song from Mother Goose" merely on account of its measured *iteration*.[4] In *that* respect it does remind one of "The House that Jack Built." But I think it is eloquent good sense, and entirely true. The Parson is too coarse for my taste, but he is the only Southern man whose utterance satisfies me.

You dear soul, how you keep harping upon our coming to Staten Island! What for do you want us to exhibit our old wrinkled phizzes, and out-of-the-world ways? I never did know very well how to behave, and I have forgotten what little I ever knew in that line. What makes the matter more hopeless is that I am too indifferent to society to take the slightest pains to conform to its regulations. Now you know you are all the time surrounded by properly behaved, stylish people; and from such people I generally have to hide, or fight. Here is good Mrs. Wyman, Dr. Hayward's sister, who has a country-seat in this town. She is the most amiable of aristocrats, and is persistently bent upon being attentive to me. I try not to be rude, but as sure as we come in contact for an hour ⟨we⟩ I explode. My last explosion was in reply to her vindication of Dr. Dewy.[5] She said his respect for the Constitution led him to say he should be willing to send his mother into slavery. Of course, the best I could do under the circumstances was not to say Damn the Constitution! If I should encounter his Highness, Howland Shaw, ten chances to one I should break one of his ribs; and if I didn't, I should afterward reproach myself for having failed in my duty.[6] Seriously, I have wonderfully little patience with people of aristocratic tendencies. They arouse in me a fierce antagonism, and if I am where I can't show it, I am made very miserable. They say people grow more conservative as they grow older; but I grow more radical. Andy Johnson's having been a tailor makes me feel a great deal worse about his disgracing himself. I rejoiced in the fact that a rail-splitter, awkward and uncouth in appearance, had in him such elements of greatness that the world could not *help* respecting him. I should have been proud to show European aristocrats that Republican institutions could make something more than "the ninth part of a man" out of a tailor. But as it is, every true lover of the country must want to creep into a knot-hole and hide himself, whenever the name of our President is mentioned. It is *so* vexatious, when there was such a fair opportunity to place the Republic on a secure and honorable foundation! I do not see how another civil war can be avoided; and if we do have one, those Fenians will come in as a terrible element. They *now* seem to be at enmity with Johnson; but their natural affinity is with the *Dim*mocratic Party, and thither they will inevitably be drawn, if it comes to an outbreak. I am for seeking a home in Switzerland, if the Democratic

[4] William G. Brownlow (1805–77), Tennessee Unionist, had published the best-seller *Parson Brownlow's Book* in 1862, denouncing the Confederate cause. In 1865 he was elected governor of Tennessee, and in 1869 he became U.S. senator.
[5] Dr. Orville Dewey, Unitarian minister of Boston, had supported the Fugitive Slave Law.
[6] Gardiner Howland Shaw was one of Frank Shaw's wealthy brothers.

Party and their allies again come into power. But David insists that he will stay and enlist; and I really fear he would, he has such prodigious veneration for old John Burns of Gettysburg.[7] It would be but a short time that poor David could stand the exposure and fatigue of camp life. He has been ill a great deal this summer. Almost every week he has to take to his bed more or less.

. . .

ALS; Houghton Library, Harvard University (microfiche 65/1738).

To Sarah Shaw

Wayland, Sep. 25'th, 1866.

Darling Sarah,

I yesterday sent to you, by Adams's Express, a Photograph Album and $20, for your Freedmen's Fair. I wrote in haste, in consequence of going to Boston suddenly, and omitted many names of people whose photographs I intended to insert, if I had filled the Album.

Angelina Grimké ought to go in; for the Anti Slavery cause derived an immense impetus from her exertions in the early days. She would make a good pendant for Lucretia Mott, both being Quakers, and working together at the same time.

Of Elijah P. Lovejoy there are only silhouette likenesses; but perhaps they have been photographed. James G. Birney deserves a place, because he early in the cause emancipated his slaves, and joined the society.

Robert Small ought to go in. Sergeant W. H. Carney, of N. Bedford, Mass. would make a good pendant to him, if a a [sic] photograph of him can be found.[1] He was the one who, at Fort Wagner, dragged his bleeding limb along, holding up the Stars & Stripes, and exclaiming, "The dear old Flag never touched the ground, boys"!

Anna Dickenson ought to go in among the later ones; and Mattie Griffith has a good claim; dont you think so?[2]   Gratz Brown and Col. Moss, the brave Southern Unionist ought to go in.[3]   If there is room, I would add to

[7] John Burns (1793–1872) became the "hero of Gettysburg" for his valiant fighting with the Union army at the Battle of Gettysburg, July 1863. He was the town constable of Gettysburg and almost seventy years old at the time.

[1] Robert Smalls, a South Carolina slave, had stolen a Confederate gunboat and handed it over to the Union navy. He was elected to five terms in Congress from South Carolina. Carney had carried the flag of Shaw's Fifty-fourth to the parapet at Fort Wagner; he survived his wounds.

[2] Anna Dickinson (1842–1932), a Philadelphia abolitionist, had won fame as a young orator during the Civil War.

[3] Benjamin Gratz Brown (1826–55) was a Missouri emancipationist. Col. Charles E. Moss, from Missouri, was an anti-Lincoln Republican.

———

the military men Gen. Birney, Gen. Wild, Gen. Thomas, Col Bowman.[4] Maj. George L. Stearns, who was so early on the ground to raise colored troops, and who worked so hard and spent so much money for the purpose might come in, if there was room. Geo. W. Curtis, too.

I thought *foreign* friends of the U.S. John Bright, Gasparin, Professor Cairnes, Garibaldi, Mazzini, Labouaye (I have forgotten how to spell his name) should go in.[5] They ought to be numbered very neatly, and the name and number of each written, in very small, plain hand, in the index. I should have done *that* part well; but I was afraid I should not be able to collect the photographs in season. I think those ought to be placed together who worked conspicuously together; thus J. Q. Adams & Giddings. Charles Sumner and Wilson. Owen Lovejoy and Geo. W. Julian.

I tried to think of some *orthodox* clergyman of *distinction*, who came out in the early time, and remained faithful; but I could remember none. They behaved shabbily.

I would put in only *prominent* helpers of the cause, whether lecturers, writers, preachers, politicians, or military men; and not one whose anti slavery was doubtful, or otherwise than hearty.

And now I have a personal favor to ask of you. I am writing a story[6] in which I wish to introduce an evening at the opera in Rome. What is the name of the principal opera house? What street is it in? Is it lighted by a chandelier in the centre? Are there foot-lights in front of the stage, arranged like ours? Are the orchestra placed in the same way? Is the interior bright with gay colors and gilding? Is the general arrangement of the boxes similar to ours? What opera did you see performed there? What airs were encored? Were the audience enthusiastic? Were there various peasant costumes mixed with the fashionably dressed, in the audience? I don't mean in the same boxes; but were the peculiar Italian costumes *there?*   I think I have given you a job to answer all those questions. I wish I could look at a map of modern Rome. I take it that Monte Pincio is in the N.E. part of the city; but I have asked several who have been there, and none can tell. I take it that Frascati can be seen from Monte Pincio, in a clear day. Can Monte Cavo, sometimes called Monte Albano, be seen from Monte Pincio? *I* see it, in imagination; but travellers in *imagination* may be deceived by Fata Morgana illusions.

[4] David Bell Birney (1825–64), Union officer, was the son of abolitionist James G. Birney. Edward Augustus Wild (1825–1901), from Massachusetts, organized black troops and in 1865 supervised the Freedmen's Bureau in Georgia. Lorenzo Thomas (1804–75) organized black regiments in the Mississippi Valley; Child may also be referring to George Henry Thomas (1816–70), the Union general from Virginia known as "the Rock of Chickamauga." Bowman may be Alexander Hamilton Bowman (1803–65), Superintendent of West Point, 1861–64.
[5] John E. Cairnes, an Englishman, was the author of *The Slave Power* (London, 1862). Edouard Laboulaye (1811–83), a French jurist, wrote *Histoire Politique des États-Unis, . . . 1620–1789* (Paris, 1855–56).
[6] *A Romance of the Republic.*

You used to think I judged W'm H. Seward too harshly. What do you think now?[7] I have for six or seven years thought him the most false and artful man out of that place Calvinists preach about. He is revengeful, too. When the Republicans nominated Lincoln instead of him, he said to a gentleman from Illinois, "I'll teach these Republicans *yet* that I am their *master*." And all along thro' the war he was insidiously trying to undermine that party. Lincoln would have gone ahead much faster, if it had not been for the dead weight of W. H. Seward's influence. Now he is leading a tipsy jackass about, on purpose to disgust people with his braying, and compel the new party to take *him* for a leader. And then we should have a tipsy fox instead of a tipsy donkey. It would be comic, were it not that such tragic consequences may be involved in it.

Did you receive the autograph letters I sent you? Yours in love,

Mariechen.

I can think of no distinguished Anti Slavery *artists*. Can you?

I have two photographs of Robert as Col of the 54th.

I send by the mail with this eight photograph cards, which you can use if you like them.

ALS; Houghton Library, Harvard University (microfiche 65/1740).

At the end of 1865, Elizabeth Cady Stanton and Susan B. Anthony had begun a petition campaign opposing the word *male* in the Fourteenth Amendment. They claimed in their *History of Woman Suffrage* (New York, 1881, II, 96) that Child's name headed a petition to Charles Sumner. Nothing in Child's papers or the National Archives collection of such petitions either supports or refutes the claim. Sumner refused to help. Like many, he believed that bringing in the issue of female suffrage would jeopardize black male suffrage. The next two letters are representative of Child's views.

To Elizabeth Cady Stanton

[Before 6 December 1866]

I am old, and, having fought through a somewhat long campaign of reform, I feel little energy for enlisting in a new war. But since you care to know my opinion of the cause you are advocating so zealously and ably, I will tell you frankly that I sympathize entirely with your views concerning woman's true position in society, and I cordially wish you God speed. I believe it to be right and just that women should vote, for many of them are taxed to support the Government, and 'taxation without representation' is contrary to the principles

[7] While Johnson's speeches and conduct in the congressional campaign of 1866 cost him all support from the Radical Republicans, Seward still clung to him.

on which our republic was founded. Women are imprisoned and hung by the laws, and therefore they have a right to a voice in *making* the laws. As for our capacity to vote as intelligently as the mass of men, *that* is a point I would scarcely condescend to argue. It is absurd, on the very face of it, that an illiterate foreigner, ignorant of our institutions, and with nothing at stake in the welfare of the country, should be allowed to vote, while a woman like Mrs. Stowe is excluded from the privilege of thus influencing the public affairs which she understands so well.[1] Grant that many women would but echo the opinions of husbands, fathers, or brothers; how is it with the crowds of ignorant foreign voters? Do they not notoriously vote according to the dictation of others? The number of women capable of forming opinions for themselves, and sufficiently independent to do so, is by no means small, and the sense of responsibility involved in voting would rapidly increase the number. I believe the effect would be to enlarge and strengthen the character of women, and all will admit that the dignity and safety of a state depends greatly on the character of its women.

. . .

L, extract; *Independent*, 6 Dec. 1866 (microfiche 66/1750).

To Theodore Tilton

[Before 17 January 1867]
Professor Lewis says, very truly, that the questions of black *men's* voting and of white *women's* voting are not analogous.[1] And I confess to a reluctance to urge the question of female suffrage upon Congress at this time, when they have so many other difficult problems to solve. That the loyal blacks of the South should vote is a present and very imperious necessity—not only for their own protection, but also for the safety of the small minority of whites who are true to the Government. This is another of those remarkable leadings of Divine Providence which have been so conspicuous throughout the war, whereby the people have been compelled to do justly for the sake of their own interest.

I will say, in passing, that there is a fallacy in the phrase "impartial suffrage," as used by many friends of the colored people. They propose that the elective franchise should not be taken away from any who have heretofore exercised it; but that hereafter only those should vote who can read and write. Thus thousands of foreigners, who cannot write their own names, or read their own votes, would be allowed to influence the elections of the country, while numerous

[1] The Irish immigrants who were Roman Catholics were viewed with alarm by the American Protestants who had arrived earlier.
[1] Child was responding to a two-part article by Tayler Lewis, called "Household Suffrage," that appeared in the *Independent* on 6 and 20 Dec. 1866. His anti-woman-suffrage stance was based on the idea that the family was divinely sanctioned and the basic unit or microcosm of society; the sovereignty of the husband meant that he was authorized to vote for his wife and unmarried daughters.

native citizens, who are ignorant because our own laws have hitherto prevented them from obtaining the rudiments of learning, would be excluded from the polls. This is *not* impartial suffrage. Either *all* voters should be required to have some degree of education, or *none* should be subject to such limitations.

I have always thought that suffrage ought to rest on an educational basis. There is no hardship in such an arrangement, in a country where the means of obtaining the requisite qualification are offered to every one at the public expense. As a stimulus to education, it would be valuable beyond measure. Probably no motive would operate so strongly on the "poor whites" of the South; and their enlightenment is greatly needed as a check to that arrogant class who led them blindfold into a worse than needless war—a class whose patriarchal tendencies make them the natural enemies of a republic, and whose boast it has been that society among them was becoming "more and more oriental." This patriarchal element would, of course, ultimately destroy our free institutions, if unimpeded in its operations. It is important for the salvation of the nation that it should be kept in check until it disappears before the advances of a higher degree of civilization; and that can only be done by the moral and intellectual improvement of the people, black and white.

The suffrage of woman can better afford to wait than that of the colored people; and they speak truly who say that a majority of women would negative the claim, if left to their decision. In a recent debate in Congress several senators declared themselves ready to grant suffrage to women whenever a considerable number of them asked for it. I smiled at this adroit way of handing over a perplexing question to their sons or grandsons. But this state of mind in women proves nothing, except that human beings are creatures of habit. If a Chinese woman should let the feet of her infant daughter grow to the natural size, and furnish her with suitable shoes to walk in the street, would she not be regarded by her own sex as a shameless innovator? That Chinese men should regard such a proceeding as threatening the disintegration of patriarchal society would be a matter of course. Yet it would be a great improvement in the condition of China if the women were allowed to let their feet grow, and were at liberty to walk with them. When Frederick the Great emancipated the serfs, many of them petitioned to be exempted from the operation of his decree. He persisted in freeing them, for their own good; and at this day Prussia is all the stronger for it.[2] One of the teachers of freedmen at the South informs us that both parents and children complain because there is no whipping in schools. "I really think I should behave better if you would whip me," said one of the boys. He had been brought up under "the patriarchal system," and could not easily get rid of the habits thus acquired.

In my former letter, I showed how women were gradually becoming accustomed to many pursuits that once seemed to them strange and inappropriate. It would be the same with their exercise of the rights of citizenship. Very few

[2] Actually, Frederick maintained serfdom but lightened the burden of the peasants.

would vote at first; but year by year the number of those interested in public affairs would increase. They would doubtless make mistakes, as all beginners do. Some of them would be easily duped, and some would be over-conceited with a little superficial information. The present enlargement of woman's sphere of action is not without such results; and the same is true of the colored people. But I think candid observers would admit that the general gain to character is much greater than the loss.

It is the theory of our government that the people govern. Women constitute half of the people. It has been legally decided that they are citizens; and, as citizens, constituting so large a portion of the people, I think they plainly have a right to vote. I believe it would be good for them to exercise the right, because all human souls grow stronger in proportion to the increase of their responsibilities, and the high employment of their faculties. For ten or twelve years I lived in the midst of Quakers; and I could not but observe that their women were superior to women in general in habits of reflection and independent modes of thinking. I remember a Quaker cobbler who was much addicted to talking, not very wisely, about public affairs. His wife would look up from her knitting, now and then, and quietly remark, "I do not agree with thee, Reuben. Thee has not got on the right principle there, Reuben." If she had voted, it certainly would have been in a manner very different from him; but I don't think there would ever have been any nearer approach to a quarrel than that frequently expressed in her calm dissent from his opinions. This staid and self-relying character in Quaker women I attribute to the fact that they share equally with men in the management of all the business of the society. Frivolous pursuits make frivolous characters. Society has done grievous wrong to the souls of women by fencing them within such narrow enclosures. And then it adds insult to injury by mocking at the meanness it has made. The literature of all nations abounds with jibes, and jeers, and degrading comparisons concerning women. This is so common that men in general probably pass it by unnoticed; but to sensible women it is a perpetual offense. "More than a thousand women is one man worthy to see the light of life," says Euripides. "Stiff ale, stinging tobacco, and a girl in a smart dress are the best things," says the tradesman in Goethe's Faust. "There are exceedingly good points about the Turks; chibouks, coffee, and as many wives as they please. Under their system women become as gentle, as docile, and as tractable as any domestic animal," says Stephens, in his "Incidents of Travel."[3] "Such a thing may happen as that the woman, not the man, may be in the right, (I mean when both are godly); but ordinarily it is otherwise," says John Bunyan. "It is not easy to keep up conversation with women. It is thought rudeness to differ with them, and it is not quite fair to ask them a *reason* for what they say," says Hazlitt.

[3] John Lloyd Stephens (1805-52) was an archeologist and travel writer. The reference is probably to his *Incidents of Travel in Egypt, Arabia, Petræa, and The Holy Land* (10th ed., New York, 1837).

And, as a compensation for this habitual tone of contempt, we are assiduously waited upon by that false, flippant shadow called gallantry; that shallow compound of frivolity and foppery, that has no basis in true respect and genuine esteem for woman. And all this comes upon us in consequence of our having been systematically excluded from the professions, the trades, the arts, the sciences, the halls of legislation; in a word, from all the pursuits that are best calculated to enlarge the mind, to occupy it profitably, and to raise it above mean and petty subjects of thought. Professor Lewis asks whether, if wives and daughters voted, their influence would be as potent and healthy as it now is. I do not think the mere act of voting would make any difference, one way or the other; but I do think the education they would gradually acquire by taking a part in public affairs would make them more instructive and more interesting as household companions. I believe the domestic bond will never reach its possible hight of perfection till women occupy their thoughts and feelings with all that occupies the thoughts and feelings of men. The astronomer and the chemist would find home more satisfactory with wives who could understand their investigations and feel interested in their discoveries. The architect would find himself both enlivened and aided by a companion who had an eye for form and color, and a talent for inventing conveniences. If mothers, wives, and daughters were more generally interested in the ethics of politics, our statesmen would not so often waste their abilities on games of compromise, risking the interests of freedom on the hazard of their play.

How many such struggles we have witnessed as this concerning admitting Colorado and Nebraska into a free republic with a deep taint of despotism in their constitutions! And how very rare are legislators like Charles Sumner, who can never be induced, by any amount of reproach or persuasion, to sacrifice eternal principles to temporary expediency! What a stainless record he is leaving for history!

There is an obvious fallacy in Professor Lewis's statement that women *do* vote in the same way that all our people vote for President: that is, they choose their elector to vote *for* them. The circumstances of the times are always changing, requiring new men and new measures, and when men vote for electors to choose a President, they vote for such electors as are suited to the present emergency. But, admitting that, when a woman marries, and thus becomes "dead in the law," she chooses an elector to vote for her; what manifold changes may take place in affairs, and in his character, if they live together twenty or thirty years! How many chances there are that he will cease to represent her views, even if he does not vote for measures that she entirely disapproves. The Professor again observes: "Women choose their electors, or he is *provided* for them by one of the most precious ordinances of God and Nature." If a husband or a father should become an atheist or an infidel, while his wife and daughters of mature age wished to give their influence and a share of their earnings to the support of evangelical churches, would the Professor decide that the husband and father was their divinely-appointed representative, and that they ought to act only through him? In large portions of Christendom people believe that heads of the Church are divinely appointed to prescribe the faith of other men. I once asked an acquaintance how he came to turn Roman Catholic; and he replied, "It is so convenient to have a bishop to think *for* me." A young lady once told me that she went to all the churches in Boston by turns, because she did not want to decide till she knew what would be the religion of the man she married. Some time afterward she married a Roman Catholic; and, having chosen him to do her believing, she joined his church. What vitality can there be in a religion assumed under such circumstances? The fact is all conclusions are fallacious based on the hypothesis that one human soul can be merged in another soul. No human being can possibly think for me, or believe for me, any more that he can eat for me, or drink for me, or breathe for me. The family is a very sacred thing; but it appears to me that in a family of true order each one would think, feel, and act, as an individual, with respectful regard to the freedom of the other members, and a conscientious feeling of duty concerning the influence exerted on their characters and happiness. I do not see why difference in voting should necessarily produce dissension between husband and wife, any more than the mere difference of opinion which so frequently exists without such result. Nor do I see why the mere circumstance of depositing a vote need to make women boisterous, or expose them to rudeness. *They* are accustomed to press through crowds to go to theaters and operas, and meetings at Faneuil Hall; they go with the throng to hear orators and statesmen, and nobody treats them uncivilly, or considers their presence an unbecoming intrusion. Their appearance at the polls would soon cease to be a novelty, and the depositing of a vote might be done as easily and as quietly as leaving a card at a hotel.

I respect the fears of kind and conscientious conservatives, like Professor Lewis, although I do not share them. There is one abiding consolation for all that class of thinkers. God has so wisely arranged the laws of the universe that great changes *cannot* come till the way is prepared for them. History plainly shows his hand continually preparing the way for the complete individualizing of the masses. Paul spoke for a much larger audience than the churches of Galatia, when he said, "There is neither Jew nor Greek, there is neither bond nor free, there is neither male nor female: for ye are all one in Christ Jesus." With increasing knowledge the work goes on with accelerated speed; but the world is far enough yet from the great festival of ALL SOULS.

L; *Independent,* 17 Jan. 1867 (microfiche 66/1760).

A Romance of the Republic was Child's fourth book to be published by Ticknor and Fields. Fields offered a flat thousand-dollar payment for the novel, which she rejected to take instead the usual 10 percent royalty. The book did not sell well, and she probably earned less than if she had accepted the flat fee.

This letter suggests awareness of Fields's current battle with Mary Abby Dodge, a writer using the pen name Gail Hamilton, who accused him of underpaying his female authors. Her claims were eventually upheld by an impartial board of arbiters.

To James T. Fields

Wayland, May 14'th, 1867.

Dear Mr. Fields,

I herewith return the contract signed.   I was not unmindful of the in-crease of percent growing out of increase of prices; but I remembered also that the *proportion* between the profits of authors and publishers remains the same as when I wrote my first book.

I wanted to know whether you offered me the same that you did other authors who were considerably known. I am not arrogant in my claims, but I thought I ought not to be put at the *foot* of the ladder, and I wanted to know whether I had been.

Of course, neither you nor I have time to discuss what ought to be the relative profits of labor and capital.

Always cordially your friend,
L. Maria Child.

I suppose nothing could be done with the English market.

ALS; James Thomas Fields Collection, Huntington Library (microfiche 67/1774).

To Samuel J. May

Wayland, Sep. 29'th, 1867

Dear Friend,

Your anti-slavery sketches carry me back pleasantly to those by-gone days when our souls were raised above the level of common life by the glorious inspiration of unselfish zeal.[1] It seems but a little while ago, yet men speak of it as a "dead subject;" so swiftly the world whirls round, carrying us, and all memory of us, with it!

In your very kind notice of me, you have exaggerated some things, and omitted others. I don't think I lost so much per-annum by espousing the Anti Slavery cause. At all events, I think the indefinite statement that my literary prospects were *much injured* by it would have been better. With regard to *society* I was a *gainer* very decidedly; for though the respectables, who had

[1] Samuel J. May's sketches, then appearing in the *Christian Register*, were republished as *Some Recollections of Our Antislavery Conflict* (Boston, 1869).

473

condescended to patronize me, forthwith sent me to "Coventry," anti slavery introduced me to the noblest and best of the land, intellectually and morally, and knit us together in that firm friendship which grows out of sympathy in a good but unpopular cause. Besides, it is impossible to estimate how much one's own character gains by a warfare which keeps the intellect wide awake, and compels one to reflect upon moral principles. I did not deserve much *credit* for espousing the anti-slavery cause, for at the outset I was altogether unconscious of the unpopularity I was about to incur, and when I became aware of it, it troubled me exceedingly little, because I really never cared much for social or literary distinction. I have forgotten most of the cuts which I received in those days; but the remarks in your article has [*sic*] brought back one to my memory.

I was quite surprised one day by a note from the Trustees of the Boston Atheneum, offering me the free use of the library, the same as if I owned a share. I had never asked such a favor, and I am not aware that any friend of mine ever solicited it. My *conjecture* was that the move was made by Professor George Ticknor, who was at that time a very kind patron of mine. ⟨It happened that I had become acquainted with Mr. Garrison a short time before, and my attention being turned toward slavery, the first use I made of my Athe——⟩ My husband was anti-slavery, and it was the theme of many of our conversations while Garrison was in prison.[2] About the time of the unexpected attention from the Trustees, Mr. Garrison came to Boston, and I had a talk with *him.* Consequently the first use I made of my Atheneum privilege was to take out several books on that subject, with a view to writing my "Appeal."
A few weeks after the "Appeal" was published, I received another note from the Trustees informing me that at a recent meeting they had passed a vote to *take away* my privilege, lest it should prove an inconvenient precedent.

. . .[3] me credit for *more* than I have done, you have omitted the most notable of all my anti-slavery doings. I mean the Letter to Governor Wise, and the Letter to Mrs. Mason in the John Brown times.[4] They had an immense circulation all over the free states, and were blazoned by all manner of anathemas in the Southern papers. The Letter to Mrs. Mason, especially, was copied by hundreds of thousands; and it is a satisfaction to me to think of it as one of the innumerable agencies that were at work to prepare the mind of the North for the final great crisis. . . .

Mr. C. unites with me in cordial greetings. Your affectionate friend, L. Maria Child.

[2] Garrison was in jail in Baltimore, Md., 17 Apr.–5 June 1830, for libel of Francis Todd of Newburyport, Mass. Garrison had publicly accused the merchant of transporting slaves from Baltimore to New Orleans.
[3] Ellipses here and subsequently indicate where half a page has been cut off, omitting about twelve lines of writing on either side. A marginal note follows.
[4] She refers to *Correspondence between Lydia Maria Child, Gov. Wise and Mrs. Mason, of Virginia* (Boston, 1860).

Are you supplied with Mr. Child's pamphlet on the "Despotism of Freedom," or do you want him to send it to you?[5] *He* was wide awake before I was.

ALS; Lydia Maria Child Papers, Anti-Slavery Collection, Cornell University (microfiche 67/1794).

Sarah Shaw

Wayland, Feb. 2d, 1868.

My dear Sarah,

Thanks for your letter. I am *not* disposed to say, "Now hold your tongue"! because you say I am entirely out of my "appropriate sphere" in Wayland. I know that, as well as you do, and it sometimes makes me a little restless.[1] But I have reflected much and often upon it, and I cannot think of anything better that lies within my power to do. My income falls short of eight hundred dollars. Out of it I annually pay $50 toward the support of Mr. Child's invalid sister; and in case of increased infirmities, I should feel it my duty to pay more. Annual taxes take up $171,,67 cts more. This leaves about $550 for *food, clothing* for us both, perpetually recurring *repairs*, replenishing of *furniture, fuel, lamp-light, medicines, stage-fare, cars*, &c.   *Here*, the sum furnishes us with every necessary physical comfort; but how could I mix with society without getting into debt? You will say I had better earn by my pen, than save by my needle and stew-pan. But at my age, it will not do to *trust* to that resource, for it *may* fail me at any moment, and *must*, in the common course of nature, fail me before many years. What should I do *then*, with increased habits of expenditure without increased means of supply? What I now earn by my pen, I use as a fund for benevolence, mostly devoted to the freedmen. During the war, I gave it *all*, outright, to soldiers' hospitals, and to freedmen; and I shall continue to give at least all the *income* of my *earnings*, unless prevented by some stern necessity; and where the claim seems strong, I shall not confine myself to the use of the *income*. I could not accomplish this, if I had not a real genius for economy. You would smile to see the record of my yearly expenses. In 1867, "Clothing for myself, $18,,6 cts.["] Hardly enough to supply Mrs. Minturn with boots. "Amusements, 50 cts;" being the admission fee to two of Bierstadt's paintings. Books, or pictures, I never buy; except now and then some little thing to give to a child. I have gone into this stupid detail, merely to convince you that I am not obstinate, and that my present mode of life is not a matter of choice, but of rational calculation of possibilities. Then in addition to limitation of income, I am weary of being knocked about, "from post to pillar," and having found a comfortable retreat, (thanks to my kind old father) I am re-

[5] (Boston, 1833).
[1] Child never moved from the Wayland home, except to spend her winters in Boston in later years.

luctant to undertake the fatigue of removal, and searching for a new home. When you are 66 years old, as I shall be next week, you will find an increase of inertia, both in body and mind. Besides, Mr. Child is nearly eight years my senior, and his health is so precarious, that if we were to "stay round" among friends, while looking out for a new residence, change of habits would be likely to bring on serious and protracted illness, which would be very troublesome to our hosts. Here, he has great simplicity in his food, great regularity in his sleep, no violent excitements, a garden to dig in, and a wood-lot to chop in. These keep him alive and cheerful, especially, as he is always planning *improvements;* which do not prove very expensive, because he makes them, to a great extent, with his own hands. If his energies had not these safe and healthy occupations, he would inevitably spend them on projects at once unprofitable and expensive. Now, as the *one* mission I have left to perform in this life is to make his old age as comfortable and happy as I can, I think I do wisely to shut myself up here. If you are not convinced, I should like to know how *you* would manage to do better, with such an income for the support of two?

    . . .

I abominate the Fenian modes of proceeding, but I am so unchristian as rather to enjoy having step-mother England a little scared.

ALS, incomplete; Houghton Library, Harvard University (microfiche 68/1811).

To John Fraser

Wayland, Feb. 13'th, 1868.

Dear Mr. Fraser,

    . . .

Do you think it is peculiar to *you* to feel as if your life might "be at last summed up as a failure"?

I have the same feeling with regard to myself very frequently; and I have never met with a person, past fifty years old, who had *not.* All who strive to live for something beyond mere selfish aims find their capacities for doing good very inadequate to their aspirations. They do so much less than they *want* to do, and so much less than they, at the outset, *expected* to do, that their lives, viewed retrospectively, inevitably look like failure. I do not indulge such moods, tho' they often intrude upon me; and I find the best mode for banishing them is to "do with my might whatsoever my hands find to do," however humble the use may seem.

In the present transition state of society, I think clergymen have less chance ⟨than others⟩ for healthy occupation, and spiritual freedom, than other men. In a greater or less degree, most of them sell themselves into bondage for a salary. For my own part, I should greatly prefer to till the ground for my food, and say what I *had* to say to my fellow creatures in the form of occasional lectures, when I felt like it. But perhaps this is one of my peculiarities.

. . .

L, transcript; Simison Papers, Beinecke Rare Book and Manuscript Library, Yale University (microfiche 68/1814).

To Sarah Shaw

Wayland, Feb. 18'th, 1868.

Dear Sarah,

. . .

With regard to Mr. Higginson, I am desirous to oblige him, from motives of personal respect; but the idea of laying open my private letters for such a purpose is excessively painful to me.[1] It is perfectly horrid to think of having the public informed of expressions uttered in the childish *abandon* of familiar friendship. I don't think anybody has a *right* to make a biography of a person who does not *wish* to have it done. It puts me in a real fret. I detest notoriety. There are plenty of people who *like* it. Let him blow the trumpet for *them*. This mousing round after my private sentiments seems to me like surgeons politely asking me to be dissected before I am dead. You will think I am cross. Well, I am. It *always* makes me cross to have the public "pervading my department, wanting to *know*."

. . .

ALS; Wayland (Mass.) Historical Society (microfiche 68/1815).

By the spring of 1868 public attention was turning to the coming presidential election. The abolitionists saw it as crucial for the cause of black suffrage. A Republican victory would guarantee that Reconstruction would move ahead. If the Democrats won, it would mean the end of Radical Reconstruction and the readmission of Southern states without black suffrage. General Grant, the military hero, had been the obvious candidate since the war's end. Radical abolitionists had doubts about his principles, but Republican leaders saw him first of all as a man who could win.

[1] T. W. Higginson was collecting material for his contributions to *Eminent Women of the Age*, ed. James Parton (Hartford, 1868).

To Samuel E. Sewall

Wayland, March 21st, 1868.

My very dear Friend,

. . .

I think, as *you* do, that taking *all* things into consideration, the nation *might* fare worse than it would be likely to in the hands of General Grant. But he is by no means my choice. I like many traits in his character; but the terms of Lee's surrender; and his never expressing any sympathy for the colored people; and his consenting to give *éclat* to Johnson, by forming a part of his mountebank exhibition in the West; these all tended to excite distrust in my mind.[1] Moreover, I am afraid that he is an habitual tippler; and we have had *enough* of that sort of thing in the White House. On the other hand, I think it very likely we should have had a *coup d état* at Washington, causing the outbreak of another war, if Grant had not behaved so patriotically and firmly as he has done. Therefore, since we *cannot* have Sumner, I know not whether we could do better than take *him*.

I am glad that Andy Johnson is impeached, at last; though I wish the terms of indictment had expressed something about the slaughter of loyal whites and blacks, and the sufferings and discouragements of the freed people, caused by his nefarious "policy."[2]

I am sorry Mrs. Stanton carries such a *Train* with her.[3] I think it is an error of judgment. The question of Woman's Right to Suffrage requires, more than any *other* reform, great care to avoid making it ridiculous; and George Francis Train certainly *is* ridiculous. He throws off some scintillations of eloquence, but his egotism amounts to insanity, and his judgment to O.

I hope you do not think, because I zealously support the Standard, that I have any *partisan* feeling concerning the unfortunate difference between Garrison & Phillips. Certainly not. I can have no other feeling than respect and regard toward two such efficient friends of freedom. But we have always agreed with Mr. Phillips in thinking that the Anti Slavery Society ought not to be disbanded, until the rights of the freed men were much more secure than they are at present; and we have not the slightest doubt that if Francis Jackson

---

[1] Radicals began to distrust Grant when he accompanied Johnson on the latter's famous speaking tour in 1866.
[2] The impeachment trial of Johnson had begun 4 Mar. Child objected to the charges as peripheral to the real issues.
[3] George Francis Train (1829–1904), author, flamboyant promoter, and Democrat, in 1867 made a speaking tour with Stanton and Anthony to promote a woman suffrage amendment in Kansas. In 1868 he funded the weekly *Revolution*, which Stanton and Anthony edited.

could have spoken, he would have ordered his bequest to be paid to that Society.[4]

. . .

ALS; Robie-Sewall Papers, Massachusetts Historical Society (microfiche 68/1819).

For more than forty years Child had shown great interest in the American Indians, expressing it in her fictional, historical, and polemical writings. When the report of the Indian Peace Commission appeared in 1868, she sought to bring it to public attention through a long letter in the *National Anti-Slavery Standard* (11 April 1868). Commending the report for its "just and humane" views, she gave several extracts from its findings. The report expressed the views of humanitarian reformers who believed that benign methods would have more success than military measures in speeding the pacification and assimilation of the tribes: "The best possible way to avoid war is to do no act of injustice," the report said. But, Child noted, "our relations with the red and black members of the human family have been one almost unvaried history of violence and fraud." She hoped that Indians and whites would learn to live together, but criticized any attempts to force the dominant culture upon the Indians. Her pamphlet entitled *An Appeal for the Indians* was published in 1868.

To Charles Sumner

Wayland, May 8'th, 1868

Dear and Honored Mr. Sumner,

. . .

My dear friend Mrs. Shaw wrote me that you had shown my letter about the Indians to Gen. Sherman.[1] I thank you. It is a subject that has long excited deep interest in my mind; and the indications of candor and humanity in the Report of the Commission filled me with unspeakable satisfaction; all the more so because so many of the signers were *military* men, and as such likely enough to be brought into intimate and very important relations with our Indian affairs. No *mere politicians* would have ventured to speak so impartially and bravely; but who *can* presume to be independent in the utterance of unflattering

[4] At the end of the Civil War, the goal of abolition having been achieved, Garrison felt that the American Anti-Slavery Society should disband. He directed that a bequest from Francis Jackson should go not to the society but to the New England Freedmen's Union Commission. The Childs had publicly joined Wendell Phillips in protesting this decision.

[1] Child's *Standard* letter had mentioned General Sherman. He was at this time next to Grant in military authority and would succeed him in command in 1869. It was the army, of course, which confronted the Indians in the West.

truths, if it be not men who have such undisputed claims on the respect and gratitude of the nation, for the important services they rendered in the hour of desperate need?   Though I believe war to be a barbarism, that will be abolished by increasing civilization, I know how to honor the men who offer their lives a willing sacrifice for the advancement of freedom and justice. I am out of all patience with the sickly sentimentality of Gerrit Smith, Horace Greely, and H. W. Beecher. They seem to me to confound all distinctions between right and wrong. Those who eulogize the bravery of Lee, and shake hands with Jeff Davis, have no right ever to touch the hands of Grant, Sherman, Sheridan, &c   I never, for one moment, wished for any greater severity toward the South than was necessary to restrain them from farther evil. But there is a right and a wrong in this matter, which ought not to be confounded by a desire to exhibit ⟨our⟩ magnanimity. Our civil war was no tournament for show; it was a death-grapple between Freedom & Despotism; and unhorsed despotism is all unworthy to receive again his sword and spurs, as if he were an honorable knight, instead of a thieving, murderous caitiff.

. . .

ALS; Houghton Library, Harvard University (microfiche 68/1827).

Harriet (Winslow) Sewall (1819–89), wife of the abolitionist Samuel E. Sewall, became Child's close friend and later edited her letters. She was active in the woman's suffrage movement in Massachusetts.

To Harriet Sewall

Wayland, July 10'th, 1868.

Dear Friend,

. . . My mind has been troubled somewhat about the letter I wrote to Edmonia, because you thought it must have been "very hard" for me to write it.[1] The fact is, I should rather have given $50, than have done it. But I have observed that she has no calculation about money; what is *received* with facility is *expended* with facility. She is not to blame for this deficiency. How could it be otherwise, when her childhood was spent with poor negroes, and her youth with wild Indians? People who live in "a jumpetty-scratch way," (as a slave described his "poor white" neighbors) cannot possibly acquire habits of balancing income and outgo. If she found all her bills for freight and marble paid, without expostulation from any quarter, she would soon send over *another* statue, in the same way. She wrote to me, some months ago, requesting

[1] The sculptor Edmonia Lewis had been in Rome three years at this time, aided by members of the American colony.

me to tell her all I knew about Pocahontas, as she wanted to make a statue of her. I complied with her request, and told her I thought it would be a good subject for her, because she had been used to *seeing young Indian girls*, and could work from *memory*, and with her *heart* in it, for her mother's sake; but I recommended it as a *practice in clay* merely, and that only a *portion* of her time should be given to it. But if marble and freight are obtained by whistling "to raise the wind," she will probably send over a marble Pocahontas, to be presented to the Chief of the Chippeways; the tribe to which her mother belonged. I think she would make a statue of an Indian better than anything else; but neither her mind or her hands are yet educated enough to work in *marble*. She should wait till her models are good enough to be *ordered* in marble. A mediocre *statue* is worse than a *painting* of the same degree of merit; for it is so conspicuous, and takes up so much room, that one knows not what to do with it.   The account given to you by a lady from Rome was a relief to my mind; though I presume it was only *partially* true. I dont believe that Charlotte Cushman has taken Edmonia "under her *protection;*" for if she had, she never would have allowed her to run in debt for marble, on the mere *supposition* that Mr. Garrison's friends would raise money to pay for it.[2] Miss Cushman is very kind-hearted, and if Edmonia was in great trouble, she would relieve her; but she is a shrewd, experienced, managing woman of the world. I have no doubt Edmonia was very poor at the time she wrote. She would take music-lessons, and hire horses, while her money lasted, and then be surprised and distressed to find herself without funds. It is absolutely necessary for her to do *something* for a living, and devote only a *portion* of her time to perfecting herself as a sculptor; which it will take years of patient labor for her to do. I have always told her that, from the outset.

. . .

. . . As for Mrs. Lewes, who writes under the *nom de plume* of George Elliott, in my estimation she stands at the head of novel-writers, and very *far* above anybody else. George Sand alone approaches her; but it is George Sand's misfortune that she was educated in France, and describes that diseased thing, French society. The noblest soul cannot come out of *such* an ordeal quite clean.

. . .

ALS; Robie-Sewall Papers, Massachusetts Historical Society (microfiche 69/1841).

When Louisa Loring died 25 May 1868, Child wrote a memoir of her for the *Standard*, 6 June 1868. Child recollected how they together held the first antislavery fair in 1833, using the law office of Samuel E. Sewall. Anna (Loring) Dresel continued being Child's correspondent, though often abroad in Germany.

[2] Charlotte Cushman (1816–76), the American actress, then retired, had made her home in Rome a center for people in the arts.

To Anna (Loring) Dresel

Wayland, August 12'th, 1868.

Dear Anna,

. . .

I have just finished reading "The Spanish Gypsy," for the third time.[1] Mrs. Sewall sent it to me, and I don't know that I ever read anything that so fascinated and thrilled me. Never was tragedy wrought up to such intensity. The characters are sketched with wondrous power, the scenery stands before you in the mild glory of a poetic atmosphere, and the language is worthy of the high thoughts it conveys. Decidedly "George Elliott" is an empress among women. She is a wonderful combination of masculine power with feminine grace; and if there is any trusting to the internal evidence of writing, her morale must be as pure and refined as her intellect is strong and discriminating. Certainly in novel-writing, whether in prose or verse, the men are distanced by women. If they could develope their faculties as *freely* as men do, I think they would equal them in *all* departments of Art. But they are bound by so many lilliputian cords, of which the most entangling and contemptibly belittling is the glossy cobweb of Fashion. The manner in which they fritter away their souls in the service of that capricious tyrant is deplorable.

. . .

ALS; Lydia Maria Child Papers, A/C 536, b, Schlesinger Library, Radcliffe College (microfiche 69/1844).

Robert Purvis (1810–98), a black living in Philadelphia, was a founder and later president of the American Anti-Slavery Society. He dedicated his life and inherited wealth to ending slavery and fighting discrimination.

To Robert Purvis

Wayland, Aug. 14th, 1868

Mr. Purvis,
Dear Sir,

I received your letter, and I thank you for it. It is gratifying to know that my efforts are appreciated by a gentleman for whom I entertain such sincere respect.

In these days of novel-reading, I thought a Romance would take more

[1] George Eliot, *The Spanish Gypsy* (Edinburgh, 1868).

hold of the public mind, than the most elaborate arguments; and having fought against Slavery, till the monster is *legally* dead, I was desirous to do what I could to undermine Prejudice.[1]   You say, "The Demon of Prejudice was never more cruel and relentless than now." I grant that it often exhibits more ferocity than ever, but I think that is merely angry resistance to a change that is seen to be inevitable. The colored people, being better protected by the laws, venture to *take* their rights more boldly, than they formerly did; and that also tends to the increase of wrath. But notwithstanding these rude manifestations on the surface, a salutary change is really going on. When I compare the state of things with what it was when I was young, the change seems to me wonderful. Another half century will see changes still more wonderful.

It is strange that anything so irrational as prejudice should be so difficult to eradicate. Consider what contempt and cruel outrages the Jews suffered for nearly two thousand years. No amount of virtue, or learning, or wealth, could protect them from treatment as contemptuous as was ever bestowed on the most abject slave. They had no security for life or property, and were subject to cruel outrages and tortures whenever the rabble took the whim. And how utterly absurd, as well as wicked, was this prejudice! for not one Jew in a million had ever *heard* of Jesus at the time he was crucified by a faction at Jerusalem.   As well might all Christendom be considered responsible for the murder of Joe Smith, when only a small fraction of them ever even heard of it. Yet, to this day, Jews are despised and persecuted in many European countries; nor have we Americans quite outgrown this unjust and narrow prejudice.[2]

But the world *does* grow; and the time *will* come when all classes will find their natural level, as freely as the waters do. I have tried to help on this good work, according to the measure of my ability; and sad as I sometimes am over the present state of public affairs, still, on the *whole*, I feel encouraged.

Whether my faith and hope would survive the restoration of the Democratic Party to power, is more than I can say.[3] They would doubtless reverse all the laws in favor of the freedmen; but if worst comes to worst, it will last only for a time. Meanwhile, all we can do is to work for the right with might and main.

Mr. Child unites with me in sincere respect and cordial good wishes.

Very truly your friend,

L. M. Child.

ALS; Clifton Waller Barrett Library, University of Virginia (microfiche 69/1847).

[1] Child refers to her novel, *A Romance of the Republic* (Boston, 1867).
[2] Child's comparison of antiblack prejudice with anti-Semitism was unusual for that time.
[3] Grant was running against the Democrat Horatio Seymour, former governor of New York.

To Lucy Osgood

Wayland, Feb. 4th, 1869.

Dear Friend,

I thank you for your long, pleasant letter. I agree with you concerning the "Radical."[1] I have seen but few numbers of it, but they seemed to me, as you say, "misty and unprofitable." But I rejoice over the organization from which it issues, because it frankly throws down *all* enclosures, and walks out free into infinite space.   I agree also, in part, with you concerning voting. I have always considered it a great mistake that foreigners, and others, were admitted to suffrage without a moderate educational qualification; but the mistake *was* made, and now there is no help for it but to make haste and educate all classes as fast as possible. Negroes are as *well* qualified to vote as the mass of Irishmen, and circumstances make it *their* interest to vote on the *right* side. Besides, negro suffrage is *forced* upon us, as a *political* necessity, just as emancipation was forced upon us, as a "military necessity." I see the same wonderful hand of Providence in both cases. He leaves us but two alternatives; either the government of the country must again be given up to slave-holding rebels, and their Democratic allies, or the loyal men of the South *must* vote; and nearly all the loyal men in that region are black. I therefore regard it as by far the most important question now at issue.   As for women, the being treated as subordinates has made them "Biddy and Molly"; and the being educated only to elegant trifling, to please their keepers, has made them "Flora M'c Flimsies." If the men for whose convenience such institutions as "Five Points" exist are granted the right of suffrage, I see no reason why the women they have ensnared should be excluded.[2] I think there is quite as much danger in granting it in one case, as in the other. The fact is, I don't believe in *classes*. I believe only in *individuals*. Human souls have been stinted for centuries, and the progress of society retarded, by arrangement into classes, by reason of sex, or sect, or color, or employments. I have long seen that the true principle is to leave to every human soul a free, open, unimpeded course to whatever goal it chooses; and when I see that a principle is *true*, I follow it without fear, knowing God has so arranged his universe that evil is never the outgrowth of truth. It is *my* mission to help in the breaking down of classes, and to make *all* men feel as if they were brethren of the same family, sharing the same rights, the same capabilities, and the same responsibilities. While my hand can hold a pen, I will use it to this end; and while my brain can earn a dollar, I will devote it to this end.

I wish to see Sam. Johnson's book, and I thank you for the offer to send

---

[1] The *Radical* was a monthly magazine "devoted to intellectual freedom and natural religion" edited by S. J. Morse and J. B. Marvin. Some of the contributors were A. Bronson Alcott, O. B. Frothingham, and T. W. Higginson.

[2] Five Points, notorious for prostitution, was a slum district below City Hall in Manhattan, crowded with newly arrived Irish and German immigrants.

it to me.[3] I will write 11th of Feb. in it, and put it among my birth-day offerings. It is very true that a philosophic religion is fit only for philosophers. But
all that each individual has to do is to follow the truth as far as *he* sees it,
without assuming that *his* boundary is necessarily the end of the universe. I
opine that we have nothing to *do* with the question whether the views that seem
to *us* true can meet the wants of the "ignorant, silly, sensuous, suffering masses."
It is *our* business to seek truth reverently, and utter it frankly, leaving it to do
its mission of educating "the masses" to a higher stand-point. It is never safe
to look *outside*, and calculate consequences, in forming our estimate of any
truths. What a muddy medley they made of Christianity, by grafting upon it
one superstition which was important to the Jewish convert, another to the
Greek, another to the Scandinavian, & so on! The Italian peasant woman is
doubtless comforted by praying to a doll dressed up in tinsel, which she worships as the "Mother of God." I would not, if I had the power, make it illegal
for her to comfort herself in that way; but shall I refrain from philosophic
utterance, lest it should make her doll fall out of its shrine? The doll *will* not,
and *cannot* fall, so long as the "ignorant, sensuous, suffering masses" have need
of her. The work that needs to be done is to bring the world into such a state
of order, that there will *be* no "ignorant sensuous, suffering masses," and consequently no further use for consecrated dolls. Meanwhile, let them comfort
themselves with their dolls. It is the business of *grown* people to lead children
gently away from the necessity of toys.   It is a long time since *Principles*
were all that commanded my implicit faith and reverence. Some would say re-
gretfully that I believed *less* than formerly; but in my inmost soul, I know that
I believe *more*.

   . . .

ALS; Lydia Maria Child Papers, Anti-Slavery Collection, Cornell University (microfiche 70/1878).

To Abigail (Kelley) Foster

Wayland, March 28'th '69

Dear Mrs. Foster,
     It is odd of you to apologize for saying such kind words to me. It is my
sincere wish to do what good I can in the world before I go hence; and it
strengthens my hands to know that others in the same state of mind, think I
am doing some good.
     The subject of Homes for the Freedmen is one that has "exercised my
mind" for a long time. I have no desire for wealth on my own account, my
personal wants being few and simple, but I *have* sometimes longed for Mr.
Peabody's power to buy millions of acres to sell again, at low prices, to those

[3] The Reverend Samuel Johnson wrote several books on Oriental religions.

poor homeless laborers.[1] I say to *sell* again, first, because I believe it is more salutary to all classes of people to *earn* a home than to have it *given* to them; and because a permanent fund could be thus obtained to furnish homes to an indefinite extent.   In the Standard of March 27'th is an article from J. M. Wood, a Quaker missionary, in Virginia, containing a proposition to form a joint-stock company to purchase wild lands and sell them to the freedmen, at low prices. I wish the idea could be carried into execution, and that agricultural teachers could be sent to instruct them how to make the most of their land. Obviously, it is the general policy of their former masters to prevent their becoming owners of the soil. Whether they shall be disheartened vagrants, or become a class of contented and useful citizens depends upon their being enabled to have homes of their own.   It did vex my spirit to have H. W. Beecher, Gerrit Smith, and Horace Greely, making such liberal donations to that proud, unprincipled Lee, when the money, used as above suggested, might have made so many happy homes for the poor freedmen. It was a great mistake. It seemed as if their desire to make a great show of magnanimity had rendered them blind to the plainest dictates of justice and common-sense.

. . .

ALS; Kelley-Foster Collection, Worcester (Mass.) Historical Society (microfiche 71/1892).

To Sarah Shaw

Wayland [September? 1869]

Dear Sarah,

. . . Responsibility and a consciousness of independence is what women need. Their higher faculties remain dormant all their lives, for want of free exercise. Though tired of battling, I cannot keep my hands off "the woman question." It is decidedly the most important question that has been before the world. But I am vexed beyond measure with those New York women. They have tried hard to draw me into their Association.[1] They seem to have no discretion; no restraining grace; several things made me distrustful of their judgment, and I was afraid to venture, though my sympathies went with the *principles* they were seeking to advance. To think of Mrs. S[tanton]'s writing an editorial with the heading, "All Wise Women will oppose the 15th Amendment"![2] The most impardonable of all her doings, in *my* eyes. Short-sighted

---

[1] George Peabody (1795–1869), U.S. financier and philanthropist, contributed more than two million dollars to promote education in the South.
[1] The National Woman Suffrage Association.
[2] Stanton and Anthony opposed both the Fourteenth and the Fifteenth amendments because they specifically disfranchised women by introducing the adjective *male* to qualify *suffrage* in the Constitution. In this transcription of Child's letter, Stanton's name was left a blank.

indeed, at *this* time, to seek to set up one principle by trampling on another! Surely we ought to have learned, by this time, that the rights of one class of people can never be secured by taking away the rights of another. In Kansas she showed a willingness to compromise with the Democrats, and give up negro suffrage, if they would favor female suffrage. The trouble is, women are only partially *developed* by reason of adverse influences for ages; just as it is with the colored race; and the consequence is, that the talented among them are usually prone "to carry too much sail for their ballast." Time will doubtless set it all right. It will take a great deal of *it*, and therefore it is all the more necessary to make a *beginning*. I intend to do what I can, *individually*, for the elevation of women; but I confess to feeling a little skittish about incurring responsibility for what they may do in *associated* movement. Perhaps the feeling is wrong, but I cannot quite free myself from it since Mrs. [Stanton]'s developments. How ashamed I was to have George Francis Train an accredited leader of the movement! . . .

L; Lydia Maria Child Papers, Anti-Slavery Collection, Cornell University (microfiche 72/1909).

To Harriet Sewall

Wayland, Oct 24th, 1869

Dear Friend,

I was indeed sorry to hear of your poor state of health. I was unaware of it, till Eliza Scudder alluded to it in a letter received the day before yours. I know nothing of "The Movement Cure." I am a great believer in movement; but I don't believe *any*thing does much good that is done *merely* for health. It makes me groan to hear of people swinging dumb-bells for exercise, when there is so much wood to be cut, and grass to be mowed, and stone-wall to be laid, and it is so difficult to find anybody to do it. I believe it is an unalterable law of our being that moral and mental health depend upon constant usefulness. Walking out into infinite space, merely for exercise, does not do either body or mind a thousandth part the good that it does to start off on some errand of business or beneficence. I have a great horror of public institutions for invalids. If I found myself among a set of incurables, I am sure I should lose the balance of my mind. I can tend upon the sick without losing either patience or cheerfulness. I even found pleasure in the performance of many offices for my aged father, which were in themselves very disagreeable; but to be a *spectator* in a congregation of sufferers would drive *me* wild; and I am sure it can not be good for a person whose nerves are in such a sensitive state as yours are.

You ask if I cannot spare you a little of my "roundness and energy." I do indeed wish I knew how to impart some of it to you. I would go through any Herculean labor to accomplish it, if it were possible.

The continuance of my health and energy I believe is mainly owing to the fact that almost every hour of my life is usefully employed; and that I cannot help putting all my soul into whatever I undertake, whether it is making pudding or patch-work, writing an article, or dressing a doll. This morning I have been at work in my garden, might and main, setting out great roots and digging up great roots. My lame foot complained loudly; but I said, "Ache or no ache, I am going to have my roots well set before the ground freezes." If I had called my good mate from his work, he would gladly have helped me; but he don't know where my multifarious roots are, and nine chances out of ten he would have done mischief. And as for my foot, it aches most of the time, whether I use it or not. You ask whether lemonade fails to keep rheumatism in check. Neither lemonade nor anything else can prevent the inroads of old age. At present, I am stoical under its advances, and hope I shall remain so. I have but one prayer at heart; and that is, to have my faculties so far preserved that I can be useful, in *some* way or other, to the last.   As for understanding the ways of Providence, I gave up trying, long ago. I see no way of solving the mysteries of this strange existence, except by regarding it as preparatory to another; and even with *that* explanation, the fate of some individuals remains an inexplicable riddle.

. . .

ALS; Robie-Sewall Papers, Massachusetts Historical Society (microfiche 72/1913).

In January 1870 Child went to Boston for a gathering of antislavery veterans. She also attended the founding meeting of the Massachusetts Woman Suffrage Association. Mary Livermore (1820–1905), from Chicago, became editor of the association's weekly, *Woman's Journal.*

To Eliza Scudder

Wayland, Feb. 6'th 1870

Dear Eliza,

. . .

I was right down vexed after I parted from you at the Depot; but, in the course of half an hour, I subsided into my long-established habit of "accepting the situation;" and finally I was glad that the accident happened; for it gave me an opportunity to hear Mrs. Livermore, at the Women's Convention. She is the most electrifying speaker I have heard for many a long year. She has a good deal of argumentative power, she introduces many little humorous anecdotes and illustrations, which contrast well with touches of genuine pathos, and even of sublimity. Mrs. Howe talks sensibly and philosophically, and her manner is lady-like and dignified; but the strait jacket of propriety, with which "elegant society" invested her in her youth, fetters the freedom of her soul.[1] Mrs. Livermore is the product of the untramelled West. I have an increasing desire to keep out of the way of *society*, which always seems to me like an enemy lying in wait to catch me and impound me, or get me into an elegant harness. So I glance at it till it comes near me, than I snort, kick up my heels at it, and scamper away. I always was rather coltish in this respect, and I think I grow wilder, rather than tamer, with years.

. . .

. . . *Reform* always seems something *outside* of me, something belonging to the *external* of my life; but the *love of beauty* is my *inmost*. It is a comfort to believe that when we pass into another sphere of being, if *any*thing remains of us, it must be the *inmost*. If so, my life hereafter will be love of *beauty* and love of *use*. . . .

. . .

When I told Mrs. Stanton that I wanted to shake Gerrit Smith, she replied good-humoredly, "Let's you and I go next summer, and shake him." Poor man! If *two* such "strong minded women" should shake him, he would be dreadfully riled.

Good bye, dear. Your affectionate friend, L. M. Child.

ALS; Lydia Maria Child Papers, Anti-Slavery Collection, Cornell University (microfiche 72/1926).

On the trip to Boston for the gathering of antislavery workers, Child heard many reports of violent attacks on freedmen and their white allies. By 1867 the Ku Klux Klan and other secret organizations had combined their terror in an attempt to destroy Radical Reconstruction. They used business pressure, vote buying, the lash, the torch, and the gun to crush the blacks and their white associates.

To Lucy Osgood

Wayland, Feb. 14'th, 1870.

My dear and honored friend,

. . .

The meeting of "the old Anti Slavery champions" was very far from being such an "ovation" as you suppose. The colored people and the loyal white people of the South, write us too many letters describing their persecutions and their dangers, and imploring us to stand by them, and say that *for* them

[1] Julia Ward Howe (1819–1910), author of "Battle Hymn of the Republic," was president of the Massachusetts association.

which they dare not say for themselves. The Southerners are no worse than other men, excepting so far as the long training of a system of violence has made them so. But I agree with Mr. Phillips and Mr. Sumner in thinking it wrong to leave the poor ignorant, timid freedmen to the tender mercies of their former masters. A very large number of those masters are determined to exterminate the colored race, rather than live on terms of civil equality with them. You would be astonished to know how many murders have been committed, and are still being committed every week. The loyal people in Virginia, white and black, have been writing to Mr. Sumner, "For mercy's sake, keep Virginia out. As soon as she has power to drive off our teachers, she will do it; and neither our property nor our lives will be safe." Walker the Gov. of Virginia, as quoted by Mr. Sumner, openly and defiantly manifests a perfectly murderous spirit toward resident Yankees, loyal Virginians, and the system of free schools. No, there is no time for "ovations." You described Mr. Phillips perhaps better than you intended, when you alluded to his "Cassandra tones"; for what Cassandra prophesied always came *true*. I was delighted with your tribute to my hero of heroes, Charles Sumner. I confess that I well nigh worship him. This arises from no partisan feeling. It arises from the fact that I have never read of, or known, any man who uniformly had such clearness of moral vision, and such earnest stedfastness in following it.   William and Ellen Crafts are very remarkable people. I send you a copy of the "Freedmen's Book,["] that you may read their romantic history. With funds that they have gathered in England and Boston, they are going to purchase land in their native state of Georgia, and collect a Colony of Freedmen, establish Industrial Schools, and, other Schools, Lyceum, Libraries, &c. They are very intelligent, perfectly upright, and have great prudence and business-faculty. I think they will do a great and good work, provided the devilish Ku Klux Klan does not murder them.[1]   I don't remember whether I sent you a copy of my "Freedmen's Book." It is adapted to *their* comprehension, not to *yours;* but you may find somebody to whom it will be useful, after you have looked it over. I prepared it, in order to stimulate and cheer the poor freedmen; and since it was first published, five years ago, I have expended one thousand two hundred dollars in getting it distributed among them, by help of the various Freedmen's Aid Societies. Their wages have been so very low, and so badly paid, that the poor creatures could not buy it, as I hoped they would, to some extent. . . .

. . .

ALS; Lydia Maria Child Papers, Anti-Slavery Collection, Cornell University (microfiche 72/1928).

[1] In 1869, back from England, the Crafts went to Georgia to manage the Southern Industrial School and Labor Enterprise on a plantation bought by Boston abolitionists and philanthropists. The freedmen attended vocational and agricultural classes and worked in the fields, saving their wages to buy land for themselves. When the Klan burned the crops and buildings in 1871, the Crafts rebuilt the school. They conducted it until 1878, when they sold tracts to the freedmen and returned to Boston.

Early in 1870 Stanton and Anthony made a six-week tour of the Midwest, encouraging new women to come into the ranks of woman suffrage groups. A local suffrage group was started in Iowa.

To the Advocates of Woman's Suffrage in Iowa

Wayland, Mass'ts, May 30'th, 1870

To the Advocates of Woman's Suffrage in Iowa,

So much has been well said and well written on "The Woman Question," that there seems little or nothing to be added. But the spirit prompts me to thank you heartily for coming forward at this time to help in the great and good work of promoting perfect equality, in all respects, between men and women. I consider it the most important of all questions ever presented to the consideration of the civilized world. The condition and character of woman would be immeasurably improved by habits of thinking and acting on subjects of grave responsibility; but men would be still more benefitted by the change. No domestic happiness is to be compared with that which results from the wife's capacity to sympathize with all the pursuits of her husband, whether in Art, science, literature, business, or politics. It was this perfect companionship of mind, as well as heart, that blessed the life of John Stuart Mill, and gave that noble man so high an idea of the capabilities of woman.[1] Men are not generally aware what high pleasures and important aid they lose by those customs of society which render wives, daughters, and sisters, either mere domestic drudges, or dressed-up dolls of fashion. If the effects of woman's subordination could be fairly shown by statistics, there would be a startling exhibition of loss to mankind, in every direction; in maternal guidance, in domestic and social companionship, and helpfulness in every department of business; to say nothing of the immense injury it does to the *moral* tone of society, which is everywhere more or less high in proportion to the elevation of woman toward that perfect partnership with man, for which the Creator designed her.

That a majority of women do not wish for any important change in their social and civil condition, merely proves that they are the unreflecting slaves of custom. It is to be presumed that in no Asiatic country could a majority of women be found who would vote to adopt European customs. To walk or ride unveiled in the streets, among men, would seem to them both dangerous and depraved; and the idea of having any voice in the selection of their husbands would be regarded by them as utterly shameless. They have been brought up so, and they are totally unconscious of what they have lost by the systematic

[1] John Stuart Mill (1806–73) had advocated in Parliament the rights of women. His *Subjection of Women* (London, 1869) was written in collaboration with his wife, Harriet.

stifling of their souls. But if you would form an estimate of what Asiatic women would gain by living under a freer system of developement, you merely need to compare the ignorant, stupid, listless women of the harems with the intelligent and capable wives and mothers of New England and the West.

It is one of the most deplorable results of a subjugated condition that it renders its victims so accustomed to their limitations and disadvantages, that they see no need of change, till they are roused from their lethargy by the appeals of a few more thoughtful and observing than the mass; and even then, the suggestion seems to them impolitic and impracticable. When Frederic (surnamed the Great by courtesy of history) proclaimed emancipation to the serfs of Prussia, many of them petitioned *not* to be emancipated. They were used to serfdom, and it had never occurred to them that freedom would be better. Very likely, they thought only of some indulgences, privileges, and exemptions, to which they had been accustomed as serfs, and which seemed to them preferable to the exercise of rights involving responsibilities. A majority of women have never had their thoughts directed toward the limitations and disadvantages of their position in the social system. It was a cunning stroke of policy in the men of Vermont to make haste and take their vote before they had time and opportunity to become awake on the subject.[2] The grand daughters will reverse the decision of their grand mothers.

I am glad to see that you are trying to waken the sleepers in Iowa. On all questions of progress, I hope and expect much from the great free West. Yours for the unshackled exercise of every faculty by every human being.

L. Maria Child.

ALS; Friends Historical Library, Swarthmore College (microfiche 73/1947).

Joseph Dugdale (1810–96), of Iowa, was a Quaker farmer and reformer.

To Joseph Dugdale

[30 May 1870]

Friend Dugdale,

I have a very pleasant recollection of our talk together, many years ago, at Friend Hopper's,[1] and since then I have often welcomed your name in connection with some good word or work. Though a good deal hurried with occupations, I have written a few words to express the fullness of my sympathy with the friends of Woman's Suffrage in Iowa and my earnest hope that their efforts may be crowned with success.

On the subject of Peace my sentiments have known no change, except a

---

[2] A state constitutional convention had that month voted 231 to 1 against a woman suffrage amendment.

[1] The home of Isaac T. Hopper.

deepening conviction of the wickedness, barbarism, and insane foolishness of war. The world will be slow in outgrowing it; but it *must* be that the progress of civilization will eventually abolish the cruel and demoralizing custom. To say nothing of the *morality* of war, as a mere question of *common sense*, it is the most absurd thing imaginable. Take away the "fuss and feathers," look at it aside from the dazzling tinsel of military glory, and what does it amount to in reality? Thousands of men, in obedience to the arbitrary orders of their rulers, stand up, rank and file, to shoot off each other's heads, legs, and arms, with the assumption that whichever can blow into fragments the greatest number of human bodies proves ⟨that the . . .[1] right on⟩ the right is on that side. Not one in a hundred of the soldiers knows what he is fighting for. Generally, the awful massacre and mutilation is done merely in blind obedience to orders, or from senseless enthusiasm for some ⟨selfish⟩ conqueror like Bonaparte, the dazzle of whose success seems to reflect glory on themselves. Even in those wars where a *principle* is involved, how few among the thousands of human machines employed in it have the least comprehension of it!

It is assumed that war settles questions of right; but the plain truth is, that nothing is ever settled by physical force. The settling has to be done afterward, by mutual treaties and laws; and it would be wiser, and cheaper, and far more kindly, to settle disputes in *that* way, with the omission of the monstrous prelude of blowing out one another's brains.

War is so manifestly discordant with the Christian religion, that I should suppose candid minds must necessarily reduce discussion to the one question whether the precepts of Christianity on this subject are *practicable*, or not. For myself, I regard them as prophetic of the highest attainments of human nature; and I deem it a duty to urge them on the attention of mankind, as one of the most efficient methods of helping the fulfilment of that high prophecy, "Peace on earth and good will toward men."

I reciprocate the kindly greeting of your "dear Ruth," and am very cordially your friend,

L. Maria Child

ALS; Friends Historical Library, Swarthmore College (microfiche 73/1948).

To Charles Sumner

Wayland, July 4'th, 1870.

Dear and Honored Mr. Sumner,

. . .

. . . I was sorry you favored Mrs. Lincoln's appeal for a pension. In the first place, I think the pensioning system ought to be very jealously guarded;

[1] Two words are cancelled and unrecovered.

493

there being great liability to abuses dangerous to our republican institutions. In the second place, Mrs. Lincoln already has property enough to live in as much style as the widow of a Republican President *ought* to live. In the third place, she is not a worthy recipient of national honors and bounties. All through the war, her influence was a drag on the movements of her husband, who was quite slow enough *without* a drag. Why should people be taxed to enrich a woman who vied with the Empress Eugenie in extravagant dressing, at a time when the country was exhausting all its resources to defend the existence of the government? a woman who sent pistols to Kentucky Rebels, and listened at the doors of State apartments, to obtain secret information to send to them? She ought to consider herself lucky that reverence for her husband's memory shields her from public execration.[1]

I thank you for your Speech on Post Office regulations. . . .[2]

. . . We have paid enormous tribute to *Slavery* in the form of Post Office expenses, as well as in other ways. That miserable system rendered small farms, owned by those who tilled them, an impossibility, and prevented the formation of villages, by dividing the land into large plantations, many miles apart. Gen. Jackson laid down the law that the mail ought to be carried, at the public expense, "to the door of every agriculturist; that *best* portion of the American population." Of course, this was intended for the especial benefit of the South; such an arrangement being quite unnecessary at the North, where farmers were clustered together in villages. He dignified the lazy, spendthrift *planters* in the South with the name of *"agriculturists"*; totally ignoring the fact that their laborers, the *real* agriculturists, who tilled the soil and produced the crops, were forbidden by law to read or write, and consequently were as little benefitted as their masters' swine by the transmission of the mails. Who had to pay for carrying a single letter through miles and miles of swamp and forest? The Free States, of course. "Issachar was a strong Ass, couching down between burdens."
Years before the war, Mr. Child used to make calculations concerning the amount of taxation on the North to carry letters and papers to the isolated plantations of the South; and the sum he made out was much larger than would have been believed. It would be a curious item of statistics if one could ascertain what proportion of the letters were from slave-traders and slave-catchers. In how many ways did this people pay perpetual tribute to Slavery, without being aware of it!

In your Speech, you say: "The oppressiveness of a tax is not to be measured by the insensibility of the people on whose shoulders it is laid. It is a curiosity of despotism that the people are too often *unconscious* of their slavery, as they

---

[1] In 1870 Congress granted Mrs. Lincoln an annual pension of three thousand dollars later raised to five thousand. Mrs. Lincoln was the target of charges of disloyalty and treachery, often levelled by Radical Republicans. No evidence supports the accusations.
[2] Sumner was pressing for a lower, one-cent postage rate to aid education and diffuse knowledge.

are *unconscious* also of bad laws. A wise and just government measures its duties, not by what the people *bear* without a murmur, but by what is most for their *welfare*."

My dear Mr. Sumner, is not the same remark applicable to the assertion that the elective franchise ought not to be bestowed on women till a majority of them require it?[3] I have been often urged to write to you on this subject; but I have forborne, because I thought your shoulders had sufficient weight to carry, strong and willing as they are. Moreover, when I have perfect confidence in the moral and intellectual insight of a man, I am not desirous to hurry his conclusions. You are so organized that I know you cannot help following *principles*, whithersoever they may lead. Therefore, sooner or later, you will see that the republican ideas you advocate so earnestly cannot be consistently carried out while women are excluded from a share in the government.   I reduce the argument to very simple elements. I pay taxes for property of my own earning and saving; and "taxation without representation" seems to me obviously unjust. As for representation by *proxy*, that savors too much of the *plantation*-system, however kind the masters may be. I am a human being and I hold that every human being has a right to a voice in the laws, by which he may be taxed, imprisoned, or hung. The exercise of *rights* always has a more salutary effect on character, than the enjoyment of *privileges*. Any class of human beings to whom a position of perpetual subordination is assigned, however much they may be petted, must inevitably be dwarfed morally and intellectually. For forty years, I have keenly felt the cramping effects of my limitations as a woman, and I have submitted to them under a perpetual and indignant protest. It is too late for the subject to be of much interest to me personally. I have walked in fetters thus far, and my pilgrimage is drawing to a close. But I see so clearly that domestic life and public life would both be greatly ennobled by the perfect equality and companionship of men and women, in *every* department of life, that I long to have it an accomplished fact, for the order and well-being of the world.

I have not seen your reasons for opposing the annexation of St Domingo, but it is one of the things for which I thank you.[4] There is great need of checking the insane rage for annexation in this country; and in this case I am particularly glad to have it checked, because I deem it exceedingly dangerous to add anything to the weight of Roman Catholic influence. Of course, I have no wish to interfere with theological doctrines. I would guard the right of every man to be as superstitious as he pleases, whether the form be Protestant or Catholic; conceiving that I have done all my duty by securing to him a full and fair chance

[3] In 1866 Sumner had voted against an amendment giving women the suffrage, saying it was "one of the great questions of the future which will be easily settled whenever the women in any considerable proportion insist that it shall be settled."
[4] Sumner opposed Grant's attempt to annex Santo Domingo, believing that it would involve the United States in empire-building.

to become more enlightened. But danger lies in the fact that the Roman Catholic Church, in its spirit and its form, is utterly antagonistic to republican institutions. Its existence depends on the masses being kept in ignorance, that they may be blindly led by an ambitious and crafty hierarchy. It is a great misfortune that this element has become so mixed up with our *politics*. Circumstances have made the protection of the colored race an instinct of self-preservation with the Republican Party. The Democratic Party are, and always have been, ready to compromise *any* principle of freedom for the sake of securing and retaining the Irish vote; and the Irish hate the negroes and their protectors. I believe the Roman priesthood, and the Catholic powers of Europe, wish, and expect, to undermine our free institutions by means of the influence of Catholic voters, who, under their guidance, will go to the death to maintain the infallibility of the Pope in *politics*, as readily as they would to maintain his infallibility in *religious* matters. The whole history of the Irish, from the first conquest of their island down to the last Fenian expedition to Canada, shows that they are very deficient in the qualities most essential to military success; but they are brutal fighters, and unscrupulous in their modes of vengeance. What they lack is leaders; and those would be furnished by that unprincipled class of American politicians, who sold themselves to slaveholders for the sake of the loaves and fishes in their gift, and who would be equally ready to serve the purposes of the Roman Catholic priesthood, if their party could thereby again control the government and secure a monopoly of offices. How can the Democratic Party do otherwise than sympathize with the Pope, when he was the only European Power that ventured upon open recognition of the Southern Confederate government? His Cardinals well understood the game they were playing, when they advised him to make that move. The question of the Bible in schools is an entering wedge to try their strength for further experiments in splitting the pillars of our Republican edifice. I have for years anxiously watched this cloud lowering on the horizon. I see that it continually grows larger and blacker. Mr. Child thinks I greatly exaggerate the importance of this subject. He says the Puritan element would find no difficulty in overpowering any attempt at Catholic usurpation. But the trouble is, the process will be insidious and undermining. The sacred name of religious freedom will be made to serve the vilest political purposes. It seems to me that no other danger to our free institutions is to be compared with this in magnitude. I think there is a great deal of suppressed feeling on this subject. The sharp altercation in Congress concerning an ambassador to Rome, is a little escape of steam, indicating how furiously the covered cauldron is boiling. The perfect *party* division on the subject was very significant.

. . .

Dear Mr. Sumner, is it possible to remedy the mischievous effects of our impolitic and wicked course toward the Indians? If we had *wished* to make them paupers and vagabonds, we could not have taken more effectual means to accomplish it than we have done. I have no romantic feelings about the Indians. On the contrary, I have to struggle with considerable repugnance toward them;

and something of the same feeling I have toward all *fighters*. War, even in its best aspects, is a barbarism; and sooner or later, the world will outgrow it. But though my efforts for the Indians are mere duty-work, I do it as earnestly, as I should if they were a people more suited to my taste. They have been, and are, outrageously wronged and there is abundant proof that they are as capable as other human beings of being developed into noble manhood by just and kindly influences. Gen. Grant has fairly gained my heart by his wise and humane course toward them.[5] I did not expect it, of a military man. In fact, Gen. Grant makes a much better President than I thought he would. If I could vote, I should vote for his re-election unless *you* were a candidate.

What a long letter! Pardon me for the long intrusion.

I thank you for the garden-seeds. They came up; which seed from Washington are not apt to do. Mr. Child unites with me in heartfelt blessings on Charles Sumner.

Yours with profoundest respect and gratitude,

L. Maria Child.

ALS; Houghton Library, Harvard University (microfiche 73/1951).

To John Greenleaf Whittier

Wayland, July 31st, 1870.

Dear Friend Whittier,

. . .

I was vexed with Henry Wilson for not standing by Charles Sumner in his efforts to have the word *white* stricken out of the Naturalization Bill. The fact is, Wilson is an ingrained demagogue. He wants to curry favor with the Anti-*Chinese* party.[1] I dislike and despise this petty "Native American" feeling. God kept this continent hidden for centuries, to make it a High School for all the nations. Let us fulfil the glorious mission, and be thankful. I welcome the Chinese. Their industry and patience will prove a blessing to this country. Let them build temples to Buddha, if they like. They would be scarcely more foreign to our thoughts and feelings than Altars to the Virgin Mary.

Yours with true respect and affection,

L. Maria Child.

ALS; Child Papers, Manuscript Division, Library of Congress (microfiche 74/1954).

[5] Under Grant, a Board of Indian Affairs, the administrators of which were often corrupt, was created and placed within the Department of Interior. The federal government began a program of enforced acculturation of the Native Americans: they were penned into reservations, shifted about at the whim of bureaucrats, starved, intimidated, and persecuted.

[1] "The Chinese Must Go!" had become a national rallying cry by this time. Both political parties, the labor movement, and even radicals like Wendell Phillips supported exclusion of the Chinese.

To Anna (Loring) Dresel

Wayland, Jan. 25th, 1871.
You Darling, Precious Child!
 . . . What you write about the German war expresses my sentiments exactly.[1] I think Wendell Phillips, and others, are blinded by the name of a Republic; and it is a mere *name;* for the French Provisional Government is just as much a *coup d'état* as the Empire was. They never have taken the vote of the people, and they are determined *not* to take it. They go on slaughtering the poor misguided masses, merely from pride of their old military prestige. They forced Prussia to *begin* the war, and they force her to *continue* it. Vanity and rage makes them insane. It is another application of the ancient saying: "Whom the gods will destroy, they first make mad." And really, from the beginning of the war, there has seemed to be the hand of Destiny in it. France has filled up, and overflowed, her measure of spoliation and robbery, and now (by the slow but sure laws of the Universal Providence) her hour of retribution has come. It provokes me to hear people say, "I took sides with Prussia at first, but I feel differently now they have *invaded* France."

Just so the English, and our own copperheads, talked when we took Richmond and Charleston. Even Lord John Russell said, "The North is fighting for empire, the South for independence." They coolly ignored the fact that the *existence* of our government was at stake, and that we had no alternative but to bombard Charleston, or have New York bombarded. France and Prussia are in a similar relative position now; and Germany can justly say of the present contest what Körner said of their resistance to the robbery and tyranny of the *First* Napoleon:

> " 's ist ja kein Kampf für die Güter
> der Erde; Das *Heiligste* schützen
> wir mit dem Schwerte."[2]

It has made me shudder to read of the intense cold in Europe; and when I read of wounded soldiers freezing to death it made me cry out with anguish. Oh, the horrid barbarism of war! When *will* the nations consent to a wiser way of proceeding? Never, while such aggressive neighbors as the French are among them. I long for a strong, United Germany. As the States will all send Representatives to the General Diet, an important step will be gained for popular rights; and I believe it will do more for the progress of human freedom, than

[1] The Franco-Prussian War had begun on 19 July 1870.
[2] "It is not a battle for the goods of the earth; the most holy things we protect with the sword."

any Republic they will ever get up in France. There is no basis in French *character* for a Republic to rest upon; but the Germans are granite pillars.

. . .

ALS; Loring Family Papers, Schlesinger Library, Radcliffe College (microfiche 74/1972).

To Thomas Wentworth Higginson

Wayland, Feb. 21st 1871.

Friend Higginson,

I thank you heartily for your pamphlet on "The Sympathy of Religions." I always like what you write; which I consider to be a sign that I am in a very healthy state of mind. But I was very particularly pleased with the aforesaid pamphlet. Such largeness of thought and of sympathy, so much learning so eloquently uttered, are rarely found. I think he is the greatest benefactor of the world, at the present day, who helps men to outgrow the sectarianism of Christianity.

Perhaps you will be tempted to ask, "Since you say you always like what I write, pray tell me how you liked my biography of yourself."[1]

To tell you the plain truth, friend Higginson, I have never read a single word of it. I have never been able to get up the courage to do it. To read my own biography seems too much like being dissected before I am dead. I have always been talking, more or less, to the public; but I have never talked about *myself*. And I am strangely sensitive about any *personal* introduction to the public. I do not pretend to defend this state of feeling; but it exists, and I cannot get rid of it.

That recalls to my memory how my exclusiveness was disturbed by your wishing to read my letters as a help to writing my biography.

How should you like to have me *leave* you my letters, as a *legacy?* I have written a great many, all improvisations, and forgotten as soon as written. I don't know whether the public would take any interest in *any* of them. It is barely possible that enough might be selected from them to make a small volume that would have a moderate sale. If so, I should like to have you edit them, and after taking reasonable compensation for your trouble, devote any sum that be left to the "Free Religious Association," or any other Association of similar purpose and tendency.[2]

[1] Higginson's sketch "Lydia Maria Child" was published in *Eminent Women of the Age*.
[2] Higginson did not receive her letters. In her will Child, among many other bequests, left $1,000 to the Free Religious Association, and her effects to her niece, Sarah M. Parsons. The text of the will is in Helene G. Baer, *The Heart Is Like Heaven* (Philadelphia, 1964), appendix.

———

It would be a pleasant thought to me that I could thus continue to help a little the cause of truth and freedom, when the hand that now obeys the impulse of my mind shall have become ashes.

Always yours, with cordial respect and affection,

L. Maria Child.

ALS; Anti-Slavery Collection, Rare Books and Manuscripts, Boston Public Library (microfiche 75/1982).

To George W. Julian

Wayland, July 12'th, 1871.

Dear Mr. Julian,

I send you an Introduction to your volume,[1] which I hope will prove satisfactory. It has at least the merit of being sincere. I wrote it *con amore*, from a heart full of gratitude for the public services you have rendered. If I have made any mistakes in dates, or misunderstood your position at any time, you can alter it by the erasure or addition of *words;* but where my name is appended to an article, I do not like to have any other than very *slight* and absolutely *necessary* alterations. I did not enter into a recapitulation of the Speeches, or into any analysis of them; because I feared it would be tedious. It would do well for an electioneering document, or for a newspaper article, to enter into such particulars; but readers are very impatient of prolix Prefaces to books.

I beg you will not speak of any compensation to me. I am sufficiently paid by what you are doing for the cause of Woman. Beside, I consider that I am not conferring a favor on *you*, but am rendering some service to the cause of *freedom*, in my small way.

Your views are similar to my own on most subjects; but there is one point on which I differ from you. My sympathies go very thoroughly and warmly with the working-men; but I consider the "eight hour law" an unjust and unwise measure.[2] For one party to a bargain to fix his own price on what he has to sell, and to fix it above the market value, and to attempt to *compel* the other party, by *legal force*, to pay it, seems to me to have an element of tyranny in it. Moreover, it is *useless* to attempt to regulate the value of money, or of labor, by legislation. There is an eternal law of supply and demand, by which they *will* keep returning to their level, whatever may be done to prevent it. In England, in France, and in Spain, government has, at different periods, tried to

[1] Julian's *Speeches on Political Questions* (New York, 1872).
[2] Not until the Fair Labor Standards Act of 1938 was an eight-hour law established. An eight-hour day for federal government employees had been established in 1868. But it and similar state laws were full of loopholes that made them impossible to enforce.

alter the price of money; to meet some emergency, they have passed a law that a ten cent piece should pass for a twenty cent piece. What was the result? The next day, every article in the market doubled its price. So the level of things was the same as before the law was passed.

It will be just so with any legal attempt to raise the value of labor above its level. If the eight hour law prevails, people will hire by the hour, and pay accordingly; and if they find difficulty in that, they will diminish their business. *Farms* cannot be carried on upon the eight-hour system. The fact is, government ought not to meddle at all with the price of either money or labor. They *will* find their own level; and any attempt to change it, merely produces confusion in business.

The only way of harmonizing the conflicting claims of Labor and Capital is to institute a system of *co-partnerships* between Labor and Capital, in all branches of business.

It may seem audacious for a little old woman of seventy to speak so authoritatively on a big subject, to a big man. But I am like you, in one respect; I form opinions decisively, on what seems to me sufficient grounds, and then I stick to them pertinaciously.

Please have my name printed as I have written it on the M.S. Introduction.

Please give my best regards to Mrs. Julian. She will see that I attended to the suggestion in her note.

Yours with great respect,
L. M. Child.

ALS; Joshua Giddings Papers, Manuscript Division, Library of Congress (microfiche 76/2003).

To Francis Shaw

Wayland, Oct. 21'st, 1871

My very Dear Friend,

. . .

The terrible disaster at Chicago excited and absorbed all my sympathies, as it did yours.[1] But it is pleasant to have so much proof that the great human family are becoming more and more like brethren. When London was so nearly destroyed by fire, the cities of the earth were almost strangers to each other. Now, if one city is ravaged by fire or pestilence, all the other cities are thrilled with sympathy. Even this sluggish little town of Wayland called a meeting, and is contributing to the sufferers more liberally than is their wont on such occasions.

[1] The Chicago Fire broke out on 8 Oct. 1871 and lasted twenty-four hours; there were more than 250 deaths, 98,500 people left homeless, 17,450 dwellings consumed, and a property loss of $200 million.

My first thought, on reading of the terrible disaster was that the fire *could* not have spread with such astonishing rapidity, so early in the night, unless incendiaries were at work with petroleum. I believe that such *was* the case; and that the incendiaries were Ku Klux, from Kentucky.[2] Hence, *another* fire took in another part of the city, and, as is now ascertained, a false cause for it was rumored; and forty men were found setting fires. I should like to know whether those forty men were residents in Chicago. I think it will turn out that they were Ku Klux. Up to this time, notwithstanding all we have suffered, very few at the North realize what a desperate, reckless, malignant set of villains are engendered by the institution of slavery. A large class at the South hate the North for its prosperity, and would gladly destroy it, without scruples as to the means.

I have but one fault to find with Gen. Grant's administration; and that is, that for the sake of conciliating these men of violence, he has allowed them to ride rough-shod over the peaceful citizens of the South.[3] I would not have had any undue severity, but I *would* have had the laws so firmly sustained and vigorously administered, that innocent men could not be murdered in their beds with impunity. It is a cruel mockery to turn such murderers over to the *civil* law, when the civil officers are themselves accomplices of the Ku Klux.

Harper's ingenuity in showing up "The Ring" seems absolutely inexhaustible. But *will* justice finally prevail? It is a herculean job to clean out the stables where such beasts have congregated. As for Nast, I have long been in love with the wonderful talent he uses for such excellent purposes.[4]

. . .

ALS; Houghton Library, Harvard University (microfiche 76/2014).

Hampton Institute, a nonsectarian, coeducational school for blacks, was opened in Virginia in 1868. It was founded by the American Missionary Society to train teachers and farmers, and Stephen Salisbury (1798–1884), a civic leader in Worcester, Massachusetts, became one of its chief patrons. Child supported the school and in her will left it two thousand dollars.

[2] There was no evidence found that the Klan had started the fire.
[3] Appeals to Grant for federal intervention against the Klan brought little relief. In Apr. 1871 Congress passed the Ku Klux Klan Act, empowering the president to declare martial law when secret organizations were deemed in rebellion against the United States. A joint congressional committee held hearings in the South that summer on the counter-Reconstruction violence.
[4] The *New York Times* began editorial attacks on Tweed rule in New York City in 1870, and both the *Times* and *Harper's Weekly* published Thomas Nast's powerful political cartoons against the Tweed Ring.

To Stephen Salisbury

Wayland, Jan. 13'th, 1872.

Mr. Salisbury,
Dear Sir,

Knowing the interest you take in the judicious, practical education of working-men, I send you a Report of the Hampton Normal Institute, to show you what they are doing in that line in Virginia. I think that Institute is the very best agency at work to improve the condition of the freedmen, and of all classes at the South.

It has the great advantage of combining *labor* with study, and of teaching intelligent *modes* of labor; a thing peculiarly needed at the South, where the wasteful system of Slavery gave birth to laziness and improvidence both in masters and slaves. I have seen a good many letters from the freedmen pleading for admission to the Institute for themselves or their children; and it is really quite touching to see how eager those poor people are for knowledge, and the means of self-support.

When you have read the Report, and the newspaper article appended to it, I will thank you to return them to me by mail.

Mr. Child has not been as well as usual for some weeks past, but is able to do much toward keeping our little nest comfortable. He desires to send you his affectionate and grateful remembrance.

Yours with great respect,
L. Maria Child.

ALS; Salisbury Family Papers, American Antiquarian Society (microfiche 77/2031*a*).

Victoria Woodhull (1838–1927) was a reformer whose advocacy of free love was being voiced in her muckraking paper, *Woodhull and Claflin's Weekly*, in the early 1870s. Stanton and Anthony invited her to address the 1871 National Woman Suffrage Association convention after they heard her speak to Congress claiming the right of woman suffrage under the Fourteenth and Fifteenth Amendments and urging appropriate legislation to ensure the right. As Child anticipated, the collaboration was a short-lived one. Anthony broke with her more theatrical coworker when she sensed that Woodhull was using the suffrage organization to further her own political ambitions. Woodhull ran for president in 1872.

To Lucy Osgood

Wayland, Feb. 12th, 1872.

My Dear and Honored Friend,

. . .

I do not know what Mrs. Stowe's views are on the "Woman Question"; so cannot tell whether she would satisfy me, or not.[1] My own faith on that subject may be summed up in very few words. I believe that every human being has a right to do whatsoever they can do *well;* and I believe that, for the good of the State, as well as for individual character, every human being ought to have a direct voice in the laws that govern them.

Mrs. Woodhull and her associates are a great blister to my spirit. They are doing immense harm to the real progress of women. It seems as if there must be a flaw in her brain. How else could she do such a preposterous thing as to personate Demosthenes?[2] Speaking of women, is it not wonderful how all the world seems to be moving on that question? Did you notice that the Pasha of Egypt has established a school for girls at Cairo?[3] What is more, he *compels* the officials of his government to send their daughters for two years, to be instructed on European subjects after the European manner. After that, he stipulates that the girls shall be left free to choose whether they will veil themselves again and return to their former Egyptian modes of life, or not. Among the Mohammedans is a sect called The Bab, meaning The Gate, or Door. It appears to be a door that opens easily; for it is very courteous about letting in other religions, and urges that women should be educated, and go about as freely as men. The Brama-Somadj is pleading for the similar emancipation and enlightenment of Hindoo women. Assuredly, the Millerites will have to wait a while. The world cannot be destroyed just yet; there is too much going on that needs to be completed.

. . .

ALS; Lydia Maria Child Papers, Anti-Slavery Collection, Cornell University (microfiche 77/2038).

By the early 1870s popular support for Radical Reconstruction began to fade. The new state governments in the South, in which blacks as well as whites could participate, had made reforms. Helped by Northern abolitionists, missionaries, and teachers, the blacks proved their equality and demonstrated their strength

---

[1] In some of her writing at this time, Stowe satirized the "new woman"—suffragists like Stanton and Anthony, and such free-love advocates as Woodhull.
[2] Woodhull was a spiritualist; she claimed for her "control" the Athenian orator Demosthenes.
[3] Ismail, who had been ruling Egypt since 1863, was introducing many reforms.

and courage. Local leaders came up from the anonymity of slavery to become makers of laws and officers of government. But faced with bitter and unrelenting opposition, they had to lean on federal troops for support. As the years passed, the troops, never very many, were steadily withdrawn. In 1872 there were already signs that Northern Republicans were losing interest in Reconstruction and turning to other problems, while the Democratic party was steadily regaining its strength and power. On 1 May 1872, a group calling themselves the Liberal Republicans, reacting against Radical Reconstruction policies in the South, as well as against the corruption staining the Grant administration, put up Horace Greeley for president and B. Gratz Brown for vice-president on a platform of civil service reform. In July the Democrats would also pick Greeley to head their slate. The regular Republicans would renominate Grant, with Henry Wilson as his running mate. In her letters of the campaign period Child discusses the issues and candidates.

To Sarah Shaw

Wayland, May 20'th, 1872.

My Darling,

I *know* you had written last, and I thought many times about answering your kind letter; but I have been in an anxious and desponding state of mind; and when I write to you, I like to be like the sun-dial, which tells of no hours but those on which the sun shines. There has been nothing new, or very especial the matter; but old age creeps upon me, and I dreadfully need a friend; a practical, working-woman friend; and such a thing is not to be found in these days. This transition-period about Labor and Capital is an evil time for old people with small income. I think, and think, and think, but can devise no feasible plan to get a little rest and freedom for my old age; or even to get anybody to help me out of the world.

You ask what I think about the Presidential election. I don't take any very lively interest in it, any way; but I do *not* want Greely to be President. He has some estimable qualities, doubtless; but he is wofully deficient in many elements of character essential to such a responsible office. The man I should prefer above all others is Charles Sumner; a man of noble bearing, of high culture, of inflexible integrity, of singular clearness of moral vision, and great experience in public affairs. But that is out of the question. He is too far in advance of the public, for them to be able to realize his greatness. Next to him, I should prefer Colfax.[1]

But, of all those that have been *named* for the office, I prefer Gen. Grant. When he was first nominated, I had no enthusiasm about him, as you may

[1] In September, Schuyler Colfax, Grant's vice-president, would be accused of misconduct in the Crédit Mobilier scandal that tainted many prominent politicians. Although he escaped formal censure, his political career was ruined.

remember. In the first place, I did not approve the tendency of Republics to deify military heroes; and in the next place, I feared his well-known habits of intemperance.

But, since he has been President, he has shown great strength of character is resisting the temptations to strong drink; and he has not acted at all like a *military* man. So far from seeking fresh laurels of that kind, he has proved himself a sincere lover of peace. He has manifested a spirit of justice and impartiality toward the colored people, and his humane policy toward the Indians delighted me, as much as it surprised me, in a *military* man. I am also grateful for his efforts to diminish the national debt. In short, I think we cannot do better than choose him again. I am aware, of course, that Charles Sumner thinks differently; but as I don't *know* his reasons, I cannot be *influenced* by them.[2]

I thank you for Miss Sedgwick's Memoirs. I will return the volume when read, as it is not a kind of book I care to keep; cordial thanks to Mr. Curtis, all the same.[3] I agree with you in thinking that any person who *apologized* for Slavery must have been deficient in moral sense. That question was an excellent test of morality. But that was not the case with Miss Sedgwick. She sincerely wished well to the negroes, but she could not bear to *contend* for them, or for anything else. She was afraid of the subject. She was very deficient in moral *courage*. She was very kind to me; wrote me many letters, called to see me often, and frequently urged me to visit her at Stockbridge. But during the Anti Slavery battle, she cooled toward me. She was *afraid* of reformers.   I had a copy of "Hope Leslie," but, two or three years ago, I gave it to some of the numerous Libraries, which are always applying to me for contributions.[4] "The Rebels,"[5] I will send soon.

Thank you for the Venus of Milo. How kind it was for you to try to procure it for me! Indeed you are *always* kind. You have always been the brightest ray of sunshine in my life. Give my true love to your dear, good Frank. Give my love to Rosa, when you see her. She is a charming woman, an inborn lady. Your "delightful book about music" excites my curiosity.

What a charming story "Middlemarch" is![6]

Yours with a heart full of love. Maria.

. . .

ALS; Houghton Library, Harvard University (microfiche 78/2048).

[2] Sumner's strong criticism of some Grant policies—annexation of Santo Domingo, feeble resistance to the Klan, despotic control of the party—were taken as personal disloyalty by the president, who used his office to retaliate. Bitterness grew on both sides.
[3] *Life and Letters of Catharine M. Sedgwick*, ed. Mary E. Dewey (New York, 1871), appeared four years after Sedgwick's death, the book sent to Child by George William Curtis, the Shaws' son-in-law.
[4] This 1827 novel by Sedgwick was published in New York.
[5] Child's 1825 novel.
[6] George Eliot's novel was published in Edinburgh in 1871–72.

To Sarah Shaw

Wayland, July 13'th, 1872.

Darling Sarah,

. . .

As you say, in this strange jumble of political affairs, it is extremely difficult to keep one's mind evenly balanced. Mr. Sumner's letters to me increase
the difficulty.[1] He declares, with such calm, sad earnestness, that he is acting
from conscientious convictions that the good of the country requires him to
pursue the course he does.

Yet, he is obviously unjust; and I have, very respectfully, told him so. For
instance, he refuses to give Grant the slightest credit for his humane policy
toward the Indians; but curtly dismisses it as one of his "failures"; because the
"massacres on the frontier still continue."

I wrote to him that he appeared to forget the formidable "Indian-ring,"
of traders, agents, land-monopolizers, &c. whose *policy* it was to excite hatred
against the Indians, even to utter extermination. They have been determined
that the President's humane policy should *not* succeed; and for that purpose,
they have done all they could to goad the poor creatures to desperation, and
then they get that ruffianly Sheridan to declare that they must be put down
by force.[2] I wrote to Mr. Sumner that he seemed to me as unjust in charging
this state of things upon President Grant, as those were who charged the blame
of the civil war upon the *abolitionists*, when it resulted from the *slaveholders'*
determined efforts to frustrate their exertions to bring about *peaceful* emancipation. I asked him what other President had ever proved his humane intentions
by sending such officials among them as that excellent Gen. Howard, and the
Quaker Samuel Janney.[3]

But Grant's enemies vilify him just as much for the *good* things he has
done, as they do for the *wrong* things. I feel just as you do. The *injustice* they
do him excites an interest in my mind, that I should not otherwise feel. How
far this will *generally* be the effect produced by it, it is impossible to foretell.
My own conviction is that there is very great danger of Greely's being elected.
And, disguise it as they may, *his* being elected is the return of the *Democratic
Party* to power, and the adoption of their old policy. I wrote that to Charles
Sumner; and added: "If the Devil himself were at the helm of the Ship of State,

[1] Child and many of Sumner's old friends—among them, Whittier, Phillips, Curtis, and
Garrison—felt that Sumner's political judgment was distorted by the personal wrongs
he had suffered from Grant.
[2] Child held Gen. Philip Sheridan (who was commanding the Department of the West)
responsible for the war of attrition against the Indians.
[3] Gen. Oliver O. Howard, who served also as head of the Freedmen's Bureau, had been
sent West by Grant as intermediary between the Indians and the army. Janney was
probably the liberal Virginia Quaker Samuel McPherson Janney (1801–80), who was
active in education affairs.

my conscience would not permit me to aid in removing him to make room for the Democratic Party."

But how artful the Rebels and Democrats have shown themselves in their Baltimore platform! They have framed it so as to deceive, if possible, "the very elect." Every distinguishing trait of democracy is laid aside, and the mask of radical republicanism is assumed. It was a hard job for them, accustomed as they are to falsehood and trickery; but, for the sake of getting into power, they nerved themselves up to professing the very principles they hate. I think there is internal evidence that Sumner's hand was largely employed in constructing that platform; and perhaps he and others will think that an honest party can be built thereon. But the Rebels and Democrats have taken care to put in some loop-holes, through which they can creep out of all they have promised. They claim "self-government for the States"; which means the "State Sovereignty" for which the Rebels fought, and hope to fight again, if they cannot attain their end by political management; which they doubtless *would* do, with Greely for their tool. They demand that "the nation should *return* to methods of *peace*, and the supremacy of civil over military authority"; which means that when the Ku Klux renew their efforts to exterminate Republicans, white and black, they shall be dealt with by *Southern* civil authorities,—that is, by Judges and Jurors who are themselves members of the Ku Klux association. I verily believe this Republic is in more imminent peril now, than it was in 1861. Oh, *can* it be that all that blood and treasure was expended in vain? *Can* all that lofty patriotism and noble self-sacrifice come to nought? Oh, Sarah, my soul is full of fearful forebodings.

What a strange, unexpected tangle! Horace Greely, once a loud-spoken herald of freedom, now a tool in the hands of Southern despots, and their unprincipled allies the democrats! And Charles Sumner placed in such an equivocal position, that one cannot attempt to shield his honored name, ⟨with⟩ without appearing to aid the Democrats, who hate him so! I did not mean ever to trouble myself about the state of public affairs again; but this perilous crisis *does* trouble me, so that I can't sleep o'nights.

I have never forgiven the Republican Party, and I never *shall* forgive them, for humoring the vindictiveness of the President by consenting to Mr. Sumner's being turned out of the Committee of Foreign Relations.[4] Both the President and the Party *deserve* to be defeated for that unjust and mean proceeding. But I earnestly hope they will *not* be defeated; because, "with all their imperfections on their heads," they are the best bulwark we have against the re-flux of the tide of despotism.

But enough of politics!

You may return "The Rebels" some time, if you please; no matter when.

---

[4] Angered because Sumner helped defeat his attempt to annex Santo Domingo, Grant influenced the Senate to remove Sumner as chairman of the Foreign Relations Committee.

It belongs to Mr. Child, and he values it for the sake of "auld lang syne." You ask me if I like it. I really do not know. I would not read it, for a great deal. When I have just written anything, it always seems to me very good; but afterward, I get to dislike and despise it. I belong to the numerous class who can *conceive* of vastly better things than they can *do*.

"The Progress of Religious Ideas" is an exception to my rule. I have an increasing respect for *that*.

George Sand's Autobiography has *not* been translated.[5] It was to me a very attractive book. I agree with you in preferring English reading; but *she* writes such beautiful French, that I love to read it. I am afraid she was "no better than she should be"; but in her biography she does not gratify the curiosity of the public about her amours; if it be just to put them in the plural number.

. . .

. . . As for Vic. Woodhull and her sister, I wish they were abed and asleep.[6] They have done great mischief to the "Woman Question." *I* think they have a screw loose.

. . .

ALS; Houghton Library, Harvard University (microfiche 78/2055).

To Francis Shaw

Wayland, Aug. 15'th, 1872.

Dear Friend,

. . .

With regard to Charles Sumner, I have for years noticed that you and Sarah did not appreciate him so highly as I did; and I have often spoken of it with David. It has not been that I thought Mr. Sumner's intellect so preeminently superior to several others. His culture is by no means so various as that of many other minds. But, until this late strange obliquity, he has been superior to all of our public men in never departing from the straight line of *principle* to try the crooked paths of *expediency*, as a shorter cut to his object. I have lost my early faith in many things, but I have never for a moment doubted that *justice* is always the best *policy*. Wilson has been continually tempted aside into paths of temporary expediency.[1] He joined the "Native American" party, because he thought it was going to be powerful; though the idea on which it was based was entirely antagonistic to the principles of our government. He

---

[5] Sand's *Histoire de ma vie* (Paris, 1848–54).
[6] Woodhull's sister and coworker was Tennessee Claflin (1845–1923).
[1] Although Henry Wilson was implicated in the Crédit Mobilier scandal, he remained on Grant's ticket and was elected vice-president.

opposed granting Suffrage to the Freedmen, because he thought it might bring the Republican Party into disrepute. Sumner, of course, went straight ahead on that question. Wilson would not sustain Sumner in trying to keep Colorado out of the Union, if she *would* insist upon having the word *"white"* in her Constitution. Wilson thought that principle had better be given up, pro tem, for the sake of having Representatives to Congress from Colorado, who would *probably* strengthen the Republican Party; also because other Bills were pending, which might be lost if they spent time in discussing the word *white*. His tendency to seek *present* popularity and advantage has always been conspicuous. I was sorry that Garrison, in his Letter, showed such a tendency to depreciate Sumner, and to put Wilson at least on a level with him, if not above him.[2]

. . .

ALS; Houghton Library, Harvard University (microfiche 78/2059).

To Harriet Sewall

Wayland, Jan 3d, 1873

My very Dear Friend,

. . .

It was not "over-work" that put me in the dumps, dear friend. I do my work by convenient instalments, and rest when I need it. Moreover, I belong to that generation of American women whose strength and energy are becoming mere traditions of the past. It makes me smile to think of your little will-o'-the wisp body, and soft baby hands bringing in pails of water, and great armfulls of green wood, and shovelling away snow from door to gate, and tossing over beds, &c as I do every day. Few women of thirty are so strong as I am.[1]

A short time ago, the rainwater hogshead froze hard out-doors, and was in danger of bursting. Mr. Child's hands were disabled, and there was nobody I could call upon within a mile. So I took an axe and broke the thick ice into atoms, and brought ten pailfulls of water and ice into the house, without stopping; and I felt none the worse for it. You see it was not *work* that made me have such a fit of the blues. The fact is, I flattered myself that Mr. Child was getting well; and there came a rain-storm, dark and chilly, and put him all back; and I got discouraged, and also felt the effects of the ungenial weather. Everything looked dark and dreary to my mental vision, and I was fool enough to write while that mood was on me.

. . .

ALS; Robie-Sewall Papers, Massachusetts Historical Society (microfiche 79/2080).

[2] In several articles Garrison bitterly attacked his old friend Sumner for supporting Greeley.
[1] Child was nearly seventy-one.

Lucy Larcom (1824–93), author of *A New England Girlhood* (Boston, 1889), was at this time editor of *Our Young Folks,* a children's magazine.

To Lucy Larcom

Wayland, March 12th, '73

Dear Lucy,

The copyright in my juvenile books has expired.

My stories for juveniles were all put into two volumes, for economy in binding. These volumes, one entitled "Flowers for Children," and the other "A *New* Flower for Children" were bought by D. L. Lathrop & Co. 38 and 40, Cornhill, Boston, who still have them for sale. The words "Bible Warehouse" are on their sign, in large letters. If I could get into Boston, I would go in and procure them for you; but Mr. Child continues to be so much disabled by severe rheumatism, that I cannot venture to leave him alone.

If I should think of anything likely to suit your purpose, I will inform you. In the juvenile literature of the present day, I decidedly think there is too great predominance of the *fairy* element. *Moral* influence is too much neglected. Of cour[s]e I do not mean the *preaching* of morals. I mean that stories should be written with a view to bring the moral emotions into *activity;* such emotions as tenderness toward the aged, kindness to animals, compassion for the poor and suffering, brotherly feeling toward all races of men, and all religions.

Of Hans Christian Andersen's stories, I think the very best is "the Ugly Duck." The *meaning* of it is, to be sure, deeper than children can understand; but they *like* it, in the same way that they ⟨like it, in the same way that they⟩ like "Pilgrim's Progress," without understanding the significance of the pilgrim's adventures.

"The Ugly Duck" is doubtless an autobiography of Hans Christian Andersen himself; but it would answer for the autobiography of *any* person of genius, struggling with poverty and uncongenial surroundings. His story of a Spruce Tree, the adventures of which culminated in being a Christmas Tree, is very pretty. I dont know whether it has been translated from the German or not. If it has not been, and you think you should like it, I will with pleasure translate it from a volume of his, in German which I own.

Remember me very affectionately to J. G. Whittier, to whom I owe a great debt of gratitude for the influence of his poetry. His memory is also very precious to me, as one of the foremost in that noble army of moral veterans who fought with the dragon of Slavery.   I thank you for your affectionate letter.

Yours cordially,
L. Maria Child.

I have written in haste, to catch a chance to send to the distant Post Office.

ALS; Lucy Larcom Collection, James Duncan Phillips Library, Essex Institute (microfiche 80/2095).

A scandal involving corrupt practices by the Crédit Mobilier, a construction company formed by the Union Pacific directors to build the railroad with great profit to themselves, was exposed by the press in the fall of 1872. Several prominent Republican politicians were charged with accepting stock in return for warding off investigation. A congressional committee reported two congressmen guilty, but the House merely censured them.

To Sarah Shaw

Wayland, March 24'th, 1873.

Best Beloved,

. . .

It seems as if universal demoralization was carrying us to ruin with a swifter impetus than has hastened the decay of preceding Republics. But when Congress has become such a Gambling Saloon, and the Tammany Ring have such great success in sacking the Treasury of the Metropolis, how can we wonder that watches and silver spoons are nowhere safe from thieves on a smaller scale? The *money* stolen from the U.S. and from New York is the smallest part of the evil; it spreads abroad a *moral contagion* worse than the bodily infection of the plague. "Credit Mobilier" fraud will kill the Republican Party, as surely as the Tammany fraud killed the Democratic Party. The only way they could save themselves was by visiting the enormous wrong with scorching indignation and severe penalties; but this they failed to do, because so *many* were implicated in the fraud. These shameful disclosures, so tamely met, write "Ichabod! Ichabod!" on the Republican Party.

Around what nucleus will the *new* party form? I have thought, this long time, that, sooner or later, the Catholic question would become as vexed a question as Slavery ever was. I don't mean as a *religious* question. The world is too old, I trust, for men to go to war about theological doctrines, or traditions. But the Church of Rome has an unbounded ambition for political power, and all that she gains in that direction she insidiously uses in the service of ignorance and despotism. She is constantly enlarging her borders and strengthening her stakes in this country; and, sooner or later, the old Puritan element, from which we derived our national strength, will have to do battle with her for an inch of ground to stand on. I am glad to see that Harper's Weekly is so bold in sounding the trumpet of alarm on this subject.

It seems as if the *Dis*credit *Imm*obilier (the permanent disgrace) had sufficiently damaged the American name, without having John C. Fremont arrested for swindling. Perhaps you remember that I was unable to join in the popular enthusiasm for him. I then thought there was good ground for *suspecting* that he appropriated to his own use and emolument a large number of horses and cattle belonging to the U.S.; and I *know*, from his own unblushing statements, that his treatment of the Indians in California was brutal.

I liked extremely what President Grant said in his Message about the Indians and the Negroes. But I am very sorry to see him so infected with the greed for annexation; and I thought it very injudicious to blurt out that prophecy about a Universal Republic. The allusion to what had been said against him also appeared to me undignified in an official document.

. . .

ALS; Manuscript Division, New York Public Library (microfiche 80/2098).

To Francis Shaw

Wayland, May 25'th, 1873.

My very dear friend,

. . .

I agree with you that there are *portions* of the Old Testament too devout and sublime to be omitted in any Bible for the human soul. But I do not remember anything in the New Testament so demoralizing as Lot and his daughters, Noah's drunkenness, Jacob's dishonest trickery, and David's conduct to Uriah. I believe the constant reading of such monstrous things, as sacred writ, from God himself, has done much more to unsettle the moral principles of mankind than is generally supposed. When I get thinking of that side of the question, with its multifarious ramifications of evil, it sometimes seems to me not easy to decide whether Christianity has done most good or evil. But with all its drawbacks, it is undoubtedly much better than what it supplanted; and it seems to be a universal law of our being that *always*, in *every*thing, there must be as much evil as good, as much shadow as light, as much death as life.   You ask if Hillel's name may not have been Jesus.[1] I should think it was not possible. Hillel was a learned Rabbi, who lived and died respected by the Jews, who are still proud of his name. My supposition is that, for some time before Jesus, the Jews were getting their ideas enlarged by intercourse with Chaldeans, Greeks, and Romans; ⟨and⟩ that Jesus grew up inhaling the freer spiritual atmosphere around him, and that the *best* of all that was afloat readily assimilated with his large, loving, sympathizing soul. You know there is a very strong similarity between his teaching and that of those old Jewish Quakers called Essenes.[2] The record we have of him leaves a great gap between his childhood and the beginning of his public ministry, when he is supposed to have been not far from 30 years old. Whether he was with the Essenes during that time,

[1] Hillel (ca. 30 B.C.–A.D. 10), Jewish scholar and spiritual leader, was the greatest sage of the Second Temple period. He taught that love of man is the essence of the Divine Law. Both Christian and Jewish scholars have noted an arresting resemblance between the ethical teachings and personality traits of Hillel and Jesus.
[2] The Essenes, members of a Jewish religious order, originated in the Second Century B.C. What Child suggests—that Jesus may have come from their sect—has never been substantiated.

or under what influences he was coming to maturity, we shall never know. Very likely the forms of prayer and the maxims read in Hillel's School were more or less adopted in the Synagogues; and that Jesus used such portions as he best liked, enlarging and improving upon them, as the Spirit moved. As for the Golden Rule, I imagine it must have been as ancient as the first dawning of a moral sense in mankind. The roughest and most ignorant boy will spontaneously rebuke offence by asking, "How would you like to have me do that to *you?*" Confucius taught it; so did Thales; so did Hillel; but probably none of them originated it.

But I have spun too long a yarn on this theme. The substance of it all is, that spiritual growth, as well as material growth, goes on by gradual developement; the evolving of one thing from another preceding thing.

. . .

ALS; Manuscript Division, New York Public Library (microfiche 80/2104).

The Seminole Wars, to which Child refers in the next letter, had been of great concern to the abolitionists. White troops fought against Indians and the blacks who had escaped from Southern slaveholders to live among the Seminole in Florida. General Andrew Jackson carried on the first war against the Seminole, which began in 1818. The second Seminole War broke out in 1835, in Jackson's second Presidential term, and lasted until 1842. In the end, four thousand Seminole were driven into exile.

To Sarah Shaw

Wayland, June 22d, 1873.

Darling Sarah,

. . .

As for the poor Indians, would to Heaven they had education and news-papers to tell *their* side of the story! The pages you enclose scarcely give a glimpse of the the [*sic*] real facts that caused the Seminole war. The Seminoles were adopting civilized modes of life. They were devoting themselves to agricul-ture, and had established a friendly relation with their neighbors. But the slave-holders of Georgia wanted to drive them out, because they coveted their lands, and still more because their slaves were prone to take refuge with them. This had been going on for generations, and the fugitives had largely intermarried with the Indians. The slaveholders not only claimed their slaves that had escaped, but their children and grand children, and great, great grand children; on their ground, that "the child follows the condition of the *mother*." It was to satisfy *them* that Jackson got up the war. It was not Osceola's wife and children *only*, that were siezed and carried into slavery. *Multitudes* of their wives and children were carried off; and you may easily conjecture that no very nice care was always taken to ascertain whether they had descended from slaves in the U.S. or not. The pages you send contain the cool remark that "the siezure of Osceola's beautiful wife was an *unfortunate affair*." God of Heaven grant me patience! What would *he* call it if the Indians had siezed and carried off *his* beautiful wife, to sell her in the markets for a mistress? I hope the writer is no relation of yours; for I have a vehement desire to cuff his ears.   As for the Seminoles not removing after they had by treaty agreed to, I do not know the real facts of the case; but this I *do* know; that Gen. Jackson was in the *habit* of making nominal treaties with *any* Indians who could be bought by grog to sign a paper, which was forthwith declared to be an *official treaty* concluded with the government of the tribe. Just the same as if the government of France or England should enter into negotiations with General Butler, or Boss Tweed, and then claim that the arrangement was binding on the government of the United States.

General Grant has disappointed me. His Indian policy looked candid and just on paper; but he does not seem to have taken adequate care that it should be carried out. The Modocs have formerly had a good name as peaceable neighbors; but they have been driven from place to place, and finally pushed into a barren corner, where the soil did not admit of their raising sufficient for a subsistence. They were driven to desperation by starvation, and wearied out with promises that were never fulfilled. Poor Captain Jack said, "To die by bullets not hurt much; but it hurts a heap to die by hunger." I regret the barbarities of Captain Jack, but not more than I regret the barbarities of Phil. Sheridan. I look upon Osceola and Captain Jack both as worthy of an historical place in the list of heroes that have died for their oppressed peoples.[1] But I may as well stop writing on this theme, for it is a hopeless task to try to delineate the "general cussedness" of governments. It is a strange thing, but it seems impossible to convince politicians that it is not "visionary" to be guided by correct principles in the administration of affairs. Their idea is, the greater the indirectness and the double dealing, the greater the statesmanship. Yet, all the time, they make loud professions of following the teaching of him who said, "Let your yea be yea, and your nay, nay." Oh, Sarah, I am so tired of shams! It is very inconvenient to be habitually direct, in such a world of indirectness.
    . . .
    I am so sorry about the Modocs! I have no doubt the poor wretches had been goaded to desperation before they committed that wanton and most impolitic assault upon the Peace Commissioners. White men have so perpetually

---

[1] The Modoc Indians, forced onto a reservation, broke free under the leadership of Chief Kintpuash, or Captain Jack. They were defeated by federal troops in 1873. Some of the Modocs were sent to Oklahoma, the others to a reservation in Oregon.

lied to them that they don't know whom, or what, to believe. And after all, we, who are so much more enlightened, and who profess to be so much more human, have again and again killed Indians who were decoyed into our power by a flag of truce. No mortal will ever know the accumulated wrongs of that poor people. No wonder they turn at bay, in their desperation and despair. . . .

ALS, incomplete; Houghton Library, Harvard University; last two paragraphs from *Letters of Lydia Maria Child*, 1882 (microfiche 80/2106).

To Sarah Shaw

Wayland [July? 1873?]

Darling Sarah,

I believe I used some strong language in my last letter. I hope you were not disgusted with it. I have no partiality for the Indians, as a race; but the injustice of our course toward them excites my indignation to an irrepressible degree; and when I see people so entirely indifferent about it, I get furious. According to all the laws which we set up for *ourselves*, the Modocs are perfectly justifiable. When we wanted to have Oregon settled, the U.S. Government, without making any treaty with the Indians, who owned the land, without *even* notifying them of what they intended to do, offered to give 640 acres of the land to every man who would settle there. When the Modocs saw thousands upon thousands of their acres taken from them in this way, they remonstrated, and the white settlers began to be afraid they would make resistance. Col. Wright a U.S. officer who was stationed in the region, invited several of the most influential Indians, among whom was a brother of Capt. Jack, to come, and dine with him, and have a peaceable conference about the adjustment of affairs. They went. He had his plans all in readiness, and when he had entrapped them, they were all shot. Since then the U.S. has packed them off, from one place to another, till finally, they were pushed into a corner where game was scarce, and the land too barren to yield them corn. In the desperation of starvation, they resolved to go back to their old home, and die, if die they must, by the graves of their fathers. And when the Peace Commissioners went to talk with them, they found they were not authorized to restore their lands, on which they could live, and they thought their smooth talk was, like all the other promises of the U.S., *sheer* humbug; and they shot them. In remembrance of what they had suffered from Col. Wright, and from a succession of rascally agents, who can blame them, especially as *they* do not *profess* a Gospel of "peace, and good will toward men." I don't know that I am sorry I swore, after all. I am inclined to think it is a *duty* to swear against such monstrous injustice, and hypocrisy.

I wish Gen. Grant would pay more *attention* to the affairs of the Indians.

I presume his intentions are good; but the reckless character of land-agents, and speculators render vigilant *watching* a necessity in those regions.

Your loving old friend
Mariquita.

L; Lydia Maria Child Papers, Anti-Slavery Collection, Cornell University (microfiche 81/2110).

On the death in 1873 of her old friend Edmund Benzon, Child received a legacy of seventy-eight hundred dollars. Investing it brought her an annual income of about four hundred dollars, which helped ease her last years.

To Harriet Sewall

Wayland, Dec. 16'th, 1873.

My Dear Friend,

. . .

. . . The walls close closer round me, as time passes on. Three intimate friends have vanished since 1873 commenced. One of them you knew nothing about. Edmund L. Benzon, partner in the house of Naylor & Co. He was a very intelligent, cultivated, and affectionate young German, who, thirty years ago, was strongly attached to me and I to him. The interests of the house required that he should remove to London, where he has resided for the last twenty years. He married, had a family, lived in a world of fashion, was immersed in business, grew very rich, and made a tremendous show. Thus we were widely separated, both by space and circumstances. I seldom heard from him in the latter years, though when I did hear, his affection seemed undiminished, and his desire to serve my worldly interests always seemed very earnest. He had always insisted that I should survive him; but as he was more than fourteen years my junior, and strikingly young in his spirits and energies, I supposed that I should pass away before him. But he died last autumn, after a brief illness; and a few weeks afterward, I was informed by his Executor that he had left me a legacy. It was paid in gold, and when changed into our currency, amounted to $7,800. I was surprised, and completely overwhelmed; for I had never dreamed of such a thing. I was deeply touched and grateful. But, alas! how much there is that money cannot buy! It cannot buy a daughter to close my eyes; it cannot buy an old, *attached* servant, such as Miss Osgood had; it cannot restore the friendships that are gone. But there is one aspect in which this unexpected addition of funds is a blessing. I have sometimes been a little uneasy lest, if I survived the ability to do for myself, my income might prove inadequate to meet necessary expenses; but dear Edmund's thoughtful generosity has removed that anxiety.

Mr. Child sends hearty greetings to you both.

———

With affectionate greetings to your good mate, I am always your loving old friend,

L. Maria Child.

ALS; Robie-Sewall Papers, Massachusetts Historical Society (microfiche 81/2123).

To Angelina (Grimké) Weld

Wayland, Feb. 4'th, 1874.

Dear Angelina,

Our affectionate and sympathizing thoughts have been much with you, since we heard of your great bereavement;[1] though, with the inertia common to old folks, we have been dilatory about writing to tell you so. David and I have talked over a great deal those memorable days when we first knew you and your good sister. From that time to this, we have always cherished the greatest respect and gratitude toward you both. How good she was! how thoroughly unselfish, kind-hearted and large-hearted! How readily she always distinguished the false and true in principles, because she habitually looked at everything in the light of conscience. It must be very sad to miss her from the dear familiar paths, where she for so many years walked side by side with you. But the *memory* of such a friend is a benediction; and souls that have grown together in such tender and sacred communion *cannot* be forever separated. The memory of the past, and the hope of the future are both full of blessing; and as for the present space of external separation, how brief it is!

Does it now sometimes seem strange to you that those exciting and eventful years, that so tried our souls and taxed our energies, have passed away into history? Chateaubriand says: "*Before* revolutions, superior men die unknown; their public has not yet arrived. *After* revolutions, superior men die neglected; their public has retired." How few now living on earth have any idea of the prayers, and tears, and inward struggles, through which you and your noble sister passed, in that arduous mission of rescuing millions of human brethren from the darkness and misery of slavery!

To the young men and women of the present day, the fiery trials and hairbreadth escapes of that stormy period have the far-off sound of traditions, like the mob that stoned Stephen, and the wild beasts let loose upon Christians in the Coliseum. But the Cross stands in the Coliseum now, and colored men are in the Halls of Congress.[2]

[1] Sarah Grimké died on 23 Dec. 1873.
[2] Twenty-two black men served in Congress during the Reconstruction era, two of them in the Senate. Nine of the fifteen ex-slave states failed to elect any black congressmen during Reconstruction; no blacks were elected to Congress from the North in this period.

"Let our *names* perish," said Lamartine, "so that our principles remain."

Mr. Child has had a great deal of ill health, of late years; but he keeps recovering from the attacks of various diseases, and manages to get a good deal of quiet comfort out of what remains to him of life. His small garden, his carpenter's tools, and his Greek and Latin investigations, keep him pleasantly and innocently occupied. My health is extremely good, and I am unusually strong for my years. The seventy-second anniversary of my birth comes round next week. I find it difficult to realize that I have been in the world so long. We keep no help, and as I do all our sewing, housework, and nursing, I have very little time for discontented thoughts. I read and study enough to keep my mind from rusting out prematurely; and there is no want of objects on which to exercise the kindly feelings. Both of us are more prone to be thankful for the blessings we have, than to repine for those we have not.

My good old mate cordially unites with me in affectionate remembrance, true respect, and heartfelt sympathy for you and your noble-hearted husband. May the evening of your lives be serene!

Your truly attached old friend,
L. Maria Child.

ALS; Weld-Grimké Papers, Clements Library, University of Michigan (microfiche 81/2133).

To Sarah Shaw

Wayland, [after 11 March] 1874.

I have been wanting to write you these many days, but I make it a rule not to write when I am sad, and my soul has been greatly troubled. Since the death of Ellis Gray Loring, no affliction has oppressed me so heavily as the death of Charles Sumner.[1] I loved and reverenced him beyond any other man in public life. He was my ideal of a hero, more than any of the great men in our national history. In fact I almost worshipped him. I see no hopes of such another man to stem the overwhelming tide of corruption in this country. But perhaps when a momentous crisis comes, the hour will bring forth the man. If so, it will be well for the nation and for the world; but for myself I can never, never again feel the implicit trust in any mortal man that I felt in Charles Sumner. A feeling akin to remorse renders my grief almost insupportable. Certainly it was not my fault, that I could not view the last election in the light he did; but I wept bitterly when he wrote to me: "It makes the tears come to my eyes to find that you do not sympathize with me in the stand I have taken from motives the most conscientious that have ever influenced my life." And now that he has gone, it seems as if it would kill me to think that my want of sympathy should ever have brought tears to his eyes. Then I have not written

[1] Charles Sumner died on 11 Mar. 1874.

to him for some months past. I often wanted to, but his mind seemed full of the old vexed topic, and I knew, however tenderly and reverentially I might write, nothing would satisfy him but the acknowledgment that he had been entirely in the right; because he never for a moment ceased to believe himself so. It is true that President Grant, since his second election, has done many things, and left still more undone, which tend to confirm Mr. Sumner's estimate of him. But, as I again and again wrote to Mr. Sumner, the question was not whether General Grant was a fitting candidate for the presidency, but whether it was safe to restore power in our national councils to Democrats and rebels. He believed that Democrats and rebels had met with a great change of heart; but I thought, and still think, there was superabounding evidence that they were still essentially in the same state of mind as ever. I thought then, and I think now, that artful politicians could not have so imposed upon Mr. Sumner if it had not been for the state of his health. If he had been in perfect physical health he would never have believed that Mr.——— had cultivated the growth of a conscience, after doing without one for half a century. But the more I am convinced that his nervous system was in a shattered and excited state, the more keenly do I regret that I did not write to him frequently and affectionately. I am aware that my letters could not have been of much consequence to him, but perhaps they might have soothed him a little. It seems as if I had been un-grateful to him for all his magnificent services to freedom and public morals. In the anguish of my heart I cry out, "Enemies wrote to him, and friends did not! And all the while he was dying by inches!"

Processions and flowers and panegyrics have become so much a matter of custom that they are generally distasteful to me, as are all things that degenerate into forms without significance. But the homage to the memory of Charles Sumner seems to be really spontaneous and almost universal. It is a great con-solation to me, not only because he richly deserved it, but because it is a good omen from the nation. There has been nothing like it except the mourning for Abraham Lincoln; and in both cases it was preeminently honesty of character to which the people paid spontaneous homage. They reverenced the men be-cause they trusted them.

L, extract; *Letters of Lydia Maria Child*, 1882 (microfiche 82/2142).

Abigail Williams May (1829–88), from a Boston abolitionist family, was active in freedmen's organizations and later was a supporter of women's rights. In 1874 she and four other women were the first women elected to the Boston School Committee. That same year she was on the executive committees of both the New England and the Massachusetts Woman Suffrage Association. She usually called herself Abby W. May.

To Abigail May

Wayland, March 15'th, 1874

Dear Miss May,

I have delayed answering your note, because it "put me in a quandary," as country folks sometimes say. I have a very strong desire to do whatever *you* ask, and also to serve the woman cause to the utmost of my power.

But the plain fact is, this refusal to pay taxes does not commend itself to my judgment. The proposed meeting on the 26th of May will probably endorse it, and if my name is on the Committee, I shall appear to endorse it also, and that I do not feel ready to do.[1]

Very likely the agitation it produces will help the cause of Woman's Suffrage. During the progress of the Anti Slavery struggle many things were done and said, which appeared to me to be wrong at the time, and still appear to me to be so; though they unquestionably helped on the cause of Anti Slavery by exciting a great deal of talk.

In all reforms there are sure to be people who are sincere and zealous workers, but who have no balance-wheel in their machinery. In the Anti-Slavery cause, I was frequently unable to act with such coadjutors. To endorse what we do not approve because we think it may help to produce the good *end* we have in view seems to me to assimilate too much to the maxim of the Jesuits.

I do not question the right of others to adopt measures that I do not feel free to make use of; but I have always resisted being drawn into an endorsement of proceedings that did not commend themselves to my own judgment, however popular they might be with my co-laborers.

With great respect and esteem, I am very cordially yours,
L. Maria Child.

ALS; May-Goddard Papers, Schlesinger Library, Radcliffe College (microfiche 82/ 2143).

To Sarah Shaw

Wayland, April 2d, 1874.

Darling Friend,
. . .
With regard to my own affairs, I will not discuss them on paper. You suggest a "cousin," as a resort. I don't know that I have any cousins. If I should discover any, I should probably find them ignorant and coarse people. I was

[1] Taxation without representation was an important issue in the women's movement at this time, and withholding taxes an increasingly popular tactic. "Tea parties" commemorating the centennial of the Boston Tea Party were held in many eastern cities in December of 1873. In May 1874 Child was chosen for the second time as one of the vice-presidents of the New England Suffrage Association.

not made of "porcelain clay"; but as my father was a baker, I may claim to have been modeled in *biscuit*. The unavoidable barrier between me and many of my family connexions, owing to a total difference of culture, has caused me frequent annoyance all my life-long. I think most of the sums in the moral arithmetic of life are hard to work out. I try not to be anxious about my future, and to feel a trust that "something will turn up." With regard to *out*-door work, something did "turn up," in a wonderful way, when David's hands became too lame to do his customary jobs. The husband of the woman who has washed and scoured for me, has for many years "acted like Cain"; drinking up all his wages, and maltreating his wife; and, at last, he set fire to a barn and burnt up a dozen cattle, because the man who had employed him hid his rum-bottle. He received the mild sentence of two years in the house of correction. I hoped he would die there. I felt as if I could never endure the sight of him again. But when he came here of an errand, the day he had served his time out, he was so timid, and his eyes had such a beseeching look, as if his soul was hungry for a friend, that I could n't stand it. I shook hands with him, and invited him in. I had a long private talk with him, and told him that though he was 60 years old, it was not too late to make a man of himself, if he would only resolve never to taste another drop of liquor; and I assured him that if he would only try, I would be a faithful friend to him. He promised me that he *would* try. It is now more than a year and a half ago. He has kept his promise, and I have kept mine. Every Sunday since he came out of prison, I prepare a good dinner for him, and give him a strong cup of tea. He works diligently, supplies his wife with everything comfortable, and makes her a present of what remains of his wages. The poor woman says she was never so happy in her life. His attentions to us are unbounded. Whenever there is a snow-storm, he is here, prime and early, with his shovel. He runs everywhere to do errands; and on Sundays, he brings wood, and water, and splits kindlings, and does everything he can find to do. He is in fact our "man Friday." If I could get such faithful, hearty service *within* doors, I should be set up for life. Of course, he *may* fall back into his old habits, but so long a time has elapsed, and I seem to be such an object of worship to him, that I cannot but hope for the best.   I have never in my life experienced any happiness to be compared to the consciousness of lifting a human soul out of the mire.[1]

. . .

With regard to living near you, darling, it would be like heaven, if one could only live without house-rent, servants, &c. as we suppose they do in heaven. I have suffered so much pecuniary embarrassments, since my marriage, that I am now "like a scalded cat, that dreads even *cold* water.["] Since Edmund's legacy, my income is $1200 a year. $100 a year I give to Mr. Child's

[1] The man Child discusses here was Charles Moulton. In her will she provided that if he survived her, he was to be paid fifty dollars annually in monthly installments so long as he abstained from intoxicating drinks.

invalid sister. $200 a year goes for taxes. Even if I should do *nothing* for others, the remainder would not be enough to live on Staten Island.

With regard to your promised visit, I can only say that the sight of you is always a refreshment to my soul; but it seems too bad for you to take so much trouble to see two such "old codgers.["]

My man Friday waits to take this to the Post Office.

With hearty love to dear Frank, I am your ever affectionate old friend,

Mariquita.

ALS; Houghton Library, Harvard University (microfiche 82/2146).

To Sarah Shaw

Wayland, July 2d, 1874.

Darling Friend,
. . .

I did not read Adams's Oration. I *never* read anything of his. I take strong antipathies, you know. My particular political antipathy was W'm H. Seward, and my next greatest antipathy is C. F. Adams.[1] Both of those men had a very blurred vision as to right and wrong; but Adams is essentially a small, mean soul. Old fogy Harvard clings to the prestige around the name of Adams; if it were not for *that*, he would be universally pronounced a man of poor calibre intellectually, with a cataract of selfishness blinding his moral vision. "Let no such man be trusted." David read his oration with infinite disgust. Hon. Henry Wilson was here the other day. He says the soldiers who heard it were indignant at being *apologized* for.

When I look at our political men, I get into a desponding state of mind. But, after all, good *is* more active than evil; and even in this corrupt age it is the *prevailing* force. Have you seen a little volume entitled "Hampton and its Students," by the wife of General Armstrong?[2] It is a very sensible and kindly book, and inspires cheerful hopes that God is taking good care of this Republic. I cannot endure the thought that this Republic may die of phlethoic disease. Great prosperity is so dangerous to States, as well as to individuals! There are many inconveniences and many dangers inevitable to a Republican form of government; but, with all its defects, it is the best means of developing human faculties, and making the most of human resources.

[1] In June 1874, Charles Francis Adams gave an address at the dedication of Harvard's Memorial Hall. In 1830, Child had unsuccessfully sought his help when David was in jail and the *Massachusetts Whig Journal* was failing.

[2] Mrs. Armstrong was the wife of Samuel Chapman Armstrong (1839–93), a Union general. He persuaded the American Missionary Association to found Hampton Institute, which he headed until his death.

I see they are trying to dethrone the young King of Bavaria.[3] I wonder whether he is really somewhat crack-brained, as they say he is, or whether he gets that name because he is suspected of sympathizing with his friend Wagner's republican proclivities. Can you understand Wagner's music? or his theory concerning the "music of the future"? It puts me in a "blue maze."

. . .

ALS; Houghton Library, Harvard University (microfiche 82/2159).

To Anna (Loring) Dresel

Wayland, Aug. 5'th, 1874.

Dear Anna,

Mr. Child has been very ill for several weeks; more ill than I have ever known him. His stomach rejected every kind of food, even bread, or gruel; and he became reduced almost to a skeleton. For some time, I feared he could not live through the summer. I urged him to consult a doctor, and told him I would send for one of *any* school he chose. He decidedly preferred Dr. Gersdorf, and we went into Boston about a week ago to consult him. I was very anxious lest the journey should prove too fatiguing for David. But I took a carriage at every step, and hired a comfortable room where he rested four hours, and took suitable refreshment. With these precautions, the journey did him no harm, and tired him but little. Dr. Gersdorf's prescriptions are working admirably. He gets better day by day, and can now eat meat and bread, without suffering for it. Vegetables and wines disagree with him. With care, I think he is now likely to be restored to his normal condition in a few weeks. *Quite* well, he will never be, of course. He was 80 years old last month; and no doctoring can entirely repair the waste of years. I am well, and remarkably strong, for my years. . . .

. . .

I do not leave David an hour, lest he should have a poor turn while I am out of the way. I have spent a good deal of the time by his bed-side looking over and arranging a great mass of papers, to save others trouble when I am gone. I have destroyed over 350 letters. Some of them were written by myself to friends now deceased. You don't know how foreign the letters seem that I wrote forty years ago! Time changes the state of our souls, even more than that of our bodies.

Lucy Ann sends her best love to you all.[1] Her heart seems to be bound up in you and yours. Good bye, dear. Your affectionate old Mariechen.

[3] Ludwig II, king of Bavaria (1864–86), was a patron and friend of Richard Wagner. Confined for insanity, Ludwig committed suicide.
[1] Lucy Ann Pickering, their houseworker, lived with the Childs.

David, who is lying down on the bed near me, sends very cordial greetings to you and Mr. Dresel.

In 1874 the Tilton-Beecher case surfaced in the press. The charge that Theodore Tilton's pastor and friend, Henry Ward Beecher, had committed adultery with Tilton's wife had been made public by Victoria Woodhull in her *Weekly*. Beecher denied the allegations and was exonerated by church investigations. He threatened to sue Tilton for defamation of character. Tilton brought suit for alienation of affections, and the trial became a national sensation. Beecher was acquitted, but by the verdict of a divided jury; Tilton's wife later made a public confirmation of her affair with Beecher.

To Sarah Shaw

Wayland, Aug. 7'th, 1874.

Dear Sarah,

. . . The spiritualists have been in the habit of sending me a great many of their publications, and I have read them with curiosity, and I believe with candor. But I must say I have never met with anything so trashy as the discourses of their trance-mediums; which *they* recommend as real golden words of inspiration. Then the communications from another world—what do they amount to? Not a thing do they tell us that has not been said a thousand times before in a far better manner. My patience has been severely tried with shallow-pated people in *this* world; and if they are so much *more* foolish there beyond, the prospect seems to me by no means attractive. Then the *sort* of indications that spirits give of their presence seems to degrade the whole subject; such as knocking tables about, and throwing down on the table a sun-flower six feet long, with the earth about its roots. There is a vast amount of imposition practised on the credulity of those who are drawn toward it, and there is a still greater amount of *self* delusion. Still, I do not think it is *all* imposition, or delusion. There are inexplicable phenomona connected with it, which render it a very curious psychological question; but the same thing is true of dreams.

With regard to the Beecher Tilton case, I sometimes veer to one side, and sometimes to the other, according to the conflicting testimony. I have, for several years, considered Tilton an unprincipled, unscrupulous man; and, for the sake of public morals, I am painfully anxious to have Beecher's reputation cleared beyond the shadow of a doubt. If he is *not* blameless, he must be awfully corrupt. A very good man may yield to a sudden temptation, and commit an act totally at variance with his real character. But to try to conceal it by falsehoods, uttered in such a religious strain, seems absolutely incredible with regard to a man whose moral teaching has uniformly been so high as that of Mr. Beecher. And yet he seems to me to give a very unsatisfactory explanation of that letter which he wrote to Tilton, saying: "I humble myself before you as before my God. I wish I was dead." And was it not *very* strange that Mrs. Tilton, with all her professed reverence for her pastor, should sign a paper accusing him of such a grievous misdemeanor as would blight him utterly if believed? If *my* husband had held a pistol to my breast, and ordered *me* to sign such a document about Revd Mr. Sears, I might *possibly* have been terrified into doing it; but I should have siezed the very first opportunity to go to a magistrate and make a formal affidavit that I had been frightened into signing an utter falsehood; and that is what would have been done by any woman of common sense and common good feeling.

I know not what to think. Certainly, there never was a case where so many people, supposed to be respectable, gave each other the lie direct, as they do in this case. The whole affair is giving me a good deal of pain, on account of the bad effects it is producing.

. . .

ALS; Houghton Library, Harvard University (microfiche 83/2170).

As Child entered her eighth decade, she began to lose old friends: Henrietta Sargent, Lucy Osgood, Sarah Grimké, Edmund Benzon, Charles Sumner. Then, on 17 September 1874, David Lee Child died. He was eighty years old, and to the end his mind was clear and active. They had been married almost fifty years. She wrote the news to several friends who responded with warm tributes to David's fine qualities. Garrison wrote, "I do not think you could have wedded a man more nobly chivalrous in spirit, more appreciative of womanly worth, or more alive to the demands of honor, justice and truth. . . ." He recalled "how totally exempt he was from all low ambition to shine."* Whittier regretted that "a brave, true and strong man has gone from us," and added that David's writing in the early antislavery years had provided "the best and fullest exposition of our principles and objects."†

Child was deeply affected by her loss. She told Sarah Shaw she felt like "a piece of wreck drifting out into the ocean."‡ After the funeral she spent a few days with the Sewalls in Melrose, then accepted the Shaws' invitation to winter with them at their Staten Island home.

* 25 Oct. 1874, Rare Books and Manuscripts, Boston Public Library.
† 23 [Sept. 1874], *John Greenleaf Whittier*, ed. Francis H. Underwood (Boston, 1884), p. 282.
‡ 7 Oct. 1874, Houghton Library, Harvard University.

To Sarah Shaw

Wayland, Sep. 18'th, 1874

Darling Sarah,

My dear, kind old mate passed away last night, at midnight. He suffered greatly during the last three days, but at last sunk to sleep in my arms, as peacefully as a tired babe.

I feel that it has been wisely and kindly ordered; for if he had lived he must have suffered. And I am *so* thankful that my earnest prayer, to be able to take care of him to the last, has been answered!

But oh, Sarah dear, no tongue can tell how desolate I feel.

Mrs. Pickering has been an inexpressible blessing; so kind, so capable, so sympathizing.

Yours in love and sadness,
L. Maria Child.

ALS; Houghton Library, Harvard University (microfiche 83/2178).

10

1875-1880

Child stayed in Staten Island with the Shaws until March of 1875 and then returned to Wayland. She remained strong in body and mind, followed political affairs with concern, and in 1878 published her last book, *Aspirations of the World*.

Francis Jackson Garrison (1848–1916), to whom the next letter is addressed, was a Boston wool merchant and a son of William Lloyd Garrison.

To Francis Jackson Garrison

Staten Island, Jan 1'st, 1875.

Dear Francis,

I should have attended to your request weeks ago, had not Mrs. Parsons[1] told me that *she* would inform you that I had sent all my Anti Slavery documents to Wendell Phillips. I sent them to him because his house was more accessible, than your father's, or Mr. Sewall's; and I was in a hurry to deposit them before I left Wayland.

Mr. Phillips said he would use them for colleges and public libraries, and that he particularly wished to complete the set for Cornell University.[2] I presume he would have distributed them ere now, if he had been able to leave the sick bed of his wife.

I may *possibly* have some scattering copies of the books you mention; but I cannot ascertain at present, because my books are packed and locked up two hundred miles off. As for "*rest*," I do not care for it here or elsewhere, being a

[1] Sarah M. Parsons.
[2] The letters and papers Phillips received from Child are deposited at Cornell University.

worker by nature, and by long habit. With best respects to your honored father, and affectionate remembrance and kind wishes to all the household, I am, very cordially, your friend

L. Maria Child.

ALS; Anti-Slavery Collection, Rare Books and Manuscripts, Boston Public Library (microfiche 84/2210).

To Lydia B. Child

> West New Brighton.
> Staten Island. N. York.
> Care of Francis G. Shaw.
> Feb. 11'th, 1875.

Dear Lydia,

. . .

Perhaps you were surprised that your brother left no other property than the $1000 bequeathed to him by his Uncle Tyler.[1] My good, darling David was the kindest, best soul alive; but the fact is, he never had any business-faculty. It was a marvel to everybody, who knew him, that a man so intelligent, so learned, so capable, so energetic, and so industrious, was *always* in pecuniary difficulty. The reason was, that he inherited his father's deficiences. He had no promptitude, no system in his affairs; hence everything went into confusion. After many years of struggling with ever-recurring pecuniary difficulties, I reluctantly became convinced that there was *no help* for these deficiences. It was always in my heart to give him the *whole* of my earnings, or my inheritance; but if I did so, I foresaw that our old age must be spent in the poor-house. So, it was agreed between us that *I* should take care of all business-concerns.

For the last 45 years, I have paid, from my own funds, all the expenses for both of us; food, clothing, washing, fuel, taxes, &c. Also, what I have given to the Freedmen, to other charities, and to you and Walter.

When he received his Uncle's legacy, he proposed to add the interest to the general household fund; but I told him I wanted him to keep it for his own especial use; to buy books, or maps, or any superfluity he took a fancy to; and he did so. Though the dear, generous, kind soul was always *offering* it to me.   I make this statement merely that you may know exactly how matters stand.

. . .

I shall leave here in the Spring. My plans for the future are all unsettled;

---

[1] Tyler Bigelow, a lawyer, had died in 1865.

but I shall not board out, if I can possibly help it. With kindest remembrance and best wishes for you all. Yrs affectionately,

L. M. Child.

ALS; Child Letters, MC 305, Schlesinger Library, Radcliffe College (microfiche 84/2217).

To Sarah Shaw

Wayland, Oct. 4th, 1875

Darling Friend,

. . .

I am very glad Mr. Curtis approves of my ideas concerning the taxation of women.[1] In the Anti-Slavery cause, I always had a tendency to take the "middle extreme["]; and I have the same tendency in the Woman cause. That women have a right to vote, and ought to have their claim allowed, has been plain to me for many years; and when I am convinced that a theory is based on a *principle* I am never afraid to see it carried into practice. I never say, "Let Truth prevail, though the heavens fall," because I am well assured that the heavens never do fall, when truth prevails. But though reforms compel my conscience, they jar upon my taste.

. . .

I went to Wendell Phillips a short time ago, to inquire whether any of my stock had fallen, in these disastrous times.[2] He said, "No; not a cent. It is all A. No. 1." Then he began to preach inflation as the only cure for hard times. I told him I thought neither my stock, nor any other stock, would hold its own, if *that* remedy was applied. He said a friend of his had been talking with Henry Wilson about it, and that Mr. Wilson regretted the Republicans had not secured such a good plank for *their* platform, instead of letting their opponents have the benefit of it. How *like* Henry Wilson! How his diplomacy *did* try the righteous soul of Charles Sumner!

. . .

ALS; Houghton Library, Harvard University (microfiche 86/2250).

---

[1] Child did not support the tactic of refusing to pay taxes.
[2] The depression which had begun in 1873 proved to be one of the biggest and worst the country ever knew. By 1877 it would engulf nearly all but the rich, and its effects would still be observable in the 1880s. Child's income from the Benzon bequest and her own frugality spared her the sufferings of others.

To Sarah Shaw

Wayland, Jan. 27'th, 1876

Meine Einzige,

. . .

. . . Miss Osgood left $2000 for the colored people, and appointed me
Trustee. I gave $1000 to the Home for Old Colored Women, and with the re-
mainder I founded a scholarship at Hampton College, Va. Soon after, I chanced
to see a letter from a young colored man in Georgia to a lady, who had been
his teacher. He had been working very industriously to earn money to go to
Hampton College, and had, for that purpose placed $300 in the Freedmen's
Bank, and lost it all by the dishonesty of the managers.[1] His letter impressed
me very favorably, not only because it was uncommonly well written, but
especially because he wrote: "Don't beg for me at the North, my good friend.
I will go to work and try again. I want to row my own boat." I sent the letter
to Gen. Armstrong, and asked that the Osgood Scholarship might be bestowed
upon him. That would defray the expense of his *education*, and if he was unable to pay for board, necessary books, &c. I agreed to be responsible therefor;
with the request that he might not *know* there was any one to help him row his
boat. A few days ago, I had a letter from Gen. Armstrong, in which he says:
"Forsyth is an uncommonly intelligent, sensible, and every way satisfactory
pupil; and I have no doubt he will make a good record of himself hereafter."
That had a very *happy-fying* influence. I have so often been unsuccessful in
my efforts to help others!   As for the Centennial, I should have liked it very
well if we had kept the anniversary or centiversary in a rational, quiet way.[2]
But I have no sympathy whatever with this "Spread-Eagle" affair. It is a manifestation of excessive national vanity, extremely distasteful to me; and I have no
patience with Congress for increasing the burden of taxes by voting for the
required appropriation of a million and a half to the Centennial.

. . .

You ask if we like the President's Message. Yes, we do. It is concise, sensible, and characterized by just and humane sentiments. His course with regard
to the Indians particularly pleases me. If such a policy had been instituted years
ago, how much bloodshed and money might have been saved! But I feel somewhat vexed with Grant for not being more vigilant in preventing the murder
of loyal people at the South. He secured a safe election in Mississippi by military protection; why didn't he do the same in Tennessee, Texas, Georgia, &c?

---

[1] The Freedman's Savings Bank and Trust Company failed in 1874 because its managers had stolen from it more than three million dollars. No one went to jail for the
crime. Child had written letters on behalf of the young man, W. A. Forsyth, two years
earlier.
[2] The Centennial Exposition of 1876 ran from 10 May to 10 Nov. in Fairmont Park,
Philadelphia.

I am glad to see that Mr. Curtis is candid enough to find fault with the Republican Party when it deserves it.[3] . . .

ALS; Houghton Library, Harvard University (microfiche 86/2261).

To Sarah Shaw

Wayland April 8'th, 1876.

Dearest Friend,

. . .

I *did* see that Mr. Curtis headed a minority against Conkling; and I thanked God for his doings, as I often do.[1] I sometimes think it is almost hopeless for men of integrity to try to stem the current of venality and trickery; but it is a solemn duty for every honest citizen to *try* to do it. Latterly, I have not attended to the doings in Congress; not having any one to whom I can read the Speeches and Debates, as I used to, with a running commentary of mutual remarks. But in the days when I did keep a look-out upon Congress, I was frequently offended by Conkling's obvious want of *fixed principles*.

There was another thing for which I thanked Mr. Curtis; and that was his claiming (in The Harper's Monthly) a place for Thomas Paine among the Heroes of the American Revolution.[2] Thomas Paine was a true friend of human freedom, and there was a good deal of moral grandeur in many things he did. His attack upon the popular theology was honest in intention, and originated in his inherent hostility to shams. But he did it in a coarse, rude way, which has always rendered his "Age of Reason" a repulsive book to me, though I do not dispute the justice of many of his statements, and respect him for his courage in making them. Like Stephen S. Foster, he has no tact; he goes to work upon a hard and knotty moral log, with might and main; but he is prone to drive in the wedge butt end foremost.[3] It is a common defect with reformers. If Thomas Paine was sensual in his later days, as they say he was, it was the natural result of public thanklessness for his great services, and the isolation into which he was forced by popular prejudice. Whatever may have been his faults, he deserves a niche in the Gallery of Centennial Heroes for the brave and honest work he did in the days of the Revolution.

With a most affectionate greeting to Frank, I am always your loving old
Mariquita.

---

[3] George W. Curtis led the reformers within the Republican party who repudiated corruption and the spoils machine.
[1] Curtis helped frustrate the presidential ambitions of Sen. Roscoe Conkling, Republican boss of New York.
[2] The Philadelphia Centennial Exposition included an exhibit devoted to these heroes.
[3] Foster was a controversial abolitionist.

I am glad you have been having such good musical times. How do you like the *White,* colored violinist?[4]

. . .

ALS; Houghton Library, Harvard University (microfiche 86/2271).

To Sarah Shaw

Wayland, June 18'th, 1876.

Darling Sarah,

. . .

James T. Fields sent me his little book about "Old Acquaintance".[1] He is a very amiable, pleasant gossip; and has earned his title of "the American Boswell." While reading "Daniel Deronda," I thought of *him,* when the sociable guest was introduced, who "could tell everything about a great philosopher or physicist, except his theories or discoveries."[2] That is a wonderful book. With what a bold and accurate hand the Jewish pictures are outlined and colored! and all the while there is an anti sectarian moral *in* the picture, because it is sketched by a large, liberal soul. I wish my good Edmund[3] were here to read it. I am afraid they have no circulating-libraries in the region where table-tippers come from.

I have been gadding unusually for me. I went to the meeting of the Free Religious Association, where I was sorely tempted to speak; because the only woman who did speak was so flippant and conceited, that I was ashamed of her.[4] In the same excursion, I spent a day and night at Concord, with the Alcotts. Mrs. Alcott was a friend of my youth, and the sister of my dear friend S. J. May.[5] We had a charming time talking over the dear old eventful times. I like Louisa and her artist-sister, May, very much.[6] Some people complain that they are brusque; but it is merely because they are very straightforward and sincere. They have a Christian hatred of lionizing; and the Leo Hunters are a very numerous and impertinent family. Moreover, they don't like con-

[4] Joseph White, a black born in Cuba, studied violin at the Paris Conservatory. His concerts were highly praised by Rossini and others. When he gave his first concerts in New York and Boston in Mar. 1876, critics said he was better than Ole Bull, Henri Wieniawski, and Henri Vieuxtemps.

[1] *Old Acquaintance: Barry Cornwall and Some of His Friends* (Boston, 1876).

[2] George Eliot, *Daniel Deronda* (London, 1876).

[3] Edmund Benzon.

[4] Child attended the Sunday meetings of the Free Religious Association, where Wendell Phillips and others lectured.

[5] Abigail May (1800–1877), sister of abolitionist Samuel J. May, married Bronson Alcott in 1830. Child knew her before either had married and in 1838 they were neighbors in Boston.

[6] Louisa May Alcott (1832–88), the writer, and Abbie May Nieriker (1840–79).

ventional *fetters* any better than I do. There have been many attempts to saddle and bridle me, and teach me to keep step in respectable processions; but they have never got the lasso over my neck *yet;* and "old hoss" as I am now, if I see the lasso in the air, I snort and gallop off, determined to be a free horse to the last, and put up with the consequent lack of grooming and stabling.

The *house* of the Alcotts took my fancy greatly.[7] When they bought the place, the house was so very old, that it was thrown into the bargain, with the supposition that it was fit for nothing but fire-wood. But Mr. Alcott has an architectural taste, more intelligible than his Orphic Sayings. He let every old rafter and beam stay in its place; changed old ovens and ash-holes into Saxon-arched alcoves; and added a wash-woman's old shanty to the rear. The result is a house full of queer nooks and corners, and all manner of juttings in and out. It seems as if the Spirit of some old architect had brought it from the Middle-Ages and dropped it down in Concord, preserving much better re-semblance to the place whence it was brought, than does the Virgin Mary's house, which the Angel carried from Bethlehem to Loretto. The capable Alcott-daughters painted and papered the interior themselves. And gradually the artist-daughter filled up all the nooks and corners with pannels on which she had painted birds, or flowers; and over the open fire-places she painted mottoes in ancient English characters. Owls blink at you, and faces peep from the most unexpected places. The whole leaves a general impression of harmony, of a medieval sort, though different parts of the house seem to have stopped in a dance that became confused, because some of the party did not keep time. The walls are covered with choice engravings, and paintings by the artist-daughter. She really *is* an artist. If you wanted a copy of some of Turner's pictures, I think hers would please you. She is an enthusiast for Turner. Those two girls are the stay and staff of the family; pecuniarily, and otherwise. I am *so* glad that Mrs. Alcott has such gifted daughters to lean upon, after all the toil and struggle of her self-sacrificing life!   Mrs. Emerson called to see me, while I was in Concord.[8] You cannot imagine how very peculiar is her personal ap-pearance. Her hair is as white as drifted snow; and she wears over it nothing but a very long scarf of the thinnest white illusion lace, without any bit of coloring whatsoever upon it. This entirely white protuberance looks like some-thing that has sprouted out of her body in the cellar. Her eyes, always large, seem larger now that her face is very thin and pale. When she entered the room about dusk, I was absolutely startled by her spectral appearance. She would make the fortune of any Spirit-Photographer.

. . .

ALS; Houghton Library, Harvard University (microfiche 87/2276).

[7] The Alcotts had been living in Orchard House, Concord, since 1858.
[8] Lidian (Jackson) Emerson (1802–92) was the second wife of Ralph Waldo Emerson; they married in 1835.

Lucy Stone (1818–93) apparently asked Child to write something for the *Woman's Journal*, weekly newspaper of the American Woman Suffrage Association, which she edited. Near the end of July, Stone invited Child to visit, but Child, more than ever the recluse, declined, thanking Stone for discouraging "lion-hunters" from invading her privacy.

To Lucy Stone

Wayland, July 1'st, 1876

Dear Lucy

My brains are so stewed by the heat, that I did n't feel as if I *could* possibly write a word. But I have scribbled something, which you can use or not, as you please

If you knew how I hate the very sight of a pen, you would appreciate my wish to oblige you. I had rather bake, brew, knit, sew, wash, scour, than to write.

Yrs truly,
L. Maria Child.

ALS; National American Woman Suffrage Association Papers, Manuscript Division, Library of Congress (microfiche 87/2278).

To Sarah Shaw

Wayland [August?] 1876

My Darling,

Oh dear! what *shall* I do, now that "Daniel Deronda" is finished? It has been the one solitary excitement of my life, since 1876 came in. What marvellous insight into human nature! What wonderful skill in the delineation of character, both in large, free outline, and minute touches in detail! How plainly I can see little Jacob in his scarlet stockings, and hands in the pockets of his knickerbockers! There is a great deal of moral beauty in the character of Deronda, especially manifested in his course toward the fascinating Gwendolen. But I was disappointed to have him sent off to the East to expend his energies in bringing back the Jews. It seems such a forlorn hope. I was disappointed in the same way to have the free spirited brilliant "Spanish Gipsy" sent off to unknown ports, to be Queen of a tribe of gipsies. In both cases, the self-abnegation is grand, but the purpose seems unworthy of the sacrifice. But, dear me, how George Elliot takes the [. . .][1] out of all other novels! Was n't that courtship of Grandecourt inimitable? I wonder how she came to know human nature so well, in so many varieties. In her "Clerical Sketches," she is perfectly at home

[1] This letter is a transcription made after Child's death; a single word in a crossed-out sentence is unrecovered.

in the poor ministers household, and knows all the difficulties about keeping silk dresses presentable, making the cream hold out for company, &c &c.[2] Truly she is a wonderful woman.—I have always been an enthusiastic admirer of George Elliot, but Daniel Deronda I think excels all her others; and nothing in it strikes me as more remarkable than her power of identifying herself so completely with the Jews,—not merely in their traditions, and customs, but in their feelings and aspirations. What a stain on Christianity is the treatment of the Jews! Millions of men, in various parts of the world, robbed, persecuted, tortured, for the crucifixion of a Jewish reformer of whom they never heard! By what queer agencies the world moves on! What could be more absurd than the "scheme of salvation"? God fore-ordained that man should fall; then was angry with him for falling; then his justice required that he should punish somebody; so he shed the blood of his innocent son; and his son was himself. Yet this rigamarole led the sons of men out of a lower kind of fetishism.

I am delighted with Mrs. Lowell's appointment.[3] The manner in which she will discharge the duties of her important trust, will do more good for the Woman Cause, than a dozen conventions.

Your affectionate old Mariquita

L; Lydia Maria Child Papers, Anti-Slavery Collection, Cornell University (microfiche 87/2284).

Early in November 1876, Child and Mrs. Pickering left Wayland to winter in two rented rooms at 7 Groton Street, Boston. Boston was much more expensive than Wayland. Child took breakfast at bakeries and had dinner in restaurants, and wrote "I like this Bohemian life better than genteel boarding."*

To Sarah Shaw

Boston [November?] 1876.
Dear Sarah

Here we are away up at the South End, above Dover St. And we are close by Cottage Place, where Frank introduced you to me. Oh, Sarah dear, what changes have come over us all, since then! Outwardly, how changed! and spiritually, still more so. Surely, the angels do not call us by the same names they did then. It seems so strange to round the circle, and come back in sight of Cottage Place, where my little minikin garden bloomed, and where dear David and I lived so lovingly and cosily, looking out on the diamond-sprinkled

[2] George Eliot, *Scenes of Clerical Life* (London, 1858).
[3] The Shaws' daughter, reformer Josephine (Shaw) Lowell (1843–1905), was appointed the first woman member of the New York State Board of Charities in 1876.
* 10 Dec. 1876, Wayland (Mass.) Historical Society.

water, that flowed between us, and South Boston. All that has happened since then, what was it *for?* What has all the toil *accomplished?* At present it seems to me a barren record; but perhaps I shall understand it better hereafter. Your loving old friend

Mariquita

L; Lydia Maria Child Papers, Anti-Slavery Collection, Cornell University (microfiche 87/2288).

To Sarah Parsons

Boston, February 10, 1877.

. . .

I think every individual, and every society, is perfected just in proportion to the combination, and cooperation, of masculine and feminine elements of character. He is the most perfect man who is affectionate as well as intellectual; and she is the most perfect woman who is intellectual as well as affectionate. Every art and science becomes more interesting, viewed both from the masculine and feminine points of view. Not of marriage only may it be justly said, "What God has joined together, let not man put asunder." I think God intended a participation of the masculine and feminine element in every relation and every duty of life. Politics form no exception to this universal rule. There are many ways in which women could do good service to their country by thoughtful and conscientious action in politics. By urging more enlightened laws, and voting for those who will sustain such laws, they may do much to shield their sons and brothers from the dangerous temptations of intemperance and licentiousness. By advocating and voting for a peaceable international settlement of difficulties, they may do much to prevent husbands, sons, and brothers from being butchered in battle. War is a horrid barbarism, which ought to cease throughout the civilized world. But even war is no exception to the rule that masculine and feminine elements should everywhere cooperate together. None can help so efficiently as women in the hospital department of war, and their usefulness might also be great in the commissary department. The more the sphere of woman's activity of thought enlarges, the more her character and capabilities enlarge. The more her attention is taken up with important subjects, the less time and thought will she expend on fashion and frivolous amusements. During the War of the Rebellion, there were sudden changes of character in mere worldly women, that seemed almost miraculous. Ladies, who had been accustomed to while away the hours of life with fancy work, manifested a degree of executive ability in the sanitary commission, and in the hospitals, which astonished their husbands and brothers. The power had always been in them, but it had not been developed, because they had not been called upon to use it. The women of Asia have the same human nature, and the same natural capabilities, that we have; but in those countries they spend their time playing with dolls and chattering with parrots. If they had been brought to New England as soon as they were born, they would have become clerks, authors, doctors, painters, and sculptors, and enlightened domestic companions for intelligent men, and sensible, judicious mothers of coming generations.

The civilization of any country may always be measured by the degree of equality between men and women; and society will never come truly into order until there is perfect equality and copartnership between them in every department of human life.

L, extract; *Letters of Lydia Maria Child*, 1882 (microfiche 87/2304).

The results of the 1876 election marked the end of Reconstruction. In the early returns the Democratic candidate backed by the South, Samuel J. Tilden, seemed to defeat the Republican, Rutherford B. Hayes; it was almost time for the president to take office before the final decision was in. A complicated dispute arose over the last crucial electoral votes, but a bipartisan electoral commission finally settled the dispute in Hayes's favor. Behind the dubious victory of the Republicans and its acceptance by the Democrats was an elaborate and secret maneuver between spokesmen for the two candidates. The Republicans got the presidency, and the Democrats got a pledge to let the South have "home rule" and the economic aid it badly needed.

When Hayes took office in March 1877, he promptly withdrew the last federal troops from the South. The white Democrats were now in complete control. As the troops marched away, the last of the Radical state governments collapsed. The Republicans, immensely strengthened in the North and Midwest, no longer needed the votes of Southern blacks to win and hold national power. Child and the abolitionists watched as, in a new South ruled by Democrats, the civil and political rights of blacks were taken away piece by piece, with the approval of Congress and the Supreme Court. The blacks sank to the bottom of a caste system.

What Child always feared—progress based upon expediency rather than idealistic conviction—came to pass. "Peace with the old master class," wrote Frederick Douglass in the early 1880s, "has been war to the Negroes. As one has risen, the other has fallen."

To Sarah Shaw

Boston, 7 Groton St. Feb 19'th, 1877.

Darling Sarah,

. . .

I have done puzzling my brains to discover who is elected President. If Hayes is elected, I am afraid they will poison him. If all the Roman Catholic Priests should be assembled on an island, and the island should plump down to the bottom of the ocean, I should not find it difficult to be reconciled to the doings of Providence. What *could* possess the German Jews to aid and abet the plans of their worst persecutors? I suppose the *word* democracy misled them, as it has many other foreigners. Speaking of Jews, did you read in the Advertiser that silly and absurd criticism of "Daniel Deronda," by Mrs. "Co-operation" Pierce? Among other things she says George Elliott never does justice to the *Christian* character; that if she introduces Christians they are of a mean type; and that if she wants an ideal, she has to go to a *Jew*. The woman seems to have forgotten Savonarola, and Romala, and Dinah the preacher, and Lyon the Preacher, and the simple devout piety of the peasant woman, in the lovely poem of "Agatha."[1] *Theological* prejudice and jealousy is at the root of much of the effort to detect flaws in George Elliott. If she was an Episcopalian, who scrupulously ⟨eat⟩ ate pancakes on Shrove Tuesday, there would be quite a different tone in the criticisms upon her. If she would sprinkle in "Father, Son, and Holy Ghost," here and there, *with* meaning, or *without* meaning, how loudly they would blow the trumpet for her! To think of the impertinence of attempting to measure a soul like hers in their theological pint pots!

. . .

ALS; Houghton Library, Harvard University (microfiche 87/2310).

Anne Whitney (1821–1915), sculptor, supported the antislavery and woman's rights movements. After the Civil War she lived several years in Europe, but in 1877 she had recently bought a house in Boston. Whitney did many portrait busts, including such figures as Garrison, Harriet Beecher Stowe, Lucy Stone, and Frances Willard. Although Child declined Whitney's offer to sculpt her, the two became warm friends.

To Anne Whitney

7 Groton St. April 8th '77

Dear Miss Whitney,

I will answer your kind note with my characteristic directness and truthfulness.

I should consider it a great honor to have my bust made by you; and if it were ever to be made by anyone, I should decidedly give you the preference.

But nature did not mould my features harmoniously. Even in my youth, their outlines could not have been fashioned into beauty; and an *old* woman

[1] Savonarola is a prominent character in *Romola* (London, 1863). Dinah is a Methodist preacher in *Adam Bede,* and Lyon an Independent minister in *Felix Holt the Radical* (Edinburgh, 1866). Eliot's poem "Agatha" had been published in the *Atlantic Monthly* in 1869.

is *always* an ugly subject for sculpture. Old *men* have the advantage of us in that respect. Old men are often nobler subjects for Art, than young men; but it is not so with women.

I admire your genius too much to have it employed on any but beautiful or noble forms; and I have too much reverence for the high mission of Art to consent to its being desecrated by the portraiture of my old visage. So please accept my most grateful acknowledgements for the offered honor, which I feel bound to decline.

I should have had the pleasure of calling upon you ere this, had not the weather been so unfavorable. I shall be glad if circumstances admit of our becoming better acquainted.

Yours very cordially,
L. Maria Child.

ALS; Anne Whitney Papers, Wellesley College (microfiche 88/2317).

To Lidian Emerson

Wayland, May 22d [1877?]

My Dear Mrs. Emerson,

That you may not feel it necessary to reserve a seat in your carriage for me, I write to say that it will not be convenient for me to carry the pleasant project into execution. I have, for many years, followed quite literally Mr. Emerson's advice to "sit at home with might and main," and as I grow older, the habit becomes a necessity, as habits are wont to do. I thank you none the less heartily for the kind and tempting invitation.

I always supposed you were a Swedenborgian. I recollect very well the first time I ever heard of you. Some one told me that Mr. Emerson was about to marry a Swedenborgian lady, who, the first time she heard him lecture, received a very strong impression that they were spiritual partners; insomuch that, on her return home, she said to a friend, "That man is certainly my predestined husband."

It seemed to me strange how a Swedenborgian should find in Mr. Emerson's lectures proofs of intimate spiritual relationship; and, therefore, I doubted the authenticity of the story.

Madame Guyon was a favorite ideal of *mine*, at one period of my life; but the older I have grown, the less and less have I been inclined to any form of asceticism.[1] My state of mind demands something more vigorous, healthy, and joyous. It seems to me that religion should not be a thing *apart* from our earthly life, nor do I see the necessity of its being *above* it. The religion that is not *in* our daily duties seems to me of little value. I have seen so much piety without

[1] Madame Guyon was the subject of one of Child's biographies in her *Ladies' Family Library* of 1832–35.

humanity, that I have long since come to the conclusion that devout tendencies have no necessary connexion with moral principles. It was not hypocrisy that led the Barons of the Middle Ages to consecrate to the Virgin part of what they robbed from their neighbors. They were *really* devout, but they were not honest. John Newton has recorded "sweet seasons of communion with God," while he was in Africa personally engaged in the Slave Trade.[2] He was *really* pious, but he was not just or humane. I give Daniel Webster credit for sincerity in the religious feelings he expressed; but he was unquestionably a very bad man. On the other hand, the two best men, in a moral point of view, with whom I have ever been acquainted, were out-and-out infidels. The fact is, devotion is merely the reverential tendency of the human mind directed toward super-natural things; and it may, or may not, co-exist with morality.

Very cordially yours,
L. Maria Child.

ALS; Houghton Library, Harvard University (microfiche 90/2389).

In July, repeated wage cuts led to the Railway Strike of 1877, the first great collision between U.S. capital and labor. In clashes between troops and workers scores were killed or wounded. With the Paris Commune of 1871 still a fright-eningly fresh memory, the press and the middle class saw the strike as "a com-munist conspiracy to overthrow the government." Police, troops, and vigilantes crushed the strike in two weeks.

To Sarah Shaw

Wayland, July 31'st, 1877.

Darling Friend,

   . . .

   . . . O! why can't the American people be universally thankful that the threatening aspect of the Presidential campaign terminated in such an honest, good, sensible Chief-Magistrate?[1] Why *need* they be passing resolutions that he was not legally elected? Since we were lucky enough to *be* at peace, why *could*'nt they *keep* the peace? I was not very much surprised at the terrible outbursts on the rail-roads; for I have long been aware that there was a volcano seething and rumbling beneath our feet, on this vexed question of Labor and Capital. But it gives one a frightful sense of insecurity to be made tangibly aware that in all our large towns there is an ignorant desperate rabble, ready for any work of destruction, whenever opportunity offers. There is no excuse

[2] The slave trader John Newton ordered prayers twice a day aboard his slave ship. He viewed the slave trade as a means of converting heathen, as well as making profit. Later he was converted to abolitionism.
[1] The effect of Hayes's withdrawal of federal protection of the blacks in the South was apparently not yet clear to Child.

for it in this country, where every man who is unjustly dealt by has ample legal means of redress. To me, one of the saddest things about it is the common remark that a "Republican form of government is not strong enough for emergencies." They seem to forget the marvellous strength it manifested in the War of the Rebellion; and they also ignore the fact that most of these reckless rioters have had their training under European governments. It grieves me to hear such remarks, because they indicated the beginning of an end I have long dreaded. No observing person can help being aware of an increasing tendency toward a strong *demarcation of classes* in this country. The genteel classes do not intermarry with the middle classes; the middle classes do not intermarry with the laboring class; nothing is *said* about it, but there is a systematic avoidance of it. Moreover, they don't intermix socially; they are as much strangers to each other, as if they lived in different countries. There are individual exceptions, like myself; cases where persons born in the middle class, and always remaining in it, still mix considerably with the classes above them; but these cases are exceptions to the general rule. And how often it has been hinted to me that I should stand a great deal better with the upper classes, if I would avoid mentioning that my father was a mechanic!   This state of feeling may be unavoidable; but if it be so, all I have to say is, that a Republic is impossible. I have long noticed that attachment to our institutions is becoming perceptibly loosened. I am sorry; for I love the Republic. Not because it is *my* country, but because its institutions are better calculated than any other to give every man a chance to develope whatever faculties are in him. Sad it is that they can't appreciate the blessing! These rioters are terribly in the wrong; and there is nothing for it but to subdue them with a strong hand.

   With love to Frank. I am always your affectionate old friend Mariquita.

ALS, incomplete?; Houghton Library, Harvard University (microfiche 88/2335).

To Sarah Shaw
                                                    Wayland, Aug. 25'th 1877.
Dear Sarah,

   To begin at the *beginning*, in answer to your queries, I will say that, for *myself*, I have very little reason to find fault with the aristocratic spirit. While I was Miss Francis, I twice or thrice met with marked discourtesy from some members of the first class of Bostonians. That I was decidedly snubbed during the Anti Slavery struggle, and since, has doubtless been owing to my reformatory and radical tendencies, and my neglect of dress, rather than to any considerations of my birth. On the other hand, I have met with a great deal of friendly attention, and cordial kindness, from people of the genteel classes. For *myself* I have no complaint to make of them.

   I am not "proud of my father's being a mechanic"; neither am I ashamed of it. It is simply a subject of which I never think, unless I am reminded of it by some one. I honor his memory; for he was a very honest, kind-hearted, industrious man, simple as a child, uneducated, but very intelligent by nature.

As for *classes*, the Vanderbilts and ⟨Stuarts⟩ Stewarts, they do not constitute a *class;* there are too few of them.[1] By the genteel class, I mean those who live in mansions of their own, with incomes varying from $5000 to $20,000 or more. By the middle class, I mean farmers and mechanics, who work with their *hands,* own a house, with or without some acres of land, with incomes, from their own labor, varying from $300 a year to $1,500.   By the laboring class, I mean those who own no dwelling, and subsist upon the proceeds of their labor upon the premises of other people.   I smiled to see you class yourself, and Mrs. Barlow, and Mr. Curtis, with the *middling* class.[2] Certainly none of you have aristocratic airs; but all of you have luxurious habits, and are unaccustomed to wait upon yourselves. If you were to find yourselves suddenly in the surroundings of the middle class, you would be like fishes out of water.

Certainly, neither your daughter, nor mine, if I had one, could marry a day-laborer; because there could be no chance for happiness where there was no congeniality of manners, habits, and tastes. But if the wood-sawyer had a *son,* of good manners, pure morals, and cultured mind, the saw-horse and saw would be as acceptable to me, as any dragon, or castle, in a field azure, for armorial bearings. Now, I do not know of a farmer in this rustic town, who would not object to his daughter's marrying the son of a day-laborer; and the daughters themselves will put up with any deprivations at home, rather than go to help a neighbor in any emergency, for a dollar, or two dollars a day. All want to crowd into employments deemed genteel; employments that do not soil the clothes, or the hands. Hence, the supply of teachers and artists is much greater than the demand, and a good deal of it not above mediocrity; while there is absolute suffering for services not deemed genteel, but which are absolutely necessary. There is no use in being blind to the fact; an unwillingness to be *known* to labor with the hands *does* pervade all classes of the community. Moreover, each class draws a line between itself and the class below it. Even the Irish shop-keeper, or provision-dealer, considers it a mésalliance to marry an Irish cook, or chambermaid. And as for the colored people, *their* "fust families," carry matters with a high hand.

The prevalence of these ideas and feelings does make me[3]

Mrs. Pickering lived in Oregon sometime. She is predisposed to favor the genteel classes; but she says the treatment of the Indians is, to her own knowledge, a sin and an outrage.

AL; Houghton Library, Harvard University (microfiche 88/2338).

---

[1] She refers probably to Alexander T. Stewart, developer of a department store in New York.
[2] Ellen Shaw, Sarah's daughter, had married wealthy lawyer Francis Channing Barlow in 1867.
[3] The rest of the letter is missing; the passage following is a marginal note.

To James T. Fields

Wayland, Oct. 28'th, 1877.

Mr. Fields,

Dear Sir, I know you are always ready to help, wherever you can; and I want you to help me with a little advice. You may perhaps remember that I once told yo[u] I wanted to make an Eclectic Bible. I am afraid to undertake *that*, lest I should get into debt; but I have made a *small* vol. on that plan; not more than a 150, or 180 duodecimo pages.

If you will have the goodness to glance over what I send, you will see that it bears no resemblance to Conway's Anthology; indeed I am not aware that there is *any* book on a similar plan.

The Free Religious writers are *scholars*, and they do not reach the *popular* mind. I aim directly at the *common people*. I have altered nothing, but I have put Oriental and Grecian ideas into a plain English dress.

I do not expect to get any money, or any reputation, by the publication of it; but I do want, before I go hence, to do something more toward loosening the fetters with which old superstitions shackle the minds of men.

I have taken up various subjects in succession, and carried them through ancient down to modern times, in the same way I have done with those I send you.   It is all finished and arranged, and if you think I can publish it *without getting into debt*, I should like to proceed immediately. If you are doubtful about it, I will lay it aside.[1]

I have taken lodgings for the winter, at 15 Ashland Place, next above East Dover St.   If nothing untoward happens, I expect to go in on Tuesday, Nov. 6th; and I will come immediately to your house to hear your opinion about the risk of publication. Meanwhile, please inform me whether it arrives safely. I have no other copy.

With affectionate remembrance to Mrs. Fields, I am

Yours cordially,
L. Maria Child.

ALS; James Thomas Fields Collection, Huntington Library (microfiche 89/2343).

Child, with Mrs. Pickering, made her annual move to Boston in November 1877, taking rooms at 15 Ashland Place. They stayed until early April.

---

[1] The book was *Aspirations of the World* (1878). Fields helped her find another publisher, Roberts Brothers of Boston.

To Sarah Shaw

15 Ashland Place. Dec. 19th, 1877.

Darling Friend,

. . .

I don't feel so sad as you do about the transition-state in which we are living. I admit that it is not so *pleasant* as a quiet adherence to old opinions and traditionary forms. But transition is necessary to *growth;* and the same universal laws of Providence take care of the souls of men in states of transition, ⟨as well⟩ as in the places where they have rested for a while. The chrysalis seems a dead thing; but there is a beautiful wingéd creature within it, and in due time it comes forth.

How very sad it must have seemed to the cultured minds of ancient Greece to see all their magnificent system of worship passing away, like a dream of the night! Men's minds seemed in a chaos; all the old land-marks gone. But noble and true characters grew through it all, and higher human ideals were evolved by the process.

In trying to remember my own spiritual progress, it does not seem to me as if what is called religion had helped it much. Reading the Bible and going to meeting seem to me like the clothes that I wore outside. The vital warmth was *within.* Something *within* me impelled me to do what was just and kind; and something *within* troubled me when I did wrong. I thought I believed the Bible to be the only inspired rule of life; but, unconsciously and habitually, my life was really far more influenced by Carlyle, Emerson &c; and by the good and true persons with whom I was brought into contact. Now that my faith in time-honored traditions has vanished, I am more conscientious than I ever was.

Through all the seeming confusion I believe there is real progress. I think your grand-children will grow up under influences better calculated to make strong, free, true characters, than the influences which educated *us.* The same universal laws of Providence that have protected *our* souls will protect *theirs.*

Trees do not die because the leaves drop when they have done the work of the season. The old foliage has helped to form a sap *within,* which will clothe the trees with new verdure. I am full of hope for the future of the world; and my faith grows ever stronger that it is governed by wise and beneficent laws.

. . .

ALS; Houghton Library, Harvard University (microfiche 89/2352).

To Sarah Shaw

[1877]

. . . The photograph of President Hayes is far the best I have seen. The head and face is good; indicating intelligence, alertness, and firmness. I am sorry to hear that he promises to sustain Wade Hampton's government of South

Carolina.[1] I know that Frank approves of it; so does Elizur Wright, and several other friends of the colored people; but it seems to me a strange forgetfulness of the lessons of the past. Certainly the government of every state ought to be administered by *intelligent* citizens. It is a misfortune and a peril to be governed by the ignorant, whether negroes or Irish. But the rulers should be men who respect the rights of the ignorant, and who sincerely aim at their welfare and improvement. Now Wade Hampton has always been the hardest of the hard, with regard to the interests of the colored people. He has always considered them animals, and has always manifested a desire to *keep* them so. Unless he has recently gone through some wonderful process of regeneration, he is totally *incapable* of doing justice to the colored citizens of South Carolina. I would as soon set a fox to take care of the geese.

. . .

L; Lydia Maria Child Papers, Anti-Slavery Collection, Cornell University (microfiche 89/2356).

James Redpath had met John Brown in Kansas and after Brown's execution had published two books about him. After he became manager of a lecture bureau, he maintained his interest in Brown. Sculptor Anne Whitney at this time modelled a head of John Brown, now unlocated.

To James Redpath

Jan. 10'th 1878
15 Ashland Place. Boston.

Mr. Redpath,
    Dear Sir,
    I see there is a proposition to make a statue of John Brown; and, feeling a great interest in it, I cannot help wishing that the first-rate artists should try who can make the best model; and that the one who makes the *best* model should have the making of the statue.
    Miss Ann Whitney of Boston has more than talent; she has decided *genius* for sculpture. She is conscientiously *thorough* in all her work; and she has an unusual faculty of putting *life* and *character* into marble. Of this, you can judge for yourself, if you look at her fine statue of Samuel Adams in the Gallery at Washington. Her model of Charles Sumner obtained the highest prize, and it is extremely satisfactory to all the friends and admirers of Mr. Sumner.
    Common *justice* required that she should have had the cutting of the statue.

---

[1] The Democrat Wade Hampton, running for governor of South Carolina, had promised to respect the rights of the blacks if elected. But once he was in office, his party used force and fraud to restore the state to white supremacy.

But they did not give it to her, simply on the ground that she was a *woman*, and as a woman was not likely to understand the anatomy of masculine figures. But she studied with great diligence four years in Europe; much of the time in *Life* Model schools; and her knowledge of anatomy is exceptionally perfect; as is sufficiently shown in her statues of Samuel Adams and Charles Sumner.

She took a warm interest in the Anti Slavery struggle; as she does in the cause of human freedom in every form.

Such mental habits are, I think, a peculiarly good preparation for imparting an heroic character to the sculptured forms of heroic people.

She is a quiet, straightforward person, incapable of lobbying, or any other kind of management, to obtain success. She places her reliance upon her genuine merits as an artist; and they are certainly very great.

I do not think a woman should be encouraged, in any department, merely because she *is* a woman. But if a woman works, in any department, as *well* as men, she ought to have an equal chance with men.

Miss Whitney is a mature, highly cultured woman, and an earnest, devoted artist.

She knows nothing of my writing this. I write it because "the spirit moves" me.

Yours very respectfully,
L. Maria Child.

ALS; Beinecke Rare Book and Manuscript Library, Yale University (microfiche 89/ 2360).

To Sarah Shaw

15 Ashland Place. Jan 20'th, 1878.

Darling Sarah,

. . .

. . . An atmosphere of sadness seems to brood over the city. "Great Bankrupt Sales" stare one in the face in every street, and thousands of unemployed men and women are clamorous for food. It has all grown out of excessive extravagance. None thought of saving a reserve fund in the days of prosperity. All lived up to their means, and multitudes lived far beyond them. It seemed as if the whole nation were on a wild race-course, determined to win the golden cup, or break their necks. I can see no relief for the present state of things, but to draw off thousands from over-crowded trade, and send them to dig farms in the West. The dear *Earth* is a good mother, and feeds her children well, if they will only seek her favors industriously. I know what *I* would do, if I had Vanderbilt's property. I would give free rail-road passage to the West for 20,000 people, and furnish them with agricultural tools and seeds, with ten years credit for the money. Frank need n't tell me that I *could n't* do it. I *would* do it. Let the good Lord give me $20,000,000, and *see* if I would n't do it!

. . .

I have been reading all sorts of books. Renan's Jesus, Herber[t] Spencer's Philosophy, Omar Kheyám, &c[1] What a very *French* Jesus Renan portrays. To think of its being all *arranged* to raise Lazarus, to produce an *effect*, because public opinion required that he should prove himself a prophet by restoring a dead man to life! How constantly Jesus does things, or avoids doing them, from motives of *policy!* O France! France! How plainly *all* your children betray their Jesuitical training! Speaking of Jesuitism, were you not amused at the Pope's mourning for Victor Emanuel?[2]

. . .

ALS; Houghton Library, Harvard University (microfiche 89/2362).

To Sarah Parsons

15 Ashland Place. Feb. 12'th, '78

Dear Sarah,
. . .

You wrote, the Sunday after Christmas, that I might expect a visit from Mr. Garrison on *that day;* but I have not seen him yet. His mind is much exercised about the condition of the freedmen; and I fear not without cause. I think President Hayes is honest, and has tried to do what he thought would be best for the welfare of the country. But I did not like the "sops to Cerburus" which he threw in his Southern tour; and I am afraid the ex-slaveholders will make use of this *excessive* spirit of conciliation to oppress the colored population, and gain control of the politics of the North.[1] It is their old game; and they are as cunning, and as aggressive, as ever.

. . .

ALS; Lydia Maria Child Papers, Anti-Slavery Collection, Cornell University (microfiche 89/2367).

[1] The references are to Ernest Renan (1823–92), French historian and critic, whose *Life of Jesus*, the first volume of his *History of the Origins of Christianity* (London, 1864), was his best-known book; Herbert Spencer (1820–1903), English philosopher; and Edward Fitzgerald's translation of the Persian poet's *Rubaiyat* (1859).
[2] Victor Emmanuel II (1820–78) was the first king of united Italy. In 1870 his troops had seized the papal states and made Rome the capital of Italy, an act protested by Pope Pius IX and his successors.
[1] In September 1877 Hayes had made a "goodwill" tour of five Southern states. He urged his "confederate friends" to "obey the whole Constitution" and assured blacks that their "rights and interests" would be safe if the "great mass of intelligent white men were let alone by the general government."

To Anne Whitney

Wayland, May 22d, 1878.

Dear Anne,

Wind and weather permitting, I propose to go to Boston on Thursday, May 30'th. I shall have to go to the Bank, to Mr. Sewall's Office, to the Bookseller's, and several other places, on business. I shall dine *en route*, and hope to arrive at your house somewhere about 3 P.M. there to abide till Friday, when I propose to attend the Free Religious Meeting, for speaking. I propose to spend Friday night with my niece in Cambridge, and on Saturday return home to Wayland. We shall have Thursday afternoon and evening to settle the affairs of the universe; which will be abundant time for us to accomplish it; considering that one of us is so well posted up in all that relates to Matter, and the other so familiar with all that relates to Spirit.

If it should storm, all my plans will be frustrated.

I don't wonder you were surprised by the low dress in my photograph; especially, considering the age at which it was taken.[1] The explanation is this: My dear old husband was as lover-like to the last year of his life, as he was during the days of courtship. He was often saying: "I fell in love with your *honest shoulders;* and I want you to have a photograph taken, on purpose for *me,* with the shoulders uncovered." So, at last, I humored the lover-like whim; and having no low dress, I folded a shawl about the bust.

Some years after it was taken, Mr. Prang[2] came here to look at photographs of me, with a view to make a picture of "Representative Women." Mr. Child showed him *his* photograph, and Mr. Prang thought it was the best that had been taken. I thought so, too; and I consented that he should copy merely *the head.* Contrary to my intention, the "honest shoulders" came to light; and I did not think it worth while to make any fuss about it. Head, shoulders, and all will be forgotten in a few years.

I am neither disgusted nor disturbed with Col. Ingersoll.[3] I believe in *unlimited* freedom to express any amount of belief or unbelief. Because he is fighting *that* battle, I am willing to "hold up his hands till the going down of the sun." I have not arrived at his conclusions; and if I had, it would not be *my* way to state them thus. But it is *his* way. He is by nature full of fun. The prevailing theological ideas seem to him ridiculous, and he makes all manner of jokes at their expense. The ideas seem to *me* as ridiculous as they do to *him;* but I have so much pity for poor human-nature, wandering in the dark, that I have not the heart to joke about *anything* that furnishes any poor starving soul with consolation or support. Yet Ingersoll and I are, to a certain extent,

---

[1] The photograph was made in the early 1870s.
[2] The lithographer.
[3] Robert G. Ingersoll (1833–99), lawyer and orator, was known as the "Great Agnostic"; his trenchant wit enraged the orthodox and sometimes irritated liberals.

doing the same work. He is *knocking* off fetters, and I am *melting* them off. Good riddance to fetters! say I. I want to see human souls stride about *freely* in search of truth. *You* are overturning superstition with the crow-bar of Science, *he* brings Fun in to give it a heave. By *all* our help, it will be rolled into the abyss of oblivion.

. . .

AL; Anne Whitney Papers, Wellesley College (microfiche 90/2390).

In the spring of 1878 Child edited and published *Aspirations of the World: A Chain of Opals.* Hoping "to exorcise the spirit of bigotry from the popular mind," Child selected passages from the religious works of many faiths and cultures, avoiding theology. *Aspirations of the World* was an expression of the same ecumenical impulse which had created her *Progress of Religious Ideas* nearly a quarter century before.

To Francis Shaw

Wayland, June 7'th, 1878.

Dear Friend,

I thank you heartily for your kind letter. I live so much alone, that a sympathizing word about my little book comforts and strengthens me greatly. I told you I did not prepare it for readers who knew as much on the subject as you do; but for the masses of minds who have adopted old traditions, without much reading, or thought. If they will read the book, I think its influence must be to loosen the bonds of their prejudices, and to expand their human sympathies. "A little leaven will leaven the whole lump," provided you can get it *into* the lump. Whether I can do this is doubtful. The book has very small sale; and the clergy of all sects will quietly do all in their power to impede its circulation.

The mistake we have made with regard to Jesus has been in supposing him to have come directly from heaven, bringing with him truths never before announced. Like all the great benefactors of the world, he was the product of antecedent progress. I think it is evident he never thought of establishing a *new* religion, but merely of purifying and reforming the *old.* His sympathies went with the poor, and his earnest, kindly spirit revolted against the pride and hypocrisy of the ruling classes. He brought the highest *teaching* of the Jews home to their consciences, in contrast with their *practices;* just as Garrison used to thunder Scripture in the ears of pious slaveholders.

I attribute the rapid spread of Christianity and Buddhism to the fact that the founders of both religions did away with all distinctions of rank, and associated freely with the poor and despised. The yearning for *equality* probably arose as soon as there were two men in the world.

What think you of the present aspect of Communism?[1] It seems to me we are approaching a very dangerous crisis. The clamor is too purely *selfish* to result in good to any class. Secluded as I am, I continually see indications of a reckless disregard of reason, or principle, which must inevitably work nothing but mischief.

. . .

ALS; Houghton Library, Harvard University (microfiche 90/2394).

To Sarah Shaw

Wayland, July 9'th, 1878.

Dear Sarah,

. . .

. . . Poor Mag![1] She was one of that host of forlorn beings, who go through life with souls gasping and perishing, for want of somebody to love them, and somebody to love. It is so hard to tell what to *do* with characters so blighted by neglect, and hardened by harshness! Every kind person is willing to make efforts to redeem them; but where to place them, after the process of redemption is begun,—that is the puzzling question. Compassion is not enough for them; they need the consciousness of being loved by somebody, and of being essential to the comfort of some one. Dear Bessie Green's rule never to separate a mother from her illegitimate child was a wise provision for this craving of human nature.[2] How to find a *home* for such outcasts as poor Mag is a very difficult problem. Public institutions are generally anything but healing to their wounded souls, and it is rare to find a family *all* the members of which are disposed to help them forget the past. In three cases, I tried the experiment of taking a cast-a-way into my own room for several months. While they were with me, all went well; but every case proved a failure after they went out into the world to earn their living; one after a probation of a few months, the other two after a term of years. I confess that if I had known human nature as well as I now know it, I never should have had courage to try such experiments. But is it not strange that some way cannot be discovered by which the elements of human society can be so harmonized as to prevent such frightful discords? Oh, Sarah, my heart is very weary striving to solve this strange problem of human

[1] The militancy of the industrial workers, a third of them foreign born and desperately poor, stirred fears of communism in many quarters.
[1] "Mag" was the main character of an otherwise unidentified story set in the South.
[2] Bessie Green, a niece of Frank Shaw's, had worked with unwed mothers; she died in a shipwreck in 1875, at the age of twenty-eight.

life. If men only *could* be convinced that selfishness is very short-sighted *policy!* If they only *would* realize that to save another soul is the only way to save their own!

. . .

ALS; Houghton Library, Harvard University (microfiche 90/2400).

To William Lloyd Garrison

Wayland, Aug. 14'th, 1878.

Friend Garrison,

Some two months ago, I sent you my little book called "Aspirations of the World." Did you receive it?

I want you to tell me what you think of Mr. Heyward, and of the justice of his sentence.[1] I remember him as a pleasing young man in the Anti Slavery cause, and, without *knowing* anything about it, I have been inclined to suppose his *motives* were clean and disinterested, however mistaken his *theories* might be. He has written to me from prison, and evidently considers himself a martyr in a good and true cause.

What is called "the social question" is exceedingly loathsome to me. It seems to me an Augean Stable, which no Hercules could cleanse. Unfortunately, I know a good deal about the present diseased state of society, and I feel utterly hopeless concerning a cure. Consequently, I dodge the question whenever its discussion is proposed.

I do not know what Mr. Heyward has really been doing; I only know that the papers accuse him of advocating unlimited "free love." If so, he proposes a remedy worse than the disease; malignant as the disease is. Transient amours would prove disastrous to human happiness and character, even if law and public opinion did not brand them as sins. There has been a good deal of boasting about the healthy working of the strange system that prevails at Oneida Institute.[2] But a writer, who seems to know about the state of things there, says the women are pale, care-worn, and discontented. How can it be otherwise, when they live under a system, which renders domestic affection impossible.

[1] Ezra Hervey Heywood (1829–93) was a radical pamphleteer and publisher of the reform journal the *Word*. He and his wife, Angela F. Tilton, formed the New England Free Love League in 1873. In June 1878 he was convicted in Boston of mailing obscene publications to Anthony Comstock. He was sentenced to a one-hundred-dollar fine and two years at Dedham jail, but a protest by six thousand people at Faneuil Hall led to his pardon by President Hayes six months later.
[2] Oneida was the experimental cooperative community founded by John Humphrey Noyes in New York State in 1848. His Perfectionists advocated full equality of the sexes and practiced "complex" marriage, dissolving the traditional roles of husband and wife into temporary sexual partnerships. For contraception, men practiced coitus reservatus (withholding orgasm); this practice also reputedly enhanced sexual pleasure for women.

I think it not unlikely that Heyward has *meant* well; and I pity him. But I am rather afraid to write to him, lest I should seem to endorse proceedings of which I am ignorant.

. . .

ALS; Anti-Slavery Collection, Rare Books and Manuscripts, Boston Public Library (microfiche 90/2405).

To George W. Julian

Wayland, Sep. 28'th, 1878.

Dear Mr. Julian,

. . .

The *rapidity* of changes in these days is somewhat bewildering. Having known the wonderful enthusiasm, self-sacrifice, and courageous daring of the early abolitionists, I find it difficult to realize how completely the anti-slavery struggle is forgotten by the people; and how even the terrible expenditure of blood and treasure, which followed it, is fast sinking into oblivion.

Wendell Phillips was telling me, the other day, of his conversation with a highly educated young citizen of Boston, 26 years old. Mr. P. alluded to the possibility of mobs. "Oh, they never have mobs in *Boston*," replied the young man. To say *that* to *Mr. Phillips*, of all men!

When Mr. P. told him there *had* been violent outbreaks in Boston, he exclaimed, "Indeed! What were the mobs *about*? I never heard of them."

If the ill-feeling of the South had passed away as easily as the moral indignation of the North, I should be glad. But the lamentable misfortune is that emancipation was not the result of a popular ⟨moral⟩ *moral sentiment,* but of a miserable *"military necessity."* It was not the "fruit of righteousness," and therefore it is not "peace."

When Charles Sumner was in the Senate, and you were in the House, I used to read all the proceedings of Congress, and I knew how every member was likely to vote on any important question. I felt my soul expanded by the large views, and lifted up by the high moral standard, which characterized some members of Congress *then.* But, alas, where are our great men *now?*

I am sorry to hear that your health is "prematurely broken down." The old machine of *my* body is worn by long use; but it continues to work well. I am very respectfully & very cordially your old friend, and admirer,

L. Maria Child.

ALS; Joshua Giddings Papers, Manuscript Division, Library of Congress (microfiche 91/2411).

For the winter of 1878–79, Child and Mrs. Pickering took rooms at 8 West Dover Street in Boston. This season Child ventured out but little, usually only to dine with her old friends the Sewalls. Boston seemed like "a great desert" to her, "lacking the advantage of stillness" (20 November 1878, Cornell University).

To Anne Whitney

8 West Dover St. Nov. 25'th, 1878

Dear Saucebox,

I dined with the Sewalls yesterday, and I expect to do it again next Sunday; and I do *not* intend to enter upon a course of promiscuous visiting. I have been a Bohemian for nearly 77 years, and I have resolved to remain a Bohemian. Society has never yet got me into harness, and there is still enough of the colt in me to run at sight of a halter. So you may hang up your lasso, my lady.

I hope you are careful about going too near your windows. *I* have no temptation to such pitch-poling myself, but as your imagination seems active on that subject, it behoves you to take care. I certainly could not throw myself out without considerable forethought and preparation. Therefore, if such a somersault should occur, you may inform the interviewers of the press that you have *my* authority for declaring that it was done on purpose.

Thereupon, paragraphs will appear, stating that Mrs. Child was the author of several books of water-color reputation, and, though a somewhat eccentric, old woman, was generally considered to have common sense; and, as it was not known that any peculiarly heavy trouble weighed upon her mind, her friends were at a loss how to explain her rash proceeding.

You perhaps, knowing that I think I have a soul (excuse the word) may conclude I was in a hurry to go and see what was to become of it.

With profound respects to old Roma, and love to Lief,[1] I remain your truly attached

Bird o' Freedom.

ALS; Anne Whitney Papers, Wellesley College (microfiche 91/2416).

Child had copies of *Aspirations of the World* mailed to George Eliot and Thomas Carlyle. Eliot replied on 30 March, saying that she valued the book and thanking Child for "stretching out your hand to me."[*]

---

[1] These were statues sculpted by Whitney.

[*] *The George Eliot Letters,* ed. Gordon S. Haight (New Haven: 1955), VII, 122.

To George Eliot

Boston, Mass'ts, Jan 26'th, 1879

Dear Mrs. Lewes,

I am now a very old woman, and during many years of my long pilgrimage, your writings have been to me like the morning light, the mountain air, the pure, sparkling stream—like all things broad, bright, refreshing, and free. Therefore, I send you a small token of my love. The little book was made solely for the enfranchisement of the popular mind, and, of course contains no ideas that have not long been familiar to you; but, as one of numerous signs of the times, it may not be altogether without interest to one who loves the human race.

The loss of your life-companion is a grief too sacred to be intermeddled with by strangers; but my heart goes out to you in affectionate sympathy.[1]

Your unknown friend,
L. Maria Child.

ALS; Beinecke Rare Book and Manuscript Library, Yale University (microfiche 91/2429).

To Abby B. Francis

Boston, February 21, 1879.

. . .

The labor question continues to seethe and grumble, like a volcano about to explode. Laborers, instead of serving their own interests by leaving off smoking and drinking, are clamoring for the expulsion of the industrious and frugal Chinese.[1] A great force is brought to bear upon Congress to procure the abolition of our treaty with China; a measure which would be dishonest and disgraceful to the United States, and extremely injurious to our trade with China.[2]

Garrison, Phillips, Ward Beecher, and others are trying their utmost to prevent such a violation of principle. H. W. Beecher, in one of his public speeches, said, in his facetious way: "It is complained that the Chinese are idolaters, and therefore not fit to associate with Christians. We have stoned them, and clubbed them, and persecuted them, and tried religion upon them in almost every shape, and still they won't embrace it!"

L, extract; *Letters of Lydia Maria Child*, 1882 (microfiche 91/2435).

[1] George Henry Lewes died on 30 Nov. 1878.
[1] Child's was almost a lone voice opposing the racist assault upon the Chinese, led by the labor movement.
[2] The Burlingame Treaty of 1868 between China and the United States allowed the people of each country to migrate freely to the other. The treaty would be amended in 1880, permitting the United States to suspend Chinese immigration when it wished. Two years later Congress passed the Chinese Exclusion Act.

To Sarah Shaw

8 Dover St. March 20'th, 1879.

Dear Sarah,

. . .

Perhaps you thought I was rude in what I wrote of "Daisy Miller," and "The International Episode."[1] I do not deny that the pictures are well sketched; but I despise the subjects. The fact is, my contempt of fashionable people is almost ferocious. In Washington St. there is a window full of dolls; some in walking-dresses, some in ball-dresses, some in bridal costume arranging their veils, coquetting with fans, &c. What a fool Raphael would have been to have made the most exquisite picture of those dolls, instead of copying genuine living beings! The writer who sketches shoddy fashionables wastes his talents, just as foolishly.

. . .

ALS; Houghton Library, Harvard University (microfiche 92/2440).

To escape terror and oppression in the late 1870s, thousands of blacks fled from the South to the North and West in what was called the Negro Exodus. The largest number went to Kansas. On 24 April 1879, in a letter to a Faneuil Hall meeting he was too ill to attend, Garrison lashed out against the "bloody misrule" in the South responsible for this exodus. It was his last published utterance.

To Samuel E. and Harriet Sewall

Wayland, April 30'th 1879.

. . .

I have felt greatly excited about the poor exiled freedmen. The practice of Slavery teaches human beings *nothing* good; not even enlightened self-interest. How I *have* wanted to let out my indignation! But not a mortal in this sleepy town cares a button what becomes of the negroes. I console myself with the thought that their forced exodus may, in the end, prove a benefit to their much-injured race. But, I tell you, if the Devil don't get our government, "there might as well be no Devil at all." It has expended all its energies in efforts to conciliate the oppressors, and has given no thought to the protection of the oppressed. Garrison's trumpet-blast to the Faneiul Hall Meeting sounded like the old times. I myself, though tamed by age, felt ready to rush into the fight

[1] Henry James, *Daisy Miller* (New York, 1877) and "An International Episode" (New York, 1878).

again. Trumpet-tones will stir the blood of an old war-horse, however long he may have been dragging round his cart-load of stones.

. . .

ALS; Robie-Sewall Papers, Massachusetts Historical Society (microfiche 92/2447).

Garrison died on 24 May 1879. Child describes his influence on her in the following letter. To Francis Jackson Garrison she observed, "My radicalism grows more pronounced, the older I grow."*

To Anne Whitney

May 25th—1879

Dear Friend,

. . .

I am glad you had such a pleasant evening with Garrison. He has been a singularly fortunate man. Fortunate in accomplishing his purposes; fortunate in drawing around him the best spirits of his time; fortunate in having an amiable sympathizing wife; fortunate in having excellent, devoted children, whose marriages have suited him, and who have lived in proximity to him; fortunate in having his energies developed by struggle in early life; fortunate in later years in being at ease in his worldly circumstances; and *most* fortunate of all in dying before his mind became weakened. Death will be to him merely passing out of one room filled with friends into another room still more full of friends.

It is wonderful how one mortal may affect the destiny of a multitude. I remember very distinctly the first time I ever saw Garrison. I little thought then that the whole pattern of my life-web would be changed by that introduction. I was then all absorbed in poetry and painting,—soaring aloft, on Psyche-wings, into the etherial regions of mysticism. He got hold of the strings of my conscience, and pulled me into Reforms. It is of no use to imagine what might have been, if I had never met him. Old dreams vanished, old associates departed, and all things became new. But the new surroundings were all alive, and they brought a moral discipline worth ten times the sacrifice they cost. But why use the word sacrifice? I was never conscious of any sacrifice. A new stimulus siezed my whole being, and carried me whithersoever it would. "I could not otherwise, so help me God"! How the same circumstances changed the whole coloring of life for Charles Sumner, and Wendell Phillips! The hour of national expiation had come, and men and women must needs obey the summons to accomplish the work, through means they could not foresee.

ALS; Anne Whitney Papers, Wellesley College (microfiche 92/2451).

* 19 June 1879, Lutz Collection, Schlesinger Library, Radcliffe College.

In 1879, for the last time, Child moved to Boston. She stayed from October until May, again at 8 West Dover Street.

To Francis Shaw

Boston, 8 Dover St. Oct. 26th '79

Dear Frank,

When I opened the envelope, I fairly shouted; the likeness is so good, and I was so glad to see it. I never get over a feeling of surprise at the wonderful discovery of photography. Only think what a help it would have been to the Egyptians in making *their* pictures! And, notwithstanding the present discouraging state of the world, I believe the advance has really been as great spiritually, as it has been in external things. I retain enough of my old Swedenborgian ideas, to believe that, on a *large* scale, the external and the internal must inevitably correspond. The world *does* slowly become wiser and better, as the centuries roll on. You and I have tried to help onward the process; and if we have accomplished ever so little, it is something to be thankful for. It seems too bad that we should be so cheated out of the benign results of emancipation. But, after all, we could not reasonably expect things to work more smoothly, in the beginning. When such a malevolent disease as slavery had lasted for generations, it must unavoidably produce disastrous effects on the characters of both masters and slaves. The colored people, with all their deficiencies, have done remarkably well, considering the circumstances in which they have been placed. Their former masters, instead of guiding them and helping them through their transition state, have been so impolitic, in their blind pride, that they have done everything to discourage and alienate them. Even under more favorable circumstances, it would naturally take generations for the poor dwarfed souls to develope to the size of ours. Only reflect how long it took the boasted Anglo Saxon race to rise from the tattoo-ing condition to the demand for House of Commons, penny postage, and Catholic emancipation!

Crowds are passing by the windows here all the time; and not a single soul of them all do I know. Cities seem to me like ant-hills. Yet each hurry-scurrying little atom has its experiences of tragedy and comedy. So have the ants, too, for that matter; for *they* also make war upon each other, and one tribe carries off another tribe as prisoners, and makes slaves of them, to do all the drudgery, while their masters are eating sugar. Their resemblance to humans is rather mortifying. But though they make slaves, they dont produce any abolitionists. Let us comfort ourselves with that reflection.

With hearty and grateful love to you all, I remain always your very affectionate old friend,

Mariquita.

ALS; Wayland (Mass.) Historical Society (microfiche 93/2475).

559

To Abby B. Francis

Boston, December 24, 1879.

I know of nothing very interesting in the literary world, except a small volume called the "Light of Asia," by the English Mr. Arnold, who married W. H. Channing's daughter.[1] It recites the well-known legends about Buddha, in a form of singular poetic beauty. He made a great mistake, that good "Lord Buddha." It would have been more wise to have taught his fellow-creatures how to raise more grain, weave more cloth, and take better care of their health, than it was to descend into beggary with them. But there is something very touching and sublime in his determination to quit regal splendor and luxury, and live among the poor and suffering like a brother. The book sells well on account of its literary merit, and is helping many other quiet influences to enable human souls to recognize their spiritual kinship.

L, extract; *Letters of Lydia Maria Child*, 1882 (microfiche 93/2484).

At the time of the following letter, Anne Whitney had sculpted a model for a statue of Charles Sumner, although not until 1902, at the age of eighty, did she complete it. The sculpture now overlooks Harvard Square in Cambridge.

To Sarah Shaw

Boston, 1879.

Dear Sarah,

. . . I hear that a copy of her Charles Sumner is at the house of Mrs. Chapman's son, in New York.[1] I hope you and Frank will see it. It seems to me to embody his *character* wonderfully. She gained the prize for it as the best model exhibited; in fact it was so *much* the best, that the general remark was that it made all the others seem mean and poor. Yet when the Committee found it was the work of a woman, they voted not to give her the cutting of the statue, because a woman could not know how to make the masculine figure. The Jackasses! By that showing, what business have men to carve feminine figures?

L; Lydia Maria Child Papers, Anti-Slavery Collection, Cornell University (microfiche 93/2488).

---

[1] *The Light of Asia* (Boston, 1861, reissued 1879), a blank verse epic dealing with the life of Buddha, was written by Edwin Arnold, English poet and journalist.
[1] Henry Grafton Chapman (1833–83) was a New York banker.

To Sarah Shaw

Boston, 8 Dover St. March 2d, 1880.

Dear Sarah,

. . .

I have been not a little excited about the Negro Exodus. Thank God *that* safety-valve is open for the poor creatures! But I am afraid they have suffered a good deal with hunger and cold.[1] I have tried to do what I could for them; but only time can ameliorate their condition. Mrs. Pickering, who does not take kindly to reforms, occasionally makes the cheering remark that they were better off in slavery. But even in my most desponding moods, I will not admit *that*. Notwithstanding the miserable blunders of our government, and the abominable knavery of politicians, there *has* been a great gain. They cannot be bought and sold in the market; they *can* emigrate; and we have made no contract to send them back. Best of all, there is now a possible *basis* for the salutary education of both races; and under the old system there *was* no such possibility.

I fully appreciate the difficulties attending the admission of women to the right of suffrage. The influence of the Catholic Church on our schools and our free institutions has been to me a very dark cloud on our horizon, for a long time. If Slave holders, Democrats, and Catholics unite their forces, the country will be in very great peril. But *every* inch of the world's progress has to be gained by a tremendous struggle. The transition from an imperfect state of things to a better is *always* accompanied with many inconveniences and dangers, and is always productive of more or less wrong. The Protestant Reformation produced a great deal of suffering, and doubtless caused much injustice. But liberty of conscience was an immense step forward in the world's progress. It was worth all that it has cost, and all it is now costing. Then how many dangers and how much suffering to *all* classes was, and *is*, involved in the abolition of chattel slavery! All we can do is to follow, patiently and fearlessly, every principle which we clearly perceive to be true. And, to my mind, no principle is more obviously and entirely true, than that which claims for *every* individual the right to have a voice in the laws by which they are governed. If he or she is not *fit* to have a voice in the government, it is because they have been wrongfully kept in subserviency; and the sooner the wrong is remedied, the better for individuals, and for society.   The work is difficult and often disagreeable, my dear friend; but every *true principle* is ultimately *safe;* and while we are trying to help others we are sure to invigorate our own characters. Justice never *does* make the heavens fall; on the contrary, it is the main pillar that sustains the heavens.

. . .

ALS; Houghton Library, Harvard University (microfiche 93/2492).

[1] Most of the Southern blacks arrived in Kansas penniless. The Freedmen's Relief Association and other groups aided the settlers with food, tools, cash, and clothing, but neither the state nor the federal government provided direct help.

To Samuel E. and Harriet Sewall

Wayland, June 15'th, 1880.

My very dear friends,

My long silence has not been owing to any deficiency of grateful memories and loving thoughts concerning you. But I have been so tormented with rheumatism, that I have spent much of my time on the bed; being unable to get ease in any other position. Mrs. Pickering also has been very poorly; and, as it was almost impossible to obtain help, the getting the house into habitable condition was a tedious job. Circumstances will compel me to sell here, and go out to board somewhere. I was in hopes to die before I was obliged to break up my home, and stow myself away in the corner of some other household. But we must all yield to necessity. When I was young, it was easy to obtain a comfortable home, if one had the pecuniary means; but in these days, comfort is starved for the sake of gentility, and everybody is too busy studying Greek, or painting china, to spare time to learn how to prepare nourishing food, or keep a room in order. It vexes me to see so much time and ingenuity uselessly frittered away, while all the real necessities of life are left to the mercy of ignorant and wasteful foreigners. But it is of no use to remonstrate with the Spirit of the Age; it is rushing us headlong on the same downward course where all other Republics have been swamped.

However, there is one thing to be thankful for; that we have escaped the hazardous precedent of a Third Term Presidency.[1] It would seem to be the beginning of a tendency toward Dictatorship. I confess, too, that a third election of Grant would have jarred somewhat on my feelings, as a contemptuous disregard of the warnings of Sumner. Before the doctors drugged his mind with opiates, he certainly had wonderful insight concerning the characters of men and the tendency of events.

. . .

ALS; Robie-Sewall Papers, Massachusetts Historical Society (microfiche 94/2505).

Angelina (Grimké) Weld died on 26 October 1879.

To Theodore Dwight Weld

Wayland, July 10'th, 1880.

Dear Friend Weld,

I thank you cordially for the interesting Memorial of your excellent wife. Such a benediction is rarely bestowed on any man as to have loved and been

[1] With Hayes declining a second term, a Republican faction tried to win for Grant a third-term nomination. But the dark horse James A. Garfield was chosen instead.

beloved by such a woman. How dim and cold all the pictures of the old saints seem, when brought into comparison with the clear light of her conscience, and the glowing warmth of her love for her fellow-creatures!

The memory of the early Anti-Slavery days is very sacred to me. The Holy Spirit *did* actually descend upon men and women in tongues of flame. Political and theological prejudices, and personal ambitions, were forgotten in sympathy for the wrongs of the helpless, and in the enthusiasm to keep the fire of freedom from being extinguished on our national altar. *All* suppression of selfishness makes the moment great; and mortals were never more sublimely forgetful of self, than were the abolitionists in those early days, before the moral force which emanated from them had become available as a political power. Ah, my friend, that is the *only* true church organization, when heads and hearts unite in working for the welfare of the human-race.

And how wonderfully everything came as it was wanted! How quick the "mingled flute and trumpet eloquence" of Phillips responded to the clarion-call of Garrison! How the clear, rich bugle-tones of Whittier wakened echoes in all living souls! How wealth poured in from the ever open hands of Arthur Tappan, Gerrit Smith, the Winslows, and thousands of others who gave even more largely in proportion to their smaller means![1] How the time-serving policy of Dr. Beecher[2] drove the bold, brave boys of Lane Seminary into the battle-field! Politicians said, "The abolitionists exaggerate the evil; they do not know whereof they affirm"; and in response, up rose Angelina and her sister Sarah, shrinking from the task imposed upon them by conscience, but upheld by the divine power of truth, to deliver this message to the world: "*We* know whereof we affirm; for we were born and bred in South Carolina; and we know that abolitionists *have* not told, and *could* not tell, half the horrors of slavery." Then, like a cloud full of thunder and lightning, Frederic Douglas loomed above the horizon. *He* knew whereof he affirmed; for he had *been* a slave. Congress seemed in danger of becoming a mere "den of thieves," when Daniel Webster walked out, with Ichabod written on his garments; and strong in moral majesty in walked Charles Sumner, a man so honest and pure, that he could not *see* any other line than a straight one. What if the pulpits were silent? Theodore Parker, that Boanerges[3] of the clerical ranks, spoke in tones strong and far-reaching as a thousand voices.

Those were indeed inspiring days. I look back lovingly upon them; and I find it very hard to realize that so much of it has passed into oblivion, and that what remains is merely the cold record of history.

Your good and great Angelina, and yourself, are prominent in these memory-pictures of a thrilling and exalting period. How well I remember her pale

---

[1] Nathan and Isaac Winslow, Quaker merchants from Maine, gave substantial financial support to *The Liberator*.
[2] Lyman Beecher.
[3] The Sons of Thunder, Saint James and Saint John.

countenance and trembling limbs, when she rose to address the Legislature of Masachusetts! The feminine shrinking was soon overcome by her sense of the duty before her, and her words flowed forth free, forcible, and well-arranged. Those who went from that Hall unconverted were those who being "convinced against their will, were of the same opinion still."

Some years ago, I wrote my impressions of that memorable scene, for the New York Tribune; but no words could do justice to the photograph in my memory.[4]

If, when we go hence, we carry with us scenes so vividly painted on the soul, what a gallery of pictures we shall have!

I did not think of writing half so much, when I sat down; but it *came*. Whence?

Yours with affectionate respect,

L. Maria Child.

I feel more warmed up about the Presidential election than I ever expected to again. Garfield comes from the Western Reserve of Ohio, and seems to have been imbued with the honest Anti Slavery spirit of that region.

ALS; Weld-Grimké Papers, Clements Library, University of Michigan (microfiche 94/ 2509).

On 6 May 1880, about six months after G. H. Lewes's death, George Eliot married the broker John Walter Cross, an old friend twenty years her junior. There was much speculation about her motive, but within eight months the marriage was ended by Eliot's death.

To Sarah Shaw

[7 August 1880]

. . .

In answer to your other questions. I answer, Yes, I was very sorry about George Elliot's marriage. There is something incongruous in such a marriage. It clashes on the imagination like discord on the ear. I conjecture how it was with her. At her age, it could not be passion, or any degree of romantic illusion. By courtesy, she had long been called Mrs. Lewes; but when he died, the law required the use of her maiden name in the legal documents employed in settling the estate. It is said she has always been a good deal saddened by her anomalous position, though it has been partially veiled from the public. But when legal documents proved that she had no right to any but her maiden name, I have no doubt that British Society made her feel very acutely the awkwardness of her situation. Very likely she might hope that marriage in church would operate

[4] Child's article was reprinted in the *National Anti-Slavery Standard*, 5 Apr. 1862.

as a sort of Protestant absolution for past offences. The man she married has long been a very intimate and devoted friend of Mr. Lewes and herself; and perhaps a feeling of chivalry led him to wish to shield her with the shelter of his name. Still, the marriage, viewed in any light, seems to me a great weakness.

I am sorry that a soul so noble should have any scar for meaner souls to point at.

This world is a hazardous pilgrimage for those who are endowed with the impressible temperament of genius. As Elizabeth Browning says: "Tis hard to carry a soul through all the spilt saltpetre of this world."

With blessings on you all, I am your loving old friend

Mariechen.

L; Lydia Maria Child Papers, Anti-Slavery Collection, Cornell University (microfiche 94/2514).

To Francis Shaw

Wayland, Aug. 10th, 1880

Dear Friend,

I thank you for the Life of Gen. Garfield. I did not think I should ever again take so much interest in a political campaign, as I do in his election. I read every word of his Speech on "Honest Money,["] eight columns long. I am not well posted up on financial questions, and have had rather a distaste for such controversies. But his statements were so very plain, that I understood every sentence; and my *common* sense, and my *moral* sense cordially responded thereto. Everything I have read of his seems to me to have the ring of true metal. I am constantly reminded of the practical good sense and sturdy honesty of Francis Jackson. I was especially pleased with the emphasis he places on the assertion that there was a right & a wrong in the war of the rebellion. I would not have one unnecessary word said, that might hurt the feelings, or wound the pride, of the South. They acted just as *we* should have acted, if we had been educated under the same institution. But their institution was bad, and the means they took to sustain and extend it were bad. I have been disgusted, and somewhat discouraged, by the "mush of concession" that has passed current under the name of magnanimity. The tendency to speak of both sides as equally in the right, because they both fought bravely, is utterly wrong in principle and demoralizing in its influence. The real question at issue was whether the free principles on which our government was founded should be maintained, or should be overthrown. Doubtless, the Southerners were honestly blinded by the prejudices of their education; but none the less were they in the wrong. Their physical bravery is of the same character as the reckless courage of Bonaparte's legions, going about robbing other nations, for what they assumed to be the glory of France.

Yes, I like Gen. Garfield; because he manifests no sectional bitterness, or prejudice, but at the same time sees clearly, and asserts manfully, that it is our duty to protect the slaves we have emancipated in the exercise of their civil rights.

I know we are very liable to be disappointed in our Presidents; but I cannot help thinking that the Republican Party, by accident, or the guidance of a superintending Providence, have fixed their choice on an honest and an able man.

I see you are about to settle a minister at your pretty little chapel on Staten Island. How can Unitarians consistently name a place of worship "The Church of the *Redeemer*," when they don't believe in redemption by the blood of Jesus? Is it altogether fair and square to use phrases in the universal meaning of which we have no belief? It seems to me that Unitarianism continually weakens itself by trying to ride two horses. I don't think anything is ever really gained, either for truth, or freedom, by a "mush of concession."

Did you see the account of Jacob Bright's (John Bright's father) experiment of managing his large manufacturing establishment on co-operative principles?[1] For years, the experiment proved eminently safe and prosperous. There is a prejudice against Associations, growing out of the grievous mistakes made by Communities. But my faith has never for a moment wavered, that co-operation is the *only* way to solve the troublesome problem between labor and capital. By a law of human-nature, men will take a more lively interest in any business where they *share the profits*, than they will where they receive *wages*, however liberal. I think mankind will continue to go through a variety of blundering experiments, till they finally hit upon a practical business plan of co-operative industry, in which none of the laws of human nature are violated.   The Shakers do violence to nature by abolishing the family relation. Oneida does the same, in a much more objectionable way. But, so far as mere *business* is concerned, both of those communities are eminently successful.   I have seen nothing this long time that interested me so much as Godin's "Social Palace", in France.[2] He seems to me to have very nearly worked out the problem. It *will* be worked out, sooner or later; of that I feel very sure. Men's highest *aspirations* are *prophecies*.

But why should I write all this to you, who knew it all before, and could express it better? I suppose I fell into this prosy utterance of my thoughts, because there is no mortal near to whom I can utter them; and, like the apothecary's owl, I "keep up a devil of a thinking."

AL, signature cut off; Houghton Library, Harvard University (microfiche 94/2515).

---

[1] Jacob Bright was a Quaker cotton miller in Rochdale, England.
[2] Jean Baptiste André Godin (1817–88) was a manufacturer and social reformer strongly influenced by Fourier. His iron works at Guise, France, were the basis for the successful Co-partnership Association formed in 1879. Based on the principle of equitable sharing of wealth among capital and labor, the association offered its workers communal homes, cooperative day care, insurance, old-age pensions, and education.

To Sarah Shaw

Wayland, Sep. 6'th, 1880.

Dear Friend,

I was very glad to know your opinion of "The Fool's Errand."[1] When I first read it, I wrote to you about it, because I was curious to know what impression it had made on your mind; but you had not then read it. That it was a true description of Southern feeling I did not doubt; for it was a corroboration of all I had been hearing, ever since the war, from teachers, and others, who had been down South. But it seemed to me intensely *Southern* in its spirit. Under the appearance of candor to both sides, there seemed to me to be a very slightly veiled *sneer* at those who believed in principles of justice and freedom. There is something of this sneer in the very *title*. It is assumed at the beginning that the man who left his home and his profession to join the army of the North was a "fool for meddling with what did not concern him"; and his final epitaph is, "By following the counsels of the wise, he became a Fool." The book made me feel so sad and discouraged, and seemed to me so calculated to undermine faith in right principles, that I laid it away, and never felt willing to lend it. But I never could find any one who took the same view of it that I did. I therefore concluded that the impression it left on my mind was peculiar to myself. Nevertheless, though I thought the book indicated a good deal of talent, I never liked its "*sphere*." (to use a Swedenborgian phrase.[)] I enclose a paragraph showing how they like it at the South.

Have you read a book called "Certain Dangerous Tendencies in American Life"?[2] I think it is a true picture of an extensive phase of thought and feeling at the *North*. In the views presented there seems to me to be a good deal of practical wisdom. The chapter on "Preaching" is the only really weak chapter. The idea of restoring declining faith by having the clergy become a holy and mysterious order, by living apart from the people, is simply preposterous. The world has had more than enough of that sort of reverence. The writer is the only one I have met with who seems to be aware of the very extensive underlying influence of "Spiritualism." That some of the alleged phenomona of "spiritualism" are real, I feel perfectly sure; and like all realities, they doubtless indicate some laws of our mysterious being. But the *traffic* in these phenomona is contemptible and injurious beyond description; whether it be intentional imposture, or the result of self-delusion. I have long thought it the most powerful and extensive, though the least noted, of the many agencies at work, shaking the foundation of things, in this transition period.

---

[1] *A Fool's Errand, by One of the Fools* (New York, 1879) by Albion W. Tourgée, an Ohio lawyer, was a fictional treatment of the author's experience in North Carolina during Reconstruction.
[2] By Jonathan Baxter Harrison, Boston, 1880.

There are stormy times ahead. But perhaps you and I will slip away before they come.

I do hope Garfield will be elected; but it seems to me there is going to be a close contest.

With love and blessing to you all, Your old friend Mariquita.

ALS; Houghton Library, Harvard University (microfiche 94/2519).

On 20 October 1880, six weeks after this letter, Child died at the age of seventy-eight. Three days later, after services in her house attended by many old friends, she was buried in the Wayland cemetery, beside David Lee Child.

Books and Pamphlets by Lydia Maria Child

Child's works are arranged here in strict chronological order by date of the first edition; titles of some later editions vary slightly, as do the contents. Besides the books and pamphlets listed below, Child published an abundance of short stories, poems, and articles for periodicals. Most of her fiction and poetry she anthologized in book form, and these collections are included. Important sources for her short works are the *Juvenile Miscellany; The Liberator;* the *Liberty Bell;* the *National Anti-Slavery Standard* and its successor, the *National Standard;* the *Boston Courier;* the *Atlantic Monthly;* and the *Independent.* Occasional articles appeared in other antislavery periodicals and in Boston and New York newspapers, and during the mid-1840s many of her stories were published in New York magazines.

Hobomok, a Tale of Early Times. Boston: Cummings, Hilliard and Co., 1824.

Evenings in New England. Boston: Cummings, Hilliard and Co., 1824.

The Rebels; or, Boston before the Revolution. Boston: Cummings, Hilliard and Co., 1825.

Emily Parker; or, Impulse, not Principle. Boston: Bowles and Dearborn, 1827.

Ed. The Juvenile Souvenir. Boston: Marsh and Capen, 1827.

Ed. Moral Lessons in Verse. Cambridge, Mass.: Hilliard and Brown, 1828.

Biographical Sketches of Great and Good Men. Boston: Putnam and Hunt, 1828.

The First Settlers of New-England; or, Conquest of the Pequods, Narragansets and Pokanokets: as Related by a Mother to Her Children, and Designed for the Instruction of Youth. Boston: Munroe and Francis, 1828.

The Frugal Housewife. Boston: Marsh and Capen, and Carter and Hendee, 1829.

The Little Girl's Own Book. Boston: Carter, Hendee and Babcock, 1831.

The Mother's Book. Boston: Carter, Hendee and Babcock, 1831.

The Coronal: A Collection of Miscellaneous Pieces, Written at Various Times. Boston: Carter and Hendee, 1831.

The Biographies of Madame de Staël, and Madame Roland. Vol. 1 of Ladies' Family Library. Boston: Carter and Hendee, 1832.

The Biographies of Lady Russell, and Madame Guyon. Vol. 2 of Ladies' Family Library. Boston: Carter, Hendee and Co., 1832.

Good Wives. Vol. 3 of Ladies' Family Library. Boston: Carter, Hendee and Co., 1833.

An Appeal in Favor of That Class of Americans Called Africans. Boston: Allen and Ticknor, 1833.

Ed. The Oasis. Boston: Allen and Ticknor, 1834.

The History of the Condition of Women, in Various Ages and Nations. Vols. 4 and 5 of Ladies' Family Library. Boston: J. Allen and Co., 1835.

Authentic Anecdotes of American Slavery. Nos. 1–2. Newburyport, Mass.: Charles Whipple, 1835.

Anti-Slavery Catechism. Newburyport, Mass.: Charles Whipple, 1836.

The Evils of Slavery, and the Cure of Slavery. Newburyport, Mass.: Charles Whipple, 1836.

Philothea: A Romance. Boston: Otis, Broaders and Co., 1836.

Ed. A Garland of Juvenile Poems. London: John Limbird, Mirror Press, 1836.

Ed.? Stories for Holiday Evenings. London: John Limbird, 1836.

The Family Nurse; or, Companion of the Frugal Housewife. Boston: Charles J. Hendee, 1837.

Authentic Anecdotes of American Slavery. No. 3. Newburyport, Mass.: Charles Whipple, 1838.

Ed. Memoir of Benjamin Lay: Compiled from Various Sources. New York: American Anti-Slavery Society, 1842.

Ed. The American Anti-Slavery Almanac. New York: American Anti-Slavery Society, 1843.

Letters from New-York, First Series. New York: Charles S. Francis and Co., 1843.

Flowers for Children, First and Second Series. New York: C. S. Francis and Co., 1844.

Letters from New-York, Second Series. New York: C. S. Francis and Co., 1845.

Fact and Fiction. New York: C. S. Francis and Co., 1846.

Flowers for Children, Third Series. New York: C. S. Francis and Co., 1846.

With M. Kendrick. The Gift Book of Biography for Young Ladies. London: Thomas Nelson, Paternoster Row; and Edinburgh, 1847.

Sturgis, Caroline. Rainbows for Children. Ed. Lydia Maria Child. New York: C. S. Francis and Co., 1848.

Rose Marian, and the Flower Fairies. New York: C. S. Francis and Co., 1850.

Sketches from Real Life. Philadelphia: Hazard and Mitchell, 1850.

Isaac T. Hopper: A True Life. Boston: J. P. Jewett and Co., 1853.

The Progress of Religious Ideas through Successive Ages. 3 Vols. New York: C. S. Francis and Co., 1855.

A New Flower for Children. New York: C. S. Francis and Co., 1856.

Sturgis, Caroline. The Magician's Showbox. Ed. Lydia Maria Child. Boston: Ticknor and Fields, 1856.

Autumnal Leaves: Tales and Sketches in Prose and Rhyme. New York: C. S. Francis and Co., 1857.

Correspondence between Lydia Maria Child and Gov. Wise and Mrs. Mason, of Virginia. Boston: American Anti-Slavery Society, 1860.

The Right Way, the Safe Way, Proved by Emancipation in the British West Indies, and Elsewhere. New York: [American Anti-Slavery Society], 1860.

Ed. The Patriarchal Institution, as Described by Members of Its Own Family. New York: American Anti-Slavery Society, 1860.

The Duty of Disobedience to the Fugitive Slave Act: An Appeal to the Legislators of Massachusetts. Boston: American Anti-Slavery Society, 1860.

Jacobs, Harriet Brent. Incidents in the Life of a Slave Girl. Ed. Lydia Maria Child. Boston, privately published, 1861.

Ed. Looking toward Sunset. Boston: Ticknor and Fields, 1865.

The Freedmen's Book. Boston: Ticknor and Fields, 1865.

A Romance of the Republic. Boston: Ticknor and Fields, 1867.

An Appeal for the Indians. New York: W. P. Tomlinson, 1868.

Ed. Children of Mt. Ida. New York: Charles S. Francis, 1871.

Ed. Aspirations of the World. A Chain of Opals. Boston: Roberts Brothers, 1878.

Letters of Lydia Maria Child, with a Biographical Introduction by John G. Whittier and an Appendix by Wendell Phillips. Boston: Houghton Mifflin Co., 1882.

The Collected Correspondence of Lydia Maria Child, 1817–1880. Ed. Patricia G. Holland, Milton Meltzer. Millwood, N.Y.: Kraus Microform, 1980.

Index

The index lists the names of all those Child wrote to, designated by *to* immediately after the name. Other references to that person follow the semi-colon. The index also includes the names of people referred to within the letters, as well as ideas, events, issues, book titles, and so on. While detailed, the index is necessarily selective. Because of Child's special interests, a few themes are so often voiced throughout the letters that they are not indexed as subjects. In place of "abolitionism," for example, see more specific items such as "American Anti-Slavery Society" and the names of individual abolitionists.

fugitive slave rescue attempts, 257, 260, 268, 269–70

fugitive slaves, 40, 52, 63–64, 88, 140, 144, 166, 221, 237, 244, 255, 256, 260, 355, 357, 358, 380–81, 383, 387, 391–92, 456

Fuller, Margaret, *to*: 10, 211; 78, 125, 134, 179, 200, 217–18, 219, 222, 227, 229, 231, 240, 249, 250, 251, 253, 460

Furness, William H., 143, 394

gag rule, 57, 139, 159

Gantt, Edward W., 438

Garfield, James A., 562, 564, 565, 568

Garrison, Francis J., *to*: 529; 558

Garrison, Helen E., 37

Garrison, Helen F., *to*: 397

Garrison, William Lloyd, *to*: 68, 119, 127, 326, 336, 456, 553; 25, 30, 37, 47, 60, 61, 65, 78, 89, 107, 108, 117, 144, 149, 159, 173, 176, 187, 197, 223, 285, 290, 304, 310, 331, 335, 367, 409, 416, 450, 474, 478, 510, 526, 549, 557, 558, 563

Gaskell, Elizabeth, 309

Gasparin, Agenor de, 392

Gates, Seth M., 168

Gay, Sidney H., *to*: 335

Gibbons, Abigail, 140

Gibbons, James, 130, 140, 143, 162, 172, 178–79, 185, 187, 190

Giddings, Joshua, 139, 164

Gilman, Caroline, 80, 234

Gilman, Samuel, 80

Godwin, Parke, *to*: 274, 330; 196

Goethe, von, Johann W., 132, 275, 289

Gold Rush, 199

Goodell, William, 165

Goodrich, Samuel G., 113

gradual emancipation, 365

Grant, U. S., 442, 444, 451, 453, 477, 478, 483, 497, 502, 505–8, 515, 516, 520, 532, 562

Great Britain, view of American Civil War, 385–86, 406–7, 414, 422, 498

Greeley, Horace, *to*: 333, 406; 217, 263, 294, 299, 333, 480, 486, 505, 507–8

Green, Bessie, 552

Griffith, Martha, 306, 307, 311, 329, 354, 409, 421

Grimké, Angelina. *See* Weld, Angelina

Grimké, Sarah, 26, 39, 61, 71, 72, 97, 123, 518

Griswold, Rufus W., *to*: 231

Gurley, Ralph R., 100

Hampton, Wade, 546–47

Hampton Institute, 502–3, 523, 532

Harper, Frances E., 338

Harpers Ferry raid, 323–24, 339

Haskins, William, *to*: 423, 427

Hayden, Lewis, 456

Hayes, Rutherford B., 539, 546, 549, 562

Hayes-Tilden Compromise, 539

Heinrich, Antony P., *to*: 219; 200, 219

Helper, Hinton R., 310, 354, 362

Henshaw, Caroline, 183

Herald of Freedom, 37

Heywood, Ezra H., 553

Hibernian Anti-Slavery Society, 167

Hicks, Thomas, 261

Higginson, Thomas W., *to*: 344, 499; 25, 297, 303, 339, 371, 424, 477

Hildreth, Richard, 60

Hillel, 513–14

Holley, Sallie, 281

home burned (LMC's), 432–33

homeopathy, 152, 461

Homestead Act, 439

Hooker, Isabella, 54

Hopedale, 150

Hopper, Isaac T., 140, 145, 163, 188, 226, 244, 264, 492

Hopper, John, 140, 142, 145, 147, 189, 195, 199, 210, 227, 236, 239

Hopper, Rosa De Wolf, 236, 239

Hosmer, Harriet, 264, 265, 313, 330, 390

household work, 12, 131–32, 133, 134, 172, 258, 277, 418, 460, 519, 522

Hovey, Charles F., 355, 443

Howard, Oliver O., 507

Howe, Julia W., 488–89

Howe, Samuel G., 339, 438

Howitt, Mary, 249

Hudson, Erasmus D., 144

Hughes, John, 167, 168, 170

Hunt, Seth, 103

Hunter, David, 424

Hyatt, Thaddeus, *to*: 328; 330

hydropathy, 181

Ida May, 278

Incidents in Life of a Slave Girl, 357, 375, 378

income (LMC's), 475

Indian Peace Commission, 479

Indians, 1, 3, 301, 327, 455, 479, 496–97, 506, 507, 512, 514–16, 544

Ingersoll, Robert G., 550–51

interracial marriage, 3, 110–11, 414
Iowa suffragists, *to*: 491
Irish, 140, 167, 169–70, 434, 440, 468, 544

Jackson, Andrew, 11, 67, 454, 514
Jackson, Francis, *to*: 361; 86, 118, 156, 244, 478
Jackson, James C., 146, 165
Jacobs, Harriet, *to*: 357, 358, 375; 364, 378, 420
James, Henry, 557
Jameson, Anna B., 235
Jane Eyre, 238, 309
Janney, Samuel M., 507
Jay, John, *to*: 221
Jay, William, 78, 86, 166, 168
Jean Paul Frederic Richter, 179, 181
Jesus, 513–14, 549, 551
Jews, 109, 124, 140, 240–41, 460, 483, 513, 534, 536–37, 540, 551
Jim Crow, 434
Johnson, Andrew, 449–50, 453, 454, 457, 463, 464, 478
Johnson, Oliver, *to*: 334, 435; 68, 84, 109, 146
Johnson, Samuel, 303, 304, 484
Journal of a Residence on a Georgia Plantation, 341, 434, 435
Journey in the Seaboard Slave States, 280–81
Julian, George W., *to*: 403, 439, 500, 554

Kansas, struggle over, 256, 282–83, 288, 290–91, 292, 294, 299, 312, 323, 324, 333
Kansas-Nebraska Bill, 268, 269
Kelley, Abigail. *See* Foster, Abigail
Kemble, Fanny, *to*: 341; 96, 264, 308–9, 340, 434, 435
Keyes, John, 11, 13, 17
Kimball, George, 54, 63
Kimball, Joseph H., 37
King, Augusta, *to*: 202, 216; 147, 258
King, John, 234, 235
King, Thomas S., 442
Knapp, Isaac, 52, 160
Kneeland, Abner, 78
Kneeland, Horace, 69, 200, 221
Know-Nothings, 293
Ku Klux Klan, 489, 490, 502, 506, 508

Lafayette, Marquis de, 234, 235

land distribution, 417, 439, 452, 463, 485
Lane, Charles, 202–4
Lane, James H., 405
Lane Theological Seminary, 54, 56, 62, 104, 563
Larcom, Lucy, *to*: 511
Leavitt, Joshua, 145, 157, 193
Lee, Robert E., 451, 452, 453, 480, 486
legacy, 517, 522
legal will (LMC's), 279, 522
Leggett, William, 196
Lesley, J. Peter, *to*: 271, 329; 264, 364
Lesley, Susan L., *to*: 264, 329; 76, 214, 215, 236, 237
"Letters from New York," 183, 201, 236
Lewis, Edmonia, 446, 480
Lewis, Tayler, 468
Liberator, The, 25, 27, 39, 52, 61, 65, 68, 84, 107, 108, 109, 122, 127, 131, 166, 170, 194, 197, 333
Liberty Bell, 277
Liberty Party, 45, 75, 112, 148, 155 f., 165, 168, 196
Lincoln, Abraham, 324, 331, 352, 367, 379, 393, 399, 401, 404, 407, 410, 412, 415, 420, 423, 436, 445, 449–50, 453, 467
Lincoln, Mary Todd, 396, 400, 404, 493–94
Lind, Jenny, 76, 274
Livermore, Mary, 488–89
Lockwood, Lewis C., 397, 400
Longfellow, Henry W., 318
Loring, Anna. *See* Dresel, Anna Loring
Loring, Ellis Gray, *to*: 33, 43, 76, 95, 113, 130, 134, 143, 146, 151, 159, 162, 164, 166, 168, 173, 178, 180, 181, 187, 188, 192, 203, 207, 245, 251, 252, 253, 258, 260, 262, 270, 273, 279, 282; 30, 53, 56, 62, 96, 145, 185, 255, 314–15, 350, 443, 450, 519
Loring, Louisa, *to*: 31, 49, 58, 63, 76, 95, 112, 218, 223, 234, 236, 242, 245, 249, 267, 294; 30, 314–15, 346, 443, 462, 481
L'Ouverture, Toussaint, 135, 459
Lovejoy, Elijah, 54, 61, 99, 353
Lovejoy, Owen, 353, 387, 404
Lowell, Charles R., 447
Lowell, James R., 188, 195, 252
Lowell, Josephine S., 447, 537
Lundy, Benjamin, 42, 43–44, 47, 48, 50, 54
Lyman, Anne J., 76, 77, 80
Lyman, Joseph, 76, 77
Lyman, Susan. *See* Lesley, Susan L.
lynch law, 366
Lyon, Nathaniel, 393

Wise, Henry A., *to*: 325; 324, 326, 332, 333, 474

Woman in the Nineteenth Century, 217, 219

"woman question," 75, 82, 114, 122–24, 461, 486, 491, 504

woman suffrage, 114–15, 459, 467–72, 484, 486, 487, 491, 495, 503, 521, 531, 561

Woman's Journal, 536

woman's rights, 26, 50, 71, 75, 78, 79, 122–24, 127–29, 168, 188, 195, 217, 282, 355, 467–72, 491

women. *See* under individual names

women, as journalists, 139

women, as lecturers, 71, 87, 123, 281, 338

women, legal inferiority of, 279

women reformers, 25, 26

women, socialization of, 461, 470, 491–92, 539

women, subordination of, 468–72, 484, 491–92, 548, 560

women's history, 12

Women's National Loyal League, 430

women's role, 12, 39, 64, 71, 82, 122–24, 217, 234, 469–70, 538

Wood, Fernando, 380

Woodhull, Victoria, 503, 504, 509

Worcester, Thomas, 143, 441

working class, 383, 392, 413, 422, 456, 500, 542–44, 552, 556

World Anti-Slavery Convention, 62

Wright, Elizur, Jr., 31, 35, 165, 547

Wright, Henry C., 168, 171, 311

writing and publishing career. *See* LMC: Works

Yamoyden, 3, 232

Yancey, William L., 373

Library of Congress Cataloging in Publication Data

Child, Lydia Maria Francis, 1802–1880.
Lydia Maria Child, selected letters, 1817–1880.

"Books and pamphlets by Lydia Maria Child": p.
Includes index.
1. Child, Lydia Maria Francis, 1802–1880—
Correspondence.   2. Authors, American—19th century—
Correspondence.   3. Social reformers—United States—
Correspondence.   I. Meltzer, Milton, 1915–
II. Holland, Patricia G.   III. Krasno, Francine.
IV. Title.
PS1293.Z5A4   1983   818′.209 [B]   82–8464
ISBN 0–87023–332–7